Prune
Appizz

Time Out

New York

timeout.com/newyork

Published by Time Out Guides Ltd, a wholly owned subsidiary of Time Out Group Ltd.
Time Out and the Time Out logo are trademarks of Time Out Group Ltd.

Previous editions 1990, 1992, 1994, 1996, 1997, 1998, 1999, 2000, 2001, 2002, 2003, 2004, 2005, 2006, 2007.

10 9 8 7 6 5 4 3 2 1

This edition first published in Great Britain in 2008 by Ebury Publishing
A Random House Group Company
20 Vauxhall Bridge Road, London SW1V 2SA

Random House Australia Pty Limited 20 Alfred Street, Milsons Point, Sydney, New South Wales 2061, Australia
Random House New Zealand Limited 18 Poland Road, Glenfield, Auckland 10, New Zealand
Random House South Africa (Pty) Limited Isle of Houghton, Corner Boundary Road & Carse O'Gowrie, Houghton 2198, South Africa

Random House UK Limited Reg. No. 954009

For further distribution details, see www.timeout.com

ISBN: 978-1-846700-48-4

A CIP catalogue record for this book is available from the British Library

Printed and bound by Firmengruppe APPL, aprinta druck, Wemding, Germany

The Random House Group Limited supports The Forest Stewardship Council (FSC), the leading international forest certification organisation. All our titles that are printed on Greenpeace approved FSC certified paper carry the FSC logo. Our paper procurement policy can be found at http://www.rbooks.co.uk/environment

Contents

Introduction 7

In Context 15

History 16
New York Today 33
Architecture 36
Art Goes Boom 45
New York Rocks! 49

Where to Stay 53

Where to Stay 54

Sightseeing 81

Introduction 82
Tour New York 88
Downtown 93
Midtown 117
Uptown 135
Brooklyn 156
Queens 167
The Bronx 172
Staten Island 177

Eat, Drink, Shop 181

Restaurants & Cafés 182
Bars 216
Shops & Services 228

Arts & Entertainment 259

Festivals & Events 260
Art Galleries 267
Books & Poetry 276
Cabaret & Comedy 279
Children 284
Clubs 291
Film & TV 298
Gay & Lesbian 301
Music 312
Sport & Fitness 333
Theatre & Dance 340

Trips Out of Town 355

Day Trips 356

Directory 365

Getting to & from NYC 366
Getting Around 368
Resources A-Z 371
Further Reference 384
Index 386
Advertisers' Index 395

Maps 397

Street Index 398
Manhattan 402
Brooklyn 410
Queens 412
Manhattan Bus Map 413
New York City Subway 414
Manhattan Subway 416

Time Out Guides Limited
Universal House
251 Tottenham Court Road
London W1T 7AB
Tel + 44 (0)20 7813 3000
Fax + 44 (0)20 7813 6001
Email guides@timeout.com
www.timeout.com

Editorial
Editor Keith Mulvihill
Consultant Editor Elizabeth Barr for *Time Out New York*
Deputy Editors Ismay Atkins, Cyrus Shahrad
Proofreader Cathy Limb
Indexer Ismay Atkins

Managing Director Peter Fiennes
Financial Director Gareth Garner
Editorial Director Ruth Jarvis
Deputy Series Editor Dominic Earle
Editorial Manager Holly Pick
Assistant Management Accountant Ija Krasnikova

Design
Art Director Scott Moore
Art Editor Pinelope Kourmouzoglou
Senior Designer Henry Elphick
Graphic Designer Gemma Doyle
Junior Graphic Designer Kei Ishimaru
Digital Imaging Simon Foster
Advertising Designer Jodi Sher

Picture Desk
Picture Editor Jael Marschner
Deputy Picture Editor Katie Morris
Picture Researcher Helen McFarland
Picture Desk Assistant Troy Bailey

Advertising
Sales Director Mark Phillips
International Advertising Manager Kasimir Berger
International Sales Consultant Ross Canadé
International Sales Executive Charlie Sokol
Advertising Sales (New York) Siobhan Shea Rossi
Advertising Assistant Kate Staddon

Marketing
Group Marketing Director John Luck
Marketing Manager Yvonne Poon
Sales and Marketing Director North America Lisa Levinson

Production
Group Production Director Mark Lamond
Production Manager Brendan McKeown
Production Controller Caroline Bradford
Production Coordinator Susan Whittaker

Time Out Group
Chairman Tony Elliott
Financial Director Richard Waterlow
Group General Manager/Director Nichola Coulthard
Time Out Magazine Ltd MD Richard Waterlow
Time Out Communications Ltd MD David Pepper
Time Out International MD Cathy Runciman
Group Art Director John Oakey
Group IT Director Simon Chappell

Contributors
History Kathleen Squires. **Architecture** Pablito Nash. **New York Today** Howard Halle. **Where to Stay** Keith Mulvihill. **Tour New York** Keith Mulvihill. **Downtown** Carmela Ciuraru. **Midtown**, **Uptown** Keith Mulvihill (Central Park Walk Eric Mendelsohn). **Brooklyn** Carmela Ciuraru. **Queens** John Roleke. **The Bronx**, **Staten Island** Kathleen Squires. **Restaurants & Cafés**, **Bars** *Time Out New York* Eat Out staff. **Shops & Services** Kelly McMasters, Helen Yun, Keith Mulvihill. **Festivals & Events** Keith Mulvihill. **Art Galleries**. Kate Lowenstein. **Books & Poetry** Michael Miller. **Cabaret & Comedy** Adam Feldman (cabaret), Jane Borden (comedy). **Children** Keith Mulvihill. **Clubs** Bruce Tantum. **Film & TV** Joshua Rothkopf. **Gay & Lesbian** Beth Greenfield. **Music** Jay Ruttenberg (popular), Steve Smith (classical). **Sport & Fitness** Keith Mulvihill. **Theatre & Dance** David Cote (theatre), Amy Norton (dance). **Trips Out of Town** Adapted from *Time Out New York* magazine.

Maps john@jsgraphics.co.uk.

Photography by Ben Rosenzeig; except: page 16 The Art Archive/Museum of the City of New York; page 17 North Wind Picture Archives; page 23 Getty Images; page 24 AP Photos; page 28 Bettmann/Corbis; page 29 Time & Life Pictures/Getty Images; page 31 Mike Segar/Reuters/Corbis; page 42 Jock Pottle ESTO; page 44 Michael Ficeto/Hearst Corporation; page 45 Image courtesy Andreas Grimm New York; page 47 Image courtesy of Sikkema Jenkins & Co; page 48 Alys Kenny; page 49 Ebert Roberts/Redferns; pages 55, 60, 61, 67, 73, 78, 175, 199, 200, 203, 212, 213, 292, 294, 354 Jonathan Perugia; page 63 Courtesy of the Bowery Hotel; page 64 Courtesy of the Plaza; page 71 Courtesy of the London NYC; page 89 Aaron M. Cohen; page 118 Design by Field Operations and Diller Scofidio + Renfro/ Courtesy the City of New York; page 214 Peter Medilek; pages 229, 284 Alys Tomlinson; page 249 Dennis Finnin; page 265 Michael Daniel; page 321 Don Perdue; page 329 Richard Termine; page 334 Courtesy of Madison Square Garden; page 356 Courtesy of Mayflower Inn & Spa; page 358 Richard Barnes, courtesy Dia Art Foundation; page 359 Historic Hudson Valley; page 363 Six Flags Theme Parks Inc.

The Editor would like to thank Elizabeth Barr, Nestor Cervantes, Melisa Coburn, Billie Cohen, Brian Farnham, Sarina Finkelstein, Brian Fiske, Gabriella Gershenson, Howard Halle, Stacy Hillegas, Killian Jordan, Eric Mendelsohn, Leslie Price, Cyndi Stivers, Drew Toal, Alison Tocci, Reed Tucker and all contributors to previous editions of the *Time Out New York Guide*, whose work forms the basis for parts of this book.

Introduction

How can it be that on such a small strip of land, only 13 miles long and three miles at its widest, so many superlatives have been racked up? New York, at one time or other, has been home to the world's tallest buildings, its longest bridges, its busiest ports, its crabbiest cabbies and its most super superheroes. Still, despite its storied past, many first-timers here are surprised at just how tiny Manhattan (the most famous borough) is. At 309 square miles, it's a pittance compared to many of the country's much less exciting suburbs. And yet, despite all this, our little island still manages to pack a formidable punch.

Indeed, Manhattan's lifeblood surges through the arteries and veins of its avenues and streets. Energy pumps continuously through the neighbourhoods of Wall Street, Times Square and the always arty, eclectic East Village. And because so many distinct and intriguing cultures, landmarks and neighbourhoods stand cheek by jowl in a few square miles, your days here take on a kaleidoscopic quality.

The phrase 'New York minute' usually refers to the pace and intensity from which the natives suffer (and of which they boast). It's seen most clearly in the fixity of purpose with which they stride the avenues or dart through traffic. Chances are you'll feel you've burned up a great deal of energy spending time in the city that never sleeps. Although the subway can get you almost anywhere (and is best for covering longer distances), many people often opt to walk. And, despite the fact that everyone appears to be in a rush, don't assume that no one has time for a quick chat. The persona of rude New Yorkers – emboldened by the dozens of gritty, urban films set here – is just that, a movie-made stereotype. For the most part, you'll finds the natives are more than willing to give directions or share the name of a nearby eaterie. Still, we'd be remiss if we didn't point out that many New Yorkers chuckled at Mayor Michael Bloomberg's gimmicky 'Just Ask the Locals' tourist-welcoming campaign, which launched towards the end of 2007. After all, it's not as if legions of would-be tour guides are just waiting to show you around.

There's an oft-repeated truism that New York offers too much to see in a single visit – even its longest-serving residents find themselves continually discovering the city anew. But even if your visit only lasts a few days, the trick is not to speed things up, but rather to slow them down. Linger over brunch in the West Village and stroll the charming cobbled streets; spend an afternoon sipping martinis at the Carlyle like it's a weekly ritual; take an early morning jaunt over the Brooklyn Bridge and discover the quaint side-streets of Brooklyn Heights or art-hearty Dumbo.

At the end of the day, the point of this book is to help you seize those special moments and make them your own. Take heart in the fact that it's written by a crew of New York diehards, each one of them eager to share their personal delight in seeking out hidden gems, unseen pleasures and places, and both the monuments and the minutiae of a city that's waiting eagerly to make you its newest admirer.

ABOUT TIME OUT CITY GUIDES

This is the 16th edition of the *Time Out New York Guide*, one of an expanding series of more than 50 guides produced by the people behind the successful listings magazines in London, New York, Chicago, Sydney and many more cities around the world. Our guides are all written and updated by resident experts who have striven to provide you with all the most up-to-date information you'll need to explore, whether you're a local or a first-time visitor.

THE LOWDOWN ON THE LISTINGS

Above all, we've tried to make this book as useful as possible. Addresses, telephone numbers, websites, transport information, opening times, admission prices and credit card details have all been included in the listings, as have details of other selected services and facilities. However, owners and managers can change arrangements at any time, and we strongly advise you to call ahead and check details in advance. While every effort has been made to ensure the accuracy of the information in this guide, the publishers cannot accept responsibility for any errors it may contain.

PRICES AND PAYMENT

Our listings detail which of the major credit cards – American Express (AmEx), Diners Club

(DC), Discover (Disc), MasterCard (MC) and Visa (V) – are accepted by individual venues. Many businesses will also accept other cards, such as Maestro and Carte Blanche, as well as travellers' cheques issued by a major financial institution.

The prices we've supplied should be treated as guidelines, not gospel. Fluctuating exchange rates and inflation can cause charges, particularly in shops and restaurants, to change rapidly. If prices vary wildly from those we've quoted, ask whether there's a good reason, and email us to let us know. We aim to give the best and most up-to-date advice, and we always want to know if you've been badly treated or overcharged.

THE LIE OF THE LAND

Most visitors find New York an extremely easy city to negotiate thanks to its famous grid system of conveniently interconnecting streets. To make both book and city easier to navigate, we've divided New York into areas and assigned each one its own section in the Sightseeing chapter of the book (*see pp81-180*).

For all addresses given in the book, we've included cross-streets, details of the nearest public transport option(s) and a reference to the series of fully indexed colour maps at the back of this guide, which start on page 402. The precise locations of hotels (❶), restaurants (❶) and bars (❶) have all been pinpointed on these maps; the section also includes local subway and bus maps and a street index.

For more information on finding your way around the city, *see pp82-87*.

TELEPHONE NUMBERS

You must dial 1 + the area code before a number, even if the place you are calling is in the same area code. The codes for Manhattan are 212 and 646; those in Brooklyn, Queens, the Bronx and Staten Island are 718 and 347; generally (but not always), 917 is reserved for mobile phones and pagers. The country code for the US is 1. For more on telephones and codes, *see p381*.

ESSENTIAL INFORMATION

For all the practical information you might need for visiting the city, including customs and immigration information, disabled access, emergency telephone numbers, the lowdown on the local transport network and a list of useful websites, turn to the Directory at the back of this guide (*see pp365-385*).

LET US KNOW WHAT YOU THINK

We hope you enjoy the *Time Out New York Guide*, and we'd like to know what you think of it. We welcome tips for places that you consider we should include in future editions, and take notice of your criticism of our choices. You can email us at guides@timeout.com.

Advertisers

We would like to stress that no establishment has been included in this guide because it has advertised in any of our publications and no payment of any kind has influenced any review. The opinions given in this book are those of Time Out writers and are entirely independent.

There is an online version of this guide, along with guides to more than 50 other international cities, at **www.timeout.com**.

Time Out
Miami
Milan
Mumbai & Goa
Naples
New Orleans
New York
Paris
Patagonia
Prague
Budapest
San Francisco
Seville & Andalucía
Shanghai
Singapore
South of France
Stockholm
Sydney
Tokyo 東京
Turin
Venice
Vienna
Washington, DC
Amsterdam
Athens
Bangkok
Barcelona
Beijing
Boston
Brussels
Budapest
Buenos Aires
California
Cape Town
Chicago
Copenhagen
Croatia
Dublin
Edinburgh
Florence
Havana
Hong Kong
Istanbul
Las Vegas
Lisbon
London
Madrid
Mallorca
Marrakech
Miami
Milan
Mumbai & Goa
Naples
New Orleans
New York
Patagonia
Prague
Rio de Janeiro
Rome
San Francisco
Seville & Andalucía
Shanghai
Singapore
South of France
Sydney
Tokyo 東京
Toronto
Turin
Venice
Vienna
Washington, DC
Amsterdam
Athens
Barcelona
Beijing
Berlin
Boston
Brussels
Budapest
Buenos Aires
California
Cape Town
Copenhagen
Croatia
Dubai
Dublin
Edinburgh
Florence
Havana
Hong Kong
Istanbul

OFF DUTY
6G69
OFF DUTY
601864

In Context

History 16
New York Today 33
Architecture 36
Art Goes Boom 45
New York Rocks! 49

Features

Cheap date 21
Greetings from Governors Island 26
Further reading 30
Key events 32
Top-billing buildings 37
Monumental mess 40
Clean streets 43
Buy now? 47
Show offs 48
Style council 50

View from the **Time Warner Center**. *See p146.*

Peter Minuit.

History

The rise of New York City – warts and all.

This skyscraper-packed metropolis wasn't built by a bunch of mild-mannered do-gooders, bending over backwards to be nice to each other, got it? No sir, it took a combination of guts, nasty language and raised voices. Sure, there were some happy types who said 'thank you' and 'have a nice day' but, all told, there were generations of ambitious (some would say back-stabbing) characters who made New York what it is. A brief look back at New York's history shows just how its residents earned their nerves-of-steel reputation, and explains why having a salty disposition has gotten them where they are today.

NATIVES AND NEWCOMERS

Members of the indigenous Lenape tribe were the original native New Yorkers. They lived among the meadows, forests and farms of the land they called Lenapehoking, pretty much undisturbed by outsiders for thousands of years – until 1524, when their idyll was interrupted by tourists from the later-named Old World. The first European sightseer to cast his eyes upon this land was Giovanni da Verrazano, an Italian explorer commissioned by the French to find a shortcut to the Orient. Instead, he found Staten Island. Recognising that he was on the wrong track, Verrazano pulled up anchor nearly as quickly as he had dropped it, never actually setting foot on dry land.

Eighty-five years later, Englishman Henry Hudson was far more favourably disposed. Commissioned by the Dutch, and with the same goal of finding out a shortcut to the Far East, Hudson sailed into Manhattan's natural deep-water harbour in September 1609, and was entranced by what lay before him. He lingered long enough to explore the entire length of the river that now bears his name, but it wasn't his fate to grow old in the place he admired and described in his logs as a 'rich and pleasant land': on a return trip in 1611, Hudson's crew mutinied and cast him adrift. Still, his tales of the lush, river-crossed countryside had captured the Dutch imagination, and in 1624 the Dutch West India Company sent 110 settlers to establish a trading post here. They planted themselves at the southern tip of the island called Mannahata and christened the colony New Amsterdam. In many bloody battles against the local Lenape, they did their best to drive the natives away from the little company town. But the Lenape were immovable.

In 1626, a man named Peter Minuit, New Amsterdam's first governor, thought he had solved the Lenape problem by pulling off the city's very first real-estate rip-off. The tribe had no concept of private land ownership, so Minuit made them an offer they couldn't refuse: he 'bought' the island of Manhattan – all 14,000 acres of it – from the Lenape for 60 guilders' worth of goods. Legend famously values the purchase price at $24, but modern historians set the amount closer to $500. (These days, that wouldn't cover a month's rent for a closet-size studio apartment.) It was a slick trick, and a precedent for countless ungracious business transactions that would occur in New York over the centuries that followed.

The Dutch quickly made the port of New Amsterdam a centre for fur trading. The population didn't grow as fast as the business, however, and the Dutch West India Company had a hard time finding recruits to move to an unknown island an ocean away. The company instead gathered servants, orphans and slaves, and other more unsavoury outcasts such as thieves, drunkards and prostitutes. The population grew to 400 within ten years, but given that one in every four structures was a tavern, drunkenness, crime and squalor prevailed. If the colony were to thrive, it needed a strong leader. Enter Dutch West India Company director Peter Stuyvesant.

THE FIRST IN-YOUR-FACE MAYOR

A one-legged, puritanical bully with a quick temper, Stuyvesant was less than popular: rudeness was a way of life for Peg-leg Pete, as he was known. But he was the colony's first effective governor. He made peace with the Lenape, formed the first policing force (consisting of nine men) and cracked down on debauchery by shutting taverns and outlawing drinking on Sunday. He also established the first school, post office, hospital, prison and poorhouse. Within a decade, the population quadrupled, and the settlement became an important trading port.

Lined with canals and windmills, and dotted with gabled farmhouses, New Amsterdam finally began to resemble its namesake city. Newcomers arrived to work in the fur and slave trades, or to farm. Soon, a dozen and a half languages could be heard in the streets – a fact that made the bigoted Stuyvesant nervous. In 1654, he attempted to quash immigration by turning away Sephardic Jews who were fleeing the Spanish Inquisition. But, surprisingly for the time, the corporate honchos at the Dutch West India Company reprimanded him for his intolerance and overturned his decision, leading to the establishment of the earliest Jewish community in the New World. That was the first time the inflexible Stuyvesant was made to bend his ways. The second time would put an end to the 40-year Dutch rule for good.

YOU SAY YOU WANT A REVOLUTION?

In late August 1664, English warships sailed into the harbour, set on taking over the now prosperous colony. To avoid bloodshed and destruction, Stuyvesant quickly surrendered. Soon after, New Amsterdam was renamed New York (after the Duke of York, brother of King Charles II), and Stuyvesant quietly retired to his farm. Unlike Stuyvesant, the English battled with the Lenape; by 1695, those members of the tribe who weren't killed off were sent packing upstate, and New York's European population shot up to 3,000. Over the next 35 years, Dutch-style farmhouses and windmills gave way to

Giovanni da Verrazano.

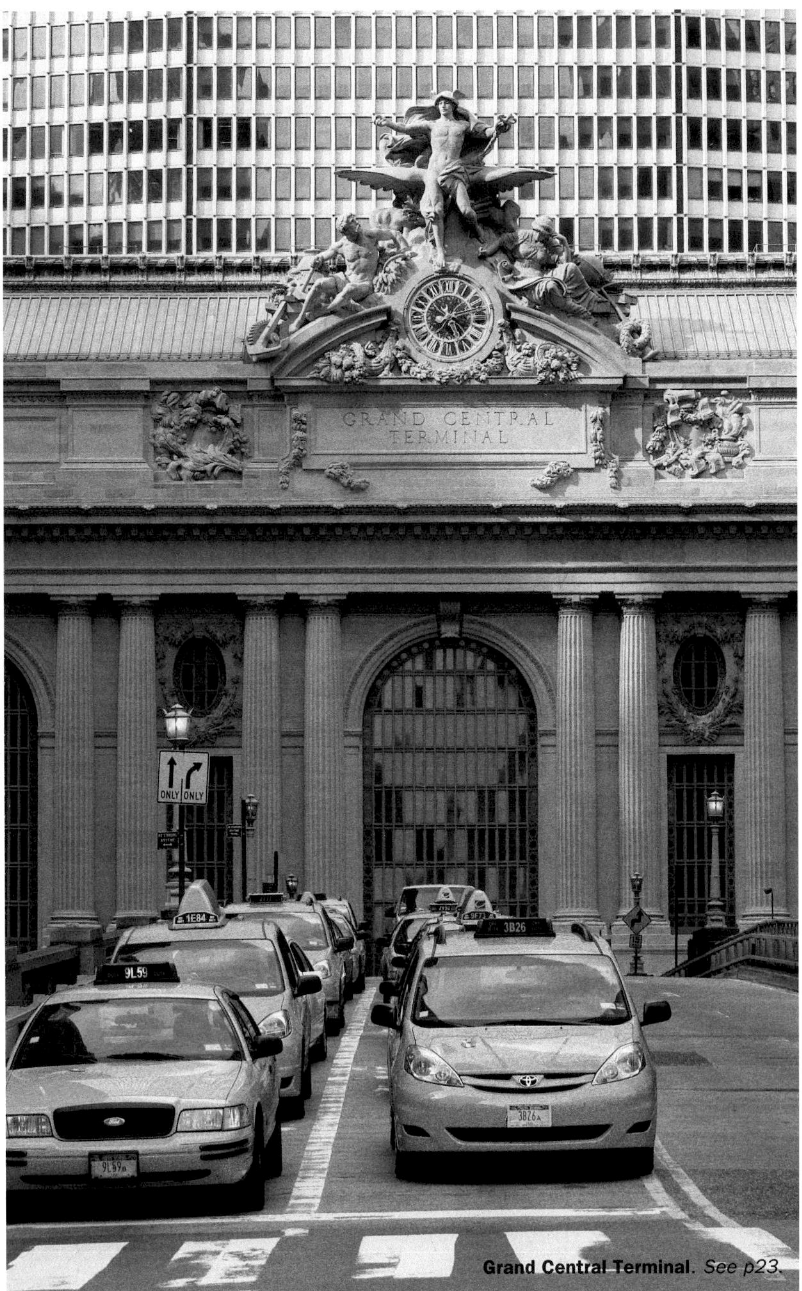

Grand Central Terminal. *See p23.*

stately townhouses and monuments to English royals. By 1740, the slave trade had made New York the third-busiest port in the British Empire. The city, now home to more than 11,000 residents, continued to be prosperous for a quarter-century more. But resentment was beginning to build in the colony, fuelled by the ever-heavier burden of British taxation.

One very angry young man was Alexander Hamilton, the illegitimate son of a Scottish nobleman. Hamilton arrived in New York from the West Indies in 1772. A fierce intellectual, he enrolled in King's College (which is now Columbia University) and became politically very active – writing anti-British pamphlets, organising an artillery company and serving as a lieutenant colonel in General George Washington's army. In these and many other ways, Hamilton played a central role in a movement that would ultimately change the city – and the country – forever.

'As the British forces left, Washington and his troops marched triumphantly down Broadway to reclaim the city as part of the new United States of America.'

Fearing the brewing revolution, New York's citizenry fled the city in droves in 1775, causing the population to plummet from 25,000 to just 5,000. The following year, 100 British warships sailed into the harbour of this virtual ghost town, carrying with them an intimidating army of 32,000 men – nearly four times the size of Washington's militia. Despite the British presence, Washington organised a reading of the Declaration of Independence, and patriots tore the statue of King George III from its pedestal. Revolution was inevitable.

The battle for New York officially began on 26 August 1776, and Washington's army sustained heavy losses. Nearly a quarter of his men were slaughtered in a two-day period. As Washington retreated, a fire – thought to have been lit by patriots – destroyed 493 buildings, including Trinity Church, the tallest structure on the island. The British found a scorched city, and a populace living in tents.

The city continued to suffer for seven long years. Eventually, of course, Washington's luck turned. As the British forces left, he and his troops marched triumphantly down Broadway to reclaim the city as a part of the newly established United States of America. A week and a half later, on 4 December 1783, the general bade farewell to his dispersing troops at Fraunces Tavern, which still stands to this day on Pearl Street.

Alexander Hamilton, for his part, got busy in the rebuilding effort, laying the groundwork for New York City institutions that remain vital to this day. He started by establishing the city's first bank, the Bank of New York, in 1784. When Washington was inaugurated as the nation's first president in 1789, at Federal Hall on Wall Street, he brought Hamilton on board as the first secretary of the treasury. Thanks to Hamilton's business savvy, trade in stocks and bonds flourished, leading to the establishment in 1792 of what would eventually be known as the New York Stock Exchange. In 1801, Hamilton founded the *Evening Post* newspaper, still in circulation today as the *New York Post*. By 1804, he had helped make New York a world-leading financial centre. The same year that his dream was realised, however, Hamilton was killed by political rival Aaron Burr in a duel in Weehawken, New Jersey.

Cheap date

This date requires a wee bit of planning: before you meet up with your date, sneak off to a market (*see p245*) and fill your backpack with picnic items, a bottle of wine and a pair of plastic cups. Grab your companion by the hand and witness the evolution of the metropolis for yourselves in *Timescapes*, a fascinating 25-minute multimedia film showing every day (every 30mins 10.15am-4.45pm) at the **Museum of the City of New York** (*see p145*). It uses animated maps, historic images and film footage to show the rise of New York City over four centuries, giving life to buildings and street corners you might otherwise breeze by. Admission to the museum is pay-what-you-wish, and the film is free.

After the flick, head out of the museum and two blocks up to 105th Street, where you'll find the **Conservatory Garden**, the only formal garden in Central Park. It's so named for the gorgeous glass conservatory that stood here from 1898 until 1934, when it was torn down. The impressive wrought-iron gate that you pass through originally stood at the opulent Vanderbilt Mansion just down the road. Today, this lush oasis with impressive floral flourishes (such as the 20,000 tulips that mark the end of winter), is a perfect retreat for some good old-fashioned hand holding.

BOOMTOWN

New York continued to grow and prosper for the next three decades. Maritime commerce soared, and Robert Fulton's innovative steamboat made its maiden voyage on the Hudson River in 1807. Eleven years later, a group of merchants introduced regularly scheduled shipping (a novel concept at the time) between New York and Liverpool on the Black Ball Line. Reflecting the city's status as America's shipping centre, the urban landscape was ringed with sprawling piers, towering masts and billowing sails. A boom in the maritime trades lured hundreds of European labourers, and the city – still entirely crammed below Houston Street – grew more and more congested. Where Dutch farms and English estates once stood, taller, far more efficient structures took hold, and Manhattan real estate became the most expensive in the world.

The first man to conquer the city's congestion problem was Mayor DeWitt Clinton, a brilliant politician and a protégé of Alexander Hamilton. Clinton's dream was to organise the entire island of Manhattan in such a way that it could cope with the eventual population creep northwards. In 1807, he created a commission to map out the foreseeable sprawl. It presented its work four years later, and the destiny of this new city was made manifest: it would be a regular grid of crossing thoroughfares, 12 avenues wide and 155 streets long.

Then Clinton literally overstepped his boundaries. In 1811, he presented a plan to build a 363-mile canal linking the Hudson River with Lake Erie. Many of his contemporaries thought it was simply an impossible task: at the time, the longest canal in the world ran a mere 27 miles. But he pressed on and, with a silver tongue to rival a certain modern-day Clinton, raised a truly staggering $6 million for the project.

Work on the Erie Canal began in 1817 and was completed in 1825 – three years ahead of schedule. It shortened the journey between New York City and Buffalo from three weeks to one, and cut the shipping cost per ton from about $100 to $4. Goods, people and money poured into New York, fostering a merchant elite that moved northwards to escape the urban crush. Estates multiplied above Houston Street even as 3,000 new buildings were erected below it – each grander and more imposing than its modest colonial forerunners. Once slavery was officially abolished in New York in 1827, free blacks became an essential part of the local workforce. In 1831, the first public transportation system began operating, pulling its passengers in horse-drawn omnibuses to the city's far reaches.

BUMMERTOWN

As the population grew (swelling to 170,000 by 1830), so did New York City's problems. Tensions bubbled between immigrant newcomers and those who could trace their American lineage back a generation or two. Crime rose and lurid tales filled the 'penny press', the city's proto-tabloids. While wealthy New Yorkers were moving as far 'uptown' as Greenwich Village, the infamous Five Points neighbourhood – the city's first slum – festered in the area now occupied by City Hall, the courthouses and Chinatown. Built on a fetid drained pond, Five Points slowly became the ramshackle home of poor immigrants and blacks. Brutal gangs with colourful names like the Forty Thieves, Plug Uglies and Dead Rabbits often met in bloody clashes in the streets, but what finally sent a mass of 100,000 people scurrying from Downtown was an outbreak of cholera in 1832. In just six weeks, 3,513 New Yorkers died.

'The rioters set fire to the Colored Orphan Asylum and vandalised black homes.'

In 1837, a financial panic left hundreds of Wall Street businesses crumbling. Commerce stagnated at the docks, the real-estate market collapsed, and all but three city banks closed down. Some 50,000 New Yorkers lost their jobs, while 200,000 teetered on the edge of poverty. The panic also sparked an era of civil unrest and violence. In 1849, a xenophobic mob of 8,000 protesting the performance of an English actor at the Astor Place Opera House was met by a militia that opened fire, killing 22 people. But the Draft Riots of 1863, known as 'the bloodiest riots in American history', were much worse. After a law was passed exempting men from the draft for a $300 fee, the (mostly Irish) poor rose up, forming a 15,000-strong force that rampaged through the city. They trashed police stations, draft boards, newspaper offices, expensive shops and wealthy homes before the chaos took a racial turn. Fuelled by anger about the Civil War (for which they blamed blacks), the rioting gangs set fire to the Colored Orphan Asylum and vandalised black homes. Blacks were beaten in the streets, and some were lynched. A federal force of 6,000 men was sent to subdue the violence. After four days and at least 105 deaths, peace was finally restored.

PROGRESSIVE CITY

Amid the chaos of the mid 19th century, the pace of progress continued unabated. Compared alongside the major Southern cities, New York

Building the **Brooklyn Bridge** over troubled waters.

emerged nearly unscathed from the Civil War. The population ballooned to two million, and new technologies revolutionised daily life. The elevated railway, for example, helped extend the population into what are now the Upper East and Upper West Sides, while other trains connected the city with upstate New York, New England and the Midwest. By 1871, train traffic had grown so much that rail tycoon Cornelius Vanderbilt built the original Grand Central Depot, which could accommodate 15,000 passengers at a time. (It was replaced in 1913 by the current Grand Central Terminal.)

One ambitious project was inspired by the harsh winter of 1867. The East River froze over, halting water traffic between Brooklyn and Manhattan for weeks. Brooklyn, by then, had become the nation's third most populous city, and its politicians, businessmen and community leaders realised that the boroughs had to be linked. Thus, the New York Bridge Company was incorporated. Its goal was to build the world's longest bridge, spanning the East River between downtown Manhattan and south-western Brooklyn. Over 16 years (four times longer than projected), 14,000 miles of steel cable were stretched across the 1,595-foot span, while the towers rose a staggering 276 feet above the river. Disasters, worker deaths and corruption dogged the project, but the Brooklyn Bridge opened in triumph on 24 May 1883. It remains one of the city's most beloved symbols.

CORRUPT CITY

As New York recovered from the turmoil of the mid 1800s, one extremely indecorous man, William M 'Boss' Tweed, was pulling the strings. Using his ample charm, the six-foot-tall, 300-pound bookkeeper, chair maker and volunteer fire-fighter became one of the city's most powerful politicians. He had been an alderman and district leader; he served in the US House of Representatives and as a state senator; and he was a chairman of the Democratic General Committee and leader of Tammany Hall, a political organisation formed by local craftsmen to keep the wealthy class's political clout in check. But even though Tweed opened orphanages, poorhouses and hospitals, his good deeds were overshadowed by his and his cohorts' gross embezzlement of city funds.

By 1870, members of the 'Tweed Ring' had created a new city charter, granting themselves control of the City Treasury. Using fake leases and wildly inflated bills for city supplies and services, Tweed and his cronies may ultimately have pocketed as much as $200 million, and caused the city's debt to triple. The work of cartoonist Thomas Nast, who lampooned Tweed in the pages of *Harper's Weekly*, helped to bring the Boss's transgressions to light. Tweed was eventually sued by the city for $6 million, and charged with forgery and larceny. In 1875, while being held in debtor's prison pending bail, he escaped. He was caught in

Spain a year later and died in the can in 1878. But before his final fall from power, Tweed's insatiable greed hurt many: as he was emptying the city's coffers, poverty spread. Then the bond market collapsed, the stock market took a nosedive, factories closed and railroads went bankrupt. By 1874, New York estimated its homeless population at 90,000. That winter, *Harper's Weekly* reported, 900 New Yorkers starved to death.

THE TWO HALVES

In September 1882, a new era dawned brightly when Thomas Alva Edison lit up half a square mile of lower Manhattan with 3,000 electric lamps. One of the newly illuminated offices belonged to a man known for brushing people aside when he strode down the sidewalks: financier JP Morgan, who was essential in bringing New York's, and America's, economy back to life. By bailing out a number of failing railroads, then merging and restructuring them, Morgan jump-started commerce in New York once again. Goods, jobs and also businesses returned to the city, and very soon aggressive businessmen with names like Rockefeller, Carnegie and Frick wanted a piece of the action (none of them, incidentally, was noted for his courtesy, either). They made New York the HQ of Standard Oil and US Steel, corporations that would go on to shape America's economic future and New York's solid reputation as the country's centre of capitalism.

A shining symbol for those less fortunate immigrants also made New York its home around that time: to commemorate America's freedom 100 years after the Declaration of Independence, and to celebrate an international friendship, the French gave the Statue of Liberty to the United States. Sculptor Frédéric-Auguste Bartholdi had created the 151-foot-tall Amazon using funds donated by French citizens, but their generosity could not cover the expense of building her base. Although the project was initially met with apathy by the US government, Hungarian immigrant and publisher Joseph Pulitzer used his *World* newspaper to encourage Americans to pay for a pedestal. When she was finally unveiled in 1886, Lady Liberty measured 305 feet high – taller than the towers of the Brooklyn Bridge.

Between 1892 and 1954, the statue ushered more than 12 million immigrants into New York Harbor. Ellis Island (*photo p28*) opened as an immigration centre in 1892, with expectations of accommodating 500,000 people annually;

Fortune's fools: traders line the streets following the 1929 **stock market crash**. *See p28.*

it processed twice that number in its first year. In the 34-building complex, crowds of would-be Americans were herded through examinations, inspections and interrogations. Fewer than two per cent were sent home, and others moved on, but four million stayed, turning New York into what British playwright Israel Zangwill called 'the great melting pot where all the races of Europe are melting and reforming'.

Many of these new immigrants crowded into dark, squalid tenements on the Lower East Side, while millionaires like the Vanderbilts were building huge French-style mansions along Fifth Avenue. Jacob A Riis, a Danish immigrant and police reporter for the *New York Tribune*, made it his business to expose this dichotomy, however impolite it may have seemed to the wealthy. Employing the then relatively new technology of photography to accompany his written observations, Riis's 1890 book, *How the Other Half Lives,* revealed in graphic terms the bitter conditions of the slums. The intrepid reporter scoured filthy alleys and overcrowded, unheated tenements, many of which lacked the barest minimum of light, ventilation and sanitation. Largely as a result of Riis's work, the state passed the Tenement House Act of 1901, which called for drastic housing reforms.

'With little land left to develop in lower Manhattan, New York embraced the steel revolution and grew steadily skywards.'

EXPANDING CITY

By the close of the 19th century, 40 fragmented governments had been formed in and around Manhattan, creating political confusion on many different levels. On 1 January 1898, the boroughs of Manhattan, Brooklyn, Queens, Staten Island and the Bronx consolidated to form New York City, America's largest city. More and more companies started to move their headquarters to this new metropolis, increasing the demand for office space. With little land left to develop in lower Manhattan, New York embraced the steel revolution and grew steadily skywards. Thus began an all-out race to build the tallest building in the world.

By 1902, New York boasted 66 skyscrapers, including the 20-storey Fuller Building (which is now known as the Flatiron Building) at Fifth Avenue and 23rd Street, and the 25-storey New York Times Tower in Longacre (now Times) Square. Within four years, these two buildings would be completely dwarfed by the 47-storey Singer Building on lower Broadway, which enjoyed the status of tallest building in the world – but for only 18 months. The 700-foot Metropolitan Life Tower on Madison Square claimed the title from the Singer Building in 1909, but the 792-foot-tall Woolworth Building on Broadway and Park Place topped it in 1913 – and amazingly held the distinction for nearly two decades.

If that weren't enough to demonstrate New Yorkers' unending ambition, the city burrowed below the streets at the same time, starting work on its underground transit system in 1900. The $35-million project took nearly four and a half years to complete. Less than a decade after opening, it was the most heavily travelled subway system in the world, carrying almost a billion passengers on its trains every year.

CITY OF MOVEMENT

By 1909, 30,000 factories were operating in the city, churning out everything from heavy machinery to artificial flowers. Brutal factory conditions worsened the situation for workers, who toiled long hours for meagre pay. Young immigrant seamstresses worked 60-plus hours for just $5 a week. Mistrusted and abused, factory workers faced impossible quotas, had their pay docked for minor mistakes and were often locked in the factories during working hours. In the end, it would take a tragedy for real changes to be made.

On 25 March 1911, a fire broke out at the Triangle Shirtwaist Company. Though it was a Saturday, some 500 workers – most of them teenage girls – were toiling in the Greenwich Village factory. Flames spread rapidly through the fabric-filled building, but as the girls rushed to escape, they found many of the exits locked. Roughly 350 made it out on to the adjoining rooftops before the inferno closed off all exits, but 146 young women perished. Many jumped to their deaths from windows on the eighth, ninth and tenth floors. Even in the face of such tragedy, justice was not served: the two factory owners, tried for manslaughter, were acquitted. The disaster did at least spur labour and union organisations, which pushed for – and won – sweeping reforms for factory workers.

Another sort of rights movement was taking hold during this time. Between 1910 and 1913, New York City was the site of the largest women's suffrage rallies in the United States. Harriet Stanton Blatch (who was the daughter of famed suffragette Elizabeth Cady Stanton, and founder of the Equality League of Self Supporting Women) and Carrie Chapman Catt (the organiser of the New York City Women's Suffrage party) arranged attention-getting demonstrations intended to pressure the state

Greetings from Governors Island

Even though Manhattan is an island, it doesn't much feel like one. Maybe it's because humans have managed to pile so much concrete, glass and steel on to such a narrow little strip of land that any sense of natural topography is all but lost. Still, anyone looking for an escape from high-octane Manhattan may be surprised to learn that another island, one offering gentle ocean breezes and many picturesque 19th-century homes, lies within easy reach.

In 1637, so the story goes, a Dutchman 'paid' the native Lenape tribe who were living on the island two axe heads, some beads and a few nails for full ownership of the tiny island. In 1664, the British put a dampener on any plans the Dutch might have had when they took over New Amsterdam and renamed it New York, eventually taking over official ownership of the island, changing the name from Nutten Island (named for its wealth of nut trees) to Governors Island.

The island's strategic location, smack-bang in the middle of New York Harbor, cemented its future as a military outpost, and for more than 200 years it was strictly off limits to the public. All that changed in the mid 1990s, when the United States Coast Guard decided to give up the high cost of island life and decamp. The island sat in limbo for several years while New Yorkers bandied over their plans. In summer 2008, the island will, for the second year, be welcoming visitors from June until 2 September.

Just a five-minute ferry ride from Manhattan, the 172-acre isle still retains a significant chunk of its military-era construction, including Fort Jay, started in 1776, and Castle Williams, completed in 1812 and for years used as a prison. The 22-acre area containing the forts and historical residences is now a national landmark, meaning that plans for casinos or expensive high-rise condos are – thankfully – out of the question. Today, the island is jointly run by the city, the state and National Park Service.

'Each year we're hoping to further expand the activities available,' explains Leslie Koch, president of the Governors Island Preservation & Education Corporation. So far, island activities include biking and a summer-long concert series on Saturday afternoons at Colonel's Row. The National Parks Service also organises free historical walking tours, during which you'll learn about the former Army base's checkered past. Governors Island has been a site for everything from 17th-century transvestites and Civil War internments to President Reagan's famous lunch summit with Mikhail Gorbachev in 1988.

The end of 2007 will see the conclusion of a landscape design competition for a new park and promenade on the island, and the winning team will begin working on the project in early 2008. 'We have a unique opportunity to create something special on Governors

into authorising a referendum on a woman's right to vote. The measure's defeat in 1915 only steeled the suffragettes' resolve. Finally, with the support of Tammany Hall, the law was passed in 1919, challenging the male stranglehold on voting throughout the country. (With New York leading the nation, the 19th Amendment was ratified in 1920.)

In 1919, as New York welcomed troops home from World War I with a parade along Fifth Avenue, the city also celebrated its emergence on the global stage. It had supplanted London as the investment capital of the world, and it had become the centre of publishing, thanks to two men: Pulitzer and Hearst. The *New York Times* had become the country's most respected newspaper; Broadway was the main focal point of American theatre; and Greenwich Village, once the home of an elite gentry, had become a world-class bohemia, where flamboyant artists, writers and political revolutionaries gathered in galleries and coffeehouses. John Reed, reporter on the Russian revolution and author of *Ten Days That Shook the World*, lived here, as did Edna St Vincent Millay, famous for her poetry and her public, unfettered love life.

The more personal side of the women's movement also found a home in New York City. A nurse and midwife who grew up in a family of 11 children, Margaret Sanger was a fierce advocate of birth control and family planning. She opened the first ever birth-control clinic in Brooklyn on 16 October 1916. Finding this unseemly, the police closed the clinic soon after and imprisoned Sanger for 30 days. She pressed on and, in 1921, formed the American Birth Control League – the forerunner of the organisation Planned Parenthood – which researched birth control methods and provided gynaecological services.

Island, a destination that preserves the island's natural beauty and our country's history,' said Dan Doctoroff, the Deputy Mayor for Economic Development.

The short walk from the ferry terminal to the charming historic grounds is like stepping into a time machine that whisks you back to 1950s small-town America, an ivy-league campus and a Revolutionary War battleground all at the same time. It has the almost surreal atmosphere of an abandoned film studio's back lot: turn one corner and you're on the set of *Pleasantville*, turn another and you're in *The Shawshank Redemption*. The script for Governors Island's third century is just waiting to be written.

● *The Governors Island Ferry is located in the Battery Maritime Building, Slip No.7, directly east of the Staten Island Ferry terminal. For tour schedule and ferry times, call 1-212 825 3045 or visit www.nps.gov/gois.*

Forward-thinking women like Sanger set the tone for the Jazz Age, a time when women, now a voting political force, were moving beyond the moral conventions of the 19th century. The country ushered in the Jazz Age in 1919 by ratifying the 18th Amendment, which outlawed the distribution and sale of alcoholic beverages. Prohibition turned the city into the epicentre of bootlegging, speakeasies and organised crime. By the early 1920s, New York boasted 32,000 illegal watering holes – twice the number of legal bars before Prohibition.

In 1925, New Yorkers elected the magnetic James J Walker as the city's mayor. A charming ex-songwriter (as well as a speakeasy patron and skirt-chaser who would later leave his wife for a dancer), Walker was the perfect match for his city's flashy style, hunger for publicity and a consequences-be-damned attitude. Fame flowed in the city's veins: home-run hero Babe Ruth drew a million fans each season to the New York Yankees' games, and sharp-tongued Walter Winchell filled his newspaper columns with celebrity titbits and scandals. Alexander Woollcott, Dorothy Parker, Robert Benchley and other writers met up daily to trade witticisms around a table at the Algonquin Hotel (*see p65*); the result, in February 1925, was *The New Yorker*.

The Harlem Renaissance blossomed at the same time. Writers such as Langston Hughes, Zora Neale Hurston and James Weldon Johnson transformed the African-American experience into lyrical literary works, and white society flocked to the Cotton Club to see genre-defining musicians like Bessie Smith, Cab Calloway, Louis Armstrong and Duke Ellington. (Blacks were not welcome here unless they were performing.) Downtown, Broadway houses were packed out, thanks to brilliant composers

Ellis Island. *See p24.*

and lyricists like George and Ira Gershwin, Irving Berlin, Cole Porter, Lorenz Hart, Richard Rodgers and Oscar Hammerstein II. Towards the end of the '20s, New York-born Al Jolson wowed audiences in *The Jazz Singer*, the first ever talking picture.

THE FALL AND RISE

The dizzying excitement ended on Tuesday, 29 October 1929, when the stock market completely crashed (*photo p24*) and hard times set in. Corruption eroded Mayor Walker's hold on the city: despite a tenure that saw the opening of the Holland Tunnel, the completion of the George Washington Bridge and the construction of the Chrysler and Empire State Buildings, Walker's lustre faded in the growing shadow of graft accusations. He resigned in 1932, as New York, caught in the depths of the Great Depression, had a staggering one million inhabitants who were out of work.

In 1934, an unstoppable force named Fiorello La Guardia took office as mayor, rolling up his sleeves to crack down on mobsters, gambling, smut and government corruption. La Guardia was the son of an Italian father and a Jewish mother. He was a tough-talking politician who was known for nearly coming to blows with other city officials, and he described himself as 'inconsiderate, arbitrary, authoritative, difficult, complicated, intolerant and somewhat theatrical'. La Guardia's act played well: he ushered New York into an era of unparalleled prosperity over the course of his three terms. During World War II, the city's ports and factories proved essential to the war effort. New Yorkers' sense of unity was never more visible than on 14 August 1945, when two million people spontaneously gathered in Times Square to celebrate the end of the war. The 'Little Flower', as La Guardia was known, streamlined city government, paid down the debt and updated the transportation, hospital, reservoir and sewer systems. Additional highways made the city more accessible, and North Beach (now La Guardia) Airport became the city's first ever commercial landing field.

Helping La Guardia to modernise the city was Robert Moses, a hard-nosed visionary who would do much to shape – and in some cases, destroy – New York's landscape. Moses spent 44 years stepping on toes to build expressways, parks, beaches, public housing, bridges and tunnels, creating such landmarks as Shea Stadium, the Lincoln Center, the United Nations complex and the Verrazano-Narrows Bridge.

'Allen Ginsberg, Jack Kerouac and their fellow Beats gathered in Village coffeehouses to create a new voice for poetry.'

THE MODERN CITY

Despite La Guardia's belt-tightening and Moses' renovations, New York began to fall apart financially. When World War II ended, 800,000 industrial jobs disappeared from the city. Factories in need of more space moved to the suburbs, along with nearly five million residents. But more crowding occurred as rural African-Americans and Puerto Ricans flocked to the metropolis in the '50s and '60s, only to meet with ruthless discrimination and a dearth of jobs. Robert Moses' Slum Clearance Committee reduced many neighbourhoods to rubble, forcing out residents in order to build huge, isolating housing projects that became magnets for crime. In 1963, the city also lost Pennsylvania Station – McKim, Mead & White's architectural masterpiece. Over the protests of picketers, the Pennsylvania Railroad Company demolished the site to make way for a modern station and Madison Square Garden. It was a wake-up call for New York: architectural changes were hurtling out of control.

But Moses and his wrecking ball couldn't knock over one steadfast West Village woman. An architectural writer and urban-planning critic by the name of Jane Jacobs organised local residents when the city unveiled its plan to clear a 14-block tract of her neighbourhood to make space for yet more public housing. Her obstinacy was applauded by many, including an influential councilman named Ed Koch (who would become mayor in 1978). The group fought the plan and won, causing Mayor Robert F Wagner to back down. As a result of Jacobs's efforts in the wake of Pennsylvania Station's demolition, the Landmarks Preservation Commission – the first such group in the US – was established in 1965.

At the dawning of the age of Aquarius, the city harboured its share of innovative creators. Allen Ginsberg, Jack Kerouac and their fellow Beats gathered in Village coffeehouses to create a new voice for poetry. A folk music scene brewed in tiny clubs around Bleecker Street, showcasing musicians such as Bob Dylan. A former advertising illustrator from Pittsburgh named Andy Warhol began turning the images of mass consumerism into deadpan, ironic art statements. Gay men and women, long a hidden part of the city's history, came out into the streets in 1969's Stonewall riots, sparked when patrons at the Stonewall Inn on Christopher Street resisted a police raid – giving birth to the modern gay rights movement.

By the early 1970s, deficits had forced heavy cutbacks in city services. The streets were dirty, subway cars and buildings were scrawled with graffiti, crime skyrocketed and the city's debt deepened to $6 billion. Despite the huge downturn, construction commenced on the World Trade Center; when completed, in 1973, its twin 110-storey towers were the world's tallest buildings. Even as the Trade Center rose, the city became so desperately overdrawn that Mayor Abraham Beame appealed to the federal government for financial assistance in 1975. Yet President Gerald Ford refused to bail out the city, a decision summed up by the immortal *Daily News* headline: 'Ford to city: drop dead'.

The President's callousness certainly didn't help matters during this time. Around the mid '70s, Times Square degenerated into a morass of sex shops and porn palaces, drug use rose and subway ridership hit an all-time low. To make situations worse, in 1977, serial killer

Buy low, sell high and leave a good-looking corpse: boom time on **Wall Street**. *See p30.*

Further reading

Herbert Asbury *The Gangs of New York: An Informal History of the Underworld*
A racy journalistic portrait of the city at the turn of the 19th century.
Robert A Caro *The Power Broker*
A biography of Robert Moses, New York's mid-20th-century master builder, and his chequered legacy.
Federal Writers' Project *The WPA Guide to New York City*
A wonderful snapshot of the 1930s by writers who were employed under FDR's New Deal.
Sanna Feirstein *Naming New York*
How Manhattan places got their names.
Mitchell Fink & Lois Mathias *Never Forget: An Oral History of September 11, 2001*
A collection of first-person accounts.
Clifton Hood *722 Miles: The Building of the Subways and How They Transformed New York*
The title adequately describes the content.
Kenneth T Jackson (ed) *The Encyclopedia of New York City*
An ambitious and useful reference guide.
David Levering Lewis *When Harlem Was in Vogue*
A study of the Harlem Renaissance.
Shaun O'Connell *Remarkable, Unspeakable New York*
A history of New York as literary inspiration.
Mitchell Pacelle *Empire*
The story of the fight to build the Empire State Building.
Jacob A Riis *How the Other Half Lives*
A pioneering photojournalistic record of squalid tenement life.
Alice Rose George (ed) *Here Is New York*
A collection of nearly 900 powerful amateur photos that document the aftermath of September 11, 2001.
Marie Salerno & Arthur Gelb *The New York Pop-up Book*
An interactive historical account of NYC.
Luc Sante *Low Life*
Opium dens and brothels in New York from the 1840s to the 1920s.
Mike Wallace & Edwin G Burrows *Gotham: A History of New York City to 1898*
The first volume in a planned mammoth history of NYC.

For other literature about New York, *see p385.*

Son of Sam terrorised the city, and a blackout one hot August night that same year, led to widespread looting and arson. The angst of the time fuelled the punk culture that rose up in downtown clubs like CBGB, where the Ramones and other bands played fast and loud. At the same time, celebrities, designers and models converged on Midtown to disco their nights away at Studio 54.

The Wall Street boom of the '80s (*photo p29*) and fiscal petitioning by then-mayor Ed Koch brought money flooding back into New York. Gentrification glamorised neighbourhoods like Soho, Tribeca and the East Village. But deeper ills persisted. In 1988, a demonstration against the city's efforts to impose a strict curfew and displace the homeless away from Tompkins Square Park erupted into a violent clash with the police. Crack use was endemic in the ghettos, homelessness was rising and AIDS became a new scourge. By 1989, citizens were restless for change. They turned to David N Dinkins, electing him the city's first African-American mayor. A distinguished, softly-spoken man, Dinkins held office for only a single term – one marked by a record murder rate, flaring racial tensions in Washington Heights, Crown Heights and Flatbush, and the explosion of a terrorist bomb in the World Trade Center that killed six, injured 1,000 and foreshadowed the catastrophic attacks of 2001.

'As cases of police brutality grabbed the headlines, crime plummeted and New York became safer than it had been in decades.'

Deeming the polite Dinkins ineffective, New Yorkers voted in former federal prosecutor Rudolph Giuliani. Like his predecessors Peter Stuyvesant and Fiorello La Guardia, Giuliani was an abrasive leader who used bully tactics to get things done. His 'quality of life' campaign cracked down on everything from drug dealing and pornography to unsolicited windshield washing. Even as multiple cases of severe police brutality grabbed the headlines, crime plummeted, tourism soared and New York became cleaner and safer than it had been in decades. Times Square was transformed into a family-friendly tourist destination, and the dot-com explosion brought a generation of young wannabe millionaires to the Flatiron District's Silicon Alley. Giuliani's second term as mayor would close, however, on a devastating tragedy.

On 11 September 2001, terrorists flew two hijacked passenger jets into the Twin Towers

Michael Bloomberg.

of the World Trade Center, collapsing the entire complex and killing nearly 2,800 people. Amid the trauma, the attack triggered a citywide sense of unity, and New Yorkers muscled together and did what they could to help their fellow citizens, from feeding emergency crews around the clock to cheering on rescue workers en route to Ground Zero.

Two months later, billionaire Michael Bloomberg was elected mayor and took on the daunting task of repairing not only the city's skyline but also its battered economy and shattered psyche. He proved adept at steering the city back on the road to health as the stock market revived, downtown businesses re-emerged and plans for rebuilding the Trade Center were drawn. True to form, however, New Yorkers debated the future of the site for more than a year until architect Daniel Libeskind was awarded the redevelopment job in 2003. His plan, called 'Memory Foundations', aims to reconcile rebuilding and remembrance, with parks, plazas, a cultural centre, a performing arts centre, a memorial and a very sleek new office tower. The foundations for David Childs' Freedom Tower were laid in late 2006 and the project should be completed by 2015. Nevertheless, conflict continues to plague every step of the project (*see also p44*).

The summer of 2003 saw a huge electricity blackout that shut down the city (and much of the eastern seaboard). New Yorkers were sweaty but calm, and again proved that they possessed surprisingly strong reserves of civility as the city's cafés set up candlelit tables and bodegas handed out free ice-cream.

And yet, despite Bloomberg's many efforts to make New York a more considerate and civil place – imposing a citywide smoking ban in bars and restaurants and a strict noise ordinance that would even silence the jingling of ice-cream vans – New Yorkers continue to uphold their hard-edged image. The 2004 Republican National Convention brought out hundreds of thousands of peace marchers who had no trouble expressing how they felt about the war in Iraq. Still, the oft-cranky citizenry swooned for Christo and Jeanne-Claude's *The Gates* – the 7,503 billowing orange fabric and metal gates that lined 23 miles of paths in Central Park for two weeks in February 2005. But just as quickly, it was back to business as usual: local belly-aching helped kill a plan to build a 75,000-seat stadium on Manhattan's West Side, squashing Bloomberg and Co's dream to bring the 2012 Olympic Games to the Big Apple. In 2007, Bloomberg jumped on the eco bandwagon and announced plans to green up NYC, aiming to reduce greenhouse emissions by 30 per cent; fight traffic jams by making motorists pay driving fees in parts of Manhattan; and ensure that every New Yorker is no more than a ten-minute walk from a park.

In true New York fashion, we can assure you that Bloomberg won't be taking any critiques lying down. But let's face it, if any of these rude, abrasive or inconsiderate people had their attitudes adjusted, New Yorkers wouldn't be where they are today: thriving in a city that is often looked upon as the capital of the world. And no doubt they would offer a big, disrespectful Bronx cheer to those who disagree.

Key events

1524 Giovanni da Verrazano sails into New York Harbor.
1624 First Dutch settlers establish New Amsterdam at the foot of Manhattan Island.
1626 Peter Minuit purchases Manhattan for goods worth 60 guilders.
1639 The Broncks settle north of Manhattan.
1646 Village of Breuckelen founded.
1664 Dutch rule ends; New Amsterdam renamed New York.
1754 King's College (now Columbia University) founded.
1776 Battle for New York begins; fire ravages the city.
1783 George Washington's troops march triumphantly down Broadway.
1784 Alexander Hamilton founds the Bank of New York.
1785 New York becomes the nation's capital.
1789 President Washington inaugurated at Federal Hall on Wall Street.
1792 New York Stock Exchange founded.
1804 New York becomes the country's most populous city, with 80,000 inhabitants; New York Historical Society founded.
1811 Mayor DeWitt Clinton's grid plan for Manhattan introduced.
1825 New York Gas Light Company completes installation of first gas lamps on Broadway; Erie Canal completed.
1827 Slavery officially abolished in New York.
1833 The *New York Sun*'s lurid tales give birth to tabloid journalism.
1851 The *New York Daily Times* (now the *New York Times*) published.
1858 Work on Central Park begins; Macy's opens.
1870 Metropolitan Museum of Art founded.
1883 Brooklyn Bridge opens.
1886 Statue of Liberty unveiled.
1890 Jacob A Riis publishes *How the Other Half Lives*.
1891 Carnegie Hall opens with a concert conducted by Tchaikovsky.
1892 Ellis Island opens.
1895 Oscar Hammerstein's Olympia Theater opens, creating Broadway theatre.
1898 The city consolidates the five boroughs.
1902 The Fuller (Flatiron) Building becomes the world's first skyscraper.
1903 The New York Highlanders (later the New York Yankees) play their first game.
1904 New York's first subway line opens; Longacre Square becomes Times Square.
1908 First ball dropped to celebrate the new year in Times Square.
1911 The Triangle Shirtwaist Fire claims nearly 150 lives, spurring unionisation.
1923 Yankee Stadium opens.
1924 First Macy's Christmas Parade held – now the Thanksgiving Day Parade.
1929 The stock market crashes; Museum of Modern Art opens.
1931 George Washington Bridge completed; the Empire State Building opens; the Whitney Museum opens.
1934 Fiorello La Guardia takes office; Tavern on the Green opens.
1939 New York hosts a World's Fair.
1946 The New York Knickerbockers debut.
1950 United Nations complex completed.
1953 Robert Moses spearheads building of the Cross Bronx Expressway; 40,000 homes demolished in the process.
1957 The New York Giants baseball team moves to San Francisco; Brooklyn Dodgers move to Los Angeles.
1962 New York Mets debut at the Polo Grounds; Philharmonic Hall (later Avery Fisher Hall), the first building in Lincoln Center, opens.
1964 Verrazano-Narrows Bridge completed; World's Fair held in Flushing Meadows-Corona Park in Queens.
1970 First New York City Marathon held.
1973 World Trade Center completed.
1975 On the verge of bankruptcy, the city is snubbed by the federal government; *Saturday Night Live* debuts.
1977 Serial killer David 'Son of Sam' Berkowitz arrested; Studio 54 opens; 4,000 arrested during citywide blackout.
1989 David N Dinkins is elected the city's first black mayor.
1993 A terrorist bomb explodes in the World Trade Center, killing six and injuring 1,000.
1997 Murder rate lowest in 30 years.
2001 Hijackers fly two jets into the Twin Towers, killing nearly 2,800 and demolishing the World Trade Center.
2004 The Statue of Liberty reopens for the first time since 9/11; the Republican National Convention brings out hundreds of thousands of protesters.
2005 Christo and Jeanne-Claude decorate Central Park with art installation *The Gates*; New York loses its bid for the 2012 Olympics.
2007 Mayor Bloomberg unveils long-term vision for a more eco-friendly New York.

New York Today

Howard Halle, *Time Out New York* magazine's editor-at-large, delivers the latest from Gotham.

Depending on how you look at things, New York is either: a) entering the sixth year of a remarkable recovery in the wake of the 9/11 attacks, or b) continuing to enjoy a 25-plus-year climb out of economic ruin that began back in the administration of Mayor Edward I Koch – one which even the World Trade Center attacks couldn't derail. One person, former mayor and current Republican presidential hopeful Rudy Giuliani, opts for c) namely, that he single-handedly rescued New York from the abyss when he assumed the mayoralty in 1993… but that's another story. Whichever the case, even as bankruptcies and home mortgage defaults rise across the country, real estate continues to rocket in Gotham, while Wall Street hedge-fund managers continue to make obscene amounts of money (unless, that is, this year's downturn in the markets finally signal the end of the party).

GOOD OL' DAYS

New York dwellers recently marked the 30th anniversaries of two events in the city's history that represent New York's modern nadir: the Son of Sam murders, and the Great Blackout of 1977, which precipitated days of looting in Harlem and the Bed-Stuy section of Brooklyn. Today, both areas are rapidly gentrifying, as moneyed elites and fashionable types transform previously sketchy streets into neighbourhoods safe enough for Starbucks. Indeed, the US Census Bureau issued a report this summer showing that the city's white population – that all-important indicator of economic good times – increased significantly over the past five years, while it's African-American population had declined. What these changes mean for the city's creative energy remains to be seen; that long-ago Summer of Sam also brought the first stirrings of hip hop culture in the Bronx.

Inevitably perhaps, given the distance of time and the comfort of fattened bank accounts, New Yorkers started to recall both the Blackout and the Son of Sam killings with a degree of nostalgic fondness, as if those twin horrors bestowed a retroactive toughness on living there – without, that is, having to deal with the inconvenience of everyday crime. Of course, plenty of things happened this year to suggest that living in New York City is still something of a crap-shoot. But the overall reduction in crime in recent years and the rise in economic good fortune has led to an overall soothing of concerns over personal safety, which in turn seems to be freeing up the minds of New Yorkers to fret over an altogether different concern: the issue of sustainability.

HOW GREEN IS NYC?

Sustainability is a hot topic of discussion in New York (as it is all over the world right now), and the prospect of global warming drastically changing the quality of human life is no joke. A torrential rainstorm in August 2007 flooded the subway, bringing trains to a halt citywide. The storm set off a tornado – the first in New York in living memory – that touched down in Bay Ridge, Brooklyn, bringing with it 135mph winds and causing hundreds of millions of dollars in property damage. New York, of course, has been visited by plagues of nature throughout its storied past (including a major hurricane – Gloria – in the '80s) but, like so many Americans, New Yorkers have become increasingly aware of global warming, and are more likely to blame it for natural disasters. It doesn't hurt either that the city in being led by the most environmentally proactive mayor in its history, Michael Bloomberg.

During 2007's Earth Day festivities, Mayor Bloomberg announced an hugely ambitious undertaking to make New York 'green' by 2030, hailing it as 'the broadest-scale attack on the causes of global warming and environmental degradation that any city has ever undertaken'. Plan NYC 2030, as it's now called, will, among other things, generate the city's electrical needs through recycled garbage; plant a million new trees; turn unsightly asphalt lots into grassy playing fields; build open plazas in every neighbourhood; allocate $15 million dollars to reclaim polluted former industrial sites for residential and commercial redevelopment; and build 1,800 miles of new bicycle paths.

But its most controversial proposal by far and away is the notion of charging drivers $8 on top of existing tolls to enter Manhattan below 86th Street. The scheme, known as congestion pricing, has been roundly denounced by outer-borough city and state representatives for saddling their constituents with an undue financial burden (as indeed it would do for Manhattanites south of 86th planning to drive off the island and back in again). Congestion pricing was almost scuttled by the New York State Assembly; only a last-minute intervention by New York State Governor Elliot Spitzer kept the scheme alive. In August 2007, the Federal government agreed to help fund the scheme if the State government finally approves it – which is no sure thing. And, many would say, it's just as well. Congestion pricing isn't likely to lighten the mood of local drivers, recently ranked second in the country after Miami for road rage incidents, according to a survey by AutoVantage, a Connecticut-based drivers club.

Sustainability ahoy on the **Science Barge**.

Aside from the mayor's plan, the biggest thing happening on the city's sustainability horizon is the 'green' skyscrapers that have recently opened or are currently rising. These towers, which include the headquarters for the Hearst publishing empire, designed by Lord Foster on West 57th Street, are among the first to obtain so-called green certification.

Of course, the building trade isn't the only outfit in the city promising a greener future. Companies as diverse as Pottery Barn and Hertz Rent-A-Car are making similar (and sometimes questionable) claims for the greenness of their services and products. The Science Barge that was parked in the Hudson River for most of 2007 also helped to fuel the citizenry's lust for ecologically-friendly practices, with demonstrations of solar power and greenhouse gardens. Still, it's important to remember a couple of obvious truisms about sustainability in New York: people build up, not out, thus avoiding the impact of suburban sprawl, and when it isn't being flooded, the city's subway does get people around town quickly, obviating the need for a car. On this basis alone, it would seem that New York may well be one of the greenest places in the entire country.

THE OTHER GREEN

Transit Authority officials are warning riders that fares are likely to go up in 2008. Whatever the increase, it's likely to be rather small beer compared to the cost of renting a New York apartment. Indeed, according to a report by the rental brokerage firm Citi Habitats, New Yorkers pay more for rent than anywhere else in the United States. It's not hard to believe when you consider the average monthly rent for a studio apartment throughout the five boroughs is now $2,000, while a one-bedroom fetches an average of $2,700. In Manhattan, the average climbs to $2,825. And if you have a family and need more room? Well, just be sure you have plenty of green in your wallet: three-bedrooms average a princely $5,534 per month!

CON ED-ACHE

People paying that kind of money for rent are at least likely to be moving into a place that has undergone some level of renovation. The city's infrastructure, on the other hand, is decidedly decrepit. This may be especially true of the facilities maintained by the city's major power company, Con Edison. In July 2007, New Yorkers were suddenly jolted by the explosion of a steam pipe running under a street near Grand Central Station during the afternoon rush hour. The hot pipe, one of many Con Ed uses to provide heat to commercial buildings below 96th Street in Manhattan, was 83 years old.

The resulting blast beneath the intersection of East 41st Street and Lexington Avenue could be heard all over Midtown and was mistaken by many for being a terrorist bomb. It shot a geyser of superheated steam, mixed with mud, rust and pavement debris, into the air, flipping a truck in the process, while killing one person and injuring 30 others, before leaving a crater measuring 35 by 40 feet. The area had to be sealed off while officials determined whether the blast had released asbestos, common in construction during the period when the pipe was laid. (It had, though only in trace amounts.)

As if that weren't bad enough, a woman nearly died a couple of months earlier when a metal grate covering a Con Ed utility box under the sidewalk gave way beneath her. She fell 15 feet into a wet mud-filled pit containing wires surging with 13,000 volts – a lethal combination that the woman miraculously escaped thanks to a rescue by the city's Fire Department. These events were just two of a string of incidents that have sullied the power giant's reputation over the past year. Since then, the Queens blackout of 2006 (during which, unlike in 1977, luckily no riots ensued) raised the question of which is the greater menace: terrorism, global warming or Consolidated Edison?

BIG BROTHER IS NOW WATCHING

Strangely enough, although 9/11 took a greater toll in lives than London's subway bombings, New York never really resorted to the same widespread use of surveillance cameras as London's 'Ring of Steel' security system, installed in the 1990s to deter IRA bombings. That is, until now.

Recently, the NYPD announced that by early 2008, the first phase of a similar network will be in place, when more than 100 surveillance cameras go online to monitor traffic moving through Lower Manhattan round the clock. At the same time, this is just the beginning of a much larger deployment, known as the Lower Manhattan Security Initiative. Once it's fully operational, the surveillance system will have expanded to include a complex web of cameras and licence-plate readers numbering in the thousands, as well as pivoting gates at certain intersections that could close in a moment's notice to stop and detain a suspect vehicle. Face recognition hardware may be also part of a package expected to be completed by 2010.

Understandably, civil liberties advocates are extremely alarmed at the idea, and worry about its high potential for abuse. They point out that London's Ring of Steel did nothing to prevent 7 July, 2005, though British authorities say it did prove invaluable in identifying and apprehending the perpetrators of those attacks. Certainly it seems fair to say that reports like the one in the summer 2007 (which proved to be unsubstantiated) of a planned Al Queda radiological attack in the Financial District will do nothing to deter the eventual installation of just such a system.

PRESIDENT MAYOR?

We've already mentioned the Presidential aspirations of former Mayor Giuliani, but the city was thrown into a veritable tizzy recently when the current Mayor, Michael Bloomberg, announced that he was switching his party affiliation from Republican to Independent – a move widely assumed to mean that Mayor Mike was planning to throw his hat into the ring. Bloomberg himself was tight-lipped about making the change, and has so far not announced plans to run for President. But as a billionaire several times over, he certainly has the means to finance a campaign. This raises the prospect of a three-way race for the White House involving Bloomberg, Giuliani and Democratic front-runner Hillary Rodham Clinton – all New Yorkers. Which means that even if the markets continue to tumble, and New York makes a return to those anarchic days of 1977, the president, at least, will know where to get a good pastrami on rye.

Grand Central Terminal. *See p38.*

Architecture

A story of the invention – and reinvention – of a skyline.

Under New York's gleaming exoskeleton of steel and glass lies the heart of a 17th-century Dutch city. It began at the Battery and New York Harbor, one of the greatest naturally formed deep-water ports in the world. The former Alexander Hamilton Custom House, now the **National Museum of the American Indian** (*see p95*), was built by Cass Gilbert in 1907 and is a symbol of the harbour's significance in Manhattan's growth. Before 1913, the city's chief source of revenue was customs duties. Gilbert's domed marble edifice is suitably monumental – its carved figures of the Four Continents are by Daniel Chester French, the sculptor of the Lincoln Memorial in Washington, DC.

The Dutch influence is still traceable in the downtown web of narrow, winding lanes, reminiscent of the streets in medieval European cities. Because the Cartesian grid that rules the city was laid out by the Commissioners' Plan in 1811, only a few samples of Dutch architecture remain, mostly off the beaten path. One of these buildings is the 1785 **Dyckman Farmhouse Museum** (4881 Broadway, at 204th Street, www.dyckmanfarmhouse.org) in Inwood, Manhattan's northernmost neighbourhood. Its decorative brickwork and gambrel roof reflect the architectural fashion of the late 18th century. The single oldest house still standing today in the five boroughs is the **Pieter Claesen Wyckoff House Museum** (5816 Clarendon Road, at Ralph Avenue, Flatbush, Brooklyn, www.wyckoffassociation.org). First erected in around 1652, it is a typical Dutch farmhouse with deep eaves and roughly shingled walls. The **Lefferts Homestead** (Prospect Park, Flatbush Avenue, Prospect Heights, Brooklyn), built between 1777 and 1783, combines its gambrel roof with column-supported porches, a hybrid style popular during the Federal period.

In Manhattan, the only building extant from pre-Revolutionary times is the stately columned and quoined **St Paul's Chapel** (*see p100*), completed in 1766 (a spire was added in 1796). George Washington, a parishioner here, was officially received in the chapel after his 1789 presidential inauguration. The Enlightenment ideals upon which the nation was founded influenced the church's highly democratic, non-hierarchical layout. **Trinity Church** (*see p100*) of 1846, one of the first and finest Gothic

Revival churches in the country, was designed by Richard Upjohn. It's difficult to imagine now that Trinity's crocketed, finialed 281-foot-tall spire held sway for decades as the tallest structure in Manhattan.

Holdouts remain from each epoch of the city's architectural history. An outstanding example of Greek Revival from the first half of the 19th century is the 1842 **Federal Hall National Memorial** (*see p100*), the mighty marble colonnade that was built to mark the site where George Washington took his oath of office. A larger-than-life statue of Washington by the sculptor John Quincy Adams Ward stands in front. The city's most celebrated blocks of Greek Revival townhouses, built in the 1830s, are known simply as the **Row** (1-13 Washington Square North, between Fifth Avenue & Washington Square West); they're exemplars of the more genteel metropolis of Henry James and Edith Wharton.

Greek Revival gave way to Renaissance-inspired Beaux Arts architecture, which itself reflected the imperial ambitions of a wealthy

Top-billing buildings

New York scores most mentions on a list of America's favourite architecture.

Back in 2007, the American Institute of Architecture (AIA) decided, as part of its 150th birthday celebrations, to find out which American buildings were the most beloved by it's citizenry. After much polling, they came up with the top 150. The good news? While Washington prevails in the top 10, New York garnered a whopping 33 buildings on the list (see below, by ranking), including classics like the **Empire State Building** (in first place) and the **Chrysler Building**, as well as the two cutting-edge **Apple** buildings, one in SoHo, an inventive reworking of a 1920s neoclassical former post office, and the newer Fifth Avenue, which opened in 2006 with an extraordinary glass cube design.

'This poll of America's Favorite Architecture confirms that architecture resonates with people,' said RK Stewart, AIA president. 'The choice of the Empire State Building [as number one] shows that when you ask people to select their favourites, they choose buildings and designs that most symbolised innovation and the spirit of their community – but also, more importantly – they choose structures that hold a place in their hearts.'

RANKING	BUILDING NAME
1	**Empire State Building** (*see p39*)
9	**Chrysler Building** (*see p39*)
11	**St Patrick's Cathedral** (*see p133*)
13	**Grand Central Station** (*see p38*)
16	**St Regis Hotel** (*2 E 55th Street, 1-212 753 4500*)
17	**Metropolitan Museum of Art** (*see p143*)
19	**World Trade Center** (*see p98*)
20	**Brooklyn Bridge** (*see p158*)
23	**Cathedral of St John the Divine** (*see p149*)
33	**Rose Center for Earth and Space** (*see p148*)
44	**Woolworth Building** (*see p39*)
46	**Waldorf Astoria** (*see p72*)
47	**New York Public Library** (*see p133*)
48	**Carnegie Hall** (*see p321*)
53	**Apple Store Fifth Avenue** (*767 Fifth Avenue, 1-212 336 1440*)
56	**Rockefeller Center** (*see p133*)
68	**New York Times Tower** (*see p41*)
71	**Hearst Tower** (*see p42*)
72	**Flatiron Building** (*see p39*)
74	**Guggenheim Museum** (*see p145*)
81	**Plaza Hotel** (*see p65*)
84	**Yankee Stadium** (*see p334*)
86	**Lincoln Center** (*see p328*)
87	**The Dakota Apartments** (*see p147*)
100	**Radio City Music Hall** (*see p319*)
105	**Time Warner Center** (*see p146*)
111	**United Nations Headquarters** (*see p39*)
115	**TWA Terminal, JFK Airport** (*see p366*)
125	**Citicorp Center** (*see p133*)
133	**Royalton Hotel** (*see p67*)
141	**Apple Store SoHo** (*103 Prince Street, 1-212 226 3126*)
143	**Penn Station** (*see p123*)
146	**Museum of Modern Art (MoMA)** (*see p131*)

Inspired: the **Chrysler Building**.

young nation during the Gilded Age of the late 19th century. Like Emperor Augustus, who boasted that he had found Rome a city of brick and left it a city of marble, the firm of McKim, Mead & White built noble civic monuments and palazzi for the rich. The best-known buildings of the classicist Charles Follen McKim include the main campus of **Columbia University** (*see p149*), which was begun in the 1890s, and the austere 1906 **Morgan Library** (*see p122*). His partner, socialite and bon vivant Stanford White (scandalously murdered by his mistress's husband in 1906) designed more festive spaces, such as the **Metropolitan Club** (1 E 60th Street, at Fifth Avenue) and the extraordinarily luxe Villard Houses of 1882, now part of the 100-year-old **New York Palace Hotel** (*see p65*).

Another Beaux Arts treasure from the city's grand metropolitan era is Carrère & Hastings's sumptuous white-marble **New York Public Library** of 1911 (*see p133*), built on the site of a former Revolutionary War battleground; the site later hosted an Egyptian Revival water reservoir and, currently, the greensward of Bryant Park. The 1913 travertine-lined **Grand Central Terminal** (*see p134* and *photo p36*) remains the elegant foyer in town, thanks to preservationists (including Jacqueline Kennedy Onassis) who saved it from the wrecking ball.

UP, UP AND AWAY

Cast-iron architecture peaked in the latter half of the 19th century, coinciding roughly with the Civil War era. Iron and steel components freed architects from the bulk, weight and cost of stone construction, and allowed them to build taller structures. Cast-iron columns – cheap to mass-produce – could support a tremendous amount of weight. The façades of many Soho buildings, with their intricate details of Italianate columns, were manufactured on assembly lines and could be ordered in pieces from catalogues. This led to an aesthetic of uniform building façades, which had a direct impact on the steel skyscrapers of the following generation and continues to inform New York's skyline today. To enjoy one of the most telling vistas of skyscraper history, gaze northwards from the 1859 **Cooper Union** building in the East Village (*see p110*), the oldest existing steel-beam-framed building in America.

The most visible effect of the move towards cast-iron construction was the way it opened up solid-stone façades to expanses of glass. In fact, window-shopping came into vogue in the 1860s. Mrs Lincoln bought the White House china at the **Haughwout Store** (488-492 Broadway, at Broome Street). The 1857 building's Palladian-style façade recalls Renaissance Venice, but its regular, open fenestration was also a portent of the future. (Look carefully: the cast-iron elevator sign is a relic of the world's first working safety passenger elevator, designed by Elisha Graves Otis in 1852.)

'The new century saw a frenzy of skyward manufacture, resulting in buildings of record-breaking height.'

Once engineers perfected steel, which is stronger and lighter than iron, and created the interlocking steel-cage construction that distributed the weight of a building over its entire frame, the sky was the limit. New York is fortunate to have one building by the great skyscraper innovator Louis Sullivan, the 1898 **Bayard-Condict Building** (65-69 Bleecker Street, between Broadway & Lafayette Street). Though only 13 storeys tall, Sullivan's building, covered with richly decorative terracotta, was one of the earliest to have a purely vertical design rather than a design that imitated the horizontal styles of the past. Sullivan wrote that a skyscraper 'must be tall, every inch of it tall.… From bottom to top, it is a unit without a single dissenting line'.

Chicago architect Daniel H Burnham's 1902 21-storey **Flatiron Building** (aka the Fuller Building; *see p120*) is another standout New York building; its height and modern design combined with traditional masonry decoration, breathtaking even today, was made possible only by its steel-cage construction.

The new century saw a frenzy of skyward manufacture, resulting in buildings of record-breaking height; the now modest-looking 30-storey, 391-foot-tall **Park Row Building** (15 Park Row, between Ann & Beekman Streets) was, when it was built in 1899, the tallest building in the world. That record was shattered by the 612-foot Singer Building in 1908 (demolished in the 1960s); the 700-foot **Metropolitan Life Tower** (1 Madison Avenue, at 24th Street) of 1909, modelled after the Campanile in Venice's Piazza San Marco; and Cass Gilbert's Gothic masterpiece, the 792-foot **Woolworth Building** (*see p102*). The Woolworth reigned in solitary splendour until William van Alen's homage to the Automobile Age, the 1930 **Chrysler Building** (*see p134*), soared to 1,046 feet, its spire still one of the city's most notable landmarks today.

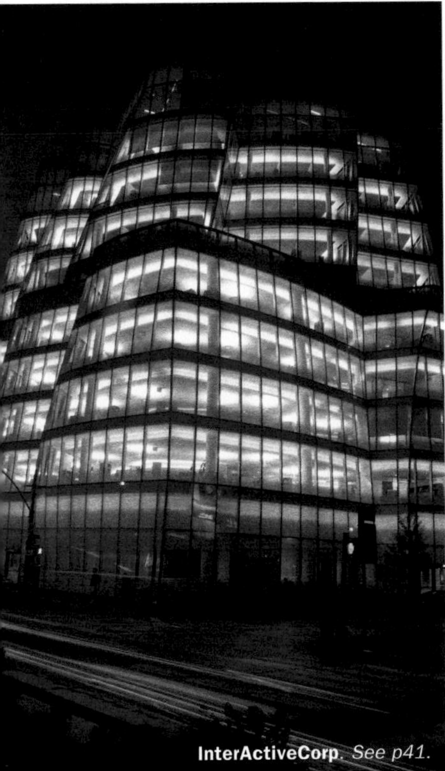

InterActiveCorp. *See p41.*

In a highly publicised race, the Chrysler was outstripped 13 months later, in 1931, by Shreve, Lamb & Harmon's 1,250-foot-tall **Empire State Building** (*see p130*), which has since lost its title to other giants: the 1,450-foot Sears Tower in Chicago (1974); in Kuala Lumpur, Malaysia, the 1,483-foot Petronas Towers (1996); and the current record holder, the 1,671-foot Taipei 101 in Taiwan (2004). But the Empire State remains the quintessential skyscraper, one of the most recognisable buildings in the world, with its broad base, narrow shaft and distinctive needled crown. (The giant ape that scaled the side might have something to do with it too.)

The Empire State's setbacks, retroactively labelled art deco (such buildings were then simply called 'modern'), were actually a response to the zoning code of 1916, which required a building's upper storeys to be tapered in order not to block out sunlight and air circulation to the streets. The code engendered some of the city's most fanciful architectural designs, such as the ziggurat-crowned 1926 **Paramount Building** (1501 Broadway, between 43rd & 44th Streets) and the romantically slender spire of the former **Cities Service Building** (70 Pine Street, at Pearl Street), illuminated from within like an enormous rare gem.

BOLD NEW WORLD

The post-World War II period saw the rise of the International Style, pioneered by such giants as Le Corbusier and Ludwig Mies van der Rohe. The style's most visible symbol was the all-glass façade, like that found on the sleek slab of the **United Nations Headquarters** (*see p134*). The International Style relied on a new set of aesthetics: minimal decoration, clear expression of construction, an honest use of materials and a near-Platonic harmony of proportions. **Lever House** (390 Park Avenue, between 53rd & 54th Streets), designed by Gordon Bunshaft of Skidmore, Owings & Merrill, was the city's first all-steel-and-glass structure when it was built in 1952 (it recently received an award-winning brush-up). It's almost impossible to imagine the radical vision this glass construction represented on the all-masonry corridor of Park Avenue, because nearly every building since has followed suit. Mies van der Rohe's celebrated bronze-skinned **Seagram Building** (375 Park Avenue, between 52nd & 53rd Streets), which reigns in imperious isolation in its own plaza, is the epitome of the architect's cryptic dicta 'Less is more' and 'God is in the details'. The Seagram's detailing is exquisite – the custom-made bolts securing the miniature bronze piers that run the length of the façade must be polished by hand annually to keep them from oxidising and turning green. With this heady combination of grandeur and attention to detail, it can truly be called the Rolls-Royce of skyscrapers.

High modernism began to show cracks in its façade during the mid 1960s. By then, New York had built too many such structures in Midtown and below, and besides, the public had never fully warmed to the undecorated style (though for those with a little insight, the best glass boxes are fully rewarding aesthetic experiences). And the International Style's sheer arrogance in trying to supplant the traditional city structure didn't endear the movement to anyone, either. The **MetLife Building** (200 Park Avenue, at 45th Street), originally the Pan Am Building of 1963, was the prime culprit, not so much because of its design by Walter Gropius of the Bauhaus, but because of its presumptuous location, straddling Park

Monumental mess

Every year, the **World Monuments Fund** (WMF) releases its list of 100 of the world's most endangered sites, helping to 'safeguard the world's irreplaceable heritage'. Most of the trouble spots announced on 2008's list were in far-off lands like Peru (Machu Picchu), Malta (Fort St Elmo) and Afghanistan (the Bamiyan Buddhas, destroyed by Taliban forces in 2001). What's surprised many, though, was the number of endangered structures on the list located in the US – seven in total, including the Salk Institute in La Jolla, California; the Frank Lloyd Wright-designed Florida Southern University Historic Campus in Lakeland, Florida; and that famed interstate of screen and song, Route 66. And one of them is right in New Yorkers' backyard: the once-famous **New York State Pavilion** (*see p171*) in Flushing, Queens, created for the 1964 World's Fair by renowned architect Philip Johnson. Hard to believe, but more than six million came to Corona Park to see the elliptical 'Tent of Tomorrow' when it opened.

The WMF notes that, back in the day, the complex was one of the few World's Fair structures not panned by critics. In fact, they cite a *New York Times* architect review that called the piece 'a runaway success, day or night... a sophisticated frivolity... seriously and beautifully constructed'. Here's how the Fund describes the situation today: 'An icon to some, an eyesore to others, this remarkable complex, including the 'Tent of Tomorrow', is endangered by neglect and indifference as much as by rust.' Harsh, but potentially very accurate.

The city has made numerous efforts to renovate the pavilion area over the past few decades – including a $24,000 partial reconstruction of the lower tower – but to date no plans to reuse the structure (with any significant amount of money attached) have materialised.

So, is the former World's Fair structure worth saving? Hop on the No.7 train to Willets Point and judge for yourself.

Avenue and looming over Grand Central. There was even a plan at the time to raze Grand Central and construct a twin Pan Am in its place. The International Style had obviously reached its end when Philip Johnson, who was instrumental in defining the movement with his book *The International Style* (co-written with Henry-Russell Hitchcock), began disparaging the aesthetic as 'glass-boxitis'.

POSTMODERNISM AND BEYOND

Plainly, new blood was needed. A glimmer on the horizon was Boston architect Hugh Stubbins's silvery, triangle-topped **Citicorp Center** (Lexington Avenue, between 53rd & 54th Streets), which utilised contemporary engineering (the building cantilevers almost magically on high stilts above street level), while harking back to the decorative tops of yesteryear. The sly old master Philip Johnson turned the tables on everyone with the heretical Chippendale crown on his **Sony Building**, originally the AT&T Building (350 Madison Avenue, between 55th & 56th Streets), a bold throwback to decoration for its own sake.

Postmodernism provided a theoretical basis for a new wave of buildings that mixed past and present, often taking cues from the environs. Some notable examples include Helmut Jahn's **425 Lexington Avenue** (between 43rd & 44th Streets) of 1988; David Childs's retro diamond-tipped **Worldwide Plaza** (825 Eighth Avenue, between 49th & 50th Streets) of 1989; and the honky-tonk agglomeration of Skidmore, Owings & Merrill's **Bertelsmann Building** (1540 Broadway, between 45th & 46th Streets) of 1990. But even postmodernism became old hat after a while. Too many architects relied on fussy fenestration and passive commentary on other styles, instead of creating vital new building façades.

The electronic spectacle of **Times Square** (*see p124*) still provided, and continues to provide, one possible direction for architects. Upon seeing the myriad electric lights of Times Square in 1922, the British wit GK Chesterton remarked: 'What a glorious garden of wonder this would be, to anyone who was lucky enough to be unable to read.' This particular crossroads of the world continues to be at the cybernetic cutting edge with the 120-foot-tall, quarter-acre-in-area NASDAQ sign; the real-time stock tickers and jumbo TV screens; the news zipper on the original **New York Times Tower** (1 Times Square, between Broadway & Seventh Avenue). The public's appetite for new images seems so insatiable that a building's fixed profile no longer suffices here – only an ever-shifting electronic skin will do. The iconoclastic critic Robert Venturi, who taught us how to learn from Las Vegas, calls this trend 'iconography and electronics upon a generic architecture'.

Early 21st-century architecture is moving beyond applied symbolism to radical new forms, facilitated by computer-based design methods. A stellar example is Kohn Pedersen Fox's stainless steel and glass 'vertical campus', the **Baruch College Academic Complex** (55 Lexington Avenue, between 24th & 25th Streets). The resulting phantasmic designs that curve and dart in sculptural space are so beyond the timid window-dressing of postmodernism that they deserve a new label.

It may be founded on a very deliberate grid, but the city's growth has been organic. In the next decade, Manhattan may come to look like a sculpture garden, as computer-aided designs bridge the gap between what is possible and what can be imagined. Among the eye-popping newcomers is the **Eyebeam** art and technology centre in staid Chelsea, to be completed in 2007 by Diller Scofidio + Renfro, known for their designs that owe as much to conceptual art as to architecture. The curvilinear walls of the planned museum are suggestive of film looping through a projector. Meanwhile, Frank Gehry's ten-storey, white-glass mirage of a building on the Lower West Side is emblematic of the radical reworking of the New York cityscape. Gehry's first ever glass building and his first office building in New York, the headquarters for Barry Diller's **InterActiveCorp** (555 W 18th Street, at West Side Highway; *photo p39*) is composed of tilting glass volumes that strikingly resemble a fully rigged tall ship.

And change is quite literally in the air on Manhattan's Lower West Side, once an ugly duckling neighbourhood of warehouses and industrial buildings, is being transformed by the much-anticipated **High Line** project, a former elevated railroad viaduct that is being reconceived as a cutting-edge urban park (part of which is due to open in summer 2008), with Diller Scofidio + Renfro's team blending nature into an urban context. The completed development will feature more than a dozen new towers and a branch of the Whitney Museum, as well as a new Standard Hotel designed by James Stewart Polshek for the hotelier Andre Balazs. French architect Jean Nouvel is also designing high-end condominiums for the hip hotelier at 40 Mercer Street. For more on the High Line, *see p118* **Walking the line**.

Lower West Side chic extends to the Tribeca neighbourhood with one of the late Philip Johnson's last designs, the **Urban Glass House** (330 Spring Street, at Washington Street; *photo p42*), which is a mini-skyscraper multiplication of his iconic Glass House in New

Cutting edge: **Urban Glass House**. *See p41.*

Canaan, Connecticut. Nearby, Mexican architect Enrique Norten's crisply planed 14-storey glass tower rises from an antebellum warehouse at **One York Street**.

The Lower East Side is also finally getting a makeover, and this goes beyond Gwathmey Siegel's undulating glass-walled apartment that stands out like a socialite among punk rockers at **Astor Place** (445 Lafayette Street, at the corner of Astor Place). One of the most startling new designs in the city is the **New Museum of Contemporary Art** (235 Bowery, at Prince Street; *see p110*) by the architects Kazuyo Sejima and Ryue Nishizawa of the Tokyo firm Sanaa. Uneven, asymmetrically staggered boxy volumes covered in aluminum mesh shake up the traditional street front of the Bowery. A mysterious oversized silhouette of a seated figure on the façade presents a challenge to the onlooker's sense of scale. Nearby, the Swiss starchitects Herzog & de Meuron have built a set of five deluxe 11-storey cast-iron and green-glass townhouses at **40 Bond Street**. The building boasts a cast-aluminum fence at street level that looks like a dense thicket of graffiti.

Ian Schrager has redone the dowdy dowager of the super-spendy **Gramercy Park Hotel** (2 Lexington Avenue, at E 21st Street, 1-212 920 3300) with the help of Julian Schnabel, who designed the OTT lobby, which contains art by Andy Warhol, Jean-Michel Basquiat, Cy Twombly and naturally Schnabel. The hotel itself has a bright Bohemian past: Babe Ruth loved its bar and Humphrey Bogart married his first wife, actress Helen Menken, there.

Among the more controversial facelifts of recent years is Brad Cloepfil's renovation of Edward Durell Stone's modernism-meets-Venetian-palazzo **2 Columbus Circle**, originally the home of A & P heir Huntington Hartford's Gallery of Modern Art. In the same way that the gallery's collection of mostly figurative painting was seen as reactionary in the face of the abstract art movement, Stone's quotation of an historicist style was laughed into apostasy. However, Stone's work is being re-evaluated as a precursor to postmodernism, and many 20th-century architecture enthusiasts lamented the loss of the original façade after a lengthy, unsuccessful battle by the Landmarks Preservation Commission.

BREAKING NEW GROUND

World-class architecture is also sprouting up in much less predictable places in town. Midtown West has become a hotbed of new construction, first with Norman Foster's elegant, 46-storey, 597-foot high crystalline addition to the art deco base of the **Hearst Magazine Building** (300 W 57th Street, at Eighth Avenue; *photo p44*). The structure is a breathtaking combination of old and new, with the massive triangular struts of the tower penetrating the façade of the base, opening up great airy spaces within.

Just before the Great Depression, the McGraw-Hill Company hoped to expand the Midtown business centre by moving its HQ further west than anybody else. The move failed, and the splendid terracotta-skinned structure by the architect Raymond Hood stood in isolation for many decades. Now, *The New York Times* has boldly made its stand at **620 Eighth Avenue** (between W 40th & W 41st Streets) with a 40-storey glass tower by Renzo Piano featuring a highly unusual see-through screen of ceramic tubing that boldly brings the antiquated business of newspaper publishing into the 21st century.

Brooklyn has craved its own skyline since the **Williamsburgh Savings Bank Tower** (which has just gone condo as One Hanson Place) was built in 1927 to lure business to downtown. Once the single tallest building in Long Island, with the largest four-sided clock tower in the world, the 34-storey, 512-foot-tall structure now stands at the heart of the $4 billion **Atlantic Yards** project to be built in the next decade over the old Vanderbilt railyards near the intersection of Atlantic and

Flatbush Avenues. The flagship for the new skyline of ten 29- to 58-storey apartment towers is a new stadium for the Nets basketball team designed by Frank Gehry. Unfortunately, Enrique Norten's sleek, glass proposal for the new Public Library for the Visual Performing Arts fell through on account of cost concerns, but Hugh Hardy is taking over the commission. The noted landscape architect Laurie Olin will also design more than seven acres of new public space.

Richard Meier has added a glass box condo at **One Prospect Park**, upsetting some of the long-standing residents in the process, most of whom preferred the unbroken vista of classic pre-war apartment buildings. At $1,200 per square foot for some of the units, Meier's building set a new real estate record for Brooklyn, even though it's not as inspired as his more elegantly thought-out apartment buildings at 173 and 176 Perry Street that overlook the Hudson River.

Spritely new museum spaces include Arquitectonica's sleek aluminium and glass addition to the **Bronx Museum of the Arts** (*see p176*), at 1040 Grand Concourse at 165th Street, which opens up to narrow strips of windows like accordion pleats.

THE FUTURE OF 'GROUND ZERO'

Despite the city's rapid pace of development, the most popular tourist attraction in the city, the foundations of the former World Trade

Clean streets

Graffiti meets its match in a fleet of tag-busting trucks.

When asked what one thing best describes 1970s Gotham, many New Yorkers, one imagines, would answer 'graffiti'. Graffiti was the visual embodiment of the city's ills back then, and its abatement has been a symbol of New York's transformation in the years since. Of course, the scrawling hasn't totally disappeared, but it is being managed, thanks in large part to **Graffiti Free NYC**, a squadron of graffiti-removal trucks. The 13-unit fleet is set to nearly double in size by early 2008.

Craig Small, of the City's Economic Development Corporation, oversees the 26-person team. He says the programme began in 1999 by focusing on graffiti-covered warehouses, but since 2003, it's also been scouring smaller businesses and homes. He adds that some owners were resistant at first, thinking that they'd be charged for the privilege. 'But once they see their neighbour's property clean and found out they didn't get a bill, they call us right up.'

In addition to more trucks, Graffiti Free NYC has added two night shifts at the request of the mayor's office. Unlike the day crews, these trucks travel in packs to take on heavily-hit areas like parks or playgrounds. Depending on the job, they'll use high-powered nozzles to wash off the marks, or paint sprayers to cover them over with a fresh coat. On a good day, they can remove a whopping 30,000 square feet of graffiti.

Center, remains little more than a construction site because of seemingly endless political infighting. David Childs effectively wrested control of the design for the central Freedom Tower from the original architect Daniel Libeskind. Because of a lack of a single, unifying vision, preliminary sketches for the Freedom Tower still have an unfinished, anonymous look to them – like designs for the car of the future that somehow always manage to look the same.

Plans for the site keep shifting according to budgets and who has the political upper hand at any given time, but the current lineup is a truly stellar array of international architects, including Norman Foster, Richard Rogers and Fumihiko Maki. The real gem of the site will not be whatever compromise is made for the tower, but rather the vivid vision of Spanish architect Santiago Calatrava for the $2 billion PATH transit hub. His oddly skeletal bird-like design opens up to the sky and contains as much space underground as Grand Central Terminal. *See also p98.*

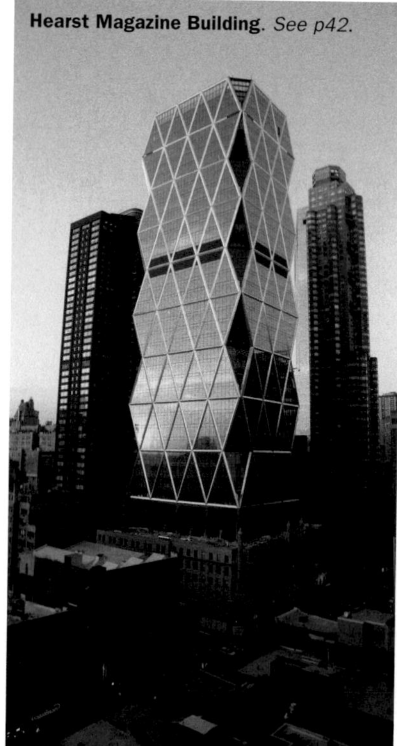

Hearst Magazine Building. *See p42.*

THE SHAPE OF BUILDINGS TO COME

Another victim of cutbacks was David Childs' revamp of the grand Beaux Arts **General Post Office** (421 Eighth Avenue, between 31st & 33rd Streets), to be renamed Moynihan Station in honour of former New York senator Daniel Patrick Moynihan. The original plan was to recreate the grandeur of the old Penn Station that once stood across the avenue with a giant glass clamshell-shaped atrium, but the new scaled-back design will still be an improvement on the current low-ceilinged station.

There's many a slip between the drawing board and completed construction, but peering into the future we still hope to see Santiago Calatrava's daringly original design for **80 South Street**, a series of 12 four-storey glass cubes standing in an almost invisible steel framework. Calatrava is also proposing a spider web-like tramway to Governors Island.

'Green, sustainable design is the watchword for the newest skyscrapers going up in New York.'

By 2009, Queens will have its own skyline care of Richard Rogers's $1 billion, six-acre, 1,000-apartment complex **Silvercup West**, next to the Queensboro Bridge. The plan also includes eight new soundstages for Silvercup Studios, where the television shows *Sex in the City* and *The Sopranos* were filmed.

Even Staten Island, long associated in the public mind with waste disposal (as referred to in 5 Boroughs Ice Cream's new flavour Staten Island Landfill), comes up smelling sweet as a rose by 2016 when it will have water courses, a wind farm, and running and biking trails.

Green, sustainable design is the watchword for the newest skyscrapers going up in New York, and Cook & Fox Architects' torqued, 54-storey tower for the headquarters of Bank of America at **1 Bryant Park** bills itself as the 'world's most sustainable skyscraper'. A wind turbine built into the top will generate electricity for the building, while insulated glass maximises daylight and prevents heat loss and an internal system recycles rainwater.

For more on the latest developments in New York's architectural renaissance – the extensive waterfront green belts planned for the next decade, say, or Renzo Piano's master plan for Columbia University's second campus Manhattanville, which will extend all the way from Broadway to Twelfth Avenue between W 125th and W 133rd Streets – visit the **AIA Center for Architecture** (*see p114*).

Dasha Shishkin. *See p47.*

Art Goes Boom

Flourishing art fairs and auctions are changing the way art is made in New York – and plumping up prices.

In 2007, at an auction at Sotheby's in London, the painting *White Canoe* by the Scottish artist Peter Doig fetched $11 million (the artist's previous high was $2 million). It was a remarkably hefty price tag for a mid-career talent, even one as well respected as Doig. Or as one New York critic put it, the sale was 'fucking obscene'. The auction house's own press release declared it to be 'the most successful contemporary sale ever staged in Europe'. The winning bid, however, illustrates a much larger phenomenon: a boom in the global art market. Plenty more evidence of this is on display at New York's major art fairs. In a city that was already in a frenzy of public art projects and had 300-plus galleries in Chelsea alone, the big-bucks art fests further inflated the unprecedented art bubble, with fat cats and newbie hedge fund managers flush and eager to spend their bonuses on wall hangings.

Other price records set recently include the diptych by Andreas Gursky, *99 Cent II*, that went for $3 million, making it the most expensive photographic work ever sold at auction. Two paintings by the late Francis Bacon racked up a whopping $95 million. And Damien Hirst became the world's most expensive living artist with the $19 million sale of *Lullaby Spring*, a stainless-steel cabinet

▶ For a guide to New York's **art galleries**, *see pp267-275.*

containing 6,136 handmade and handpainted pills. (With this sale, Hirst promptly dethroned previous auction record-holder Jasper Johns, whose *Figure 4* netted $17 million at Christie's just a month earlier.)

'"Money talks," notes Robert Storr, "but generally, when it comes to art's substance, it doesn't have much to say."'

What this means to the artists and dealers is more exposure and more money. What this means for art hounds visiting New York is an unprecedented opportunity to see the entire world of cutting-edge art right here in town. What it means for the art work itself, however, is less clear. The value of art isn't supposed to be purely monetary, after all. So are these works being marketed at the expense of their meaning? As Robert Storr, dean of the Yale School of Art, has wryly noted, 'Money talks, but generally, when it comes to art's substance, it doesn't have much to say.'

The commercialisation of art is a hot topic in the art world right now – in large measure because there's precious little else to talk about. The isms of the past century's art have become wasms, as artists seem to retreat more and more into their own subjectivity or treat art history as if it were the food court at the mall. 'The relationship of art and money is something that critics and curators have been in denial about forever,' says Walter Robinson, editor of artnet, an online magazine. 'Now everyone's trying to deal with it. Criticality is out of the window – market standards rule,' he adds, not so much as a complaint, but as a statement of fact. As if in response, a show at P.S.1 (*see p168*) in Queens called 'Not for Sale', was a riposte to the spread of art fairs, presenting a mixed bag of unsold works by artists, with little in common except that none were available for purchase.

Blue-chip dealer Marianne Boesky (whose own Chelsea gallery represents artists such as Barnaby Furnas, Sarah Sze and Takashi Murakami) disagrees with the dark assessment, saying that the huge gush of cash affords more opportunities for artists at all levels: 'It allows me to mount shows of critical work that I know won't sell.' She argues that more money means more interest, not only in artists in their 20s and 30s, but in those over 40 as well.

Painter Amy Sillman, 51, whose own work landed last year on the cover of *Artforum* for the first time, is one of the beneficiaries of this overheated market. 'I guess it is a case of a rising tide lifting all boats,' Sillman allows, before noting that she knows plenty of talented artists who can't find galleries to show their work, let alone sell it. Sillman admits to feeling pressure when her dealers ask for paintings to exhibit at art fairs and she can't provide them. 'I make six to ten paintings a year, period,' she says, 'and I still teach because I choose to.' And Sillman says that the graduate students she encounters at Bard and Columbia continue to deal with the critical questions, first raised in the '60s and '70s, about the efficacy of the market-ready object as a mode of expression.

'At top grad schools, dealers and collectors now regularly scour campuses, hungry to discover the next art star.'

At top grad schools like Columbia and Yale, dealers and collectors now regularly scour campuses, hungry to discover the next art star. That means more career options (and ego-gratification) for MFA (Master of Fine Arts) students, but the practice of headhunting young artists – often before their talents and styles are fully developed – also invites overexposure, or simply premature exposure, to the marketplace.

Some argue that certain young artists have already figured out how to play the game – by Disneyfying conceptual art. An installation in spring 2007 at the Whitney by Terence Koh, 30, consisted of a blinding light radiating out of a gallery. However anti-art it may have been as a gesture, the piece was also pure showmanship – the sort of thing that gets an artist noticed in the feverish environment of an art fair. 'What happens at fairs is that you look at ten works a second,' says one critic who writes regularly about the state of the art world. 'Your take has got to be fast.'

Given the factors contributing to the boom (the growth of markets in places like India, Russia and China; and the increasing frequency of auctions), the fairs look set to stay. Though there's no denying the benefits they've brought to artists and to New York City, there's really no disputing the fact that money changes everything. The effect may not be evident now, but all this frenetic activity may have an impact on the quality of the art you'll be seeing in the future.

'Ten years ago, when we first opened the gallery, you could sit with someone for an hour and have a conversation about art,' says Boesky. 'Now we're too busy.' She pauses. 'The boom has been a plus. But do I miss those conversations? Certainly.'

Buy now?

Four New York-based artists to watch.

Joe Fig

Using doll's houses as his inspiration, Fig creates amazing cabinets of curiosities that serve as miniature replicas of artists' studios. These painstakingly (sometimes obsessively) accurate sculptural models, based on Fig's visits to the workspaces of notables such as April Gornick, Chuck Close and Ross Bleckner, catch artists in the act of art-making and allow viewers a rare glimpse into an artist's most private and hallowed room.

Spencer Finch

The Rhode Island School of Design grad was included in the 2004 Whitney Biennial; his ambitious works (drawings, sculptures, photographs, videos and paintings) explore colour, light, perception and memory. A huge solo exhibit, *What Time Is It on the Sun?* (at Massachusetts Museum of Contemporary Art, MASS MoCA, through spring 2008) is sure to raise Finch's profile even further.

Wangechi Mutu

The arresting collage paintings by this Kenyan-born artist, usually depicting the female body, take on fashion, cultural identity, mythology and sexuality. Mutu is a rapidly rising star in the art world, and rightly so.

Dasha Shishkin

Just 30 years old, Moscow-born Shishkin graduated from Columbia University's prestigious School of the Arts in 2004, and her dream-like, figurative work, which incorporates drawing and painting, has already found a place in the collections of the Whitney and MoMA. *Photo p45.*

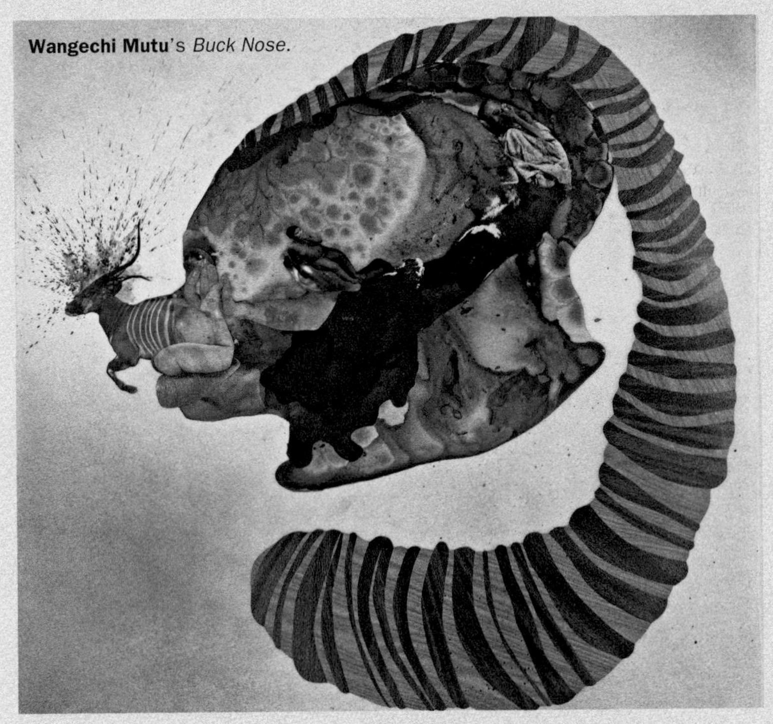

Wangechi Mutu's *Buck Nose.*

Show offs

Five alternative art fairs screw with the norm.

The Art Show of the ADAA

Now celebrating its 20th year, the Art Dealers Association of America (ADAA) show is a classy event featuring mostly museum-quality pieces. Here, organisers go for a sleeker design and lots of contemporary art. Still, you come here for the gravitas: yes, that is a Diego Rivera landscape having its US debut.
Perfect for Artgoers who secretly prefer the MoMA to Chelsea.
www.artdealers.org. **Date** 21-25 Feb.

DiVA New York

This small fair is dedicated exclusively to digital and video art. A handful of galleries take rooms on a floor of a hotel, while another group are represented in bare shipping containers parked up and down the streets of Chelsea.
Perfect for Wii lovers and webheads.
www.divafair.com/ny_07. **Date** late Feb.

PULSE

This indie alternative to the Armory throws down at the site of the original Armory Show, where Marcel Duchamp rocked the art world with *Nude Descending a Staircase* in 1917. Look out for quality painters like Karen Arm of the New York-based P.P.O.W gallery.
Perfect for Indie kids who hate labels. And their hippie dads.
The 69th Regiment Armory, 68 Lexington Avenue, at 26th Street (www.pulseart.com/ny). **Date** late Feb.

Red Dot

Forget conventional framing techniques: at this relatively new fair, look out for work lying on mattresses, leaning up against the wall or hanging out in the loo. 'People should realise that art's a tangible commodity,' said one exhibitor last year. 'It doesn't have to seem so precious.'
Perfect for Anyone who's ever ducked the guard to get up close.
www.reddotfair.com. **Date** late Feb.

Scope New York

At last year's sprawling affair, participants showed off works as weird as a hairstyling service; a floor installation of moving cloth inspired by the Red Sea; and a performance by Gabriel Martinez, who appeared in a skintight suit, sporting a 12-foot Vegas-style headdress.
Perfect for Fans of performance art (and drag queens, and *Jackass*).
www.scope-art.com. **Date** late Feb.

New York Rocks!

Time Out New York magazine's music editors mull over the city's greatest 20 musicians of all time.

1 The Velvet Underground

Forget, for a moment, the surly genius of Lou Reed and his songs. Forget John Cale's experimental background. Forget that the classic Velvet Underground lineup lasted just three years. Forget that Cale and Reed were living and recording on Ludlow Street three decades before it seemed like a good idea. Forget Warhol and the Factory, forget Mo Tucker's stand-up drumming, forget the shades and the heroin. Just play any of the first three albums. They still sound impossibly cool. The Velvets were born in the space after the Beats and before the hippies, and represented a stern, aloof rejoinder to everything California was spewing at the time. They midwifed the love child of rock and the avant-garde. They remain the ultimate NYC band.
Must-own album *The Velvet Underground & Nico* (1967)

2 Duke Ellington

Call him the blueprint, the godfather of the 20th century. On some level, the sound, substance and style of Duke Ellington set in motion the idea of New York City as a place where nonconformity is well nurtured and auspicious things are born. Like the man said: 'It don't mean a thing if it ain't got that swing.'
Must-own album *The Far East Suite* (1966)

3 Chic

Living and recording on erstwhile musical nexus 52nd Street, Chic transformed big-band discipline, elemental funkiness and hedonistic disco aesthetics into a glorious dance machine. Led by former Black Panther Nile Rodgers on guitar, the band, which once opened a bill including Blondie and the Clash at the now-defunct Bond's on 44th Street, embodied the mix of genres that defined 1970s NYC.
Must-own album *Risqué* (1979)

4 Miles Davis

For a long time, Left Coast jazz was stamped 'cool', but in the '40s trumpeter Miles Davis presided over the 'birth of the cool' here

► Looking for the next big thing on the New York music scene? *See pp312-332* for the lowdown on the city's best **music venues**.

Style council

New York didn't just produce its own legendary musicians – it also gave birth to whole musical genres.

Tin Pan Alley Around the turn of the last century, composers and publishers (the music industry in those pre-radio days) were squeezed into a single, cacophonous block of 28th Street. Many of the songs were novelties, but the best of them – by the likes of George M Cohan, Irving Berlin and George Gershwin – still provide the subconscious soundtrack for America.

Broadway Some of New York's richest and most enduring music made its entrance on the musical-theatre stage, from the likes of Cole Porter and Rodgers and Hart, through to the later innovations of Rodgers and Hammerstein, Leonard Bernstein and Stephen Sondheim.

Greenwich Village folk Everyone thinks of Dylan when this early '60s post-Beats scene is discussed, but a host of lesser-known stars made the Washington Square neighbourhood the place to be for much of the decade. The folk establishment embodied by Ramblin' Jack Elliott, Dave Van Ronk and Oscar Brand rubbed shoulders with youngsters Fred Neil, Joan Baez and Phil Ochs in venues like the Bitter End and Café Wha? – both still firmly in business today.

The Brill Building sound In the late '50s and early '60s, the epicentre of American pop was a building on Broadway and 49th Street. It's there that songwriters such as Gerry Goffin and Carole King, Jeff Barry and Ellie Greenwich, Barry Mann and Cynthia Weil, and Burt Bacharach and Hal David toiled nine to five in little offices, concocting hits that evoked the dreams, joys and heartache of young people in love.

The New York School and Minimalism Classical music took a radical turn towards expressive freedom with the music of the New York School, a loosely knit cabal that centred on John Cage in the '50s. Cage favoured anarchy and Zen; Morton Feldman patterned vast musical expanses after Oriental rugs and Color Field paintings. Minimalism arrived in the '60s with La Monte Young, but it was Philip Glass and Steve Reich who brought this busy, hypnotic style to fruition in the late '70s.

New York Hardcore After the wreckage of punk's late '70s flame-out settled, some weren't willing to give up the idea of liberation through hard, fast rock. Their answer? Make the music harder, faster and more violent. While LA's Black Flag is generally considered the first hardcore band, a cadre of lifers, including Agnostic Front and Murphy's Law, have reimagined punk in New York as the ultimate working-class music.

in New York on 52nd Street. That's where the mystique began, and for the next 40-plus years, no one signified the city's cutting-edge spirit with more bad-ass bravado and panache.
Must-own album *Kind of Blue* (1959)

5 Public Enemy

The best hip hop group ever scared the shit out of mainstream America in the late '80s – partly because the mainstream was such a huge part of PE's fan base. Yet Chuck D & co were (and still are) more punk than punk itself. Courtesy of the Bomb Squad production team (whose work could never be replicated in our copyright-sensitive times), every song sounds like an emergency.
Must-own album *It Takes a Nation of Millions to Hold Us Back* (1988)

6 Billie Holiday

They called her Lady Day, but her music seemed at one with the night. Her brutal life dragged her from one tragic identity to another: rape victim, prostitute, drug addict, prisoner. Malcolm X remembered her hanging tough at Harlem's Lenox Lounge during his thug days. Transmuted into music, this pain gave a raw beauty to everything she sang.
Must-own album *Lady Day – The Best of Billie Holiday*

7 Tito Puente

The mambo was Cuba's gift to the world, so it's no small feat that Puente, a Nuyorican, ended up wearing the title of Mambo King. Tito's bands ruled Latino music mecca the Palladium in the '50s, but his reputation was assured once Santana covered Puente's classic 'Oye Como Va'.
Must-own album *Dance Mania, Vol 1* (1958)

8 Run-DMC

Straight out of Hollis, Queens, Joseph 'Run' Simmons and Darryl McDaniels (backed by Jason 'Jam Master Jay' Mizell) turned the entire world on its ear with their literate

rhymes, hard-edged delivery and social consciousness, paving the way for Public Enemy, N.W.A and everything that followed. The group's signature sound – booming beats hitched to heavy-metal guitars – ignited hip hop's explosive chart domination.
Must-own album *Raising Hell* (1986)

9 Al Jolson

Al Jolson was the first real pop music superstar. His Broadway career lasted 30 years (1911-1940), but he also shook up the nascent movie industry – in 1927's *The Jazz Singer* he kicked off the age of the talking picture with his catchphrase 'You ain't heard nothin' yet!'. Jolson is largely forgotten today – or derided for performing in blackface – but we haven't stopped hearing him yet.
Must-own album *The Golden Years of Al Jolson*

10 Ella Fitzgerald

At 17 she won an amateur night competition at the Apollo Theater, and for the next six decades Fitzgerald was *the* voice of American jazz – first as a swing goddess, then as a bebop scat queen and finally as the smoothest interpreter of gold standards.
Must-own album *The Best of the Songbooks*

11 The Ramones

Gabba, gabba, we accept you!
Must-own album *Rocket to Russia* (1977)

12 Barbara Streisand

Before the hair and the politics and the fingernails, there was the brash, goofy, endearing Brooklyn girl who wowed the world in *Funny Girl*. The ugly duckling opened her mouth to sing, and bam! A swan was born.
Must-own album *Greatest Hits*

13 Ornette Coleman

A maverick alto saxophonist from Fort Worth by way of Los Angeles, Coleman introduced the concept of free jazz during a lengthy run at Manhattan's Five Spot in 1959. His freewheeling music polarised audiences then; now, it sounds like the inevitable offspring of country-blues it always was.
Must-own album *The Shape of Jazz to Come* (1959)

14 Blondie

Blondie often gets lumped with the blank generation, but the band – sexy, tough and aloof – always had broader ambitions. When it turned to disco and hip hop in the late '70s, Blondie maintained its cred while helping these styles jump from NYC's arty-gritty underground on to the broader American stage.
Must-own album *Parallel Lines* (1978)

15 Grandmaster Flash

One of the architects of rap music, Grandmaster Flash was also its first master technician. Alongside his posse of MCs, the Furious Five, the Bronx native refined the art of DJing at the Harlem World Disco and the occasional Midtown ballroom – thus making the next generation of NYC rap stars want to copy and improve his blueprint.
Must-own album *The Message* (1982)

16 Thelonious Monk

There are standards and then there are Monk tunes – some of the most vibrant, nuanced and witty compositions ever produced in the jazz idiom. Though the pianist had a hand in the Harlem bebop revolution, he's rightly best remembered for his dogged musical originality.
Must-own album *Brilliant Corners* (1957)

17 Sonic Youth

These four shaggy bohemians mixed post-punk dynamics, art-school leanings and a taste for bubblegum pop into one of rock's most influential sounds, becoming underground demigods in the process – and inadvertently dragging Nirvana into the spotlight.
Must-own album *Daydream Nation* (1988)

18 Dizzy Gillespie

Dizzy Gillespie's stage antics sometimes obscured his genius. He was the prime mover in two huge revolutions happening in 1940s NYC: bebop, which nailed shut the coffin of the swing era; and its cousin Cubop, which invited Cuba's Chano Pozo and other latinos to the party.
Must-own album *Something Old, Something New* (1963)

19 Talking Heads

Though they formed in Rhode Island, Talking Heads quickly moved to NYC, landing at the junction between punk and new wave. The brainy quartet discovered a holy ground where art, rock and commercial pop met, and was among the first local combos to incorporate African polyrhythms.
Must-own album *Fear of Music* (1979)

20 Afrika Bambaataa

That a black kid from the Bronx in the late '70s held Germany's Kraftwerk as his favourite band isn't even the most surprising thing about Afrika Bambaataa – though it did lead to 1982's *Planet Rock*, which birthed electro and still manages to atomise dancefloors to this day. Bambaataa's more important social contribution to NYC came when he transformed his street gang into the Zulu Nation.
Must-own album *Looking for the Perfect Beat: 1980-1985*

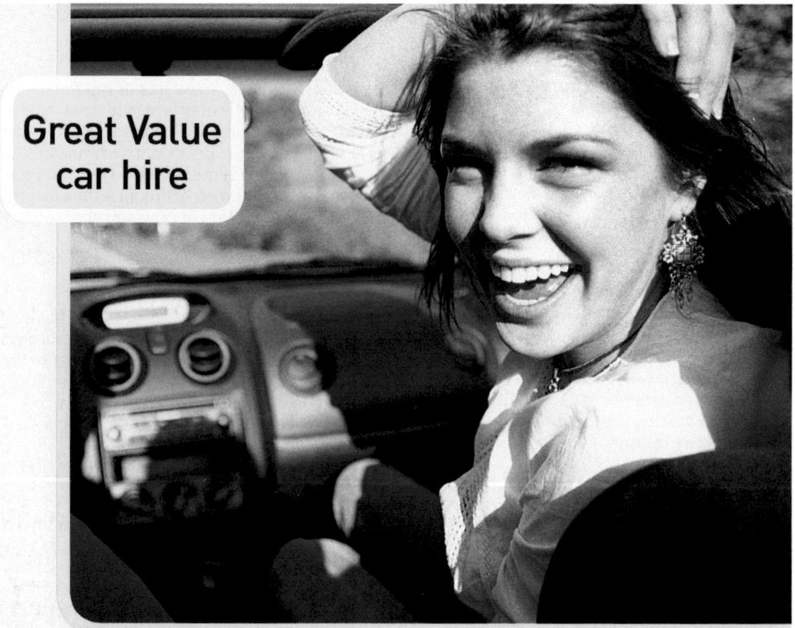

Where to Stay

Where to Stay **54**

Features

The best Hotels 54
Cheap date 57
Centenarian comeback 64
High times 72

Mercer. *See p58.*

Where to Stay

Prepare to part with a bunch of $$$s for your zzzs.

We hate to be the bearers of bad news, but here goes: the average nightly rate for a hotel room on the island of Manhattan has recently topped $300. It seems the market for nothing-special hotel rooms has simply spun out of control. In the past five years, hotel occupancy rates have shot up to just over 85 per cent, the highest level seen in more than a decade. Needless to say, stats like these have been turning heads in the hotel industry, and a staggering 13,000 new (or newly renovated) hotel rooms are expected by 2010, with a mini hotel explosion forecast for lower Manhattan (of the 70-odd hotels slated to open over the next two years, nearly 40 per cent will be located below 23rd Street). Whether or not the influx of new rooms will do anything to make this town a little friendlier on the wallet is anyone's guess.

Still, if you have deep pockets you're in luck: gobs of stylish upmarket hotels roll out the red carpet monthly – recent openings include the **London NYC** (*see p69*), where Gordon Ramsey opened his first state-side eaterie to much fanfare. Something more trendy? Check out the **Bowery Hotel** (*see p59*), located downtown, on the Bowery; the famously seedy street is known for its flophouses (which you can still find there), but the new hotel offers its guests a decidedly more upscale retreat, starting with a fantastically shabby-chic lobby space. On top of that, the views from the rooms of the otherwise rather shabby neighbourhood are, well, none too shabby.

One light in the darkness for those on a budget is the bright **Pod Hotel** (*see p75*), which debuted not too long ago in the old Pickwick Arms Hotel on Midtown's east side. If you book well in advance, rooms can be had here for around $200 dollars a night – plus you'll be within walking distance of the MoMA and Rockefeller Center.

The best Hotels

For views to die for

The **Bowery Hotel** (*see p59*), **Hotel on Rivington** (*see p60*) and the **Maritime Hotel** (*see p69*).

For celebrity spotting

The **Four Seasons** (*see p63*), **Hotel Gansevoort** (*see p57*) and the **Mercer** (*see p58*).

For style on the cheap

The **Hudson** (*see p66*), **Marrakech** (*see p79*) and the **Pod Hotel** (*see p75*).

For cosy comfort

Blue Moon (*see p59*), the **Harlem Flophouse** (*see p79*) and the **Inn on 23rd Street** (*see p67*).

For drama queens on a budget

The **Americana Inn** (*see p75*), the **Broadway Inn** (*see p72*) and the **Big Apple Hostel** (*see p76*).

PRICES AND TAXES

The best way to begin your hotel search is to choose the price range and neighbourhood that interests you. Accommodation prices can vary quite wildly within a single property (and we really mean wildly), and the rates quoted here, obtained from the hotels, reflect that disparity. We've classified hotels within each area heading (Downtown, Midtown, Uptown and Brooklyn) according to the price of a mid-season double room per night, beginning with the most expensive. The prices quoted are not guaranteed, but they should give a good indication of the hotel's average rack rates. And if you follow the tips below, you're likely to find slashed room prices, package deals and special promotions. Make sure to include New York's 13.625 per cent room tax and a $2 to $6 per-night occupancy tax when planning your travel budget.

Weekend travellers should be warned that many smaller hotels adhere to a strict three-night-minimum booking policy.

HOTEL RESERVATION AGENCIES

Pre-booking blocks of rooms allows reservation companies to offer reduced rates. Discounts cover most price ranges, including economy; some agencies claim savings of up to 65 per cent, though 20 per cent is more likely. If you simply want the best deal, mention the rate you're willing to pay, and see what's available. The following agencies are free of charge, though a few require payment for rooms at the time the reservation is made.

Up, up and away from it all at the **Hotel Gansevoort**. *See p57*.

Hotel Reservations Network
Suite 400, 10440 North Central Expressway, Dallas, TX 75231 (1-214 369 1264/1-800 246 8357/www.hotels.com).

Quikbook
3rd Floor, 381 Park Avenue South, New York, NY 10016 (1-212 779 7666/1-800 789 9887/ www.quikbook.com).

www.timeoutny.com
The *Time Out New York* website offers online reservations at more than 300 hotels. You can search for availability by arrival date or hotel name. (Full disclosure: *Time Out New York* receives a commission from sales made through our partner hotel reservation sites.)

APARTMENT RENTALS AND B&BS
Thousands of B&B rooms are available in New York, but in the absence of a central organisation, some are hard to find. Many B&Bs are unhosted, and breakfast is usually continental (if it's served at all), but the vibe is likely to be more personal in a B&B than a hotel. A sales tax of 8.625 per cent is added on hosted rooms (but not on unhosted apartments) if you stay for more than seven days. For a longer visit, it can be cheaper and more convenient to rent a place of your own; several of the agencies listed below specialise in short-term rentals of furnished apartments. For gay-friendly B&Bs (where straight guests are often welcome too), *see p305*.

CitySonnet
Village Station, PO Box 347, New York, NY 10014 (1-212 614 3034/www.citysonnet.com). **Rates** *B&B room* $90-$175. *Unhosted loft* $155-$600. *Private apartment* $150-$275. **Credit** AmEx, Disc, MC, V.
This artist-run agency specialises in downtown locations. B&B rooms and short-term apartment rentals are priced according to the room size, number of guests and whether bathrooms are private or shared.

New York Habitat
Suite 306, 307 Seventh Avenue, between 27th & 28th Streets (1-212 255 8018/www.nyhabitat.com). **Rates** *Unhosted studio* $115-$225. *Unhosted 1-bed apartment* $155-$325. *Unhosted 2-bed apartment* $250-$470. **Credit** AmEx, DC, Disc, MC, V.
A variety of services are offered, from hosted B&Bs to short-term furnished apartment rentals, which can be paid for by the day, week or month.

STANDARD HOTEL SERVICES
In the categories Luxury, Expensive and Moderate, hotels generally have the following services: alarm clock, cable TV with pay movies, currency exchange, dry-cleaning service, fax machine, hairdryer, in-room safe, laundry, minibar, radio, room service and voicemail. Hotels in these categories also provide concierge services (in many cases the front desk staff double as concierge). All hotels have air-conditioning unless otherwise noted.

Most hotels, in all categories, have access for the disabled, non-smoking rooms (and smoking rooms, at least on request) and an iron with ironing board in the room or on request. One or more computers with high-speed internet access for guest use (free or for a small fee) are almost always available on the premises. Call ahead to confirm. 'Complimentary breakfast' may mean either pastries, coffee, tea, juice, cereal and milk or a more generous continental spread. Note that while many hotels claim 'multilingual' staff, that term may be used loosely.

The vast majority of hotels in New York do not have on-site parking. There are hundreds of pay parking lots and parking garages around town. If you are driving into the city it's best to call ahead and inquire about the nearest lot; in some cases it may be right next door or on the same block as the hotel. Prices vary between areas, and weekdays and weekends, but expect to pay between $25 and $45 for 24 hours.

Cheap date
You really want to show someone a good time? Start as you mean to go on with a high-class aphrodisiac at the **Grand Central Oyster Bar & Restaurant** (Lower level, Grand Central Terminal, 42nd Street, at Park Avenue, 1-212 490 6650). After you've had your fill of the city's best oysters, stand (in opposite corners) of the station's **Whispering Gallery** and murmur your filthy intentions to your blushing lover, who will hear you clearly from 20 feet away (luckily no one else will so don't be shy). Next, make good on your promises and check into a short-stay motel. **La Semana Hotel** (25 W 24th Street, between Fifth & Sixth Avenues, 1-212 255 5944) provides rooms with large, two-person jacuzzis at surprisingly reasonable rates ($85/3hrs).

Downtown

Luxury

Hotel Gansevoort
18 Ninth Avenue, at 13th Street (1-212 206 6700/ 1-877 726 7386/www.hotelgansevoort.com). Subway A, C, E to 14th Street; L to Eighth Avenue. **Rates** $435-$475 double. **Rooms** 187. **Credit** AmEx, DC, Disc, MC, V. **Map** p403 C28 ❶

It's hard to miss this commanding hotel – a soaring 14-floor contemporary structure that stands out against the cobbled streets and warehouse storefronts of the Meatpacking District. Opened in early 2004 and blueprinted by Stephen B Jacobs, this full-service luxury hotel gets strong marks for style. The hotel announces itself by way of the world's tallest revolving door and the entrance features four 18ft light boxes, which change colour throughout the evening. Inside the rooms, colour gets less play, but the quarters are spacious and come with original photography from local artists and Molton Brown bath products. The private roof garden features a pool with underwater music and 360-degree views of the city. Jeffrey Chodorow's glossy Japanese eaterie Ono has a covered terrace, private dining huts and a robatayaki bar – all behind a red velvet rope. When it comes to evening entertainment, guests have their pick of the rooftop bar Plunge, or the subterranean spa that is transformed into the chic nightclub, G-Spot each evening. *Photos p55.*
Bars (3). Business centre. Gym. Internet (wireless; free). Pool (1 outdoor). Restaurant. Spa.

Mercer

147 Mercer Street, at Prince Street (1-212 966 6060/1-888 918 6060/www.mercerhotel.com). Subway N, R, W to Prince Street. **Rates** $595-$820 double. **Rooms** 75. **Credit** AmEx, DC, Disc, MC, V. **Map** p403 E29 ❷

Although now over seven years old, Soho's first luxury boutique hotel still has nice touches that keep it a notch above nearby competitors, which is perhaps why Marc Jacobs takes up residence here when he returns to New York. The lobby, appointed with oversized white couches and chairs, and shelves lined with colourful books, acts as a bar, library and lounge – open exclusively to hotel guests. Rooms are large by New York standards and feature furniture by Christian Liagre, enormous washrooms with tubs for two and Face Stockholm products. The restaurant, Mercer Kitchen (1-212 966 5454), serves Jean-Georges Vongerichten's stylish version of casual American cuisine.
Bar. Internet (wireless; free). Restaurant.

60 Thompson

60 Thompson Street, between Broome & Spring Streets (1-212 431 0400/1-877 431 0400/www.60thompson.com). Subway C, E to Spring Street. **Rates** $550-$1,500 double. **Rooms** 97. **Credit** AmEx, DC, Disc, MC, V. **Map** p403 E30 ❸

Don't be surprised if you have to walk through a photo shoot when you enter this stylish hotel – it's a favoured location for fashionistas. A60, the exclusive guests-only rooftop bar, offers commanding city views and is particularly magazine-spread-worthy. Designed by Thomas O'Brien of Aero Studios, 60 Thompson has been luring chic jet-setters since it opened six years ago. The modern rooms are dotted

Settle down to a lounge life less ordinary at the **Mercer**.

with pampering details such as pure down duvets and pillows, and a 'shag bag' filled with fun items to get you in the mood. The highly acclaimed restaurant Kittichai serves a sumptuous spread of creative Thai cuisine beside a pool filled with floating orchids. In warmer months, make sure to request a table on the sidewalk terrace.
Bars (2). Gym. Internet (wireless; free). Restaurant.

SoHo Grand Hotel

310 West Broadway, between Canal & Grand Streets (1-212 965 3000/1-800 965 3000/www.sohogrand.com). Subway A, C, E, 1 to Canal Street. **Rates** $400-$630 double. **Rooms** 336. **Credit** AmEx, DC, Disc, MC, V. **Map** p403 E30 ❹
Right in the heart of Downtown, and regarded by many as Soho's living room, the Grand makes good use of industrial materials like poured concrete, cast iron and bottle glass (used for the staircase). Built in 1996, Soho's first high-end boutique hotel features Bill Sofield-designed rooms, which include two spacious penthouse lofts, use a restrained palette of greys and beiges, and sport photos from local galleries. Sip cocktails in the Grand Bar and Lounge, or dine on haute macaroni and cheese in the Gallery.
Bar. Business centre. Gym. Internet (wireless; $11/day). Restaurant.
Other locations: Tribeca Grand Hotel, 2 Sixth Avenue, between Walker & White Streets, Tribeca (1-877 519 6600).

Expensive

Blue Moon

100 Orchard Street, between Delancey & Broome Streets (1-212 533 9080). Subway F to Delancey Street. **Rates** $320-$480 double. **Rooms** 22. **Credit** AmEx, DC, Disc, MC, V. **Map** p403 F30 ❺
Right next door to the Lower East Side Tenement Museum (*see p109*), this eight-storey hotel (three floors were added to the original five-storey building) aims to evoke old-world charm. There are not a lot of amenities for the price but the location is great. Orchard Street and the surrounding area offer dozens of excellent restaurants, bars and clubs. Some rooms come with views of the nearby Williamsburg Bridge. *Photos pp60-61.*
Internet (wireless; free).

The Bowery Hotel

335 Bowery, at E 3rd Street (1-212 505 9100/www.theboweryhotel.com). Subway B, D, F, V to Broadway-Lafayette Street; 6 to Bleecker Street. **Rates** $375-$750 double. **Rooms** 135. **Credit** AmEx, DC, Disc, MC, V. **Map** p403 F29 ❻
The renaissance of the formerly grungy area continues apace, and the arrival of this fanciful new boutique hotel (which garnered a glowing profile in *Vanity Fair*) from Eric Goode and Sean MacPherson (the team behind the Maritime Hotel; *see p69*) is sure

to raise the profile of the burgeoning Bowery scene. Shunning the minimalist hotel mode, Goode and MacPherson have created plush rooms that conjure up the old world, with aged oriental rugs, wood-beamed ceilings and dashes of cast iron. Floor to ceiling windows offer stunning views of the neighbourhood. The buzz will no doubt keep city scene-seekers lining up to eat (Italian restaurant Gemma), drink (Lobby Bar) and sleep here. If you're lucky enough to pop in during a lull, cosy up by the fire in the wood-panelled lobby. *Photo p63.*
Bars (2). Internet (wireless; free). Restaurant.

Hampton Inn Manhattan-Seaport

320 Pearl Street, between Dover & Peck Slip Streets (1-212 571 4400). Subway A, C, 2, 3, 4, 5 to Fulton Street-Broadway Nassau. **Rates** $250-$599 double. **Rooms** 65. **Credit** AmEx, Disc, MC, V. **Map** p402 F32 7

This new hotel caters to business travellers but weekenders might also enjoy the spot for its easy strolls to Tribeca and Chinatown. Try to bag a room with a view of the Brooklyn Bridge. *Photos p67.*
Gym. Internet (wireless; free).

Hotel on Rivington

107 Rivington Street, between Essex & Ludlow Streets (1-212 475 2600/www.hotelonrivington.com). Subway F to Delancey Street; J, M, Z to Delancey-Essex Streets. **Rates** $350-$550 double. **Rooms** 110. **Credit** AmEx, Disc, MC, V. **Map** p403 G29 8

Hotel on Rivington has a sky-high cool factor to match its trendy Lower East Side locale. Floor to ceiling windows are a theme throughout: the second-floor lobby overlooks the storefronts of Rivington Street, and every super-slick India Mahdavi-designed room has an unobstructed city view. Annie O (*see p234*), the hotel gift shop, sells high-end trinkets. For the more sexually adventurous guest, wood-panelled drawers hide binoculars and an 'intimacy kit' stocked with surprises from nearby Toys in Babeland (*see p255*).
Bar. Gym. Internet (wireless; free). Restaurant.

Wall Street District Hotel

15 Gold Street, at Platt Street (1-212 232 7700/www.wallstreetdistrict.com). Subway A, C to Broadway-Nassau Street; J, M, Z, 2, 3, 4, 5 to Fulton Street. **Rates** $300-$600 double. **Rooms** 138. **Credit** AmEx, DC, Disc, MC, V. **Map** p402 F32 9

This small, tech-savvy hotel is great value for business travellers, effortlessly fusing comfort with amenities such as automated check-in kiosks and minimising fuss from the moment you arrive. For an additional $50, you can upgrade to a deluxe room with higher-tech features (PCs with free internet, white-noise machines); things to help prepare you for the big meeting (shoe shiner, trouser press, complimentary breakfast); and a few low-tech mood lifters (gummy bears!). The hotel's restaurant and bar, San Marino Ristorante, serves casual Italian cuisine with gusto.
Business centre. Internet (wireless; $10/day). Restaurant.

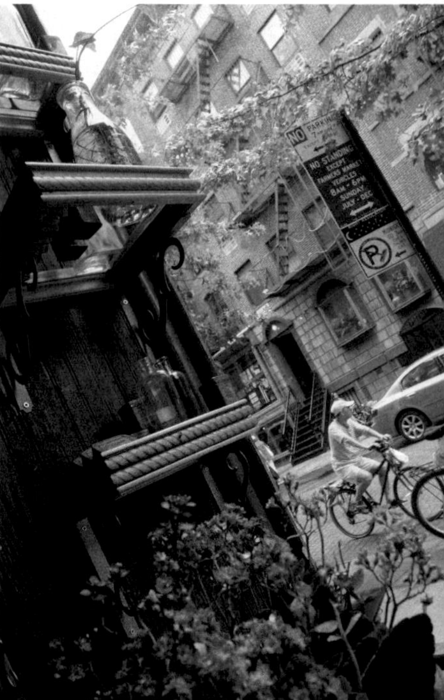

Wall Street Inn

9 South William Street, at Broad Street (1-212 747 1500/www.thewallstreetinn.com). Subway 2, 3 to Wall Street; 4, 5 to Bowling Green. **Rates** $320-$400 double. **Rooms** 46. **Credit** AmEx, DC, Disc, MC, V. **Map** p402 E33 10

The area surrounding this boutique hotel in the Financial District has seen a reincarnation in recent years, sprouting new pâtisseries, bars and restaurants along its cobblestoned streets. The Wall Street Inn started a trend back in 1998 by transforming the 1830s Lehman Brothers Bank building into tastefully appointed rooms with marble bathrooms (deluxe rooms feature jacuzzis), and these days guests are met with fresh cut flowers and free internet. To lure travellers beyond financiers, the hotel offers hefty discounts on weekends.
Business centre. Gym. Internet (free).

Moderate

Abingdon Guest House

13 Eighth Avenue, between Jane & W 12th Streets (1-212 243 5384/www.abingdonguesthouse.com). Subway A, C, E to 14th Street; L to Eighth Avenue. **Rates** $199-$240 double. **Rooms** 9. **Credit** AmEx, DC, Disc, MC, V. **Map** p403 D28 11

Blue Moon. *See p59.*

This charming, homely B&B (without the breakfast) is a good option if you want to be located near to the Meatpacking District but can't afford to stay in the Gansevoort (*see p57*). Named after nearby Abingdon Square, this nine-room townhouse offers European ambience at reasonable prices. Each room is painted a different colour and has plush fabrics, four-poster beds and private bath. The popular Brewbar coffeehouse doubles as a check-in desk and café, and you can sip your latte in the trellised garden if you're lucky enough to be in the garden room.
Internet (wireless; free).

Cosmopolitan

95 West Broadway, at Chambers Street (1-212 566 1900/1-888 895 9400/www.cosmohotel.com). Subway A, C, 1, 2, 3 to Chambers Street. **Rates** $179-$279 double. **Rooms** 125. **Credit** AmEx, DC, MC, V. **Map** p402 E31 ⓬

Despite the name, you won't find any trendy pink cocktails at this well-maintained hotel (or even a bar to drink them in). That's because the Cosmopolitan is geared towards travellers with little need for luxury. Open continuously since the 1850s, it remains a tourist favourite for its Tribeca address, clean rooms and reasonable rates.
Internet (wireless; free).

Off-Soho Suites Hotel

11 Rivington Street, between Bowery & Chrystie Street (1-212 979 9808/1-800 633 7646/www.offsoho.com). Subway B, D to Grand Street; F, V to Lower East Side-Second Avenue; J, M, Z to Bowery. **Rates** $129-$339 double. **Rooms** 45. **Credit** AmEx, MC, V. **Map** p403 F30 ⓭

These no-frills suites became a great deal more popular after the reclusive hip destination restaurant Freemans (*see p188*) opened at the end of the alley across the street. The suites are decent value for the thriving Lower East Side (a couple of blocks from Soho). Rooms are bland but clean and spacious, and they have fully equipped kitchens.
Gym. Internet (wireless; $7).

Pioneer of SoHotel

341 Broome Street, between Elizabeth Street & Bowery (1-212 226 1482/www.sohotel-ny.com). Subway J, M, Z to Bowery; 6 to Spring Street. **Rates** $139-$161 double. **Rooms** 150. **Credit** AmEx, DC, Disc, MC, V. **Map** p403 F30 ⓮

The Pioneer lives up to its name – it's the only hotel in Nolita, a rapidly developing area known for its boutiques and cafés. This European-style hotel recently got a complete overhaul and, though rooms are small and basic, they have large framed paintings and hardwood floors; most have private baths. Larger rooms have charming stucco walls and vaulted ceilings. Morning complimentary coffee is served in the lobby.
Internet (wireless; free).

St Mark's Hotel

2 St Mark's Place, at Third Avenue (1-212 674 0100/www.stmarkshotel.net). Subway 6 to Astor Place. **Rates** $130-$140 double. **Rooms** 64. **No credit cards**. **Map** p403 F28 ⓯

Positioned among all the tattoo parlours and piercing shops of St Mark's Place, this small hotel is unexpectedly bright, clean and understated (and the staff were surprisingly tattoo-free when we visited). The basic rooms have double beds with private baths. St Mark's biggest asset is its location – it's perfectly situated for immersing yourself in the East Village's historic punk-rock culture and new-found restaurant scene. Note that the hotel is in a pre-war walk-up building (no elevators).

Washington Square Hotel

103 Waverly Place, between MacDougal Street & Sixth Avenue (1-212 777 9515/1-800 222 0418/www.washingtonsquarehotel.com). Subway A, B, C, D, E, F, V to W 4th Street. **Rates** $215-$220 double. **Rooms** 155. **Credit** AmEx, MC, V. **Map** p403 E28 ⓰

This quintessential Greenwich Village hotel has been a haven for writers and artists for decades, and also has something of a rock 'n' roll past: Bob Dylan and Joan Baez both lived here back when they sang for change in nearby Washington Square Park. Today, the century-old hotel remains popular with travellers aiming to soak up Village life. Recently, the deluxe rooms were expanded into larger chambers decked out with art deco furnishings and leather headboards. The cosy bar-lounge serves

afternoon tea and light fare. Rates include a complimentary continental breakfast – or you can splurge on the Sunday jazz brunch at North Square (1-212 254 1200), the hotel's restaurant.
Bar. Gym. Internet (wireless; free). Restaurant.

Budget

East Village Bed & Coffee

110 Avenue C, between 7th & 8th Streets (1-212 533 4175/www.bedandcoffee.com). Subway F, V to Lower East Side-Second Avenue; L to First Avenue. **Rates** $90-$130 double. **Rooms** 9. **Credit** AmEx, MC, V. **Map** p403 G28 ⑰

Popular with European travellers, this unassuming East Village B&B (breakfast meaning coffee) is a great place in which to immerse yourself in downtown culture without splashing too much cash. The nine guest rooms come with eclectic furnishings and quirky themes, such as the Black and White Room and the 110 Downing Street room. Shared areas include three separate loft-like living rooms, bathrooms and fully equipped kitchens. In nice weather, sip your complimentary java in the private garden.
Internet (wireless; free).

Other locations: Second Home on Second Avenue, 221 Second Avenue, between 13th & 14th Streets, East Village (1-212 677 3161/www.secondhome.citysearch.com).

Larchmont Hotel

27 W 11th Street, between Fifth & Sixth Avenues (1-212 989 9333/www.larchmonthotel.com). Subway F, V to 14th Street; L to Sixth Avenue. **Rates** $109-$129 double. **Rooms** 60. **Credit** AmEx, DC, Disc, MC, V. **Map** p403 E28 ⑱

Housed in a 1910 Beaux Arts building, the attractive, affordable Larchmont Hotel may be the best-value place in the heart of Greenwich Village. The decor (wicker furniture, floral bedspreads) recalls the set of *The Golden Girls*, but with prices this reasonable, you can accept low marks for style. All of the bathrooms are shared, but rooms come equipped with a washbasin, a robe and a pair of slippers.
Internet (wireless; free).

Union Square Inn

*209 E 14th Street, between Second & Third Avenues (1-212 614 0500/www.nyinns.com). Subway L to Third Avenue; N, Q, R, W, 4, 5, 6 to 14th Street-*Union Square. **Rates** $89-$149 single/double. **Rooms** 45. **Credit** AmEx, MC, V. **Map** p403 F27 ⑲

For review, *see p76* **Murray Hill Inn**.

Hostels

Bowery's Whitehouse Hotel of New York

340 Bowery, between 2nd & 3rd Streets (1-212 477 5623/www.whitehousehotelofny.com). Subway B, D, F, V to Broadway-Lafayette Street; 6 to Bleecker Street. **Rates** $66 double. **Rooms** 100. **Credit** AmEx, Disc, MC, V. **Map** p403 F29 ⑳

The Bowery Hotel. *See p59.*

Even though the Bowery progressively looks more sleek than seedy, with pricey restaurants and flashy clubs popping up in recent years, the unapologetically budget Whitehouse Hotel remains steadfastly basic. Built in 1919 as housing for railroad workers, the renovated hotel offers semi-private cubicles (ceilings are an open latticework, so be warned that snorers or sleep talkers may interrupt your slumber) at unbelievably low rates. Towels and linens are provided. A microwave and large-screen TV are available in the lounge at all times.
Internet (wireless; $5/day).

Midtown

Luxury

Four Seasons

57 E 57th Street, between Madison & Park Avenues (1-212 758 5700/1-800 332 3442/www.fourseasons.com). Subway N, R, W to Lexington Avenue-59th Street; 4, 5, 6 to 59th Street. **Rates** $695-$915 double. **Rooms** 368. **Credit** AmEx, DC, Disc, MC, V. **Map** p405 E22 ㉑

New York's most quintessential hotel hasn't slipped a notch from its heyday. Everybody who's anybody, from music-industry executives to political figures, continue to drop in for a dose of New York luxury. Renowned architect IM Pei's sharp geometric design (in neutral cream and honey tones) is sleek and modern, and rooms are among the largest in the city (the three-bedroom Royal Suite measures 2,000 sq ft). From the higher floors, the views of the city are superb. The hotel is known for catering to the guest's every need; your 4am hot-fudge sundae is only a room-service call away.

Bar. Business centre. Gym. Internet (wireless; $10/day). Restaurants (2). Spa.

Inn at Irving Place

56 Irving Place, between 17th & 18th Streets (1-212 533 4600/1-800 685 1447/www.innatirving.com). Subway L, N, Q, R, W, 4, 5, 6 to 14th Street-Union Square. **Rates** $445-$595 double. **Rooms** 11. **Credit** AmEx, DC, Disc, MC, V. **Map** p403 F27 ㉒

Centenarian comeback

October 2007 marked the 100th birthday of one of the grandest dames of New York society, **The Plaza Hotel** (*see opposite*). Like all celebrated ladies of her rarefied rank, she isn't taking it lying down. After more than two years of nipping, tucking and lifting, this New York classic is poised to regain its rightful place in the social spotlight. A recent walk through the Plaza's lobbies and corridors revealed that the battalion of construction workers have done a stupendous job and, best of all, that the splendid interiors are still intact. The original mosaic floors, with their elaborate motifs, shine like new.

Since it opened in 1907, the Plaza has starred in movies (*North by Northwest, The Way We Were*); been written about (*The Great Gatsby*, the Eloise books); and has hosted some of the most unforgettable high-society galas (such as Truman Capote's noted Black and White Ball in 1966). But despite its towering reputation, the Plaza found itself struggling in recent years. Taking advantage of out-of-control property values, the five-star has now converted most of its hotel rooms into luxury condominiums – many of which have been snapped up for many millions of dollars. All told, the $350 million renovation of the French Renaissance-style building will have 182 luxury residences and 282 hotel rooms. Posh retail outlets and smart restaurants are slated for the low mezzanine. But visitors hoping to get a taste of the glory days won't be disappointed. Eight of the hotels most revered public spaces – including the Oak Room, Palm Court and Grand Ballroom – have been designated as landmarks. What's more, features such as the Palm Court's intricate stained-glass ceiling have been recreated in the neo-classical style that architect Henry Hardenburgh intended (the original was painted over in the 1940s). Ladies and gentlemen, we give you... the Plaza.

Inn at Irving Place may admittedly be one of Manhattan's smallest hotels, but it is also one of its most endearing. Housed in a pair of brownstones near Gramercy Park, the place is liberally dotted with fresh flowers and antique furnishings. While some rooms are petite, each is decorated with turn-of-the-19th-century elegance. Leave the little ones at home (children under 12 are not permitted). At Lady Mendl's (1-212 533 4466, reservations required), the inn's pretty tearoom, damask love seats and a lavish tea and dessert menu create the perfect spot for brushing up on your manners. Edith Wharton would feel right at home.
Bars. Internet (wireless; free).

New York Palace Hotel

455 Madison Avenue, between 50th & 51st Streets (1-212 888 7000/1-800 697 2522/www.newyorkpalace.com). Subway E, V to Fifth Avenue-53rd Street. **Rates** $445-$620 double. **Rooms** 896. **Credit** AmEx, DC, Disc, MC, V. **Map** p404 E23 ㉓
Stepping inside the Palace is like stepping into a fairytale, with red carpet, twinkling lights and fancy tea parties, so it's hard to believe that the hotel was once owned by recently deceased real-estate tycoon (and former jailbird) Leona Helmsley. Designed by McKim, Mead & White, the cluster of mansions now holds nearly 900 rooms decorated in an art deco or neoclassical style. Triplex suites have a top-tier terrace, solarium and private rooftop garden. The famous restaurant Le Cirque 2000 has now moved from here, but you can still sip a Manhattan in the extravagant Gilt, a new bar and lounge, and you can sample New American fare and exotic cocktails at the elegant Istana Restaurant.
Bars (2). Business centre. Gym. Internet (wireless; free). Restaurants (2). Spa.

The Pierre

2 E 61st Street, at Fifth Avenue (1-212 838 8000/1-800 743 7734/www.tajhotels.com). Subway N, R, W to Fifth Avenue-59th Street. **Rates** $475-$995 double. **Rooms** 201. **Credit** AmEx, DC, Disc, MC, V. **Map** p405 E22 ㉔
A long-standing landmark of New York glamour, the Pierre marked its 75th birthday in 2005. In the same year, the Taj Hotels group took over – and at press time, a $6 million renovation was on the cards. In the meantime, the old-time glamour remains intact: a black-and-white-checkered sidewalk leads up to the gleaming gold lobby; front-facing rooms overlook Central Park; and wares from fancy neighbouring stores are on display in the lobby. There are three separate restaurants in the building, including the opulent Café Pierre. *Photo p68.*
Bars (2). Business centre. Gym. Internet (wireless; $10/day). Restaurant (3).

The Plaza Hotel

768 Fifth Avenue, at Central Park South (1-212 759 3000/1-800 759 3000/www.fairmont.com). Subway N, R, W to Fifth Avenue-59th Street. **Rates** from $725 double. **Rooms** 282. **Credit** AmEx, DC, Disc, MC, V. **Map** p405 E22 ㉕
Built in 1907 and renowned for its sprawling baroque splendour, the Plaza Hotel counts some of Fifth Avenue's most exclusive stores among its immediate neighbours. This landmark building has recently undergone a dazzling restoration and is set to reopen for its 100th birthday in late 2007; *see opposite* **Centenarian comeback**.
Bars (2). Business centre. Gym. Internet (wireless; free). Restaurants (2). Spa.

Expensive

The Algonquin

59 W 44th Street, between Fifth & Sixth Avenues (1-212 840 6800/www.thealgonquin.net). Subway B, D, F, V to 42nd Street-Bryant Park; 7 to Fifth Avenue. **Rates** $299-$700 double. **Rooms** 174. **Credit** AmEx, DC, Disc, MC, V. **Map** p404 E24 ㉖
This landmark hotel with a strong literary past (greats like Alexander Woollcott and Dorothy Parker gathered in the infamous Round Table Room to gossip) is beautifully decked out with upholstered chairs, old lamps and large paintings of key figures of the Jazz Age. In 2004, renovations spiffed up the small quarters with new bed spreads and mahogany furniture, and many rooms now have flat-screen TVs. But there's still a sense of old New York; hallways are covered with wallpaper printed with *The New Yorker* cartoons (to commemorate Harold Ross, who secured funding for the magazine over long meetings at the Round Table). Quarters are on the small side and the décor can feel a little dated, but the feel is still classic New York. You can catch readings by local authors on some Mondays, and cabaret performers take over in the Oak Room (*see p281*) Tuesday through Saturday. The lobby still buzzes with a buttoned-up after-work crowd looking to wet their whistle in style.
Bar. Gym. Internet (wireless; $10/day). Restaurant.

Bryant Park Hotel

40 W 40th Street, between Fifth & Sixth Avenues (1-212 642 2200/www.bryantparkhotel.com). Subway B, D, F, V to 42nd Street-Bryant Park; 7 to Fifth Avenue. **Rates** $309-$675 double. **Rooms** 129. **Credit** AmEx, DC, MC, V. **Map** p404 E24 ㉗
This midtown hotel has seen a lot more action since Koi (*see p207*), the East Coast branch of the splashy Los Angeles restaurant, opened on site in spring 2005. Ian Schrager's partner Philip Pilevsky converted the 1924 American Radiator Building into his first New York property. The Bryant Park has all the right accessories to lure a modish crowd (including a gorgeous 70-seat screening room with red velour chairs and built-in desks) and, thanks to the hotel's close proximity to Bryant Park, a well-heeled clientele checks in each year during Fashion Week. And yet, despite all this, the rooms can occasionally feel a little stark, and – casting aside the LCD TVs – a little IKEA-esque. You can always head downstairs for a cocktail in the vaulted Cellar Bar, however, to redress the balance.
Bar. Gym. Internet (wireless; $10/day). Restaurant.

Casablanca Hotel

147 W 43rd Street, between Sixth Avenue & Broadway (1-212 869 1212/1-800 922 7225/www.casablancahotel.com). Subway B, D, F, V to 42nd Street-Bryant Park; N, Q, R, W to 42nd Street; S, 1, 2, 3, 7 to 42nd Street-Times Square. **Rates** $279-$365 double. **Rooms** 43. **Credit** AmEx, DC, MC, V. **Map** p404 D24 ㉘

Run by the same people who own the Library Hotel (*see p69*), this 48-room boutique hotel has a cheerful Moroccan theme throughout. The main lobby is an oasis in the middle of Times Square, with plenty of greenery and walls that are adorned with blue and gold Mediterranean-style tiles. The theme is somewhat diluted in the basic rooms, but wicker furniture, wooden shutters and new carpets and sofas warm up the space. Rick's Café serves free wine and cheese to guests Monday to Saturday. Breakfast is complimentary, as is your copy of *Casablanca* and a pass to a nearby gym.

Bar. Internet (wireless; free). Restaurants.

Dream Hotel

210 W 55th Street, between Broadway & Seventh Avenue (1-212 247 2000/1-866 437 3266/www.dreamny.com). Subway N, Q, R, W to 57th Street. **Rates** $275-$575 double. **Rooms** 216. **Credit** AmEx, Disc, MC, V. **Map** p405 D22 ㉙

In 2004, hotelier Vikram Chatwal, who brought us the Time hotel (*see p68*), enlisted bold-faced names to turn the old Majestic Hotel into a luxury lodge with a trippy slumberland theme. New York architect and designer David Rockwell decked out the restaurant, an outpost of Italian Serafina, with an interior inspired by Fellini films; and bestselling new-age author Deepak Chopra conceived the Ayurvedic spa. The lobby sums up the whimsical aesthetic – walls are cloaked in Paul Smith-style stripes, a crystal boat dangles from the ceiling and an enormous gold statue of Catherine the Great stands guard. The rooms are more streamlined, with white walls, satin headboards and an ethereal blue backlight that glows under the bed. Luxurious touches include feather-duvet-topped beds, plasma TV with movies on demand and an iPod – loaded with ambient music – featuring cutting-edge Bose speakers. Ava, the rooftop bar, wows drinkers with its panoramic views of the city beyond.

Bars (2). Gym. Internet (wireless; free). Restaurant. Spa.

Flatotel

135 W 52nd Street, between Sixth & Seventh Avenues (1-212 887 9400/www.flatotel.com). Subway N, R, W to 49th Street; 1 to 50th Street. **Rates** $300-$489 double. **Rooms** 293. **Credit** AmEx, DC, MC, V. **Map** p404 D23 ㉚

Upon entrance, the Flatotel seems to have a hip swagger: techno beats pump through the granite lobby, where dimly lit nooks and cowhide couches are filled with guests drinking cocktails. Rooms are less cutting-edge, however, although they still modern and very spacious, and some rooms have impressive views of the city. A slew of reality television shows, including *America's Next Top Model*, has been filmed in the penthouse suites. The in-house restaurant, Moda (1-212 887 9880), serves Italian-inspired fare; in temperate weather, catch a breeze with your cocktail in the restaurant's alfresco atrium. For private imbibing, call the martini butler, who will mix the drink in your room.

Bar. Business centre. Internet (wireless; free). Restaurant.

Hotel Chandler

12 E 31st Street, between Fifth & Madison Avenues (1-212 889 6363/www.hotelchandler.com). Subway 6 to 33rd Street. **Rates** $325-$425 double. **Rooms** 125. **Credit** AmEx, DC, Disc, MC, V. **Map** p404 E25 ㉛

Rooms at this delightful hotel are certainly a touch style-conscious, with black-and-white photographs of New York streetscapes on the walls, chequered carpeting, and Frette robes and Aveda products in the bathroom. The in-house 12:31 bar offers cocktails and light nibbles. And the affable turndown service means a chocolate on your pillow and a next-day weather forecast.

Bar. Gym. Internet (wireless; free).

Hotel Elysée

60 E 54th Street, between Madison & Park Avenues (1-212 753 1066/www.elyseehotel.com). Subway E, V to Lexington Avenue-53rd Street; 6 to 51st Street. **Rates** $295-$465 double. **Rooms** 101. **Credit** AmEx, DC, Disc, MC, V. **Map** p405 E22 ㉜

The Hotel Elysée is a well-preserved piece of New York's Jazz Age: quarters are appointed with a touch of romance (period fabrics, antique furniture), and some rooms have coloured-glass conservatories and terraces. Elysée is popular with publishers and literary types, who convene over complimentary wine and cheese in the evening. Downstairs is the Steakhouse at Monkey Bar (1-212 838 2600), where a well-coiffed clientele dines on fine cuts.

Bar. Internet (wireless; free). Restaurant. Spa.

Hotel 41

206 W 41st Street, between Seventh & Eighth Avenues (1-212 703 8600/www.hotel41.com). Subway N, Q, R, W to 42nd Street; S, 1, 2, 3, 7 to 42nd Street-Times Square. **Rates** $280-$320 double. **Rooms** 47. **Credit** AmEx, Disc, MC, V. **Map** p404 D24 ㉝

Although its look is cool, this tiny boutique hotel feels comfy-warm: reading lamps extend from dark-wood headboards, and triple-glazed windows effectively filter out the cacophony from the streets below. The penthouse suite has a large private terrace with potted trees and views of Times Square. Bar 41 serves breakfast, lunch and dinner.

Internet (wireless; free).

Hudson

356 W 58th Street, between Eighth & Ninth Avenues (1-212 554 6000/www.hudsonhotel.com). Subway A, B, C, D, 1 to 59th Street-Columbus Circle. **Rates** $399-$469 double. **Rooms** 805. **Credit** AmEx, DC, Disc, MC, V. **Map** p405 C22 ㉞

Business meets pleasure at the **Hampton Inn Manhattan-Seaport**. *See p60.*

The Hudson might have miniscule rooms but it certainly gets points for looks. The verdant courtyard is shaded with enormous potted trees, a rooftop terrace overlooks the Hudson River, and the glass-ceilinged lobby (with imported English ivy), the Hudson Cafeteria and the three on-site bars are crawling with beautiful people. This is the third New York palace in Ian Schrager's hip-hotel kingdom, which also includes Morgans and the Royalton.

Bars (2). Business centre. Gym. Internet (wireless; $10/day). Restaurant.

Other locations: Morgans, 237 Madison Avenue, between 37th & 38th Streets, Midtown (1-212 686 0300/1-800 334 3408); Royalton, 44 W 44th Street, between Fifth & Sixth Avenues, Midtown (1-212 869 4400/1-800 635 9013).

Inn on 23rd Street

131 W 23rd Street, between Sixth & Seventh Avenues (1-212 463 0330/www.innon23rd.com). Subway A, C, E to 14th Street; L to Eighth Avenue.

Rates $209-$279 double. **Rooms** 14. **Credit** AmEx, MC, V. **Map** p404 D26 35

This real-deal B&B in the heart of Chelsea gives you a warm and fuzzy feeling from the moment that you enter. Owners and innkeepers Annette and Barry Fisherman renovated a 19th-century townhouse into a homely inn with 14 themed rooms (all accessible by elevator and each with a private bathroom). Rooms are exceptionally plush: pillow-topped mattresses, double-glazed windows and white-noise machines will ensure a decent night's sleep.

Internet (wireless; free).

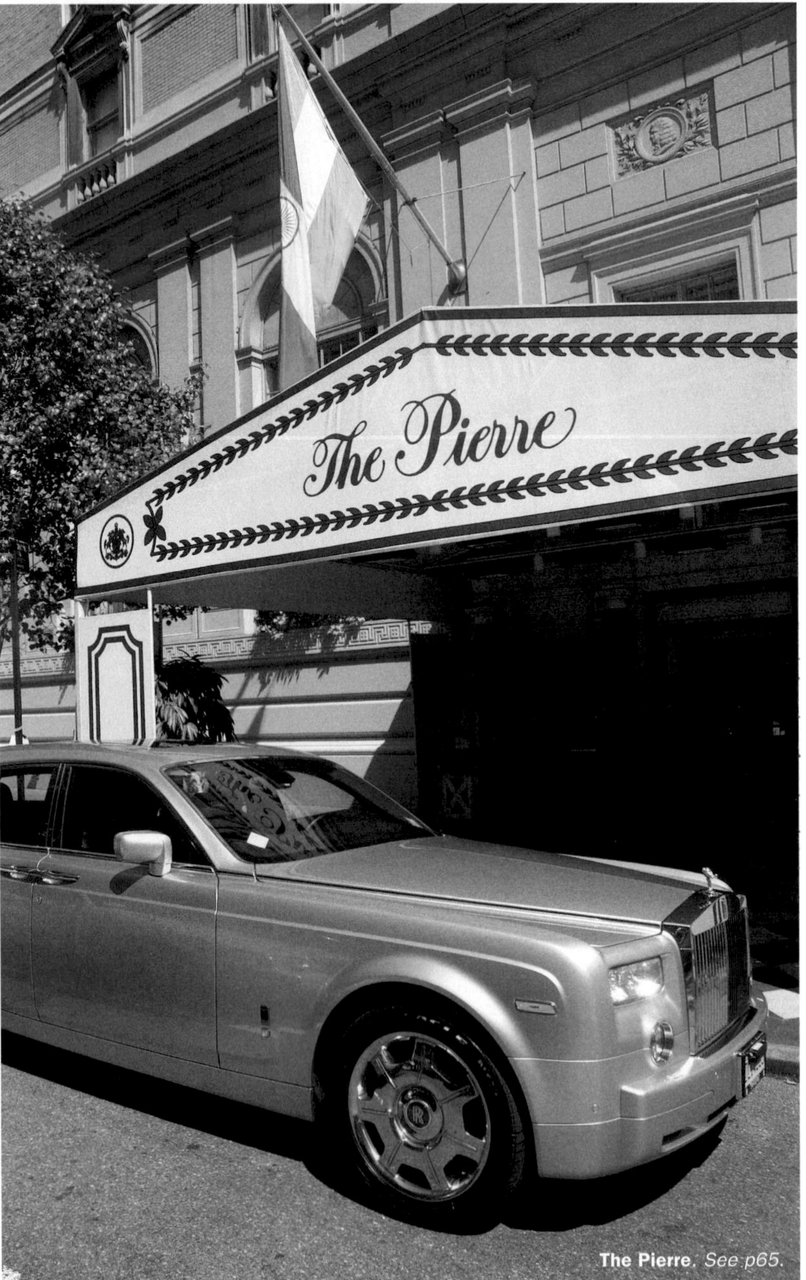

The Pierre. *See p65.*

Library Hotel

299 Madison Avenue, at 41st Street (1-212 983 4500/www.libraryhotel.com). Subway 42nd Street S, 4, 5, 6, 7 to 42nd Street-Grand Central; 7 to Fifth Avenue. **Rates** $400 double. **Rooms** 60. **Credit** AmEx, DC, MC, V. **Map** p404 E24 36

More than 6,000 books were handpicked from indie fave the Strand Book Store (*see p231*) to match the theme of the rooms they adorn at this literary-inspired boutique hotel. Even before you enter, you'll see quotes from famous authors inscribed in the sidewalk. Lodgings are organised according to the Dewey decimal system and furnished by subject (Botany, Fairy Tales). For instance, the Love Room is strewn with rose petals, and Casanova's autobiography sits on a bedside table in the Erotica Room. Rates include breakfast, evening wine and cheese gatherings in the second-floor Reading Room, and access to the mahogany-lined writer's den (which has a lovely tiny terrace and a glowing fireplace). The casual seafood destination, Branzini, is located in the lobby. Hotel Giraffe, meanwhile, which is a sister hotel to the Library, manages to embody modern European style 15 blocks south.

Business centre. Internet (wireless; free). Restaurant.

Other locations: Hotel Giraffe, 365 Park Avenue South, at 26th Street, Flatiron District (1-212 685 7700/1-877 296 0009/www.hotelgiraffe.com).

The London NYC

151 W 54th Street, between Sixth & Seventh Avenues (1-866 690 2029/www.thelondonnyc.com). Subway B, D, E to Seventh Avenue. **Rates** $299-$529 double. **Rooms** 562. **Credit** AmEx, DC, Disc, MC, V. **Map** p405 D22 37

Formerly the Rihga Royal Hotel, this 54-storey high-rise was completely overhauled and reopened as the chic London NYC in early 2007. With luxury at every turn and an on-site concierge service, the London promises to provide guests with any indulgence no matter how great or small. If you can't afford the sky-high rates you can always pop in for a look-see: the inviting lobby is done up as a grand London residence. The spot also boasts the London Bar and Gordon Ramsay at The London (*see p205*) – the first ever US eaterie for the UK's favourite bad boy chef. *Photo p71.*

Bar. Business centre. Gym. Internet (wireless; $13/day). Restaurant. Spa.

Maritime Hotel

363 W 16th Street, between Eighth & Ninth Avenues (1-212 242 4300/www.themaritimehotel.com). Subway A, C, E to 14th Street; L to Eighth Avenue. **Rates** $325-$425 double. **Map** p403 C27 38

What are porthole windows doing on a hotel in Chelsea? Well, it's not *all* for show – the building is the former headquarters of the Maritime Union. In 2002, owners Eric Goode and Sean MacPherson took this nautical theme and spun it into the high-gloss Maritime Hotel, blending the look of a luxury yacht with a chic 1960s airport lounge. The lobby is a bit dark, but the rooms are much more eye-catching. Modelled after ship cabins, with a chic retro look, each has one large porthole window and lots of glossy teak panelling. For more space, book one of the two penthouses, which have their own private terrace with an outdoor shower. The hotel offers four food and drink spaces: Matsuri, a gorgeous Japanese restaurant; La Bottega (*see p199*), an Italian trattoria with a lantern-festooned patio; Cabana, an airy rooftop bar; and Hiro, a basement lounge that regularly draws a buzzing crowd.

Bars (3). Business centre. Gym. Internet (wireless; free). Restaurants (2).

Night Hotel

132 W 45th Street, between Sixth & Seventh Avenues (1-212 835 9600/www.nighthotelny.com). Subway N, Q, R, W to 42nd Street; S, 1, 2, 3, 7 to 42nd Street-Times Square. **Rates** $325-$400 double. **Rooms** 70. **Credit** AmEx, DC, Disc, MC, V. **Map** p404 D24 39

At Midtown's Night Hotel, the new 72-room night-themed boutique property from Vikram Chatwal (of Dream Hotel and Time; *see p66 & p71*), guests will see the city through the romantic lens of 'modern Gothic Gotham'. A nightcrawler's roost, the hotel's stylish black-and-white motif extends beyond the loungey lobby to the sultry and handsome rooms. The Addams Family would love it. *Photo p73.*

Bar. Internet (wireless; $10/day). Restaurant.

Park South Hotel

124 E 28th Street, between Park Avenue South & Lexington Avenue (1-212 448 0888/1-800 315 4642/www.parksouthhotel.com). Subway 6 to 28th Street. **Rates** $250-$350 double. **Rooms** 141. **Credit** AmEx, DC, Disc, MC, V. **Map** p404 E26 40

Everything about this quaint boutique hotel says 'I love New York'. The mezzanine library is crammed with books on historic Gotham, and the walls are covered with images from the New York Historical Society. Rooms are handsomely appointed in warm amber and brown tones, and some have dazzling views of the Chrysler Building. Bathrooms are stocked with essential oil products and thick terry-cloth bathrobes. The hotel's bar-restaurant, Black Duck (1-212 204 5240), provides live jazz music to accompany a laid-back brunch.

Bar. Business centre. Gym. Internet (wireless; free). Restaurant.

Roger Smith

501 Lexington Avenue, between 47th & 48th Streets (1-212 755 1400/1-800 445 0277/www.rogersmith.com). Subway E, V to Lexington Avenue-53rd Street; 6 to 51st Street. **Rates** $300-$295 double. **Rooms** 136. **Credit** AmEx, DC, Disc, MC, V. **Map** p404 F23 41

The spacious chambers at this arty spot make it a good option for families with a little cash to spare. Each room is decorated with unique furnishings and colourful wallpaper. The Roger Smith Gallery hosts rotating exhibitions, and a few interesting pieces by artist James Knowles (whose family owns the hotel) adorn the lobby.

Bar. Internet (wireless; free). Restaurant.

Time

224 W 49th Street, between Broadway & Eighth Avenue (1-212 320 2900/1-877 846 3692/www.thetimeny.com). Subway C, E, 1 to 50th Street; N, R, W to 49th Street. **Rates** $349-$559 double. **Rooms** 162. **Credit** AmEx, DC, Disc, MC, V. **Map** p404 D23 42

Ever wondered what it would be like to feel, taste and smell colour? Adam Tihany, of Night and Dream Hotels (*see p69 and p66*), designed this boutique hotel with the idea of stimulating the senses through a single primary colour (guest rooms are furnished in either red, yellow or blue). Expect to find your room replete with matching duvets, jellybeans and reading materials, as well as a chromatically inspired scent.

Bar. Internet (wireless; $11/day). Restaurant.

W New York-Times Square

1567 Broadway, at 47th Street (1-212 930 7400/1-877 976 8357/www.whotels.com). Subway N, R, W to 49th Street; 1 to 50th Street. **Rates** $300-$579 double. **Rooms** 509. **Credit** AmEx, DC, Disc, MC, V. **Map** p404 D23 43

'Whatever, whenever' is the motto of this luxury boutique chain, and the hotel's concierge is always at the ready to fill your bathtub with champagne, chocolate or whatever else your heart desires. NYC's fifth and flashiest W location has a street-level vestibule with a waterfall (reception is on the seventh floor). To your right, the Living Room is a sprawl of white leather seating. Every private room features a floating-glass desk and a sleek bathroom stocked with Bliss spa products, but it's the bed-to-ceiling headboard mirror and sexy room service menu that really get the mind racing. Steve Hanson's Blue Fin (1-212 918 1400) serves a combination of stellar sushi and superb cocktails.

Bars (2). Business centre. Gym. Internet (wireless; $17/day). Restaurant. Spa.

Other locations: W New York, 541 Lexington Avenue, at 49th Street, Midtown (1-212 755 1200); W New York-The Court, 130 E 39th Street, between Park Avenue South & Lexington Avenue, Midtown (1-212 685 1100); W New York-The Tuscany, 120 E 39th Street, between Park Avenue South & Lexington Avenue, Midtown (1-212 686 1600); W New York-Union Square, 201 Park Avenue South, at 17th Street, Midtown (1-212 253 9119).

Waldorf-Astoria

301 Park Avenue, at 50th Street (1-212 355 3000/1-800 925 3673/www.waldorf.com). Subway E, V to Lexington Avenue-53rd Street; 6 to 51st Street. **Rates** $300-$450 double. **Rooms** 1,215. **Credit** AmEx, DC, Disc, MC, V. **Map** p404 E23 44

First built in 1893, the Waldorf-Astoria was the city's largest hotel (and birthplace of the Waldorf salad), but it was demolished to make way for the Empire State Building. The current art deco Waldorf opened in 1931 and now has protected status as a historic hotel. The rooms, with wingback chairs, love

The London NYC. *See p69.*

seats, rich colours and layered fabrics, feel like they were decorated by Upper East Side socialites of yore. In addition to history, it has spent $2 million on making 24 rooms into 12 reconfigured 'Astor Suites' – larger than many New York apartments. As ever, the Waldorf-Astoria caters to the high and mighty; guests have included Princess Grace, Sophia Loren and a long list of US presidents. Double-check your attire before entering the hotel – you won't be allowed in if you're wearing a baseball cap, T-shirt or even trendy ripped jeans.
Bar. Business centre. Gym. Internet (wireless; free). Restaurants (4). Spa.

Warwick New York Hotel

65 W 54th Street, at Sixth Avenue (1-212 247 2700/ 1-800 223 4099/www.warwickhotels.com). Subway E, V to Fifth Avenue-53rd Street; F to 57th Street.
Rates $325-$475 double. **Rooms** 426. **Credit** AmEx, DC, MC, V. **Map** p405 E22 45

You'd never know it from its dated façade, but the grand Warwick was frequented by Elvis and the Beatles during their tours, and the top-floor suite with a wraparound balcony was once the home of actor Cary Grant. Built by William Randolph Hearst in 1927, the Warwick is listed by the National Trust for Historic Preservation. Rooms are exceptionally large by Midtown standards, and have feminine touches such as floral curtains and bedspreads. The Murals on 54 restaurant – with a range of murals by Dean Cornwell – has been recently refurbished by designer Pierre Court.
Bars (2). Business centre. Gym. Internet (wireless; $12/day). Restaurant.

Moderate

Broadway Inn

264 W 46th Street, at Eighth Avenue (1-212 997 9200/1-800 826 6300/www.broadwayinn.com). Subway A, C, E to 42nd Street-Port Authority.
Rates $265-$350 double. **Rooms** 40. **Credit** AmEx, DC, Disc, MC, V. **Map** p404 D23 46

Theatre junkies should take note: this endearing little hotel can arrange a 35-40 per cent discount on theatre tickets; it also offers several good Broadway dinner-and-show combos. The warm lobby has exposed-brick walls, ceiling fans and shelves that are loaded with bedtime reading material, and the fairly priced basic guest rooms and suites get lots of natural light. On the downside, there are no elevators, and the hotel is strict about its three-night minimum policy on weekends and holidays.
Internet (wireless; free).

High times

Raise a glass at one of these happening hotel bars in the sky.

The **Time Warner Center** (*see p146*) might be little more than a glorified shopping mall, but even jaded New Yorkers can't deny that the location, overlooking Columbus Circle, provides some stellar views. One prime spot to enjoy them is from the comfort of a leather chair at the **Mandarin Oriental Hotel**'s (Time Warner Center, 80 Columbus Circle, at 60th Street, 1-212 805 8800) Lobby Lounge, perched 35 floors above the south-west corner of Central Park. Naturally, the drinks aren't exactly cheap (signature cocktails are $17 apiece), but the Fifth Avenue and Central Park South skylines, glittering through walls of windows, make those extra bucks worthwhile.

Plunge, the rooftop bar over at the **Hotel Gansevoort** (*see p57*) with access to the adjacent pool, is where you'll find bikini-clad hotel guests. You, of course, will have to wear clothes if you want to make it through the posh lobby and up to the penthouse, but you can strip down once you get there and sunbathe, caipirinha, mojito or margarita in hand. Prices are sky-high but Plunge's $15 Mango Lime Rickey will at least have you tapping into the trendy soundtrack. Nearby, at the **Maritime Hotel** (*see p69*), preppy striped banquettes give Cabanas a yacht-ish vibe. This rooftop bar offers comfy alfresco couches, exotic drinks served by model-like cocktail waitresses and a canopy of paper lanterns to help set the mood.

Ava Lounge, at the **Dream Hotel** (*see p66*), is a chic, bi-level space offering gorgeous, nearly wraparound views across Midtown, including an electric vista of Times Square. Equal parts safari, French Riviera and old-school Miami Beach, this spot is a superb perch, and Broadway theatre-goers should keep it in mind for pre- or post-show drinks.

Everybody knows that Downtown is simply the coolest part of town, and it doesn't really get any cooler than A-60, the rooftop bar at **60 Thompson** (*see p58*), where good-looking media types gather to celebrate their wonderfulness in a sleek, shimmering lounge. The snag? It is for hotel guests only, but if you're looking gorgeous and it's slightly off-hours, you might be able to squeeze in for drinks and a killer view.

Chelsea Hotel

222 W 23rd Street, between Seventh & Eighth Avenues (1-212 243 3700/www.hotelchelsea.com). Subway C, E, 1 to 23rd Street. **Rates** $239 double. **Rooms** 100. **Credit** AmEx, DC, Disc, MC, V. **Map** p404 D26 47

Built in 1884, the Chelsea has a long (and infamous) past: Nancy Spungen was allegedly murdered in Room 100 by her boyfriend, Sex Pistol Sid Vicious. This funky hotel has seen an endless parade of noteworthy guests: in 1912, *Titanic* survivors stayed here; other former residents include Mark Twain, Dee Dee Ramone, Thomas Wolfe and Madonna. Rooms are generally large with high ceilings, but certain amenities, like large flat-panel TVs, washer-dryers and marble fireplaces, vary. Make no mistake, you're paying for the hotel's sordid (if not grungy) past – the rooms aren't exactly gleaming.

Internet (wireless; free).

414 Hotel

414 W 46th Street, between Ninth & Tenth Avenues (1-212 399 0006/www.414hotel.com). Subway A, C, E to 42nd Street-Port Authority. **Rates** $209-$229 double. **Rooms** 22. **Credit** AmEx, MC, V. **Map** p404 C23 48

This small hotel's shockingly affordable rates and reclusive location make it feel like a secret you've been lucky to stumble upon. Immaculate rooms are tastefully appointed with suede headboards, vases full of colourful roses and framed black-and-white photos of the city. There's a glowing fireplace and computer available to guests in the lobby and a leafy courtyard outside.

Internet (wireless; free).

Hotel Edison

228 W 47th Street, at Broadway (1-212 840 5000/1-800 637 7070/www.edisonhotelnyc.com). Subway N, R, W to 49th Street; 1 to 50th Street. **Rates** $190-$210 double. **Rooms** 800. **Credit** AmEx, DC, Disc, MC, V. **Map** p404 D23 49

Theatre lovers flock to this recently renovated art deco hotel for its affordable rates and convenient location. Rooms are of a standard size but are decidedly spruced up. Café Edison (1-212 840 5000), a classic diner just off the lobby, is a long-time favourite of Broadway actors and their fans – Neil Simon was so smitten that he put it in one of his plays.

Bar. Business centre. Gym. Internet (wireless; $10/day). Restaurant.

Hotel Metro

45 W 35th Street, between Fifth & Sixth Avenues (1-212 947 2500/1-800 356 3870/www.hotelmetronyc.com). Subway B, D, F, N, Q, R, V, W to 34th Street-Herald Square. **Rates** $275-$365 double. **Rooms** 179. **Credit** AmEx, DC, MC, V. **Map** p404 E25 50

It's not posh, but the Metro has good service and a retro vibe. Black-and-white portraits of Hollywood legends adorn the lobby, and the tiny rooms are clean. Take in views of the Empire State Building from the rooftop bar of Metro Grill.

Night Hotel. *See p69.*

Bar. Business centre. Gym. Internet (wireless; free). Restaurant.

Hotel Pennsylvania

401 Seventh Avenue, between 32nd & 33rd Streets (1-212 736 5000/1-800 223 8585/www.hotelpenn.com). Subway A, C, E, 1, 2, 3 to 34th Street-Penn Station. **Rates** $199-$299 double. **Rooms** 1,700. **Credit** AmEx, DC, Disc, MC, V. **Map** p404 D25 51

One of the city's largest hotels, the Pennsylvania's reasonable rates and convenient location (directly opposite Madison Square Garden and Penn Station) make it extremely popular with tourists. Rooms are basic but pleasant. The hotel's Café Rouge Ballroom once hosted such greats as Duke Ellington and the Glenn Miller Orchestra.

Bar. Business centre. Gym. Internet (wireless; $10/day). Restaurants (2).

Hotel QT

125 West 45th Street, between Sixth & Seventh Avenues (1-212 354 2323/www.hotelqt.com). Subway N, Q, R, W to 42nd Street; S, 1, 2, 3, 7, 9 to 42nd Street-Times Square. **Rates** $225-$425 double. **Rooms** 139. **Credit** AmEx, Disc, MC, V. **Map** p404 D23 52

Celebrity hotelier André Balazs has mastered almost every type of property, from hip LA hotels (the Standard) to art deco resorts (the Raleigh) in Miami to luxury condominiums in Manhattan. In 2006, he had a go at a 'youth hostel chic', albeit one with Egyptian cotton sheets, flat-panel TVs and a lobby pool with underwater music. Rooms start at pretty low prices for a Midtown hotel. This brand new stylish hotel for the budget-minded traveller is the last thing you'd expect to find in the middle of Times Square. The trippy corridors get smaller as you get to your room – which is also likely to be narrow, but with a range of fittings well adapted to the space.

Bar. Gym. Internet (wireless; free). Pool (1; indoor).

Hotel Thirty Thirty

30 E 30th Street, between Madison Avenue & Park Avenue South (1-212 689 1900/1-800 497 6028/www.thirtythirty-nyc.com). Subway 6 to 28th Street. **Rates** $249-$350 double. **Rooms** 250. **Credit** AmEx, DC, Disc, MC, V. **Map** p404 E25 53

Before it became a smart hotel, Thirty Thirty was a residence for single women, and 60 tenants still live here. Ambient music sets the tone in the spare, very fashionable, block-long lobby. Rooms are small but sleek and complemented by clean lines and textured fabrics. Executive-floor rooms are slightly larger, with nifty workspaces and slate bathrooms thrown into the mix. The hotel's restaurant, Zanna, serves a range of upmarket Mediterranean fare.

Bar. Internet (wireless; $10/day). Restaurant.

Marcel

201 E 24th Street, at Third Avenue (1-212 696 3800/www.hotelmarcelnewyork.com). Subway 6 to 23rd Street. **Rates** $197-$347 double. **Rooms** 97. **Credit** AmEx, DC, Disc, MC, V. **Map** p404 F26 54

Frequented by fashion-industry types because of its easy access to the Flatiron and Garment Districts, the Marcel features compact rooms with nice touches such as modern wood furniture and multicoloured padded headboards. An added bonus is the complimentary espresso bar in the lobby that's always open. You'll find the same chic perks and low prices at Marcel's four sister establishments: Ameritania Hotel, Amsterdam Court, the Moderne and the Bentley Hotel (*see p78*).

Internet (wireless; $10/day). Restaurant.

Other locations: Ameritania Hotel, 230 W 54th Street, at Broadway, Midtown (1-888 664 6835); Amsterdam Court, 226 W 50th Street, between Broadway & Eighth Avenue, Midtown (1-888 664 6835); Moderne, 243 W 55th Street, between Broadway & Eighth Avenue, Midtown (1-888 664 6835).

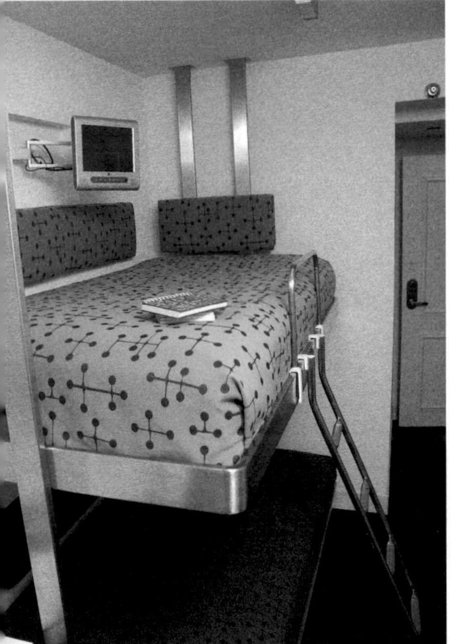

Good things, small packages: inner space explored at **The Pod Hotel**.

The Pod Hotel

230 E 51st Street, at Third Avenue (1-212 355 0300/ www.thepodhotel.com). Subway E to Lexington Avenue-53rd; 6 to 51st Street **Rates** $249 double. **Rooms** 349. **Credit** AmEx, DC, MC, V. **Map** p404 F23 55

This stylish new hotel opened in early 2007, offering bright and affordable rooms perfect for people who want a little style and a convenient location without parting with their life savings for the privilege. A short walk away you'll find the Museum of Modern Art, Rockefeller Center and plenty of splurge-worthy shopping on Fifth Avenue.

Internet (wireless; free).

Budget

Americana Inn

69 W 38th Street, at Sixth Avenue (1-212 840 6700/ www.newyorkhotel.com). Subway B, D, F, N, Q, R, V, W to 34th Street-Herald Square; B, D, F, V to 42nd Street. **Rates** $145 double. **Rooms** 54. **Credit** AmEx, MC, V. **Map** p404 E24 56

This budget hotel near Times Square has a speakeasy feel: the signage is discreet and you'll have to ring the doorbell to enter. What the Americana might lack in ambience (with its linoleum floors and fluorescent lighting), it makes up for in location (a rhinestone's throw from the major Broadway shows) and reasonable prices (rooms start at just under $100). And although all bathrooms are shared, rooms come with a mini-sink and large walk-in closets.

Internet (wireless; $10/day).

Carlton Arms Hotel

160 E 25th Street, at Third Avenue (1-212 679 0680/www.carltonarms.com). Subway 6 to 23rd Street. **Rates** $99-$115 double. **Rooms** 54. **Credit** MC, V. **Map** p404 F26 57

The Carlton Arms Art Project started in the late 1970s, when a small group of creative types brought new paint and fresh ideas to a run-down shelter. Today, the site is home to a Bohemian, tastefully decorated and very clean hotel with themed spaces (check out the English cottage room). Discounts are offered for students, overseas guests and patrons on weekly stays. Most guests share baths; tack on $15 for a private toilet. Rooms are booked early, so be sure to reserve well in advance.

Internet ($1/10mins).

Chelsea Lodge

318 W 20th Street, between Eighth & Ninth Avenues (1-212 243 4499/www.chelsealodge.com). Subway C, E to 23rd Street. **Rates** $129-$150 double. **Rooms** 26. **Credit** AmEx, DC, Disc, MC, V. **Map** p403 D27 58

If Martha Stewart decorated a log cabin, it would end up looking something like this 22-room inn, which is housed in a landmark brownstone. All of

the rooms (including the four suites down the block at 334 West 20th Street) have new beds, televisions, showers and air-conditioning. Although most are fairly small in size, the rooms are so incredibly charming that reservations fill up quickly. There's no sign outside, so be sure to write down the address before you set out.
Internet (wireless; free).

Chelsea Star Hotel

300 W 30th Street, at Eighth Avenue (1-212 244 7827/1-877 827 6969/www.starhotelny.com). Subway A, C, E to 34th Street-Penn Station. **Rates** $30 per person dorms; $69-$105 single/double/triple/quad with shared bath; $109-$199 double with private bath. **Rooms** 30. **Credit** AmEx, MC, V. **Map** p403 D25 59

Tired of sleeping in a boring beige box? Check in to this whimsical place, where your quarters might be decked out with Japanese paper screens (the Madame Butterfly) or huge wall paintings (the Dalí). The 16 themed rooms are a little on the small side (though also less pricey), and lavatories are shared. A recent renovation more than doubled the hotel's size; there are now 18 superior rooms and deluxe suites with mahogany furnishings, flat-screen TVs and private baths. Ultra-cheap, shared hostel-style dorm rooms are also available.
Internet (wireless; free)

Gershwin Hotel

7 E 27th Street, between Fifth & Madison Avenues (1-212 545 8000/www.gershwinhotel.com). Subway N, R, W, 6 to 28th Street. **Rates** $30-$60 per person in 4- to 8-bed dorm; $109-$329 for 1-3 people in private room. **Rooms** 60 beds in dorms; 135 private. **Credit** AmEx, MC, V. **Map** p404 E26 60

Works by Lichtenstein line the hallways, and an original Warhol soup-can painting hangs in the lobby of this funky pop art-themed budget hotel. Rates are extremely reasonable for a location just off Fifth Avenue. All rooms received a facelift in 2005, which brought in new chairs and upholstery. If you can afford a suite, book the Lindfors (named after the building's designer), which has screen-printed walls and a sitting room. Just off the lobby, but unaffiliated with the hotel itself, is Gallery at the Gershwin, a bar and lounge with glowing counter-tops and mod Lucite orbs.

Hotel 17

225 E 17th Street, between Second & Third Avenues (1-212 475 2845/www.hotel17ny.com). Subway L to Third Avenue; N, Q, R, W, 4, 5, 6 to 14th Street-Union Square. **Rates** $150 double. **Rooms** 120. **Credit** MC, V. **Map** p403 F27 61

Equivalent to a good dive bar, Hotel 17's grungy cachet is the draw here, and has been for some time now. Except for a recent sprucing up of the lobby, the place remains a little rough and funky. The hotel has been used for numerous films (Woody Allen shot scenes from *Manhattan Murder Mystery* here) and magazine shoots. Labyrinthine corridors lead to tiny high-ceilinged rooms filled with discarded dressers and mismatched 1950s wallpaper. Expect to share the hallway bathroom with other guests. The affiliated Hotel 31 (*see below*) has less ambience, but it suffices as a Gramercy budget hotel.

Hotel 31

120 E 31st Street, between Park Avenue South & Lexington Avenue (1-212 685 3060/www.hotel31.com). Subway 6 to 33rd Street. **Rates** $140-$180 double. **Rooms** 60. **Credit** MC, V. **Map** p404 E25 62
For review, *see above* Hotel 17.

Murray Hill Inn

143 E 30th Street, between Lexington & Third Avenues (1-212 683 6900/1-888 996 6376/www.nyinns.com). Subway 6 to 28th Street. **Rates** $89-$99 double with shared bath; $129 single/double with private bath. **Rooms** 50. **Credit** AmEx, MC, V. **Map** p404 F25 63

A recent renovation at the Murray Hill Inn added hardwood floors and new bathrooms (most of which are private). Discounted weekly and monthly rates are available for longer stays. Be sure to book well in advance, or try the sister locations: Amsterdam Inn (*see p79*), Central Park Hostel (*see p80*) and Union Square Inn (*see p63*).
Internet (wireless; $7/day).

Hostels

Big Apple Hostel

119 W 45th Street, between Sixth & Seventh Avenues (1-212 302 2603/www.bigapplehostel.com). Subway B, D, F, V to 42nd Street; N, Q, R, S, W, 1, 2, 3, 7 to Times Square-42nd Street. **Rates** $35-$60 dorm; $120 private room. **Rooms** 112 dorm beds; 11 private. **Credit** AmEx, DC, Disc, MC, V. **Map** p404 D23 64

Increasingly popular with backpackers, this very basic hostel is lacking in frills, but rooms are spotless and as cheap as they come. The Big Apple puts you just steps from the Theater District and Times Square. Beware if you're travelling in August: dorm rooms aren't air-conditioned and can easily start to feel a little overheated. That said, you can always take refuge in the breezy back patio, equipped with a grill for summer barbecues. Linens are provided, but remember to pack a towel.
Internet ($1/10mins).

Chelsea Center

313 W 29th Street, between Eighth & Ninth Avenues (1-212 643 0214/www.chelseacenterhostel.com). Subway A, C, E to 34th Street-Penn Station; 1 to 28th Street. **Rates** $35 per person in dorm. **Beds** 20. **Map** p404 D25 65

One for the ladies and a lot of fun for it, the Chelsea Center lets you relive your student days in a small, women-only hostel with shared rooms and a communal kitchen and living area. Bathrooms are clean, and there's a patio garden out back. The (non-smoking) rooms lack air-con, but the rate includes breakfast.
Internet (wireless; free).

Marrakech. *See p79.*

102Brownstone.

Uptown

Expensive

Bentley Hotel
500 E 62nd Street, at York Avenue (1-212 644 6000/1-888 664 6835/www.hotelbentleynewyork.com). Subway F to Lexington-63rd Street; 4, 5, 6 to 59th Street. **Rates** $427-$447 double. **Rooms** 197. **Credit** AmEx, DC, Disc, MC, V. **Map** p405 G22 66
It's hard to notice anything in the Bentley's sleek rooms other than the fantastic sweeping vistas from the floor-to-ceiling windows. Converted from an office building in 1998, this effortlessly slender 21-storey hotel is an ideal getaway for weary execs, with a decent night's sleep helped on by solid soundproofing and blackout shades. Sip cappuccinos in the mahogany-panelled library or take in even more views from the glittering rooftop restaurant.
Bar. Internet (wireless; $10/day). Restaurant.
Other locations: Ameritania Hotel, 230 W 54th Street, at Broadway, Midtown (1-888 664 6835); Amsterdam Court, 226 W 50th Street, between Broadway & Eighth Avenue, Midtown (1-888 664 6835); Marcel (*see p74*); Moderne, 243 W 55th Street, between Broadway & Eighth Avenue, Midtown (1-888 664 6835).

Moderate

Country Inn the City

270 W 77th Street, between Broadway & West End Avenue (1-212 580 4183/1-800 572 4969/www.countryinnthecity.com). Subway 1 to 79th Street. **Rates** $150-$210 double. **Rooms** 4. **No credit cards**. **Map** p405 C19 67

The name of this charming B&B on the West Side is pretty accurate. Four-poster beds, flagons of brandy and moose heads in the hallways make this intimate inn a special retreat in the middle of the city.

Internet (wireless; free).

Beacon Hotel

2130 Broadway, between 74th & 75th Streets (1-212 787 1100/1-800 572 4969/www.beaconhotel.com). Subway 1, 2, 3 to 72nd Street. **Rates** $295 double. **Rooms** 265. **Credit** AmEx, DC, Disc, MC, V. **Map** p405 C20 68

The Hotel Beacon offers very good value in a desirable residential neighbourhood that's only a short walk from Central and Riverside Parks. Rooms are clean and spacious, and include stylish marble bathrooms. The classic diner Viand Café downstairs has plenty of cheap eats.

Business centre. Internet (wireless; $10/day).

Hotel Belleclaire

250 W 77th Street, at Broadway (1-212 362 7700/www.hotelbelleclaire.com). Subway 1 to 79th Street. **Rates** $189-$329 double. **Rooms** 200. **Credit** AmEx, DC, Disc, MC, V. **Map** p405 C19 69

Housed in a landmark building near Lincoln Center and Central Park, the sleek Belleclaire is a steal for savvy budget travellers. Rooms feature goose-down comforters, sleek padded headboards and mod lighting fixtures. Every room comes with a refrigerator – perfect for chilling your protein shake while you're hitting the state-of-the-art fitness centre.

Gym. Internet (wireless; $10/day).

Marrakech

2688 Broadway, at 103rd Street (1-212 222 2954/www.marrakechhotelnyc.com). Subway 1to 103rd Street. **Rates** $209-$349 double. **Rooms** 125. **Credit** AmEx, DC, Disc, MC, V. **Map** p406 C16 70

Nightclub and restaurant designer Lionel Ohayon (Crobar, Koi) was enlisted to make over this Upper West Side hotel, formerly the Hotel Malibu. As the name implies, rooms are warm-toned with simple Moroccan embellishments. This is a clean no-frills hotel that is most likely to appeal to twentysomethings who are not that interested in amenities (which are few and far between), or bothered by the fact that there is no elevator. *Photos p77.*

Bar. Internet (wireless; free).

On the Ave Hotel

222 W 77th Street, between Broadway & Amsterdam (1-212 362 1100/1-800 509 7598/www.ontheave-nyc.com). Subway 1 to 79th Street. **Rates** $200-$250 double. **Rooms** 266. **Credit** AmEx, DC, Disc, MC, V. **Map** p405 C19 71

Stylish additions to On the Ave include industrial-style bathroom sinks, CD players, HDTVs and 310 count Egyptian cotton bed linen. Penthouse suites have fantastic balcony views of Central Park (all guests have access to a garden balcony on the 16th floor of the hotel). On the Ave's Citylife Hotel Group sibling is Hotel Thirty Thirty (*see p74*).

Business centre. Internet (wireless; $10/day).

102Brownstone

102 W 118th Street, between Malcolm X Boulevard (Lenox Avenue) & Adam Clayton Powell Jr Boulevard (Seventh Avenue) (1-212 662 4223/www.102brownstone.com). Subway 2, 3 to 116th Street. **Rates** $175-$250. **Rooms** 6. **Credit** AmEx, MC, V. **Map** p407 D14 72

Located near Marcus Garvey Park on a landmark, tree-lined street, 102 features five substantial suites, all renovated and individually themed by lively proprietor Lizette Lanoue, who owns and lives in the 1892 Greek Revival row house with her husband. She says 102 is 'not your typical B&B. We aren't up in your face. We want to give you the experience of what it would be like to live here in Harlem, in your own apartment'.

Internet (free).

Budget

Amsterdam Inn

340 Amsterdam Avenue, at 76th Street (1-212 579 7500/www.amsterdaminn.com). Subway 1 to 79th Street. **Rates** $109-$169 double. **Rooms** 30. **Credit** AmEx, MC, V. **Map** p405 C19 73

For review, *see p76* **Murray Hill Inn**.

Efuru Guest House

106 W 120th Street, at Malcolm X Boulevard (Lenox Avenue) (1-212 961 9855/www.efuru-nyc.com). Subway 2, 3 to 116th Street. **Rates** $95-$135 double with shared or private bath. **Rooms** 3. **Credit** MC, V. **Map** p407 D14 74

Efuru, a Nigerian word meaning 'daughter of heaven', is the brainchild of Lydia Smith, who bought the once-abandoned property through a lottery system in the late 1990s, and then endured a five-year renovation process. The result is a homey inn where guests can enjoy total privacy (each garden-level room has an entrance and patio) or mingle in a communal living room decorated with antique couches and a working fireplace. The three suites, painted in serene hues of green and blue, are basic but clean and comfy. All have queen beds and refrigerators, most have private baths and some have a kitchenette to boot.

Internet (free).

Harlem Flophouse

242 W 123rd Street, between Adam Clayton Powell Jr Boulevard (Seventh Avenue) & Frederick Douglass Boulevard (1-212 662 0678/www.harlemflophouse.com). Subway A, C, B, D to 125th Street. **Rates** $100-$150 single/double with shared bath. **Rooms** 4. **Credit** MC, V. **Map** p407 D14 75

The dark-wood interior, moody lighting and lilting jazz make the Flophouse feel more like a 1930s speakeasy than a 21st-century B&B. The airy suites have restored tin ceilings, glamorous chandeliers and working sinks in antique cabinets. For $15 per person ($25 per couple), you can eat a home-cooked breakfast in the communal dining room or garden. Don't want the hassle of having to change out of your PJs? Fear not: an amiable staff member will bring your meal to your room.

Hostels

Central Park Hostel

19 W 103rd Street, at Central Park West (1-212 678 0491/www.centralparkhostel.com). Subway B, C to 103rd Street. **Rates** $29-$45 bed in shared room; $109-$149 private room with shared bath. **Beds** 250. **Credit** MC, V. **Map** p406 D16 76

Housed in a recently renovated brownstone, this tidy hostel offers dorm-style rooms that sleep four, six or eight people; private chambers with two beds are also available. All baths are shared.

Internet ($2/20mins).

Hostelling International New York

891 Amsterdam Avenue, at 103rd Street (1-212 932 2300/www.hinewyork.org). Subway 1 to 103rd Street. **Rates** $29-$40 dorm rooms; $120 family rooms; $135 private room with bath. **Beds** 624. **Credit** AmEx, DC, MC, V. **Map** p406 C16 77

This budget lodging is actually the city's only 'real' hostel (being a completely not-for-profit accommodation that belongs to the International Youth Hostel Federation), but it's also one of the most architecturally stunning. The gabled, Gothic-inspired brick-and-stone building spans the length of an entire city block, and is much admired of locals as well as those staying here. The immaculate rooms are admittedly rather spare but at least air-conditioned, and there is a shared kitchen and a large backyard.

Internet ($2/20mins).

International House

500 Riverside Drive, at Tiemann Place (1-212 316 8436/www.ihouse-nyc.org). Subway 1 to 125th Street. **Rates** $120-$130 single; $150-$160 double/suite. **Rooms** 11. **Credit** MC, V. **Map** p407 B13 78

Primarily a dormitory for foreign graduate students, this housing facility is a good reliable bet for short-term summer travellers (when all the students have checked out). Located on a peaceful block overlooking Grant's Tomb and the small but well-tended Sakura Park, this hostel has simple rooms with private bathrooms and refrigerators.

Bar. Internet (wireless; free).

Jazz on the Park Hostel

36 W 106th Street, between Central Park West & Manhattan Avenue (1-212 932 1600/www.jazzonthepark.com). Subway B, C to 103rd Street. **Rates** $20-$32, 4- to 12-bed dorm; $65-$90 2-bed dorm (max 2 people); $125-$200 private room with bath. **Beds** 310. **Credit** MC, V. **Map** p406 D16 79

Jazz on the Park might be the trendiest hostel in the city – the lounge is kitted out like a space-age techno club, and sports a piano and pool table. But some visitors have been known to complain about the customer service, so make sure to double-check your room type and check-in date before you arrive. In summer, the back patio hosts a weekly barbecue. Linens and a continental breakfast are complimentary, while lockers come with a surcharge.

Internet ($2/20mins).

Other locations: Jazz on the Town Hostel, 307 E 14th Street, between First & Second Avenues, East Village/Gramercy Park (1-212 228 2780); Jazz on Harlem, 104 W 128th Street, between Adam Clayton Powell Jr Boulevard (Seventh Avenue) & Malcolm X Boulevard (Lenox Avenue), Harlem (1-212 222 5779).

Brooklyn

Moderate

Akwaaba Mansion

347 MacDonough Street, between Lewis & Stuyvesant Avenues, Bedford-Stuyvesant (1-718 455 5958/www.akwaaba.com). Subway A, C to Utica Avenue. **Rates** $100-$165 double. **Rooms** 3. **Credit** MC, V. **Map** p410 W10 80

Akwaaba means 'welcome' in Ghanaian, a fitting name for this gorgeous restored 1860s mansion with a wide screened-in porch and flower gardens. The individually themed rooms are decorated with African artefacts and textiles. A hearty Southern-style breakfast and complimentary afternoon tea are served in the dining room or on the porch.

Awesome Bed & Breakfast

136 Lawrence Street, between Fulton & Willoughby Streets, Downtown Brooklyn (1-718 858 4859/www.awesome-bed-and-breakfast.com). Subway A, C, F to Jay Street-Borough Hall; M, R to Lawrence Street; 2, 3 to Hoyt Street. **Rates** $99-$130 double. $140-$150 triple/quad. **Rooms** 7. **Credit** AmEx, MC, V. **Map** p410 T10 81

'Awesome' isn't normally a word employed to describe a B&B, but this colourful themed rooms could well be a setting for MTV's *The Real World*, with details like giant daisies and purple drapes. The equally snazzy bathrooms are communal, and a complimentary breakfast is delivered to your door promptly at 8am. Plans to double the capacity of the hotel are currently in the works.

Bed & Breakfast on the Park

113 Prospect Park West, between 6th & 7th Streets, Park Slope (1-718 499 6115/www.bbnyc.com). Subway F to Seventh Avenue. **Rates** $165-$295 double. **Rooms** 7. **Credit** AmEx, MC, V (cheques preferred). **Map** p410 T12 82

Staying at this 1895 parkside brownstone is like taking up residence on the set of *The Age of Innocence*. The parlour floor is crammed with antique furniture, and guest rooms are furnished with love seats and canopy beds swathed in French linens.

Sightseeing

Introduction	**82**
Tour New York	**88**
Downtown	**93**
Midtown	**117**
Uptown	**135**
Brooklyn	**156**
Queens	**167**
The Bronx	**172**
Staten Island	**177**

Features

New York at a glance	83
What price vice?	85
Walkie talkie	89
Walk it out Night crawler	96
New dork city	104
Chinatown's secret city	108
Walking the line	118
Cheap date	120
Eyes on the size	124
Sleeper hit	128
Light fight	131
Bethesda reborn	137
Walk it out Garden variety	140
The empire strikes back	144
Fall of the wild	151
Cheap date	157
Walk it out The other Fifth Avenue	160
Cheap date	168
A little Italy	175

Rockefeller Center. *See p133.*

Introduction

Bewitched, bothered and bewildered? Get your bearings here.

Most newcomers arriving in New York City have a pretty good idea what they're in for – which is to say non-stop sightseeing, shopping, eating and drinking. Then there's dancing, art gazing and people-watching. Visiting New York is not for the easily winded, and you'll fare better if you devise even a basic plan of attack.

Start by jotting down a few of your must-see and -do destinations. Remember, whole days can be spent wandering such enormous institutions as the **Metropolitan Museum of Art** (*see p143*) or the **American Museum of Natural History** (*see p148*). But if you are looking to see as much as possible on your trip then plan on spending just a few hours at your museum of choice taking in the highlights. Take a walk across the **Brooklyn Bridge** (*see p158*), take in the jaw-dropping view at the top of the **Rockefeller** (*see p133*) or stroll through **Central Park** (*see p140* **Walk it out**). Then, catch your breath: hang out at a café or raise a glass at a neighbourhood bar. And, for God's sake, don't be shy – New Yorkers aren't, and just maybe a conversation you strike up could lead you to one of the city's countless hidden gems.

For our guide to the best of New York's many **tours**, *see pp88-91*.

THE LIE OF THE LAND

New York City is made up of five boroughs: Brooklyn, the Bronx, Manhattan, Queens and Staten Island. What the island of **Manhattan** lacks in land mass (it's the smallest of the bunch), it more than makes up for in cultural and commercial power; it is bordered by New Jersey, just over the Hudson River, to the west; **Brooklyn** and **Queens** (*photo p87*) are east, on the other side of the East River; the **Bronx** is just to the north, above the Harlem River; and **Staten Island** is south, at the mouth of New York Harbor. Within each borough, areas of varying size are broken down into neighbourhoods like Midtown, Chinatown and the Upper East Side (*see p83* **New York at a glance**), all marked on the maps that you'll find at the back of this book.

STREET SMARTS

Setting out into New York's teeming streets, we guarantee that you're going to feel hugely overwhelmed, if not downright lost. Take heart: although much of Manhattan is laid out on a

New York at a glance

Broadway & Times Square (p124)
Night-time under the world's most famous array of twinkling lights is positively thrilling.

Chelsea (p117)
The city's gayest neighbourhood is also home to hundreds of art galleries west of Tenth Avenue, between 19th and 26th Streets.

Chinatown (p106)
You'll feel like you are in another country walking among the Asian restaurants and groceries here. Canal Street offers myriad designer knock-offs.

East Village (p110)
Tompkins Square Park (just off Avenue A) is the heart of this young, edgy 'hood. No traditional tourist destinations to note (aside from now-defunct CBGB), but a great deal of fun to wander nonetheless.

Fifth Avenue (p129)
The well-heeled still shop here (at Tiffany's, Cartier, Bergdorf Goodman), but mall stores are beginning to nudge in on the action. Landmarks aplenty, among them the Empire State Building, Rockefeller Center and St Patrick's Cathedral.

Greenwich Village (p113)
Come for leafy streets and highly Bohemian Washington Square Park, where folks prefer a slower pace. Literary associations abound.

Harlem (p150)
Broad, sunny boulevards with many stunning examples of late 19th- and early 20th-century architecture. And soul food galore.

Lower East Side (p107)
See how waves of immigrants lived at the Lower East Side Tenement Museum. Hip young things have recently opened up all kinds of indie boutiques and hot new bars, but the delis and pickle shops remain.

Midtown East (p133)
Lots of office buildings and bustling streets, but it's the United Nations and Grand Central Terminal that beckon.

Soho (p103)
The city's former art district is now a must-see stop for trendy shoppers. Helpfully, there are also tons of smart cafés and restaurants in which to cool your heels.

Tribeca (p103)
Actor Robert De Niro put this area on the map when he debuted the Tribeca Film Festival here in 2002. Chic bars and restaurants nestle among warehouses (now loft apartments).

Upper East Side (p138)
Rich and important, and full of embassies and billionaires. Museums such as the Met and the Guggenheim up the culture quotient.

Upper West Side (p146)
Lovely turn-of-the-century architecture and lush green havens on either side (Central Park to the east, Riverside Park to the west).

Wall Street (p99)
The oldest area of the city and the epicentre of capitalism. Offers a glimpse of traders and a chance to stroll narrow streets darkened by skyscrapers. Home of the New York Stock Exchange and Trinity Church.

West Village & Meatpacking District (p114)
Quiet, cobblestoned streets offer plenty of opportunities to peer into picturesque 19th-century brownstones. The trendy restaurants and bars on Ninth Avenue buzz at night.

Beyond Manhattan
Particularly worth the trip over to Brooklyn are **Williamsburg** (*see p164*), with dozens of über-hip cafés, bars and shops; **Brooklyn Heights** (*see p156*), with its views; and **Coney Island**'s boardwalk and carnival-like atmosphere, perfect for a summer's day (*see p166*).

Chinatown.

Sightseeing

New York Botanical Garden.

grid system, even New Yorkers get turned around and frequently can't remember which way is which. The older streets of Lower Manhattan, in particular, can cause confusion. Your best bet is to take a few moments to study our maps on pages 402-412, and to read the **Getting Around** section (*see pp368-370*) at the back of this book before setting out on the streets themselves.

VISITING MUSEUMS

Visiting several venues in a single day can be exhausting. Similarly, it's self-defeating to attempt to hit all the major collections during one visit to an institution as large as the Met or the American Museum of Natural History. So plan, pace yourself, and don't forget to eat: a host of excellent museum cafés and restaurants afford convenient breaks. Delicious spots for refuelling include Sarabeth's at the **Whitney Museum of American Art** (*see p145*); the elegant Café Sabarsky at the **Neue Galerie** (*see p145*); the **Jewish Museum**'s Café Weissman (*see p143*); and a more formal option, the Modern, at the **Museum of Modern Art** (MoMA; *see p131*). It may be tempting to save museums for a rainy day, but remember that most sites offer cool, air-conditioned relief on sticky summer days and cosy warmth come winter.

If the weather is too gorgeous to stay indoors all day, keep in mind that several gardens adjoin New York museums. The Brooklyn Museum abuts the **Brooklyn Botanic Garden** (*see p164*), which has a Japanese garden complete with pavilion, wooden bridges and a Shinto shrine; there's also the **New York Botanical Garden** in the Bronx (*see p176*). The **Cloisters** (*see p155*), in Manhattan's Fort Tryon Park, was John D Rockefeller's gift to New York. The reconstructed monastery houses the Met's stellar collection of medieval art. In summer, bring a picnic and relax on the lush grounds (admission free of charge), with spectacular views of the Hudson River.

Brace yourself for local admission prices; they tend to be steep (tickets to the recently renovated MoMA cost $20 per adult). This is because most of the city's museums are privately funded and receive little or no government support. Even so, a majority of them, including MoMA, the Whitney and the Guggenheim, either waive admission fees or make them voluntary at least one evening a week. Most museums also offer discounts to students and senior citizens with valid IDs. And although the Met suggests a $20 donation for adults, you can, in fact, pay whatever you wish for your visit.

What price vice?

Don't do the crime if you can't pay the fine!

New York's anything-goes era is long gone, but some New Yorkers still insist on behaving naughtily in plain view. To better weigh up the risks of blowing that spliff on a park bench, consider these penalties for the most popular public transgressions. Note to foreigners: in addition to the fine, you just might find yourself deported, never to return again. The lesson? Judge wisely!

Open container of alcohol – $25
It's a mere $25 ticket, payable by mail – that is, if you're not too drunk to find the nearest mailbox for posting it.

Smoking a cigarette inside a bar – $100
The law allows for up to a $100 fine, but this ticket is rarely issued.

Playing your music too loudly – $250
Disturbing the peace is one of the most common charges in the city, and can mean 15 days in the slammer or $250 straight out of your pocket.

Sex on the beach – $500
The law calls it 'public lewdness'. It's $500, plus three months behind bars.

Smoking a joint – $500
A class-B misdemeanour that can cost you up to three months in the pokey, not to mention $500 up in smoke.

Jumping the subway turnstile – $1,000
That's called stealing city services, a class-A misdemeanour, punishable by up to a year in jail and a $1,000 fine.

Urinating in public – up to $2,000
Depending on what violation the cop decides to hit you with, fines range from $50 all the way to $2,000.

Shooting off fireworks – $10,000
The NYPD declared zero tolerance for fireworks in 2006, and getting caught could cost you between $1,000 and $10,000, or up to 30 days in the slammer.

Jackson Heights' large Indian community brings **Queens** to life. *See p82.*

Discovering the secrets of a new museum on your own can be exciting, but many institutions offer tours that are both entertaining and educational. For example, the audio tour at the **Ellis Island Immigration Museum** (*see p95*) and the (mandatory) guided tours at the **Lower East Side Tenement Museum** (*see p109*) and the **Museum of Jewish Heritage** (*see p99*) offer insights into NYC's immigrant roots.

Most New York museums are closed on major US holidays (*see p376*). Nevertheless, some institutions are open on certain Monday holidays, such as Columbus Day and Presidents' Day. A few places, like **Dia:Beacon** (*see p357*) and the **Queens Museum of Art** (*see p171*), change their hours seasonally; it's therefore wise to call ahead before setting out.

Security has been severely tightened at most museums. Guards at all public institutions will ask you to open your bag or backpack for inspection; umbrellas and large bags must be checked (free of charge) at a cloakroom.

Most museums are accessible to people with disabilities and offer free wheelchairs.

PACKAGE DEALS

If you're planning to take in multiple museums – and you're likely to add a Circle Line tour (*see p89*) or a visit to a major attraction – consider buying a nine-day **CityPass** for $65 ($49 12-17s). Similarly, the **New York Pass** covers entry to over 40 of the city's top attractions and cultural institutions, and gives discounts on shopping, eating and other activities. The card is $65 for the day ($45 5-12s) and $155 for the week ($120 5-12s). You can compare benefits between the two and buy online at www.citypass.com and www.newyorkpass.com.

Tour New York

Do it your way.

There are simply too many must-see attractions to cram into a single visit to New York. But, thankfully, there's also a wide plethora of tour options to help you pack them in. You can sit back and enjoy the ride on a double-decker bus, rickshaw or ferry. If you need more personal control, rent a bike or take a walking tour. For additional inspiration, refer to the Around Town section of *Time Out New York* magazine, with its weekly listings for urban outings.

By bicycle

For more on cycling, *see p336*.

Bike the Big Apple

1-877 865 0078/www.bikethebigapple.com. **Tours** call or visit website for schedule. **Tickets** $49-$69 (incl bicycle & helmet rental). **Credit** MC, V.

Licensed guides take cyclists through both historic and newly hip neighbourhoods. Half- and full-day rides are family-friendly and gently paced.

Bite of the Apple Tours

Bite of the Apple Tours (1-212 541 8759/www.centralparkbiketour.com). **Tours** *Apr-Oct* 9am, 10am, 11am, 1pm, 4pm daily. *Nov-Mar* by reservation only. **Tickets** $35; $20 under-15s (incl bicycle rental). **Credit** AmEx, Disc, MC, V.

Bite of the Apple focuses its attentions on Central Park. The main tour visits the John Lennon memorial at Strawberry Fields, Belvedere Castle and the Shakespeare Garden. Dedicated film buffs will especially enjoy the Central Park Movie Scenes Bike Tour (10am, 1pm, 4pm Sat, Sun), passing locations from *When Harry Met Sally...* and *Wall Street.* Most tours run at a leisurely two hours, but serious cycling enthusiasts might consider enrolling on the three-hour Manhattan Island Bicycle Tour ($45, by appointment only).

By boat

Adirondack

Chelsea Piers, Pier 59, 18th Street, at the Hudson River (1-646 336 5270/www.sail-nyc.com). Subway C, E to 23rd Street. **Tours** *1 Apr-15 Oct* 1pm, 3.30pm, 6pm, 8.30pm daily. **Tickets** $40 day sails; $50 eve & Sun brunch sails. **Credit** AmEx, MC, V.

Built in 1994, the *Adirondack* is a beautiful three-masted replica of a classic 19th-century, 80-foot schooner. Trips on board are the essence of laidback luxury: sip your complimentary glass of wine (or beer, if you prefer) as the ship sails slowly from Chelsea Piers to Battery Park, past Ellis Island, to the Statue of Liberty and around to Governors Island and the Brooklyn Bridge.

Circle Line Cruises

Pier 83, 42nd Street, at the Hudson River (1-212 563 3200/www.circleline.com). Subway A, C, E to 42nd Street-Port Authority. **Tours** call or visit website for schedule. **Tickets** $29/3hrs; $24 seniors; $16 children. **Credit** AmEx, DC, Disc, MC, V. **Map** p404 B24.

Circle Line's famed three-hour guided circumnavigation of Manhattan is a fantastic way to see the city's sights. The themed tours include a New Year's Eve cruise, a DJ dance party or an autumn foliage ride to Bear Mountain in the Hudson Valley. From April to October, there's also a fun 30-minute speedboat ride on *The Beast* (*photos p91*).

Other locations: South Street Seaport, Pier 16, by Burling Slip & Fulton Street, Downtown (1-212 630 8888).

NY Waterway

Pier 78, 38th Street, at the Hudson River (1-800 533 3779/www.nywaterway.com). Subway A, C, E to 42nd Street-Port Authority. **Tours** times vary; call or visit website for schedule. **Tickets** $23 90min cruise; $19 seniors; $13 children. **Credit** AmEx, Disc, MC, V. **Map** p404 B24.

Walkie talkie

Tour guide **Gideon Levy** reflects on his street-smart career path.

Your tour company, the Levys' Unique New York, is a family act. What's it like to work with your dad and older brother?

It's intense – we're all very loud and there's a lot of energy and creativity. Turning that into productivity can sometimes be a challenge. No more than two of us are allowed in the office at the same time.

What's the most popular tour you offer?

The 'Hey Ho! Let's Go! Punk Rock on the Bowery' tour, based on my brother's thesis that the punk rockers of 1977 can be traced to the Bowery Boys of the 1840s and '50s.

How do you prepare for a tour like that?

Luc Sante's book *Low Life* was invaluable in giving us the backstory. We have a big New York library at my dad's house; Edwin Burrows and Mike Wallace's *Gotham* is our overall bible. Scorsese's *Gangs of New York* was also illuminatingly brilliant. It really kick-started my love for the city's history. Our tours are very story-based, rather than being just a lot of facts and figures – that's what makes us unique.

In your opinion, what is the most underrated area in New York?

The neighbourhood of Brooklyn Heights, definitely. Most tourists, and even New Yorkers, will just walk across the Brooklyn Bridge and turn around once they reach the Brooklyn side. Get off the bridge and explore this neighbourhood! Cranberry and Orange Streets have some of the most beautiful homes in the city and the Brooklyn Heights Promenade (*see p157*) is amazing.

And the most overrated?

Times Square – it is saturated with traffic and billboards. Go if you must, but don't linger.

What's your favourite novel about New York?

I love *Time and Again*, by Jack Finney. It's a time-trave romance that takes place in the Dakota apartment building (*see p147*) on the Upper West Side – it's magical.

What's the dumbest question anyone's ever asked you?

On one of our bus tours, someone asked, 'Does this bus stop at the Statue of Liberty?'.

● For more on **The Levys' Unique New York**, *see p91*.

The scenic 90-minute harbour tour makes a complete circuit around Manhattan's landmarks, and another 90-minute tour focuses on the skyline of lower Manhattan. Other tours are also available – check the website for more information.
Other locations: World Financial Center Pier, Pier 11, Wall Street, Downtown.

Pioneer

South Street Seaport Museum, 12 Fulton Street, between Water & South Streets (1-212 748 8786/ www.southstreetseaportmuseum.org). Subway A, C to Broadway-Nassau Street; J, M, Z, 2, 3, 4, 5 to Fulton Street. **Tours** call for schedule. **Tickets** $25; $15 under-12s. **Credit** AmEx, MC, V. **Map** p402 F32.
Built in 1885, the 102ft *Pioneer* is the only iron-hulled merchant sailing ship still in existence. Sails billow as you cruise the East River and New York Harbor. A range of highly educational children's programmes are also offered.

Shearwater Sailing

North Cove, Hudson River, between Liberty & Vesey Streets (1-212 619 0885/1-800 544 1224/www. shearwatersailing.com). Subway R, W to City Hall; A, C, 2, 3, 4, 5 to Fulton Street/Broadway-Nassau Street. **Tours** *15 Apr-15-Oct* 5 times daily; call for schedule. **Tickets** $45-$50; $25 children. **Credit** AmEx, Disc, MC, V. **Map** p402 D32.
Set sail on the *Shearwater*, an 82ft luxury yacht built all the way back in 1929. The champagne brunch ($79) or full-moon ($50) sail options are lovely ways to take in the skyline.

Staten Island Ferry

Battery Park, South Street, at Whitehall Street (1-718 727 2508/www.siferry.com). Subway 1 to South Ferry; 4, 5 to Bowling Green. **Open** 24hrs daily. **Tickets** free. **Map** p402 E34.
During this commuter barge's 25-minute crossing, you get superb panoramas of lower Manhattan and the Statue of Liberty. Boats leave South Ferry at Battery Park. Call or see the website for schedules and more information.

By bus

Gray Line

777 Eighth Avenue, between 47th & 48th Streets (1-212 445 0848/1-800 669 0051 ext 3/www.graylinenewyork.com). Subway A, C, E to 42nd Street-Port Authority. **Tours** call or visit website for schedule. **Tickets** $25-$125. **Credit** AmEx, Disc, MC, V. **Map** p404 D23.
This is your grandma's classic red double-decker tour (the line runs other buses too), but with something to interest everyone. Gray Line offers more than 20 bus tours, from a basic two-hour ride (with more than 40 hop-on, hop-off stops) to the guided Manhattan Comprehensive, which lasts eight and a half hours and includes lunch, admission to the United Nations tour, and a boat ride to Ellis Island and the Statue of Liberty.

By helicopter, carriage or rickshaw

Liberty Helicopter Tours

Downtown Manhattan Heliport, Pier 6, East River, between Broad Street & Old Slip (1-212 967 6464/ 1-800 542 9933/www.libertyhelicopters.com). Subway R, W to Whitehall Street; 1 to South Ferry. **Tours** 9am-7pm daily. **Tickets** $69-$186. **Credit** AmEx, MC, V. **Map** p402 E34.
There'll be no daredevil swooping and diving (Liberty's helicopters provide a fairly smooth flight), but the views are excitement enough. Even a five-minute ride (durations vary) is long enough to get a thrilling look at the Empire State Building.
Other locations: VIP Heliport, Twelfth Avenue, at 30th Street, Midtown.

Manhattan Carriage Company

200 Central Park South, at Seventh Avenue (1-212 664 1149/www.ajnfineart.com/mcc.html). Subway N, Q, R, W to 57th Street. **Tours** 10am-2am Mon-Fri; 7pm-2am Sat, Sun. **Tickets** from $40/20min ride (extended rides by reservation only). Hours and prices vary during holidays. **Credit** AmEx, MC, V (reserved tours only). **Map** p405 D22.
The beauty of Central Park seems even more romantic from the seat of a horse-drawn carriage. Choose your coach from those lined up on the streets along the southern end of the park, or book in advance.

Manhattan Rickshaw Company

1-212 604 4729/www.manhattanrickshaw.com. **Tours** noon-midnight Tue-Sun & by appointment. **Tickets** $10-$50, depending on duration and number of passengers. **No credit cards**.
Manhattan Rickshaw Company's pedicabs operate in Greenwich Village, Soho, Times Square and the Theater District. If you see one that's available, hail the driver, but determine your fare before you jump in. For a pre-arranged pick-up, make reservations at least 24 hours in advance.

On foot

Adventure on a Shoestring

1-212 265 2663. **Tours** daily; call for schedule and reservations. **Tickets** $5. **No credit cards**.
The motto of this organisation, now in its 45th year, is 'Exploring the world within our reach... within our means', and founder Howard Goldberg is dedicated to revealing the 'real' New York. Walks take you from one charming neighbourhood to another, and topics can include Millionaire's Row and Haunted Greenwich Village. Special celebrity theme tours, including tributes to Jackie O, Katharine Hepburn and Marilyn Monroe, are also available.

Big Onion Walking Tours

1-212 439 1090/www.bigonion.com. **Tours** *Sept-May* 11am, 1pm & major holidays. *June-Aug* 1pm, 5pm Mon, Wed-Sun. **Tickets** $15; $12 seniors; $10 students. **No credit cards**.

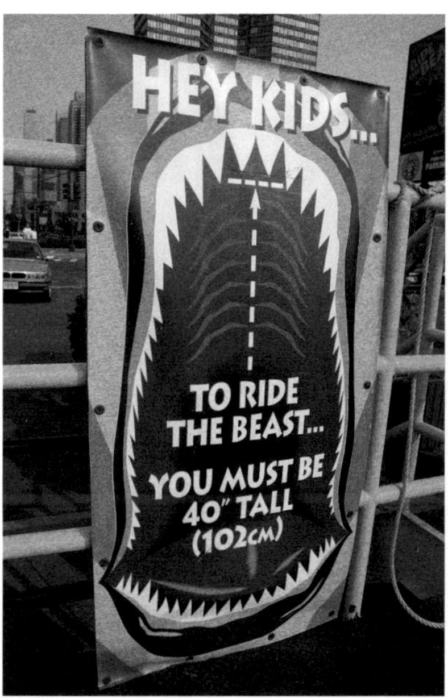

Just when you thought it was safe to go back in the water. *See p89* **Circle Line Cruises**.

Sightseeing

New York was known as the Big Onion before it became the Big Apple. The tour guides will explain why, and they should know – all guides hold advanced degrees in history (or a related field). Check the website for meeting locations. Private tours are also available.

Greenwich Village Literary Pub Crawl

1-212 613 5796/www.geocities.com/newensemble. Tour meets at the White Horse Tavern, 567 Hudson Street, at 11th Street. Subway 1 to Christopher Street-Sheridan Square. **Tours** 2pm Sat (reservations requested). **Tickets** $15; $12 seniors, students (not incl drinks). **No credit cards**.

Local actors from the New Ensemble Theatre Company take you to the past haunts of famous writers. Watering stops include Chumley's (a former speakeasy) and Cedar Tavern, where Jack Kerouac and a generation of abstract expressionist painters, including Jackson Pollock, drank with their peers.

Harlem Heritage Tours

1-212 280 7888/www.harlemheritage.com. **Tours** call or visit website for schedule & meeting points. **Tickets** $20-$100 (reservations required). **Credit** AmEx, MC, V.

Now operating more than 15 bus and walking tours, Harlem Heritage aims to show visitors the soul of the borough. The Harlem Song, Harlem Nights tour takes tourists to landmarks like the Apollo Theater. The Renaissance tour walks you to Prohibition-era speakeasies, clubs and one-time residences of artists, writers and musicians.

The Levys' Unique New York

1-718 287 6177/www.levysuniqueny.com. **Tours** call or visit website for schedule & meeting locations. **Tickets** from $25 (reservations may be required for some tours). **No credit cards**.

This family tour company not only features walking tours lasting between an hour and 90 minutes – the Levys go the extra mile with their speciality four-hour comprehensive Manhattan tours. 'Starring New York', for example, dazzles its walkers with a relentless slew of TV show and movie spots. *See also p89* **Walkie talkie**.

Municipal Art Society Tours

1-212 935 3960/recorded info 1-212 439 1049/ www.mas.org. **Tours** call or visit website for schedule & meeting points. **Tickets** $12-$15 weekends; $10-$12 weekdays (reservations may be required for some tours). **No credit cards**.

The Municipal Art Society (MAS) organises bus and walking tours in New York and even New Jersey. Many – like Art Deco Midtown – reflect the society's focus on contemporary architecture, urban planning and historic preservation. There's also a guided walk going through Grand Central Terminal on Wednesdays at 12.30pm (suggested donation $10). Private tours are available by appointment.

Downtown

Glimpses of New York's beginnings – and an eyeful of its future.

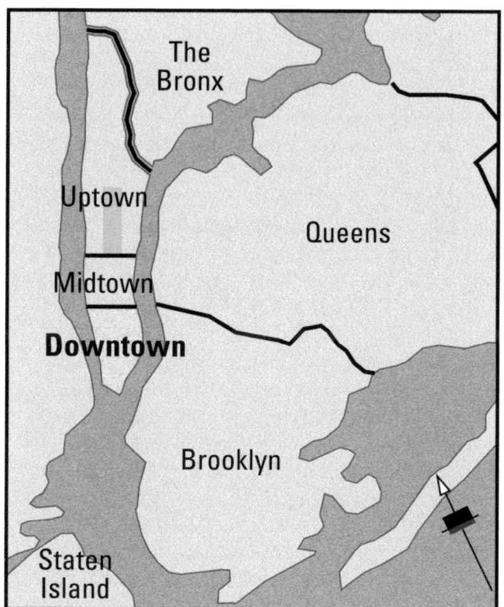

Maps p402 & p403

Welcome to the epicentre – and epitome – of New York cool. Some of Downtown's famed edginess and bohemia may have been smoothed over with the inevitable revitalisation of its neglected areas and the surge in commercial rents and housing prices, but many trends in music, fashion and design still begin here and spread the world over. The manic gentrification of the area is showing no signs of slowing down, which means that indie shops and struggling artists are increasingly forming part of downtown's past. Meanwhile, hedge-funders, trust-funders, high-end retailers, celebrity-chef-owned eateries and million-dollar (st)architect-designed condos (Gehry, Nouvel, Meier, Stern, et al) point empathically to its future. Still, diehards argue that everything you might need or desire can still be found below 14th Street – and many of them joke that they'll never venture north of that sacred dividing line.

Manhattan's downtown neighbourhoods are a microcosm of nearly everything that's going on in the rest of the city. Developments such as the swankification of the shops in the West Village; the condo-isation of the Lower East Side and the East Village; the rejuvenation of Chinatown; and the rebirth of the area around Ground Zero mirror similar debates and changes taking place in all five boroughs. But here, like nowhere else in the rest of the city, the small, amorphously shaped neighbourhoods bump against each other, and in some cases overlap like jigsaw pieces – the product of the city's early, unplanned and somewhat disorganised growth, and the uniquely ungridded street layout that went with that.

Battery Park

Until you reach its southern tip, Manhattan doesn't feel much like an island. Atlantic Ocean breezes remind you how millions of people once travelled to New York on overcrowded, creaking sailing ships. Trace their journey past the golden torch of the **Statue of Liberty**, through the immigration and quarantine centres of **Ellis Island** (for both, *see p95*) and, finally, to the statue-dotted **Battery Park promenade**. In summertime, this strip – the closest thing the largely green area has to a main drag – will pull you back to the present as you take in a harbour filled with jet-skiers and sailing boats, and sidewalks crowded with hurried urbanites who are ferried to work from their Staten Island homes.

The bench-lined promenade is a good spot for quiet contemplation, and also a stage for applause- (and money-) hungry performers, who entertain crowds waiting to hop on to the boats to the Statue of Liberty and Ellis Island. The park itself plays host to a wide variety of events, including the always fantastic **River to River Festival** (*see p262*) in September, a celebration of downtown culture featuring free outdoor events, from music and movies to comedy and kids' programmes on summer evenings. **Castle Clinton**, in the park, is an intimate, open-air setting for concerts. Built in 1812 to defend against attacks by the British, the castle, really a former fort, has been a theatre and an aquarium; it now also serves as a visitors' centre and ticket booth for Statue of Liberty and Ellis Island tours.

As you join the throngs making their way to Lady Liberty, you'll head south-east along the shore, where several ferry terminals jut into the harbour. The Whitehall Ferry Terminal is the boarding place for the famous **Staten Island Ferry** (*see p90*). Constructed in 1907, it has been completely rebuilt in recent years, after

The **Statue of Liberty**: flipping brilliant.

being damaged by fire in 1991. The new terminal opened in 2005, and it's the place to catch one of the city's three new ferry boats: the *Guy V Molinari*, named after the former Staten Island borough president; the *Sen John J Marchi*, honouring the veteran Republican legislator; and the *Spirit of America*, which commemorates the teamwork of Staten Islanders on 9/11. The 25-minute ride to the Staten Island shore is one of the few things in New York City that is free; quite a result, considering it offers unparalleled views of the downtown Manhattan skyline and a close look at the iconic statue. In the years before the Brooklyn Bridge was built, the **Battery Maritime Building** (11 South Street, between Broad & Whitehall Streets) served as a terminal for the ferry services between Manhattan and Brooklyn. Get a spectacular view of the harbour, cocktail in hand, from the terrace of the Rise Bar, located on the 14th floor of the luxe Ritz-Carlton New York Battery Park (2 West Street, 1-917 790 2626); it's especially glorious as the sun goes down.

In summer, you can take a ferry from the Battery Maritime Building across to tranquil **Governors Island**. For many years, the island was military-owned and off-limits, but it now welcomes visitors in summer to its historical forts and homes. For more information, *see p26* **Governors Island**.

Just north of Battery Park you'll find the triangular **Bowling Green**, the city's oldest park and the recipient of a hugely expensive makeover completed in 2004. This garden spot is also the front lawn of the 1907 Beaux Arts Alexander Hamilton Custom House, now home to the **National Museum of the American Indian** (*see p95*). On its northern side, sculptor Arturo DiModica's muscular bronze bull is intended to represent the potent capitalism of the Financial District.

Other interesting historical sites are close by: the rectory of the **Shrine of St Elizabeth Ann Seton** (7 State Street, between Pearl & Whitehall Streets, 1-212 269 6865, www.setonshrine.org), a 1790 Federal building dedicated to the first American-born saint, and the **Fraunces Tavern Museum** (*see below*), a restoration of the alehouse where George Washington celebrated his victory over the British. After a pint, you can examine the Revolution-era relics displayed in the tavern's period rooms. The **New York Vietnam Veterans Memorial** (55 Water Street, between Coenties Slip & Hanover Square) stands one block to the east. Erected in 1985, and refreshed with a newly designed plaza a few years ago, it features the Walk of Honor – a pathway inscribed with the names of the 1,741 New Yorkers who lost their lives fighting in the South-east Asian conflict – and a touching monument etched with excerpts from letters, diary entries and poems written during the war. The newest memorial in the area is the **British Memorial Garden** at Hanover Square (at William & Pearl Streets), which was completed in summer 2007 (landscaping is ongoing, and quite impressive thus far). Hanover is one of the city's oldest public squares, named in 1714 for King George I, Elector of Hanover. The garden was created to commemorate the 67 Britons who died in New York on September 11, 2001, and the new park space features hand-carved stone from Scotland, plants from Prince Charles's estate and iron bollards from London. HRH Princess Anne also donated heirloom seeds to the garden, from the privy gardens of Henry VIII and William III.

Nearby, the **Stone Street Historic District** is built around one of Manhattan's oldest roads, a mini cobblestoned street closed to traffic. Office workers and tourists now frequent its restaurants and bars, including the boisterous Ulysses (95 Pearl Street, at Stone Street, 1-212 482 0400) and Stone Street Tavern (52 Stone Street, near Broad Street, 1-212 785 5658), in an 1836 building with comfort food and rustic décor.

Fraunces Tavern Museum

54 Pearl Street, at Broad Street (1-212 425 1778/www.fraucestavernmuseum.org). Subway J, M, Z to Broad Street; 4, 5 to Bowling Green. **Open** noon-5pm Tue-Fri; 10am-5pm Sat. **Admission** $4; $3 seniors, 6-18s; free under-6s. **No credit cards.** **Map** p402 E33.

This 18th-century tavern was George Washington's watering hole and the site of his famous farewell to the troops at the Revolution's close. During the mid to late 1780s, the building housed the fledgling nation's departments of war, foreign affairs and treasury. In 1904, Fraunces became a repository for artefacts collected by the Sons of the Revolution in the State of New York. Ongoing exhibits include 'George Washington: Down the Stream of Life', which examines America's first ever President. The tavern and restaurant (1-212 968 1776) serve hearty fare at lunch and dinner from Monday to Saturday.

National Museum of the American Indian

George Gustav Heye Center, Alexander Hamilton Custom House, 1 Bowling Green, between State & Whitehall Streets (1-212 514 3700/www.nmai.si.edu). Subway R, W to Whitehall Street; 1 to South Ferry; 4, 5 to Bowling Green. **Open** 10am-5pm Mon-Wed, Fri-Sun; 10am-8pm Thur. **Admission** free. **Map** p402 E33.

This branch of the Smithsonian Institution displays its collection around the grand rotunda of the 1907 Custom House, at the bottom of Broadway (which, many moons ago, began as an Indian trail). The life and culture of Native Americans is presented in rotating exhibitions – from intricately woven fibre Pomo baskets to beaded buckskin shirts – along with contemporary artwork. On show until 23 September 2008 is 'Beauty Surrounds Us', a collection of musical instruments, games and ceremonial clothing that celebrates the importance of decorative art in native cultures. The Diker Pavilion for Native Arts & Culture, opened in 2006, has already made its mark on the cultural life of the city by offering the only dedicated showcase for Native American visual and performing arts. The Diker's 6,000 square feet contain ten exhibition cases set into niches between a series of sloping walls all panelled in a wonderfully rich cherry wood.

Statue of Liberty & Ellis Island Immigration Museum

Statue of Liberty (1-212 363 3200/www.nps.gov/stli). R, W to Whitehall Street; 1 to South Ferry; 4, 5 to Bowling Green; then take Statue of Liberty ferry (1-866 782 8834), departing every 25mins from gangway 4 or 5 in southernmost Battery Park. **Open** ferry runs 8.30am-4.30pm daily. Purchase tickets at Castle Clinton in Battery Park. **Admission** $11.50; $9.50 seniors; $4.50 3-12s; free under-3s. **Credit** AmEx, MC, V.

Trust us, even if your blood doesn't run red, white and blue you will not be underwhelmed by either of these two landmarks. But, contrary to some mistaken notions, the mother of all American statues is not on Ellis Island, though that historic place and its resident Ellis Island Immigration Museum can both be reached by the same ferry.

Frédéric-Auguste Bartholdi's *Liberty Enlightening the World*, a gift from the people of France, was unveiled in 1886. Although security concerns placed the statue off-limits after 9/11, Lady Liberty's insides were reopened for guided tours (reservations required, call 1-866 782 8834) in 2004. However, you still can't climb up to the crown, and backpacks and luggage are not permitted on the island. Still, you

Putting faces to the huddled masses at **Ellis Island Immigration Museum**.

Sightseeing

Walk it out Night crawler

Some of New York's sights are best seen after dark.

Bridge Café.

Start Fulton Street, at Front Street. Subway A, C to Broadway-Nassau Street; J, M, Z, 2, 3, 4, 5 to Fulton Street.
End Staten Island Ferry Terminal. Subway 1 to South Ferry.
Distance 3.75 miles
Time 3.5 hours

New York after dark needn't be X-rated to be interesting. Many neighbourhoods are monumentally serene at night, a time when the city relaxes and opens itself up to easy exploration. Chinatown and the Financial District, which teem with shoulder-to-shoulder crowds during the day, are both peaceful by moonlight – and are steeped in rich city history. Start at the South **Street Seaport** (Fulton Street, at South Street, Pier 17). Its annoying mall-like nature fades at night – even the mime knocks off around 10 – and it's easier to enjoy the docked schooners and views of an illuminated Brooklyn Bridge.

Walk up Fulton Street and take a right on **Front Street**, where inviting bars and restaurants are nestled in old brick buildings. You'll come to Dover Street, where the **Bridge Café** (279 Water Street, at Dover Street, 1-212 227 3344) occupies the site of the city's oldest continuously operating bar. Along with a drink, try the blue cheese soufflé.

Continue up Dover and hang a right on Pearl, which will take you into Chinatown, then bear right at St James Place. Whiffs of seafood and over-ripe lychee signal the change of 'hood. On East Broadway, stop at **White Swan Bakery** (at Forsythe Street) for Asian pastries and all your fish-oil needs. Keep chugging up East Broadway to **169 Bar** (169 East Broadway, at Rutgers Street, 1-212 473 8866), formerly known as the 'Bloody Bucket' for its frequent fisticuffs. These days, the crowd is docile and eclectic, and there's live music every night. Head west toward the Bowery and start walking further downtown. On Pell Street you can get a 'foot rub' as late as 1am – at **Foot Heaven** (16 Pell Street, between Bowery & Mott Street, 1-212 962 6588). Note: you must call before 11pm to line up your massage. Take a quick right on to Mott, then a quick left on to Bayard. Linger for a moment – or a song – at karaoke bar **Winnie's** (104 Bayard Street, 1-212 732 2384); across the street on Baxter, you even might see perps getting dragged into a police holding cell by the fuzz.

Next, wander south then west on to Centre Street and walk downtown until you reach **City Hall Park**. The southern gates are open all night, offering visitors a surprisingly scenic respite amid the soft glow of oil lamps above the central fountain.

If you want to remember and reflect on 9/11 at **Ground Zero**, walk east one block to Church Street and hang a left. With its screened fences and ultra-sanitised memorial photos, the site is no longer the emotional gut-punch it once was. Still, it draws hundreds of curious onlookers each week. In 2008, city officials expect the new Freedom Tower

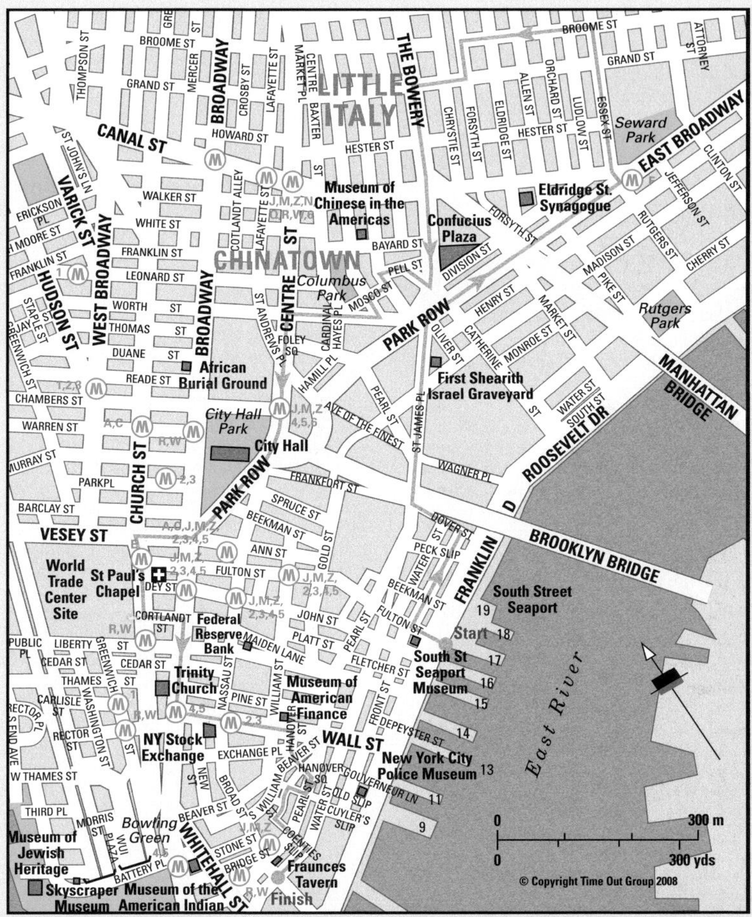

(*see p98*) to start rising. One block east on Broadway, behind designer duds shop Century 21 (*see p238*), is an area that was once the Fifth Avenue of its day, a snazzy commercial stretch frequented by the finest turn-of-19th-century ladies. Now, sadly, it is more Burger King territory.

Walk south on Broadway, passing **Trinity Church** (89 Broadway) and the graveyard where politician Alexander Hamilton is buried. Across from Trinity Church, head to **Wall Street**; at night, the famous street is an impressive urban canyon. George Washington, memorialised in bronze sculpture outside Federal Hall (No.26), took his first oath of office here. Say hello to the security guard who stands watch at the **New York Stock Exchange** (No.11) from 6pm to 6am.

Meander south, glancing at **Fraunces Tavern**, where George Washington bid a final farewell to his soldiers during the Revolutionary War. Stop when you reach the **South Ferry Ferry Terminal**, at the tip of the island. Hardcore insomniacs should take the **Staten Island Ferry** over and back. It runs every half hour (or every hour from 1.30am to 5.30am), and from the water the skyline rises before you in spectacular fashion.

can take in the carving on the pedestal, which features the 1883 Emma Lazarus poem with the renowned lines 'Give me your tired, your poor/your huddled masses yearning to breathe free'.

On the way back to Manhattan, the ferry will stop at the popular Immigration Museum, on Ellis Island, once an immigration depot through which more than 12 million people entered the country between 1892 and 1954. The exhibitions are a moving tribute to the immigrants from so many different countries who made the journey to America, dreaming of a better life. The $6 audio tour, narrated by Tom Brokaw, is informative and inspiring.

Battery Park City & Ground Zero

The streets around **Ground Zero**, the former site of the **World Trade Center**, have been drawing crowds since the terrorist attacks of 2001. Not that there's been much to see. The site of the worst attack on US soil, on 11 September 2001, took nearly three thousand lives and left a hole where one of the most recognisable American icons, the Twin Towers, had been. It took five years of bureaucratic red tape, but construction on the site is well under way and moving steadily forward. Completion of the entire project, including the much-debated and redesigned Freedom Tower (a 1,776-foot spire planned as the world's tallest building but stalled by security issues in 2005) and the memorial, is expected in around 2010. Eventually, five towers will also be built at the new World Trade Center complex.

In July 2007, the Port Authority announced that the Freedom Tower's steel frame will rise in 2008, a significant sign of progress. Concrete for the foundation has already been poured, and many of the building's initial structural steel columns have been installed. Next, about 43,000 tons of steel will be used to create the frame, which will soar high on the city's skyline. The redesigned tower will be set further back from the street, to increase protection from a terrorist attack, and it will taper into eight tall isosceles triangles, forming an octagon at its centre. There will be an observation deck at 1,362 feet above the ground, and the building will offer 2.6 million square feet of office and retail space, upscale restaurants and below-ground access to the subway and World Financial Center.

As we went to press, it looked as though the **World Trade Center Memorial & Museum** (for which construction began in spring 2006) were on track to open in the next few years. Tentatively, the memorial is due to open on 11 September, 2009, with the museum itself to open one year later. Titled *Reflecting Absence*, the memorial will consist of two 'void' spaces representing the footprints of the original towers. The voids will be surrounded by oak trees, with cascading water falling into illuminated reflecting pools. The adjacent museum will use artefacts and exhibitions to tell the story of both the 26 February 1993 bombing and 9/11. Visitors will be able to view a large portion of the slurry wall that held back the Hudson River during the attacks.

Immediately to the west of Ground Zero, the city-within-a-city **World Financial Center** (*see p99*) is a pretty place for a walk-through. To the east of Ground Zero, serious shopaholics can sift through the seemingly endless stock at the enormous discount designer duds vault Century 21 (*see p238*).

Just west of the World Financial Center lies **Battery Park City**, devised by Nelson A Rockefeller (the governor of New York from 1959 to 1973) as a site of apartment housing (some of it certified 'green') and schools in an area that is otherwise all business. Home to roughly 9,000 people, the self-contained neighbourhood includes restaurants, cafés, shops and a marina amid 92 glorious riverside acres. Sweeping views of the Hudson River and close proximity to the downtown financial scene have also made this an ideal spot for office space. Still, the most impressive aspects of BPC are its esplanade, a paradise for bikers, skaters and joggers, and the strolling park (officially called Nelson A Rockefeller Park), both of which run along the Hudson River north of the Financial Center and connect to Battery Park at the south. Close by the marina is the 1997 **Police Memorial** (Liberty Street, at South End Avenue), a granite pool and fountain that symbolically trace the lifespan of a police officer through the use of moving water, with names of the fallen etched into the wall. The **Irish Hunger Memorial** (Vesey Street, at North End Avenue) is here too, paying a silent tribute to those who suffered so greatly during the terrible Irish Famine.

One of the larger chunks of grass along this stretch is Rockefeller Park's sprawling **North Lawn**. This spot, located adjacent to the well-respected Stuyvesant High School, has a veritable beach vibe in summer, when sunbathers, kite fliers and soccer players vie for turf. Basketball and handball courts, concrete tables inlaid with chess and backgammon boards, and playgrounds with swings are some of the built-in recreation options.

Situated between Battery Park City and Battery Park are the inventively designed **South Cove**; **Teardrop Park**, a two-acre space designed to evoke the Hudson River Valley; and **Robert F Wagner Jr Park**, where an observation deck offers fabulous

Money talks: the Downtown Alliance information kiosk at the **World Financial Center**.

views of both the harbour and the Verrazano-Narrows Bridge. New York City's Holocaust remembrance archive, the **Museum of Jewish Heritage** (*see below*), is tucked in amid the green spots, and the entire park area is dotted with sculptures, including Tom Otterness's whimsical *The Real World*, which, by the way, has nothing to do with MTV's long-running reality show of the same name, although both debuted in 1992. Just across the street sits the **Skyscraper Museum** (*see below*), where you can learn about the high-rise buildings that have made the city's iconic skyline, and explore the World Trade Center Dossier, a moving exhibit about the fallen towers and what will ultimately replace them.

The **Battery Park City Authority** (1-212 417 2000, www.batteryparkcity.org) website lists events taking place and has a very useful map of the area.

Museum of Jewish Heritage

Robert F Wagner Jr Park, 36 Battery Place, at First Place (1-646 437 4200/www.mjhnyc.org). Subway 1, 9 to South Ferry; 4, 5 to Bowling Green. **Open** 10am-5.45pm Mon-Tue, Thur, Sun; 10am-8pm Wed; 10am-3pm Fri, eve of Jewish holidays (until 5pm in the summer). **Admission** $10; $7 seniors; $5 students; free under-12s. Free 4-8pm Wed. **Credit** AmEx, MC, V. **Map** p402 E34.

Opened in 1997 and expanded in 2003, this museum offers one of the most moving cultural experiences in the city. Exploring Jewish life and detailing the horrific attacks on it over the past century, the collection consists of 24 documentary films, 2,000 photographs and 800 cultural artefacts, many donated by Holocaust survivors and their families. The Memorial Garden features English artist Andy Goldsworthy's permanent installation *Garden of Stones*, 18 fire-hollowed boulders, each planted with a dwarf oak sapling.

Skyscraper Museum

39 Battery Place, between Little West Street & 1st Place (1-212-968-1961/www.skyscraper.org). Subway 4, 5 to Bowling Green. **Open** noon-6pm Wed-Sun. **Admission** $5; $2.50 seniors, students. **Map** p402 E34.

In just 5,000sq ft – very modest by institutional standards – this space manages to evoke both the mighty scale and aspirations of its subject matter.

World Financial Center & Winter Garden

From Albany to Vesey Streets, between the Hudson River & West Street (1-212 945 2600/www.worldfinancialcenter.com). Subway A, C to Broadway-Nassau Street; E to World Trade Center; J, M, Z, 2, 3, 4, 5 to Fulton Street. **Map** p402 D32.

Completed back in 1988, Cesar Pelli's four glass-and-granite postmodern office towers, each crowned with a different geometric form, surround an upscale retail area and a series of restaurant-lined plazas that ring the marina, where private yachts and water taxis for New Jersey are docked. The Winter Garden hosts a series of concerts. Visit the website to access the calendar of free events, covering everything from folk concerts to silent-film festivals.

Wall Street

Since the city's earliest days as a fur-trading post, wheeling and dealing has been New York's main activity, and commerce the backbone of its prosperity. The southern tip of Manhattan is generally known as the **Financial District** because, in the days before telecommunications, banks established their headquarters here to be near the city's active port. Although this neighbourhood is bisected vertically by the ever-bustling Broadway, it's that east–west thoroughfare Wall Street (or 'the Street' in trader lingo) that is synonymous with the world's greatest den of capitalism.

Wall Street, which took its name from a defensive wooden wall built by the Dutch in 1653 to mark what was then the northern limit of New Amsterdam, is big on legend despite being less than a mile long (it's truncated by Broadway on its western end, and therefore only spans about half the width of the island). Here at Broadway rises the Gothic Revival spire of **Trinity Church** (89 Broadway, at Wall Street, 1-212 602 0872, www.trinitywallstreet.org). This Episcopalian house of worship was the island's tallest structure when it was completed in 1846 (the original burned down in 1776; a second was demolished in 1839). A set of gates north of the church on Broadway allows access to the adjacent cemetery, where cracked and faded tombstones mark the final resting places of many dozens of city dwellers, including signatories of the Declaration of Independence and the Constitution. The church is also home to the Trinity Church Museum, which displays a large assortment of historic diaries, photographs, sermons and burial records. **St Paul's Chapel** (*see below*), a satellite of Trinity Church, is an oasis of peace in the midst of frantic business activity and one of the finest Georgian structures in the country. Miraculously, both landmark churches survived the World Trade Center attack. Although mortar fell from their façades, the steeples remained intact.

A block east of Trinity Church, the **Federal Hall National Memorial** is a rather august Greek Revival building and – in a previous incarnation – the site of George Washington's inauguration in 1789. It was along this stretch that corporate America made its first audacious architectural statements, and a continued walk eastwards offers much evidence of what money can buy. Notable structures include **40 Wall Street** (between Nassau & William Streets), which went head to head with the Chrysler Building in 1929, battling for the title of 'world's tallest building' (the Empire State Building trounced them both a year later), and the former **Merchants' Exchange** at 55 Wall Street (between Hanover & William Streets), with its stacked rows of Ionic and Corinthian columns, giant doors and a remarkable 12,000-square-foot ballroom inside. Back around the corner is the **Equitable Building** (120 Broadway, between Cedar & Pine Streets), whose greedy use of vertical space helped instigate the zoning laws now governing skyscrapers (stand across the street from the building to get the best view).

The nerve centre of the US economy is the **New York Stock Exchange** (11 Wall Street, between Broad & New Streets). For security reasons, the Exchange is no longer open to the public, but the street outside offers an endless pageant of brokers, traders and their minions. For a lesson on Wall Street's influence over the years, visit the **Museum of American Finance** (*see below*) in its new home in the old Bank of New York building.

A few blocks from the East River end of Wall Street, on Old Slip, is the **New York City Police Museum** (*see below*).

Federal Reserve Bank

33 Liberty Street, between Nassau & William Streets (1-212 720 6130/www.newyorkfed.org). Subway 2, 3, 4, 5 to Wall Street. **Open** 9am-5pm Mon-Fri. **Tours** every hr on the half-hour, last tour 2.30pm; must be arranged at least 1wk in advance; tickets are sent by mail. Phone for reservations. **Admission** free. **Map** p402 E33.

Here's your chance to descend 80ft below street level and commune with the planet's most precious metal. Roughly a quarter of the world's gold (more than $100 billion dollars) is stored here in a gigantic vault that rests on the bedrock of Manhattan Island.

Museum of American Finance

48 Wall Street, at William Street (1-212 908 4110/www.financialhistory.org). Subway 2, 3, 4, 5 to Wall Street; 1 to Rector Street. **Open** 10am-4pm Tue-Sat. **Admission** $8; $5 seniors, students; free under-6s. **Credit** AmEx, MC, V. **Map** p402 E33.

In September 2007, the museum packed up its loot and moved into the former headquarters of the Bank of New York. The newly renovated Banking Hall makes an excellent place to view the museum's permanent collection, which traces the history of Wall Street and America's financial markets. You'll see the ticker tape from the morning of the big crash of 29 October 1929, an 1867 stock ticker and the earliest known photograph of Wall Street.

New York City Police Museum

100 Old Slip, between South & Water Streets (1-212 480 3100/www.nycpolicemuseum.org). Subway 2, 3 to Wall Street; 4, 5 to Bowling Green. **Open** 10am-5pm Mon-Sat. **Admission** suggested donation $5; $3 seniors; $2 6-18s; free under-6s. **No credit cards**. **Map** p402 F32.

The NYPD's self-tribute features exhibits on its history, as well the tools and transportation of the trade. You can also buy official NYPD paraphernalia.

St Paul's Chapel

209 Broadway, between Fulton & Vesey Streets (1-212 233 4164/www.saintpaulschapel.org). Subway A, C to Broadway-Nassau Street; J, M, Z, 2, 3, 4, 5 to Fulton Street. **Open** 10am-6pm Mon-Sat; 9am-4pm Sun. **Map** p402 E32.

The chapel here is the New York's only extant pre-Revolutionary building (it dates from 1766) and one of the nation's most valued Georgian structures.

South Street Seaport

Although New York's importance as a port has diminished, its initial fortune rolled in on the swells that crash into its deep-water harbour.

The city was perfectly situated for trade with Europe; after 1825, goods from the Western Territories arrived via the Erie Canal and the Hudson River. By 1892, New York had become the point of entry for millions of immigrants, and so its character was shaped not only by commodities but also the waves of humanity that arrived at its docks. The South Street Seaport is the best place to appreciate this seafaring heritage.

If you enter the Seaport area from Water Street, the first thing that you're likely to notice is the whitewashed **Titanic Memorial Lighthouse**, originally erected on top of the Seaman's Church Institute (Coenties Slip & South Street) in 1913, the year after the great ship sank. The monument was moved to its current location in 1976. Check out the views of magnificent **Brooklyn Bridge** that this corner of the neighbourhood offers.

The **South Street Seaport**, redeveloped in the mid 1980s, is lined with reclaimed and renovated buildings that have been converted to shops, restaurants, bars and a museum. It's not an area that New Yorkers often visit, despite its rich history. The Seaport's public spaces, including blocks of both Fulton and Front Streets, where cars are barred, are a favourite for street performers. At 11 Fulton Street, the **Fulton Market** (open daily), with its gourmet food stalls and seafood restaurants, is a great place for people-watching and for oyster-slurping. Familiar national-chain stores such as J Crew and Abercrombie & Fitch line the surrounding thoroughfares. The shopping area of **Pier 17**, admittedly little more than a picturesque mall by day and an after-work watering hole by night, is nevertheless worth a quick walk-through.

Outdoor concerts in summer attract locals, and may justify a sit-down, even for the most determined of sightseers. Antique vessels are docked at neighbouring piers. The street right in front of Pier 17 used to support the famous Fulton Fish Market, a bustling, early morning trading centre that dated back to the mid 1800s, where much of the city's food industry once purchased fresh seafood for their daily menus. In 2006, the market was relocated to a larger, more modern and sanitary facility in the Hunts Point area of the Bronx, making it the second-largest fish market in the world (second only to Tokyo); it is, however, no longer open for tours. Plans for the former site are up in the air, although cynical New Yorkers suspect the historic site, one of the last vestiges of the city's working waterfront, will probably be turned into condos, instead of, say, being annexed by the **South Street Seaport Museum** (*see below*), which details New York's maritime history. The museum is located inside the restored 19th-century buildings of Schermerhorn Row (2-18 Fulton Street, 91-92 South Street & 189-195 Front Street).

South Street Seaport Museum

Visitors' Center, 12 Fulton Street, at South Street (1-212 748 8600/www.southstseaport.org). Subway A, C to Broadway-Nassau Street; J, M, Z, 2, 3, 4, 5 to Fulton Street. **Open** *Apr-Oct* 10am-6pm Tue-Sun. *Nov-Mar* 10am-6pm Fri-Sun. **Admission** $8; $6 seniors, students; $4 5-12s; free under-5s. **Credit** AmEx, MC, V. **Map** p402 F32.

Set in 11 blocks along the East River, this museum is an amalgam of galleries, historic ships, 19th-century buildings and a visitors' centre. Wander around the rebuilt streets and pop in to see an exhibition on marine life and history before climbing aboard the four-masted 1911 *Peking*. The seaport is generally thick with tourists, but it's still a lively place to spend an afternoon, especially for families with children, who will enjoy the atmosphere and intriguing seafaring memorabilia. In summer 2008, the museum launches 'World Port New York', an ambitious exhibition highlighting the economic and social importance of New York's bustling seaport to the city, country and world beyond.

Civic Center & City Hall

The business of running New York occurs in the many grand buildings of the **Civic Center**, an area that formed the budding city's northern boundary in the 1700s. **City Hall Park** was treated to an extensive renovation just before the millennium, and the pretty landscaping and abundant benches make it a popular weekday lunching spot for local office workers. At the southern end you'll find a granite 'time wheel' tracking the park's history. Like the steps of City Hall, the park has been the site of press conferences and political protests for years. Under former mayor Rudy Giuliani, the steps were closed to such activities unless they were approved by Hizzoner's office. A federal district judge subsequently declared the ban unconstitutional in April 2000, after a celebration of the Yankees' World Series victory took place, but an event commemorating World AIDS Day was snuffed.

City Hall (*photo p102*), at the northern end of the park, houses the mayor's office and the chambers of the City Council, and is therefore usually buzzing with preparations for VIP comings and goings. When City Hall was completed in 1812, its architects were so confident the city would grow no further north that they didn't bother to put any marble on its northern side. The building, a beautiful blend of Federalist form and French Renaissance detail, is closed to the public (except for scheduled

City Hall. See p101.

group tours; *see p103*). Facing City Hall, the much larger, golden-statue-topped **Municipal Building** contains other civic offices, including the marriage bureau; note the nervous, blushing brides- and grooms-to-be awaiting their various ceremonies, particularly in the early morning.

Park Row, east of City Hall Park, is now lined with cafés, electronics shops and the campus of **Pace University**. It once held the offices of 19 daily papers and was affectionately known as Newspaper Row (these days, the many scoop-driven crime reporters from all the major newspapers share just one cramped office, popularly known as 'the Shack', which is located nearby at 1 Police Plaza).

Facing the park from the west is Cass Gilbert's famous **Woolworth Building** (233 Broadway, between Barclay Street & Park Place), a vertically elongated Gothic cathedral-style office building considered by many to be the Mozart of skyscrapers (and alternatively nicknamed the Cathedral of Commerce). Be sure to cast your eyes skywards as you face the striking façade.

The houses of crime and punishment are also located in the **Civic Center**, near Foley Square, which was once a pond and later the site of the city's most notorious 19th-century slum, Five Points. These days, you'll find the State Supreme Court in the **New York County Courthouse** (60 Centre Street, at Pearl Street), a hexagonal Roman Revival building; the beautiful rotunda is decorated with the mural *Law Through the Ages*. The **United States Courthouse** (40 Centre Street, between Duane & Pearl Streets) is a Corinthian temple crowned with a golden pyramid.

Next to City Hall, on Chambers Street, is the 1872 Old New York County Courthouse, more popularly known as the **Tweed Courthouse**, a symbol of the runaway corruption of mid-19th-century municipal government. William 'Boss' Tweed (*see p23*), leader of the political machine Tammany Hall, famously pocketed some $10 million of the building's huge $14 million construction budget. What he didn't steal bought a beautiful edifice, with exquisite Italianate detailing. These days, the Tweed houses the city's Department of Education, a considerably less lucrative machine.

The **Criminal Courts Building & Manhattan Detention Complex** (100 Centre Street, between Leonard & White Streets) is still known as 'the Tombs', despite its official renaming by former mayor Rudy Giuliani in December 2001. The 881-bed jail is commonly called 'the Tombs' after the original 1838 Egyptian Revival building, or for the grimness of the environment, depending on whom you ask. It's true that the hall's architecture – great granite slabs and looming towers guarding the entrance – is downright Kafkaesque. There's an interesting drama behind the renaming: Giuliani had declared it the Bernard B Kerik Complex, in honour of his own NYC Police Department Commissioner. But that was five years before Kerik was disgraced after pleading guilty to accepting free home renovations and failing to report a hefty loan from a real estate developer. That's why in July 2006, less than 48 hours after Kerik's court plea, Mayor Michael Bloomberg swiftly had his name stripped from the building. Bloomberg had workers remove Kerik's name between 1am and 3am, so that the new name would appear later that same morning. Each of these courts is open to the public on weekdays from 9am to 5pm. Your best bet for legal drama is the Criminal Courts. If you can't slip into a trial, you can at least observe legal eagles and their clients, or observe the pleas at the Arraignment Court (until 1am).

Nearby, a stunning archaeological find, the **African Burial Ground** (*see below*), was officially designated a National Monument by President Bush in 2006.

African Burial Ground

Duane Street, between Broadway & Centre Streets, behind 290 Broadway (1-212 637 2019/www.nps.gov/afbg). Subway N, Q, R, W to Canal Street; J, M, Z to Chambers Street; 4, 5, 6 to Brooklyn Bridge-City Hall. **Open** 9am-4pm Mon-Fri. **Admission** free. **Map** p402 E31.

A major archaeological discovery, the African Burial Ground is a small remnant of a five-and-a-half-acre cemetery where between 10,000 and 20,000 African men, women and children were buried. The cemetery, which closed in 1794, was unearthed during the construction of a federal office building in 1991 and designated a National Monument. In October 2007, a dedication ceremony was held for the newly erected stone memorial designed by architect Rodney Leon, a 37-year-old African-American New Yorker. The two-storey-tall curved monument draws heavily on African architecture and contains a spiral path leading to an ancestral chamber. There is a visitor centre located inside 290 Broadway.

City Hall

City Hall Park, from Vesey to Chambers Streets, between Broadway & Park Row (1-212 788 3000/www.nyc.gov). Subway J, M, Z to Chambers Street; 2, 3 to Park Place; 4, 5, 6 to Brooklyn Bridge-City Hall. **Map** p402 E32.

For group tours only; call two weeks in advance.

Tribeca & Soho

Tribeca (the Triangle Below Canal Street; *photos p105*) is a textbook example of the gentrification process in lower Manhattan. A few pockets still appear abandoned – the cobblestones crumbling, the cast-iron buildings chipped all and unpainted – but watch this space. Derelict areas like these are transformed seemingly overnight with deluxe makeovers.

The rich and famous weren't here first, but they are certainly here now. Many big-name celebs (Robert De Niro, Christy Turlington) and established, successful artists (Richard Serra) live in the area. JFK Jr also lived for years on North Moore Street until his premature death. There's a host of haute eateries here, including top-notch **Nobu** (105 Hudson Street, at Franklin Street, 1-212 334 4445), and the long-running Odeon (145 West Broadway, at Duane Street, 1-212 233 0507), immortalised by Jay McInerney in his famous 1984 novel *Bright Lights, Big City*, remains a hotspot for the beautiful people.

Many of the buildings in Tribeca are large, hulking former warehouses; those near the river, in particular, are rapidly being converted into modern condos, but fine small-scale cast-iron architecture still stands along **White Street** and the parallel thoroughfares. You'll find galleries, salons, furniture stores, spas and other businesses here that cater to the neighbourhood's stylish residents. Architecture star Frank Gehry designed the multi-million-dollar interior for the Tribeca **Issey Miyake** boutique (119 Hudson Street, at North Moore Street, 1-212 226 0100). **Bouley Bakery & Market** (*see p183*) opened at 130 Broadway a few years ago to much fanfare, thanks to celeb chef David Bouley, who is often credited with putting Tribeca on the culinary map. Here, French pastries are elevated to fine art (and the prices reflect that feat).

Tribeca is also the unofficial headquarters of New York's film industry. Robert De Niro's **Tribeca Film Center** (375 Greenwich Street, at Franklin Street) houses screening rooms and production offices in the old Martinson Coffee Building; his restaurant, Tribeca Grill, is on the ground floor. A few blocks away, his recently acquired **Tribeca Cinemas** (54 Varick Street, at Laight Street, 1-212 966 8163, www.tribecacinemas.com) hosts film premières and glitzy parties when it isn't serving as a venue for the **Tribeca Film Festival** (*see p260*), which gets bigger every year.

It's hard to believe that **Soho**, the most popular (and packed) downtown shopping destination, was once an industrial zone known as Hell's Hundred Acres. In the 1960s, the neighbourhood was earmarked for destruction, but its signature cast-iron warehouses were saved by the artists who inhabited them. Urban-planning theorist Chester A Rapkin coined the name Soho, for South of Houston Street, in a 1962 study of the neighbourhood. The **King and Queen of Greene Street** (respectively, 72-76 Greene Street, between Broome & Spring Streets, and 28-30 Greene Street, between Canal & Grand Streets) are both fine examples of the area's beloved architectural landmarks.

Not surprisingly, as loft living became fashionable and buildings were renovated for residential use, landlords sniffed the potential for profits, and Soho subsequently morphed into a playground for the young, beautiful and rich. It can still be a pleasure to stroll around the cobblestoned streets on weekday mornings, but large chain stores have now moved in among the boutiques and bistros, bringing with them

New dork city

New York, capital of hip, has a secret geeky side just waiting to be explored.

If you think this is a joke, think again – New York is a hotbed of bespectacled smartypants. Don your best pocket protector and check out one of the city's many geeky gatherings. The monthly gatherings at **Café Scientifique** (Rialto, 265 Elizabeth Street, between E Houston & Prince Streets, 1-212 334 7900, www.sciencecafenyc.org) see speakers from one of New York's many research institutions dazzle the crowd with their latest and greatest findings; the best bit is often the lively Q&A session that follows.

If the idea of 'people doing strange things with electricity' appeals to you, then check out **Dorkbot-NYC**, a monthly meeting of designers, engineers, students and science boffs (see www.dorkbot.org for schedule and locations). Over at Cornelia Street Café (29 Cornelia Street, 1-212 989 9319, www.corneliastreetcafe.com), Nobel laureate Roald Hoffmann curates a monthly gathering on the first Sunday of the month (6pm) called **Entertaining Science**, when science groupies pack the joint to hear informal readings from the likes of esteemed science and medical writer Dr Oliver Sacks, and physics and maths writer KC Cole.

Nerds looking for something a little out of the ordinary won't want to miss the monthly concert party featuring 'chiptune' sounds derived from rewiring hacked Nintendo gaming consoles. 'It's the folk music of a new digital era,' enthuses organiser Mike Rosenthal. 'A lot of experimental music is hard for people to get into, but this has a real playful element to it.' Tribeca's media venue the **Tank** (279 Church Street, at Franklin Street, 1-212 563 6269, www.thetanknyc.org) plays host.

Not afraid to show off your high IQ? Join the throngs of know-it-alls who know how to spell really hard words and head out to Brooklyn where Pete's Candy Store (709 Lorimer Street, between N 10th & 11th Streets, 1-718 302 3770) hosts **Williamsburg Spelling Bee**. Compete for prizes such as Broadway show tickets or the chance to be included in one of two prestigious finals. Rather than single-error elimination, 'it's three strikes and you're out,' says comedian/host Jennifer Dziura. 'It's a little less pressure.' And whether you're competing for free booze, prestige or serious prizes, quiz nights are the perfect outlet for your inner dork.

The gold standard in useless trivia is the **Big Quiz Thing** (www.bigquizthing.com), held every other Monday at the **Slipper Room** (*see p296*). It's one of the few places where you can see cool brainiacs vie for cold hard cash – and the occasional cookie. You've got to love any competition where you can earn Smart-Ass Points for a wrong answer that makes the host laugh.

Now for something completely different. Thanks to Nasty Canasta, Jonny Porkpie and the **Pinchbottom** crew (www.pinchbottom.com), your perverted genre fantasies could come shimmying to life. The Pinchbottom dancers recently served up a sci-fi theme (boobified Godzilla, we won't forget you), and the group promises 'more geek-tastic burlesque' in the coming months, including nights devoted to superheroes.

a shopping-mall-at-Christmas-style crush on weekends. The commercialism and crowds have caused a number of more exclusive shops to head to other neighbourhoods, and most of the galleries that made Soho an art mecca in the 1970s and '80s have decamped to cheaper (and now much trendier) neighbourhoods such as West Chelsea and Brooklyn's Dumbo and Williamsburg. Surprisingly, some garment factories remain in Soho, especially near Canal Street, though many of the very same elegant buildings now house design studios, magazine publishers and record labels.

Many upscale hotels like the **Mercer**, **60 Thompson** (for both, *see p58*) and the **SoHo Grand Hotel** (*see p59*) keep the famous people flocking to the area; high-end clothing stores include Prada, Issey Miyake, Miu Miu, Paul Smith and Agnès b; and swanky home furnishings rule at Euro-cool design stores such as Moss and Cappelletti. And the goods aren't all that's worldly in these parts. At weekends, you're as likely to hear French, German and Italian as you are to catch a blast of Long Island. One museum in Soho that makes for a worthwhile detour is the **New York City Fire Museum** (*see p105*), a former fire station that now houses a collection of antique engines dating from the 1700s.

Just west of West Broadway, tenement- and townhouse-lined streets contain remnants of the Italian community that once dominated the area. Elderly men and women stroll slowly along Sullivan Street to the **St Anthony of Padua Roman Catholic Church** (No.155, at W Houston Street), which was dedicated in 1888. You'll still find old-school neighbourhood flavour in local businesses such as Joe's Dairy (No.156, between Houston & Prince Streets, 1-212 677 8780), Pino's Prime Meat Market (No.149, between Houston & Prince Streets, 1-212 475 8134) and Vesuvio Bakery (160 Prince Street, between Thompson Street & West Broadway, 1-212 925 8248), whose eminently old-fashioned façade has appeared in dozens of commercials over the years.

New York City Fire Museum

278 Spring Street, between Hudson & Varick Streets (1-212 691 1303/www.nycfiremuseum.org). Subway C, E to Spring Street; 1 to Houston Street. **Open** 10am-5pm Tue-Sat; 10am-4pm Sun. **Admission** suggested donation $5; $2 seniors, students; $1 under-12s. **Credit** AmEx, DC, Disc, MC, V. **Map** p403 D30.

An active firehouse from 1904 to 1959, this museum is filled with gadgetry and pageantry, from late 18th-century hand-pumped fire engines to present-day equipment. The museum also houses a permanent exhibit commemorating firefighters' heroism after the attack on the World Trade Center.

Little Italy & Nolita

Little Italy, which once ran from Canal to Houston Streets, between Lafayette Street and the Bowery, hardly resembles the insular community portrayed in Martin Scorsese's 1973 classic *Mean Streets*. Many Italian families have long since fled Mott Street and gone to the suburbs, Chinatown has crept north, and rising rents have forced mom-and-pop businesses to surrender to the stylish boutiques of Nolita: North of Little Italy (a misnomer, since it technically lies within Little Italy). Another telling change in the 'hood: **St Patrick's Old Cathedral** (260-264 Mulberry Street, between Houston & Prince Streets) holds services in English and Spanish, not in Italian, as it once did. Completed in 1809 and restored after a fire in 1868, this was New York's premier Catholic church until it was demoted, upon consecration of the Fifth Avenue cathedral of the same name. But ethnic pride remains. Italian-Americans flood in from the outer boroughs to show their love for the old neighbourhood during the 10-day **Feast of San Gennaro** (*see p264*) every September. Tourist-oriented Italian cafés and restaurants line Mulberry Street between Canal and Houston Streets, but nearby pockets of the past still linger. Elderly locals (and in-the-know young ones) buy olive oil and fresh pasta from venerable shops such

Tribeca. *See p103.*

Sightseeing

...io's Fine Foods (200 Grand Street, at Mott ..., 1-212 226 1033) and sandwiches packed ... salami and cheeses at the Italian Food Center (186 Grand Street, at Mulberry Street, 1-212 925 2954).

Of course, Little Italy is also the site of several notorious **Mafia landmarks**. The brick-fronted store occupied by accessories boutique Amy Chan (247 Mulberry Street, between Prince & Spring Streets) was once the Ravenite Social Club, Mafia kingpin John Gotti's HQ from the mid 1980s until his arrest (and imprisonment) in 1990. Mobster Joey Gallo was shot to death in 1972 while celebrating a birthday at Umberto's Clam House, which has since moved around the corner to 178 Mulberry Street, at Broome Street (1-212 431 7545). The various restaurants in the area are mostly undistinguished grill-and-pasta houses, but two reliable choices are Il Cortile (125 Mulberry Street, between Canal & Hester Streets, 1-212 226 6060) and La Mela (167 Mulberry Street, between Broome & Grand Streets, 1-212 431 9493). Drop in for dessert at Caffè Roma (385 Broome Street, at Mulberry Street, 1-212 226 8413), which opened in 1891.

Chichi restaurants and shops owned by fledgling and established designers have taken over **Nolita**. Elizabeth, Mott and Mulberry Streets, between Houston and Spring Streets, in particular, are now the source of everything from perfectly cut jeans to handblown glass. Hip shops like Cath Kidston, Steven Alan and Paul Frank are in abundance now. The young, the insouciant and the vaguely European still congregate outside hip eateries like Bread (20 Spring Street, between Elizabeth & Mott Streets, 1-212 334 1015) and Café Habana (*see p184*). For a more low-key, old-school experience, there's always the coal-fired pizzeria Lombardi's (32 Spring Street, at Mott Street, 1-212 941 7994), still going strong after more than 100 years; it claims to be the first pizzeria in the United States.

Chinatown

Take a walk in the area south of Broome Street and west of Broadway, and you'll feel as though you've entered a completely different continent. You won't hear much English spoken along the crowded streets of **Chinatown**, lined by fish-, fruit- and vegetable-stocked stands and home to vendors along Canal Street selling bootleg CDs and DVDs, as well as counterfeit Louis Vuitton and Kate Spade handbags. This is a bargain-hunter's paradise, but many of the goods are being sold illegally – so consider yourself warned. Manhattan's Chinatown is among the largest Chinese communities outside Asia. Some residents eventually decamp to one of the four other Chinatowns in the city (two each in Queens and Brooklyn), but a steady flow of new arrivals keeps this hub full to bursting, with thousands of both legal and illegal residents packed into the area surrounding East Canal Street. Chinatown's busy streets get even wilder during the **Chinese New Year** festivities, in February (*see p266*).

Food is everywhere. The markets on Canal Street sell some of the best and most affordable seafood and fresh produce in the city – you'll see buckets of live eels and crabs, stacks of greens and piles of hairy rambutans (cousins of the lychee). Street vendors sell satisfying snacks such as pork buns and sweet egg pancakes by the bagful. Mott Street, between Kenmare and Worth Streets, is lined with restaurants representing the cuisine of virtually every province of mainland China and Hong Kong; the Bowery, East Broadway and Division Street are just as diverse. Adding to the mix are myriad Indonesian, Malaysian, Thai and Vietnamese eateries and stores.

One site of historical interest is **Wing Fat Shopping**, a strange little subterranean mall with its entrance at Chatham Square (No.8, to the right of the OTB parlour), rumoured to have been a stop on the Underground Railroad 25 years before the Chinese began populating this area in the 1880s.

A statue of the Chinese philosopher of the same name marks **Confucius Plaza**, at the corner of the Bowery and Division Street. In Columbus Park, at Bayard and Mulberry Streets, elderly men and women gather around card tables to play mah-jong and dominoes (you can hear the clacking tiles from across the street), while more agile youngsters practise martial arts. The **Museum of Chinese in the Americas** (*see p107*) hosts exhibitions and events that explore the Chinese immigrant experience in the western hemisphere. Over in the **Eastern States Buddhist Temple of America** (64 Mott Street, between Bayard & Canal Streets, 1-212 966 6229), you'll be dazzled by the glitter of hundreds of Buddhas and the aroma of wafting incense. Donate $1 and you'll receive a fortune slip.

For a different perspective on the area's culture, visit the noisy, dingy **Chinatown Fair** (at the southern end of Mott Street), an amusement arcade where some of the East Coast's best Street Fighter players congregate. Older kids hit Chinatown to eat and drink at Joe's Shanghai (9 Pell Street, between Bowery & Mott Street, 1-212 233 8888), known for its soup dumplings, boiled pillows of dough filled with pork and broth; Jing Fong (20 Elizabeth Street, between Bowery & Canal Streets, 1-212 964

5256), a classic destination for dim sum; and Happy Ending (302 Broome Street, between Eldridge & Forsyth Streets, 1-212 334 9676), a hip nightspot for denizens of every ethnicity, occupying a former massage parlour (the bar's seemingly innocuous name is actually a rather unabashed nod to its sexually charged roots).

For more on everything that Chinatown has to offer, *see p108* **Chinatown's Secret City**.

Museum of Chinese in the Americas

2nd Floor, 70 Mulberry Street, at Bayard Street (1-212 619 4785/www.moca-nyc.org). Subway J, M, N, Q, R, W, Z, 6 to Canal Street. **Open** noon-6pm Tue-Sun. **Admission** suggested donation $2; $1 seniors, students; free under-12s. Free Fri. **No credit cards**. **Map** p402 F31.

In the heart of downtown Manhattan's Chinatown, a century-old former schoolhouse holds a two-room museum focused on Chinese-American history and the Chinese immigrant experience. The huge archive holds thousands of rare and important papers and artefacts. Call for details about walking tours of the neighbourhood.

Lower East Side

The **Lower East Side** was shaped by New York's immigrants, as millions upon millions poured into the city from the late 19th century onwards. The resulting patchwork of dense communities is great for dining and expoloring – though today you'll that find the Lower East Side is less dominated by Asian, Jewish and Latino families, and increasingly ruled by chic boutiques, restaurants and the stylish types who frequent them. Early inhabitants of this area were mostly Eastern European Jews, and mass tenement housing was built to accommodate the 19th-century influx of immigrants, which included many German, Hungarian, Irish and Polish families. The unsanitary, airless and overcrowded living conditions suffered by these people were documented near the end of that century by photographer and writer Jacob A Riis in *How the Other Half Lives*; the book's publication fuelled reformers, who then prompted the introduction of building codes. To better understand how these immigrants lived, tour the fascinating **Lower East Side Tenement Museum** (*see p109*).

Between 1870 and 1920, literally hundreds of synagogues and religious schools were established. Various Yiddish newspapers and associations for social reform and cultural studies flourished, as did vaudeville and classic Yiddish theatre. (The Marx Brothers, Jimmy Durante, Eddie Cantor, and George and Ira Gershwin were just a few of the entertainers who once lived in the district.) Currently, only about ten per cent of the LES population is Jewish. The **Eldridge Street Synagogue** (12 Eldridge Street, between Canal & Division Streets, 1-212 219 0888, www.eldridgestreet.org, admission $5) often has a hard time rounding up the ten adult men required to conduct a service. Still, the synagogue has not missed a Sabbath or holiday service in more than 115 years. **First Shearith Israel Graveyard** (55-57 St James Place, between James & Oliver Streets), on the southern edge of Chinatown, is the burial ground of the country's first Jewish community. It has gravestones that date from 1683, including those of Spanish and Portuguese Jews who fled the Inquisition. Puerto Ricans and Dominicans began to move to the Lower East Side after World War II. Colourful awnings still mark the area's various bodegas, and many restaurants serve a range of hearty Caribbean standards.

In the 1980s a new breed of immigrant began moving in: young artists and musicians attracted by the low rents. Bars, boutiques and music venues sprang up on and around Ludlow Street, creating an annex to the East Village. This scene is still thriving, though rents have risen like mercury in August. The area is now rife with luxury condos and boutique hotels. One casualty was the Luna Lounge, a Ludlow Street stalwart that offered free concerts and cheap comedy shows, both of which were breeding grounds for big names. It was torn down in 2005 to make way for, you guessed it, a luxury apartment building. Another recent victim was Tonic, which shut its doors in the spring of 2007. After serving as a thriving experimental music venue for nearly a decade, it could no longer afford the increasingly exorbitant rent. For live music, you can still check who's playing at **Arlene's Grocery** (95 Stanton Street, between Ludlow & Orchard Streets, 1-212 995 1652) or at the **Bowery Ballroom** (*see p314*). The sign at **Pianos** (*see p319*), a bi-level music bar, is itself a remnant from the piano store it once was.

These days, the biggest draw to the **Bowery**, at least for culture lovers, is not so much music but art: in December 2007, New York's only museum devoted entirely to contemporary art, the **New Museum of Contemporary Art** (*see p110*) opened its $50 million, 60,000-square-foot home. No doubt this institution will lift the local art scene that has recently taken root here. **Rivington Arms** (First Floor, 4 East 2nd Street, at Bowery, 1-646 654 3213) and **Participant Inc** (95 Rivington Street, between Orchard & Ludlow Streets, 1-212 254 4334) are storefront galleries in the neighbourhood showcasing young artists.

Chinatown's secret city

New York's Chinatown – one of the largest Chinese communities outside Asia – conjures up images of exotic-looking restaurants and crowds scurrying through streets packed with fish shops, fruit vendors and dumpling mongers. Chinatown has all these things, but look beyond the fish stalls and dim sum and you'll discover plenty of lesser-known diversions in this thriving, dynamic district.

First timers should head straight for **Mott Street** (between Worth & Grand Streets) to experience classic Chinatown. At No.64, slip into the **Eastern States Buddhist Temple of America** (*see p106*). Founded in 1962, this is the oldest Buddhist temple on the East Coast. Contemplate the meaning of your fortune for a $1 donation. Or if you'd rather put that dollar bill to another use, head over to the games arcade **Chinatown Fair** at No.8.

Chinatown is packed with no-frills joints that offer manipulative therapy (*tui na*), breathing work (*qi gong*) and traditional massage (*shiatsu*) – last-minute appointments are usually no problem and the prices are always reasonable. At **Fishion Herb Center** (107 Mott Street, at Hester Street, 1-212 966 8771), ten bucks gets you 15 minutes of acupressure bliss, albeit in less-than-luxe surroundings. Over at **Back and Foot Rub** (185 Mulberry Street, between Kenmare & Broome Streets), steel-fingered women go at your back (or feet) in a darkened communal room. It sure ain't glamorous, but it's cheap ($7/10mins) and it hurts so good.

The Lower East Side's reputation as a haven for political radicals lives on at the prolific and hugely popular arts centre ABC No Rio (156 Rivington Street, between Clinton & Suffolk Streets) with its **SOS: Sunday Open Series** (*see p278*), which was first established in 1980 after a group of squatters first took over an abandoned ground-floor space; it now houses a gallery and performance space. Meanwhile, luxe apartment complexes have also moved in. The flashy **Hotel on Rivington** (*see p60*), a 21-storey glass tower, is one of the new crop of high-rise buildings in this low-rise 'hood, and therefore difficult to miss.

Despite the trendy shops that have cropped up along the block, Orchard Street below Stanton Street remains the very heart of the **Orchard Street Bargain District**, a row of stores selling utilitarian goods. This is the place for cheap hats, luggage, sportswear and T-shirts. In the 1930s Mayor Fiorello La Guardia forced pushcart vendors off the streets and into large indoor marketplaces. Although many of these bazaars are a thing of the past, **Essex Street Markets** (120 Essex Street, between Delancey & Rivington Streets) is still going strong and is packed with purveyors of all sorts of things Latino, Jewish and Chinese.

Many New Yorkers have yet to learn that sometimes working out one's kinks can be as easy as grabbing a paddle and a small plastic ball. Nothing seedy, mind – we're talking about ping pong. Today, fans of the sport pack the **New York Table Tennis Foundation** (384 Broadway, Lower Level, between Walker & White Streets, 1-212 966 2922) for fast-paced (and cheap) paddle action all hours of the day. The NYTTF offers lessons by appointment, and hosts a tournament every Friday night.

Naturally, Chinatown is also about great food. One of our budget favourites is **New Bo Ky Restaurant** (80 Bayard Street, between Mott & Mulberry Streets, 1-212 406 2292), a noodle joint where broths zing with flavour, and the dozens of toppings will have your taste buds humming; we love the teochew chilli paste (just say 'number 47'), served on flat noodles with a slice of lemon. Don't be intimidated by the lack of English spoken here; you can always point to what you want on the picture menu. The peach-tiled interior isn't especially pretty, but the prices and flavours more than make up for it. **Vegetarian Dim Sum House** (24 Pell Street, between Bowery & Mott Streets, 1-212 577 7176) makes a perfect pit stop for vegetarians – and anyone else worn down by the sight of all the local shop displays of dead birds and fish. The menu at this meat-free haven offers excellent mock dishes including 'shrimp' dumplings (made with rice flour, yams and tofu), sesame 'chicken' (deep-fried bean curd skin) and Peking 'spare-ribs' (make that 'spare-yams'), plus great fresh fruit shakes.

Another vestige of the neighbourhood's Jewish roots remains: Katz's Delicatessen (205 E Houston Street, at Ludlow Street, 1-212 254 2246) sells some of the best pastrami in New York (and Meg Ryan's famous 'orgasm' scene in *When Harry Met Sally…* was filmed here). Lox lovers are devoted to Russ & Daughters (179 East Houston Street, at Orchard Street, 1-212 475 4880), serving its famous herring, caviar and smoked salmon since 1914.

The Lower East Side is truly a carb-craver's paradise. Pay tribute to the area's Eastern European origins with a freshly baked bialy from Kossar's Bialystoker Kuchen Bakery (367 Grand Street, between Essex & Norfolk Streets, 1-212 473 4810). For something sweet, head a few doors over to the Doughnut Plant (379 Grand Street, between Essex & Norfolk Streets, 1-212 505 3700), for high-quality organic doughnuts.

Lower East Side Tenement Museum

108 Orchard Street, at Broome Street (1-212 431 0233/www.tenement.org). Subway F to Delancey Street; J, M, Z to Delancey-Essex Streets. **Open** *Visitors' centre* 11am-5.30pm Mon; 11am-6pm Tue-Fri; 10.45am-6pm Sat, Sun. **Admission** $15; $11 seniors, students. **Credit** AmEx, MC, V. **Map** p403 G30.

Housed in an 1863 tenement building (along with a gallery, a shop and a video room), this fascinating museum is accessible only by guided tour. The tours, which regularly sell out (book ahead), explain the daily life of typical tenement-dwelling immigrant families. From April to December, the museum also leads walking tours of the Lower East Side.

New Museum of Contemporary Art

353 Bowery, between Prince & Stanton Streets (1-212 219 1222/www.newmuseum.org). Subway F, V Second Avenue-Lower East Side. **Open** noon-6pm Wed, Sat, Sun; noon-10pm Thur, Fri. **Admission** $12; $8 seniors; $6 students; free under-18s. **Credit** MC, V. **Map** p403 F29.

As we went to press, this bold seven-storey building (*see p42*), designed by the cutting-edge Tokyo architectural firm Sejima + Nishizawa/SANAA, was poised to open in December 2007 with galleries, a theatre, a café and roof terraces. It's the first new art museum ever constructed from the ground up below 14th Street – and marks a major contribution to the continuing revitalisation of downtown Manhattan. The focus here is on emerging media and surveys of important but under-recognised artists, which is further evidence of its pioneering spirit. The inaugural exhibition, entitled 'Unmonumental: The Object in the 21st Century', running until 6 April 2008, features works by 30 international artists, including Isa Genzken and Nobuko Tsuchiya.

East Village

Scruffier than its genteel western counterpart, the **East Village** has a long history as a countercultural hotbed. Originally considered part of the Lower East Side, the neighbourhood boomed in the 1960s, when writers, artists and musicians moved in, transforming it into the hub for the period's social revolution.

Clubs and coffeehouses thrived, including the **Fillmore East**, on Second Avenue, between 6th and 7th Streets (the theatre has since been demolished), and the **Dom** (23 St Marks Place, between Second & Third Avenues), where the Velvet Underground often headlined (the building is now a condo). In the '70s, the neighbourhood took a dive as drugs and crime prevailed – but that didn't stop the influx of artists and punk rockers. In the early '80s, East Village galleries were among the first to display the work of groundbreaking artists Jean-Michel Basquiat and Keith Haring. The nabe's past as an alt-scene nexus of arts and politics gets a nod with **Howl!** (*see p264*), a late-summer festival organised by the Federation of East Village Artists. Poetry, music and film events celebrate the community's vibrant heritage.

The area east of Broadway between Houston and 14th Streets is less edgy today (the arrival of faux-hippie supermarkets Whole Foods and Trader Joe's signal the creeping influx of suburban perks), but remnants of its spirited past endure. A generally amiable population of ravers, punks, yuppies, hippies, homeboys, vagrants and trustafarians (those wannabe bohos funded by family money) has crowded into the neighbourhood's tenements, alongside a few elderly holdouts from previous waves of immigration. Check out the indie record shops, bargain restaurants, grungy bars, punky clubs and funky, cheap clothing stores.

Looking for a portal into the 19th century? Make a social call at the **Merchant's House Museum** (*see p113*), at No.29 E 4th Street. Built in 1832, the home is the best example of domestic life of the period.

For a historical and cultural tour of the neighbourhood, start on the corner of 10th Street and Second Avenue. Here, on the eastern end of historic Stuyvesant Street (one of only a few streets in this area that break the grid), sits the East Village's unofficial cultural centre: **St Mark's Church in-the-Bowery**. St Mark's was built in 1799 on the site of Peter Stuyvesant's farm, and the old guy himself, one of New York's first governors, is buried in the adjacent cemetery. The Episcopal church holds regular services, and also hosts arts groups, such as the experimental theatre troupe Ontological at St Mark's (1-212 533 4650).

St Marks Place (8th Street, between Lafayette Street & Avenue A) is the East Village's main drag. In 1917, the Bolshevik Leon Trotsky ran a printing press at No.77 (between First & Second Avenues), and poet WH Auden lived at the address from 1953 to 1972. Lined with stores, bars and street vendors, St Marks stays packed until the wee hours with crowds browsing for bargain T-shirts, records and books. Since tattooing became legal again in New York City in 1997 (it had been banned in 1961), a number of parlours have opened up, including the famous Fun City (94 St Marks Place, between First Avenue & Avenue A, 1-212 353 8282), whose awning advertises cappuccino and tattoos.

Astor Place, with its 1970s balanced-cube sculpture – which made news in 2005, when it disappeared overnight (turns out the Parks Department took it away for cleaning) – is always swarming with young skateboarders and other modern-day street urchins. It is also the site of Peter Cooper's **Cooper Union**; home to schools of art, architecture and engineering, it bears the distinction of being the only full-scholarship (as in free) private college in the United States. During the 19th century, Astor Place marked the boundary between the slums to the east and some of the city's most fashionable homes. **Colonnade Row** (428-434

Lafayette Street, between Astor Place & E 4th Street) faces the distinguished Astor Public Library building, which theatre legend Joseph Papp rescued from demolition in the 1960s. Today, the old library is the **Public Theater** (*see p349*), a haven for first-run American plays, the headquarters of the **Shakespeare in the Park** festival (*see p262*), held in Central Park, and the trendy **Joe's Pub** (*see p315*).

Below Astor Place, Third Avenue (one block east of Lafayette Street) becomes the **Bowery**. For decades, the street languished as a seedy flophouse strip and the home of missionary organisations catering to the down and out. In recent years, however, it's become increasingly sanitised, and has been invaded by swanky restaurants and clubs. It is also home to fancy new hotel the **Bowery** (*see p59*).

Even the hallowed CBGB, the birthplace of American punk, got the boot. The club's devotees, both young and old, considered it both outrageous and tragic that its phenomenal pedigree couldn't protect it from rising rents. The seminal club – once host to legends such as the Ramones, Talking Heads and Patti Smith – had been embroiled in a legal battle with its landlord for several months, and was finally evicted in October 2006. Owner Hilly Kristal has said that he will search for another location for the venue, but no firm plans have been made.

Regardless, other bars and clubs in the East Village still successfully apply the cheap-beer-and-loud-music formula, including favourites like **Cake Shop** (*see p314*) and the **Mercury Lounge** (*see p317*). And the **Bowery Poetry Club** (*see p278*) – at 308 Bowery, at Bleecker Street – is a colourful joint that shows its roots in the poetry-slam scene, but also regularly offers jazz, folk, hip hop and improv theatre.

Elsewhere in the neighbourhood, **East 7th Street** is a Ukrainian stronghold, of which the focal point is the Byzantine St George's Ukrainian Catholic Church at No.30. Across the street, there's often a long line of beefy fraternity types waiting to enter McSorley's Old Ale House (15 E 7th Street, between Second & Third Avenues, 1-212 473 9148), which touts itself as the city's oldest pub in a single location (1854); it still serves just one kind of beer – its own brew, available in light and dark formulas. For those who would rather shop than sip, the boutiques of young designers and vintage-clothing dealers dot 7th, 8th and 9th Streets.

Curry Row, on E 6th Street, between First & Second Avenues, is one of several Little Indias in New York. Roughly two dozen Indian restaurants sit side by side (contrary to an oft-told joke, they do not share a single kitchen), and they remain popular with diners on an extremely tight budget. The line of shiny Harleys on 3rd Street, between First & Second Avenues, tells you that the New York chapter of the Hell's Angels is based here.

Alphabet City, so-called because of the way it occupies Avenues A, B, C and D, stretches towards the East River. The once largely working-class Latino (and in particular, Puerto Rican) population has been overtaken by those young professionals able to pay higher rents. Avenue C is also known as Loisaida Avenue, a rough approximation of 'Lower East Side' when pronounced with a Spanish accent. An important cultural melting pot in the 1970s and '80s, the area has lost some of its unprocessed energy in recent years with the change in demographics, but gentrification has brought cleaner streets and lower crime rates, and the neighbourhood's link with the drug trade is now mostly a thing of the past. Two churches on 4th Street are built in the Spanish colonial style: **San Isidro y San Leandro** (345 E 4th Street, between Avenues C & D) and **Iglesia Pentecostal Camino Damasco** (289 E 4th Street, between Avenues B & C). The noted **Nuyorican Poets Café** (*see p278*), a more than 30-year-old clubhouse for espresso-drinking beatniks, is famous for its poetry slams, in which performers do lyric battle before a score-keeping audience.

Dating from 1837, **Tompkins Square Park** (from 7th to 10th Streets, between Avenues A & B; *photos p112*), honours Daniel D Tompkins, governor of New York from 1807 to 1817, and vice-president during the tenure of the Monroe administration. Over the years, this 10.5-acre park has been a site for demonstrations and rioting. The last major uprising was about 16 years ago, when the city evicted squatters from the park and renovated it to suit the area's increasingly affluent residents. It now boasts lovely landscaping and dozens of 150-year-old elm trees (some of the oldest in the city), along with basketball courts, three playgrounds and two dog runs. Despite the drastic changes in and around the park over the past two decades – including plummeting crime and rising housing prices – this is a place where bongo beaters, acoustic guitarists, punky squatters, khaki-wearing yuppies and the homeless all mingle. The square also plays host to the city's on-again, off-again drag celebration Wigstock.

North of Tompkins Square, around First Avenue and 11th Street, are remnants of earlier communities: discount fabric dealers, Italian cheese shops, Polish butchers and two great Italian coffee-and-cannoli houses: De Robertis (176 First Avenue, between 10th & 11th Streets, 1-212 674 7137) and Veniero's Pasticceria and Caffè (342 E 11th Street, at First Avenue, 1-212 674 7264).

Tompkins Square Park. *See p111.*

Merchant's House Museum

29 E 4th Street, between Lafayette Street & Bowery (1-212 777 1089/www.merchantshouse.org). Subway B, D, F, V to Broadway-Lafayette Street; 6 to Bleecker Street. **Open** noon-5pm Thur-Mon. **Admission** $8; $5 seniors, students. **Credit** AmEx, MC, V. **Map** p403 F29.

New York City's only preserved 19th-century family home is an elegant, late Federal-Greek Revival house stocked with the same furnishings and decorations that filled its rooms when it was inhabited from 1835 to 1933 by the noted hardware tycoon Seabury Treadwell and his descendants.

Greenwich Village

Stretching from Houston Street to 14th Street, between Broadway and Sixth Avenue, **Greenwich Village**'s leafy streets have inspired bohemians for almost a century. Now, having become one of the most expensive (and exclusive) neighbourhoods in the city, it also attracts plenty of wealthy types and Hollywood celebrities. Yet, it's still a fine place for idle wandering, candlelit dining in out-of-the-way restaurants, and for hopping between bars and cabaret venues. Sip a fresh roast in honour of the Beats – Jack Kerouac, Allen Ginsberg and their buddies – as you sit in one of their former haunts. Kerouac's favourite was Le Figaro Café (184 Bleecker Street, at MacDougal Street, 1-212 677 1100), a popular hangout for NYU students. The Cedar Tavern (82 University Place, between 11th & 12th Streets, 1-212 929 9089), which was originally at the corner of 8th Street, is where leading figures of abstract expressionism and the so-called New York School poets discussed how best to apply paint; Jackson Pollock, Larry Rivers, Willem de Kooning, Frank O'Hara and Kenneth Koch drank under this banner in the 1950s.

The hippies who tuned out in **Washington Square Park** (*photos p115*) are still there in spirit, and often in person as well. The park hums with musicians and street artists, though the once-ubiquitous pot dealers have largely disappeared, largely thanks to the NYC Police Department's hidden surveillance cameras. In warmer months, this 9.75-acre Village landmark is one of the best people-watching spots in the city; many locals consider this spot the heart and soul of Greenwich Village. The dog run is a very popular hangout – crowds stand around the fenced-in perimeter, taking in the free show as dogs of all shapes and sizes frolic and chase each other. Chess hustlers and students from New York University are a ubiquitous presence in the park, along with hip hop kids, who drive down to West 4th Street in their booming Jeeps, and Generation-Y skateboarders, who clatter around the fountain and near the base of the Washington Arch, a modestly sized replica of Paris's Arc de Triomphe, built in 1895 to honour George Washington.

The NYC Parks Department has proposed a $16 million redesign of the park, which is causing uproar among community activists. At least five lawsuits have been filed against the city thus far. Locals fear that some aspects of the plan, such as altering the central plaza, will ruin the park's bohemian vibe. One of the more controversial parts of the proposal is the transformation of the iconic fountain from a theatre-in-the-round to ornamental showpiece – one with a spray so strong that no one could sit in or around it. Historically, the fountain has served as a prized spot for spontaneous public gatherings and dance performers. The plan also calls for a fence around the park, and a reduction in the size of the central plaza so significant that an estimated 5,000 fewer people will be able to gather in it. For now, the Parks Department's intentions are tied up in court and in numerous ongoing public hearings, and as went to press Washington Square's final fate had yet to be determined.

In the 1830s, the wealthy began building handsome townhouses around the Square. A few of those properties are still privately owned and occupied; many others have become part of the ever-expanding **New York University** campus. NYU also owns the Washington Mews, a row of charming 19th-century buildings that were once stables; they line a tiny cobblestoned alley just to the north of the park between Fifth Avenue and University Place. Several famed literary figures, including Henry James, Herman Melville and Mark Twain, lived on or near the square. In 1871, the local creative community founded the **Salmagundi Club** (*see p114*), America's oldest artists' club, now situated north of Washington Square on Fifth Avenue.

Greenwich Village continues to change with the times, for better and for worse. Eighth Street is currently a long procession of piercing parlours, punky boutiques and shoe stores; in the 1960s, it was the closest New York got to San Francisco's Haight Street. Jimi Hendrix's Electric Lady Studios is still at 52 W 8th Street, between Fifth & Sixth Avenues.

Once the more dingy but colourful stomping ground of Beat poets as well as folk and jazz musicians, the very well-trafficked strip of **Bleecker Street**, between La Guardia Place and Sixth Avenue, is now an overcrowded stretch of poster shops, cheap restaurants and music venues for the college crowd. Bob Dylan lived at and owned 94 MacDougal Street (on a row of historic brownstones near Bleecker Street) through much of the 1960s, performing in Washington Square Park and at clubs such as Cafe Wha? on MacDougal Street, between Bleecker and West 3rd Streets. The famed Village Gate jazz club once stood at the corner of Bleecker and Thompson Streets; it's been carved up into a CVS pharmacy and a small theatre, though the Gate's sign is still in evidence. The **AIA Center for Architecture** (*see below*), a comprehensive resource for building and planning in New York, is just up the street, on La Guardia Place.

In the triangle formed by Sixth Avenue, Greenwich Avenue and 10th Street, you'll see the Gothic-style **Jefferson Market Library** (a branch of the New York Public Library); the lovely flower-filled garden facing Greenwich Avenue once held the art deco Women's House of Detention (Mae West did a little time there in 1926, on obscenity charges stemming from her Broadway show *Sex*), which was torn down in 1974. On Sixth Avenue at West 4th Street, join the crowd of spectators standing in front of 'the Cage' – outdoor basketball courts where outstanding schoolyard players showcase their fast, high-flying moves. Across the street (at 323 Sixth Avenue) lies the state-of-the-art **IFC Center** (*see p298*), an indie cinema. In 2005, after four years of renovation, the IFC took the place of the grungy and subsequently long-abandoned Waverly Cinema.

AIA Center for Architecture

536 La Guardia Place, between Bleecker & W 3rd Streets (1-212 683 0023/www.aiany.org). Subway A, B, C, D, E, F, V to W 4th Street. **Open** 9am-8pm Mon-Fri; 11am-5pm Sat. **Admission** free. **Map** p403 E29.

After five years of planning, the Center for Architecture opened to acclaim in autumn 2003. Founded in 1867, the organisation languished for years on the sixth floor of a Lexington Avenue edifice, far out of sight (and mind) of all but the most devoted architecture aficionados. In 1997, recognising its isolation and perceived insularity, the American Institute of Architects (AIA) began searching Soho and the Village for new digs, finally opting for a vacant storefront in an early-20th-century industrial building. After a major design competition, Andrew Berman Architect was chosen to transform the space into a fitting home for architectural debate. The sweeping, light-filled design is a physical manifestation of AIA's goal of promoting transparency in both its access and programming. Berman cut away large slabs of flooring at the street and basement levels, converting underground spaces into bright, museum-quality galleries. He also installed a glass-enclosed library and conference room – open to the public – on the first floor, and a children's gallery and workshop on the mezzanine level. The building is New York's first public space to use an energy-efficient geothermal system. Water from two 1,260ft wells is piped through the building to help heat and cool it.

Salmagundi Club

47 Fifth Avenue, at 12th Street (1-212 255 7740/www.salmagundi.org). Subway L, N, Q, R, W, 4, 5, 6 to 14th Street-Union Square. **Open** *Exhibitions* 1-5pm daily; phone for details. **Admission** free. **Map** p402 E28.

America's oldest artists' club, founded as the New York Sketch Club in 1871, is set in a landmark building and hosts exhibitions, lectures and art auctions.

West Village & Meatpacking District

In the early 20th century, the West Village was largely a working-class Italian haven. These days, it is home to a wide range of celebrities (Sarah Jessica Parker and hubby Matthew Broderick live here, as does former NYC mayor Ed Koch, and the trio of Richard Meier towers at the end of Perry and Charles Streets houses A-listers galore), but a low-key, everyone-knows-one-another feel remains.

The area west of Sixth Avenue to the Hudson River, from 14th Street to Houston Street, possesses the quirky geographical features that moulded the Village's character. Only in this neighbourhood could West 10th Street cross West 4th Street, and Waverly Place cross… Waverly Place. The West Village's layout doesn't follow the regular grid pattern but rather the original horse paths that settlers used to navigate it. Locals and tourists fill bistros along Seventh Avenue and Hudson Street (aka Eighth Avenue) and the neighbourhood's main drags, and patronise the increasingly high-rent shops, including three Marc Jacobs boutiques, three Ralph Lauren outposts and so-trendy-it-hurts boutique Intermix (365 Bleecker Street, 1-212 929-7180, www.intermixonline.com), at the newly hot end of Bleecker Street.

The north-west corner of this area is known as the **Meatpacking District**. In the 1930s, it was primarily a wholesale meat market; until the 1990s, it was also a choice haunt for prostitutes, many of them transsexual. In recent years, however, the atmospheric cobbled streets of this landmark district have seen the arrival of a new type of tenant. The once-lonely Florent (69 Gansevoort Street, between Greenwich & Washington Streets, 1-212 989 5779), a 24-hour French diner that opened in 1985, is now part of a chic scene that includes some swinging watering holes and restaurants such as Pastis (9 Ninth Avenue, at Little W 12th Street, 1-212 929 4844), 5 Ninth (5 Ninth Avenue; *see p221*) and Spice Market (403 W 13th, at Ninth Avenue, 1-212 675 2322). When the swanky boutique Hotel Gansevoort (*see p57*) opened in 2004, it cemented the area's hotspot reputation. The hotel's G Spa & Lounge is a kooky blend of bar

Washington Square Park. *See p113.*

and spa, in which the treatment rooms become VIP coves at night. The district also lures the fashion faithful with hot spots such as Jeffrey New York, Diane Von Furstenberg, Alexander McQueen and Stella McCartney. As local rents skyrocketed in recent years, many of the meatpacking plants were forced out to make space for trendy shops, but on sweltering summer days, you can still get a whiff of the meat dealers that remain.

The neighbourhood's bohemian population may have dwindled years ago but several historic nightlife spots soldier on (at least for the time being) to the south in the West Village. The **White Horse Tavern** (567 Hudson Street, at 11th Street, 1-212 989 3956) is where poet Dylan Thomas went on his last drinking binge before his death, in 1953. Earlier in the century, John Steinbeck and John Dos Passos passed time at **Chumley's** (1-212 675 4449), a still-unmarked Prohibition-era speakeasy at 86 Bedford Street. Note that, at press time, the beloved bar was closed due to a partially collapsed chimney. It is expected to make a (fairly) complete recovery but call before heading out. Writer Edna St Vincent Millay lived at 75 1/2 Bedford Street, built in 1873, from 1923 to 1924; subsequent inhabitants were Cary Grant and John Barrymore. Only nine and a half feet wide, it's the narrowest house in the entire city. In its early years, the tiny building was a cobbler's shop and a candy-maker's home. On and just off Seventh Avenue South are jazz and cabaret clubs, including the **Village Vanguard** (*see p324*).

The West Village is internationally renowned as a major gay mecca, though the gay scene is far more happening in Chelsea these days (*see p117*). The **Stonewall Inn** (*see p308*), on Christopher Street, is next to the original, the site of the 1969 rebellion that marked the birth of the modern gay-liberation movement. Same-sex couples stroll along Christopher Street (from Sheridan Square to the Hudson River pier), and most of the area's many shops, bars and restaurants are out, loud and proud. The Hudson riverfront features grass-covered piers, food vendors, picnic tables and volleyball courts – ideal for warm-weather dawdling by folks of any sexual persuasion.

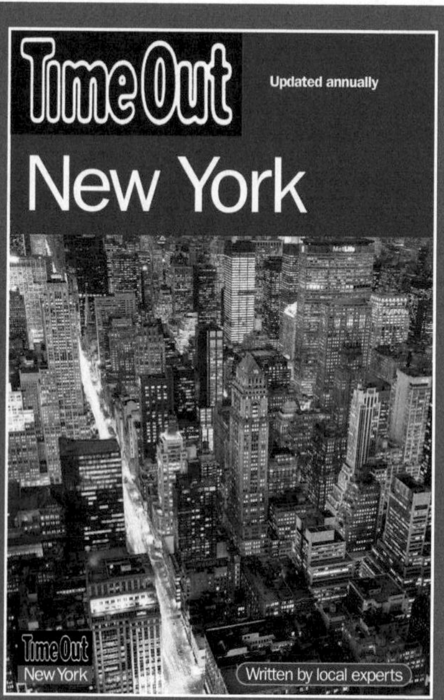
Time Out
Updated annually
New York
Time Out
New York
Written by local experts

Midtown

Mingle with the madding crowds.

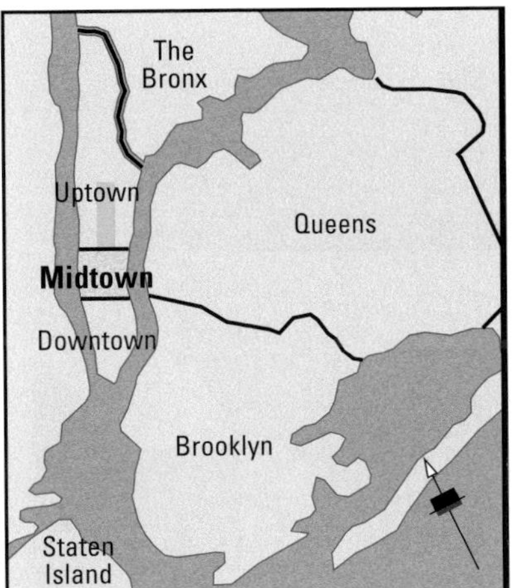

Maps pp403-405

By day, the streets of Midtown – from 14th to 59th Streets, but especially above 34th Street – are strictly business. The area is famous for its towering office buildings and the working stiffs that pack the sidewalks by the thousands between 8am and 6pm. The simple experience of walking cheek to jowl with the hordes of pedestrians brings the term 'rat race' vividly to life. You'll also find dozens of large hotels, numerous department stores and, of course, countless tourists milling about. It's the place where, in July 2007, a steam pipe dating back to the 1920s exploded, sending a geyser of steam and debris nearly four storeys high into the air – only to rain down on hundreds of bystanders who couldn't flee fast enough.

Some of the city's most prized landmarks are located in Midtown, a fact that we hope may induce the powers that be to upgrade ageing pipes sooner rather than later. You'll see such icons as **Empire State Building**, the **Chrysler Building**, **Times Square**, **Rockefeller Center** and **Grand Central Terminal**. But there's more to Midtown than glistening towers and high-octane commerce. You can take refuge from the masses in a number of cultural heavyweights such as the **Museum of Modern Art**, **Broadway**, the **Theater District**, **New York Public Library** and **Carnegie Hall**. You'll also find the **Union Square Greenmarket**, an agrarian oasis, and the quaint tree-lined streets of **Chelsea**, **Tudor City** and **Gramercy Park**.

If city life is for you, you've come to the right place. Anyone hoping to avoid the crowds are advised to cruise through the area after 10pm. Late in the evening, when the empty sidewalks are ablaze with the dozens of colourful neon signs and flashing lights, Midtown exudes a calmer urban charm.

Chelsea

Up until the 1980s, Chelsea was a mostly working-class and industrial neighbourhood. Now it's the epicentre of the city's gay life, but residents of all types inhabit the blocks between 14th and 29th Streets, west of Fifth Avenue. There's a generous assortment of bars and restaurants, most of which are clustered along Eighth Avenue, the main hub of all the activity. Various pioneers in the gallery world, such as Dia:Chelsea, led the art crowd northwards from Soho, and the whole western edge of Chelsea is now the city's hottest gallery zone. As we went to press, **Dia:Chelsea** (548 W 22nd Street, between Tenth & Eleventh Avenues, 1-212 989 5566, www.diachelsea.org) had moved its collection to Dia:Beacon (*see p357*) while it looked for a new Manhattan gallery space; the headquarters are to remain in Chelsea.

This far-west warehouse district is now a nesting ground for fashionable lounges and nightclubs, and has become much more residential in recent years. The most exciting thing to happen in Chelsea of late is a plan to turn a defunct elevated train, known as the **High Line**, into a 1.5-mile-long promenade and urban park (*see p118* **Walking the line**).

Don't miss the weekend flea markets tucked between buildings in parking lots on 25th Street, between Sixth Avenue and Broadway, or the rummage-worthy **Garage** (*see p252*). Ornate wrought-iron balconies distinguish the **Chelsea Hotel** (*see p73*), which has been a magnet for international bohemians since the 1950s. In the '60s and '70s, Andy Warhol's superstars (the Chelsea Girls) made the place infamous, and punk rock conferred its notoriety in the '80s, when Nancy Spungen was stabbed to death by boyfriend Sid Vicious in Room 100.

Walking the line

The much-anticipated High Line promenade gears up to open in 2008.

It's been more than a year since ground was broken for the inspired new public park that is taking shape along the inoperative elevated High Line freight-train tracks, built in the 1930s. Below and above it, new residential buildings and hotels are rising in a breathtaking transformation of a neighbourhood heretofore known solely for its auto body shops and art galleries. The first section of the park, which will run from Gansevoort Street to W 20th Street, is scheduled to open in summer 2008 and, in a recent development, the Whitney Museum of American Art (*see p145*) signed to build a satellite museum at the southern end of the High Line.

Time Out recently caught up with Joshua David, co-founder of Friends of the High Line, a not-for-profit group of community activists that spearheaded the campaign to turn the defunct elevated train track into a lush walkway. 'The progress we are making is just amazing,' says David. 'Having the Whitney anchor one side of the park ensures its art-oriented identity. Both artists and local gallery owners were extremely supportive of the project from the beginning. They really understood the aesthetic and creative vision, and got us off to a strong start within the local community, so we are thrilled to have such a strong cultural and artistic presence.'

The last train to use the elevated High Line was back in the early 1980s. Then, for more than two decades, this 22-block-long, three-storey-high ribbon of rail on Manhattan's far west side, between Gansevoort Street in the Meatpacking District and 34th Street in Midtown, was abandoned – an urban afterthought made lush by nature.

'What attracted us to saving the High Line was exactly that strangeness – this steel structure with wild flowers growing on top of it, in the middle of the city,' says Robert Hammond, who in 1999 founded the Friends of the High Line with David. The two Chelsea residents started pitching a simple concept to anyone who would listen: save the High Line and turn it into an elevated, urban oasis.

In May 2007, David Bowie curated the first ever **High Line Festival** (*see p261*), an art fest celebrating High Line.

Stop by for a peek at the lobby artwork and the grunge-glamorous guests, and linger over a drink in the luxe basement lounge, Serena. Occupying the long stretch of 23rd Street, between Ninth and Tenth Avenues, **London Terrace** is a distinctive 1920s Tudor-style apartment complex that's home to some rather famous names, including Debbie Harry, Chelsea Clinton and Teri Hatcher (she of *Desperate Housewives* fame).

Of Chelsea's cultural offerings, the **Joyce Theater** (*see p353*) is a brilliantly renovated art deco cinema that presents better-known contemporary dance troupes. The **Dance Theater Workshop** (*see p353*) performs at the Bessie Schönberg Theater (219 W 19th Street, between Seventh & Eighth Avenues, 1-212 691 6500), and towards the river on 19th Street is the **Kitchen** (*see p354*), a pioneering experimental arts centre. Looking to kick-start your libido? Head to Fifth Avenue and check out the **Museum of Sex** (*see below*).

One of the most talked-about additions to the neighbourhood is the beautifully billowing nine-storey glass-sheathed **InterActiveCorp** building (555 W 18th Street, at the West Side Highway), designed by Frank Gehry. The building is the East Coast headquarters for media and e-commerce mogul Barry Diller.

Cushman Row (406-418 W 20th Street, between Ninth & Tenth Avenues), in the Chelsea Historic District, is an example of how the area looked when it was developed in the mid 1800s (although its grandeur was later affected by the intrusion of noisy elevated railways). Just to the north is the block-long **General Theological Seminary of the Episcopal Church** (175 Ninth Avenue, between 20th & 21st Streets, 1-212 243 5150, www.gts.edu), whose gardens (closed Sun) offer a pleasant respite. The seminary's land was part of the estate known as Chelsea, owned by the poet Clement Clarke Moore (best known for ''Twas the night before Christmas').

The former Nabisco plant on Ninth Avenue, where the first Oreo cookie was made in 1912, has been renovated and is now home to the **Chelsea Market** (75 Ninth Avenue, between 15th & 16th Streets, www.chelseamarket.com). The former factory site is a conglomeration of 18 structures built between the 1890s and the 1930s. The ground-floor food arcade offers artisanal bread, lobster, wine, hand-decorated cookies and imported Italian foods, among other treats. The upper floors house several major media companies, including the Oxygen Network and the highly popular Food Network studios, where shows such as *Emeril Live* and *30 Minute Meals with Rachel Ray* are recorded.

Chelsea's art galleries, occupying former warehouses on streets W 20th to W 29th, west of Tenth Avenue, draw an international audience, especially at weekends. Many of the major galleries that were priced out of Soho (replaced by retail shops) found new homes here; bars and restaurants on the prowl for cheaper space followed suit. Evolving much as Soho did, the area has become similarly pricey.

On Seventh Avenue, at 27th Street, is the Fashion Institute of Technology (www.fitnyc.edu), a state college for those who aspire to vie with renowned alumni, including Calvin Klein. Fashionistas won't want to miss the school's **Museum at FIT** (*see below*), a block away, which mounts great free exhibitions.

You can watch the sunset from one of the spectacular Hudson River piers, which were once terminals for the world's grand ocean liners. Many other city piers remain in a state of ruin, but the four between 17th and 23rd Streets have been transformed into the mega sports centre and TV- and film-studio complex called **Chelsea Piers**. When you're down by the river, the **Starrett-Lehigh Building** (601 W 26th Street, at Eleventh Avenue) comes into view. The stunning 1929 structure was left in disrepair until the dot-com boom of the late '90s, when media companies, photographers and fashion designers snatched up its loft-like spaces.

Museum at FIT

Seventh Avenue, at 27th Street (1-212 217 5800/ www.fitnyc.edu/museum). Subway 1 to 28th Street. **Open** noon-8pm Tue-Fri; 10am-5pm Sat. **Admission** free. **Map** p404 D26.

The Fashion Institute of Technology houses one of the world's most important collections of clothing and textiles, curated by the influential fashion historian Valerie Steele. Incorporating everything from extravagant costumes to sturdy denim work clothes, the exhibitions explore the role fashion has played in society since the beginning of the 20th century.

Museum of Sex

233 Fifth Avenue, at 27th Street (1-212 689 6337/ www.mosex.org). Subway R, W, 6 to 28th Street. **Open** 11am-6pm Mon-Fri, Sun; 11am-8pm Sat. **Admission** $14.50; $13.50 seniors, students. Under-18s not admitted. **Credit** AmEx, MC, V. **Map** p404 E26.

Despite the subject matter, don't expect too much titillation at this museum, which opened in 2002 to mixed reviews. Instead, you'll find presentations of historical documents and items – many of which were too risqué to be made public in their own time – that explore prostitution, burlesque, birth control, obscenity and fetishism. Still, the museum boasts an extensive collection of pornography from a retired Library of Congress curator (apparently, he applied his professional knowledge to recreational pursuits as well). Thus, the Ralph Whittington Collection features thousands of items, such as 8mm films, videos, blow-up dolls and other erotic paraphernalia.

Flatiron District & Union Square

The Flatiron District, which extends from 14th to 29th Streets, between Fifth and Park Avenues, gives Downtown a run for its money in terms of cachet – and cool. This chic enclave is full of retail stores that are quite often less expensive but just as stylish as those below 14th Street. The area is compact enough that tourists can hit all the sights on foot and then relax with a cocktail at a local watering hole.

The district has two public commons: Madison and Union Squares. **Madison Square** (from 23rd to 26th Streets, between Fifth & Madison Avenues) was the site of PT Barnum's Hippodrome and the original Madison Square Garden – the scene of the scandalous murder of its architect, Stanford White (recounted in EL Doctorow's novel *Ragtime*, also adapted as a film). After years of neglect, the statue-filled **Madison Square Park** (www.madisonsquarepark.org), sheltered in the grand shadow of the landmark Flatiron Building, finally got a facelift in 2001. But it's been a relative newcomer to the scene, **MAD Sq. Art**, that's helped to transform the formerly neglected spot of parkland into a real must-see destination. MAD Sq. Art, an adjunct of the Madison Square Park Conservancy, has in the past couple of years presented outdoor video works by Tony Oursler, and work by sound artist Bill Fontana. In autumn 2007, MAD Sq. Art helped the park go to the dogs with the help of William Wegman. The artist placed a series of monitors around the park with videos of his loveable canines engaging in various park-related activities, like reading the newspaper on a park bench. During warmer months, stop by **Danny Meyer's Shake Shack** (south side of Madison Square Park, near 23rd Street, at Madison Avenue, 1-212 889 6600), a hot-dog, hamburger and ice-cream stand where you can eat alfresco, surrounded by lush foliage.

Just south of Madison Square is a famously triangular Renaissance palazzo, the **Flatiron Building** (175 Fifth Avenue, between 22nd & 23rd Streets). The 22-storey edifice is clad in white terracotta, and its light colour was revealed again by intensive cleaning and restoration in the early 1990s. The surrounding neighbourhood was christened in honour of the structure, which had the honour of being the world's first ever steel-frame skyscraper.

In the 19th century, the neighbourhood went by the moniker of Ladies' Mile, thanks to the ritzy department stores that lined Broadway and Sixth Avenue to the west. These huge retail palaces attracted the carriage trade, wealthy women who bought the latest imported fashions and household goods. By 1914, most of the department stores had moved north, leaving their proud cast-iron buildings behind. Today, the area is peppered with bookshops and photo studios and labs (it was known as New York's photo district well into the 1990s), as well as supermodels. The area has also reclaimed its fashionable history and is once again a prime shopping destination. Broadway between 14th and 23rd Streets is a tasteful home furnishings strip; be sure to take a spin through the eclectic, expensive six-storey home-design store **ABC Carpet & Home** (*see p252*). Fifth Avenue below 23rd Street is a clothing mecca; many upscale shops, including the exclusive Paul Smith outpost, showcase the latest designs. In the mid 1990s, big internet companies began colonising the lofts on Fifth Avenue and Broadway, and the district was dubbed Silicon Alley, a name that stuck even after the boom flattened out.

Union Square (from 14th to 17th Streets, between Union Square East & Union Square West) is named after neither the Union of the Civil War nor the lively labour rallies that once took place here, but simply for the union of Broadway and Bowery Lane (now Fourth Avenue). From the 1920s until the early 1960s, Union Square had a reputation as the favourite location for rabble-rousing political oratory, from AFL-CIO rallies to anti-Vietnam War protests. Following 9/11, the park became a focal point for the city's outpouring of grief. Today, it's probably best known as the home of the **Union Square Greenmarket** (*see p121*), an excellent farmers' market fast becoming a New York institution.

The buildings flanking Union Square are used for a variety of commercial purposes. They include the W New York-Union Square hotel, the giant Zeckendorf Towers residential complex (1 Irving Place, between 14th & 15th Streets), a Virgin Megastore and a Barnes & Noble bookstore. Facing south, look up (and slightly east) and marvel at what three million bucks can buy: the ugly sculpture-wall before you, called *Metronome,* was installed in 1999 and remains one of the largest private commissions of public art in the city's history. But what on earth is it? 'The entire work symbolises the intangibility of time,' according to its makers (artists Kristin Jones and Andrew

Cheap date

Strike your best John Travolta moves at groove studio **Dancesport**'s half-hour private tutorial (fourth floor, 22 W 34th Street, between Fifth & Sixth Avenues, 1-212 307 1111). An instructor will school you and your beloved on the hustle's smooth disco stylings and continuous head-spinning turns. Or, if you prefer to cop Antonio Banderas's latin rhythm, you can try tango or salsa. After all, when you're cheek to cheek in an Argentine strut, your crush won't be able to see the lack of coordination in your feet. After your lesson, skip the tourist-laden doldrums of Midtown for Koreatown's 24-hour **Han Bat** (*see p207*). Warm your bellies with *gob dol bibimbab*, veg and barbecued beef topped rice served in a stone pot – a hearty way to refuel after cutting a rug.

From political protests to old-fashioned fooling around at **Union Square**.

Ginzel). Reading from left to right, the digital read-out on the installation's main panel displays the current time. If you have time to kill, join the throngs that laze about on the steps facing 14th Street and enjoy the parade of passers-by.

Union Square Greenmarket

From 16th to 17th Streets, between Union Square East & Union Square West (1-212 788 7476/www.cenyc.org). Subway L, N, Q, R, W, 4, 5, 6 to 14th Street-Union Square. **Open** 8am-6pm Mon, Wed, Fri, Sat. **Map** p403 E27.
Shop elbow-to-elbow with top chefs for all manner of regionally grown culinary pleasures.

Gramercy Park & Murray Hill

You need a key to enter **Gramercy Park**, a tranquil, gated green square at the bottom of Lexington Avenue (between 20th & 21st Streets). Who gets a key? Only the lucky people who live in the beautiful townhouses and apartment buildings that ring the park. Anyone, however, can enjoy the charms of the surrounding district. Gramercy Park was developed in the 1830s to resemble a London square. The Players (16 Gramercy Park South, between Park Avenue South & Irving Place), a private club and residence, is housed in an 1845 brownstone formerly owned by actor Edwin Booth; the 19th-century superstar was the brother of Abraham Lincoln's assassin, John Wilkes Booth. Edwin had the interior revamped as a club for theatre professionals. Next door (No.15) is the Gothic Revival Samuel Tilden House, which now houses the **National Arts Club** (15 Gramercy Park South, between Park Avenue South & Irving Place, 1-212 475 3424, www.nationalartsclub.org), whose members often donate their work in lieu of annual dues. The busts of famous writers (Shakespeare, Dante) along the façade were chosen to reflect Tilden's library, which, along with his fortune, helped create the New York Public Library.

Irving Place, a strip leading south from the park to 14th Street, is named after author Washington Irving. Near the corner of 15th Street, **Fillmore New York at Irving Plaza** (*see p314*), a medium-sized live music venue that has been around since the early 1990s, hosts everyone from old-timers like Van Morrison to newer acts like Lily Allen. At the corner of Park Avenue South and 17th Street stands the final headquarters of the once-omnipotent Tammany Hall political machine. Built in 1929, the building now houses the New York Film Academy and a theatre.

A few blocks away, the **Theodore Roosevelt Birthplace** (*see p123*), a national historic site, holds a small museum. The low, fortress-like **69th Regiment Armory** (68 Lexington Avenue, between 25th & 26th Streets), now used by the New York National Guard, hosted the sensational 1913 Armory Show, which introduced Americans to Cubism, Fauvism and Dadaism. The tradition continues at the annual **Armory Show** (*see p260*).

The largely residential area bordered by 23rd and 30th Streets, Park Avenue and the East River is known as **Kips Bay**, named after Jacobus Henderson Kip, whose farm covered the area in the 17th century. Third Avenue is the neighbourhood's main thoroughfare, and a locus of ethnic restaurants representing a variety of eastern cuisines, including Afghan, Tibetan and Turkish, along with nightspots such as the **Rodeo Bar & Grill** (*see p326*), a Texas-style roadhouse that offers food and live roots music. Lexington Avenue, between 27th and 30th Streets, is known as Curry Hill because of its many Indian restaurants and groceries.

Murray Hill spans 30th to 40th Streets, between Third and Fifth Avenues. Townhouses of the rich and powerful were once clustered around Madison and Park Avenues. While it's still a fashionable neighbourhood, only a few streets retain the elegance that made Murray Hill so distinctive. **Sniffen Court** (150-158 E 36th Street, between Lexington & Third Avenues) is an unspoilt row of 1864 carriage houses located within earshot of the Queens Midtown Tunnel's ceaseless traffic. One of the area's most impressive attractions, the **Morgan Library & Museum** (*see below*), also located on 36th Street, reopened in 2006 after much extensive renovation. The charming exhibition space occupies two buildings (one of which was J Pierpont Morgan's personal library) and holds books, manuscripts, prints, and silver and copper collections accumulated by the famously acquisitive banker. If contemporary European culture interests you more, visit the nearby **Scandinavia House: the Nordic Center in America** (*see p123*).

Morgan Library & Museum

225 Madison Avenue, at 36th Street (1-212 685 0008/www.themorgan.org). Subway 6 to 33rd Street.
Open 10.30am-5pm Tue-Thur; 10.30am-9pm Fri; 10am-6pm Sat; 11am-6pm Sun. **Admission** $12; $8 12-16s, seniors, students; free under-12s. **Credit** AmEx, MC, V. **Map** p404 E25.

In April 2006, the expanded Morgan, designed by Pritzker Prize-winning architect Renzo Piano, reopened, doubling the amount of exhibition space and adding a number of new amenities. Thanks to the expansion, the museum is now able to display more of its 350,000 objects than ever. You'll see drawings by Michelangelo, Rembrandt and Picasso; a first edition of Malory's King Arthur tales from 1485; a copy of *Frankenstein* annotated by Mary Shelley herself; manuscripts by Dickens, Poe, Twain, Steinbeck and Wilde; and sheet music drafts by the likes of Beethoven and Mozart.

The homey atmosphere of the Morgan, with its small, digestible galleries, unusual artworks (ancient Mesopotamian seals, anyone?) and historical display of Pierpont Morgan's home library is a rare treat. The buildings are so pretty, warm and crowd-free that they feel like an oasis for those in the know.

Morgan Library & Museum.

Scandinavia House: The Nordic Center in America

58 Park Avenue, between 37th & 38th Streets (1-212 879 9779/www.scandinaviahouse.org). Subway 42nd Street 4, 5, 6, 7, S to 42nd Street-Grand Central. **Open** noon-6pm Tue-Sat. **Admission** suggested donation $3; $2 seniors, students. **Credit** AmEx, MC, V. **Map** p404 E24.

You'll find all things Nordic, from IKEA designs to the latest Finnish film, at this modern centre, the leading cultural link between the US and the five Nordic countries (Denmark, Finland, Iceland, Norway and Sweden). As well as exhibitions, it stages films, concerts, lectures, symposia and readings, plus kid-friendly programming. The in-house AQ Café is a bustling lunch spot with an innovative menu by NYC's most famous Swedish chef, Marcus Samuelsson.

Theodore Roosevelt Birthplace

28 E 20th Street, between Broadway & Park Avenue South (1-212 260 1616/www.nps.gov/thrb). Subway 6 to 23rd Street. **Open** 9am-5pm Tue-Sat. **Tours** 10am-4pm Tue-Sat; tours depart on the hr. **Admission** $3; free under-18s. **No credit cards**. **Map** p403 E27.

The 26th President of America's actual birthplace was demolished in 1916, but it has since been fully reconstructed, complete with a vast amount of authentic period furniture (some of it collected and restored from the original house) and a trophy room. Roosevelt lived here from his birth in 1858 until he was 14 years old.

Herald Square & Garment District

The heart of America's multibillion-dollar clothing industry is New York's **Garment District** (roughly from 34th to 40th Streets, between Broadway & Eighth Avenue), where platoons of designers – and thousands of workers – create the clothes we'll be wearing next season. The main drag, Seventh Avenue, has a fitting (though rarely used) moniker, Fashion Avenue. Although most garment manufacturing has left Manhattan, the area is still gridlocked by delivery trucks and workers pushing racks of clothes up and down the streets. Trimming, button and fabric shops line the sidewalks, especially on 38th and 39th Streets. At the north-east corner of 39th Street and Seventh Avenue, you'll spy a gigantic needle and button sculpture, signalling that you are in the fashion centre. The **Fashion Center Information Kiosk** alongside the sculpture provides spools of information to professional and budding fashion designers, buyers and manufacturers. A once-thriving fur market is in retreat, now occupying only 28th to 30th Streets, between Seventh and Eighth Avenues.

Beginning on 34th Street, at Broadway, and stretching all the way to Seventh Avenue, **Macy's** (*see p230*) is still the biggest – and busiest – department store in the world. Across the street, at the junction of Broadway and Sixth Avenue, is **Herald Square**, named after a long-gone newspaper, surrounded by a retail wonderland. The area's lower section is known as **Greeley Square**, after Horace Greeley, owner of the *Herald*'s rival, the *Tribune* (which famously employed Karl Marx as a columnist); the previously grungy square now offers bistro chairs and rest areas for weary pedestrians. To the east, the many restaurants and shops of **Koreatown** line 32nd Street, between Broadway and Madison Avenue.

The giant circular building on Seventh Avenue, between 31st and 33rd Streets, is the sports and entertainment arena **Madison Square Garden** (*see p333*). It occupies the site of the old Pennsylvania Station, a McKim, Mead & White architectural masterpiece that was razed in the 1960s – an act so soulless, it spurred the creation of the Landmarks Preservation Commission. The railroad terminal, now known as **Penn Station**, lies beneath the Garden and serves approximately 600,000 people daily – more than any other station in the country. Fortunately, the aesthetic tide has turned. The city has approved a $788 million restoration-and-development project to move Penn Station across the street, into

Eyes on the size

Enacting big change often takes a measured approach, especially when you're trying to reform a behemoth like Broadway. But this is exactly what Nation of Size cofounder Peter Meluso hopes to achieve, as he nudges theatre owners along the Great White Way towards expanding seating for a plus-size set.

Recently, Meluso and business partner Ed Dintrone attended 11 shows, ranging from *Hairspray* to *Tarzan*, with tape measures in hand to prove just how narrow theatre seats actually are. Titled 'Petey's Tush Tour', the survey also pulled ticket holders into the act. 'I stood outside the theatres with my tape-measuring kits and handed them out to audience members,' laughs Meluso.

He first realised there was concern after repeated pleas for more spacious seating were ignored when he bought tickets through Telecharge or Ticketmaster. 'No one was ever rude,' notes Meluso. 'But no one addressed the issue either.' And that's when Meluso decided to size up the situation himself. Based on the collected data, so far Meluso and Dintrone figure that the typical width of a Broadway seat is approximately 18.2 inches, uncomfortable for anyone whose body mass index is north of 25. But they know they need about 10 separate measurements per theatre to have any kind of worthwhile data.

In the meantime, Meluso is proposing what he calls a workable solution: converting three seats in each theatre to accommodate two theatre-goers of size. Meluso believes that even if a premium were charged, the response would be overwhelming.

the **General Post Office** (formally known as the James A Farley Post Office Building; 421 Eighth Avenue, between 31st & 33rd Streets, 1-800 275 8777), another McKim, Mead & White design. The project will connect the post office's two buildings with a soaring glass-and-nickel-trussed ticketing hall and concourse. When the new Penn Station is finally completed (no earlier than 2012), Amtrak services will roll in (along with rail links to Newark, La Guardia and JFK airports); the current Penn Station will remain a hub for New Jersey Transit and the Long Island Rail Road.

Broadway & Times Square

Around 42nd Street and Broadway, an area sometimes called 'the crossroads of the world', the night is illuminated not by the moon but by acres of glaring neon and sweeping arc lamps. Even native New Yorkers are electrified by this larger-than-life light show of corporate logos. No area better represents the city's glitter than **Times Square**, where zoning laws actually require businesses to include a certain level of illuminated signage on their façades. For information, stop in at the **Times Square Information Cente**r (*see p127*).

Originally called Longacre Square, Times Square was renamed after the *New York Times* moved to the site in the early 1900s; it announced its arrival with a spectacular New Year's Eve fireworks display. At the 1 Times Square building (formerly the Times Tower), the *Times* erected the world's first ticker sign, and the circling messages – the stockmarket crash of 1929, JFK's assassination, the 2001 World Trade Center attack – have been known to stop the midtown masses in their tracks. The Gray Lady, as *The New York Times* is nicknamed, is now living in a new $84 million tower on Eighth Avenue, between 40th and 41st Streets. However, the sign remains at the original locale, on 43rd Street, between Seventh and Eighth Avenues, and marks the spot where New Year's Eve is traditionally celebrated.

Times Square is really just the elongated intersection of Broadway and Seventh Avenue, but it's also the heart of the **Theater District**. More than 40 stages showcasing extravagant dramatic productions are situated on the streets that cross Broadway. Times Square's once-famous sex trade is now relegated to short stretches of Seventh and Eighth Avenues (just north and south of 42nd Street).

The Theater District's transformation first began in 1984, when the city condemned many properties along 42nd Street ('the Deuce'), between Seventh and Eighth Avenues. A few years later, the city changed its zoning laws, making it harder for adult entertainment establishments to operate. The results include places like **Show World** (669 Eighth Avenue, between 42nd & 43rd Streets), formerly a noted sleaze palace that now gets by with X-rated video sessions instead of live 'dance' shows.

The streets to the west of Eighth Avenue are filled with eateries catering to theatre-goers, especially along **Restaurant Row** (46th Street, between Eighth & Ninth Avenues). This stretch

Times Square.

Turning grey cells green at glorious **Bryant Park**. *See p129.*

is also popular after the theatres let out, when the street's bars host stand-up comedy and gleefully campy drag cabaret.

The area's office buildings are filled with entertainment companies: recording studios, record labels, theatrical agencies and screening rooms. The **Brill Building** (1619 Broadway, at 49th Street) has long been the headquarters of music publishers and producers, and such luminaries as Jerry Lieber, Mike Stoller, Phil Spector and Carole King wrote and auditioned their hits here. Both visiting rock royalty and aspiring musicians drool over the selection of new and vintage guitars (as well as other instruments) for sale along **Music Row** (48th Street, between Sixth & Seventh Avenues). Eager teenagers congregate under the windows at MTV's home base (1515 Broadway, at 45th Street), hoping for a wave from a guest celebrity like Beyoncé from the second-floor studio above. The glittering glass case that serves as headquarters to the magazine-publishing giant Condé Nast (Broadway, at 43rd Street) gleams at 4 Times Square – which is home to *Vogue*, *GQ* and *The New Yorker*, among other titles. The notorious NASDAQ electronic stock market is housed in the very same building, and its **MarketSite Tower**, a cylindrical eight-storey video screen, dominates Times Square.

Glitzy attractions strive to outdo one another in ensnaring the endless throngs of tourists. **Madame Tussaud's New York** (*see p127*), a Gothamised version of the London-based wax-museum chain, showcases local legends such as Woody Allen and Jennifer Lopez. On Broadway, the noisy **ESPN Zone** (1472 Broadway, at 42nd Street, 1-212 921 3776) offers hundreds of video games and enormous TVs showing all manner of sporting events, and the 110,000-square-foot **Toys 'R' Us** flagship boasts a 60-foot-tall indoor Ferris wheel.

Make a brief detour uptown on Seventh Avenue for a glimpse of the great classical music landmark **Carnegie Hall** (*see p321*), on 57th Street, two blocks south of Central Park. Nearby is the famous Carnegie Deli (854 Seventh Avenue, at 55th Street, 1-212 757 2245), master of the Reuben sandwich. **ABC Television Studios**, at 7 Times Square, draw dozens of early-morning risers hoping to catch a glimpse of the *Good Morning America* crew.

West of Times Square, in the vicinity of the Port Authority Bus Terminal (on Eighth Avenue) and the Lincoln Tunnel's always traffic-knotted entrance, is an area historically known as **Hell's Kitchen**, where a gang- and crime-ridden Irish community scraped by during the 19th century. Italians, Greeks, Puerto

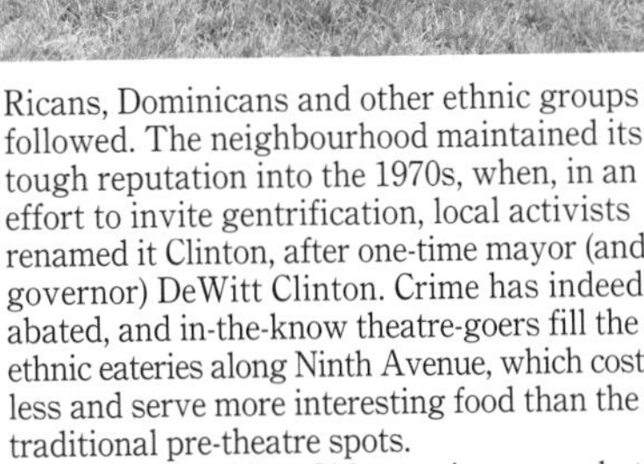

Ricans, Dominicans and other ethnic groups followed. The neighbourhood maintained its tough reputation into the 1970s, when, in an effort to invite gentrification, local activists renamed it Clinton, after one-time mayor (and governor) DeWitt Clinton. Crime has indeed abated, and in-the-know theatre-goers fill the ethnic eateries along Ninth Avenue, which cost less and serve more interesting food than the traditional pre-theatre spots.

The extreme West Side remains somewhat desolate, but in the past year a burgeoning theatre scene has taken root. Plans for a new stadium in the neighbourhood, along with the refurbishment and expansion of the unlovely **Jacob K Javits Convention Center** (Eleventh Avenue, between 34th & 39th Streets), were stalled in 2006, but there is some hope they may be revived in 2008. Still, the massive black glass structure draws huge crowds to its various trade shows. Maritime enthusiasts will appreciate the area along the Hudson River between 46th and 52nd Streets. The **Intrepid** (*see below*), a retired naval aircraft carrier, houses a sea, air and space museum (and a Concorde jet), and big crowds flock to the river whenever cruise ships dock at the terminal near 50th Street. The huge naval ship is in dry dock in nearby New Jersey getting much-needed repairs and is expected to be welcoming visitors again in autumn 2008. During Fleet Week (the last week of May), the West Side fills with white-uniformed sailors on shore leave. The Circle Line Terminal is over on 42nd Street, at Pier 83.

Intrepid Sea-Air-Space Museum

USS Intrepid, Pier 86, 46th Street, at the Hudson River (1-212 245 0072/www.intrepidmuseum.org). Subway A, C, E to 42nd Street-Port Authority, then M42 bus to Twelfth Avenue. Closed until autumn 2008. **Map** p404 B23.

The retired aircraft carrier is closed for renovations and repairs; it will reopen in autumn 2008.

Madame Tussaud's New York

234 W 42nd Street, between Seventh & Eighth Avenues (1-800 246 8872/www.nycwax.com). Subway A, C, E to 42nd Street-Port Authority; N, Q, R, W to 42nd Street; S, 1, 2, 3, 7 to 42nd Street-Times Square. **Open** 10am-8pm Sun-Thur; 10am-10pm Fri, Sat. **Admission** $29; $26 seniors; $23 4-12s; free under-4s. **Credit** AmEx, MC, V. **Map** p404 D24.

A must if you are a fan of frozen life-sized celebs; every few months the place rolls out a new posse of freshly waxed victims.

Times Square Information Center

1560 Broadway, between 46th & 47th Streets, entrance on Seventh Avenue (1-212 869 1890/www.times squarenyc.org). Subway N, R, W to 49th Street; 1 to 50th Street. **Open** 8am-8pm daily. **Map** p404 D23.

Run by the not-for-profit Times Square Alliance, this handy centre has a large amount of free leaflets, merchandise and tourist information.

Sleeper hit

Catch 40 winks at one of the city's dedicated nap centres.

LED lights operational? Check. Zero-gravity chair in optimal position? Check. Audio transmission engaged? Check. Not a trip to outer space but rather a visit to la-la-land care of **MetroNaps** (Empire State Building, Suite 2210, 350 Fifth Avenue, between 33rd & 34th Streets, 1-212 239 3344, www.metronaps.com). Visitors enter a pod chamber, basically a darkened room, filled with a half-dozen 'EnergyPods' – futuristic chairs straight out of *2001: A Space Odyssey*. An oversized, bubble-shaped visor lowers over your head and soothing, sleep-inducing sounds lull you. 'We get all kinds of people in here,' says the attendant. 'Mostly overworked business people and tourists seeking a little quiet time.'

A few blocks away, the recently opened **Yelo** (315 W 57th Street, between Eighth & Ninth Avenues, 1-212 245 8235, www.yelonyc.com) promises lowered stress levels, increased productivity and improved health via 20- to 40-minute power-nap sessions and concurrent reflexology massages. Inside your Yelocab, a futuristic 60-square-foot private cabin, you'll repose on a leather chair that reclines until feet are above the heart (which lowers the heart rate). A cashmere blanket adds a touch of cosiness. When our intrepid (OK, exhausted and sleep-deprived) reporter recently had a go on it, she was immediately won over. 'Since I'm the sort of person who can nod off at the dentist's, I immediately felt drowsy, and as whales sang to me from speakers in the ceiling, I dipped into a light sleep,' she said. After a standard 20-minute session the rooms at Yelo undergo a soothing sunrise: you can choose your hue, which brightens until you're awake. Still, you may suffer the same problem that many have every morning at home: the miserable feeling of getting out of a warm, comfortable bed. To ease you into a lucid state MetroNaps offers Wake Stations with reviving face misters, warm towelettes, mints and moisturiser.

When our guinea pig finally rose from her brief slumber, the pre-pay approach and no-tipping policy at Yelo ensured that her calmer, more refreshed state wasn't befouled.

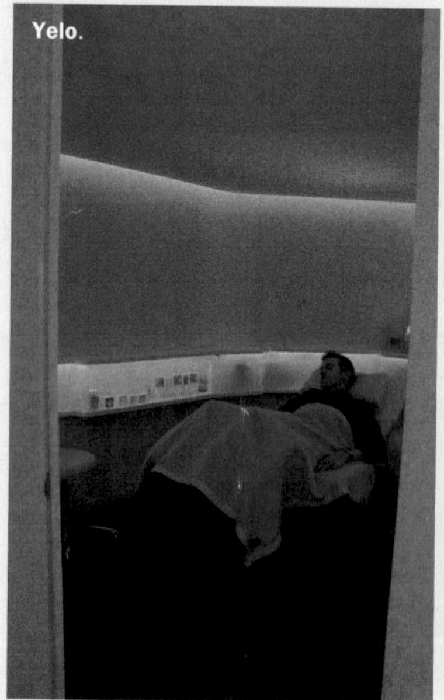

Yelo.

Sightseeing

Fifth Avenue

Synonymous with the chic and the moneyed, Fifth Avenue caters to the elite; it's also the main route for the city's many public parades: National Puerto Rican Day (*see p262*), St Patrick's Day (*see p260*), Gay & Lesbian Pride March (*see p263*), and many more. Even without a parade, the street hums with activity with the sidewalks full of people from all walks of life, from gawking tourists to smartly dressed society matrons.

The **Empire State Building** (*see p130*), located smack-bang in the centre of Midtown, is visible from most parts of the city and beyond. At night, it's lit in showy colours to celebrate a holiday or a special event in progress; *see p131* **Light fight**. Craning your neck at the corner of 34th Street to see storey after storey extend into the sky gives a breathtaking perspective of the gargantuan structure. The building's 86th-floor observation deck offers brilliant views in every direction; go at sunset to glimpse the longest urban shadow you'll ever see, cast from Manhattan all the way across the river to Queens. For a weekday break from sightseeing, catch a few winks in a cosy **MetroNaps** pod (*see opposite* **Sleeper hit**), located in the famous skyscraper. This new company welcomes midtown executives and others looking to recharge with a quick powernap.

Impassive stone lions, dubbed Patience and Fortitude by Mayor Fiorello La Guardia, guard the steps of the humanities and science collection of the **New York Public Library** (*see p133*), a beautiful Beaux Arts building at 41st Street; there's a lovely library gift shop just across Fifth Avenue. The Rose Main Reading Room, on the library's top floor, is a hushed sanctuary of 23-foot-long tables and matching oak chairs. Situated behind the library is **Bryant Park** (*photos pp126-127*), a green space that hosts a dizzying schedule of free entertainment during the summer (*see p261*), when it also attracts outdoor internet users with its free wireless access. The luxury **Bryant Park Hotel** (*see p65*) occupies the former American Radiator Building on 40th Street. Designed by architect Raymond Hood in the mid 1920s, and recently renovated, the structure is faced with near-black brick and trimmed in gold leaf. Alexander Woollcott, Dorothy Parker and friends held court and traded barbs at the **Algonquin** (*see p65*); the lobby is still a great place to meet for a drink. Just north of the park, on Sixth Avenue, is the always thought-provoking **International Center of Photography** (*see p130*).

Veer off Fifth Avenue into the 19 buildings of **Rockefeller Center** (*see p133*) and you'll see why this interlacing of public and private space is so lavishly praised. After plans for an expansion of the Metropolitan Opera on the site fell through in 1929, John D Rockefeller Jr, who had leased the land on behalf of the Met, set about creating a complex to house radio and television corporations. Designed by Raymond Hood and many other prominent architects, the 'city within a city' grew over the course of more than 40 years, with each new building conforming to the original master plan and art deco design. In autumn 2005, the legendary observation deck atop 30 Rockefeller Plaza reopened after 20 years.

As you stroll through the Channel Gardens from Fifth Avenue, the magnificent **General Electric Building** gradually appears above you. The sunken plaza in the complex is the winter home of an oft-packed ice-skating rink; an enormous Christmas tree looms above it each holiday season. The plaza is the most visible entrance to the restaurants and shops in the underground passages that link the buildings. It is also home to the famous art auction house **Christie's** (*see p130*). The centre is filled with murals, sculptures, mosaics and other artwork. Perhaps the most famous pieces are the rink-side *Prometheus* sculpture, by Paul Manship, and José María Sert's murals in the GE Building. But wander around, and you'll be treated to many more masterworks.

On weekday mornings, a (mainly tourist-filled) crowd gathers at the **NBC** television network's glass-walled, ground-level studio (where the *Today* show is shot), at the south-west corner of Rockefeller Plaza and 49th Street. When the show's free concert series in the plaza hosts big-name guests such as Norah Jones, Sting and Queen Latifah, the throng swells mightily.

Radio City Music Hall (*see p319*), on Sixth Avenue, at 50th Street, was the world's largest cinema when it was built in 1932. This art deco jewel was treated to a $70 million restoration in 1999; it's now used for music concerts and for traditional Christmas and Easter shows featuring renowned precision dance troupe the Rockettes. The backstage tour (11am-3pm daily, $17) is one of the best in town

Facing Rockefeller Center is the beautiful **St Patrick's Cathedral** (*see p133*), the largest Catholic cathedral in the United States. A few blocks north, you will find a clutch of museums – such as the **American Folk Art Museum** (*see p130*), the **Paley Center for Media** (formerly the Museum of Television & Radio, *see p133*), and the fabulously renovated **Museum of Modern Art** (*see p131*). Swing Street, or 52nd Street, between Fifth and Sixth Avenues, is a row of 1920s speakeasies; the only venue still open from that period is the '21' Club (21 W 52nd Street, between Fifth & Madison Avenues, 1-212 582 7200). The bar buzzes at night; upstairs, the restaurant is a popular power-lunch spot.

The blocks off Fifth Avenue, between Rockefeller Center and Central Park South, showcase expensive retail palaces bearing names that were famous long before the concept of branding was developed. Along the stretch between **Saks Fifth Avenue** (49th to 50th Streets; *see p230*) and **Bergdorf Goodman** (at 58th Street; *see p229*), the rents are the highest in the world; tenants include Cartier, Versace, Tiffany & Co and Gucci. Fifth Avenue is crowned by **Grand Army Plaza** at 59th Street. A gilded statue of General William Tecumseh Sherman presides over this public space; to the west stands the elegant **Plaza Hotel** building (which celebrated its 100th birthday in October 2007; *see p65*); to the north lies the luxe **Pierre Hotel** (*see p65*). From here, you can access **Central Park** (*see p135*), where the perpetual city din mercifully gives way to relative serenity.

Sightseeing

American Folk Art Museum

45 W 53rd Street, between Fifth & Sixth Avenues (1-212 265 1040/www.folkartmuseum.org). Subway E, V to Fifth Avenue-53rd Street. **Open** 10.30am-5.30pm Tue-Thur, Sat, Sun; 10.30am-7.30pm Fri. **Admission** $9; $7 seniors, students; free under-12s. Free to all 5.30-7.30pm Fri. **Credit** AmEx, Disc, MC, V. **Map** p404 E22.

Celebrating traditional craft-based work is the American Folk Art Museum (formerly the Museum of American Folk Art). Designed by architects Billie Tsien and Tod Williams, the architecturally stunning eight-floor building is four times larger than the original Lincoln Center location (now a branch of the museum) and includes a café. The range of decorative, practical and ceremonial folk art encompasses pottery, trade signs, delicately stitched log-cabin quilts and wind-up toys.

Other locations: 2 Lincoln Square, Columbus Avenue, between 65th & 66th Streets, Upper West Side (1-212 595 9533).

Christie's

20 Rockefeller Plaza, 49th Street, between Fifth & Sixth Avenues (1-212 636 2000/www.christies.com). Subway B, D, F, V to 47-50th Streets-Rockefeller Center. **Open** 9.30am-5.30pm Mon-Fri. **Admission** free. **Map** p404 E23.

Dating from 1766, Christie's joins Sotheby's as one of New York's premier auction houses, its name known throughout the world for its high-profile sales of some seriously upmarket items. The building is worth a visit purely for the architecture, in particular to see the cavernous three-floor lobby featuring a specially commissioned mural by Sol LeWitt. Most auctions are open to the public, with viewing hours scheduled in the days leading up to the sale. Hours vary with each exhibition; call or visit the website for information.

Empire State Building

350 Fifth Avenue, between 33rd & 34th Streets (1-212 736 3100/www.esbnyc.com). Subway B, D, F, N, Q, R, V, W to 34th Street-Herald Square. **Open** 8am-2am daily (last elevator at 1.15am). **Admission** *86th-floor observatory* $17; $15 seniors, 12-17s; $11 6-11s; free under-5s. *102nd-floor observatory* additional $15. **Credit** AmEx, DC, Disc, MC, V. **Map** p404 E25.

In late 2005, the 102nd-floor observatory was reopened to the public and reigns as the city's highest lookout. The view from the 86th floor isn't too shabby either, from where, on a clear day, you can see all five boroughs and five states. (Night owl alert: the roof deck now remains open until 2am.) Be warned that queues can take as long as two hours on busy days; we recommend buying your tickets online to save time. If you have money to burn, you can take advantage of the express ticket option ($42), which gets you to the 86th floor in about 20 minutes. The informative (but hokey) audio tour is worth the extra seven bucks if you want more than an eyeful.

The Empire State Building was financed as a speculative venture by General Motors executive John J Raskob; builders broke ground in 1930. It sprang up in 14 months with amazing speed, completed more than a month ahead of schedule and $5 million under budget. The 1,250ft tower snatched the title of world's tallest building from under the nose of the months-old, 1,046ft Chrysler Building (*see p134*), conveniently showing up Raskob's Detroit-based rival Walter P Chrysler.

International Center of Photography

1133 Sixth Avenue, at 43rd Street (1-212 857 9700/www.icp.org). Subway B, D, F, V to 42nd Street-Bryant Park; N, Q, R, W, 42nd Street S, 1, 2, 3, 7 to 42nd Street-Times Square. **Open** 10am-6pm Tue-Thur, Sat, Sun; 10am-8pm Fri. **Admission** $12; $8 seniors & students; free members & under-12s. 5-8pm Fri pay what you wish. **Credit** AmEx, Disc, MC, V. **Map** p404 D24.

The library here at the International Center of Photography – a major photographic resource – houses back issues of photography magazines, and thousands of biographical and photographic files. Founded in the 1960s as the International Fund for Concerned Photography, ICP has work by photojournalists Werner Bischof, Robert Capa and Dan Weiner, all of whom were killed on assignment. Photojournalism remains an important part of the centre's programme, which also includes contemporary photos and video. In 2003, the first-ever ICP Photo Triennial further solidified ICP's presence on the contemporary photography scene. The two floors of exhibition space often showcase retrospectives devoted to single artists; recent shows have focused on the work of Sebastião Salgado, Weegee and Garry Winogrand.

Museum of Modern Art (MoMA)

11 W 53rd Street, between Fifth & Sixth Avenues (1-212 708 9400/www.moma.org). Subway E, V to Fifth Avenue-53rd Street. **Open** 10.30am-5.30pm Mon, Wed, Thur, Sat, Sun; 10.30am-8pm Fri. **Admission** (incl admission to film programmes) $20; $16 over-65s; $12 full-time students; free under-16s (must be accompanied by an adult). Free to all 4-8pm Fri. **Credit** AmEx, MC, V. **Map** p404 E23.

MoMA contains the world's finest and most comprehensive holdings of 20th-century art, and, thanks to a sweeping redesign by architect Yoshio Taniguchi, completed in 2004, it is now able to show off much more of its immense permanent collection in serene, high-ceilinged galleries that almost outshine the art on display. Highlights like Van Gogh's *The Starry Night* may be what keeps the tourists flocking to the Museum of Modern Art, but even the most jaded New Yorkers swoon when they enter the spacious galleries and the soaring five-storey atrium, the central artery for the six curatorial departments: Architecture and Design, Drawings, Painting and Sculpture, Photography, Prints and Illustrated Books, and Film and Media. Works include the best creations from the hands of Matisse, Picasso, Van Gogh, Giacometti, Lawrence, Pollock, Rothko and Warhol, among many others.

Outside, Philip Johnson's sculpture garden has been restored to its original, larger plan from 1953, and its powerful minimalist sculptures and sheer matte black granite and glass wall are overlooked by the Modern, the sleek high-end restaurant and bar run by Midas-touch restaurateur Danny Meyer; for a more affordable, but no less impressive, dining experience, try the Bar Room at the Modern (*see p204*). The museum's eclectic exhibition of design objects is a must-see, with examples of art nouveau, the Bauhaus and Vienna Secession alongside a vintage 1946 Ferrari and architectural drawings from the likes of Rem Koolhaas and Mies van der Rohe.

Planned exhibitions for 2008 include 'Lucian Freud: The Painter's Etchings', until 10 March; 'Color Chart' (2 Mar-12 May), a celebration of the paradox and beauty that results when artists assign colour decisions to chance, a ready-made source or an arbitrary system; and 'Joan Miró: Painting and Anti-Painting 1927-1937' (3 Nov-12 Jan 2009).

Light fight

Last year, the **Empire State Building** (*see p130*) hosted a covert battle between two lighting companies hoping to win a contract to bring a new style of illumination to the iconic skyscraper. As we went to press, representatives were tight-lipped about the outcome of their experiment (and the debut date of the lighting overhaul), but we're betting that it's only a matter of time before the top of this building is festooned with elaborate, glowing patterns.

Originally illuminated with a single large searchlight in 1932 to herald Franklin D Roosevelt's presidential election, the Empire State Building presently requires nearly 1,400 lights for its romantic nightly display. White light remains the ESB staple, though coloured lights were introduced in 1976, during the bicentennial, to bathe the tower in patriotic red, white and blue. The pizza-sized coloured gels take four hours to fit and are used in dozens of colour combinations to celebrate holidays (red and green at Christmas) and charity causes (pink for breast-cancer awareness). Lights come on at sundown and turn off, Cinderella style, at the stroke of midnight each night except New Year's Eve, New Year's Day, St Patrick's Day, Christmas Eve and Christmas Day. On these nights, the edifice becomes the world's largest night-light, shining on until 3am.

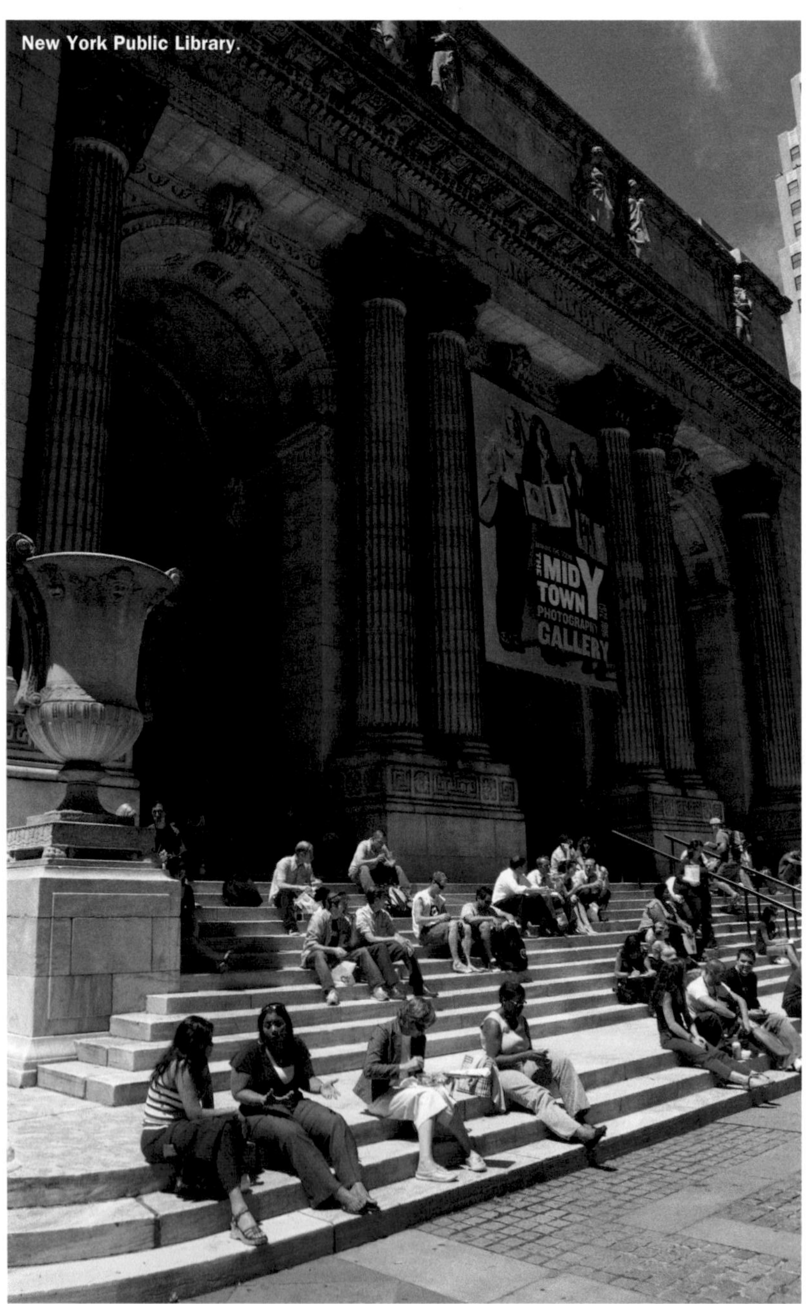

New York Public Library.

NBC Studio Tour

30 Rockefeller Plaza, 49th Street, between Fifth & Sixth Avenues (1-212 664 3700/www.nbc.com). Subway B, D, F, V to 47-50th Streets-Rockefeller Center. **Admission** $18.50; $15.50 seniors, groups of 15 or more, 6-12s. Under-6s not admitted. **Tours** call for times. **Credit** AmEx, MC, V. **Map** p404 E23.

Peer through the *Today* show's studio window with a horde of fellow onlookers, or pay admission (at the NBC Experience Store, www.shopnbc.com) for a guided tour of the studios. The tours are led by pages, many of whom – Ted Koppel, Kate Jackson, Michael Eisner, Marcy Carsey and others – have gone on to bigger and better things in showbiz. For information on NBC recordings, *see p300.*

New York Public Library

455 Fifth Avenue, at 42nd Street (1-212 930 0830/ www.nypl.org). Subway B, D, F, V to 42nd Street-Bryant Park; 7 to Fifth Avenue. **Open** 11am-7.30pm Tue, Wed; 10am-6pm Thur-Sat. **Admission** free. **Map** p404 E24.

When people mention the New York Public Library, most are referring to this imposing Beaux Arts building. (In fact, it houses only NYPL's humanities and social sciences collection; for other locations, *see p375.*) Two massive stone lions, dubbed Patience and Fortitude by former mayor Fiorello La Guardia, flank the main portal. Free guided tours (at 11am and 2pm) stop at the beautifully renovated Rose Main Reading Room and the Bill Blass Public Catalog Room, which offers free internet access. Lectures, author readings and special exhibitions are definitely worth checking out.

Paley Center for Media (formerly the Museum of Television & Radio)

25 W 52nd Street, between Fifth & Sixth Avenues (1-212 621 6600/www.paleycenter.org). Subway B, D, F, V to 47-50th Streets-Rockefeller Center; E, V to Fifth Avenue-53rd Street. **Open** noon-6pm Tue-Sun; noon-8pm Thur. **Admission** $10; $8 seniors, students; $5 under-14s. **No credit cards. Map** p404 E23.

This nirvana for boob-tube addicts and pop-culture junkies contains an archive of more than 100,000 radio and TV programmes. Head to the fourth-floor library to search the computerised system for your favourite *Star Trek* or *I Love Lucy* episodes, then walk down one flight to take a seat at your assigned console. (The radio listening room operates the same way.) There are also screenings of modern cartoons, public seminars and special presentations.

Rockefeller Center

From 48th to 51st Streets, between Fifth & Sixth Avenues (1-212 332 6868/tickets 1-212 664 7174/www.rockefellercenter.com). Subway B, D, F, V to 47-50th Streets-Rockefeller Center. **Open** 7am-11pm daily. *Tours* every hr 11am-5pm Mon-Sat; 11am-4pm Sun. *Observation deck* 8am-midnight daily. **Admission** free. *Tours* $12; $10 seniors & children. Under-6s not admitted. *Observation deck* $17.50; $16 seniors; $11.25 6-12s; free under-6s. **Map** p404 E23.

NBC, Simon & Schuster, McGraw-Hill and other media giants inhabit this art deco city within a city. Exploring the centre is free, and guided tours of the complex are available daily (call 1-212 664 3700). Top of the Rock, Rockefeller Center's observation deck, offers seriously fantastic views of the city below (www.topoftherocknyc.com). *Photo p134.*

St Patrick's Cathedral

Fifth Avenue, between 50th & 51st Streets (1-212 753 2261). Subway B, D, F to 47-50th Streets-Rockefeller Center; E, V to Fifth Avenue-53rd Street. **Open** 6.30am-8.45pm daily. **Admission** free. **Tours** call for tour dates & times. **Map** p404 E23.

St Patrick's adds Gothic grace to Fifth Avenue. The diocese of New York bought the land for an orphanage in 1810, but then, in 1858, it switched gears and began construction on what would become the country's largest Catholic church. Today, the white marble spires are dwarfed by Rockefeller Center, but, inside, visitors are treated to a still-stunning array of vaulted ceilings, stained-glass windows from Charres and altars by Tiffany & Co.

Midtown East

The area east of Fifth Avenue may seem less appealing to visitors than Times Square or Rockefeller Center, but the neighbourhood is home to some of the city's most recognisable landmarks (the United Nations, Grand Central Terminal and the Chrysler Building). The grid of busy, businesslike streets is lined with large, imposing buildings, and the area is a little thin on plazas and street-level attractions, but it compensates with a dizzying array of world-class architecture.

Grand Central Terminal (*see p134*), a 1913 Beaux Arts train station, is the city's most spectacular point of arrival, even though it isn't a national gateway (unlike Penn Station, Grand Central is used only for commuter trains). The station stands at the junction of 42nd Street and Park Avenue, the latter rising on a viaduct that curves around the terminal. The station houses a number of fancy bars, restaurants and shops.

Rising like a phoenix behind Grand Central, the **MetLife Building**, formerly the Pan Am Building, was once the world's largest office tower. Now its most celebrated tenants are the peregrine falcons that nest on the roof and feed on pigeons snatched mid-air. On Park Avenue is the famed **Waldorf-Astoria** hotel (*see p71*), formerly located on Fifth Avenue but rebuilt here in 1931, after the original was demolished to make way for the Empire State Building. Other must-see buildings around the area include **Lever House** (390 Park Avenue, between 53rd & 54th Streets), the **Seagram Building** (375 Park Avenue, between 52nd & 53rd Streets), **Citicorp Center** (from 53rd

Rockefeller Center in bloom. *See p133.*

Street to 54th Street, between Lexington & Third Avenues) and the stunning art deco skyscraper that anchors the corner of Lexington Avenue and 51st Street, formerly the **General Electric Building** (and before that, the RCA Victor Building). A Chippendale crown tops Philip Johnson's postmodern icon, the **Sony Building** (550 Madison Avenue, between 55th & 56th Streets), formerly the AT&T Building. Inside, the **Sony Wonder Technology Lab** (*see p288*) delivers a hands-on thrill zone of science in action.

Along the river to the east lies **Tudor City**, a pioneering 1925 residential development and a high-rise version of England's Hampton Court, which boasts a charming park perfect for respites from the rush of traffic below. The neighbourhood is dominated by the **United Nations Headquarters** (*see below*), with its sculpture-heavy grounds and famous glass-walled Secretariat building. But right across First Avenue is **Dag Hammarskjöld Plaza** (47th Street, between First & Second Avenues), named for the former UN secretary general. Here, you can stroll through a lovely garden honouring Katharine Hepburn (who used to live nearby in Turtle Bay Gardens, a stretch of townhouses on 48th and 49th Streets, between Second and Third Avenues).

East 42nd Street has even more architectural distinction, including the Romanesque Revival hall of the former **Bowery Savings Bank** (No.110) and the art deco details of the **Chanin Building** (No.122). Completed in 1930, the gleaming **Chrysler Building** (at Lexington Avenue) pays homage to the automobile. Architect William Van Alen outfitted the main tower with colossal radiator-cap eagle 'cargoyles' and a brickwork relief sculpture of racing cars complete with chrome hubcaps. A needle-sharp stainless-steel spire was added to the blueprint so the finished product would be taller than 40 Wall Street, which was under construction at the same time. The **Daily News Building** (No.220), another art deco gem designed by Raymond Hood, was immortalised in the *Superman* films. Although the namesake tabloid no longer has its offices here, the lobby still houses its giant globe.

Grand Central Terminal

From 42nd to 44th Streets, between Vanderbilt & Lexington Avenues (www.grandcentralterminal.com). Subway 42nd Street S, 4, 5, 6, 7 to 42nd Street-Grand Central. **Tours** call 1-212 697 1245 for information. **Map** p404 E24.

The city's most glamorous station played an important role in the nation's historic preservation movement, after a series of legal battles that culminated in the 1978 Supreme Court decision affirming NYC's landmark laws. Since its 1998 renovation, the terminal has become a destination in itself, with classy restaurants and bars, such as the Campbell Apartment cocktail lounge (off the West Balcony, 1-212 953 0409) and the expert and attitudinous Grand Central Oyster Bar & Restaurant (Lower Concourse, 1-212 490 6650). The Lower Concourse food court spans the globe with its fairly priced lunch options. One notable oddity: the constellations on the Main Concourse ceiling are drawn in reverse, as if seen from heaven.

United Nations Headquarters

UN Plaza, First Avenue, between 42nd & 48th Streets (1-212 963 7710/tours 1-212 963 8687/www.un.org). Subway 42nd Street S, 4, 5, 6, 7 to 42nd Street-Grand Central. **Admission** $13; $9 seniors; $8.50 students; $7 5-14s. Under-5s not admitted. **Tours** *Mar-Dec* 9.30am-4.30pm Mon-Fri; 10am-4.30pm Sat, Sun. *Jan, Feb* 9.30am-4.45pm Mon-Fri. **Credit** AmEx, MC, V. **Map** p404 G24.

Although you don't need a passport, you will be leaving US soil when you enter the UN complex – it's an international zone, and the vast buffet at the Delegates Dining Room (fourth floor, 1-212 963 7626) fittingly puts cultural diversity on the table. The grounds and the Peace Garden along the East River are off-limits for security reasons. Unless you pay for a guided tour, the only accessible attractions are the exhibitions in the lobby, and the bookstore and gift shop on the lower level.

Uptown

New York's back garden.

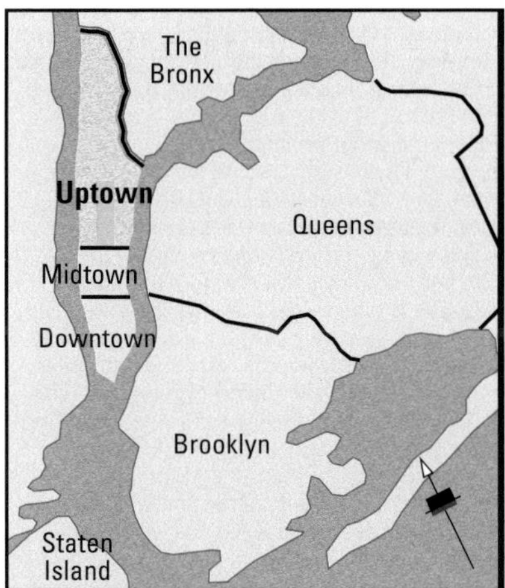

Maps pp405-409

If we've heard it once, we've heard it a thousand times: Uptown is where the rich people live. It's certainly true that above 57th Street, the Upper East Side and Upper West Side (the neighbourhoods bordering Central Park) boast an array of millionaire residents (and a few billionaires), but there's definitely more to this part of Manhattan than well-heeled socialites. The area is positively brimming with truly first-rate cultural institutions: **Lincoln Center**, the **Metropolitan Museum of Art**, the **Guggenheim** and the **Studio Museum in Harlem** all call Uptown home.

Once a bucolic getaway for 19th-century New Yorkers living at the southern tip of the island, much of this area can still feel blissfully serene. This is largely thanks to the presence of Manhattan's largest garden, **Central Park**. At the northernmost tip, near the Cloisters (*see p155*), you can also get a slice of the old wilderness in **Inwood Hill Park**. Pretty trees and flowers figure large in Uptown, but if you came to New York to escape the peace, you won't have trouble finding urban pleasures. The shopping scene, most especially along the infamously celebrity-strewn Madison Avenue, is the epitome of high chic. Further north, increasingly diverse Harlem offers myriad jazz bars and a dynamic nightlife.

Central Park

An emerald, 843-acre rectangle, this patch of nature was the first man-made public park in the US. In 1853, the newly formed Central Park Commission chose landscape designer Frederick Law Olmsted and architect Calvert Vaux to turn a vast tract of rocky swampland into a rambling oasis of lush greenery. The commission, inspired by the great parks of London and Paris, imagined a place that would provide city dwellers with respite from the crowded streets. A noble thought, but one that required the eviction of 1,600 mostly poor or immigrant inhabitants, including residents of Seneca Village, the city's oldest African-American settlement. But clear the area they did, and the rest is history.

The park celebrated its 150th anniversary in 2003, and it has never looked better, thanks to the Central Park Conservancy, a private, not-for-profit civic group formed in 1980 that has been instrumental in the park's restoration and maintenance. A horse-drawn carriage is still the sightseeing vehicle of choice for many tourists (and even a few romantic locals, though they'd never admit to it); plan on paying $34 for a 20-minute tour. (You can usually hail a carriage on Central Park South, where they line up between Fifth Avenue and Columbus Circle.) If walking is more your speed, *see p140* **Walk it out**.

The park is dotted with landmarks. **Strawberry Fields**, near the West 72nd Street entrance, memorialises John Lennon, who lived in the nearby Dakota Building. Also called the International Garden of Peace, this sanctuary features a mosaic of the word 'imagine', donated by the Italian city of Naples. More than 160 species of flowers and plants from all over the world bloom here (including strawberries, of course). The statue of Balto, a heroic Siberian husky (East Drive, at 67th Street), is a favourite sight for tots. Slightly older children appreciate the statue of Alice in Wonderland, just north of the Conservatory Water at the East 74th Street park entrance.

In winter, ice skaters lace up at **Wollman Rink** (midpark, at 62nd Street; *see also p338*), where the skating comes complete with a picture-postcard view of the fancy hotels surrounding the park. A short stroll to about 64th Street brings you to the **Friedsam Memorial**

Central Park. *See p135.*

Carousel, still a bargain at $1.50 a ride. At 65th is the old **Dairy** (*see p137*), which now houses the Central Park Conservancy's information centre. Nearby **Central Park Zoo** (*see p137*), between 63rd & 66th Streets, is another surefire hit with children; for more park activities for kids, *see p288*.

Come summer, kites, Frisbees and soccer balls seem to fly every which way across **Sheep Meadow**, the designated quiet zone that begins at 66th Street. The sheep are gone (they grazed here until 1934), now replaced by sunbathers improving their tans and scoping out the throngs. The hungry (and affluent) can repair to the glitzy **Tavern on the Green** (Central Park West, at 67th Street, 1-212 873 3200), which sets up a grand outdoor café in the summer, complete with a 40-foot bar made with trees from city parks. However, picnicking alfresco (or snacking on a hot dog from one of the park's food vendors) is the most popular option. East of Sheep Meadow, between 66th and 72nd Streets, is the **Mall**, where you'll find volleyball courts and plenty of in-line skaters. East of the Mall's Naumburg Bandshell is Rumsey Playfield – site of the annual **Central Park SummerStage** series (*see p261*), an eclectic roster of free and benefit concerts held from Memorial Day weekend to Labor Day weekend. One of the most popular meeting places in the park is the grand **Bethesda Fountain & Terrace**, near the midpoint of the 72nd Street Transverse Road. The terrace and impressively tiled arcade here has recently undergone a $7 million facelift (*see p137* **Bethesda reborn**). *Angel of the Waters*, the sculpture in the centre of the fountain, was created by Emma Stebbins, the first woman to be granted a major public-art commission in New York. North of it is the **Loeb Boathouse** (midpark, at 75th Street), where you can rent a rowing boat or gondola to take out on the lake, which is crossed by the elegant Bow Bridge. The bucolic park views enjoyed by diners at the nearby **Central Park Boathouse Restaurant** (midpark, at 75th Street, 1-212 517 2233) make it a lovely place for brunch or drinks.

Further north is the popular **Belvedere Castle**, a restored Victorian building that sits atop the park's second-highest peak. It offers excellent views and also houses the **Henry Luce Nature Observatory** (*see p137*). The open-air Delacorte Theater hosts **Shakespeare in the Park** (*see p262*), a summer run of free performances of plays by the Bard and others. The **Great Lawn** (midpark, between 79th & 85th Streets) is a sprawling stretch of grass that doubles as a rally point for political protests and a concert spot for just about any act that can rally six-figure audiences, as well as free shows by the Metropolitan Opera and the New York Philharmonic during the summer. (At other times, it's the favoured spot of seriously competitive soccer teams and much less cut-throat teams of Hacky Sackers and their dogs.) Several years ago, the **Reservoir** (midpark, between 85th & 96th Streets) was renamed in honour of the late Jacqueline Kennedy Onassis, who used to jog around it.

Next to the Harlem Meer, in the northern reaches of the park, is the **Charles A Dana Discovery Center** (*see below*), with a roster of enjoyable activities.

Central Park Zoo

830 Fifth Avenue, between 63rd & 66th Streets (1-212 439 6500/www.wcs.org). Subway N, R, W 6 to Fifth Avenue-59th Street. **Open** *Apr-Oct* 10am-5pm Mon-Fri; 10am-5.30pm Sat, Sun. *Nov-Mar* 10am-4.30pm daily. **Admission** $8; $4 seniors; $3 3-12s; free under-3s. **No credit cards. Map** p405 E21.

This is the only place in New York City where you can see a polar bear swimming underwater, and kids tend to love it as a direct result. The Tisch Children's Zoo was recently spiffed up with a series of tot-friendly play areas to mark its tenth anniversary, and the roving characters on the George Delacorte Musical Clock delight children every half-hour.

Charles A Dana Discovery Center

Park entrance on Malcolm X Boulevard (Lenox Avenue), at 110th Street (1-212 860 1370/www.centralparknyc.org). Subway 2, 3 to 110th Street-Central Park North. **Open** 10am-5pm Tue-Sun. **Admission** free. **Map** p406 E15.

Stop by for weekend family workshops, cultural exhibits and outdoor performances on the plaza next to the Harlem Meer. From April to October, the centre lends out fishing rods and bait, and on selected Thursday mornings park rangers lead birdwatching walks. Call ahead for the schedule.

Dairy

Park entrance on Fifth Avenue, at 65th Street (1-212 794 6564/www.centralparknyc.org). Subway N, R, W to Fifth Avenue-59th Street. **Open** 10am-5pm daily. **Admission** free. **Map** p405 D21.

Built in 1872 to show city kids where milk comes from (cows, in this case), the Dairy is now the Central Park Conservancy's information centre, complete with interactive exhibits, videos explaining the park's history and a gift shop.

Henry Luce Nature Observatory

Belvedere Castle, midpark, off the 79th Street Transverse Road (1-212 772 0210). Subway B, C to 81st Street-Museum of Natural History. **Open** 10am-5pm Tue-Sun. **Admission** free. **Map** p405 D19.

During the spring and autumn hawk migrations, park rangers discuss the various birds of prey found in the park and help visitors spot raptors from the castle roof. You can also borrow binoculars, maps and bird-identification guides.

Bethesda reborn

Back in 1869, when Frederick Law Olmstead and Calvert Vaux, the men behind Central Park, completed **Bethesda Terrace & Arcade** – the highly ornate passageway that connects the plaza around the famed Bethesda Fountain to the elm-lined promenade to the south – it was deemed the architectural centrepiece of Manhattan's most treasured urban getaway, boasting a stunning tile ceiling designed by English-born Jacob Wrey Mould.

After decades of weathering – and a bursting city budget that had no room for extravagant repairs – the 16,000 intricately patterned Minton clay tiles (imported from Stoke-on-Trent, England) from the ceiling were put in crates and carted off to storage in the 1980s. Now, three years and $7 million dollars later, the painstaking (and long-overdue) restoration has returned this treasure to its former glory and made the arcade essential Central Park viewing once more.

Bethesda Terrace, Central Park, enter by 72nd Street. **Map** p405 D20.

Upper East Side

Gorgeous pre-war apartments owned by blue-blooded socialites, soigné restaurants filled with the Botoxed-ladies-who-lunch set… this is the picture most New Yorkers have of the Upper East Side, and you'll certainly see a lot of supporting evidence on Fifth, Madison and Park Avenues. There's history behind this reputation. Encouraged by the opening of Central Park in the late 19th century, the city's more affluent residents began building mansions on Fifth Avenue; by the beginning of the 20th century, even the superwealthy had warmed to the idea of giving up their large homes for smaller quarters – provided they were near the park. As a result, flats and hotels began springing up. (A few years later, working-class folks settled around Second and Third Avenues, following construction of an elevated East Side train line.) Architecturally speaking, the overall look of the neighbourhood, especially from Fifth to Park Avenues, remains remarkably homogeneous. Along the expanse known as the Gold Coast – Fifth, Madison and Park Avenues from 61st to 81st Streets – you'll see the great old mansions, many of which are now foreign consulates. The structure at 820 Fifth Avenue (at 64th Street) was one of the earliest luxury apartment buildings on the avenue. New York's ultimate gingerbread house is 45 East 66th Street (between Madison and Park Avenues). Stanford White designed 998 Fifth Avenue (at 81st Street) in the image of an Italian Renaissance palazzo. Some wonderful old carriage houses adorn 63rd and 64th Streets.

Philanthropic gestures made by the moneyed classes over the past 130 years have helped to create a cluster of art collections, museums and cultural institutions. In fact, Fifth Avenue from 82nd to 104th Streets is known as Museum Mile because it is flanked by the **Metropolitan Museum of Art** (*see p143*); the Frank Lloyd Wright-designed **Solomon R Guggenheim Museum** (*see p145*); the **Cooper-Hewitt** (*see below*), which houses the **National Design Museum** inside Andrew Carnegie's former mansion; the **Jewish Museum** (*see p143*); the **Museum of the City of New York** (*see p145*) and **El Museo del Barrio** (*see p139*).

Madison Avenue from 57th to 86th Streets is New York's world-class ultra-luxe shopping strip. The snazzy department store **Barneys New York** (*see p229*) offers chic designer fashions and witty, sometimes audacious, window displays. For a post-spree pick-me-up, order a cup of divinely rich hot chocolate and a Paris-perfect pastry at **La Maison du Chocolat** (*see p245*). While bars and restaurants dominate most of the north–south avenues, hungry sightseers can also pick up a snack (or picnic supplies) at the well-stocked Grace's Market Place (1237 Third Avenue, between 71st & 72nd Streets, 1-212 737 0600) or at the Italian gourmet food shop Agata & Valentina (1505 First Avenue, at 79th Street, 1-212 452 0690). If weather permits, savour your meal on a park bench along the East River promenade leading to **Carl Schurz Park**. This seriously ritzy neighbourhood is also home to the **Asia Society & Museum**, the **China Institute** (*for both, see below*), the **Frick Collection** (*see p139*), the **Goethe-Institut New York/German Cultural Center** (*see p143*), the **Neue Galerie** (*see p145*) and the **Whitney Museum of American Art** (*see p145*).

Asia Society & Museum

725 Park Avenue, at 70th Street (1-212 288 6400/ www.society.org). Subway 6 to 68th Street-Hunter College. **Open** 11am-6pm Tue-Thur, Sat, Sun; 11am-9pm Fri. **Admission** $10; $7 seniors; $5 students; free under-16s. Free 6-9pm Fri. **No credit cards.** **Map** p405 E20.

The Asia Society sponsors study missions and conferences while promoting public programmes in the US and abroad. The headquarters' striking galleries host major exhibitions of art culled from dozens of countries and time periods – from ancient India and medieval Persia to contemporary Japan – and assembled from public and private collections, including the permanent Mr and Mrs John D Rockefeller III collection of Asian art. A spacious, atrium-like café, with a pan-Asian menu, and a beautifully stocked gift shop, make the society a one-stop destination for anyone who has even a passing interest in Asian art and culture.

China Institute

125 E 65th Street, between Park & Lexington Avenues (1-212 744 8181/www.chinainstitute.org). Subway F to Lexington Avenue-63rd Street; 6 to 68th Street-Hunter College. **Open** 10am-5pm Mon, Wed, Fri, Sat; 10am-8pm Tue, Thur. **Admission** $5; $3 seniors, students; free under-12s. Free 6-8pm Tue, Thur. **Credit** AmEx, MC, V. **Map** p405 E21.

Consisting of just two small galleries, the China Institute is somewhat overshadowed by the nearby Asia Society. But its rotating exhibitions, including works by female Chinese artists and selections from the Beijing Palace Museum, are compelling. The institute offers lectures and courses on myriad subjects such as calligraphy, Confucius and cooking.

Cooper-Hewitt, National Design Museum

2 E 91st Street, at Fifth Avenue (1-212 849 8400/ www.cooperhewitt.org). Subway 4, 5, 6 to 86th Street. **Open** 10am-5pm Tue-Thur; 10am-9pm Fri; 10am-6pm Sat; noon-6pm Sun. **Admission** $12; $9 seniors, students; free under-12s. **Credit** AmEx, Disc, MC, V. **Map** p406 E18.

Harnessing creative energy at the **Metropolitan Museum of Art**. *See p143.*

The Smithsonian's National Design Museum was once the home of industrialist Andrew Carnegie (there is still a lovely lawn behind the building, his former garden). Now it's the only museum in the US dedicated to domestic and industrial design, boasting a fascinating roster of temporary exhibitions.

El Museo del Barrio

1230 Fifth Avenue, between 104th & 105th Streets (1-212 831 7272/www.elmuseo.org). Subway 6 to 103rd Street. **Open** 11am-5pm Wed-Sun. **Admission** $6; $4 seniors, students; free under-12s when accompanied by an adult. Seniors free Thur. **Credit** AmEx, MC, V. **Map** p406 E16.

Located in Spanish Harlem (aka El Barrio), the 8,000-piece El Museo del Barrio collection is dedicated to the work of Latino artists who reside in the US, as well as Latin American masters.

Frick Collection

1 E 70th Street, between Fifth & Madison Avenues (1-212 288 0700/www.frick.org). Subway 6 to 68th Street-Hunter College. **Open** 10am-6pm Tue-Sat; 11am-5pm Sun. **Admission** $15; $10 seniors; $5 students, 10-18s (under-16s must be accompanied by an adult; under-10s not admitted). Voluntary donation 11am-1pm Sun. **Credit** AmEx, Disc, MC, V. **Map** p405 E20.

Walk it out Garden variety

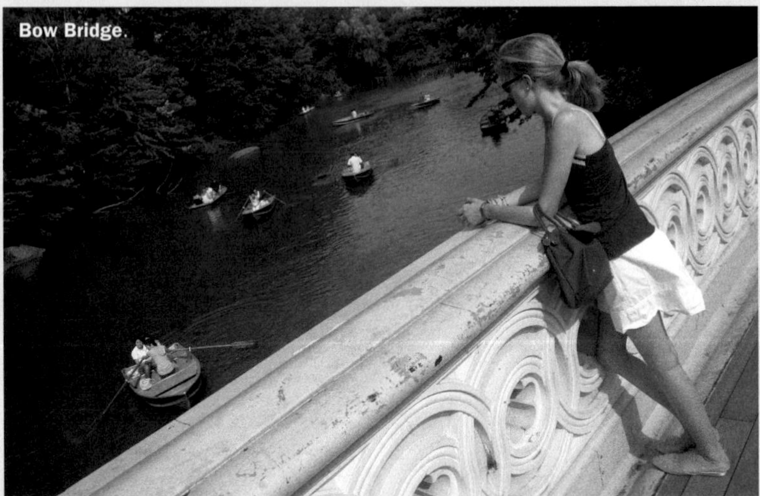

Bow Bridge.

Start Columbus Circle. Subway A, B, C, D, 1 to 59th Street-Columbus Circle.
Finish Metropolitan Museum of Art.
Distance about 1.5 miles.
Time about 3hrs.

Winners of the modestly named 'Central Park Design Competition' in 1857, Calvert Vaux and Frederick Law Olmsted set about creating a park where 'every tree and bush, every arch, roadway and walk, has been fixed where it is with a sense of purpose'. Welcome to New York City's own 843-acre backyard, where history, scenery and boundless opportunities await for 'leisurely contemplation'.

Your day begins at **Columbus Circle**, located at the south-west corner of the park. This 1892 monument got a makeover in 2005 but the real reason to celebrate is the (newish) neighbour to the west – the **Time Warner Center** (*see p146*) – a hub of shops including a big Whole Foods market in the basement and French bistro and boulangerie **Bouchon Bakery** (*see p209*) on the third floor, perfect for a coffee and a croissant before setting off into the woods.

Enter the park through its south-west gate (called the Merchants Entrance), diagonally across the street from the looming statue of Christopher Columbus, and look for the welcoming arms of a gilt-covered woman atop the imposing entry monument. Walking straight ahead (east) you'll hit the roadway that snakes through much of the park. Follow this to the right until you come to Heckscher Playground, the city's largest and oldest playground. Head past the restrooms and go north (a left turn) and you'll soon hit another kid-friendly attraction, the **Central Park Carousel** (aka the Friedsam Memorial Carousel), operated on the same site in one form or another since 1871. A masterpiece of 1900s folk art, it sports 58 of the largest handcarved horses ever constructed. The original calliope still cranks out organ music, and there's even a rather psychotic frieze of Cupid shooting rabbits.

Leave the spinning horses behind, make a sharp left, and head north up a small hill, where you will soon discover the park's undisputed spot for great city views, **Sheep Meadow** (*see p136*). The sheep were evicted in the 1930s, replaced by city sunbathers who pack in, sardine-like, on warm days. Follow the meadow around to the west and you'll find the Mineral Springs Café, a snack bar. Passing by the café, keep to your right and soon you'll come to a roadway. Cross over, and look for the statue of Daniel Webster, American politician and orator, before you come to the celebrated **Strawberry Fields**, a memorial to John Lennon with the word 'imagine' inscribed in a marble mosaic.

A short walk west takes you out of the park and straight up to the **Dakota** apartment building (*see p147*). Built in 1884, it's the last home (and murder site) of John Lennon. The German Renaissance-styled structure has not only been home to Lauren Bacall and Yoko Ono, but it's also the exterior for Roman Polanski's film *Rosemary's Baby* and a crucial setting in Jack Finney's novel *Time and Again*.

A jaunt up smart Central Park West will take you past the **New-York Historical Society** (*see p148*), which has exhibitions celebrating New York's compelling past. But if you like your history to come with more bite, keep looking for the towering medieval turret of the **American M** (*see p148*), with of dinosaur skeletons.

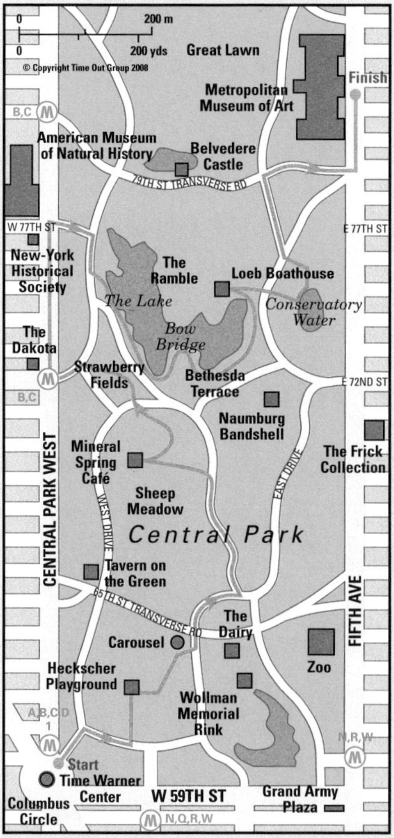

Dip back into the park at 77t follow the entry path down to the roadwa then cross it and head south (a right turn). You'll be treated to a view of water opening up on your left-hand side; follow it for some time until you arrive at **Cherry Hill Fountain**. Head down to the water's edge to witness the lake, the park's most expansive panorama.

In the distance you will soon see the cast-iron **Bow Bridge**. Stroll past it down to the undisputed heart of the park, the **Bethesda Fountain** (*see p136*), with its winged 'Angel of the Waters' statue. The only statuary commissioned for the original park's design, it also featured in the film *Angels in America*.

Following the path closest to the water's edge, head up and over a small hill leading to the **Loeb Boathouse** (*see p136*), which has boat rentals and a famed restaurant (plus a cheaper snack bar); it's also the spot where Carrie Bradshaw of *Sex and the City* made a big splash attempting to kiss Mr Big. A lone bench in the snack bar area is the designated location for the **Central Park Bird Log**, an obsessive communal diary detailing sightings of everything from warblers and green herons to swooping red-tailed hawks.

Stuffed and sated, exit the Boathouse and head straight down to the roadway. Cross over and follow the small footpath to another icon of the park's seemingly endless supply, the **Conservatory Water** (*see p135*), better known as the Boat Pond. Used by generations of Manhattan's children to sail toy ships, it is flanked on two sides by well-loved statues. One is of Hans Christian Andersen, but it's the other – featuring a certain Mad Hatter, a White Rabbit and an infamous blonde – that gets worldwide attention.

Make a beeline north and follow the path to the **Metropolitan Museum of Art** (*see p142*). Turn right and exit out on to Fifth Avenue – the museum is just north. Once inside, head to the Roof Garden (ask the nearest guard for directions; open May to late autumn, weather permitting), where you can order some wine and, on the right day, get drunk on a brilliant sunset. The view manages to be every single Woody Allen movie rolled into one impossibly long Manhattan panorama of trees, buildings and a seemingly endless sky.

…arner Center. *See p146.*

The opulent residence that houses this private collection of great masters (from the 14th to the 19th centuries) was originally built for industrialist Henry Clay Frick. The firm of Carrère & Hastings (which designed the New York Public Library) created the 1914 structure in an 18th-century European style, with a beautiful interior court and reflecting pool. The permanent collection boasts world-class paintings, sculpture and furniture by the likes of Rembrandt, Vermeer, Renoir and French cabinet-maker Jean-Henri Riesener.

Goethe-Institut New York/ German Cultural Center

1014 Fifth Avenue, at 82nd Street (1-212 439 8700/www.goethe.de/ins/us/ney). Subway 4, 5, 6 to 86th Street. **Open** *Gallery* 10am-5pm Mon, Wed, Fri, Sat; 10am-7pm Tue, Thur. *Library* noon-7pm Tue, Thur; noon-5pm Wed, Fri, Sat. **Admission** free. **Map** p405 E19.

The Goethe-Institut New York is a branch of the international German cultural organisation founded in 1951. Housed in a landmark Fifth Avenue mansion across from the Metropolitan Museum of Art, the institute mounts shows featuring German-born contemporary artists, and presents concerts, lectures and also film screenings. German-language books, videos and periodicals are available in the library.

Jewish Museum

1109 Fifth Avenue, at 92nd Street (1-212 423 3200/www.thejewishmuseum.org). Subway 4, 5 to 86th Street; 6 to 96th Street. **Open** 11am-5.45pm Mon-Wed, Sun; 11am-9pm Thur; 11am-3pm Fri. Closed on Jewish holidays. **Admission** $12; $10 seniors, $7.50 students; free under-12s when accompanied by an adult. Voluntary donation 5-8pm Thur. **Credit** AmEx, MC, V. **Map** p405 E18.

The Jewish Museum, in the 1908 Warburg Mansion, contains a fascinating collection of over 28,000 works of art, artefacts and media installations. A two-floor permanent exhibit, called 'Culture and Continuity: The Jewish Journey', studies Judaism's survival and the essence of Jewish identity.

Metropolitan Museum of Art

1000 Fifth Avenue, at 82nd Street (1-212 535 7710/ www.metmuseum.org). Subway 4, 5, 6 to 86th Street. **Open** 9.30am-5.30pm Tue-Thur, Sun; 9.30am-9pm Fri, Sat. No strollers Sun. **Admission** suggested donation (incl same-day admission to the Cloisters) $20; $10 seniors, students; free under-12s. **Credit** AmEx, DC, Disc, MC, V. **Map** p405 E19.

Many locals shuddered in anger in summer 2006, when the Met announced that its suggested fee would be jumping up to $20. We say, chill out – it's only a suggested amount, after all. And thank heavens it is, since it would take many, many visits to cover all of the Met's 2 million sq ft of gallery space. Besides the enthralling temporary exhibitions, there are excellent collections of African, Oceanic and Islamic art, along with more than 3,000 European paintings from the Middle Ages up to the fin-de-siècle period, including major works by Titian, Brueghel, Rembrandt, Vermeer, Goya and Degas, as well as the controversial *Madonna and Child* (stop by and decide whether you think the $45 million piece is the handiwork of medieval master Duccio, or some latter-day forger, as one historian recently claimed). Egyptology fans should head straight for the glass-walled atrium housing the Temple of Dendur. The Greek and Roman halls reopened in 2007 after receiving an elegant makeover (*see p144* **The empire strikes back**), and the incomparable medieval armour collection – a huge favourite with adults and children – was recently enriched by gifts of European, North American, Japanese and also Islamic armaments.

The Met has also made significant additions to its modern-art galleries, including major works by American artist Eric Fischl and Chilean surrealist Roberto Matta. Contemporary sculptures are displayed each year in the Iris and B Gerald Cantor Roof Garden (May to late autumn, weather permitting). If you're in town for a long holiday weekend, don't despair. The Met opens its doors on Monday holidays, including Martin Luther King Day, Presidents' Day, Memorial Day, and the Monday between Christmas and New Year's Day.

A large, round desk in the Great Hall (staffed by volunteers who speak multiple languages) is the hub of the museum's excellent visitors' resources (foreign-language tours are available; call 1-212 570 3711 for information). Once you've had an eyeful of the type of art that interests you most, from Greek kouroi to colourful Kandinskys, we recommend making the most of the Met's various tranquil spots. The Engelhard Court, which borders Central Park, has benches, a trickling fountain, trees, ivy and stunning examples of Tiffany stained-glass to encourage contemplation. (And if you'd like to grab a drink or a snack in less-than-hectic surroundings, try the recently opened American Wing Café.) Astor Court, on the second floor, is a garden modelled on a Ming dynasty scholar's courtyard. Wooden paths border a naturally lit, gravel-paved atrium. The nearby Asian galleries, full of superb bronzes, ceramics and rare wooden Buddhist images, seldom get heavy foot-traffic. At the western end of the museum, rest on a bench in the Robert Lehman Wing, then commune with Botticelli's *Annunciation.*

For the Cloisters, which houses the Met's permanent medieval art collection, *see p155.*

Planned 2008 exhibitions: 'Eternal Ancestors: The Art of the Central African Reliquary' (until 2 March), a presentation of some of the most celebrated creations of African masters in a new light; 'The Art of Time: European Clocks & Watches from the Collection' (until 27 April), which will draw upon the Metropolitan Museum's extensive holdings of English, Dutch, French, German and Swiss horology, ranging in date from the 16th through the 18th century; 'Jasper Johns: Gray' (5 Feb-4 May), an examination the use of the colour grey by the American artist Johns between the mid 1950s and the present; the first full retrospective of the 19th-century French

The empire strikes back

Greek and Roman art gets new digs at the Met.

Years ago, a visit to the **Metropolitan Museum of Art** (*see p143*) wasn't complete without a cafeteria lunch in the grand, dimly lit atrium around the big sunken pool – where the kids in E L Konigsburg's classic *From the Mixed-Up Files of Mrs Basil E Frankweiler* bathed. The pool was a post-war addition; McKim, Mead and White had designed the space, intended to evoke the garden of a Roman villa, for the display of sculpture.

Now a marble floor, similar to the purple stone in the Pantheon, has replaced the pool as part of the just-completed, 15-year redesign and reinstallation of the museum's truly stellar Greek and Roman collections. Standing in the luminous double-storey atrium with its newly raised glass roof, surrounded by monumental figures of Hercules and Dionysus, it's hard to imagine why the space was ever turned into a restaurant. Christopher Lightfoot, the Met's associate curator of Roman art, who supervised the project with the curator in charge, Carlos Picon, says it was mainly because of increased tourism after the war. 'At the time, the Greek and Roman period was not considered to be of prime importance,' Lightfoot says. 'The idea of the Roman Empire in 1950 wasn't one Western democracies wanted to promote.'

Times change, and the Met's director, Philippe de Montebello, has clearly made the period a priority by devoting $220 million to reworking the wing. He moved his own office and others to create room for the new Hellenistic and Roman galleries on the ground floor, and the Etruscan galleries and Greek and Roman Study Collection on the mezzanine. The renovation yielded in excess of 30,000 square feet of new space, almost doubling the area devoted to classical art.

Most of the 5,300 or so objects on view had been in storage for decades – for example, the imposing pair of Hercules statues that flank the sculpture court. Elswhere, the Met's holdings of Roman wall paintings – buried in the eruption of Vesuvius in AD 79 and excavated from two villas near Pompeii – are being shown together for the first time, and a frescoed bedroom, on view in the museum's main hall since the 1960s, now joins the rest of the group in the side galleries on the first floor.

Meanwhile, the contemporary role of antiquities is undergoing its own renovation of sorts, with ongoing controversies about whether museums have acquired works looted from Italy and Greece. De Montebello took the high road in 2006 by negotiating the return of 21 pieces in response to claims brought by the Italian Culture Ministry. But in late March 2007, another allegation, this one made by an Umbrian town without the backing of the Italian government, hit the news: the centrepiece of the new Etruscan galleries, a bronze chariot purchased in 1903 and recently restored, was sold illegally. Worse, news reports in August 2007 – unconfirmed as we went to press – reported that the piece may, in fact, be fake.

Asked about the impact such controversy has had on the project, Lightfoot – standing in front of a vitrine filed with Hellenic silver, slated for return to Italy in 2010 – insists 'it hasn't affected us a great deal.' He puts a positive spin on the subject, noting the museum's gratitude to the Italian government and European museums for loans. 'It's nice to feel part of a wider community,' he says. 'I'm hoping people will see these displays and then want to go and visit Pompeii or the Coliseum in Rome. This is a great advertisement for their cultural heritage.'

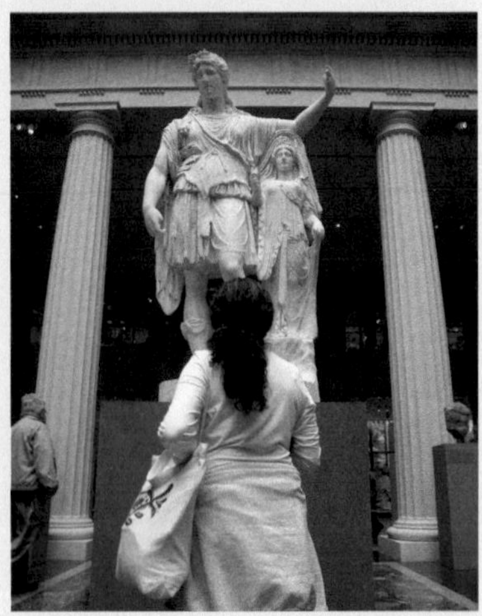

artist Gustave Courbet (27 Feb-18 May) in 30 years, which will present some 100 works by this pioneering figure in the history of modernism; and 'Radiance from the Rain Forest: Featherwork in Ancient Peru' (28 Feb-1 Sept) promises to be a brilliantly colourful spectacle. *Photos p139.*

Museum of the City of New York

1220 Fifth Avenue, between 103rd & 104th Streets (1-212 534 1672/www.mcny.org). Subway 6 to 103rd Street. **Open** 10am-5pm Tue-Sun. **Admission** suggested donation $9; $5 seniors, students, children; $20 families. **Credit** AmEx, MC, V. **Map** p405 E16.

Located at the northern end of Museum Mile, this institution contains a wealth of city history and includes paintings, sculptures, photographs, military and naval uniforms, theatre memorabilia, manuscripts, ship models and rare books. The extensive toy collection, full of New Yorkers' playthings dating from the colonial era to the present, is especially well loved. Toy trains, lead soldiers and battered teddy bears share shelf space with exquisite bisque dolls (decked out in extravagant Paris fashions) and lavishly appointed dolls' houses. Don't miss the amazing Stettheimer Dollhouse, created during the 1920s by Carrie Stettheimer, whose artist friends recreated their masterpieces in miniature to hang on the walls. Look closely and you'll even spy a tiny version of Marcel Duchamp's famous *Nude Descending a Staircase*. Don't miss the museum's *Timescapes*, a 25-minute multimedia film that tells NYC's glorious story from 1624 to the present. The film is shown free with admission and screenings are held regularly throughout the day.

Neue Galerie

1048 Fifth Avenue, at 86th Street (1-212 628 6200/ www.neuegalerie.org). Subway 4, 5, 6 to 86th Street. **Open** 11am-6pm Mon, Sat, Sun; 11am-9pm Fri. **Admission** $15; $10 seniors, students, 12-16s (must be accompanied by an adult); under-12s not admitted. **Credit** AmEx, MC, V. **Map** p405 E18.

This elegant museum is devoted entirely to late 19th- and early 20th-century German and Austrian fine and decorative arts. The creation of the late art dealer Serge Sabarsky and cosmetics mogul Ronald S Lauder, it has the largest concentration of works by Gustav Klimt and Egon Schiele outside Vienna. There's also a bookstore, a chic design shop and Café Sabarsky, serving updated Austrian cuisine and ravishing Viennese pastries.

Solomon R Guggenheim Museum

1071 Fifth Avenue, at 89th Street (1-212 423 3500/ www.guggenheim.org). Subway 4, 5, 6 to 86th Street. **Open** 10am-5.45pm Mon-Wed, Sat, Sun; 10am-8pm Fri. **Admission** $18; $15 seniors, students with a valid ID; free under-12s (must be accompanied by an adult). Half-price for all 5.45-8pm Fri. **Credit** AmEx, MC, V. **Map** p406 E18.

Even if your hectic museum-hopping schedule won't allow time to view the collections, you must get a glimpse (if only from the outside) of this dramatic spiral building, designed by Frank Lloyd Wright. In addition to works by Manet, Kandinsky, Picasso, Chagall and Bourgeois, the museum owns Peggy Guggenheim's trove of cubist, surrealist and also abstract expressionist works, along with the Panza di Biumo Collection of American minimalist and conceptual art from the 1960s and '70s. In 1992, the addition of a ten-storey tower provided space for a sculpture gallery (with views of the park), plus an auditorium and a café.

In summer 2007, the museum mounted a brief exhibition detailing the ongoing restoration and preservation of its façade, which has been plagued with cracks almost from the time it opened in 1959. The team of experts hopes to finish their work in time for the beloved institution's 50th anniversary, which falls in 2009.

Planned 2008 exhibition: a Cai Guo-Qiang (Feb-May) retrospective, the most comprehensive survey of the artist's extraordinary scope to date.

Whitney Museum of American Art

945 Madison Avenue, at 75th Street (1-212 570 3676/1-800 944 8639/www.whitney.org). Subway 6 to 77th Street. **Open** 11am-6pm Wed, Thur, Sat, Sun; 1-9pm Fri. **Admission** $15; $10 seniors, students; free under-12s. Voluntary donation 6-9pm Fri. **Credit** AmEx, MC, V. **Map** p405 E20.

Like the Guggenheim, the Whitney is set apart by its unique architecture: it's a Marcel Breuer-designed grey granite cube with an all-seeing upper-storey 'eye' window. When Gertrude Vanderbilt Whitney, a sculptor and art patron, opened the museum in 1931, she dedicated it to living American artists. Today, the Whitney holds about 15,000 pieces by nearly 2,000 artists, including Alexander Calder, Willem de Kooning, Edward Hopper (the museum holds his entire estate), Jasper Johns, Louise Nevelson, Georgia O'Keeffe and Claes Oldenburg. Still, the museum's reputation rests mainly on its temporary shows, particularly the exhibition everyone loves to hate, the Whitney Biennial. Held in even-numbered years, the Biennial remains the most prestigious (and controversial) assessment of contemporary art in America. The Whitney's small midtown Altria branch, located in a corporate atrium space across the street from Grand Central Terminal, mounts solo commissioned projects. At the main building, there are free guided tours daily and live performances on select Friday nights. Sarabeth's, the museum's café, is open daily till 4.30pm, offering sandwiches and the like. In 2007, the Whitney confirmed plans to open a separate museum outpost in the new High Line park (*see p118* **Walking the line**).

Planned 2008 exhibitions: 'Kara Walker: My Complement, My Enemy, My Oppressor, My Love' (through 3 Feb), the artist's first full-scale American museum survey, features works ranging from her signature black-paper silhouettes to film animations and more than 100 of her works on paper; 'Chimneys and Towers: Charles Demuth's Late Paintings of Lancaster' (23 Feb-27 Apr); the 2008 Biennial

Exhibition (Mar-May), the Museum's signature survey of contemporary American art, which will be led by Henriette Huldisch and Shamim M Momin. **Other locations**: Whitney Museum of American Art at Altria, 120 Park Avenue, at 42nd Street, Midtown (1-917 663 2453).

Yorkville

Not much remains of the old German and Hungarian immigrant communities that filled Yorkville with delicatessens, beer halls and restaurants. One flashback is the nearly 62-year-old **Heidelberg** (1648 Second Avenue, at 85th Street, 1-212 650 1385), where dirndl-wearing waitresses serve steins of Spaten and platters of sausages from the wurst-meisters at nearby butcher shop Schaller & Weber.

Gracie Mansion (*see below*), at the eastern end of 88th Street, is the only Federal-style mansion in Manhattan, and it's served as New York's official mayoral residence since 1942 – the current mayor, billionaire Michael Bloomberg, famously eschewed this traditional address in favour of his own Beaux Arts mansion at 17 East 79th Street (between Fifth & Madison Avenues).

The **Henderson Place Historic District** (at East End Avenue, between 86th & 87th Streets), one block from Gracie Mansion, consists of two dozen handsome Queen Anne row houses, which were commissioned by furrier and noted real-estate developer John C Henderson. Twenty-four of the 32 houses remain, with the original turrets, double stoops and slate roofs. Nearby, you can also check out what's for sale at the world-famous **Sotheby's** auction house (*see below*).

Although the city is home to approximately 400,000 Muslims, the hugely dramatic **Islamic Cultural Center** (1711 Third Avenue, at 96th Street, 1-212 722 5234), built in 1990, is New York's first major mosque.

Gracie Mansion Conservancy

Carl Schurz Park, 88th Street, at East End Avenue (1-212 570 4751). Subway 4, 5, 6 to 86th Street. **Tours** *Mar-mid Nov* 10am, 11am, 1pm, 2pm Wed. **Admission** $7; $4 seniors, students; free under-12s. Reservations required. Tours last 45mins; same-day reservations not permitted. **No credit cards**. **Map** p406 G18.

The green-shuttered yellow edifice, built in 1799 by Scottish merchant Archibald Gracie, was originally constructed as a country house for the wealthy businessman. Today, the stately house is the focal point of tranquil Carl Schurz Park, named in honour of the German immigrant who became a newspaper editor and US senator. In 2002, Gracie Mansion's living quarters were opened up to public tours for the first time in 60 years. The site is hugely popular with the public, and reservations are a must.

Sotheby's

1334 York Avenue, at 72nd Street (1-212 606 7000/www.sothebys.com). Subway 6 to 68th Street-Hunter College. **Open** 10am-5pm Mon-Sat (hrs change seasonally, call ahead). **Admission** free. **Map** p405 G20.

Sotheby's, with offices from London to Singapore, is the world's most famous auction house. The New York branch regularly holds public sales of antique furniture and jewellery in one lot, and pop-culture memorabilia in another. Spring and autumn see the big sales of modern and contemporary art. Public viewings are held prior to each auction; call or visit Sotheby's website for details of dates and times.

Upper West Side

Housing a population that's older than Downtown's, but more bohemian than the Upper East Side's, this four-mile-long stretch west of Central Park is culturally rich and cosmopolitan. As on the UES, New Yorkers were drawn here during the late 19th century, after the completion of Central Park, the opening of local subway lines and Columbia University's relocation to Morningside Heights. In the 20th century, many central Europeans found refuge here; in the 1960s, Puerto Ricans settled along Amsterdam and Columbus Avenues. These days, a rash of new real-estate development is reducing eye-level evidence of old immigrant life, and the neighbourhood's long-standing intellectual, politically liberal spirit has waned a little as apartment prices have risen. Still, sections of Riverside Drive, West End Avenue and Central Park West continue to rival the grandeur of the East Side's Fifth and Park Avenues.

The gateway to the UWS is **Columbus Circle**, where Broadway meets 59th Street, Eighth Avenue, Central Park South and Central Park West – a rare rotary in a city of right angles. The architecture around it could make anyone's head spin. A 700-ton statue of Christopher Columbus, positioned at the entrance to Central Park, goes almost unnoticed under the **Time Warner Center** (*photo p142*) across the street, which houses the offices of the media conglomerate, along with luxury apartments, hotel accommodation and **Jazz at Lincoln Center**'s (*see p321*) stunning Frederick P Rose Hall. The first seven levels of the enormous glass complex are filled with high-end retailers and gourmet restaurants, including **Per Se** (*see p209*), the four-star venture of celebrated chef Thomas Keller. In autumn 2008, the **Museum of Arts & Design** (*see p148*) plans to open its new digs on the south side of the circle. The circle also bears Donald Trump's signature: he stuck his name on the former Gulf & Western Building when he converted it into the predictably glitzy **Trump International Hotel & Tower**.

The Upper West Side's seat of highbrow culture is **Lincoln Center**, a complex of concert halls and auditoriums built in the 1960s. It is home to the New York Philharmonic, the New York City Ballet and the Metropolitan Opera, along with a host of other notable arts organisations. The big circular fountain in the central plaza is a popular gathering spot, especially in summer, when amateur dancers converge on it to dance alfresco at **Midsummer Night Swing** (*see p263*). Lincoln Center has begun a billion-dollar overhaul that includes a redesign of public spaces, refurbishment of the various ageing halls and construction of new buildings. Nearby you can also check out the **New York Public Library for the Performing Arts** (*see p148*).

The other, much less formal cultural venues on the Upper West Side include the **Makor/Steinhardt Center** (35 W 67th Street, between Central Park West & Columbus Avenue, 1-212 601 1000, www.makor.org), where the public can attend lectures, films, readings and live music performances, often with a folky or Jewish flavour; **Symphony Space** (*see p331*), where the World Music Institute programmes music and dance performances, and rated actors read short stories aloud as part of the Selected Shorts programme; and the **El Taller Latino Americano** (2710 Broadway, at 104th Street, 1-212 665 9460, www.tallerlatino.org), which offers a full range of lively Latin American-oriented cultural events.

Around Sherman and Verdi Squares (from 70th to 73rd Streets, where Broadway and Amsterdam Avenue intersect) classic early 20th-century buildings stand cheek-by-jowl with newer, often mundane high-rises. The jewel is the 1904 **Ansonia Hotel** (2109 Broadway, between 73rd & 74th Streets). Over the years, Enrico Caruso, Babe Ruth and Igor Stravinsky have lived in this Beaux Arts masterpiece, which was also the site of the Continental Baths (the gay bathhouse and cabaret where Bette Midler got her start) and Plato's Retreat (a swinging '70s sex club). On Broadway, the crowded 72nd Street subway station, which opened in 1904, is notable for its Beaux Arts entrance. The **Beacon Theatre** (*see p313*), formerly Manhattan's only rococo 1920s movie palace, is now one of the city's premier mid-size concert venues, presenting an eclectic menu of music, African-American regional theatre and headliner comedy events in its rolling programme.

Once Central Park was finally completed, magnificently tall residential buildings rose up along Central Park West to take advantage of the views. The first of these great buildings was the **Dakota** (at 72nd Street). The fortress-like 1884 luxury apartment building is known as the setting for *Rosemary's Baby* and the site of John Lennon's murder in 1980 (Yoko Ono still lives here). You might recognise **55 Central Park West** (at 66th Street) from the movie *Ghostbusters*. Built in 1930, it was the first art deco building on the block. Heading north on Central Park West, you'll spy the massive twin-towered **San Remo Apartments** (at 74th Street), which also date from 1930. A few blocks north, the **New-York Historical Society** (*see p148*) is the city's oldest museum, built in 1804. Across the street, the glorious **American Museum of Natural History** (*see p148*) has been given an impressive facelift, making even the fossils look fresh again. Dinosaur skeletons, a permanent rainforest exhibit and an IMAX theatre (which shows Oscar-winning nature documentaries) lure adults and school groups. Perhaps most popular is the museum's newest wing, the amazing, glass-enclosed Rose Center for Earth & Space, which includes the totally retooled Hayden Planetarium.

The sizeable cluster of classic groceries and restaurants lining the avenues of the neighbourhood's northern end is where the Upper West Side shops, drinks and eats. To see West Siders in their natural habitat, get in line at the perpetually jammed smoked fish counter at gourmet market **Zabar's** (*see p246*). **Café Lalo** (201 W 83rd Street, between Amsterdam Avenue & Broadway, 1-212 496 6031) is famous for its lavish desserts; **H&H Bagels** (2239 Broadway, at 80th Street, 1-212 595 8003, open 24hrs) is the city's largest bagel purveyor; and the legendary (if scruffy) restaurant and deli **Barney Greengrass** ('the Sturgeon King', 541 Amsterdam Avenue, at 86th Street, 1-212 724 4707) has specialised in smoked fish and what may be the city's best chopped liver, since 1908.

Designed by Central Park's Frederick Law Olmsted, **Riverside Park** is a sinuous stretch of riverbank that starts at 72nd Street and ends at 158th Street, between Riverside Drive and the Hudson River. The stretch of park below 72nd Street, called Riverside Park South, includes a pier and beautiful patches of grass with park benches, and is a particularly peaceful city retreat. You'll probably see yachts, along with several houseboats, berthed at the 79th Street Boat Basin; in the summertime, there's an open-air café in the adjacent park, where New Yorkers unwind with a beer and watch the sun set over the Hudson River. Several sites provide havens for quiet reflection. The **Soldiers' and**

Sailors' Monument (89th Street, at Riverside Drive), built in 1902 by French sculptor Paul EM DuBoy, honours Union soldiers who died in the Civil War, and a 1908 memorial (100th Street, at Riverside Drive) pays tribute to fallen firemen. **General Grant National Memorial** (aka Grant's Tomb), the mausoleum of former president Ulysses S Grant, is also located in the park. Across the street stands the towering Gothic-style **Riverside Church** (Riverside Drive, at 120th Street, 1-212 870 6700, www.theriversidechurchny.org), built in 1930. The tower contains the world's largest carillon: 74 bells, played every Sunday at 10.30am.

Sightseeing

American Museum of Natural History/Rose Center for Earth & Space

Central Park West, at 79th Street (1-212 769 5100/www.amnh.org). Subway B, C to 81st Street-Museum of Natural History. **Open** 10am-5.45pm daily. **Admission** suggested donation $14; $10.50 seniors, students; $8 2-12s; free under-2s. **Credit** AmEx, MC, V. **Map** p405 C/D19.

Home to the largest and arguably most fabulous collection of dinosaur fossils in the world, AMNH's fourth-floor dino halls have been blowing people's minds for decades. Roughly 80% of the bones on display were actually dug out of the ground by Indiana Jones types. The thrills begin when you cross the threshold of the Theodore Roosevelt Rotunda, where you're confronted with a towering barosaurus that's rearing high on its hind legs to protect its young from an attacking allosaurus – an impressive welcome to the world's largest museum of its kind. During the museum's mid 1990s renovation, several specimens were remodelled to incorporate discoveries made during that time. The Tyrannosaurus rex, for instance, was once believed to have walked upright, Godzilla-style; it now stalks prey with its head lowered and tail raised parallel to the ground.

The rest of the museum is equally dramatic. The newly opened Hall of Human Origins boasts a fine display of your old cousins, the Neanderthals. The Hall of Biodiversity examines world ecosystems and environmental preservation, and a life-size model of a blue whale hangs from the cavernous ceiling of the Hall of Ocean Life. The impressive Hall of Meteorites was brushed up and reorganised in 2003. The space's focal point is Ahnighito, the largest iron meteor on display anywhere in the world, weighing in at 34 tons (more than 30,000kg).

The spectacular $210 million Rose Center for Earth & Space – dazzling to come upon at night – is a giant silvery globe where you can discover the universe via 3-D shows in the Hayden Planetarium and light shows in the Big Bang Theater. An IMAX theatre screens larger-than-life nature programmes, and you can always learn something new from the innovative temporary exhibitions, an easily accessible research library (with vast photo and print archives), several cool gift shops and friendly, helpful staff.

General Grant National Memorial

Riverside Drive, at 122nd Street (1-212 666 1640). Subway 1, 9 to 125th Street. **Open** 9am-5pm daily. **Admission** free. **Map** p407 B14.

Who's buried in Grant's Tomb? No one, as it turns out – the crypts of Civil War hero and 18th president Ulysses S Grant and his wife, Julia, are in full above-ground view. Note: the memorial is closed on Thanksgiving, Christmas and New Year's Day.

Museum of Arts & Design

From autumn 2008: 2 Columbus Circle, at Broadway (1-212 956 3535/www.madmuseum.org). Subway A, B, C, D, 1 to 59th Street-Columbus Circle. **Opens** autumn 2008. **Map** p404 C22.

Formerly the American Crafts Museum, this is the country's leading museum of contemporary crafts in clay, cloth, glass, metal and wood. It changed its name to emphasise the harmonious relationships between art, design and craft. The museum plans eventually to move to this new home in the former Huntington Hartford building on Columbus Circle in autumn 2008, which will give it double the exhibition space and also a new study centre.

New-York Historical Society

170 Central Park West, between 76th & 77th Streets (1-212 873 3400/www.nyhistory.org). Subway B, C to 81st Street-Museum of Natural History. **Open** 10am-6pm Tue-Sun. **Admission** $10; $5 seniors, students; free under-12s when accompanied by an adult. **No credit cards**. **Map** p405 D20.

New York's oldest museum, founded in 1804, was one of America's first cultural and educational institutions. Highlights in the vast Henry Luce III Center for the Study of American Culture include George Washington's Valley Forge camp cot, a complete series of the extant watercolours from Audubon's Birds of America and the world's single largest collection of Tiffany lamps.

Planned 2008 exhibitions: 'French Founding Father: Lafayettes' Return to Washington's America' (until August 2008).

New York Public Library for the Performing Arts

40 Lincoln Center Plaza, at 65th Street (1-212 870 1630/www.nypl.org). Subway 1 to 66th Street-Lincoln Center. **Open** noon-6pm Tue, Wed, Fri, Sat; noon-8pm Thur. **Admission** free. **Map** p405 C21.

One of the world's great research centres for the performing arts, this institution houses a seemingly endless collection of films, letters, manuscripts, video, plus half a million sound recordings. Visitors can browse through books, scores and recordings, or attend a concert or lecture.

Morningside Heights

Morningside Heights runs from 110th Street (also known west of Central Park as Cathedral Parkway) to 125th Street, between Morningside Park and the Hudson River. The Cathedral

The **American Museum of Natural History**: rattling dem bones since 1869.

Church of St John the Divine and the campus of Columbia University exert considerable influence over the surrounding neighbourhood.

One of the oldest universities in the US, **Columbia** was initially chartered in 1754 as King's College (the name changed after the Revolutionary War). It moved to its present location in 1897. Thanks to the large student population of Columbia and its sister school, Barnard College, the area has an academic feel, with bookshops, inexpensive restaurants and coffeehouses lining Broadway between 110th and 116th Streets. **Mondel Chocolates** (2913 Broadway, at 114th Street, 1-212 864 2111) was the chocolatier of choice for the late Katharine Hepburn, and **Tom's Restaurant** (2880 Broadway, at 112th Street, 1-212 864 6137) served as a backdrop during exterior shots for the countless diner scenes on TV's perennially popular sitcom *Seinfeld*.

If you wander into Columbia's campus entrance at 116th Street, you won't fail to miss the impressive **Low Memorial Building**: it's the only one modelled on Rome's Pantheon. The former library, completed in 1897, is now an administrative building. The real attraction, however, is the student body sprawled out on its steps (or lawns out front), catching rays and relaxing between classes.

The **Cathedral Church of St John the Divine** (*see below*) is the seat of the Episcopal Diocese of New York. Known affectionately by locals as St John the Unfinished, the enormous cathedral (already larger than Notre Dame in Paris) will undergo hammering and chiselling well into this century. Just behind is the green expanse of **Morningside Park** (from 110th to 123rd Streets, between Morningside Avenue & Morningside Drive) and across the street is the **Hungarian Pastry Shop** (1030 Amsterdam Avenue, between 110th & 111th Streets, 1-212 866 4230), a great place for coffee, dessert and mingling with cute Columbia co-eds.

Cathedral Church of St John the Divine

1047 Amsterdam Avenue, at 112th Street (1-212 316 7540/www.stjohndivine.org). Subway B, C, 1 to 110th Street-Cathedral Parkway. **Open** 8am-6pm daily. **Admission** suggested donation $5; $4 seniors, students. **Credit** MC, V. **Map** p406 C15.

Construction on 'St John the Unfinished' began in 1892 in Romanesque style, was put on hold for a Gothic Revival redesign in 1911, then ground to a halt in 1941, when the US entered World War II. It resumed in earnest in 1979, but a fire in 2001 destroyed the church's gift shop and damaged two 17th-century Italian tapestries, which has delayed completion further. In addition to Sunday services, the cathedral hosts concerts and tours. It bills itself as a place for all people – and it means it. Annual events include both winter and summer solstice celebrations; the Blessing of the Animals during the Feast of St Francis, which draws pets and their people from all over the city; and (would you believe it?) the Blessing of the Bikes, which actually kicks off the bicycle season each spring. *Photo p150.*

On Earth as it is in Heaven at the **Cathedral Church of St John the Divine**. *See p149.*

Harlem

Decades after the '20s stopped roaring and the Depression consumed the '30s, a story still periodically breaks about a 'New Harlem Renaissance'. As with most rumours of second comings, it's often driven by wishful thinking. After all, Harlem has had its ups and downs since its golden age, when jazz was king and the neighbourhood's clubs and ballrooms were the most throbbing in the city. Yet Harlem's stock has risen noticeably in the past decade. The infusion of money is obvious just from a walk along 125th Street, where the sidewalk vendors have (for the most part) been roughly supplanted by chain stores, and from the increasing number of refurbished brownstones. This financial jolt has also invigorated the neighbourhood's nightlife, as seen in the variety of bars and clubs that have opened, reopened or been renovated in the past few years. Anyone who feels hemmed in by the Meatpacking District's velvet ropes or has grown weary of Williamsburg as NYC's alternative stomping ground really should investigate Harlem. Here, ancestral beats bounce between hip hop, zouk and reggae. Sundays spill sweet gospel sounds and enticing biscuit aromas on to house-front steps that have seen poets, prophets, preachers and even Presidents come and go.

Harlem has long been the cultural capital of black America and home to such luminaries as Duke Ellington, Thurgood Marshall and Jacob Lawrence. The neighbourhood – which runs from the East River to the Hudson and from 110th Street to the 160s – saw its once-glorious reputation overshadowed by images of poverty and crime during the second half of the 20th century. Today, Harlem can no longer be described as the neglected 'raisin in the sun', as it was in Langston Hughes's famous poem 'Harlem: A Dream Deferred' (1959). The poet's line inspired Lorraine Hansberry's eponymous groundbreaking play, the first black work on Broadway. And it was not just the powder keg of the 1960s that his words presaged, either. The Harlem Renaissance of the 1920s and '30s – the cultural explosion that gave us the likes of Langston Hughes, Zora Neale Hurston and Duke Ellington – continues to live on in the collective memory and has helped spur a new Harlem renaissance, jump-started largely by a rash of private real-estate investment and government support for local entrepreneurs and business development.

Harlem first began life as a suburb for well-to-do whites in the 19th century, after the West Side railroad was built. Around 1900, plans to extend the subway along Lenox Avenue to 145th Street triggered a housing boom that went bust just a few years later. White landlords, previously unwilling to lease to blacks, were now desperate for tenants, and, slowly but surely, changed their leasing habits. Blacks reportedly paid up to $5 more per month than whites at this time to rent similar flats. Yet it was a watershed for the city's resident African-American community: for the first time in NYC's history they had an opportunity to live in well-built homes in a stable community. By 1914, the black population of Harlem had risen well above 50,000.

The area is blessed with stately brownstones in varying stages of renovation, often right next to blocks of towering public housing. Thanks to a thriving black middle-class community, Harlem's cultural and religious institutions are seeing renewed interest and funding, and new commercial enterprise abounds. Yet, the neighbourhood's history remains visible. Some of the fabled locations from the original Harlem Renaissance have been restored, and while many stages in the celebrated jazz clubs, theatres and ballrooms have been replaced by pulpits, the buildings still stand.

West Harlem

West Harlem, between Fifth and St Nicholas Avenues, is the Harlem of popular imagination, and 125th Street ('the one-two-five') is easily its most vital lifeline. Start at the crossroads: the 274,000-square-foot **Harlem USA Mall** (300 W 125th Street, between Adam Clayton Powell Jr Boulevard/Seventh Avenue & Frederick Douglass Boulevard/Eighth Avenue, www.harlem-usa.com). The mall features a Magic Johnson multiplex movie theatre (1-212 665 6923) and the well-stocked Hue-Man Bookstore (1-212 665 7400), specialising in African-American titles, plus the usual retail megastores. Across the street is the Apollo Theater, which still hosts live concerts, a syndicated television programme and the classic Amateur Night held every Wednesday. A few blocks west, other touches of old Harlem linger: **Showman's Bar** (375 W 125th Street, between St Nicholas & Morningside Avenues, 1-212 864 8941), a mecca for jazz lovers, and the reconstituted **Cotton Club** (656 W 125th Street, at Riverside Drive, 1-212 663 7980), which hosts gospel brunches and evening jazz and blues sessions.

To the east of the mall is the **Lenox Lounge** (*see p323*), still cooking with old-school jazz. A well-regarded fine arts centre, the **Studio Museum in Harlem** (*see p152*) exhibits work by many local artists. Just a block away is the vibrant **Harlem Lanes** (*see p336*); there are 24 gleaming lanes here and you aren't likely to find cheaper bowling anywhere in Manhattan. The first-floor family area caters

Fall of the wild

Every autumn, sharp-eyed park strollers might notice a slight upturn in the number and variety of their fauna sightings. Sara Hobel, director of the Urban Park Rangers, calls it the back-to-school syndrome. 'Summer is over and people no longer want the burden of maintaining an animal,' she says. 'So in the fall, we see a lot of them dumped in the park.' Lest you think that by 'animal' Hobel means Fido and Kitty, she points out that there is a veritable Animal Planet of exotic creatures lurking in New York city parks – an underworld of abandoned animals. Most were once pets that fell out of favour with their owners or grew too big to keep. Compared with them, Hobel notes, the city's feral dogs and cats seem downright manageable.

There are ferrets (which are illegal in New York), ball pythons and boa constrictors. Even the American alligator (an endangered species) has been known to make a rare appearance. The scale of the problem was made clear for Hobel when the pool at W 103rd Street was drained during its restoration: 'Oh my God! We were talking 15-pound koi. And huge, huge crayfish!'

These 'non-natives' can prove tricky to round up, according to Matthew Brown, supervisor of Central Park's Soil & Water Lab. He mentions one of the more peculiar incidents from last year, when a full-grown male iguana was spotted sunning on a rock in the 59th Street lake, near the shore. To snare the lazing lizard, some of Brown's crew approached it from one side in a boat, while the rest waited on land in case the beast made a mad dash for it. 'It was just chillin',' Brown recalls before noting that the team proceeded with due caution nevertheless. 'When an iguana gets going with its claws, you don't want to get in its way.'

Hobel has observed that another dramatic jump in the parks' animal population takes place about six weeks after Valentine's Day. 'People break up and then they don't want the pet,' she says, explaining that this usually means puppies that haven't been spayed or neutered. Still, they find the occasional caiman. Brown feels that, in fairness, people may actually be trying to do the right thing: 'They probably think it's better than flushing them down the toilet.'

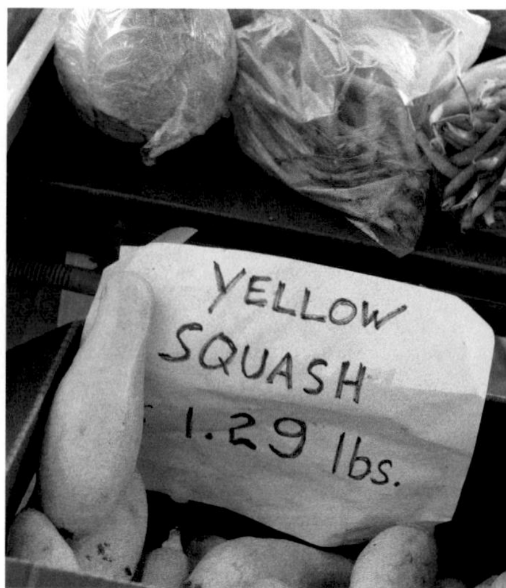

mostly to birthday parties. If you don't have kids in tow, head upstairs to the grown-ups' lounge: it's hip and cosy, featuring a bar, plush jewel-toned banquettes and exposed brick.

The luxurious offices of former president Bill Clinton are at 55 W 125th Street (between Fifth Avenue & Malcolm X Boulevard/Lenox Avenue). Harlem's rich history is preserved in the archives of the **Schomburg Center for Research in Black Culture** (*see below*). This branch of the New York Public Library contains more than five million documents, artefacts, films and prints relating to the cultures of peoples of African descent, with a strong emphasis on the African-American experience. Nearby, the **Abyssinian Baptist Church** (*see below*) is celebrated for its history, political activism and rousing gospel choir.

Feeling a touch hungry? Be sure to sample the smothered pork chops and collard greens with fatback at **Sylvia's** (328 Malcolm X Boulevard/Lenox Avenue, between 126th & 127th Streets, 1-212 996 0660), Harlem's tourist-packed soul-food specialist.

Walk off some of your meal with a stroll around **Marcus Garvey Park** (aka Mount Morris Park, 120th to 124th Streets, between Madison Avenue & Mount Morris Park West), where the brownstone revival is in full swing.

Abyssinian Baptist Church

132 W 138th Street, between Malcolm X Boulevard (Lenox Avenue) & Adam Clayton Powell Jr Boulevard (Seventh Avenue) (1-212 862 7474/www.abyssinian.org). Subway 2, 3 to 135th Street. **Open** 9am-5pm Mon-Fri. **Admission** free. **Map** p407 E11.

One of Harlem's most famous churches, the Abyssinian was where Harlem's charismatic and controversial congressman Adam Clayton Powell Jr preached in the 1960s. It harbours a small museum dedicated to Powell, the first black member of New York's City Council.

Schomburg Center for Research in Black Culture

515 Malcolm X Boulevard (Lenox Avenue), at 135th Street (1-212 491 2200). Subway 2, 3 to 135th Street. **Open** noon-8pm Tue, Wed; noon-6pm Thur, Fri; 10am-6pm Sat. **Admission** free. **Map** p407 D12.

An extraordinary trove of vintage literature and historical memorabilia relating to black culture and the African diaspora is housed in this institution first founded in 1926 by its curator, bibliophile Arturo Alfonso Schomburg. The centre also hosts jazz concerts, films, lectures and tours.

Studio Museum in Harlem

144 W 125th Street, between Malcolm X Boulevard (Lenox Avenue) & Adam Clayton Powell Jr Boulevard (Seventh Avenue) (1-212 864 4500/www.studiomuseum.org). Subway 2, 3 to 125th Street. **Open** noon-6pm Wed-Fri, Sun; 10am-6pm Sat. Guided tours by appointment. **Admission** suggested donation $7; $3 seniors, students; free under-12s. Free 1st Sat of mth. **No credit cards**. **Map** p407 D13.

When the Studio Museum opened in 1968, it was the first black fine-arts museum in the country, and it remains the place to go for historical insight into African-American art and that of the African diaspora. Under the leadership of director Lowery Stokes Sims (formerly of the Met) and chief curator Thelma Golden (formerly of the Whitney), this favourite has evolved into the city's most exciting showcase for African-American artists. *Photos pp154-155.*

Harlem. *See p150.*

Mount Morris & Strivers' Row

Harlem's historic districts continue to gentrify. The **Mount Morris Historic District** (from 119th to 124th Streets, between Malcolm X Boulevard/Lenox Avenue & Mount Morris Park West) contains charming brownstones and a collection of religious buildings in a variety of architectural styles. These days, new boutiques, restaurants and pavement cafés dot the walk down the double-wide **Malcolm X Boulevard** (Lenox Avenue). **Harlemade** (No.174, between 118th & 119th Streets, 1-212 987 2500, www.harlemade.com) sells T-shirts with Afro- and Harlem-centric messages and images, plus postcards other neighbourhood memorabilia.

Another area with a rich and varied historic past is **Strivers' Row**, also known as the **St Nicholas Historic District**. Running from 138th to 139th Streets, between Adam Clayton Powell Jr Boulevard (Seventh Avenue) and Frederick Douglass Boulevard (Eighth Avenue), these blocks of majestic houses were developed in 1891 by David H King Jr and designed by three different architects, including Stanford White. In the 1920s, prominent members of the black community, the legendary Eubie Blake and WC Handy among them, lived in this area. Now, more upwardly mobile strivers are moving in, and so are stylish boutiques such as **N** (114 W 116th Street, between Malcolm X Boulevard/Lenox Avenue & Adam Clayton Powell Jr Boulevard/Seventh Avenue, 1-212 961 1036, www.nharlemnewyork.com), which sells contemporary clothing and accessories, some by African-American designers. Along the way, there's plenty of good eating: **Londel's Supper Club** (2620 Frederick Douglass Boulevard/Eighth Avenue, between 139th & 140th Streets, 1-212 234 0601), owned by former police officer Londel Davis, serves some of the best blackened catfish in town. The neighbourhood comes alive after dark, especially at the not-to-be-missed **St Nick's Pub** (773 St Nicholas Avenue, at 149th Street, 1-212 283 9728), where you can hear live jazz pumping every night (except Tuesday) for a small cover charge.

Heading east on West 116th Street, you'll pass through a dizzying smörgåsbord of cultures. There's a West African flavour between Malcolm X and Adam Clayton Powell Jr Boulevards (Lenox & Seventh Avenues), especially at the Senegalese restaurant **Le Baobab** (No.120, 1-212 864 4700). On the north side of the street is one of the Reverend Al Sharpton's favourite restaurants, **Amy Ruth's** (No.113, 1-212 280 8779). While tour buses may favour nearby Sylvia's, locals who know better head to this cosy restaurant instead. Each dish is named after a prominent African-American New Yorker; try the Terry Rivers, honey-dipped fried chicken. Continue east, past the silver-domed **Masjid Malcolm Shabazz** (No.102, 1-212 662 2200), the mosque of Malcolm X's ministry, to the **Malcolm Shabazz Harlem Market** (No.52, 1-212 987 8131), an outdoor bazaar that buzzes with vendors, most from West Africa, selling clothes, jewellery, sculpture and other traditional goods from covered stalls.

East Harlem

East of Fifth Avenue is East Harlem, sometimes called Spanish Harlem but better known to its primarily Puerto Rican residents as El Barrio. North of 96th Street and east of Madison Avenue, El Barrio moves to a different beat. Its main east–west cross-street, East 116th Street, shows signs of a recent influx of Mexican immigrants. From 96th to 106th Streets, a little touch of East Village-style bohemia can be detected in such places as **Carlito's Café y Galería** (1701 Lexington Avenue, between 106th & 107th Streets, 1-212 534 7168), which presents music, art and poetry performances. Nearby is the **Graffiti Hall of Fame** (106th Street, between Madison & Park Avenues), a schoolyard that celebrates great old- and new-school 'writers'. Be sure to check out **El Museo del Barrio** (*see p139*), Spanish Harlem's community museum.

Hamilton Heights

Hamilton Heights (named after Alexander Hamilton, who owned a farm and estate here in 1802) extends from 125th Street to the Trinity Cemetery at 155th Street, between Riverside Drive and St Nicholas Avenue. The former factory neighbourhood developed after the West Side elevated train was built in the early 20th century. Today, it's notable for the elegant turn-of-the-20th-century row houses in the **Hamilton Heights Historic District**, running from 140th to 145th Streets, between Amsterdam and Edgecomb Avenues – just beyond the Gothic Revival-style campus of the City College of New York (Convent Avenue, at 138th Street).

Washington Heights & Inwood

The area from West 155th Street to Dyckman (200th) Street is called Washington Heights; venture north of that and you're in Inwood, Manhattan's northernmost neighbourhood, where the Harlem and Hudson Rivers converge. An ever-growing number of artists and young families are relocating to these parts, attracted by the art deco buildings, big parks, hilly streets and (comparatively) low rents.

The area's main claim to fame is the **Morris-Jumel Mansion** (*see p155*), a stunning Palladian-style mansion that served as a swanky headquarters for George Washington during the autumn of 1776.

Since the 1920s, waves of immigrants have settled in Washington Heights. In the post-World War II era, many German-Jewish refugees (including among them Henry Kissinger, Dr Ruth Westheimer and Max Frankel, a former executive editor of *The New York Times*) moved to the western edge of the neighbourhood. Broadway once housed a sizeable Greek population – opera singer Maria Callas lived here in her youth. But in the last few decades, the southern and eastern parts of the area have become predominantly Spanish-speaking due to a large population of Dominican settlers. The **Hispanic Society of America** (*see p155*) has its headquarters here.

A trek along Fort Washington Avenue, from about 173rd Street to Fort Tryon Park, puts you in the heart of what is now called **Hudson Heights** – the posh area of Washington Heights.

Start at the **George Washington Bridge**, the city's only bridge across the Hudson River. A pedestrian walkway (also a popular route for cyclists) allows for dazzling Manhattan views. Under the bridge on the New York side is a diminutive lighthouse – those who know the children's book *The Little Red Lighthouse and the Great Gray Bridge*, by Hildegarde Swift, will recognise it immediately. When the 85-year-old landmark wasn't needed any more (after the bridge was completed) fans of the book rallied against plans to put it up for auction. To see it up close, look for the footpath on the west side of the interchange on the Henry Hudson Parkway at about 170th Street. If you need to

refuel, stop at **Bleu Evolution** (808 W 187th Street, between Fort Washington & Pinehurst Avenues, 1-212 928 6006) for a downtown-style vibe, or hold out for the lovely **New Leaf Café** (1 Margaret Corbin Drive, near Park Drive, 1-212 568 5323) within the Frederick Law Olmsted-designed Fort Tryon Park.

At the northern edge of the park are the **Cloisters** (*see below*), a museum built back in 1938 using segments of five medieval cloisters shipped from Europe by the Rockefeller clan. It houses the Metropolitan Museum of Art's permanent medieval art collection, including the exquisite Unicorn Tapestries (c1500).

Inwood stretches from Dyckman Street up to 218th Street, the last residential block in Manhattan. Dyckman buzzes with streetlife and nightclubs from river to river, but, north of that, the island narrows considerably and the parks along the western shoreline culminate in the seclusion of **Inwood Hill Park**, another Frederick Law Olmsted legacy. Some believe that this is the location of the legendary 1626 transaction between Peter Minuit and the Native American Lenapes for the purchase of a strip of land called Manahatta – a plaque at the south-west corner of the ballpark near 214th Street marks the purported spot. The 196-acre refuge contains the island's last swathes of virgin forest and salt marsh. Today, with a bit of imagination, you can hike over the hilly terrain, liberally scattered with massive glacier-deposited boulders (called erratics), and picture Manhattan as it was before development. In recent years, the city's Parks Department has used the densely wooded area as a fledging spot for newly hatched bald eagles.

Studio Museum in Harlem. *See p152.*

The Cloisters

Fort Tryon Park, Fort Washington Avenue, at Margaret Corbin Plaza (1-212 923 3700/www.metmuseum.org). Subway A to 190th Street, then M4 bus or follow Margaret Corbin Drive north, for about the length of 5 city blocks, to the museum. **Open** *Mar-Oct* 9.30am-5.15pm Tue-Sun. *Nov-Feb* 9.30am-4.45pm Tue-Sun. **Admission** suggested donation (incl admission to the Metropolitan Museum of Art on the same day) $20; $10 seniors, students; free under-12s (must be accompanied by an adult). **Credit** AmEx, DC, Disc, MC, V. **Map** p409 B3.

Set in a lovely park overlooking the Hudson River, the Cloisters houses the Met's medieval art and architecture collections. A path winds through the peaceful grounds to a castle that seems to have survived from the Middle Ages. It was built a mere 70 years ago, using pieces of five medieval French cloisters. Be sure to check out the famous Unicorn Tapestries, the 12th-century Fuentidueña Chapel and the *Annunciation Triptych* by Robert Campin.

Hispanic Society of America

Audubon Terrace, Broadway, between 155th & 156th Streets (1-212 926 2234/www.hispanicsociety.org). Subway 1 to 157th Street. **Open** 10am-4.30pm Tue-Sat. **Admission** free. **Map** p408 B9.

The Hispanic Society has the largest assemblage of Spanish art and manuscripts outside Spain. Look for two portraits by Goya and the lobby's bas-relief of Don Quixote. The collection is dominated by religious artefacts, including 16th-century tombs from the monastery of San Francisco in Cuéllar, Spain. Also on display are decorative art objects and thousands of black-and-white photographs that document life in Spain and Latin America from the mid 19th century to the present. Bear in mind that the library is closed on Sundays.

Morris-Jumel Mansion

65 Jumel Terrace, between 160th & 162nd Streets (1-212 923 8008/www.morrisjumel.org). Subway C to 163rd Street-Amsterdam Avenue. **Open** 10am-4pm Wed-Sun. **Admission** $4; $3 seniors, students; free under-12s. **No credit cards**. **Map** p408 C8.

Built in 1765, Manhattan's only surviving pre-Revolutionary manse was originally the heart of a 130-acre estate that stretched from river to river (on the grounds, a stone marker points south with the legend 'new york, 11 miles'). George Washington planned the Battle of Harlem Heights here in 1776, after the British colonel Roger Morris moved out. The handsome 18th-century Palladian-style villa offers fantastic views. Its former driveway is now Sylvan Terrace, which boasts the single largest continuous stretch (one block in total) of old wooden houses in all of Manhattan.

Brooklyn

Cross the East River for a jaunt into a blooming and booming borough.

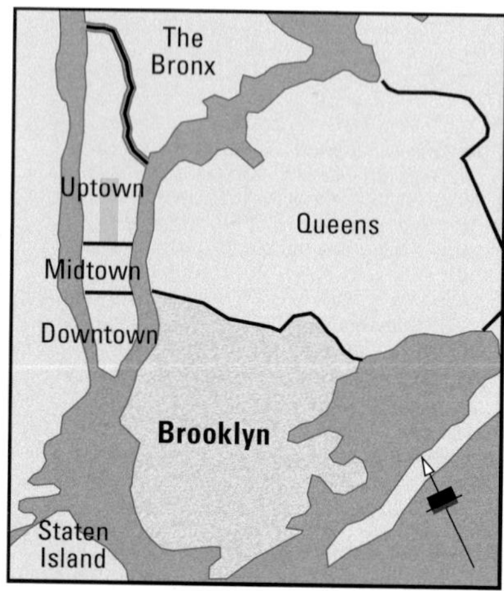

Maps p410 & p411

It's hard to believe that there was a time when Brooklyn, at least to Manhattanites, was akin to a distant relative you visited rarely, if ever. Now many consider this booming borough (which would be America's fourth-largest city if it were still independent) to be New York City's own Left Bank – a haven for novelists, poets, musicians and anyone else with artistic inclinations. Even though Brooklyn is no longer a much cheaper place to live than Manhattan (rents have been skyrocketing over the past five years), people are still flocking to its beautiful, tree-lined neighbourhoods, which have enough historical charm, cultural riches, and dining, drinking and shopping options to make Manhattanites a bit envious. In fact, many areas, especially Williamsburg and Cobble Hill, have become destinations for residents citywide, looking to explore beyond their own familiar nabes.

Thanks in large part to a hot real estate market, Brooklyn is a borough on the move – in both good and bad ways. Large-scale developments are under way everywhere. The biggest (and most controversial) project is **Atlantic Yards** (*see p43*), a real-estate venture designed by Frank Gehry for developer Bruce Ratner. For now, the development has the municipal green light, which has outraged thousands of locals, many of whom have been bought out of their homes and businesses by Ratner's company. His project is to be situated between Prospect Heights and Fort Greene, and is set to feature 16 new skyscrapers and an 18,000-seat stadium for the New York Nets team. Though some residents view projects like Atlantic Yards as a welcome example of the area's economic, social and cultural growth, others are fearsome of the resulting traffic, congestion and crowds.

Progress, though, has been in Brooklyn's lifeblood since Europeans first settled here in the early 1600s. Brooklyn (originally the Dutch settlement of Breuckelen) was an independent city from 1834 until 1898, when it became an official borough. Today, the region's diversity is still reflected in its long-standing neighbourhoods. From Russian enclaves in Brighton Beach and the Polish residents of Greenpoint to the Italians in Bensonhurst, Chinese expats in Sunset Park, and both Arab and Puerto Rican immigrants in Cobble Hill, Brooklyn is a multi-ethnic borough, with almost 40 per cent of its residents born outside the United States.

For more details on what the borough has to offer, contact the **Brooklyn Tourism & Visitor Center** (Brooklyn Borough Hall, 209 Joralemon Street, between Court & Adams Streets, 1-718 802 3846, www.visitbrooklyn.org).

Brooklyn Heights & Dumbo

One of the borough's toniest areas, **Brooklyn Heights**, developed a reputation early on as an aristocratic neighbourhood, known for its elite customs and manners. It has been historically populated by prominent bankers and lawyers, who came here partly due to the proximity to Wall Street. That's still true today, although many others flock here because of its stunning architectural beauty. This neighbourhood has had its fair share of famous residents, including Norman Mailer, Truman Capote, Arthur Miller, WH Auden and Bob Dylan.

The streets within **Brooklyn Heights** – particularly Cranberry, Hicks, Pierrepont and Willow – are lined with leafy trees and well-preserved, picturesque Greek Revival and Italianate row houses dating from the 1820s, a legacy of the area having been designated the borough's first historic district in 1965. The entire neighbourhood is so gorgeous, so seemingly untouched by time, that it resembles a film set. It's hard to imagine a more perfect scene for a stroll, romantic or otherwise.

Both Henry and Montague Streets are crammed with shops, restaurants and bars. At the very end of Montague, the **Brooklyn Heights Promenade** offers spectacular waterfront views of Manhattan, especially on the Fourth of July when the Macy's firework display lights up the entire harbour sky. Just a short jaunt away is the venerable **Brooklyn Bridge** (*see p158*), a marvel of 19th-century engineering that connected two cities and became an important symbol of progress. The first to use steel suspension cables, the bridge was the vision of German-born civil engineer John Augustus Roebling, who died before it was completed. The 5,989-foot-long transverse, which connects downtown Brooklyn with Manhattan, offers striking views of the Statue of Liberty and New York Harbor. If time permits, it's well worth a walk or bike ride across the pedestrian walkway. If you prefer your history beneath street-level, a stop at the **New York Transit Museum** (*see p158*) – housed in a former subway station – is a must. Visitors can learn about the complex engineering and construction feats that helped establish the city's century-old subway system.

More remnants of bygone Breuckelen are at the **Brooklyn Historical Society** (*see p158*) building, which, when completed in 1881, was the first in New York to use locally produced terracotta on its façade. The seat of local government, the grand **Borough Hall** (209 Joralemon Street, at Court Street, www.brooklyn-usa.org), stands as a monument to Brooklyn's past incarnation as an entirely independent municipality. Completed in 1851, the Greek Revival edifice – later crowned with a Victorian cupola – was renovated in the late 1980s. The building is linked to the **New York State Supreme Court** (360 Adams Street, between Joralemon Street & Tech Place) by **Cadman Plaza** (from Prospect Street to Tech Place, between Cadman Plaza East & Cadman Plaza West). Close by, at the junction of Court and Remsen Streets, you can buy fresh produce and flowers on Tuesdays, Thursdays and Saturdays throughout most of the year.

Nearby, in contrast to the stately, historic Heights is the always gritty (but increasingly gentrified) waterside neighbourhood of **Dumbo** (Down Under the Manhattan Bridge Overpass). Once a community of starving artists and warehouse businesses, these days Dumbo is filled, for better or worse, with million-dollar apartments and high-end design shops. Yet it has maintained its character, at least thus far, and the area's spectacular views remain the same, of course – of the Statue of Liberty, the lower Manhattan skyline, and the Brooklyn and Manhattan Bridges – which are most stunning at sunset. It's no wonder that so many fashion photographers flock to shoot their models here.

First-rate views are to be had below the Brooklyn Bridge at the **Fulton Ferry Landing**, which juts out over the East River at Old Fulton and Water Streets, and is close to two lovely refurbished parks: **Empire-Fulton Ferry State Park** and **Brooklyn Bridge Park** (riverside, between the Manhattan & Brooklyn Bridges). Also at the water's edge is a dock for the **New York Water Taxi** (1-212 742 1969, www.nywatertaxi.com), an affordable and picturesque way to travel from Manhattan to Williamsburg, Red Hook and points between.

Along the same pier is the posh and pricey **River Café** (1 Water Street, at Old Fulton Street, 1-718 522 5200); and the **Brooklyn Ice Cream Factory** (Fulton Ferry Landing, 1 Water Street, 1-718 246 3963), located in a 1920s fireboat house and surely one of the best ice-cream spots in NYC. Right next to the Factory, docked at the pier, is one of the borough's great

Cheap date

New Yorkers have been crossing the **Brooklyn Bridge** since 1883 – now it's your turn. Standing in City Hall Park, just outside the Brooklyn Bridge-City Hall subway entrance, face east and head for the pedestrian walkway. Two hours before sunset is the most romantic time to go. The 3,460ft suspension bridge was the first to use steel for its stunning web of cable wires and was the longest suspension bridge in the world when it opened. As you near the Brooklyn side the path splits; stay to the right and go down the stairs to the street. You'll come out on Cadman Plaza West. Stay to the right and walk (back towards Manhattan) to Old Fulton Street. Now for your reward: on the north side of Old Fulton Street you'll find Brooklyn stalwart **Grimaldi's Pizza** (No.19, 1-718 858 4300, www.grimaldis.com). A pie from the 800-degree, brick-walled coal oven at this old-fashioned place is a favourite among locals. Further down check out the **Brooklyn Ice Cream Factory** (Old Fulton Street, at Water Street, 1-718 246 3963); the parlour's recipe is as old-fashioned as its 1920s fireboat-house building – all cream and no eggs.

cultural jewels, **Bargemusic** (Fulton Ferry Landing, 1-718 624 2083). For the past 30 years, chamber music has been performed year-round on this 100-foot steel barge, which dates to 1899.

The visual artists who flocked en masse to the cobblestone streets and red-brick warehouses of **Dumbo** in the 1970s and '80s can still be found here today – and you can still get lost among the area's quiet side streets. And there are galleries to visit, most of which support the work of emerging artists, including **Smack Mellon** (92 Plymouth Street, at Washington Street, 1-718 834 8761) and **Wessel + O'Connor Fine Art** (111 Front Street, Suite 200, between Washington & Adams Streets, 1-718 596 1700). There's also the worthy **dumbo arts center** (30 Washington Street, between Plymouth & Water Streets, 1-718 694 0831), which continues to promote community artists through its gallery and sponsorship of the **d.u.m.b.o. art under the bridge** festival (*see p265*), held mid October. **St Ann's Warehouse** (38 Water Street, between Dock & Main Streets, 1-718 254 8779).

Dining in the area is a treat, with restaurants such as the famous **Grimaldi's** (19 Old Fulton Street, between Front & Water Streets, 1-718 858 4300), where pizza lovers can share a pie from the coal-fired oven. Look across the street from Grimaldi's and you'll see the original building of the *Brooklyn Daily Eagle*, founded in 1841, with the first few floors used as the Eagle Warehouse (it's now a luxury loft condo building). The poet Walt Whitman worked at the newspaper until he was finally fired for his lefty political views, and he also printed the first ten pages of his influential *Leaves of Grass* here.

For more substantial, upscale fare in the nabe, head to **Five Front** (5 Front Street, 1-718 625 5559), tucked under the Brooklyn Bridge, for jumbo lump crab-cake or goat's cheese gnocchi. **Bubby's** (1 Main Street, 1-718 222 0666) is right on the waterfront and offers comfort food in a cavernous, kid-friendly setting. **Superfine** (126 Front Street, 1-718 243 9005) is both a first-rate restaurant and a chic bar, but if you prefer sweets to sweet vermouth, head down to the always-packed **Jacques Torres Chocolate Heaven** shop (*see p245*) for its fabulous cocoa or one of the premium chocolates, made right on the premises. (Drool as you observe the baking and decorating process through a glass window.) Across the street, **Almondine** (67 Water Street, between Main & Dock Streets, 1-718 797 5026) serves up divine pastries, including croissants, brioches and tarts. Since it opens early (7am, except Sundays, when it opens at 10am), you could start your morning here, then head out for a walking tour of the neighbourhood.

Brooklyn Bridge

Subway A, C to High Street; J, M, Z to Chambers Street; 4, 5, 6 to Brooklyn Bridge-City Hall. **Map** p411 S8, S9.

The stunning views and awe-inspiring web of steel cables will take your breath away. As you cross its wide wood-planked promenade, look for plaques detailing the history of the bridge's construction.

Brooklyn Historical Society

128 Pierrepont Street, at Clinton Street, Brooklyn Heights (1-718 222 4111/www.brooklynhistory.org). Subway A, C, F to Jay Street-Borough Hall; M, R to Court Street; 2, 3, 4, 5 to Borough Hall. **Open** noon-5pm Wed-Sun. **Admission** $6; $4 seniors, students, 12-18s; free under-12s. **Credit** AmEx, MC, V. **Map** p411 S9.

Founded in 1863, the society is located in a landmark four-storey Queen Anne-style building and houses numerous permanent and ongoing exhibits, including 'It Happened in Brooklyn', highlighting local links to crucial moments in American history. A major photo and research library – featuring historic maps and newspapers, notable family histories, and archives from the area's abolitionist movement – are accessible by appointment. Boat tours of the waterfront in summer are fun and fascinating.

New York Transit Museum

Corner of Boerum Place & Schermerhorn Street, Brooklyn Heights (1-718 694 1600/www.mta.info/mta/museum). Subway A, C, G to Hoyt-Schermerhorn. **Open** 10am-4pm Tue-Fri; noon-5pm Sat, Sun. **Admission** $5; $3 seniors, 3-17s; free under-3s. **No credit cards. Map** p410 S10.

Brooklyn Bridge.

Located in an authentic 1930s subway station, the Transit Museum allows visitors to climb aboard an exceptional collection of vintage subway and El cars, explore a working signal tower and check out ongoing exhibitions such as 'The Triborough Bridge: Robert Moses & the Automobile Age'.
Other locations: New York Transit Museum Gallery Annex & Store, Grand Central Terminal, adjacent to stationmaster's office, Main Concourse, 42nd Street, at Park Avenue, Midtown (1-212 878 0106).

Boerum Hill, Carroll Gardens, Cobble Hill & Red Hook

By far one of the most striking examples of Brooklyn's lightning-fast gentrification can be found on **Smith Street**, stretching from **Boerum Hill** to **Carroll Gardens** and known as the neighbourhood's **Restaurant Row**. This strip was targeted for urban renewal in the 1990s, receiving a facelift that included wrought-iron streetlamps and new sidewalks. It boasts charming, walkable historic districts lined with mid-19th-century Greek Revival and Italianate homes and storefronts. Today, pricey restaurants and cafés have replaced most of tiny bodegas and discount shoe stores.

Hot eateries along trendy **Smith Street** include classic bistro Bar Tabac (No.128, at Dean Street, Boerum Hill, 1-718 923 0918); Robin des Bois (No.195, between Baltic & Warren Streets, 1-718 596 1609); the Grocery (No. 288, between Sackett & Union Streets, Carroll Gardens, 1-718 596 3335); and New American favourite, Chestnut (No.271, between DeGraw & Sackett Streets, Carroll Gardens, 1-718 243 0049). Many of the shops offer wares by local artists and designers that rival the most stylish boutiques in Soho or the Meatpacking District. Playful, trendy women's clothing is for sale at Bird (No.220, at Butler Street, 1-718 797 3774); Dear Fieldbinder (No.198, between Sackett & Union Streets, Carroll Gardens, 1-718 852 3620); and Flirt (No.252, between Baltic & Warren Streets, 1-718 858 7931). Check out Flight 001 (No.132, at Dean Street, 1-718 243 0001) for fashionable travel accessories that will give your journey a dash of style.

Along nearby **Atlantic Avenue** are haute home furnisher City Foundry (No.365, between Bond & Hoyt Streets, Boerum Hill, 1-718 923 1786); ultramodern Rico (No.384, between Bond & Hoyt Streets, 1-718 797 2077), which sells art, lighting and furnishings; and stylish women's clothier Butter (No.389, between Bond & Hoyt Streets, 1-718 260 9033). On the western fringes of Cobble Hill and Brooklyn Heights, Magnetic Field (No. 97, between Henry & Hicks Streets, 1-718 834 0069) draws cool crowds with its campy Western theme and edgy live acts.

The mile-long stretch of Atlantic Avenue between Henry and Nevins Streets, affectionately nicknamed the **Fertile Crescent**, was once crowded with Middle Eastern restaurants and markets, though gentrification and geo-political tensions now threaten the community's cohesion. The granddaddy of them all still exists: Sahadi Importing Company (No.187, between Clinton & Court Streets, Cobble Hill, 1-718 624 4550) is a 60-year-old neighbourhood institution that sells olives, spices, cheeses, nuts and other gourmet treats, and attracts fans from around the city. Atlantic Avenue is also considered the northern border of **Cobble Hill**, a quaint neighbourhood with a small-town feel. Less restaurant-heavy than nearby Smith Street (though that's slowly changing), shady **Court Street** is dotted with cafés and shops, such as local fave Book Court (No.163, between Pacific & Dean Streets, 1-718 875 3677), which carries the latest fiction and non-fiction, as well as Brooklyn guidebooks and histories. Be sure to stop by the hugely charming Sweet Melissa (No.276, between Butler & Douglass Streets, 1-718 855 3410), which serves lunch, pastries and afternoon tea in a pretty back garden.

Further south, you'll cross into the still predominantly Italian-American **Carroll Gardens**. Pick up a prosciutto loaf from the Caputo Bakery (No.329, between Sackett & Union Streets, Carroll Gardens, 1-718 875 6871) or an aged soppressata salami from Esposito and Sons (No.357, between President & Union Streets, 1-718 875 6863); then relax in **Carroll Park** (from President to Carroll Streets, between Court & Smith Streets) and watch the old-timers play bocce (lawn bowling). Walk over the Brooklyn-Queens Expressway to the industrial waterfront of **Cobble Hill** and the corner building housing Mexican bistro **Alma** (*see p214*). The rooftop dining area has a great view of the East River and lower Manhattan.

To the south-west of Cobble Hill and Carroll Gardens, the rough-and-tumble industrial neighbourhood of **Red Hook** has long avoided urban renewal, but the arrival of luxury condos and gourmet mega-grocer Fairway (1-718 694 6868, www.fairwaymarket.com) on Van Brunt Street has put it on the path to inevitable gentrification – and real estate prices reflect that. Still, 'There's no subway and the buses are inadequate,' says John McGettrick, co-chair of the local civic association, which makes this area still feel somewhat like a well-kept secret. Otherwise, Red Hook might become the new Williamsburg, which is to say awash in tapas bars and sleek boutiques. Yet, for the past 50 years, the neighbourhood has maintained its independence and identity: a down-on-its-luck peninsula isolated from the rest of Brooklyn.

Walk it out The other Fifth Avenue

There's no Saks on this more multi-ethnic Fifth Avenue.

Start Subway D, M, N, R to Pacific Street; 2, 3 to Bergen Street.
End Subway R to 95th Street.
Distance 5.8 miles.
Time 3.5 hours.

Think of Manhattan's Fifth Avenue, and you'll likely picture museums, fur coats and a whole lot of tourists. For a true cross-section of New York life, stroll Brooklyn's Fifth Avenue from beginning to end. Eastern European, Mexican, Middle Eastern, Italian... the neighbourhoods blend seamlessly together, but each is quite distinct. Start your walk by going all Irish at **O'Connor's** (39 Fifth Avenue, between Bergen & Dean Streets, 1-718 783 9721), the landmark bar that has been cheerfully pouring cheap pints since 1931.

Wander down the tree-lined avenue past disparate storefronts – a sleek yoga centre next to an old-school shop selling Jesus figurines – until you reach **Apropos** (186 Fifth Avenue, between DeGraw & Sackett Streets, 1-718 230 7605). This elegant little café and wine bar serves potent iced coffee ($2) made with roasted Danesi beans.

When you hit JJ Byrne Memorial Park on 3rd Street, head in and visit the **Old Stone House** (1-718 768 3195), a reconstruction (using

Sightseeing

Green-Wood Cemetery.

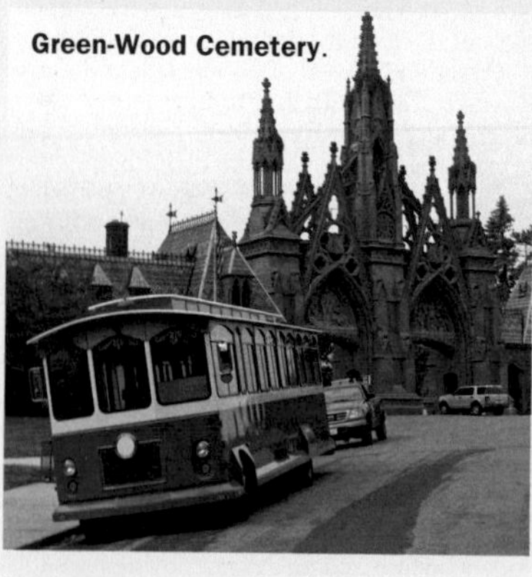

the original stones) of the Dutch domicile that stood near this site, which was occupied by the British during the Revolutionary War's key Battle of Brooklyn in 1776.

Just past Prospect Expressway, you'll find **Eagle Provisions** (628 Fifth Avenue, at 18th Street, 1-718 499 0026), a nod to the neighbourhood's pocket of Eastern Europeans. Hanging kielbasa and a room full of cheap international brews are reminiscent of Beerfest – and we mean that in a good way.

Although **Green-Wood Cemetery** (500 25th Street, 1-718 768 7300, www.green-wood.com) is alone worth an in-depth tour, its dramatic entrance at 25th Street entices with a magical Gothic archway laden with birds' nests. Hike a few steep steps to Artemesia Path, which overlooks stunning mausoleums.

At 41st Street, climb the hilly staircase up to **Sunset Park**, one of Brooklyn's highest points, and look far beyond the commercial chaos for calming views of the East River.

A slew of Mexican restaurants line the stretch around 58th Street. Refuel at authentic **Cinco Estrellas** (5724 Fifth Avenue, at 57th Street, 1-718 499 1212), where you can plop down in a pink booth and listen to upbeat Spanish music. An enormous plate of chilaquiles ($6.95) comes with a spicy salsa verde and smoky refried beans.

Around 68th Street, you'll notice storefronts adorned with Arabic lettering and hookah pipes beckoning from the windows. At Lebanese-owned **Sweet Delights** (6818 Fifth Avenue, between Bay Ridge Avenue & 68th Street, 1-718 491 5885), you can pick up boxes of baklava and Saudi Arabian dates, or freshly baked, walnut-filled maamoul cookies from one of the trays. Bathroom break? At the 86th Street shopping mecca, you can choose between Circuit City and Brooklyn's far less-crowded Century 21.

Come 95th Street, Fifth Avenue unites with Fourth and you're almost at the Verrazano Bridge. Cross the Belt Parkway to the **Shore Parkway Promenade** and you'll get a truly spectacular view of New York Bay. Or, if you're tired, rest on the grass at **John Paul Jones Park** (between Shore Road & 101st Street), named for the American patriot born and raised in... Scotland.

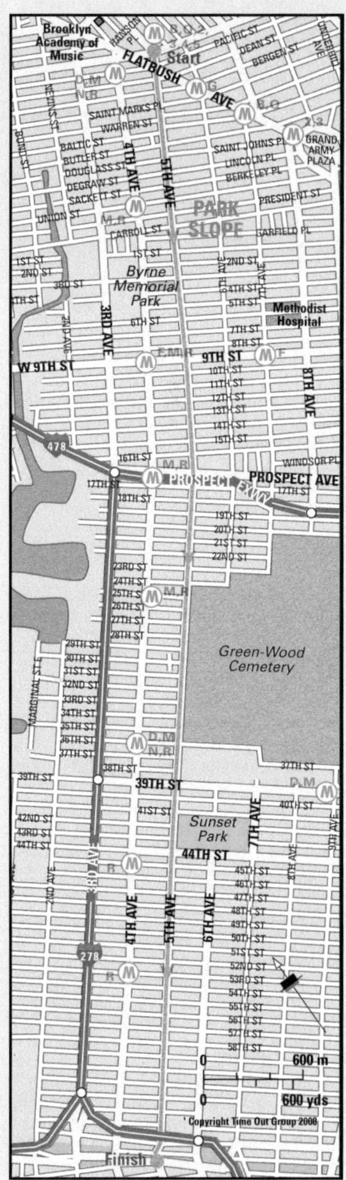

The area offers singular views of New York Harbor from **Valentino Pier**, and has an eclectic selection of artist studios, bars and eateries. Hope & Anchor (347 Van Brunt Street, at Wolcott Street, 1-718 237 0276) is a retro bar and grill that opened in 2002, when the stretch was still a bit of a culinary wasteland. Similarly pioneering was 360 (360 Van Brunt Street, between Sullivan & Wolcott Streets, 1-718 246 0360). When Alsace native Arnaud Erhart opened it in 2003, he had just one motive: to feed friends and family. Now the place has become so popular that a table is hard to score without a reservation.

Though progress gallops apace (a 346,000 sq ft outpost of Swedish furniture superstore IKEA is planning to open in late 2008), you can still catch a glimpse of the neighbourhood's time-warp charm. Its decaying piers are an appropriately moody backdrop for massive cranes, empty warehouses and trucks clattering over cobblestone streets. To check out the work of local artists, look for the word 'Gallery' hand-scrawled in block letters on the doors of the **Kentler International Drawing Space** (353 Van Brunt Street, between Sullivan & Wolcott Streets, 1-718 875 2098), or visit the **Brooklyn Waterfront Artists Coalition**'s 25,000-foot exhibition space (499 Van Brunt Street, at Beard Street Pier, 1-718 596 2507) in a Civil War-era warehouse on the pier just south of Fairway. BWAC hosts large group shows in the spring and autumn. For more information on events and developments in Red Hook, visit **B61 Productions** (www.b61productions.com).

GETTING THERE

Getting to Red Hook is indeed a challenge – from the F and G subway station at Smith-9th Street, it's either a long walk or a transfer to the B77 bus. The **New York Water Taxi** (1-212 742 1969, www.nywatertaxi.com) has improved the situation somewhat by adding stops to the Beard Street Pier, behind Fairway.

Park Slope & Prospect Heights

Though it is largely home to young families, sleepy Victorian brownstones and stoop sales galore, **Park Slope** is also home to Hollywood actors (Jennifer Connelly, John Turturro and others) and famous authors (Paul Auster, Jonathan Safran Foer). The neighbourhood's intellectual, artistic and lefty political heritage is well known. It boasts the nation's oldest working food cooperative, which has a die-hard following and is known for its fresh, organic food and wholesale prices. Only members can go in, unfortunately, but many admire it from afar as another example of the area's progressive-mindedness.

Fifth Avenue (*see p160* **Walk it out**) is the prime locale for restaurants and hip bars. Locals flock to the beloved, always-packed Venetian mainstay **al di là** (248 Fifth Avenue, at Carroll Street, 1-718 783 4565); the late-night favourite **Blue Ribbon Brooklyn** (*see p189*); and kid-friendly Peruvian sensation **Coco Roco** (No.392, between 6th & 7th Streets, 1-718 965 3376). Innovative boutiques can be found all along Fifth Avenue too, including eco-friendly home furnisher **3r Living** (No.276, between Garfield Place & 1st Place, 1-718 832 0951); **Matter** (227 5th Avenue, at President Street, 1-718 230 1150), offering cutting-edge design objects, jewellery, books and a mini art gallery out the back; cool urban gear depot **Brooklyn Industries** (No. 206, at Union Street, 1-718 789 2764), with its artist-designed T-shirts; and **Beacon's Closet** (No.220, at Union Street, 1-718 230 1630), great for vintage clothing.

Park Slope's lesbian community is one of the Big Apple's strongest: explore Sapphic lore at the **Lesbian Herstory Archives** (*see p303*), then do field research at **Cattyshack** or **Ginger's Bar** (for both *see p309*). Both welcome boys, but Park Slope's gay gents

Game for anything: **Park Slope** bringing playtime to the concrete streets.

usually occupy **Excelsior** (390 5th Avenue, 1-718 832 1599), a low-key bar with a vibrant jukebox and lush backyard garden. And whether you're straight or gay, boy or girl, you'll want to go slightly off the beaten path to the wildly popular **Union Hall** (*see p227*). The bar's front half is lined with old books and portraits of upper-crust gentlemen, as well as having a cosy fireplace. The back has its very own indoor bocce courts, comfy chairs and sofas, and board games. In addition to drinks, you can order delicious bite-size pub food, including chicken-pot stickers, Guinness-soaked burgers, and homemade cookies and milk for dessert.

Seventh Avenue is the Slope's main commercial district (between President Street & 12th Street) – it's a bit boring and generic, good for practical needs (pharmacy, grocery store and so on) but you'll find a few places worth stopping by: **Community Bookstore** (No.143, between Garfield & Carroll Streets, 1-718 783 3075), a local treasure with an ardent following; the **Clay Pot** (No.162, between Garfield & 1st Streets, 1-718 788 6564), which sells designer jewellery, watches, pottery and more; and eclectic gift shop **Loom** (115 7th Avenue, between Carroll & President Streets, 1-718 789 0061). Also worth a visit is the outdoor **P.S. 321 Flea Market** (No.180, between 1st & 2nd Streets), which operates year-round on weekends and is great for finding used clothing, estate jewellery, furniture and knick-knacks. Prices are generally reasonable, and you're welcome to haggle.

The western edge of Prospect Park is a section of the landmarked **Park Slope Historic District**. Brownstones and several fine examples of Romanesque Revival and Queen Anne residences grace these streets. Particularly charming are the brick edifices that line Carroll Street, Montgomery Place and Berkeley Place. Spielberg filmed parts of his *War of the Worlds* on these blocks just a few years ago. Writer-director Noah Baumbach, who grew up in these parts, filmed the 2005 indie darling *The Squid and the Whale* here too.

Central Park may be bigger and far more famous, but **Prospect Park** (main entrance at Grand Army Plaza, Prospect Heights, 1-718 965 8999, www.prospectpark.org) has a more rustic quality. It's entirely possible to take a short stroll into its lush green expanse and forget you're in the midst of a bustling metropolis. This masterpiece, which designers Frederick Law Olmsted and Calvert Vaux said was more in line with their vision than Central Park (their previous project), is a great spot for bird-watching, especially with a little guidance from the **Prospect Park Audubon Center at the Boathouse** (park entrance on Ocean Avenue, at Lincoln Road, Prospect Heights, 1-718 287 3400). Or pretend you've left the city altogether by boating or hiking amid the waterfalls, pools and wildlife habitats of the **Ravine District** (park entrances on Prospect Park West, at 3rd, 9th & 15th Streets, Park Slope). The rolling green park was created with equestrians in mind; you can saddle a horse at the nearby Kensington Stables (*see p337*) or hop on a bike and pedal alongside rollerbladers and runners. Children enjoy riding the handcarved horses at the park's antique Carousel (Flatbush Avenue, at Empire Boulevard) and playing with animals in the **Prospect Park Zoo** (park entrance on Flatbush Avenue, near Ocean Avenue, Prospect Heights, 1-718 399 7339).

A 15-minute walk from Prospect Park is the verdant necropolis of **Green-Wood Cemetery** (*see p164*). A century ago, this site vied with Niagara Falls as New York State's greatest tourist attraction. Filled with Victorian mausoleums, cherubs and gargoyles, Green-Wood is the resting place of some half-million

New Yorkers, among them Jean-Michel Basquiat, Leonard Bernstein and Mae West. The hugely spectacular, soaring arches of the main gate are carved from New Jersey brownstone. Intricate details of death and resurrection, carved in Nova Scotia sandstone, are the work of John Moffit. **Battle Hill**, the single highest point in Brooklyn, is on cemetery grounds.

Near the main entrance to Prospect Park sits the massive Civil War memorial arch at **Grand Army Plaza** (intersection of Flatbush Avenue, Eastern Parkway & Prospect Park West) and the central branch of the **Brooklyn Public Library** (Grand Army Plaza, Prospect Heights, 1-718 230 2100). The library's central Brooklyn Collection includes thousands of artefacts and photos tracing the borough's history. Just around the corner are the tranquil **Brooklyn Botanic Garden** and also the **Brooklyn Museum** (for both, *see below*), which has a renowned Egyptology collection. In the past few years, the museum has also hosted hugely successful exhibits of major contemporary artists, including Jean-Michel Basquiat, Annie Leibovitz and William Wegman, all of which drew sell-out crowds.

Brooklyn Botanic Garden

900 Washington Avenue, at Eastern Parkway, Prospect Heights (1-718 623 7200/www.bbg.org). Subway B, Q, Franklin Avenue S to Prospect Park; 2, 3 to Eastern Parkway-Brooklyn Museum. **Open** *Apr-Sept* 8am-6pm Tue-Fri; 10am-6pm Sat, Sun. *Oct-Mar* 8am-4.30pm Tue-Fri; 10am-4.30pm Sat, Sun. **Admission** $8; $4 seniors, students, over-12s. Free Tue; 10am-noon Sat; Sat, Sun mid Nov-Feb. **Credit** MC, V. **Map** p410 U11.

This 52-acre haven of luscious greenery was founded in 1910. April is when Sakura Matsuri, the annual Cherry Blossom Festival, takes place, when prize buds and Japanese culture are in full bloom. The recently renovated Eastern Parkway entrance and the Osborne Garden – an Italian-style formal garden – are also well worth a peek.

Brooklyn Museum

200 Eastern Parkway, at Washington Avenue, Prospect Heights (1-718 638 5000/www.brooklyn museum.org). Subway 2, 3 to Eastern Parkway-Brooklyn Museum. **Open** 10am-5pm Wed-Fri; 11am-6pm Sat, Sun; 11am-11pm 1st Sat of mth (except Sept). **Admission** $8; $4 seniors, students; free under-12s (must be accompanied by an adult). Free 5-11pm 1st Sat of mth (except Sept). **Credit** AmEx, MC, V. **Map** p410 U11.

Brooklyn's premier institution is a tranquil alternative to Manhattan's bigger-name spaces; it's rarely crowded. Among the museum's many assets is a rich, 4,000-piece Egyptian collection, which includes a gilded-ebony statue of Amenhotep III and, on a ceiling, a large-scale rendering of an ancient map of the cosmos. You can even view a mummy preserved in its original coffin.

Masterworks by Cézanne, Monet and Degas, part of an impressive European painting and sculpture collection, are displayed in the museum's skylighted Beaux-Arts Court. On the fifth floor, American paintings and sculptures include native son Thomas Cole's *The Pic-Nic* and Louis Rémy Mignot's *Niagara*. Don't miss the renowned Pacific Island and African galleries (this was actually the first American museum to display African objects as art).

In spring 2007, the museum opened the Elizabeth A Sacker Center for Feminist Art. The metaphorical and physical core of the new centre is Judy Chicago's monumental sculpture *The Dinner Party*. Made in 1979, the piece is arguably feminism's single most famous work of art.

Green-Wood Cemetery

Fifth Avenue, at 25th Street, Sunset Park (1-718 768 7300/www.green-wood.com). Subway M, R to 25th Street. **Open** 8am-5pm daily. **Admission** free. **Map** p410 S13.

Fort Greene & Williamsburg

Fort Greene, with its stately Victorian brownstones and other grand buildings, has undergone a major revival over the past decade. It has long been a centre of African-American life and business – Spike Lee, Branford Marsalis and Chris Rock have all lived here. **Fort Greene Park** (from Myrtle to DeKalb Avenues, between St Edwards Street & Washington Park) was conceived in 1846 at the behest of poet Walt Whitman (then editor of the *Brooklyn Daily Eagle*); its masterplan was fully realised by the omnipresent Olmsted and Vaux in 1867. At the centre of the park stands the Prison Ship Martyrs Monument, erected in 1909 in memory of 11,000 American prisoners who died on British ships that were anchored nearby during the Revolutionary War.

Despite the implications of its name, the 34-storey **Williamsburgh Savings Bank**, located at the corner of Atlantic and Flatbush Avenues, is in Fort Greene, not Williamsburg. The 512-foot-tall structure is the tallest in the borough and, with its four-sided clocktower, doubtlessly the most recognisable feature of the Brooklyn skyline. Now the 1927 building has been renamed One Hanson Place, and converted into (what else?) luxury condominiums.

Though originally founded in Brooklyn Heights, the **Brooklyn Academy of Music** (*see p327*) moved to its current site on Fort Greene's southern border in 1901. BAM is America's oldest operating performing arts centre. It once hosted the likes of Edwin Booth and Sarah Bernhardt and was the home of the Metropolitan Opera until 1921; now it's known for ambitious cultural performances of all varieties. BAM is host to cutting-edge dance,

Fort Greene by name, green by nature.

theatre, literary, music and film programmes that draw big audiences from throughout the metropolitan area. From October to December, the centre hosts the **Next Wave Festival** (*see p264*). Also world-famous – if to different people – is the cheesecake at Junior's Restaurant (386 Flatbush Avenue, at DeKalb Avenue, 1-718 852 5257), just a few blocks away.

A slew of popular hangouts (and some truly funky shops) can be found on or near **DeKalb Avenue**, including the funky South African i-Shebeen Madiba (No.195, at Carlton Avenue, 1-718 855 9190); lively bistro Chez Oskar (No.211, at Adelphi Street, 1-718 852 6250); and the Francophilic iCi (No. 246, at Vanderbilt Avenue, 1-718 789 2778). If you really need to satisfy a shopping fix, visit the recently opened Stuart & Wright (85 Lafayette Avenue, between South Elliott Place & South Portland Avenue, 1-718 797 0011). Everything in this small but very well-stocked shop is beautiful, and much of it suitably pricey. Still, you'll be getting limited-edition clothing, and supporting local and indie designers in the process.

Williamsburg is the epicentre of Brooklyn hipsterdom, especially if you're 22, have a blog or a band, and are sufficiently pierced. It's Brooklyn's bustling version of the East Village in its heyday, full of energy and a thriving, youthful spirit. In fact, it's just one subway stop from the East Village (on the L line), and **Bedford Avenue** is the neighbourhood's main thoroughfare. You'll also find plenty of restaurants and nightspots along North 6th Street and Grand Avenue too. Thanks to rising rents, retailers and eateries are spreading to South Williamsburg as well, which is still largely the home of a Hasidic Jewish community.

During the day, **Verb Café** (218 Bedford Avenue, between North 4th & 5th Streets, 1-718 599 0977) is one of the neighbourhood's prime slacker hangouts; at night, the scene moves to eateries like the Thai palace **SEA** (*see p215*); **DuMont** (432 Union Avenue, between Devoe Street & Metropolitan Avenue, 1-718 486 7717), with its pressed-tin ceilings, wooden bar and retro brown-leather booths; and diner **Relish** (225 Wythe Ave, at North 3rd Street, 1-718 963 4546), housed in a formerly abandoned railcar. Locals with mortgages prefer neighbourhood fixture **Peter Luger** (*see p215*), which grills what some carnivores consider to be the best steak in the entire city.

The area also has dozens of boutiques and art galleries (such as the local fave Pierogi; *see p274*). But the core of the art scene is the **Williamsburg Art & Historical Center** (135 Broadway, at Bedford Avenue, 1-718 486 7372, www.wahcenter.org), housed in a landmark 1929 bank building. The music scene rocks, too; worth-a-trip spaces include **Galapagos Art Space** (*see p315*), **Music Hall of Williamsburg** (*see p318*), **Pete's Candy Store** (709 Lorimer Street, 1-718 302 3770) and **Warsaw** (261 Driggs Avenue, at Eckford Street, 1-718 387 0505), which doubles as the Polish National Home. Formerly a community swimming hole, **McCarren Park Pool** (www.thepoolparties.com; *photo p166*), at Lorimer Street and Driggs Avenue, is now a distinctive outdoor concert venue hosting both local and national acts alike.

But long before the trendsetters invaded, Williamsburg's waterfront location made it ideal for industry; after the Erie Canal linked the Atlantic Ocean to the Great Lakes in 1825,

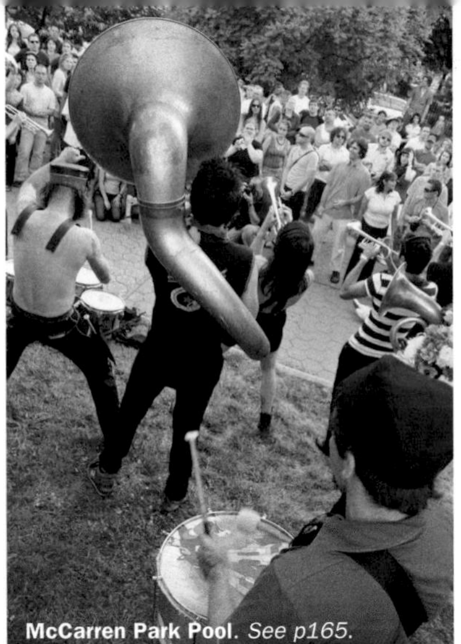
McCarren Park Pool. *See p165.*

the area became an even more bustling port. Companies such as Pfizer and Domino Sugar started here, but by the late 20th century businesses began to abandon the area's huge industrial spaces. A sign of the area's rapid gentrification, the Domino refinery finally closed in 2004, though its signature sign is still a local landmark. The beloved **Brooklyn Brewery** (79 North 11th Street, between Berry Street & Wythe Avenue, 1-718 486 7422, www.brooklynbrewery.com) took up residence in a former ironworks. Visit during the happy 'hour' (Fridays from 6pm to 11pm) for $3 drafts or take a tour on Saturdays from noon to 5pm.

Coney Island

Coney Island is mainly a summertime destination, nearly deserted in off-season. After decades of tattered decay, this odd community – known for its amusement park, beach and boardwalk – has made a comeback and is rapidly changing. NYC's Parks Department estimates that more than 15 million people visited the beach and boardwalk in the past year, a spike of over five million in three years.

It remains to be seen how much of its weird, wonderful spirit will stay intact as massive redevelopment (and demolition) takes place in this ethnically diverse community. Some residents are wary of the imminent changes to come: the old-timers remember Coney Island in its heyday, an expanse of rides, hot-dog stands, a six-storey hotel shaped like an elephant and amusement parks (Dreamland, Luna Steeplechase and Astroland, the only survivor). By 1966, nearly everything was gone, due to the wrecking ball, fire and a long, steady economic downturn.

In 2005, a developer bought up about half of the area's entertainment district and is looking to pour some $2 billion into its rejuvenation – calling for new hotels, restaurants, shops, arcades and cinemas on the site. Since the 3.3 acres underneath the Astroland were also purchased, many worry, with good reason, that the beloved park will be razed. Municipal planners have vowed to protect the amusement district as much as possible, and a few of the attractions are landmarks (including the vintage wooden rollercoaster, the Cyclone, built in 1926) and cannot be torn down. Although no formal agreement has been reached, it appears (sadly) that 2007 was Astroland's final summer, at least in its current form. For the latest details, visit www.coneyisland.com.

Thus far, it's safe to say that the only truly uncontroversial improvement to Coney Island is the seaside **KeySpan Park**, which opened in 2001. Home to the **Brooklyn Cyclones** (*see p333*), a minor league baseball affiliate of the New York Mets, the park has brought professional baseball back to the borough, making Brooklynites and sports fans proud.

The **New York Aquarium** (*see p290*) is the nation's oldest marine preserve and home to more than 350 aquatic species, including the California sea lions who perform daily at the outdoor, 1,600-seat Aquatheater. Don't forget to look up: various local artists have focused their energy on adding some colour to the signage.

The always captivating **Sideshows by the Seashore** is put on by **Coney Island USA** (1208 Surf Avenue, at W 12th Street, Coney Island, 1-718 372 5159, www.coneyisland usa.com), an organisation that keeps the torch burning for early 20th-century Coney living. You won't want to miss a minute of the show, which includes legendary freaks like human pincushion Scott Baker (aka the Twisted Shockmeister), pain-proof Eak the Geek and the heavily tattooed Insectavora, who dines on flames and climbs the dangerous Ladder of Swords. The **Mermaid Parade** (*see p262*) and **Nathan's Famous Fourth of July Hot Dog Eating Contest** (held annually since 1916) are two quirky summertime rituals at Coney. In 2007, Californian Joey Chestnut defeated the six-time world champ Takeru Kobayashi by downing 66 hot dogs – complete with buns – in a mere 12 minutes. (Kobayashi's record is 63.) Another popular annual ritual is the **Siren Music Festival** every July, which has been going for seven years; past indie rock line-ups have included the Yeah Yeah Yeahs, Modest Mouse and Death Cab for Cutie. And on Friday evenings throughout the summer, the local fireworks display is the perfect nightcap to a day of sandy adventures.

Queens

The American melting pot defined.

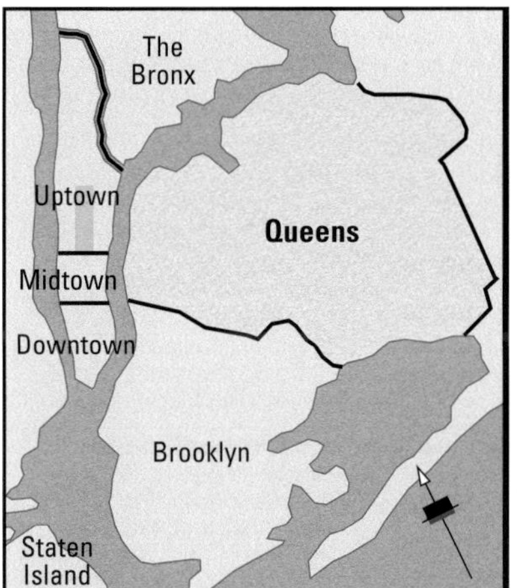

Map p412

Almost 200,000 people come to Queens every day via JFK and La Guardia airports. Yet most visitors are in such a rush to get to Manhattan that they don't realise they're missing parts of the city that many would describe as the 'real New York'. Multi-ethnic, middle-class but not yuppified, and definitely rough around the edges, Queens is a great day trip for those wanting to experience the full flavour of New York City's melting pot.

Queens is the city's huge eastern borough. It's the largest borough in terms of size, and demographers predict it will also surpass Brooklyn as the most populous in a matter of years. Its tremendous recent growth is due largely to a tidal wave of immigration – notable even by New York standards. The borough is the most diverse urban area the country has ever seen, with almost half the 2.2 million residents hailing from another land.

Except for the US Open and possibly a Mets game, haughty Manhattanites don't dare waggle a foot east of the East River, to the homeland of dysfunctional TV characters like *Seinfeld*'s George Costanza. But what do they know? Just minutes from Midtown, the borough has cutting-edge art at **P.S.1** (*see p168*), jazz history at **Louis Armstrong House** (*see p171*), and cheap, delicious ethnic eats.

As in the rest of New York, it's all about the neighbourhoods in Queens. Take a truly globetrotting tour on the elevated 7 subway, called the International Express for the microcosm of nations you find represented beneath its tracks. And that's no joke; like the Appalachian Trail, the 7 train is a designated National Millennium Trail. Get a MetroCard and head out to Queens for lunch to enjoy whichever cuisine gets your mouth watering. There is French bistro fare in Long Island City, Irish pub grub and Turkish kebabs in Sunnyside, knock-your-socks-off Thai curry in Woodside, more curry in Jackson Heights' Little India, Indonesian satay in Elmhurst, hearty steaks and tacos in pan-Latino Corona, and Chinese dumplings and Korean barbecue in Flushing, the train's last stop.

The word is out about Queens, and a steady flow of New Yorkers priced out of Manhattan and Brooklyn have moved into immigrant neighbourhoods, pushing up prices. A few years ago, the trailblazers were artists looking for cheap spaces in Long Island City's factories, followed by MoMA's temporary visit in 2003 while its midtown home was being expanded. Since then the many row houses and pre-war apartment buildings of western Queens have been staked out by young college grads and professionals ready to start families. With them they've brought new tastes, which means you'll find fries served with garlic aïoli in Long Island City, iPods on parade in Astoria and Bugaboo strollers in Jackson Heights.

Long Island City

Long Island City is undergoing the most radical transformation of all the borough's nabes, on its way from being a land of serious industry to an extension of Midtown Manhattan, with multiple residential apartment towers rising on the East River waterfront, where a Queens tour normally starts. Get off the 7 subway at its first stop, Vernon Boulevard-Jackson Avenue, to see old and new Queens at the same address. Nothing says new Queens like the **Watertaxi Beach** (2-03 Borden Avenue, at 2nd Street, Long Island City, www.watertaxibeach.com; *photo p169*), a man-made beach on the East River. The views of Midtown Manhattan look even better when you're chomping on a burger and downing cold draught beer with your toes in the sand. Next door (but with the same address) you'll find Long Island City history in the boxing-themed **Waterfront Crabhouse** (2-3 Borden Avenue, at 2nd Street, 1-718 729 4862), an old-time saloon and oyster bar. If you'd prefer a more sedate setting for Manhattan gazing, try **Gantry Plaza State Park** (48th Avenue, at Center Boulevard), named after the hulking 19th-century railroad gantries that transferred cargo from ships to trains. Both these watery outposts are directly across the East River from the United Nations, offering postcard-worthy views of the skyline.

Sightseeing

A few blocks east on Jackson Avenue is the **P.S.1 Contemporary Art Center** (*see below*), a progressive cultural outpost affiliated with MoMA that highlights the work of up-and-coming art stars. Cross the street for a close-up of the graffiti-covered building that is **5 Pointz** (Crane Street & Jackson Avenue). Art studios now inhabit this former warehouse, but it's the outdoor canvas that you'll want to inspect. Close by, a well-preserved block of 19th-century row houses in an array of styles constitutes the **Hunters Point Historic District** (45th Avenue, between 21st & 23rd Streets).

Hop back aboard the 7 subway and you'll get treated to a view of the Manhattan skyline through the elegant spans of the **59th Street Bridge** (aka Queensboro Bridge). Completed in 1909, it signifies glamorous New York in everything from F Scott Fitzgerald's novel *The Great Gatsby* to Woody Allen's film *Manhattan* to Simon & Garfunkel's hit 'The 59th Street Bridge Song (Feelin' Groovy)'.

Back when Los Angeles was a sleepy orange grove, western Queens was America's film capital, and these days it buzzes with cinematic goings-on once more. The mounted 'Silvercup' sign visible from the Queensboro Plaza subway platform announces **Silvercup Studios**, once a bakery and today a TV and film production stage, where both *Sex and the City* and *The Sopranos* were made. WC Fields and the Marx Brothers clowned at Famous Players/Lasky Studios, now called Kaufman Astoria Studios, which houses the **Museum of the Moving Image** (*see below*). Dub your voice into *The Wizard of Oz*, learn what creative minds are fashioning out of video games, and check out classic, foreign and experimental films. To get there, you'll need to transfer to the N or W trains at Queensboro Plaza.

Museum of the Moving Image

35th Avenue, at 36th Street, Astoria (1-718 784 0077/www.movingimage.us). Subway G, R, V to Steinway Street. **Open** 11am-5pm Wed, Thur; 11am-8pm Fri; 11am-6.30pm Sat, Sun. **Admission** $10; $7.50 seniors, students; $5 5-18s; free under-5s. Free 4-8pm Fri. No strollers. **Credit** AmEx, MC, V. **Map** p412 W4.

Only 15 minutes by subway from Midtown, MMI is one of the city's most dynamic institutions. Located in the restored complex that once housed the original Kaufman Astoria Studios, it offers daily film, video and video game programming. The museum also displays famous movie props, including the chariot driven by Charlton Heston in *Ben-Hur* and the Yoda puppet used in *The Empire Strikes Back*.

P.S.1 Contemporary Art Center

22-25 Jackson Avenue, at 46th Avenue, Long Island City (1-718 784 2084/www.ps1.org). Subway E, V to 23rd Street-Ely Avenue; G to 21st Street-Jackson Avenue; 7 to 45th Road-Court House Square. **Open** noon-6pm Mon, Thur-Sun. **Admission** suggested donation $5; $2 seniors, students. **Credit** AmEx, MC, V. **Map** p412 V5.

Cutting-edge shows and an international studio programme make each visit to this contemporary art space a treasure hunt, with artwork turning up in every corner. In a Romanesque Revival building (a former public school), the MoMA affiliate mounts shows for both art fans and open-minded neophytes.

Astoria

The N or W train also chugs north to Astoria, a lively neighbourhood – of Greeks, but also Brazilians, Egyptians and just about everyone else – that's favoured by post-grads sharing row-house digs. You can alight at Broadway

Cheap date

After a recent face-lift, Flushing Meadows-Corona Park's **Panorama of the City of New York** (*see p170*) – a 9,335 sq ft foam and wood model of NYC – is ready for visitors. A mini airplane takes off from La Guardia, bleating horns mimic the daily city soundtrack and a neat timed lighting system even replicates both sunrise and sunset. Best of all, entry to this off-the-beaten path museum is just $5. After you've had your fill of Lilliputian New York, grab some grub: just one stop away on the 7 train, Malaysian spot **Sentosa's** (*see p215*) exotic, dark-wood interior makes for a posh alternative to the nabe's ambience-free dim sum parlours. The tropical fare is warm and welcoming, and the coconut juice served in its shell the ultimate in refreshment. On our visit, we liked the *roti telur*, Indian-style egg-and-onion pancakes, and 'volcano' spare ribs that arrive ablaze.

Balls to the city: net gains galore at man-made **Watertaxi Beach**. *See p167.*

for a hike to the indoor-outdoor **Noguchi Museum** (*see below*), which shows works by the visionary Japanese sculptor and others. Nearby is the **Socrates Sculpture Park** (Broadway, at Vernon Boulevard, Long Island City, www.socratessculpturepark.org), a riverfront art space given to concerts and summer film screenings on Wednesday nights. At the end of the subway line (Astoria-Ditmars Boulevard), walk west to Astoria Park (from Astoria Park South to Ditmars Boulevard, between Shore Boulevard & 19th Street) for its dramatic views of two bridges: the **Triborough Bridge**, Robert Moses's automotive labyrinth connecting Queens, the Bronx and Manhattan; and the 1916 **Hell Gate Bridge**, a single-arch steel tour de force that was the template for the Sydney Harbour Bridge in Australia.

As New York's premier Greek-American stronghold, Astoria is well known for Hellenic eateries specialising in impeccably grilled seafood. **Taverna Kyclades** (33-07 Ditmars Boulevard, between 33rd & 35th Streets, 1-718 545 8666) offers a breezy Aegean atmosphere and a smoker-friendly patio. Lovely **Agnanti** (19-06 Ditmars Boulevard, between 19th & 21st Streets, 1-718 545 4554) is adjacent to Astoria Park, and serves meze and grilled catch of the day. One of the city's last central European beer gardens, **Bohemian Hall** (29-19 24th Avenue, at 29th Street, 1-718 274 4925), hosts Czech-style dining and drinking on weeknights and weekends. Better arrive early on weekends to get a table in the linden tree-shaded courtyard. South of Astoria Boulevard, you can try shisha – a (legal) hookah pipe – with thick Turkish coffee in the Egyptian cafés along Steinway Street. Over at **Steinway & Sons** (1 Steinway Place, between 19th Avenue & 38th Street, 1-718 721 2600), you can glimpse piano artisans at work on a tour of the still-thriving red-brick 1871 factory; call for tour schedule.

Noguchi Museum

9-01 33rd Road, between Vernon Boulevard & 10th Street, Long Island City (1-718 204 7088/ www.noguchi.org). Subway N, W to Broadway, then bus Q104 to 11th Street; or 7 to Vernon Boulevard-Jackson Avenue, then Q103 bus to 10th Street. **Open** 10am-5pm Wed-Fri; 11am-6pm Sat, Sun. **Admission** $10; $5 seniors, students. No strollers. **No credit cards. Map** p412 V3.

In addition to his famous lamps, artist Isamu Noguchi (1904-88) created large-scale sculptures of supreme simplicity and beauty. The museum is located in an original 1920s-era factory, where the various galleries surround a serene sculpture garden designed by Noguchi himself. The second-floor galleries are devoted to Noguchi's interior design, and boast a new café and a shop. A shuttle service from Manhattan is available on weekends (call or see the website for more information).

Jackson Heights

Find your way back to an E, F, G, R or 7 train and ride to the 74th Street-Broadway stop. This is the crossroads of Jackson Heights, a dizzyingly multicultural neighbourhood even by Queens standards, and a cheap-eats paradise. Step off the subway into **Little India**. Dosa Diner (35-66 73rd Street, between 35th & 37th Avenues, 1-718 205 2218) is packed on weekends with families feasting on the south Indian dosa crêpe specialities. Ashoka's fresh all-you-can-eat buffet is unfurled at lunch and dinner (74-14 37th Avenue, between 74th & 75th Streets, 1-718 898 5088). Shops selling saris, spices, Bollywood DVDs and intricate gold jewellery line 74th Street, between Roosevelt and 37th Avenues.

Jackson Heights claims a roughly 30-square-block landmark district of notable mock Tudor and neo-Gothic-style co-op apartment buildings, with attached houses characterised by tree-dotted lawns and park-like courtyards.

Outstanding examples of these 1920s beauties are found on 70th Street, between 34th Avenue and Northern Boulevard, and on 34th Avenue, between 76th and 77th Streets, and 80th and 81st Streets.

Jackson Heights and its various adjoining 'hoods have welcomed successive waves of Latin American immigrants and their cuisines. Colombians and Argentinians are old-school in these parts: get a taste of Buenos Aires at **La Fusta** (80-32 Baxter Avenue, between Broadway & Layton Street, Elmhurst, 1-718 429 8222), a convivial steakhouse. Thatch-covered **Gran Rancho Jubilee** (23-04 94th Street, at 23rd Avenue, East Elmhurst, 1-718 335 1700) lies just a block from the airport, but offers a full ride into Dominican life, with home cooking and live merengue shows.

Flushing

At the end of the 7 train lies historic Flushing. Egalitarian Dutchmen staked their own claim to 'Vlissingen' in the 1600s and were shortly joined by pacifist Friends, or Quakers, seeking religious freedom in the New World. These liberal settlers promulgated the Flushing Remonstrance, a groundbreaking 1657 edict extending 'the law of love, peace and liberty' to Jews and Muslims. It is now regarded as a forerunner of the United States Constitution's First Amendment.

The plain wooden **Friends Meeting House** (137-16 Northern Boulevard, between Main & Union Streets), built in 1694, creates a startling juxtaposition to the prosperous Chinatown – New York's second largest – that now surrounds its weathered wooden walls. Religious freedom is still a draw in the neighbourhood, which boasts hundreds of active temples and churches used by immigrants from Korea, China and south Asia. **St George's Church** (Main Street, between 38th & 39th Streets, 1-718 359 1171), an Episcopalian steeple chartered by King George III, was once a dominant site on Main Street, but now competes for attention with a parade of local shops and restaurants, including a major shopping development that opened just across the street in 2007. The interior of St George is worth a brief visit if only to see the two examples of Queens-made Tiffany stained glass – and to hear church services in Caribbean-accented English, Chinese and Spanish. Ambitious explorers will want to make the jaunt south to the **Hindu Temple Society** (*see p171*), a Ganesh temple whose ornate stone exterior was hand-carved in India.

The restaurants and dumpling stalls of Flushing's **Chinatown** are another way to commune with the divine, with delicious lamb specialities from northern China and Malaysian savoury *roti canai* just a couple of examples of the hundreds of heavenly options on offer. Teenagers tend to love the unique bubble tea – sweet, milky tea loaded with tapioca balls – that you can find in cafés like doughnut-serving Sago (39-02 Main Street, 1-718 353 2899) or tea-specialists Ten Ren (135-18 Roosevelt Avenue, 1-718 461 9305). For brunch at the weekend, sit side by side with local families for dim sum at banquet-sized, chandelier-lit Gum Fung (136-28 39th Avenue, 1-718 762 8821).

Flushing Town Hall (*see p171*), built during the Civil War in the highly fanciful Romanesque Revival style, showcases local arts groups, and hosts jazz concerts, chamber music and multimedia exhibits. It's hard to believe the gorgeous exterior survived utter abandonment in the early 1980s, when the building was overrun by derelicts. Here you can catch the **Queens Jazz Trail** (*see p171*), a monthly trolley tour of the homes of jazz legends who have resided in the borough, including Louis Armstrong, Count Basie, Ella Fitzgerald, Dizzy Gillespie, Billie Holiday and John Coltrane. The tour's centrepiece is the **Louis Armstrong House** in Corona (*see p171*), a modest brick home in a working-class community that 'Satchmo' never abandoned, despite his global fame.

The site in Queens that gets the most visitors every year is rambling **Flushing Meadows-Corona Park** (*see p171*), where the 1939 and 1964 World's Fairs were held. Larger than Central Park, Flushing Meadows is home to the **Queens Zoo**, where natural environments include a lush parrot habitat; **Queens Theatre in the Park**, an indoor amphitheatre designed by the late Philip Johnson; the **New York Hall of Science** (*see p171*), an acclaimed interactive museum; the **Queens Botanical Garden**, a 39-acre cavalcade of greenery; and also the **Queens Museum of Art** (*see p171*), which exhibits increasingly avant-garde shows that tie art to the local immigrant experience – fittingly enough for the building that was the first home of the United Nations. The museum's utterly mesmerising pièce de résistance is the **Panorama of the City of New York** (*see also p168* **Cheap date**), a 9,335-square-foot, 895,000-building scale model (1 inch equals 100 feet) of all five boroughs.

Flushing Meadows also encompasses **Shea Stadium**, home base of the Mets baseball team (*see p333*); the USTA (United States Tennis Association) National Tennis Center, where the US Open (*see p336*) raises a racket at summer's end (the general public can play here during the other 11 months of the year);

and the 140-foot-high Unisphere, a mammoth steel globe that became famous as the symbol of the 1964 World's Fair (and the final battle scene between humans and aliens in the first *Men in Black* movie). Also visible here are the remnants of the **New York State Pavilion**, erected 43 years ago for the 1964 World's Fair. The Pavilion was placed on the World Monuments Fund's 2008 list of 100 endangered sites (*see p40* **Monumental mess**).

For a true 'I can't believe this is New York' experience, take the E or F express subways out to 71st Avenue and stroll through **Forest Hills Gardens**, the remarkably preserved (and ritzy) 'garden city' developed in 1910 and inspired by the English Arts and Crafts movement. The planned community is a stroke of genius in the history of suburban development. At the end of boutique-heavy Austin Street is another neighbourhood genius – Nick's Pizza (108-26 Ascan Avenue, at Austin Street, 1-718 263 1126), a fine place to sample a New York pizza pie.

Rap fans should continue on the E or F trains out to **Jamaica** and **Hollis**, the hometowns of Run-DMC, LL Cool J and 50 Cent. The teenagers of Jamaica Avenue are hip hop taste-makers, and you'll find the latest fashions from Baby Phat and more near 164th Street. It's about as far as you can get from Manhattan by subway, but you'll find tons of New York attitude.

The website **Queens.about.com** is a great source of cultural and entertainment information, and **www.discoverqueens.info** is the official tourism website for Queens.

Flushing Meadows-Corona Park

From 111th Street to Van Wyck Expressway, between Flushing Bay & Grand Central Parkway (1-718 760 6565/Queens Zoo 1-718 220 5100/ www.queenszoo.com). Subway 7 to Willets Point-Shea Stadium.

Most people come out to these parts to catch a game at Shea Stadium, home of the New York Mets, but don't overlook the 1964 World's Fair sculptures. Flushing Meadows-Corona Park also contains the New York Hall of Science (*see below*) and the Queens Museum of Art (*see below*).

Flushing Town Hall/ Queens Jazz Trail

137-135 Northern Boulevard, at Linden Place, Flushing (1-718 463 7700/www.flushingtownhall.org). Subway 7 to Main Street. **Open** 9am-5pm Mon-Fri; noon-5pm Sat, Sun. **Admission** *Exhibits* free. *Jazz Trail* $35; 10am first Sat of the mth; reservations recommended. **Credit** AmEx, MC, V.

Jazz diehards will love the three-hour Queens Jazz Trail trolley tour that stops by Addisleigh Park and showcases haunts of jazz greats like Louis Armstrong, Ella Fitzgerald, Billie Holiday and Dizzy Gillespie. The 35 buck entrance fee also gets you a cool illustrated guide.

Hindu Temple Society

4557 Bowne Street, between Holly & 45th Avenues, Flushing (1-718 460 8484/www.nyganeshtemple.org). Subway 7 to Main Street. **Open** 8am-9pm Mon-Fri; 7.30am-9pm Sat, Sun. **Admission** free.

Dutch colonists in the area who stood up for religious freedom in the New World would be surprised and satisfied to see this ornate stone façade dedicated to the Hindu deity Ganesh. This was the first Hindu temple in the US. After visiting, try the dosas at next door's tiny Dosa Hutt.

Louis Armstrong House

34-56 107th Street, between 34th & 37th Avenues, Corona (1-718 478 8274/www.satchmo.net). Subway 7 to 103rd Street-Corona Plaza. **Open** 10am-5pm Tue-Fri; noon-5pm Sat, Sun. *Tours* 10am-4pm Tue-Fri, on the hr; noon-4pm Sat, Sun, on the hr. **Admission** $8; $6 seniors, students; free under-4s. **Credit** MC, V ($15 minimum).

Jazz lovers will have little choice but to make the pilgrimage, but should bear in mind that although this was indeed Louis' house, it was actually his wife Lucille who dealt with its day-to-day upkeep – with the end result that her decor can somewhat overshadow the legendary life of Armstrong.

New York Hall of Science

47-01 111th Street, at 47th Avenue, Flushing Meadows-Corona Park (1-718 699 0005/www.nyscience.org). Subway 7 to 111th Street. **Open** *July, Aug* 9.30am-5pm Mon-Fri; 10am-6pm Sat, Sun. *Sept-June* 9.30am-2pm Mon-Thur; 9.30am-5pm Fri; 10am-6pm Sat, Sun. **Admission** $11; $8 seniors, students, children. Free 2-5pm Fri Sept-June. Science playground extra $3 (open summer only). **Credit** AmEx, DC, Disc, MC, V.

The fun-for-all-ages New York Hall of Science, built for the 1964 World's Fair and recently expanded, demystifies its subject matter through colourful hands-on exhibits, with topics such as 'Marvelous Molecules' and 'The Realm of the Atom'. Children can burn off excess energy – and learn a thing or two – in the 30,000 sq ft outdoor science playground, which manages to entertain while it educates.

Queens Museum of Art

New York City Building, park entrance on 49th Avenue, at 111th Street, Flushing Meadows-Corona Park (1-718 592 9700/www.queensmuseum.org). Subway 7 to 111th Street, then walk south on 111th Street, turning left on to 49th Avenue; continue into the park & over Grand Central Parkway Bridge. **Open** *26 June-5 Sept* 1-8pm Wed-Sun. *6 Sept-25 June* 10am-5pm Wed-Fri; noon-5pm Sat, Sun. **Admission** $5; $2.50 seniors, students; free under-5s. **No credit cards**.

Located in the grounds of the 1939 and 1964 World's Fairs, the QMA holds one of the area's most amazing sights: a 9,335sq ft scale model of New York City, accurate down to the square inch (at least up to 1994, the date of its last major renovation). Contemporary and outsider exhibits have grown more bold and inventive here, garnering increasing acclaim.

The Bronx

Movin' on up.

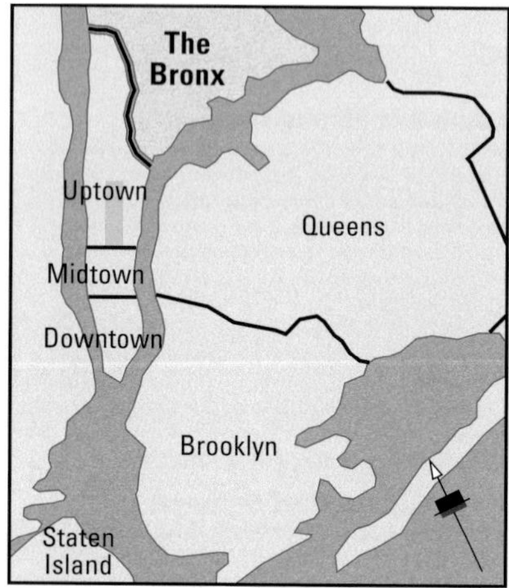

Change doesn't come easy in the Bronx. This probably has to do with the sad truth that it contains one of the poorest Congressional districts in the country. But many are hoping that the renaissance it has been promised for years will finally be realised, following an influx of cash and community support, and as an army of people seeking more affordable housing flees Manhattan and Brooklyn. In fact, so much activity is afoot that the Bronx should be called the 'hard-hat' borough, as cranes and scaffolding dominate the skyline.

In 2006, Mayor Bloomberg announced the South Bronx Initiative, which has the aim of developing and revitalising the area. Organisations like Sustainable South Bronx (www.ssbx.org) are also pledging to make way for more parks. The area was even hailed as one of the five hot markets in the country by local real-estate guru Barbara Corcoran, causing her peers to nickname the area 'SoBro'. New condos are sprouting up, old warehouses are being redeveloped, once-crumbling tenements are being refurbished and, inevitably, chain stores are moving in. Young families are snapping up the stately townhouses on Alexander Avenue and furnishing them from the thoroughfare's rejuvenated antique stores, while industrial lofts on Bruckner Boulevard are becoming homes to artistic types.

An especially thriving corner of the area is **Hunts Point**, which may still look like an industrial wasteland, but has become increasingly popular as a live-work destination for artists. In 1994, a group of artists and community leaders converted an entire 12,000-square-foot industrial building into the **Point Community Development Corporation** (940 Garrison Avenue, at Manida Street, 1-718 542 4139, www.thepoint.org), a performance space, gallery and business incubator. The Point also leads lively walking tours (call for reservations) exploring the history of locally born music genres, such as mambo and hip hop. Creative types stage performances at the nearby **Bronx Academy of Arts & Dance** (BAAD; *see p176*), and more than a dozen painters and sculptors work in the academy's studios. Those wanting a closer look at the up-and-coming arts scene should hop on the **Bronx Culture Trolley** (*see p176*), a free shuttle that visits the area's most happening galleries, performance spaces and museums. In November 2005, after much delay, Hunts Point also became the new home for the city's **Fulton Fish Market** (1-718 378 2356, www.newfultonfishmarket.com), which is housed in a modern, temperature-controlled $86 million indoor facility. Visitors can explore the place for $2-$5.

Settled in the 1630s by the family of Jonas Bronck, a Swedish farmer who had a 500-acre homestead in what is now the south-eastern Morrisania section, the area became known as 'the Broncks' farm. Over the centuries, the name stuck, though the spelling was altered. The area was originally part of Westchester County, but like the other boroughs, it was incorporated into New York City in 1898.

Throughout the early 1900s, the Bronx, like Queens and Brooklyn, drew much of its population from the ever-expanding pools of Irish, German, Italian and Eastern European Jewish immigrants who flocked to the area for its cheap rents and open spaces. After World War II, as the borough grew more urbanised, the descendants of the European immigrants moved further out to the suburbs of Long Island and Westchester, and fresh waves of newcomers, hailing from Central America, Puerto Rico, Albania and Russia, as well as Hispaniola and other points in the West Indies, took their places.

Along with the population shifts, from the late 1940s until the early '70s the Bronx probably witnessed more upheaval than the other areas of the city combined, baring the brunt of city planner Robert Moses's drastic remaking of the city. Thousands of residents saw their old apartment buildings razed to make room for the Whitestone and Throgs Neck Bridges, the east-to-west Cross Bronx Expressway and the north-to-south Bruckner Boulevard extension of the New England Thruway. Many neighbourhoods fell into neglect, a condition swiftly exacerbated by the economic and social downturns that plagued the entire city in the 1960s and '70s. The local community felt (rightly so) cut off, forgotten and left to rot by the authorities.

The Bronx always drew sightseers for its long-standing gems like **Yankee Stadium** (*see p334*), located at 161st Street and River Avenue. Baseball's most famous legends made history on its diamond, from Babe Ruth and Joe DiMaggio to Derek Jeter. When there isn't a day game, the Yankees organisation gives tours of the clubhouse, the dugout and the famous centre-field **Monument Park**. Enjoy 'the house that Ruth built' while you can: in 2009, the Yankees will move to their new home – a brand new $800 million stadium across the street. When George Steinbrenner unveiled the plan in 2005, he put an end to years of threats of abandoning the borough for Manhattan or New Jersey, finally ensuring that the Bombers will remain in the Bronx. The new stadium met with some opposition by groups concerned about it encroaching on parkland. Ground-breaking began, however, in summer 2006. The original will be torn down and replaced by a park.

Just under the Major Deegan Expressway, south of Yankee Stadium, lies the site of another controversial development – the former **Bronx Terminal Market**, once the largest wholesale market of ethnic and tropical produce on the East Coast. It closed in 2006 after 80 years of business; plans for replacing the cluster of buildings with a one-million-square-foot shopping mall are under way. The $400 million project is one of the largest private investments in the borough's history.

A few blocks east lies the six-and-a-half-mile **Grand Concourse**, which is also undergoing a facelift as its centennial approaches (2009). Around $18 million has now been set aside to rebuild the area near Yankee Stadium. Plans include adding a terraced park, planting new trees and flowers, installing new streetlights, paving a bike lane and laying down cobblestones. Once the most prestigious drag in the Bronx, it's still a real must for lovers of architecture. Engineer Louis Risse designed the boulevard, which stretches from 138th Street to Mosholu Parkway, in 1892, patterning it after Paris's Champs-Elysées. Starting at 161st Street and heading south, look for the permanent street plaques that make up the **Bronx Walk of Fame**, honouring famous Bronxites from Regis Philbin to Colin Powell to Afrika Bambaataa.

Heading north, the buildings date mostly from the 1920s to the early '40s, and display the country's largest array of art deco housing. Erected in 1937 at the corner of 161st Street, **888 Grand Concourse** has a large concave entrance of gilded mosaic and is topped by a curvy metallic marquee. Inside, the mirrored lobby's central fountain and sunburst-patterned floor could rival those of any hotel on Miami's Ocean Drive. But the grandest building on the Concourse is the landmark **Andrew Freedman Home**, a 1924 French-inspired limestone palazzo between McClennan and 166th Streets. Freedman, a millionaire subway contractor, set aside the bulk of his $7 million estate to build a poorhouse for the rich – those who lost their fortunes, that is. It now plays host to the Family Preservation Center (FPC), a community-based social service agency. Across the street, the **Bronx Museum of the Arts** (*see p176*), established in 1971 in a former synagogue, exhibits high-quality contemporary and historical works by Bronx-based artists, including many of African-American, Asian and Latino heritage. Near the intersection of Fordham Road, keep an eye out for the freshly refurbished **Loew's Paradise Theater** (2403 Grand Concourse, between Elm Place and E 188th Street, 1-718 220 6143, www.theparadisetheater.com), with its recently landmarked interior. The Italian rococo exterior of the building was landmarked in 1997.

Due north to Kingsbridge Road, lovers of literature will enjoy the **Edgar Allan Poe Cottage** (*see p176*), a small wooden farmhouse where the writer lived from 1846 to 1849. Moved to the Grand Concourse from its original spot on Fordham Road in 1913, the museum has period furniture and details about Poe and his work. Nearby, a neighbourhood enjoying a notable resurgence is Bronx's **Little Italy**, centred on Arthur Avenue (*see p175* **A little Italy**), lined with many Italian delis, restaurants, markets and cafés. Browse and nibble at the **Arthur Avenue Retail Market** (Crescent Avenue, at 186th Street), an indoor bazaar built in the 1940s when former mayor Fiorello La Guardia campaigned to get the pushcarts off the street. The market is closed on Sundays. Inside is **Mike's Deli** (2344 Arthur Avenue, between Crescent Avenue & E 186th Street, 1-718 295 5033), where you can try the trademark schiacciata sandwich of grilled vegetables, or Big Mike's Combo, a roll loaded with provolone cheese and cold cuts. If you're more in the mood for a full meal, try old-style red-sauce joints **Mario's** (2342 Arthur Avenue, between Crescent Avenue & E 186th Street, 1-718 584 1188) or the charming **Roberto's** (603 Crescent Avenue, between Hughes & Arthur Avenue, 1-718 733 9503).

The serene 250 acres of the **New York Botanical Garden** (*see p176*) are a magical respite from cars and concrete, comprising 50 gardens and plant collections, including the Rockefeller Rose Garden, the Everett Children's Adventure Garden and the last 50 original acres of a forest that once covered all of New York City. In springtime, the gardens are frothy with pastel blossoms, as clusters of lilac, cherry, magnolia and crab apple trees burst into bloom, followed in autumn by vivid foliage in the oak and maple groves. On a rainy day, you can stay warm and sheltered inside the Enid A Haupt Conservatory, a striking glass-walled greenhouse – the nation's largest – built in 1902. It offers seasonal exhibits, as well as the World of Plants, a series of environmental galleries that will send you on an eco-tour through tropical rainforests, deserts and a palm-tree oasis.

Next door is the borough's most famous attraction, the **Bronx Zoo** (*see p176*), opened in 1899 by Theodore Roosevelt in an attempt to preserve game. At 265 acres, it's the largest urban zoo in the US. The zoo shuns cages in favour of indoor and outdoor environments that mimic the natural habitats of more than 4,000 mammals, birds and reptiles. Nearly 100 species, including monkeys, leopards and tapirs, live inside the lush, steamy Jungle World, a re-creation of an Asian rainforest inside a 37,000-square-foot building. The super-popular Congo Gorilla Forest has turned six and a half acres into a dramatic Central African rainforest habitat. A glass-enclosed tunnel winds through the forest, allowing visitors to get close to the dozens of primate families in residence, including 26 majestic western lowland gorillas. For those who prefer cats, Tiger Mountain has six adult Siberian tigers, who look particularly regal on snowy days. The zoo's newest additions include African wild dogs; an aquatic aviary; a butterfly garden, featuring 1,000 colourful flutterers; and the adjacent Bug Carousel.

Pelham Bay Park (take the 6 train to Pelham Bay), in the borough's north-eastern corner, is NYC's biggest park, once home to the Siwonay Indians. Take a car or a bike if you want to explore the 2,765 acres. Get a map at the Ranger Nature Center, near the entrance on Bruckner Boulevard at Wilkinson Avenue. The **Bartow-Pell Mansion Museum** (*see p175*), in the park's south-eastern quarter, overlooks Long Island Sound. Finished in 1842, the elegantly furnished Greek Revival building faces a reflecting pool ringed by gardens. The park's 13 miles of coastline skirt the Hutchinson River to the west and the Long Island Sound and Eastchester Bay to the east. In summer, locals hit sandy **Orchard Beach**; set up in the 1930s, this 'Riviera of New York' is a rare Robert Moses project loved by all.

Riverdale, along the north-west coast of the Bronx, reflects the borough's suburban past. Huge homes perch on narrow, winding streets overlooking the Hudson River. Theodore Roosevelt, Mark Twain and Arturo Toscanini have all resided at **Wave Hill House** (*see p176*), an 1843 stone mansion set on a former private estate that is now both a cultural and environmental centre. The 28 acres of cultivated gardens and woodlands provide fine views of the river, especially at sunset. The in-house art gallery shows nature-themed exhibits, and the organisation presents year-round concerts and performances, t'ai chi classes and events like the 'barefoot dancing' series. If you need a day outdoors, try walking or cycling the quiet pathways of the Hudson River-hugging **Riverdale Park**. Enter this swath of forest preserve along Palisade Avenue, between 232nd and 254th Streets.

The nearby 1,146-acre **Van Cortlandt Park** (entrance on Broadway, at 244th Street) often hosts cricket teams made up mostly of West Indians. You can hike through a 100-year-old forest, play golf on the nation's first municipal course or rent horses at stables in the park.

Van Cortlandt House Museum (*see p176*), a fine example of pre-Revolutionary Georgian architecture, was built by Frederick van Cortlandt in 1748 and was used as a headquarters for George Washington in the Revolutionary War. It was donated to the city by the van Cortlandt family, and is the oldest building in the borough. Abutting the park is **Woodlawn Cemetery**, which houses over 300,000 bodies, including Elizabeth Cady Stanton, Duke Ellington, Miles Davis, FW Woolworth and Damon Runyon. Maps are available at the visitors' entrance at Webster Avenue and E 233rd Street. About five blocks south on Bainbridge Avenue, history buffs will also enjoy stopping in at the Bronx Historical Society's **Museum of Bronx History** (*see p176*), set in a lovely 1758 stone farmhouse.

Despite all the recent redevelopment, there is an organised effort to retain the unique New England-like charm of **City Island**. Located just east of Pelham Bay Park and ringed by the waters of Eastchester Bay and the Long Island Sound, City Island was settled in 1685 and was

A little Italy

Arthur Avenue's Italian hub, in the heart of working-class Belmont, is small and very utilitarian-looking – just six blocks, densely packed with a colourful collection of third- and fourth-generation Italian restaurants, butchers, bakers, fishmongers and grocers. These days, Albanian and Spanish signage has also become common as the local demographic shifts, but the neighbourhood remains the city's single best source for everything Italian – from St Francis medals for pets (Catholic Goods Center, 630 E 187th Street, between Hughes & Belmont Streets) to Sicilian salt-packed capers and Francesconi canned tomatoes sold by the case (Teitel Brothers, 2372 Arthur Avenue). By day, the various wares spill out on to the sidewalks, among them homemade lemon, chocolate and cremolata ices, and curbside raw bars manned by waiters in crisp white aprons. Meat vendors display skinned rabbits and baby lambs dangling on hooks over bins piled high with tripe and trotters.

Pop into **Mike's Deli** (2344 Arthur Avenue, between 183rd & 186th Streets, 1-718 295 5033), located in the city's most beloved food and kitchen supplies market. The glossy menu may paralyse you with indecision – it lists more than 50 different sandwiches.

Albanians increasingly populate these streets, but the flavour of the old country is more intact here than it is in Manhattan's stage-set Little Italy or in Brooklyn's rapidly gentrifying Carroll Gardens. In fact, Belmont's ambience has been carefully preserved for more than 80 years by those who originally came to find refuge here, not only from the poverty of Eastern Europe, but also the choked tenements of Mulberry Street. Before leaving, grab a cannoli in classic Italian-American pastry shop **Edigio's** (622 E 187th Street, at Hughes Street, 1-718 295 6077).

T-shirts on sale in the neighbourhood boldly proclaim Belmont to be 'New York's real Little Italy'. We think they have a point.

For more, visit www.arthuravenuebronx.com.

once a prosperous shipbuilding centre with a busy fishing industry. Its history is reflected in the Victorian captains' houses that line its streets. Nautical activity still abounds, especially in the summer, but recreational boating is the main industry now. The island's main drag, City Island Avenue, brims with art galleries and antique shops, while seafood restaurants, marine-themed bars, yacht clubs and sail-makers crowd the docks.

Join the warm-weather hordes at **Johnny's Famous Reef Restaurant** (No.2, at Belden Street, 1-718 885 2086) for steamed clams, cold beer and great views. Few commercial fishermen remain, but you'd hardly know it at **Rosenberg's Boat Livery** (No.663, 1-718 885 1843), a bait-and-tackle shop that rents motorboats by the day. The Livery also doubles as a bustling bar. Timeless treasures like these prove that the lure of the Bronx never really went away – they just need to be dusted off and discovered by a new generation.

Bartow-Pell Mansion Museum

895 Shore Road North, at Pelham Bay Park (1-718 885 1461/www.bartowpellmansionmuseum.org). Subway 6 to Pelham Bay Park, then take the Bee-Line bus 45 (ask driver to stop at the Bartow-Pell Mansion; bus does not run on Sun), or take a cab from the subway station. **Open** noon-4pm Wed, Sat, Sun. **Admission** $5; $3 seniors, students; free under-6s. Free Wed. **No credit cards**.

Operating as a museum since 1946, this stunning estate dates from 1654, when Thomas Pell bought the land from the Siwonay Indians. It was Robert Bartow, publisher and Pell descendant, who added the Grecian-style stone mansion.

Bronx Academy of Arts & Dance (BAAD)

2nd Floor, 841 Barretto Street, between Garrison & Lafayette Avenues (1-718 842 5223/www.bronxacademyofartsanddance.org). Subway 6 to Hunts Point Avenue. **Open** check website for performances & prices.

A myriad dance, theatre and visual arts events including OUT LIKE THAT!, the borough's only fest celebrating works by lesbian, gay, bisexual and transgender artists; and BAAD! ASS WOMEN, a cultural celebration of works by women.

Bronx Culture Trolley

The Bronx Council on the Arts, 15738 Hone Avenue (1-718 931 9500 ext 33/www.bronxarts.org). Subway 2, 4, 5 to 149th Street-Grand Concourse. **Open** *Feb-Aug, Oct-Dec* 1st Wed of mth 5.30pm, 6.30pm & 7.30pm from the Longwood Art Gallery at the Hostos Center for the Arts & Culture (450 Grand Concourse). **Admission** free.

The trolley in question is a replica of an early 20th-century trolley that shuttles you (for free!) to a whole host of galleries and performing arts venues around the Bronx. It also takes riders to the Artisans Marketplace, a giant craft fair with all sorts of attractive handmade wares. Visit the website for a full schedule of seasonal events.

Bronx Museum of the Arts

1040 Grand Concourse, at 165th Street (1-718 681 6000/www.bxma.org). Subway B, D to 167th Street Grand Concourse; 4 to 161st Street-Yankee Stadium. **Open** noon-9pm Wed; noon-6pm Thur-Sun. **Admission** $5; $3 seniors, students; free under-12s. Free Wednesday. **No credit cards**.

Founded in 1971 and featuring more than 800 works, this multicultural art museum shines a spotlight on 20th- and 21st-century artists of African, Asian and Latin American ancestry.

Bronx Zoo/Wildlife Conservation Society

Bronx River Parkway, at Fordham Road (1-718 367 1010/www.bronxzoo.org). Subway 2 to Pelham Parkway, then walk two blocks, turn left at Boston Road and bear right to the zoo's Bronxdale entrance; or Metro-North's Harlem Line to Fordham, then take the Bx9 bus south to the zoo entrance, or the Bx12 bus east to Southern Boulevard, and walk east to the zoo entrance. **Open** *Apr-Oct* 10am-5pm Mon-Fri; 10am-5.30pm Sat, Sun, holidays. *Nov-Mar* 10am-4.30pm daily. **Admission** $14; $12 seniors; $10 3-12s; free under-2s. Voluntary donation Wed. (Some rides and exhibitions cost extra.) **Credit** AmEx, DC, Disc, MC, V.

Home to more than 4,500 creatures, including African wild dogs (the latest additions). For visitors who want a bird's-eye view, the Skyfari, an aerial tram ride over the zoo itself, is excellent. Highlights include an underwater viewing area; the Congo Gorilla forest; Tiger Mountain, which educates visitors about tigers and the conservation issues surrounding them; and an indoor Asian rainforest.

Edgar Allan Poe Cottage

2640 Grand Concourse, at Kingsbridge Road (1-718 881 8900/www.bronxhistoricalsociety.org). Subway D, 4 to Kingsbridge Road. **Open** 10am-4pm Sat; 1-5pm Sun. **Admission** $3; $2 seniors, students. **No credit cards**.

Pay homage to Poe in the very house where he wrote literary gems including *Annabel Lee* and *The Bells*. A presentation film and guided tour are available.

Museum of Bronx History

Valentine-Varian House, 3266 Bainbridge Avenue, between Van Cortlandt Avenue & E 208th Street (1-718 881 8900/www.bronxhistoricalsociety.org). Subway D to Norwood-205th Street. **Open** 10am-4pm Sat; 1-5pm Sun. **Admission** $3; $2 seniors, students & children. **No credit cards**.

Operated by the Bronx County Historical Society, the Museum of Bronx History is located in the Valentine-Varian House, a Federal-style fieldstone residence built in 1758. The society offers tours that explore the neighbourhoods and historic periods.

New York Botanical Garden

Bronx River Parkway, at Fordham Road (1-718 817 8700/www.nybg.org). Subway B, D to Bedford Park Boulevard, then take the Bx26 bus to Garden gate; or Metro-North (Harlem Line local) from Grand Central Terminal to Botanical Garden. **Open** *Apr-Oct* 10am-6pm Tue-Sun, Mon federal holidays. *Nov-Mar* 10am-5pm Tue-Sun. **Admission** $18; $16 seniors, students; $5 2-12s; free under-2s. *Grounds only* $6; free 10am-5pm Wed; noon-5pm Sat. **Credit** AmEx, DC, MC, V.

Make yourself at home among these 250 acres of flora. If you're coming from Manhattan, look into specials from Metro-North's Harlem line train from Grand Central Terminal, which may include a round-trip ticket with admission.

Van Cortlandt House Museum

Van Cortlandt Park, entrance on Broadway, at 246th Street (1-718 543 3344/www.vancortlandthouse.org). Subway 1 to 242nd Street-Van Cortlandt Park. **Open** 10am-3pm Tue-Fri; 11am-4pm Sat, Sun. **Admission** $5; $3 seniors, students; free under-12s. Free Wed. **No credit cards**.

A one-time wheat plantation that has since been turned into an interesting colonial museum.

Wave Hill House

W 249th Street, at Independence Avenue (1-718 549 3200/www.wavehill.org). Rail Metro-North (Hudson Line local) from Grand Central Terminal to Riverdale. **Open** *Mid Apr-May, Aug-mid Oct* 9am-5.30pm Tue-Sun. *June, July* 9am-5.30pm Tue, Thur-Sun; 9am-9pm Wed. *Mid Oct-mid Apr* 9am-4.30pm Tue-Sun. **Admission** $4; $2 seniors, students; free under-6s. Free all day Tue, 9am-noon Sat. **No credit cards**.

Laze around in these 28 lush acres overlooking the Hudson River at Wave Hill, a former estate that has housed Mark Twain, Teddy Roosevelt and conductor Arturo Toscanini. It's now a spectacular nature preserve and conservation centre, where you can see art exhibits and dance and music performances.

Staten Island

Go for the ferry ride, stay for a slower pace and a slew of sights.

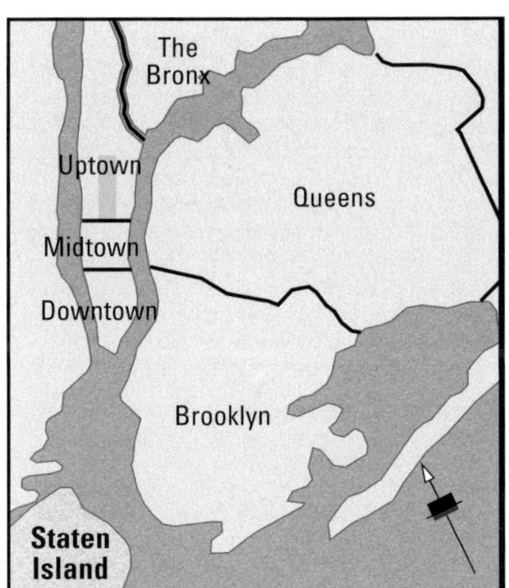

In May 2006, New York was rocked by a shocking crime on Staten Island. A woman ambushed a man at the doorstep of his home, shooting him four times. What surprised New Yorkers wasn't so much the crime, though, but the nature of the man's dwelling – in a 90-person commune known only as 'Ganas'. A free-loving, toothpaste-sharing, tree-hugging counterculture in Staten Island? Looking past the working-class neighbourhoods and the ordinary strip malls, maybe it shouldn't be a shock – Staten Island has, one way or another, long struggled to establish a utopia amid the urban sprawl.

The first visitor looking to drop out and tune in to a bucolic new world was Giovanni da Verrazano, who set down his anchor on the island in 1524. But the spot wasn't named until 1609, when Henry Hudson sailed in and christened it *Staaten Eylandt* (Dutch for 'State's Island'). Early settlements were repeatedly decimated by Native Americans, the island's first true preservationists. But the Dutch finally took hold in 1661, establishing shipping and manufacturing communities on the northern shore, and farms and small hamlets in the south. Despite being made one of the five boroughs in 1898, the predominantly rural area remained a somewhat isolated Eden until 1964, when the Verrazano-Narrows Bridge joined the island to Brooklyn's Bay Ridge neighbourhood.

The **Staten Island Ferry** (*see p90* and *photo p179*) is the borough's best-known connection to the rest of the city, linking lower Manhattan to the island's St George terminal, which was revamped in 2005 in honour of its 100th birthday. Once a dreary through-station, the terminal is now marked by floor-to-ceiling glass, providing commuters with panoramic views of the harbour and lower Manhattan's skyline. A new outdoor promenade surrounding the area is in the works, slated for completion by summer 2008, to provide easier access to the neighbourhood's many attractions, including *Postcards*, a sculpture by Japanese architect Masayuki Sono – a memorial to the 253 Staten Islanders lost on 9/11.

Along Richmond Terrace lies the **Richmond County Savings Bank Ballpark**, home of three-time minor league champions the Staten Island Yankees (www.siyanks.com), a great place to catch a game and a harbourside view. Across the street, look for the **Borough Hall**'s (10 Richmond Terrace) distinctive clocktower and step inside for a peek at the *Works Progress Administration* murals depicting local history. Also well worth popping into is the Spanish baroque-styled lobby of the newly restored **St George Theater** (35 Hyatt Street, 1-718 442 2900, www.stgeorgetheater.com), just two blocks inland. You can expect exhibits on anything from baseball cards to beetles at the **Staten Island Museum** (75 Stuyvesant Place, 1-718 727 1135, www.statenislandmuseum.org), the city's only general-interest museum, just another two blocks north. Continuing north and then west along Richmond Terrace to Westervelt Avenue, then uphill two blocks to St Marks Place, you'll come upon the **St George-New Brighton Historic District**, a landmark neighbourhood full of Queen Anne and Colonial Revival buildings dating from the early 1830s. Moving south to Bay Street near Victory Boulevard, vintage fashion fans will enjoy the various thrift shops dotting the strip.

Dozens of pastoral attractions lie further inland. You can spend an entire day looking around the 83-acre **Snug Harbor Cultural Center** (*see p179*), just a short bus ride west along Richmond Terrace. Stately Greek Revival structures form the nucleus of the former maritime hospital and sailors' home dating from 1833. The centre was converted in the

Sightseeing

1970s into a visual and performing arts complex that includes the **Art Lab and Newhouse** art galleries, the **Staten Island Children's Museum** and the verdant **Staten Island Botanical Garden** (for all, *see p179*), as well as the Noble Maritime Collection, with various artworks by **John A Noble** (1-718 447 6490, www.noblemaritime.org). Slightly further inland, the **Staten Island Zoo** (*see p179*), adjacent to the Clove Lakes Park, boasts an aquarium, a rainforest and one of the East Coast's largest reptile collections.

Buses and the single-line Staten Island Railroad depart from St George for destinations along the eastern half of the island. Along Hylan Boulevard, one of Staten Island's major arteries, lies photographer **Alice Austen**'s house (*see below*), a 15-minute bus ride east of the ferry. The 18th-century cottage has breathtaking harbour views and 3,000 of Austen's glass negative photos. At the east end of Bay Street, historic **Fort Wadsworth** (*see p178*) is one of the oldest military sites in the nation. There, visitors can explore the Civil War-era gun batteries or take in the vista of the Verrazano bridge and downtown Manhattan from one of NYC's highest points. Further along the eastern coast, residents and tourists stroll along the two-mile **FDR Boardwalk** of South Beach, the fourth longest in the world. It's also a great area for picnicking, cycling and fishing.

Right in the centre of the island, over on Lighthouse Avenue, many seek refuge at the **Jacques Marchais Museum of Tibetan Art** (*see p179*), a reproduction of a Himalayan mountain temple with tranquil meditation gardens, and a small collection of Tibetan and Buddhist objects of interest. The museum also hosts meditation workshops. Nearby, guides in period garb offer tours of **Historic Richmond Town** (*see p179*), the island's one-time county seat. Among them is Voorlezer's House (the nation's oldest former schoolhouse circa 1695). Just a stone's throw away, **High Rock Park** (*see below*) is the entry point for more than 30 miles of hiking trails. It's part of the 2,800-acre **Greenbelt** (www.sigreenbelt.org) and includes golf, archery, bird watching and a nature centre.

The island's south-eastern coast (a 40-minute ride on the S78 bus) is especially pleasant in the summer, when you can swim, picnic and fish at **Wolfe's Pond Park** (Cornelia Avenue, at Hylan Boulevard, 1-718 984 8266). A little further south, the historic **Conference House** (*see below*) was the site for a failed attempt at peace between American and British forces in 1776, and is now a museum of colonial life. A short walk away, you'll find yourself at the very tip of the island on Tottenville Beach. Here, you can relax and admire the passing sailboats.

Staten Island's areas for rural respite are growing with the addition of the **Fresh Kills Park**, a 2,200-acre parcel of land that was once the city's garbage dump and which is now slated to become the city's largest park, at almost three times the size of Central Park. While the project's completion is 30 years away, parts of the park are scheduled to open in 2008, and the Parks Department currently offers guided tours of the site twice a month (visit www.nycparks.org for more info). The finished park will include a sports stadium, cycling trails and a monument to the World Trade Center on the site where its wreckage rested after 9/11.

Still, another new development for the island was halted after drawing fierce opposition from evironmentalists – NYC's very own NASCAR track, proposed for 450 acres near the Goethals Bridge. After all, you don't have to be part of a tree-hugging commune to cherish, and preserve, some of the city's most idyllic charms.

Alice Austen House

2 Hylan Boulevard, between Bay & Edgewater Streets (1-718 816 4506/www.aliceausten.org). From the Staten Island Ferry, take the S51 bus to Hylan Boulevard. **Open** *Mar-Dec* noon-5pm Thur-Sun. Closed major holidays. **Admission** suggested donation $2. **No credit cards**.

History buffs will marvel at Austen's beautiful turn-of-the-19th-century photographs. The restored house and grounds often host concerts and events.

Conference House (Billopp House)

7455 Hylan Boulevard, at Craig Avenue (1-718 984 2086/www.theconferencehouse.org). From the Staten Island Ferry, take the S78 bus to Craig Avenue. **Open** *1 Apr-15 Dec* 1-4pm Fri-Sun. **Admission** $3; $2 seniors, children. **No credit cards**.

Britain's Lord Howe parleyed with John Adams and Benjamin Franklin in this 17th-century manor house in 1776 while trying to stop the American Revolution.

Fort Wadsworth

East end of Bay Street (1-718 354 4500). From the Staten Island Ferry, take the S51 bus to Fort Wadsworth on weekdays, Von Briesen Park on weekends. **Open** dawn-dusk daily. *Visitors' Center* 10am-5pm Wed-Sun. **Tours** phone for schedule. **Admission** free.

Explore the fortifications that guarded NYC for almost 200 years, or take one of several themed tours, like the popular evening lantern-light tours.

High Rock Park

200 Nevada Avenue, at Rockland Avenue (1-718 667 2165/www.sigreenbelt.org). From the Staten Island Ferry, take the S62 bus to Manor Road, then the S54 bus to Nevada Avenue. **Open** dawn-dusk daily. *Greenbelt Nature Center Visitors' Center (1-718 351 3450)* 10am-5pm Tue-Sun. **Admission** free.

At the 90-acre High Rock Park visitors may hike the mile-long Swamp Trail, climb Todt Hill or explore trails through forests, meadows and wetlands.

Staten Island Ferry. See p177.

Historic Richmond Town

441 Clarke Avenue, between Richmond Road & St Patrick's Place (1-718 351 1611/www.historicrichmondtown.org). From the Staten Island Ferry, take the S74 bus to St Patrick's Place. **Open** *8 Jan-30 June & Sept-Dec* 1-5pm Wed-Sun. *July-Aug* 10am-5pm Wed-Fri; 1-5pm Sat, Sun. Closed major holidays and 1-7 Jan. **Admission** $5; $4 seniors; $3.50 5-17s; free under-5s. **No credit cards.**

A colonial era 'living museum' with 15 restored buildings, including residences, public buildings and a museum. Tours are available alongside a range of activities from pumpkin picking to quilting.

Jacques Marchais Museum of Tibetan Art

338 Lighthouse Avenue, off Richmond Road (1-718 987 3500/www.tibetanmuseum.org). From the Staten Island Ferry, take the S74 bus to Lighthouse Avenue. **Open** 1-5pm Wed-Sun. **Admission** $5; $3 seniors, students, 6-12s; free under-6s. **Credit** AmEx, MC, V.

This tiny museum contains a formidable Buddhist altar, lovely gardens and a large collection of Tibetan art. An excellent Tibetan cultural festival takes place each October.

Staten Island Zoo

614 Broadway, between Glenwood Place & West Raleigh Avenue (1-718 442 3100/www.statenislandzoo.org). From the Staten Island Ferry, take the S48 bus to Broadway. **Open** 10am-4.45pm daily. Closed major holidays. **Admission** $7; $5 seniors; $4 3-14s; free under-3s. Free 2-4.45pm Wed (but suggested donation $2). **No credit cards.**

This is the home of 'Staten Island Chuck', NYC's very own furry Groundhog Day forecaster, but the zoo also holds one of the largest reptile and amphibian collections on the East Coast.

Snug Harbor Cultural Center

Art Lab

Snug Harbor Cultural Center, Building H (1-718 447 8667/www.artlab.info). **Open** 9am-8pm Mon-Thur; 9am-5pm Fri-Sun. **Admission** free.

This not-for-profit space runs classes in fine arts, crafts, and photography for children and adults. The Art Lab Gallery exhibits the work of a different local artist every month.

Newhouse Center for Contemporary Art

Snug Harbor Cultural Center, Building C (1-718 448 2500/www.snug-harbor.org/newhouse). **Open** 10am-5pm Tue-Sun. **Admission** $3; $2 seniors, under-12s. **Credit** AmEx, MC, V.

Staten Island's premier space for contemporary art.

Snug Harbor Cultural Center

1000 Richmond Terrace, between Snug Harbor Road & Tysen Street (1-718 448 2500/tickets 1-718 815 7684/www.snug-harbor.org). From the Staten Island Ferry, take the S40 bus to the north gate (tell the bus driver). **Open** *Galleries* 10am-5pm Tue-Sun. **Admission** $3; $2 seniors, under-12s. **Credit** AmEx, MC, V.

In addition to the venues that are listed here, Snug Harbor also houses a 400-seat auditorium and the city's oldest concert venue.

Staten Island Botanical Garden

Snug Harbor Cultural Center, Building H (1-718 273 8200/www.sibg.org). **Open** dawn-dusk daily. **Admission** *Chinese Scholar's Garden* $5; $4 seniors, students, children. *Grounds & other gardens* free. **Credit** AmEx, MC, V.

Stroll through more than 20 themed gardens, from the White Garden (based on Vita Sackville-West's creation at Sissinghurst Castle) and the tranquil, pavilion-lined Chinese Scholar's Garden to the delightful Secret Garden, complete with child-size castle, maze and a secluded walled garden.

Staten Island Children's Museum

Snug Harbor Cultural Center (1-718 273 2060/www.statenislandkids.org). **Open** *School year* noon-5pm Tue-Fri; 10am-5pm Sat-Sun. *Summer* 10am-5pm Tue; 10am-8pm Wed; 10am-5pm Thur-Sun. **Admission** $5. **Credit** AmEx, MC, V.

This museum's hands-on exhibits, workshops and after-school programmes entertain kids of all ages.

Eat, Drink, Shop

Restaurants & Cafés **182**
Bars **216**
Shops & Services **228**

Features

The best Restaurants 182
And the winner is... 185
Tax and tipping 189
How sweet it is 192
The upper crust 206
Gallic in Gotham 214
And the winner is... 217
Craft night 220
Lighting up 227
Where to shop 228
Green scene 232
Treasure hunt 240
Sweet love 247
Holiday helpers 255

Monkey Bar. *See p223.*

Restaurants & Cafés

The world on your plate.

The past year or so hasn't been easy for restaurant owners in New York City. City government has been more involved in what, how and where New Yorkers eat and drink than at any other time in recent memory. There was a ban placed on trans fats (perhaps the most dramatic example of a trend to improve the local eating habits); an especially public (and nasty) liquor-licence tug-of-war; and the Department of Health's energetic rampage to close eateries with seemingly only minor infractions. Still, rest assured that fine dining in NYC is doing just fine. And so too are the cheap eats – and everything in between. The parade of new openings has not ceased to amaze even the most jaded, seen-it-all New Yorkers. Today, more than ever, diners want to know where their food comes from, how it was produced and if it's in season. Restaurants like **Telepan** *(see p209)*, **Cookshop** *(see p198)* and **Applewood** *(see p213)* flaunt local, organic and sustainable ingredients like badges of honour.

One thing that hasn't changed: the burger joint and steakhouse mania that has swept the town is showing no sign of abating in red meat-crazed New York (anyone would think this was Chicago!). Topping the list is **Craftsteak** *(see p198)*, which won the 2007 *Time Out New York*'s 'Readers' Choice Eat Out' award for best new steakhouse (*see p185* **And the winner is...**). At this enormous steakhouse the meat line-up reads like a wine list – diners can select by cattle breed, type of feed, cut and time spent ageing. Also new to the meat scene are **Kobe Club** (*see p203*), and **Porter House New York** (*see p209*). Just be warned: a genuinely hearty appetite for spending is a must at these highly chic beef emporiums. Burger mavens are encouraged to indulge at the new **BLT Burger** (*see p195*) or **BRGR** (*see p198*).

The invasion of the meat mavericks has been matched only by the invasion of new restaurants in the Meatpacking District, which at long last appears to be running out of space. Mario Batali's upscale Italian joint, **Del Posto** (*p199*), caused quite a splash, but neighbouring restaurants – especially Asian-themed examples like **Morimoto** (*see p201*), **Buddakan** (*see p199*) and **Buddha Bar** (*see p198*) – have stolen some of the thunder.

New Yorkers have always had a sweet tooth but the past year has undeniably been the year of the pastry-chef-turned-restaurateur. It's hard to pinpoint when the sugar rush began, but it was clear this was a serious trend when two major dessert makers – **Pichet Ong** (formerly of Spice Market and 66) and **Sam Mason** (formerly of wd-50) – decided to open their own joints (*see p192* **How sweet it is**).

If pizza is more your style, you're in luck – we've rooted out some of the best spots for your dining pleasure (*see p206* **The upper crust**).

The best Restaurants

For burgers and fries
BLT Burger (*see p195*), **BRGR** (*see p198*) and **Corner Bistro** (*see p197*).

For cheap eats
Dojo West (*see p196*), **Gray's Papaya** (*see p209*) and **Peanut Butter & Co** (*see p196*).

For dining alfresco
La Bottega (*see p199*), **Central Park Boathouse Restaurant** (*see p211*) and **DuMont** (*see p213*).

For late-night grub
Blue Ribbon (*see p189*), **Empire Diner** (*see p199*) and **Pre:Post** (*see p199*).

For the hippest scene
Café Habana (*see p184*), **Ditch Plains** (*see p198*) and **Rapture Café & Books** (*see p190*).

For vegetarian
Blossom (*see p201*), **Caravan of Dreams** (*see p195*) and **Pure Food & Wine** (*see p202*).

For weekend brunch
Balthazar (*see p190*), **Clinton Street Baking Company** (*see p187*) and **Freemans** (*see p188*).

TABLE TALK

The hardest part about eating out in New York City is the simple fact that there are hundreds, no, make that thousands, of choices. It's virtually impossible even for locals to try to keep up with all the new places while still trying to visit old favourites. Naturally, with

A dog is for life at the **New York City Hot Dog Company**. *See p184.*

all the foodie madness, snagging reservations can be difficult, so always be sure to call ahead. Super-trendy spots can be fully booked weeks in advance, though luckily the vast majority require only a few days' notice, or less. Most restaurants fill up between 7pm and 9pm and it's harder to bag reservations on weekends than weekdays. If you don't mind eating early (5pm) or late (after 10pm), your chances of getting in somewhere popular will improve greatly. Alternatively, you can try to nab a reservation by calling at 5pm on the day you want to dine and hoping for a last-minute cancellation. Dress codes are rarely enforced any more, but some ultra-fancy eateries do require men to don a jacket and tie. If in doubt, simply call ahead and ask. But take heart: after all, you can never really overdress in this town.

Note that prices given for restaurants in this chapter are averages.

LIGHTING UP

A strict citywide smoking ban (now in its sixth year) has changed the carousing habits of many smokers: some go to bars and restaurants that allow smoking, but these are very few and far between. The only legal indoor places to smoke are either venues that largely cater to cigar smokers (and actually sell cigars and cigarettes) or spaces that have created areas specifically for smokers, and that somehow pass legal muster. For a few of our favourite spots, *see p224* **Lighting up**.

Downtown

Tribeca & South

American

Bouley Bakery & Market
130 West Broadway, at Duane Street (1-212 608 5829). Subway A, C, 1, 2, 3 to Chambers Street.
Open *Bakery* 7.30am-7.30pm daily. *Restaurant* 6-11pm Tue-Sat. **Main course** $19. **Sandwich** $9. **Credit** AmEx, DC, Disc, MC, V. **Map** p402 E31 ❶
Chef David Bouley's bakery has pastries, breads, sandwiches, salads and pizza on the ground floor; a cellar full of seafood, produce, meats and cheeses; and, on the first floor, a dining room with a sushi bar and cocktails by mixologist Albert Trummer.

► ❶ Purple numbers given in this chapter correspond to the location of each restaurant and café as marked on the street maps. *See pp402-412.*

New York City Hot Dog Company

105 Chambers Street, at Church Street (1-212 240 9550). Subway A, C to Chambers Street. **Open** 10am-10pm Mon-Fri ; 10am-7pm Sat. **Hot dogs** $3. **No credit cards. Map** p402 E31 ❷

The theme here is haute-dog. You can have turkey, kobe, tofu or classic beef. Toppings cover a wide spectrum. Blue cheese anyone? Eat in or take dogs for a walk in nearby City Hall Park. *Photos p183.*

Cafés

Jack's Stir Brew Coffee

222 Front Street, between Beekman Street & Peck Slip (1-212 227 7631). Subway A, C to Broadway-Nassau Street. **Open** 6am-7pm daily. **Coffee** $2. **Credit** MC, V. **Map** p402 F32 ❸

Java fiends rejoiced upon the arrival of this caffeine spot that brought organic, shade-grown beans and a homey vibe. Coffee is served by chatty, quick-to-grin espresso artisans with a knack for oddball concoctions, such as the super-silky Mountie latte, infused with maple syrup.

Tribeca Treats

94 Reade Street, between Church Street & West Broadway (1-212 571 0500). Subway A, C, 1, 2, 3 to Chambers Street. **Open** 10am-7pm Mon-Sat. **Desserts** $3. **Credit** MC, V. **Map** p403 E31 ❹

This sprawling and spanking new 12,000 sq ft bakery and boutique offers an array of made-on-the-premises sweets, including peanut butter and jelly cupcakes and chocolate truffles. Oven mitts and dessert cookbooks are also sold.

French

Landmarc

179 West Broadway, between Leonard & Worth Streets (1-212 343 3883). Subway 1 to Franklin Street. **Open** noon-2am Mon-Fri; 11am-2am Sat, Sun. **Main course** $23. **Credit** AmEx, DC, Disc, MC, V. **Map** p402 E31 ❺

Chef Marc Murphy has a great kids' menu, which helps to ensure that the grown-ups have time to savour the really good stuff: tender braised lamb shanks, steaks grilled in an open hearth, mussels steamed with chorizo and onions. The wine list is enticing and, in an unusual but very welcome feature, each wine is also offered as a half bottle. The $3 tasting portions of desserts such as blueberry crumble and crème brûlée will put smiles on the faces of hardened calorie-counters.

Italian

Adrienne's Pizza Bar

54 Stone Street, between Mill Street & Coenties Alley (1-212 248 3838). Subway A, C, E to Canal Street. **Open** 11am-11pm Mon-Thur; 11am-midnight Fri; 10.30am-midnight Sat, Sun. **Main course** $20. **Credit** AmEx, DC, MC, V. **Map** p402 F33 ❻

A bright, modern pizzeria on a quaint, cobbled pedestrian street. You can get pizza by the slice or a thin-crust pie, and wolf it down at the infamous standing-room bar, or savour it in the sit-down dining area. Dinner guests will find an extended menu of small plates and entrées. There's also plenty of al fresco seating for dining in the great outdoors.

Other locations: Bread, 20 Spring Street, between Elizabeth & Mott Streets, Little Italy (1-212 334 1015).

Chinatown, Little Italy & Nolita

American

Barmarché

14 Spring Street, at Elizabeth Street (1-212 219 2399). Subway N, R, W to Prince Street; 6 to Spring Street. **Open** 11am-2am Mon-Fri; 9am-2am Sat, Sun. **Main course** $15. **Credit** AmEx, MC, V. **Map** p403 F30 ❼

Peer inside this bright, white-on-white brasserie, and you'll be tempted to go in and join the party: the dining room is often filled with beautiful people and lively groups, and the kitchen keeps them happy and well-fed with generous portions of reliable bistro classics. The menu is American in the melting-pot sense, covering all the greatest hits and no-nonsense dishes from around the world: homemade fettuccine with pesto, thick gazpacho with a dollop of guacamole, tuna tartare with grated Asian pear and citrus ponzu, and a made-in-the-USA juicy burger.

Chinese

Golden Bridge

50 Bowery, between Bayard & Canal Streets (1-212 227 8831). Subway B, D to Grand Street; J, M, N, Q, R, W, Z, 6 to Canal Street. **Open** 9am-11pm daily. **Dim sum** $2. **Credit** AmEx, DC, Disc, MC, V. **Map** p402 F31 ❽

Dim sum devotees often pick places in Flushing, Queens over Manhattan options, but this serious Cantonese venue is well worth a look. An armada of carts offers flavourful standards like clams in black-bean sauce, plus unusual items like egg tarts with a soft taro crust. Look for the elusive cart filled with an irresistible, lightly sweetened tofu.

Cuban

Café Habana

17 Prince Street, at Elizabeth Street (1-212 625 2001). Subway N, R, W to Prince Street; 6 to Spring Street. **Open** 9am-midnight daily. **Main course** $10. **Credit** AmEx, MC, V. **Map** p403 F29 ❾

Hipsters storm this café day and night for its addictive grilled corn doused in butter and rolled in grated cheese and chilli powder. Other staples include crisp

And the winner is...

Every year *Time Out New York* recognises the best offerings of the city's thousands of restaurants. The combination of our culinary experts and the votes of our *Time Out New York* readers, results in a list of outstanding eateries. Below, some of the winners from the 2007 awards:

Best new burger joint

BLT Burger (*see p195*).

Best new steakhouse

Craftsteak (*see p201*).

Best new restaurant of the year

A Voce (*see p202*).

Most hype-worthy

Momofuku Ssäm Bar (*see p193*).

Best new alt coffeeshop

Joe at Alessi (*see p190*).

Best kids' food for grown-ups

Ditch Plains (*see p198*).

Best new Asian

Buddakan (*see p199*).

Joe at Alessi.

beer-battered catfish *tortas*, and juicy marinated skirt steak with rice and black beans.
Other locations: 757 Fulton Street, at South Portland Avenue, Fort Greene, Brooklyn (1-718 858 9500); Café Habana to Go, 229 Elizabeth Street, between Houston & Prince Streets, Soho (1-212 625 2002).

Eclectic

Public

210 Elizabeth Street, between Prince & Spring Streets (1-212 343 7011). Subway N, R, W to Prince Street; 6 to Spring Street. **Open** 6-11.30pm Mon-Fri; 6pm-12.30am Sat; 6-10.30pm Sun. **Main course** $20. **Credit** AmEx, MC, V. **Map** p403 F29 ⑩
This gorgeous industrial space, designed by AvroKo, is high on concept: machine-age glass lamps, pre-war office doors and a library card catalogue make sly references to public spaces. Chef Brad Farmerie, who worked at London's acclaimed Providores, has created the menu with Providores colleagues New Zealanders Anna Hansen and Peter Gordon. Look for a Kiwi influence in dishes such as grilled kangaroo on coriander falafel, and New Zealand venison with pomegranates and truffles.

Mexican

La Esquina

106 Kenmare Street, at Lafayette Street (1-646 613 7100). Subway 6 to Spring Street. **Open** 6pm-midnight daily. **Main course** $18. **Credit** AmEx, MC, V. **Map** p403 F30 ⑪
Many first-time diners here stand on the corner of Lafayette and Kenmare Streets staring at the deli sign, wondering if they wrote down the wrong address. After watching dozens of people who don't look like employees walk through a door marked 'employees only', it becomes clear that the Mexican restaurant does lurk within. Dishes like sirloin with poblano chillies, Mayan shrimp coated in a chipotle glaze and grilled fish with avocado salsa somehow taste even better when served amid exposed brick, wrought iron and wax-dripping candelabras.

Pan-Asian

Kitchen Club

30 Prince Street, at Mott Street (1-212 274 0025). Subway N, R, W to Prince Street; 6 to Spring Street. **Open** 12.30-4pm, 5.30-11.30pm Mon-Sat; 12.30-4pm, 5.30-10.30pm Sun. **Main course** $21. **Credit** AmEx, MC, V. **Map** p403 F29 ⑫
The quasi host of this inviting pan-Asian spot is diminutive Chibi, a French bulldog who defers only to chef-owner Marja Samsom. Eclectic dishes with a Japanese tinge are carefully made and prettily presented. The dumplings are a justifiable source of pride, with tasty, inventive fillings, including salmon tartare and tofu with chrysanthemum. Meat eaters will find sweet bliss in venison glazed with a raspberry sauce and sprinkled with huckleberries.

Lovely Day

196 Elizabeth Street, between Prince & Spring Streets (1-212 925 3310). Subway J, M, Z to Bowery; 6 to Spring Street. **Open** noon-11pm Mon-Thur; noon-midnight Fri; 11am-midnight Sat; 11am-11pm Sun. **Main course** $10. **Credit** AmEx. **Map** p403 F30 ⑬
Cash-strapped twentysomethings pack this inexpensive Nolita eaterie to gossip and dine on an assortment of Thai-themed curries and noodle dishes. If you're looking for a little heat, try the ginger-fried chicken served with spicy aïoli and lime sauce. The laid-back decor of simple red booths is matched at times by slow service. Relax and hold out for the crispy banana rolls served with vanilla ice-cream, honey and sesame – you'll be glad you did.

Pizza

Lombardi's

32 Spring Street, between Mott & Mulberry Streets (1-212 941 7994). Subway 6 to Spring Street. **Open** 11.30am-11pm Mon-Thur; 11.30am-midnight Fri, Sat; 11.30am-10pm Sun. **Large pizza** $15. **No credit cards. Map** p403 F30 ⑭
Lombardi's is the city's oldest pizzeria, established in 1905, and offering pies at their best – made in a coal-fired oven and with a chewy, thin crust. The pepperoni is fantastic, as are the killer meatballs. The setting is classic pizza parlour, with wooden booths and red-and-white checked tablecloths.

Vietnamese

Doyers Vietnamese Restaurant

11 Doyers Street, between Bowery & Pell Street (1-212 513 1521). Subway J, M, N, Q, R, W, Z, 6 to Canal Street. **Open** 11am-10pm Mon-Thur, Sun; 11am-11pm Fri, Sat. **Main course** $8. **Credit** AmEx. **Map** p402 F31 ⑮
The search to find this restaurant is part of the fun: it's tucked away in a basement on a zigzagging Chinatown alley. The 33 appetisers include balls of grilled minced shrimp wrapped around sugarcane sticks and a delicious Vietnamese crêpe filled with shrimp and pork. Hot-pot soups, served on a table-top stove, are made with an exceptionally good fish-broth base and brim with vegetables. For maximum enjoyment, come with a six-pack of Singha in tow (the restaurant is BYOB).

Lower East Side

American creative

Clinton Street Baking Company

4 Clinton Street, between Houston & Stanton Streets (1-646 602 6263). Subway F to Delancey Street; J, M, Z to Delancey-Essex Streets. **Open** 8am-11pm Mon-Fri; 10am-4pm, 6-11pm Sat; 10am-4pm Sun. **Main course** $13. **Credit** AmEx, DC, MC, V. **Map** p403 G29 ⑯

The warm buttermilk biscuits here are reason enough to face the brunchtime crowds; if you want to avoid the onslaught, however, the homey Lower East Side spot is just as reliable at lunch and dinner, when locals drop in for fish tacos, grilled pizzas and a daily $10 beer-and-burger special: 8oz of Black Angus topped with Swiss cheese and caramelised onions, served with a Brooklyn lager. To better your odds for getting a table at brunch (the best in town), show up between 9am and 10am, when a delicious range of coffee and pastries are served before the rest of the kitchen officially opens.

Freemans

2 Freeman Alley, off Rivington Street, between Bowery & Chrystie Street (1-212 420 0012). Subway F, V to Lower East Side-Second Avenue; J, M, Z to Bowery. **Open** 5pm-midnight Mon-Fri; 11am-4pm, 6pm-midnight Sat, Sun. **Main course** $22. **Credit** AmEx, DC, Disc, MC, V. **Map** p403 F29 17

Once you eventually find this secret restaurant (hidden at the end of Freeman Alley) you will feel as though you have stepped into a ski lodge on a mountaintop in Aspen, Colorado. Those in the know feast on affordable dishes like juicy trout, warm artichoke dip, rich wild-boar terrine and perfect batches of mac and cheese, plus a few retro oddities like 'devils on horseback' (prunes stuffed with blue cheese and wrapped in bacon), all served under the gaze of mounted animal heads. Brunch, when raised waffles with banana-maple syrup are served and the sun streams through the front windows, is a rather more tranquil affair. This is also a popular spot for cocktails both classic and forward thinking.

Cafés

Brown

61 Hester Street, between Essex & Ludlow Streets (1-212 477 2427). Subway F to East Broadway. **Open** 9am-11pm Tue-Sat; 9am-6pm Sun. **Main course** $12. **Credit** AmEx. **Map** p403 G30 18

Owner Alejandro Alcocer opened this small café to compensate for the lack of a decent cup of joe in the 'hood. Not only can you get a mean latte here, but now you can also choose from more than 20 entrées made from organic ingredients. Daily specials, scribbled on the front-door glass, usually include a soup, a frittata and a cheese-and-fruit plate, and sandwiches are also available. Alcocer recently started serving beer and wine, and introduced a dinner menu to boot. Sculpted wooden-plank tables, benches and stump-like stools give the place the feel of an afternoon picnic straight from the glossy pages of *Surface* magazine.

Cocoa Bar

21 Clinton Street, between Houston & Stanton Streets (1-212 677 7417). Subway F, J, M, Z to Delancey-Essex Streets. **Open** 8am-midnight Mon-Wed, Sun; 8am-2am Thur-Sat. **Dessert** $6. **Credit** MC, V. **Map** p403 G29 19

See p192 **How sweet it is**.

Chinese

Congee Village

100 Allen Street, between Broome & Delancey Streets (1-212 941 1818). Subway F to Delancey Street; J, M, Z to Delancey-Essex Streets. **Open** 10.30am-2am daily. **Main course** $12. **Credit** AmEx, MC, V. **Map** p403 F30 20

If you've never indulged in the starchy comfort of congee, you'll find this mainly Cantonese restaurant a fine place to be initiated. The rice porridge, cooked to bubbling in a clay pot over a slow fire, is at its best early in the day; pick a chunky version from the 30 or so options on offer, such as the treasure-laden seafood or sliced fish. Crab is impeccably fresh, as is the well-seasoned whole fish served over glistening Chinese broccoli. Rice and noodle dishes are also available, with rice dishes served in bamboo pots, and there's a good range of dim sum. It may seem incongruous, but the Congee does a great pina colada and it will only cost you $3 during the always popular weekday happy hour (4-7pm).

Eclectic

Schiller's Liquor Bar

131 Rivington Street, at Norfolk Street (1-212 260 4555). Subway F to Delancey Street; J, M, Z to Delancey-Essex Streets. **Open** 11am-4am Mon-Fri; 10am-4am Sat, Sun. **Main course** $12. **Credit** AmEx, MC, V. **Map** p403 G29 21

Decorated with old mirrors and antique subway tiles, Keith McNally's latest is a playful all-day bohemian hangout that attracts a variety show of a clientele, from suits to drag queens and artfully tousled locals. No dish, except steak, costs more than $16. The menu is a mix of French bistro classics (steak-frites), British pub faves (Welsh rarebit) and laid-back Louisiana lunch choices (oyster po'boys). Traversing the house wine list is a cinch: it weighs in at a mere six bottles long, with the choices designated 'cheap', 'decent' or 'good' to make life easier. Desserts are mandatory. *See also p218.*

Stanton Social

99 Stanton Street, between Ludlow & Orchard Streets (1-212 995 099). Subway F, V to Lower East Side-Second Avenue. **Open** 11am-4am Mon-Fri; 10am-4am Sat, Sun. **Main course** $14. **Credit** AmEx, DC, Disc, MC, V. **Map** p403 G29 22

Plenty of trendy spots have opened on the LES, but none with as much eye candy as this. Chandeliers, lizard-skin banquettes and retro booths are all part of the 1940s-inspired elegance of the three-level restaurant. Chris Santos has created 40 shareable, international plates (light dishes followed by heavier ones) that all receive special treatment. French onion soup comes in dumpling form; red-snapper tacos are covered with a fiery mango and avocado salsa. The only discernible miss is the Peking duck quesadilla, a needlessly sweet fusion of Asian and Spanish flavours that's best left alone.

Tax and tipping

Negotiating the slings and arrows of another nation's tipping etiquette can make a nightmare of even the most innocuous night out. In New York, however, things are mercifully straightforward. Most restaurants don't add a service charge to the bill unless there are six or more people in your party. So it's customary to give 15 to 20 per cent of the total bill as a tip. The easiest way to figure out the amount is to double the 8.625 per cent sales tax. Complain – preferably to a manager – if you feel the service is under par, but only in the most extreme cases should you completely withhold a tip. Remember that servers are paid far below minimum wage and rely on tips to pay the rent. Bartenders get tipped, too; $1 a drink should ensure friendly pours until last call.

Italian

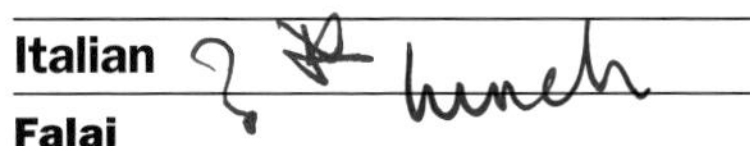

Falai

68 Clinton Street, between Rivington & Stanton Streets (1-212 253 1960). Subway F, J, M, Z to Delancey-Essex Streets. **Open** 6-11pm Tue-Thur; 6pm-midnight Fri-Sun. **Main course** $20. **Credit** AmEx, MC, V. **Map** p403 G29 23

Former Bread Tribeca chef Iacopo Falai has opened his own eaterie, and it's much smaller and more precious than his last spot: just 40 seats, in an all-white room. You'll see hints of his past, though, like a boisterous, fashionable crowd, a modern Italian menu and a sexy location (on the LES's restaurant row). Portions are fairly small but prices are reasonable and dishes both inspired and very well-executed. *See p192* **How sweet it is**.

Japanese

Cube 63

63 Clinton Street, between Rivington & Stanton Streets (1-212 228 6751). Subway F to Delancey Street; J, M, Z to Delancey-Essex Streets. **Open** 5pm-midnight Mon-Thur, Sun; 5pm-1am Fri, Sat. **Sushi meal** $19. **Credit** MC, V. **Map** p403 G29 24

This glowing lime-green dining room is tiny, but the inventive flavours created by sushi chefs Ben and Ken Lau (brothers who worked at Bond Street) are bigger than you'll find just about anywhere else. Jumbo speciality rolls are the main draw: shrimp tempura hooks up with eel, avocado, cream cheese and caviar in the Tahiti roll; the volcano is crab and shrimp topped with spicy lobster salad then set aflame with a blowtorch in an eruption of flavours.

Spanish

Oliva

161 E Houston Street, at Allen Street (1-212 228 4143). Subway F, V to Lower East Side-Second Avenue. **Open** 5.30pm-midnight Mon-Thur; 5.30pm-1am Fri; 11.30am-3.30pm, 5.30pm-1am Sat, Sun. **Main course** $17. **Tapas** $5. **Credit** AmEx. **Map** p403 F29 25

A bright red *toro* (bull) is stencilled on each table at Oliva. Young downtowners read the daily selections from an inscribed mirror over the bar; *pintxos* change daily. Serrano ham croquettes or tortilla are a tasty prelude to heartier dishes, such as seafood-heavy paella. On Wednesday and Sunday, sangria flows freely while a Latin band keeps the place jumping until after midnight.

Suba

109 Ludlow Street, between Delancey & Rivington Streets (1-212 982 5714). Subway F to Delancey Street; J, M, Z to Delancey-Essex Streets. **Open** 6pm-2am Mon-Thur; 6pm-4am Fri, Sat; 6pm-midnight Sun. **Main course** $24. **Credit** AmEx, MC, V. **Map** p403 G30 26

Down the suspended steel staircase from the loud tapas bar is another scene entirely. Suba fuses traditional Spanish dishes with modern techniques. Duck breast with white-peach coulis and cinnamon sauce is undeniably sexy, especially when followed by the sultry dark-chocolate almond cake or a truly delectable lime-pie cocktail.

Soho

American

Blue Ribbon

97 Sullivan Street, between Prince & Spring Streets (1-212 274 0404). Subway C, E to Spring Street. **Open** 4pm-4am Tue-Sun. **Main course** $22. **Credit** AmEx, DC, MC, V. **Map** p403 E30 27

Where else in the ciy, at 3am, can you slurp down just-shucked oysters and smear bone marrow on toast? The city's off-duty chefs long ago elected this Soho sleeper to be their post-work playhouse, and it's still an industry favourite. Every night past midnight, the Bromberg brothers' flagship restaurant begins filling up with a *Who's Who* of the restaurant biz. You might need patience landing even a perch at the bar. Ask for a menu while you wait and decide whether you're going to go upscale (sevruga caviar) or down (matzo-ball soup).

Other locations: Blue Ribbon Brooklyn, 280 Fifth Avenue, between Garfield Place & 1st Street, Park Slope, Brooklyn (1-718 840 0404).

Fanelli's Café

94 Prince Street, at Mercer Street (1-212 226 9412). Subway N, R, W to Prince Street. **Open** 10am-2.30am Mon-Thur; 10am-3am Fri, Sat; 11am-12.30am Sun. **Main course** $10. **Credit** AmEx, MC, V. **Map** p403 E29 28

Deemed the second-oldest restaurant in New York, Fanelli's has stood at this cobblestoned intersection since 1847, and local artists and worldly tourists pour into the lively landmark for perfectly charred beef patties on toasted onion rolls. The long bar, prints of boxing legends and checked tablecloths add to the charm. Specials, such as pumpkin ravioli or grilled mahimahi with lime and coriander, are surprisingly good in a sea of pub grub. *See also p218.*

Cafés

Joe at Alessi

130 Greene Street, between Houston & Prince Streets (1-212 941 7330). Subway B, D, F, V, 6 to Broadway-Lafayette Street; R, W to Prince Street. **Open** 7am-7pm Mon-Fri; 8am-7pm Sat; 8am-6pm Sun. **Coffee** $3. **Credit** MC, V. **Map** p403 E29 ㉙

In 2007, this burgeoning coffee-lover's chain spawned its sleekest branch to date – complete with a molto authentic espresso bar – inside Soho's Alessi store. Baristas proffer rich, nutty cups with an expert foam for those who want it – from the glorious $14,000 La Marzocco machine. *Photos p185.*

French

Balthazar

80 Spring Street, between Broadway & Crosby Street (1-212 965 1414). Subway N, R, W to Prince Street; 6 to Spring Street. **Open** 7.30-11.30am, noon-5pm, 6pm-1am Mon-Wed; 7.30-11.30am, noon-5pm, 6pm-1.30am Thur; 7.30-11.30am, noon-5pm, 6pm-2am Fri; 10am-4pm, 6pm-2am Sat; 10am-4pm, 5.30pm-midnight Sun. **Main course** $21. **Credit** AmEx, MC, V. **Map** p403 E30 ㉚

Not only is Balthazar still trendy, but the kitchen rarely puts a foot wrong. At dinner, the place is perennially packed with rail-thin lookers in head-to-toe Prada. The bread is great, the food good and the service friendly. The three-tiered seafood platter casts the most impressive shadow of any appetiser in town. The *frisée aux lardons* is exemplary, roasted chicken on mash for two, *délicieux.*

Turkish

Antique Garage

41 Mercer Street, between Broome & Grand Streets (1-212 219 1019). Subway J, M, N, Q, R, W, Z, 6 to Canal Street. **Open** noon-midnight daily. **Main course** $11. **Credit** AmEx, MC, V. **Map** p403 E30 ㉛

Formerly an auto-repair shop, the Antique Garage has good acoustics and ample Turkish carpeting to control the volume of its garrulous crowd, which comes for the live music as well as the food. Other assets: faded paintings and peeling mirrors on the walls, heirloom plates and antique chandeliers (all of which are for sale). The kitchen manages to live up to the decor with decent portions of borek (feta-stuffed filo), creamy houmous with fried toast points, and seared tuna doused in red pepper purée.

East Village

Cafés

ChikaLicious

203 E 10th Street, between First & Second Avenues (1-212 995 9511). Subway L to Third Avenue; 6 to Astor Place. **Open**: 3-5pm, 7-10.45pm Wed-Fri; 3-10.45pm Sat, Sun. **Dessert prix fixe** $12. **Credit** AmEx, MC, V. **Map** p403 F28 ㉜

See p192 **How sweet it is.**

Rapture Café & Books

200 Avenue A, between 12th & 13th Streets (1-212 228 1177). Subway L to First Avenue. **Open** 10am to 10pm daily. **Sandwiches** $5. **Credit** MC, V. **Map** p403 G28.

This spot hopes to bring a little bit of the old-time East Village back from the dead – a place for artists, writers and musicians (and the people who love them) to hang out and entertain each other – and to a large extent it manages to do exactly that. A tiny stage gives ample room for readings, performances and general showing-off. The menu, meanwhile, covers the usual café standards.

Cuban

Cafecito

185 Avenue C, at 12th Street (1-212 253 9966). Subway L to First Avenue. **Open** 6-10pm Tue, Thur, Sun; 6pm-2am Fri, Sat. **Main course** $12. **No credit cards. Map** p403 G28 ㉝

The relaxed outdoor bar is just one of the authentic touches at Cafecito ('tiny coffee'). You can sip a Mojito and nibble on green plantain chips as you contemplate menu choices: the *aborcito de Cuba* gives you a taste of each of the small hot appetisers – the best of which are the *bollos*, corn and black-bean fritters. In addition to blackboard specials such as chargrilled skirt steak with chimichurri sauce, the place does a perfectly pressed Cuban sandwich, which is always spot on.

Indian

Spice Cove

326 E 6th Street, between First & Second Avenues (1-212 674 8884). Subway F, V to Lower East Side-Second Avenue. **Open** 11.30am-midnight Mon-Fri; 11.30am-12.30am Sat, Sun. **Main course** $12. **Credit** AmEx, DC, Disc, MC, V. **Map** p403 F28 ㉞

Its reputation hasn't always been formidable, but Curry Row is beginning to look considerably less rough around the edges as new restaurants like this one, with snazzy decor and a refined menu, replace the old garish curry houses. Bright orange walls, stone archways and candles provide a seductive setting; St Germain stands in for sitar music; and in place of an insipid all-you-can-eat buffet are chef Muhammed Ahmed Ali's specialities. Expect properly spiced dishes, such as chickpeas stir-fried with

Seoul food: **Momofuku Ssäm Bar** has the Korean burrito all wrapped up. *See p193.*

coriander, cumin and cinnamon, and fenugreek-scented Atlantic salmon crowned with tomato masala. A genuine delight.

Italian

Aroma

36 E 4th Street, between Bowery & Lafayette Street (1-212 375 0100). Subway 6 to Astor Place. **Open** 5pm-midnight Tue-Thur; 6pm-1am Fri; 12.30-3.30pm, 6pm-2am Sat; 5pm-1am Sun. **Main course** $18. **Credit** AmEx, DC, MC, V. **Map** p403 F29 35

This enchanting, slender wine bar has been carved out of a former streetwear boutique. Raindrop crystal chandeliers hang from the ceiling, olives are laid out single file in porcelain vessels, and a long brick wall displays the Italian wines (including Gragnano, a rare sparkling red). Chef Christopher Daly's dishes are carefully conceived: a duck salad is loaded with *lardons*, wild chicory and a soft-poached egg. The excellent 'lamb three ways' consists of a tower of braised shoulder, a patty of neck meat, pine nuts, raisins and capers, and a juicy, rosemary-rubbed chop for those with stomach to spare.

How sweet it is

The city's sweet centre presents a persuasive argument for skipping dinner.

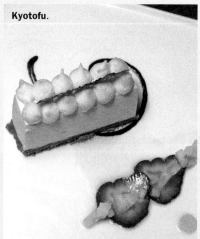

Kyotofu.

Think of three celebrity chefs. Easy, right? Now try to do the same with pastry chefs. Not so simple. But in New York, as several pastry chefs open their own joints, the divide between the two titles – revered executive chef and obscure dessert-maker – may finally begin to diminish.

At the root of this movement seems to be a desire for independence. 'When you're a pastry chef in a restaurant, you have to follow the courses that preceded,' says Pichet Ong, formerly of Spice Market. 'At Spice Market, I had to do desserts that both made sense and were Asian, and at RM restaurant, the desserts had to make sense with a seafood meal. But now I'll just serve whatever I want.' This time around, Ong, who will occupy the role of executive chef for the first time at **P*ONG** (*see p197*), takes his inspiration from the Union Square Greenmarket, which is walking distance from the restaurant. The menu is divided into sections like Savoury, Sweet-Savoury and Sweet. 'In Asia, sugar is just one of the seasonings, like salt and pepper, chilli and spices,' says Thai-born Ong, who grew up in Singapore, Japan and Hong Kong. 'Generally, a pinch is always added just to round out the flavour profile of the dish.' Ong's coveted desserts include pineapple tiramisu, chevre cheesecake with walnut croquette and a sublime Vietnamese espresso tapioca affogato.

Korean

Momofuku Ssäm Bar

207 Second Avenue, at 13th Street (1-212 254 3500). Subway L to First or Third Avenues; N, Q, R, W, 4, 5, 6 to 14th St-Union Square. **Open** 11am-2am daily. **Main course** $16. **Credit** AmEx, MC, V. **Map** p403 F27 ㊱

Chef David Chang's latest feels like two restaurants fused into one: a Korean Chipotle, and a self-aware joint serving designer ham and pricey platters. Chefs create concoctions priced to sample, including the pork-belly steamed bun with hoisin sauce, and the house *ssäm* (Korean for 'wrap'), which might just be the finest burrito in the city. *Photos p191.*

Mexican

Mercadito

179 Avenue B, between 11th & 12th Streets (1-212 529 6493). Subway 6 to Astor Place. **Open** 5pm-midnight Mon-Thur; noon-4pm, 5pm-1am Fri; 11.30am-4pm, 5pm-1am Sat; 11.30am-4pm, 5-11pm Sun. **Main course** $11. **Credit** AmEx, MC, V. **Map** p403 G28 ㊲

As we went to press, sweet specialist Sam Mason (formerly of wd-50) was also gearing up to launch the much-anticipated **Tailor** at 525 Broome Street; details were scarce at press time but word has it this sweet spot will feature a selection of very different desserts.

Iacopo Falai (previously of Le Cirque), is a proven success as a pastry-chef-turned-restaurateur. He opened the classy Italian restaurant **Falai** (*see p189*) in February 2005; needless to say, we advise you to leave room for afters. Falai credits dessert-only eateries like **ChikaLicious** (*see p190*) with breaking new ground for the current round of pastry-chef-owned venues. 'The customers realised how interesting it is to have a different option on the dessert menu,' notes Falai. 'People are tired of eating just a slice of cheesecake.'

Over in Hell's Kitchen, dining at **Kyotofu** (*see p205*), a Japanese 'dessert bar', can be a surreal experience – the windowless dining room, appointed in minimalist white on white, is tucked away out of view. The menu is equally unusual. Ritsuko Yamaguchi (previously of Daniel) combines French technique with Japanese ingredients to tempting effect, swapping milk and cream for tofu in dishes such as a large shot glass filled with black sugar syrup and silky tofu – the perfect eggless crème caramel.

It is, of course, only right that chocolate should have its place in this sweet revolution. Enter husband-and-wife team Liat Cohen and Yaniv Reeis, who turned their three favourite things – chocolate, coffee and wine – into a lifestyle by opening luxe café **Cocoa Bar** (*see p188*). You can drop in for early-morning coffee drinks and chocolatey breakfast treats (like chocolate-chip challah); at night, the place becomes a sit-down affair offering 40 wines paired with decadent chocolate desserts or rich Belgian confections. Thanks to people like Cohen and Reeis, life in New York just got a little sweeter.

Cocoa Bar.

Welcome To
BLT
BURGER
Soup : Field Green Salad
App : pigs in a Blanket
Sandwhich : Soft Shell Crab
Shake : Coffee Cake

BLT Burger.

This Mexican newcomer features wood, tiles and stucco from Mexico, a thatched roof inside the dining room and an elaborate hacienda-style courtyard outside. In the kitchen, chef Patricio Sandoval creates dishes inspired by the cuisine of southern Mexico, like smoked mahimahi ceviche, ribeye steak with cactus salad and tomatillo-avocado chimichurri, plus six kinds of tacos sold by weight. At brunch, breakfast tacos and Mexican sausage are a welcome break from bacon and eggs and understandably popular with those recovering slowly from the night before.

Pizza

Una Pizza Napoletana

349 E 12th Street, between First & Second Avenues (1-212 477 9950). Subway L to First Avenue. **Open** 5-11pm Thur-Sun. **Pizza** $16. **Credit** MC, V. **Map** p403 F28 38

See p206 **The upper crust**.

Seafood

Mermaid Inn

96 Second Avenue, between 5th & 6th Streets (1-212 674 5870). Subway F, V to Lower East Side-Second Avenue. **Open** 5.30-11pm Mon-Thur; 11.30pm-midnight Fri, Sat; 5-10pm Sun. **Main course** $20. **Credit** AmEx, DC, Disc, MC, V. **Map** p403 F28 39

The menu at the Mermaid Inn changes seasonally, but there's always the award-winning overstuffed lobster roll and spaghetti with spicy shrimp, scallops and calamari, topped with rocket. Everything tends to taste even better in summer, when you can sit in the back garden and enjoy your seafood under the sun. The only non-maritime menu item is the complimentary dessert, which is whatever the chef feels like making. This Mermaid's lure is irresistible, so make reservations or suffer in the queue.

Thai

Pukk

71 First Avenue, between 4th & 5th Streets (1-212 253 2740). Subway F, V to Lower East Side-Second Avenue. **Open** 11am-11pm daily. **Main course** $7. **Credit** MC, V. **Map** p403 F29 40

Strip this groovy little hole in the wall of its East Village clientele and you might mistake it for an empty pool: some of the stools and tables are crafted from concrete and small circular tiles (they grow out of the walls like pool steps), and the space basks in a mysterious yellow-green glow. The folks behind Highline and Peep have opened this third spot with a twist: they're cooking only vegetarian Thai dishes. So instead of pork and duck, you'll get your thrills from sweet breaded-and-fried tofu, seriously spicy tom yum soup, linguine in yellow curry and more.

Vegetarian

Caravan of Dreams

405 E 6th Street, between First Avenue & Avenue A (1-212 254 1613). Subway F, V to Lower East Side-Second Avenue; 6 to Astor Place. **Open** 11am-11pm Mon-Fri, Sun; 11am-midnight Sat. **Main course** $15. **Credit** AmEx, MC, V. **Map** p403 F28 41

Vegetarians, vegans and raw-foodists unite! A long-time East Village hangout now offers both regular meat-free dishes – grilled seitan nachos, black-bean chilli, stir-fries – and 'live foods' made from uncooked fruits, vegetables, nuts and seeds. Live 'houmous' (whipped up from cold-processed tahini and raw almonds instead of the usual chickpeas) can be scooped up with pressed flaxseed 'chips'; the live love boat pairs almond-Brazil nut 'meatballs' with mango chutney and cool marinara sauce on a napa cabbage leaf. Naturally, there are loads of salads and some macrobiotically balanced rice-and-seaweed combos. The kitchen is kosher-certified.

Venezuelan

Caracas Arepa Bar

93 E 7th Street, at First Avenue (1-212 228 5062). Subway F, V to Lower East Side-Second Avenue; 6 to Astor Place. **Open** noon-11pm Tue-Sat; noon-10pm Sun. **Arepa** $4. **Credit** AmEx, DC, Disc, MC, V. **Map** p403 F28 42

This endearing little Venezuelan spot, with flower-patterned, vinyl-covered tables, zaps you straight to South America. The secret is in the arepas; each golden patty is made from scratch daily. The golden pitta-like pockets are stuffed with a choice of 18 fillings, such as chicken and avocado or mushrooms with tofu. The simplest ones, like plain butter or nata (Venezuelan sour cream), are the best. Top off your snack with a *cocada*, a thick and creamy milkshake made with freshly grated coconut and cinnamon.

Greenwich Village/Noho

American

BLT Burger

470 Sixth Avenue, between 11th & 12th Streets (1-212 243 8226). Subway A, B, C, D, E, F, V to West 4th Street. **Open** 11.30am-11pm daily. **Burger** $12. **Credit** AmEx, MC, V. **Map** p403 D28 43

The no-frills house burger – seven ounces of sirloin, short rib, chuck and brisket – not only comes on a cookout-worthy white bun, but it's wrapped in wax paper and served with fries in a plastic basket that evokes the drive-in. Still, more esoteric items, like a spicy patty made of lamb merguez and the $62 Japanese kobe burger, make it abundantly clear that chef Laurent Tourondel has not forgotten the haute that got him here. All told, this is comfort food with a touch of genuine class.

Dojo West

14 W 4th Street, between Broadway & Mercer Street (1-212 505 8934). Subway B, D, F, V to Broadway-Lafayette Street; N, R, W to 8th Street-NYU; 6 to Bleecker Street. **Open** 11am-midnight daily. **Main course** $7. **No credit cards**. **Map** p403 E29 44

Vegetarians will find plenty of choices and carnivores can get beef or turkey burgers. Dojo's soy burger, a power-packed protein patty that's fried, then shoved inside a salad-lined pitta, has been brain food for NYU kids for 16 years. Drench the delicious mess with a generous helping of tahini dressing, and spend the meal pondering how so much tasty sustenance can possibly cost so little.

American creative

Blue Hill

75 Washington Place, between Washington Square West & Sixth Avenue (1-212 539 1776). Subway A, B, C, D, E, F, V to W 4th Street. **Open** 5.30-11pm Mon-Sat; 5.30-10pm Sun. **Main course** $25. **Credit** AmEx, DC, MC, V. **Map** p403 E28 45

This beloved gourmand destination has a knack for scoring the best local produce all year round. Chefs Dan Barber and Michael Anthony succeed consistently with their dishes thanks to their solid foundation in classical French cooking. When in season, Blue Hill's strawberries have more berry flavour, and its heirloom tomatoes are juicier than anyone's. The poached foie gras, duck breast in beurre blanc, tender roasted chicken and mango sorbet are sublime.

Cafés

Peanut Butter & Co

240 Sullivan Street, between Bleecker & W 3rd Streets (1-212 677 3995). Subway A, B, C, D, E, F, V to W 4th Street. **Open** 11am-9pm Mon-Thur, Sun; 11am-10pm Fri, Sat. **Sandwich** $6. **Credit** AmEx, DC, Disc, MC, V. **Map** p403 E29 46

To Americans, nothing brings on an attack of 'happy childhood' nostalgia like a peanut butter sandwich. Every day, the staff at Peanut Butter & Co grind out a fresh batch of peanut butter, which is used in mood-pacifiers like the Elvis – the King's infamous grilled favourite of peanut butter, banana and honey. Owner Lee Zalben confesses to a weakness for the warm sandwich of cinnamon-raisin peanut butter, vanilla cream cheese and tart apple slices. Goober-free menu items, like tuna melts and bologna sandwiches, continue the brown-bag theme.

Italian

Il Buco

47 Bond Street, between Lafayette Street & Bowery (1-212 533 1932). Subway B, D, F, V to Broadway-Lafayette Street; 6 to Bleecker Street. **Open** 6pm-midnight Mon; noon-4pm, 6pm-midnight Tue-Thur; noon-4pm, 6pm-1am Fri, Sat; 5pm-midnight Sun. **Main course** $28. **Credit** AmEx, MC, V. **Map** p403 F29 47

The old-world charm of well-worn communal tables and flickering lamps may help explain why a 12-year-old restaurant is still tough to get into on a Saturday night. Seasonal produce shapes chef Ed Witt's menu (whose previous credits include Daniel and River Café). Dunk the warm country bread in Umbrian olive oils produced exclusively for Il Buco. *Primi* include a thin-crust pizza with fresh porcini, shallots and aged Asturian goat's cheese; entrées include an excellent suckling pig snuggled into warm polenta. Book a table in the candlelit wine cellar for a rustic, charming vibe.

La Lanterna di Vittorio

129 MacDougal Street, between 3rd & 4th Streets (1-212 529 5945). **Open** 10am-3am Mon-Thur, Sun; 10am-4am Fri, Sat. **Main course** $28. **Pizza** $9. **Credit** AmEx, DC, Disc, MC, V. **Map** p403 E29 48

Woo your darling by the fire or under the stars at a romantic Village spot that has been helping to smooth the course of true love for 28 years. The 200-year-old garden was once owned by politician Aaron Burr; its history is heard in the wind rustling through the dense green canopy of apple and cherry trees, and the worn walls are strung with ivy. In wintertime, four fireplaces spark your courting. Choose a bottle from the extensive wine list to go with light café eats such as panini, crostini, smoked duck breast with salad, or thin-crust pizza.

Lupa

170 Thompson Street, between Bleecker & Houston Streets (1-212 982 5089). Subway A, B, C, D, E, F, V to W 4th Street. **Open** noon-3pm, 5-11.30pm Mon-Fri; 11.30am-2.30pm, 5-11.30pm Sat, Sun. **Main course** $14. **Credit** AmEx, MC, V. **Map** p403 E29 49

Fans of this 'poor man's Babbo' (celeb-chef Mario Batali's pricier restaurant around the corner) keep coming back for more. Here's the ritual they recommend: first, a cutting-board of fatty-delicious cured meats like tender prosciutto and spirited coppi. Move on to sublime pasta, like the ricotta gnocchi with sausage and fennel. Then choose a meaty main, like oxtail alla vaccinara or a classic saltimbocca. By the time the panna cotta with apricot arrives, you'll be ready to become a regular too.

Pan-Asian

Chinatown Brasserie

380 Lafayette Street, at Great Jones Street (1-212 533 7000). Subway B, D, F, V to Broadway-Lafayette Street; 6 to Bleecker Street. **Open** 11.30am-3.30pm, 5-11.30pm Mon-Thur; 11.30am-3.30pm, 5pm-12.30am Fri; 5pm-12.30am Sat; 5-11.30pm Sun **Main course** $19. **Credit** AmEx, Disc, MC, V. **Map** p403 F29 50

Many of the dishes on the menu here could appear at some spot with Wok or Empire in its name, except that the prices run about 50% higher. While the menu lists fried-egg rolls, wok-fried noodles and fried rice, this brasserie really specialises in dim sum. The decor is stunning: dark brocade curtains, wooden room dividers and red-and-yellow silk lanterns greet you upstairs, while a downstairs lounge shoots for tiki cool with the help of a koi pond and low to the ground lounge chairs.

Thai

Prem-On Thai

138 W Houston Street, between Sullivan & MacDougal Streets (1-212 353 2338). Subway C, E to Spring Street. **Open** noon-11.30pm Mon-Fri; noon-midnight Sat, Sun. **Main course** $17. **Credit** AmEx, DC, MC, V. **Map** p403 E29 ⑤①

In one of several stylish rooms (Prem-On Thai is refreshingly bamboo-free), you'll watch in awe as dramatically presented Thai dishes and cocktails are carried through the dining room. Prem-On Thai doesn't hold back visually or with the seasoning: a whole fried sea bass fillet is served upright and loaded with basil and roasted chilli paste sauce. Red snapper is smothered with a sweet pineapple and lychee sauce, and pork rolls are a mighty trio of towers with a punchy sesame-chilli rice-vinegar sauce.

West Village & Meatpacking District

American

Corner Bistro

331 W 4th Street, at Jane Street (1-212 242 9502). Subway A, C, E to 14th Street; L to Eighth Avenue. **Open** 11.30am-4am daily. **Burgers** $5. **No credit cards**. **Map** p403 D28 ⑤②

There's only one reason to come to this legendary pub: it serves up the city's best burgers – and beer is just $2 a mug (well, that makes two reasons). The patties here are cheap, delish and no-frills, served on a flimsy paper plate. To get one, you may have to queue for a good hour, especially on weekend nights. Fortunately, the game is on the tube, and a jukebox covers everything from Calexico to Coltrane.

Cafés

P*Ong

150 W 10th Street, at Waverly Place (1-212 929 0898). Subway A, B, C, D, E, F, V to W 4th Street-Washington Square. **Open** 5.30pm-midnight Tue-Thur; 11am-4pm, 5.30pm-1am Fri, Sat; 11am-4pm, 5.30pm-midnight Sun. **Dessert** $15. **Credit** AmEx, MC, V. **Map** p403 D28 ⑤③

See p192 **How sweet it is**.

Eclectic

Employees Only

510 Hudson Street, between Christopher & W 10th Streets (1-212 242 3021). Subway 1 to Christopher Street-Sheridan Square. **Open** 6pm-4am daily. **Main course** $22. **Credit** AmEx, MC, V. **Map** p403 D28 ⑤④

The psychic palm-reader in the window is part of the high-concept decor, inspired by the speakeasies of yore. Peek behind the purple curtain in the foyer and you'll see mahogany walls, a working fireplace, a shiny tin ceiling, and a collection of vintage cocktail books and bottles – inspiration for co-owner Jason Kosmas's interesting drinks. The 'rustic European' menu features butternut squash rigatoni and house-cured gravlax. Swing by late at night, and you can nosh on a feast of oysters, baked brie and veal goulash until 4am.

5 Ninth

5 Ninth Avenue, between Gansevoort & Little W 12th Streets (1-212 929 9460). Subway A, C, E, L to 14th Street. **Open** noon-midnight Mon-Thur; noon-1am Fri, Sat; 11am-midnight Sun. **Main course** $15. **Credit** AmEx, MC, V. **Map** p403 C28 ⑤⑤

This spare, brick-walled duplex of dining rooms has a hotter-than-hot location smack bang in the middle of the Meatpacking District. Chef Zak Pelaccio's Asian-inflected instincts are as sharp as ever: thick chips of bacon teeter atop four tiny oysters, each on a spoonful of vivid-green sweet pea purée. Poached lobster in a ginger beurre blanc and the kobe ribeye in chunky coconut chutney are too good to share. In the summer, sip a cocktail on the peaceful back deck for the ultimate in tipsy tranquility. *See also p221.*

Spotted Pig

314 W 11th Street, at Greenwich Street (1-212 620 0393). Subway A, C, E to 14th Street; L to Eighth Avenue. **Open** noon-2am Mon-Fri; 11am-2am Sat, Sun. **Main course** $15. **Credit** AmEx, MC, V. **Map** p403 D28 ⑤⑥

Brick archways, a pressed-tin ceiling and retro farm-animal pictures make this perpetually jammed two-room pub feel like a piece of England. Most of the beer is brewed in Brooklyn, and the menu… well, it's actually quite Italian, thanks to consultant Mario Batali and chef April Bloomfield, a British import from London's highly regarded, Italian-inspired River Café. The small menu changes daily but always includes Bloomfield's melt-in-your-mouth ricotta gnudi and rich smoked haddock chowder, as well as a handful of heartier dishes such as pork sausages with polenta, a sly spin on more conventional bangers and mash.

Italian

Barbuto

775 Washington Street, between Jane & W 12th Streets (1-212 924 9700). Subway A, C, E to 14th Street; L to Eighth Avenue. **Open** noon-11pm Mon-Fri; noon-midnight Sat; noon-10pm Sun. **Main course** $18. **Credit** AmEx, Disc, MC, V. **Map** p403 C28 ⑤⑦

For such an industrial-chic space (housed in a former garage), this bright corner restaurant serves surprisingly rustic food. Owner Fabrizio Ferri (who runs the Industria Superstudio complex upstairs) teamed with chef Jonathan Waxman to create a seasonal kitchen anchored by both a brick and a wood

Eat, Drink, Shop

oven. Marvellously light calamari comes in a perfectly complimentary lemon-garlic sauce; *chitarra all'aia* mixes fresh pasta with crushed walnuts, garlic, olive oil and parmesan; Vermont veal, meanwhile, is immaculately fried. In the summer months, the garage doors go up and a refreshing breeze sweeps through the airy dining room.

Japanese

EN Japanese Brasserie

435 Hudson Street, at Leroy Street (1-212 647 9196). Subway 1 to Houston Street. **Open** 5pm-2am Mon-Sat; 5pm-midnight Sun. **Main course** $15. **Credit** AmEx, DC, Disc, MC, V. **Map** p403 D29 ⑱

On the main floor of the multi-level space, Bunkei and Reika Yo have built tatami-style rooms; on the mezzanine level, they've recreated the living room, dining room and library of a Japanese home from the Meiji era (1868-1912). Chef Koji Nakano runs with the theme by offering handmade miso paste, tofu and *yuba* (soya-milk skin) in a range of delicious dishes such as Berkshire pork belly braised in sansho miso and foie gras and poached daikon steak with a helping of white miso vinegar.

Pan-Asian

Buddha Bar

25 Little W 12th Street, between Ninth Avenue & Washington Street (1-212 647 7314). Subway A, C, E to 14th Street; L to Eighth Avenue. **Open** 6pm-4am daily. **Main course** $35. **Credit** AmEx, MC, V. **Map** p403 C28 ⑲

The irony is obvious: Buddhism emphasises moderation, and Buddha Bar is a temple of excess. Statues line the entrance tunnel. A glass-encased smoking room spares puffers from having to walk outside. As a nightclub party spot, Buddha Bar succeeds on many levels. It's visually stimulating, very Vegas and the lounge scene bustles. Feasting on the pan-Asian menu, however, requires a certain amount of patience. The entrées come out whenever they are ready, but are always worth the wait.

Pizza

Joe's Pizza

7 Carmine Street, between Bleecker & Sixth Avenue (1-212 366 1182). Subway A, C, E, B, D, F, V to W 4th Street. **Open** 9am-5am daily. **No credit cards**. **Map** p403 D29 ⑳

See p206 **The upper crust**.

Seafood

Ditch Plains

29 Bedford Street, at Downing Street (1-212 633 0202). Subway A, B, C, D, E, F, V to W 4th Street; 1 to Houston Street. **Open** 7am-2am daily. **Main course** $12. **Credit** AmEx, MC, V. **Map** p403 D29 ㉑

Ditch Plains, named after a favourite surfing spot off Long Island, is a casual oyster bar and fish shack fitted with yellow pine tabletops, sheet-metal walls and flat-screen TVs showing aquatic-themed films. Breakfast plates, like eggs Benedict with chorizo or blood sausage, are available all day long. Think of it as a surfer special.

Spanish

Las Ramblas

170 W 4th Street, between Cornelia & Jones Streets (1-646 415 7924). Subway A, B, C, D, E, F, V to W 4th Street-Washington Square. **Open** 4pm-2am daily. **Small plate** $8. **No credit cards**. **Map** p403 D28 ㉒

The authenticity of Las Ramblas (the chef's from Pamplona) is apparent in every *centímetro* of the place; three flavours of sangria are mixed to order; and the intimate space fosters interaction. Food portions (aged serrano ham, grilled chorizo, *patatas bravas*, Spanish cheeses) are just the right size, and price, for sharing with a friend.

Vegetarian

'sNice

45 Eighth Avenue, between Horatio & Jane Streets (1-212 645 0310). Subway A, C, E to 14th Street: L to Eighth Avenue. **Open** 7.30am-10pm Mon-Fri; 8am-10pm Sat, Sun. **No credit cards**. **Map** p403 D28 ㉓

Someone who hasn't eaten meat for 20 years is bound to know a thing or two about what vegetarians like to eat. Mike Walter opened this sandwich shop as a haven for the happy herbivore – a simple spot to spend a few hours reading, snacking or working leisurely on a laptop.

Midtown

Chelsea

American

BRGR

287 Seventh Avenue, between 26th & 27th Streets (1-212 488 7500). Subway 1 to 28th Street. **Open** 11am-11pm daily. **Burgers** $8. **Credit** AmEx, MC, V. **Map** p404 D26 ㉔

This vowel-challenged spot riffs on the fast-food formula while adding gourmet flourishes such as organic beef and inventive shakes. Wood beams and ceiling fans give a honky-tonk texture to a do-it-yourself dining experience.

Cookshop

156 Tenth Avenue, at 20th Street (1-212 924 4440). Subway C, E to 23rd Street. **Open** noon-midnight daily. **Main course** $22. **Credit** AmEx, MC, V. **Map** p403 C27 ㉕

A meat-free meeting of minds at **'sNice**.

Vicki Freeman and chef-husband co-owner Marc Meyer want Cookshop to be a platform for sustainable ingredients from independent farmers. True to its mission, Cookshop's ingredients are consistently top-notch – and the menu changes daily. *See also p271* **Cheap date**.

Empire Diner

210 Tenth Avenue, at 22nd Street (1-212 243 2736). Subway C, E to 23rd Street. **Open** 24hrs daily. **Main course** $13. **Credit** Disc, MC, V. **Map** p404 C26 66

It's three in the morning and you're hungry – do you know where your middle-of-the-night grub is? This Fodero-style diner provides the answer for those who find themselves in Chelsea and in need of sustenance. It looks like a classic diner – gleaming stainless-steel walls and rotating stools – but few other hash houses have candlelight, sidewalk café tables and a pianist playing dinner music. Fewer still attempt such dishes as sesame noodles with chicken, and linguine with smoked salmon, watercress and healthy kick of garlic.

Pre:Post

547 W 27th Street, between Tenth & Eleventh Avenues (1-212 695 7270). Subway C, E to 23rd Street. **Open** 5pm-5am Tue-Thur; 5pm-7am Fri, Sat. **Main course** $19. **Credit** AmEx, MC, V. **Map** p404 B26 67

There's a seating option for every kind of customer here: cabanas for table-service types, regular tables for quiet wallflowers and private birch-wood log booths for couples that don't mind sitting far apart from one another. The menu wisely sticks to classic comfort food – burgers, sandwiches, meat loaf and chicken – and regular customers can't seem to get enough of the place as a result. As a general rule, the greasier the dish is, the better it tends to taste.

Chinese

Buddakan

75 Ninth Avenue, between 15th & 16th Streets (1-212 989 6699). Subway A, C, E to 14th Street; L to Eighth Avenue. **Open** 5pm-midnight Mon-Wed, Sun; 5pm-1am Thur-Sat. **Main course** $20. **Credit** AmEx, MC, V. **Map** p403 C27 68

Buddakan relies almost entirely on the shock and awe of 16,000 stunning square feet of space. Open the giant gate of a door and you are greeted by a hotel-style line-up of hosts. Continue inside and you pass a bustling front bar, dominated by giant square tables, a birdcage filled with taxidermy, Buddha pictures and European tapestries, all leading to a grand staircase that descends into a soaring, golden-hued main room with a 35ft ceiling and a long communal table. The food – yes, there is food here too – sounds more fancy, by the descriptions on the menu, than it really is. The range of both noodle and rice dishes offer great bang for your buck.

Italian

La Bottega

Maritime Hotel, 88 Ninth Avenue, at 17th Street (1-212 243 8400). Subway A, C, E to 14th Street; L to Eighth Avenue. **Open** 7-11.30am, 5pm-1am Mon, Tue; 7-11.30am, 5pm-2am Wed, Thur; 7-11.30am, 5pm-3am Fri; 11am-4pm, 5pm-3am Sat; 11am-4pm, 5pm-1am Sun. **Main course** $18. **Credit** AmEx, DC, Disc, MC, V. **Map** p403 C27 69

Given how inordinately popular this space is – especially during the summer, when the vast lantern-lit terrace is jam-packed with a fashionable Euro crowd – the reasonably priced chow is much better than it needs to be. La Bottega has the classic trattoria mix, its menu teeming with fresh pasta, meat, fish and pizzas, and is open for breakfast and lunch, as well as dinner.

Del Posto

85 Tenth Avenue, between 15th & 16th Streets (1-212 497 8090). Subway A, C, E to 14th Street; L to Eighth Avenue. **Open** 5.30-11.30pm Tue-Sat. **Main course** $28. **Credit** AmEx, MC, V. **Map** p403 C27 70

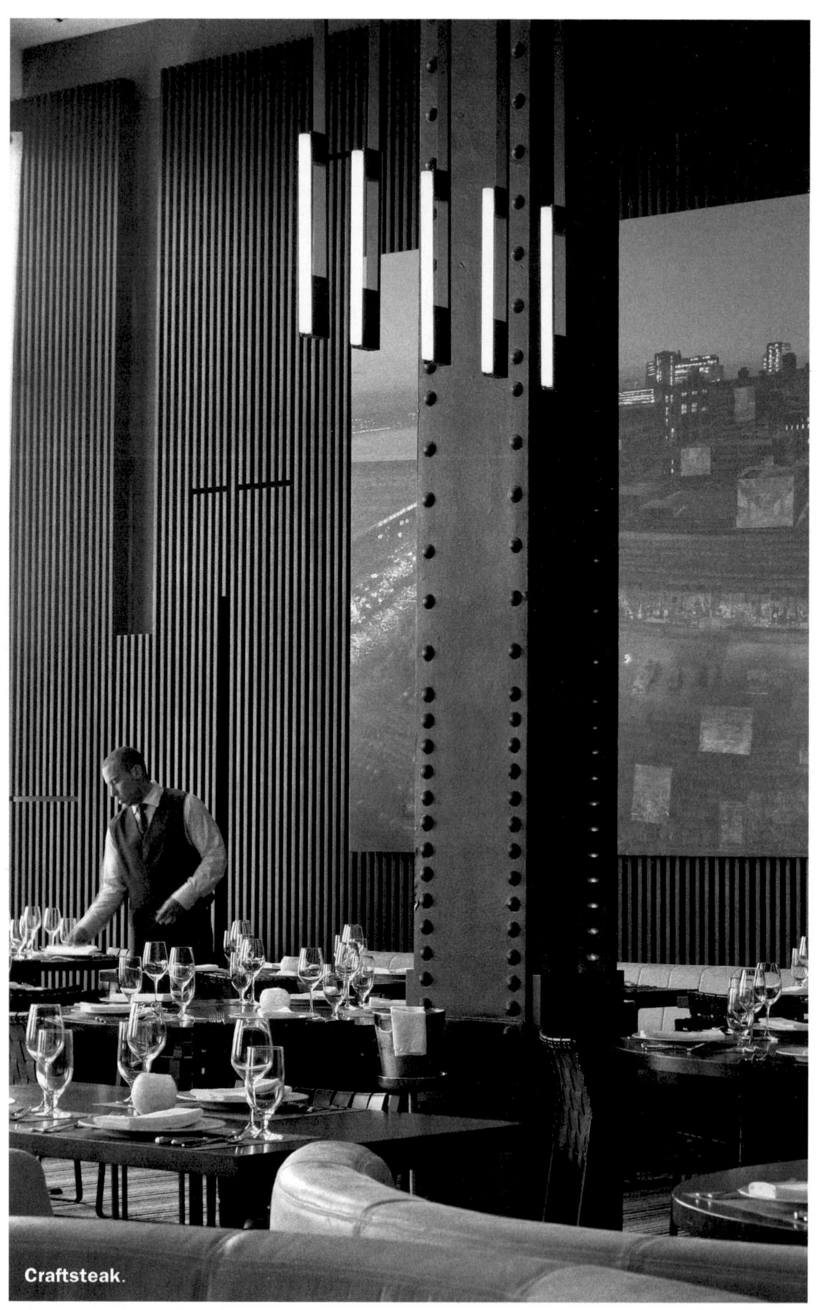

Craftsteak.

Del Posto is a huge deal in every sense of the word. The 24,000 sq ft space is backed by heavyweights Mario Batali, Mark Ladner, and Lidia Bastianich and her son, Joseph. It has a basement for private banquets, a main floor with a 60-seat dining room and a 40-seat lounge, a mezzanine with opera house-like balcony tables and a 50,000-bottle wine cellar. The menu features high-end modern Italian cuisine, such as house-made salami, pasta and bread. Big meaty dishes featuring lamb, venison and halibut are carved up tableside.

Japanese

Morimoto

88 Tenth Avenue, between 15th & 16th Streets (1-212 989 8883). Subway A, C, E to 14th Street; L to Eighth Avenue. **Open** 5pm-midnight Mon-Thur, Sun; 5pm-1am Fri, Sat. **Main course** $36. **Credit** AmEx, MC, V. **Map** p403 C27 71

This space reportedly cost $12 million to build – and it shows. You'll see undulating ceilings and a two-storey tower made from 17,000 water bottles. But the food is the real show at this Vegas-style Meatpacking restaurant from Philly restaurateur Stephen Starr. Chef Morimoto, of Iron Chef fame, successfully incorporates Western ingredients into his innovative Japanese dishes. He cures yellowtail like pastrami, places buffalo mozzarella alongside sashimi and replaces the main ingredient in chawan mushi, a traditional egg custard, with foie gras.

Naka Naka

458 W 17th Street, between Ninth & Tenth Avenues (1-212 929 8544). Subway A, C, E to 14th Street; L to Eighth Avenue. **Open** 6pm-midnight Tue-Sat. **Main course** $13. **Credit** AmEx, MC, V. **Map** p403 C27 72

Naka Naka's kitchen produces tasty traditional dishes, starting with spicy lotus root, delicate mixed-vegetable tempura and dense shrimp dumplings. The sushi is neither phenomenal nor disappointing, but considering how difficult it is to find a peaceful dinner in this part of town, we can't complain.

Pan-Asian

Rickshaw Dumpling Bar

61 W 23rd Street, between Fifth & Sixth Avenues (1-212 924 9220). Subway F, N, R, V, W to 23rd Street. **Open** 11.30am-9.30pm Mon-Sat; 11.30am-8.30pm Sun. **Dumplings** $5 (for 6). **Credit** AmEx, MC, V. **Map** p404 E26 73

Annisa chef Anita Lo has designed a simple menu consisting of six different dumplings, each inspired by an Asian cuisine and matched with its own dipping sauce: classic Chinese pork and chive with a soy vinegar, for instance, or Thai chicken with peanut satay. Large appetites can pair your dumplings with a big bowl of noodle soup, then top it all off with a green-tea milkshake or a dessert dumpling of molten chocolate in a mochi wrapper.

Spanish

Tia Pol

205 Tenth Avenue, between 22nd & 23rd Streets (1-212 675 8805). Subway C, E to 23rd Street. **Open** noon-3pm, 5pm-midnight Mon-Thur; noon-3pm, 5pm-1am Fri, Sat; 11am-3pm, 6pm-midnight Sun. **Small plate** $7. **Credit** AmEx, MC, V. **Map** p404 C26 74

This tiny tapas restaurant keeps things simple with traditional tapas such as sautéed cockles and razor clams. Other dishes showcase unlikely combinations: tomato-covered bread with lima bean purée, and chorizo and chocolate on bread rounds.

Steakhouse

Craftsteak

85 Tenth Avenue, between 15th & 16th Streets (1-212 400 6699). Subway A, C, E to 14th Street; L to Eighth Avenue. **Open** 5.30-10pm Mon-Thur, Sun; 5.30-11pm Fri, Sat. **Main course** $35. **Credit** AmEx, MC, V. **Map** p403 C27 75

Tom Colicchio's 10,000 sq ft steakhouse is about as open and bright as a beef emporium can possibly be: 16ft ceilings and giant windows lend it a luxurious airiness. The meat line-up, meanwhile, is impressively specific: diners can choose the cattle breed, the feed, the cut of meat and age. The Hawaiian grass-fed Angus steak has a clean, herbaceous quality. The sides – a fondue-like potato puree, Vidalia onion rings and six types of mushrooms – are as unconventional as the beef itself.

Vegetarian

Blossom

187 Ninth Avenue, between 21st & 22nd Streets (1-212 627 1144). Subway C, E to 23rd Street. **Open** 11.45am-3.30pm, 5-10.30pm Mon-Sat; noon-3.30pm, 5-10pm Sun. **Main course** $16. **Credit** AmEx, DC, Disc, MC, V. **Map** p404 C26 76

Blossom offers a big surprise: all the egg-free pastas and mock meats actually taste pretty good. For vegans, it's a candlelit godsend. Try the pan-seared seitan medallions, unusually satisfying mock veal with capers, served with broccoli rabe and buttery-tasting polenta (without butter, of course). Or consider the fake-chicken mole, seitan steak or a tofu BLT. The South Asian lumpia – a chickpea pancake starter with curried potato – would be right at home in a good Indian restaurant. *Photos p203.*

Gramercy & Flatiron

American creative

Country

Carlton Hotel, 90 Madison Avenue, at 29th Street (1-212 889 7100). Subway 6 to 28th Street. **Open** 5.30-11pm Mon-Sat. **Prix fixe** $85. **Credit** AmEx, MC, V. **Map** p404 F25 77

Geoffrey Zakarian's Carlton Hotel restaurant is an enthrallingly sophisticated addition to the Flatiron dining scene. The prix-fixe menu (which changes frequently) draws heavily on French influences, but adds American and Italian elements. The dress code here is formal; jackets are required for men. A more casual café serves less expensive fare in the subterranean basement.

Craftbar

900 Broadway, at 20th Street (1-212 461 4300). Subway N, R, W, 6 to 23rd Street. **Open** noon-11pm Mon-Thur, Sun; noon-midnight Fri, Sat. **Main course** $25. **Credit** AmEx, DC, Disc, MC, V. **Map** p403 E27 78

Tom Colicchio's flashy spin-off of his upscale restaurant Craft recently moved to a bigger and brighter space around the corner from the original Craftbar. The dining room is still positively raucous, and the busy bar is jammed with chatty, wine-swigging groups. Appetisers rate highest, especially the lavish platter of Italian, Spanish and house-cured meats, and the addictive pork-stuffed sage leaves. Desserts such as the chocolate pot de crème and the steamed lemon pudding are sheer heaven.

Other locations: Craft, 43 E 19th Street, between Broadway & Park Avenue South, Flatiron District (1-212 780 0880); 'wichcraft, 49 E 19th Street, between Broadway & Park Avenue South, Flatiron District (1-212 780 0577).

French

Le Express

249 Park Avenue South, at 20th Street (1-212 254 5858). Subway 6 to 23rd Street. **Open** 24hrs daily. **Main course** $13. **Credit** AmEx, MC, V. **Map** p403 E27 79

It's 3am, and, if you want to dodge that hangover, you'd better eat something. So why not consider this bustling bistro, which stays open 24 hours a day, seven days a week? You're likely to find it as crowded in the wee hours as it is at 8pm. Bistro standards such as steak au poivre, seared tuna steak, along with monkfish and chorizo brochettes, are satisfying at any hour of the day or night.

Indian

Dévi

8 E 18th Street, at Fifth Avenue (1-212 691 1300). Subway N, R, W, 6 to 23rd Street. **Open** noon-2.30pm, 5.30-10.30pm Mon-Thur; noon-2.30pm, 5.30-11pm Fri, Sat; 5.30-10.30pm Sun. **Main course** $21. **Credit** AmEx, Disc, MC, V. **Map** p403 E27 80

Dangling from the ceiling like clusters of shiny hard candies, ornate multicoloured lanterns cast a warm glow over diners, who are surrounded by gauzy saffron draperies in the split-level dining room. Start your evening with a citrusy Dévi Fizz cocktail, nibble on some crisp samosas, then pamper yourself with inspired Indian dishes such as the velvety yam dumplings in a spiced tomato gravy; stuffed baby aubergine bathed in spicy peanut sauce; or moist chunks of chicken with pistachios, coriander and green chillies.

Italian

A Voce

41 Madison Avenue, entrance on 26th Street, between Madison Avenue & Park Avenue South (1-212 545 8555). Subway N, R, W, 6 to 23rd Street. **Open** 11.30am-3pm, 5.30-11pm daily. **Main course** $22. **Credit** AmEx, DC, MC, V. **Map** p404 E26 81

The space, located off Madison Square Park, is a big, loud glass cube decorated with stainless steel, lacquer and Eames swivel aluminum chairs. It's hardly run-of-the-mill from an aesthetic point of view, nor is the menu an obvious crowd-pleaser at first glance; it is remarkably light on fish and heavy on game meat. That said, when head chef Andrew Carmellini hits his marks, he produces some truly awesome culinary winners. *Photos pp204-205.*

Spanish

Casa Mono/Bar Jamón

Casa Mono: 52 Irving Place, at E 17th Street. Bar Jamón: 125 E 17th Street, at Irving Place (1-212 253 2773). Subway L to Third Avenue; N, Q, R, W, 4, 5, 6 to 14th Street-Union Square. **Open** *Casa Mono* noon-midnight daily. *Bar Jamón* 5pm-2am Mon-Fri; noon-2am Sat, Sun. **Tapas** $9. **Credit** AmEx, MC, V. **Map** p403 F27 82

Part of Mario Batali's ever-expanding restaurant spread, this busy and tiny tapas restaurant (Bar Jamón is the equally teeny wine bar around the corner) specialises in making 'difficult' meats irresistible. Fried sweetbreads in a nutty batter, oxtail-stuffed piquillo peppers, baby squid with plump white beans, tripe with sausage – it's all good, especially with a glass of wine or sherry from the extensive Iberian-heavy list.

Vegetarian

Pure Food & Wine

54 Irving Place, between 17th & 18th Streets (1-212 477 1010). Subway L, N, Q, R, W, 4, 5, 6 to 14th Street-Union Square. **Open** 5.30-11pm Mon-Sat; 5.30-10pm Sun. **Main course** $23. **Credit** AmEx, DC, MC, V. **Map** p403 F27 83

The dishes delivered to your table – whether out in the leafy patio or inside the ambient dining room – are minor miracles, not only because they look gorgeous and taste terrific, but also due to the fact that they come from a kitchen that lacks a stove. Everything here is raw and vegan – from the pad thai appetiser to the lasagne, a rich stack of zucchini, pesto and creamy 'cheese' made from cashews. Wines, mostly organic, are top-notch, as are the desserts, especially the confoundingly fudgy and effortlessly comforting chocolate layer cake.

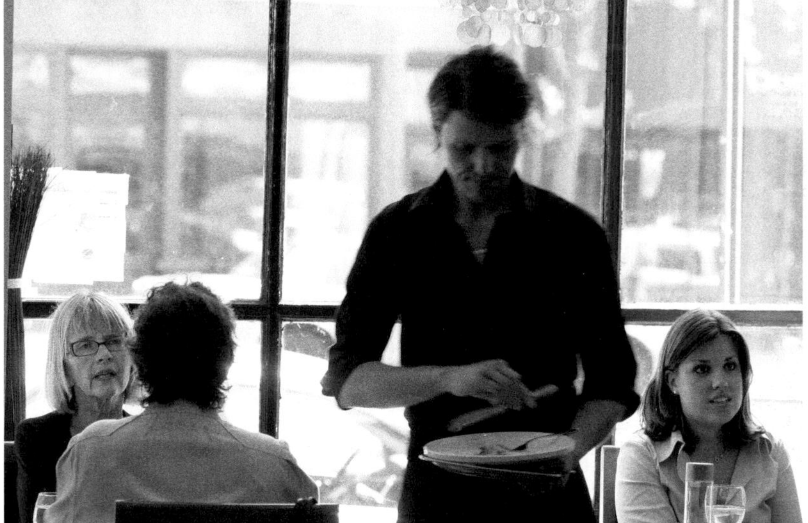

Where's the beef? Who cares? Vegan dining with decorum at **Blossom**. *See p201*.

Midtown West

American

Dave & Busters

3rd Floor, 234 W 42nd Street, between Seventh & Eighth Avenues (1-646 495 2015). Subway N, Q, R, S, W, 1, 2, 3 to 42nd Street-Times Square. **Open** 11am-12am Mon-Thur, Sun; 11am-2am Fri, Sat. **Main course** $15. **Credit** AmEx, MC, V. **Map** p405 D24 84

The latest addition to Times Square's restaurant collection of giant theme-park eateries is this behemoth food-entertainment venue, which offers virtual reality simulators, video games galore and Skee-Ball – plus Philly cheese steaks, salads and burgers.

Kobe Club

68 W 58th Street, between Fifth & Sixth Avenues (1-212 644 5623). Subway F to 57th Street; N, R, W to Fifth Avenue-59th Street. **Open** 5.30pm-midnight Mon-Wed; 5.30pm-2am Thur-Sat. **Main course** $35. **Credit** AmEx, MC, V. **Map** p405 E22 85

This is Jeffrey Chodorow's latest place (he was the evil partner in NBC's short-lived TV reality series *The Restaurant*). Framed with a wall of leather strings and 2,000 samurai swords on the high ceiling, the dark bar area is perfect for the S&M fetishist. Up-selling here is virtually nonstop – there are three varieties of raw shellfish (the most expensive costs $160) for example – and it's near impossible to leave without dropping $300 per couple. Chef

A Voce. *See p202.*

Russell Titland offers a definitive tour of all that is wagyu – including real-deal kobe from Japan, as well as varieties from Australia and the USA – ordered either à la carte or in a sampler for $190. The more risk-averse diner can stick with familiar American Prime steaks, although that does kind of defeat the object of coming here in the first place. *Photos p210.*

Market Café

496 Ninth Avenue, between 37th & 38th Streets (1-212 967 3892). Subway C, E to 34th Street. **Open** 11am-11pm daily. **Main course** $12. **No credit cards. Map** p404 C24 86

Park yourself at one of the formica tables and prepare to eat downright delicious seasonal food, and plenty of it. House-made gnocchi are bathed in chunky tomato sauce with peas, ham and fresh ricotta; plump seared scallops sit on a bed of whipped potatoes drizzled with brown butter; and some of the best houmous in town comes with triangles of char-grilled flatbread. There is also a range of simple but awesomely effective pizzas, while desserts include a sour cherry ricotta tart.

American creative

Bar Americain

152 W 52nd Street, between Sixth & Seventh Avenues (1-212 265 9700). Subway 1 to 50th Street; N, R, W to 49th Street. **Open** noon-11pm daily. **Main course** $28. **Credit** AmEx, DC, Disc, MC, V. **Map** p404 D23 87

Bobby Flay, the high-spirited, red-headed grill guy from the Food Network, opened this flashy eaterie in April 2005, 15 years after he opened his last NYC restaurant, Mesa Grill. The menu is a good ol' boy's take on a traditional European brasserie: rack of pork comes with apple-ginger chutney, creamed corn and sour mash; barbecued lamb gets hominy flecked with yellow peppers. The place gets suitably crowded at peak times, but never fear: while you're waiting for a table, you can take a seat at the stylish bar and sip one of 50 classic cocktails, all expertly made.

Bar Room at the Modern

9 W 53rd Street, between Fifth & Sixth Avenues (1-212 333 1220). Subway E, V to Fifth Avenue-53rd Street. **Open** noon-2.15pm, 6-9.30pm Mon-Thur; noon-2.15pm, 5.30-10.30pm Fri; 5.30-10.30pm Sat. **Main course** $16. **Credit** AmEx, DC, Disc, MC, V. **Map** p405 E22 88

The main culinary attraction at the new MoMA opened a little after the museum itself, but for fans of chef Gabriel Kreuther, the Modern was worth the wait. Those who can't afford to drop a pay cheque at the formal dining room should drop into the equally stunning and less pricey Bar Room (which shares the same kitchen). From the 30 savoury dishes on the menu (which features several small and medium size plates), standouts include Arctic char tartare and sweetbread ravioli in a balsamic-sage sauce. Desserts come courtesy of pastry chef Marc Aumont, and the wine list is extensive to say the least.

Cafés

Kyotofu

705 Ninth Avenue, between 48th & 49th Streets (1-212 974 6012). Subway C, E at 50th Street. **Open** noon-12.30am Sun, Tue, Wed; noon-1.30am Thur-Sat. **Dessert** $8. **Credit** AmEx, MC, V. **Map** p404 C23 89

See p192 **How sweet it is.**

Eclectic

Gordon Ramsay at the London

151 W 54th Street, at Seventh Avenue (1-212 468 8888). Subway B, D, E at Seventh Avenue; N, Q, R, W at 57th Street. **Open** noon-2pm, 5.30-10.30pm daily. **Prix fixe** $80-$110. **Credit** AmEx, DC, MC, V. **Map** p405 D22 90

The 12 tables that occupy the dining room of celebrity chef Gordon Ramsay's first stateside restaurant are infamously difficult to score. Ramsay's take on French cuisine is always interesting: the signature dish, cannon of lamb, is like a deconstructed stew; roast leg medallions and confit share the plate with candied onions, shallots, tomatoes and exotic spices. Desserts are just as important: the exceptionally fluffy apricot soufflé required advance ordering, and a bonbon trolley peddled toothsome cotton candy, caramel popcorn and fruit jellies. Potty-mouthed Ramsay may be accused of many things, but being half-hearted certainly isn't one of them.

French

Marseille

630 Ninth Avenue, at 44th Street (1-212 333 3410). Subway A, C, E to 42nd Street-Port Authority. **Open** noon-3pm, 5.15-11.30pm Mon-Fri; 11am-3pm, 5.15-11.30pm Sat; 11am-3pm, 5.15-10pm Sun. **Main course** $23. **Credit** AmEx, MC, V. **Map** p404 C24 91

This bustling corner restaurant with floor-to-ceiling windows, proscenium arches, a weathered bar and damask wallpaper will instantly transport you to France's notorious port city. While Marseille's version of bouillabaisse is not textbook, it is undeniably tasty: haddock, skate, cod and mussels are cooked separately, then added to a light broth with a generous dose of garlic. As well as main course dishes, the extensive menu also features a huge selection of salads, sandwiches, starters and brunch fodder. Sipping and snacking are encouraged in the bar: you can order every meze on the menu for only $24.

Seppi's

123 W 56th Street, between Sixth & Seventh Avenues (1-212 708 7444). Subway F, N, Q, R, W to 57th Street. **Open** noon-2am Mon-Sat; 10.30am-2am Sun. **Main course** $21. **Credit** AmEx, DC, Disc, MC, V. **Map** p405 D22 92

We can't decide what we like best about this classic French bistro: the decor is spot on (black-and-white booths, pressed-tin ceilings); the hours are rare for Midtown (order until 2am nightly); the steak au poivre is properly peppery; and then there's Bob

The upper crust

Pizza is the great equaliser. Everyone likes the stuff – food snobs, undiscerning drunks, old folks, picky kids, carnivores, vegetarians. But no one can agree on who makes the best slice or pie. If you ask New Yorkers to name their favourite pizzerias, they'll either rattle off the most famous joints (Grimaldi's, John's on Bleecker Street, Lombardi's) or tell you about some hole-in-the-wall down the block. So we asked dozens of food writers, friends and relatives to share their top pizza picks from the five boroughs – and then we visited as many as we could. Here are some of the best.

The perfect pizza, in our opinion, is made at **Di Fara Pizza** (*see p215*) in a one-room pizza shop by a man named Domenico DeMarco, who was born just outside Naples and has been making pies here for more than 40 years. His movements are slow and deliberate: he stretches the dough into an irregular, oblong shape, dresses it with sauce he makes from both fresh and canned San Marzano tomatoes, carves his own slices of mozzarella over each pie, then eases the uncooked pizza on to a wooden paddle and into the heat. Prepare to wait for a slice: he's not about to rush things now.

Unlike most pizzerias in New York, slices at **Sullivan Street Bakery** (*see p245*) are rectangular, don't have a shred of mozzarella and taste best lukewarm. Baker Jim Lahey makes masterful half-pan, thin-crust pizzas, as well as doughier six-foot-long pizza biancas. He converts basic ingredients – durum wheat, water, sea salt and yeast – into crusts and dresses his Roman-style pizzas with simple toppings like razor-thin potato slices. The pizza bianca looks like bread to the naked eye, but one bite reveals an amazing flavour, redolent of salt, olive oil and rosemary. It's available to go only – and it goes fast.

Una Pizza Napoletana (*see p195*) doesn't take reservations, but pizza fans happily line up outside for as long as an hour – in a neighbourhood full of slice joints – for owner Anthony Mangieri's pies. This purist uses only the best ingredients (dough made of stone-ground wheat berries mixed with Sicilian sea salt, tomatoes from San Marzano, extra-virgin olive oil from Southern Italy and buffalo mozzarella from Naples), cooked in a wood-burning brick oven. The resulting pizza is thin, slightly chewy, lightly charred and crunchy at the outer edge – with a bit of softness at the centre of the pie. With each bite, you taste a combination of olive oil, sweet tomatoes, pungent basil and mild, creamy mozzarella.

Most of the best old-school pizza joints sell by the pie only – no slices. **Joe's Pizza** (see *p198*) is that rare exception; it's a haven for thin-crusted, crunchy slices, and it doesn't load on too much cheese or serve reheated gunk (the kitchen goes through pizzas as fast as it makes them, anyway). Owner Pino Pozzuoli prepares sauce every six hours from fresh tomatoes, adds mozzarella (he'll put fresh mozzarella on a slice if you want it) and bakes in a 1960s oven that produces flavors only an oven that old can. Boozers, take note: it's open until 4am (5am on weekends).

Prior to opening **Totonno's** (*see p215*) in 1924, Anthony 'Totonno' Pero worked at the original Lombardi's (before it was sold and moved to its current location) – said to be the first pizza parlour in America. Today, pie makers here make the stuff the same way it has always been made – with fresh dough, Brooklyn-sourced mozzarella, Italian canned tomatoes, romano cheese and olive oil.

If your grandma made pizzas, they might look something like the ones at **Lazzara's Pizza Café** (*see p207*), a Garment District gem. The super-thin crusts are rectangular and have crisp, raised edges, with ample char and some nuttiness. Each slice is covered with delicious, tangy sauce and a perfect square of melted mozzarella. Those in the know order the plain pie and try to snag a crunchy corner slice before anyone else does.

Una Pizza Napoletana.

Baxter, an 85-year-old suspenders-sportin' magician who stops by your table late at night. Chocoholics come on Sundays to indulge in the divine $24 prix-fixe chocolate brunch, which starts with a chocolate mimosa and follows with a buffet of decadent chocolate delicacies.

Italian

Abboccato

138 W 55th Street, between Sixth & Seventh Avenues (1-212 265 4000). Subway F, N, Q, R, W to 57th Street. **Open** 6.30-10.30am, noon-3pm, 5.30-10pm Mon; 6.30-10.30am, noon-3pm, 5.30-11pm Tue-Thur; 6.30-10.30am, noon-3pm, 5.30pm-midnight Fri, Sat; 6.30-10.30am, noon-10pm Sun. **Main course** $28. **Credit** AmEx, DC, Disc, MC, V. **Map** p405 D22 93

Each dish at Jim Botsacos's Sinatra-esque restaurant (low ceilings, circular leather banquettes) is associated with a region of Italy: there's Umbrian-style quail, and octopus with Sicilian oregano. Carbonara subs in flavourful duck eggs for a richer sauce. His *vaniglia e cioccolato*, meanwhile, combines two classic dishes into one: vanilla-scented veal cheeks and wild boar stewed in red wine, spices and chocolate. It's dinner and dessert rolled into one.

Lazzara's Pizza Café

Second floor, 221 W 38th Street, between Seventh & Eighth Avenues (1-212 944 7792). Subway 1, 2, 3 to 34th Street. **Open** 11.30am-4pm Mon; 11.30am-3pm, 3.30-8.45pm Tue-Fri. **Pizzas** $13. **Credit** MC, V. **Map** p404 D24 94

See p206 **The upper crust**.

Japanese

Koi

Bryant Park Hotel, 40 W 40th Street, between Fifth & Sixth Avenues (1-212 642 2100). Subway B, D, F, V to 42nd Street-Bryant Park; 7 to Fifth Avenue. **Open** noon-2.30pm, 6-10pm Mon, Sun; noon-2.30pm, 5.30-11pm Tue-Sat. **Main course** $23. **Credit** AmEx, Disc, MC, V. **Map** p404 E24 95

Trendy Koi is a spin-off of the sceney LA Japanese restaurant. The decor embodies the four elements of feng shui: earth (bamboo stalks), wind (a ceiling installation modelled after a fluttering fishnet), fire (chandeliers of amber glass) and water (a fountain at the entrance). Chef Sal Sprufero, who worked at Ilo, put his own spin on Koi's menu, adding a white asparagus salad with crab, ossetra and watercress pesto, rock shrimp tempura and a wonderfully tender duck breast with green-tea soba.

Nobu 57

40 W 57th Street, between Fifth & Sixth Avenues (1-212 757 3000). Subway F to 57th Street; N, R, W to Fifth Avenue-59th Street. **Open** 11.45am-2.15pm, 5.45-10.15pm Mon-Fri; 5.45-10.15pm Sat, Sun. **Main course** $23. **Sushi** $6. **Credit** AmEx, DC, Disc, MC, V. **Map** p405 E22 96

Tables at this soaring new midtown location are almost as hard to come by as at the venerable Tribeca mothership – and that's on any night of the week. Chef Nobu Matsuhisa continues his sushi revolution with paper-thin slices of seared fish with a hint of yuzu. The salmon-skin roll is as stellar as its reputation: slices of cucumber enfold salty salmon skin and pieces of fish, along with avocado, pickled burdock, shiso and rice so fresh it has a translucent sheen. A heaping bowl of rock-shrimp tempura with ponzu or Nobu's special creamy, spicy dipping sauce are truly irresistible. If you can't get a table here for love or money, you can always try your luck at the downtown Next Door Nobu, the no-reservations sibling (105 Hudson Street, at Franklin Street, 1-212 334 4445).

Korean

Han Bat

53 W 35th Street, between Fifth & Sixth Avenues (1-212 629 5588). Subway B, D, F, V, N, Q, R to 34th Street-Herald Square; R to 28th Street. **Open** 24hrs daily. **Main course** $12. **Map** p404 E25 97

You have your pick of barbecue joints in Koreatown, but 24-hour diner Han Bat has one key advantage: you won't leave smelling of smoked meat. At this reliable spot, your order is ready when it leaves the kitchen – no grilling at the table. The menu isn't logically divided into courses, so the descriptions are indispensable – and often intriguing. The pajun, a scallion pancake with seafood chunks, is a great starter. *Kimchi chi gae*, juicy pieces of pork in a broth with tangy kimchi and vegetables, is plenty for two.

See also p120 **Cheap date**.

Mexican

El Centro

824 Ninth Avenue, at 54th Street (1-646 763 6585). Subway C, E to 50th Street. **Open** 5-11pm Mon, Tue, Sun; 5pm-midnight Wed-Sat. **Main course** $12. **Credit** AmEx, DC, MC, V. **Map** p405 C22 98

To start the party right, indulge in one of the frozen margaritas, available with guava or raspberry. The menu's tried-and-true offerings – tacos, burritos, enchiladas, fajitas and so on – are all extremely solid. Especially good is the quesadilla with fat chunks of shrimp and melted monterey jack cheese, and a tostada appetiser with a seriously hearty mix of black beans, lettuce, tomato, sour cream and thick, juicy slices of grilled skirt steak.

Russian

Russian Tea Room

150 W 57th Street, between Sixth & Seventh Avenues (1-212 581 7100). Subway F, N, Q, R, W to 57th Street. **Open** 11.30am-3.30pm, 5-11.30pm Mon-Fri; 11am-3pm, 5-11.30pm Sat, Sun. **Main course** $40. **Credit** AmEx, DC, MC, V. **Map** p405 D22 99

This recently reborn socialite centre has never looked – or tasted – better. Nostalgia buffs will be happy to hear that nothing's happened to the gilded-bird friezes or the famously tacky crystal-bear aquarium. The food, thankfully, has not been frozen in time. Chef Marc Taxiera has modernised the menu, looking to former Soviet republics for culinary inspiration and finding it in spades.

Midtown East

American

PS 450

450 Park Avenue South, between 30th & 31st Streets (1-212 532 7474). Subway 6 to 33rd Street. **Open** 11.30am-4am daily. **Main course** $15. **Credit** AmEx, MC, V. **Map** p404 E25.

This is what happens when a distinctly unsexy, quiet neighbourhood gets a big new playground: the place is almost always packed. An admirable selection of finger food is paired nicely with decent cocktails, including tasty duck-confit taquitos with tomatillo and pear salsa, tender pulled-pork sliders, and satisfying entrées such as a wood-grilled hangar steak sliced over chorizo hash with lobster butter. Chef Dominic Giuliano's food is better than you'd find at most lounges and clubs – just don't plan on a quiet meal and you won't be disappointed.

Cafés

Penelope

159 Lexington Avenue, at 30th Street (1-212 481 3800). Subway 6 to 28th Street. **Open** 8am-11pm daily. **Main course** $9. **No credit cards**. **Map** p404 F25 100

This pretty little café and wine bar is the last thing you'd expect to find in Curry Hill, with its generic hot-table curry houses. The kitchen here cranks out dishes with care: creamy houmous with toast, chicken potpies and a terrific grilled cheese are just a few of the homespun dishes. The soup of the day is listed on a chalkboard and is served with chunks of good, earthy bread; the skins are left on the hand-cut french fries. Penelope is also a popular brunch spot; you may have to wait for a table, but you'll be extremely glad you did.

French

Brasserie

100 E 53rd Street, between Park & Lexington Avenues (1-212 751 4840). Subway 6 to 33rd Street. **Open** 7am-midnight Mon-Thur; 7am-1am Fri; 11am-1am Sat; 11am-10pm Sun. **Main course** $23. **Credit** AmEx, DC, Disc, MC, V. **Map** p405 E23 101

The trouble with cutting-edge design is that it soon becomes passé. Such is the case with Brasserie's high-concept interior. So it's a good thing that the food holds its own. Old-school French classics (steak-frites, escargots) never go out of style, and mix well with more inventive dishes, like an appetiser of tuna tartare with mango-chilli marmalade. Those heady days when Brasserie stayed open all night are long gone, but at least it still serves food after most of the neighbourhood has shut down for the evening. *See also p223.*

Indian

Mint

150 E 50th Street, between Lexington & Third Avenues (1-212 644 8888). Subway E, V to Lexington Avenue-53rd Street; 6 to 51st Street. **Open** 11.30am-3pm, 5-11pm daily. **Main course** $19. **Credit** AmEx, MC, V. **Map** p404 F23 102

At this Indian eaterie, chefs pull all sorts of traditional baked goods from the fiery clay oven – fluffy nan, roti and kulcha – but the best in our opinion is the sublime aloo paratha: warm, chewy, slightly charred rounds with a layer of soft, spicy potato in the middle. The secret's in the seasoning and the precisely heated oven.

Japanese

Megu Midtown

845 UN Plaza, Trump World Tower, First Avenue, at 47th Street (1-212 964 7777). Subway E, V to Lexington Avenue-53rd Street; 6 to 51st Street. **Open** 5.30-10.30pm Mon-Wed; 5.30-11.30pm Thur-Sat. **Main course** $32. **Prix fixe** $70 (4 courses). **Map** p404 F24 103

The 115-seat dining room has 24ft ceilings, 16ft-long lampshades, black wood panelling, a monumental mural of white tigers and a Buddha ice sculpture. Visually it's a case of pushing all the right buttons, which is something that can also be said for the food. From the open kitchen, an army of chefs produces pristine sushi and meat dishes (kobe beef, foie gras) the likes of which you'll be hard pressed to find elsewhere. If the $70 prix-fixe menu isn't enough to impress, ask about the 'wagon service', featuring rare ingredients, jetted in daily. *Photos p212-213.*

Pan-Asian

Tao

42 E 58th Street, between Madison & Park Avenues (1-212 888 2288). Subway N, R, W to Fifth Avenue-59th Street. **Open** 11.30am-midnight Mon, Tue; 11.30am-1am Wed-Fri; 5pm-1am Sat; 5pm-midnight Sun. **Main course** $22. **Credit** AmEx, DC, MC, V. **Map** p405 E22 104

A magnificent, scenic palace, Tao is packed with glowing Chinese lanterns, wealthy businesspeople, trendy Manhattanites and intrepid tourists. The restaurant bar is always packed, and the stunning dining room has an over-the-top Far Eastern vibe, thanks to curly bamboo, Asian art and a 16ft stone Buddha. The menu offers generic small plates (dumplings, satay) and decent entrées.

Uptown

Upper West Side

American

Bouchon Bakery 

3rd Floor, Time Warner Center, 10 Columbus Circle, at Broadway (1-212 823 9366). Subway A, B, C, D, 1 to 59th Street-Columbus Circle. **Open** 11.30am-5.30pm Mon, Tue; 11.30am-9pm Wed-Sat. **Main course** $12. **Credit** AmEx, MC, V. **Map** p405 D22 105

It has taken chef Thomas Keller, of Per Se (*see below*), three years to open the New York outpost of his famous French bistro and boulangerie, Bouchon Bakery. The sleek 60-seat café is on the third floor of the mall; a chic takeaway shop sits around the corner. The menu – served throughout the space whether you sit at the espresso/wine bar, the communal table or a marble-topped table – includes savoury tartines, hearty soups, rustic pâtés, chocolate tarts and other affordable treats.

Gray's Papaya

2090 Broadway, at 71st Street (1-212 799 0243). Subway 1, 2, 3 to 72nd Street. **Open** 24hrs. **Hot dog** 95¢. **No credit cards. Map** p405 C20 106

A great number of New Yorkers think Gray's Papaya exemplifies the classic New York dog. The meat itself (all beef) boasts the ever-alluring combination of salty and sweet. It is cooked on a flat grill that renders the exterior slightly crunchy. You'll find mustard, sauerkraut, sautéed onions and ketchup on the counter. At 95 cents apiece, the price is right.

Porter House New York

4th Floor, Time Warner Center, 10 Columbus Circle, at Broadway (1-212 823 9335). Subway A, B, C, D, 1 to 59th Street-Columbus Circle. **Open** 5-10.30pm Mon-Thur; noon-4.30pm, 5-11pm Fri; 5-11pm Sat; 5-10pm Sun. **Main course** $30. **Credit** AmEx, MC, V. **Map** p405 D22 107

The latest restaurant from chef Michael Lomonaco joins the all-star line-up at the Time Warner Center. Portions are large and prices fair, all things considered. The steaks get a glorious char, though it can overpower the flavour of the meat. The wine list didn't offer much on the lower end of the price spectrum, but there are plenty of half bottles.

Telepan

72 W 69th Street, at Columbus Avenue (1-212 580 4300). Subway B, C to 72nd Street; 1 to 66th Street. **Open** 5-11pm Tue; 11.30am-2.30pm, 5-11pm Wed, Thur; 11.30am-2.30pm, 5pm-midnight Fri; 11am-2.30pm, 5pm-midnight Sat; 11am-2.30pm, 5-10.30pm Sun. **Main course** $28. **Prix fixe** $55. **Credit** AmEx, Disc, MC, V. **Map** p405 C21 108

This place isn't fancy, but it gets things right. Diners can customise their $55 prix-fixe dinners by selecting three dishes from any three columns; they can ask for assistance and get smart feedback; and they can count on a fresh, Greenmarket-inspired menu featuring ingredients such as hen-of-the-woods mushrooms, brook trout and organic lamb.

Cafés

Alice's Tea Cup

102 W 73rd Street, at Columbus Avenue (1-212 799 3006). Subway B, C, 1, 2, 3 to 72nd Street. **Open** 8am-8pm Mon-Thur; 8am-10pm Fri; 10am-10pm Sat; 10am-8pm Sun. **Sandwich** $8. **Credit** AmEx, Disc, MC, V. **Map** p405 C20 109

Wander into this basement and you'll be transported to the end of a rabbit hole. This quirky *Alice in Wonderland*-themed boutique-cum-bakeshop is the perfect refuge for afternoon tea. Choose from scrumptious scones and muffins, overstuffed sandwiches like curried chicken salad and croque-monsieur, and sprightly salads like warm lentil with ginger dressing. Or you can have the full teatime treatment (charmingly dubbed the Mad Hatter) for $27 ($7 extra to share).

Eclectic

Per Se

4th Floor, Time Warner Center, 10 Columbus Circle, at Broadway (1-212 823 9335). Subway A, B, C, D, 1 to 59th Street-Columbus Circle. **Open** 5.30-10pm Mon-Thur; 11.30am-1.30pm, 5.30-10.30pm Fri, Sat; 11.30am-1.30pm, 5.30-10pm Sun. **Prix fixe** $125-$150. **Credit** AmEx, MC, V. **Map** p405 D22 110

Rules are meant to be broken – unless you're Thomas Keller, and then they're not. Keller insists on perfection at Per Se. All he asks in return is that diners rise to the occasion and dress for it. Truth be told, a few guests are let off the hook. Mick Jagger got to wear jeans, and an occasional VIP is allowed to dine in a button-down without being forced to don the house jacket. Otherwise, those who are lucky or patient enough to get a reservation willingly suit up for the meal without making a fuss. For doing so, they're treated to nearly flawless, epic tasting menus, from the crunch of the classic opening bite – Keller's salmon-topped tuile cone – to the last little macaroon on the petits fours tray.

French

Nice Matin

201 W 79th Street, at Amsterdam Avenue (1-212 873 6423). Subway 1 to 79th Street. **Open** 8am-3.30pm, 5.30pm-midnight daily. **Main course** $18. **Credit** AmEx, DC, MC, V. **Map** p405 C19 111

Nice Matin draws mature locals seeking a relaxed night out. Chef Andy D'Amico's southern French fare isn't particularly inventive, but it's tasty and well executed. The optical-illusion wallpaper and carousel-top columns make for date-friendly surroundings. If only the waitstaff's attention didn't wander quite so much.

Kobe Club. *See p203.*

Greek

Kefi

222 W 79th Street, between Amsterdam Avenue & Broadway (1-212 873 0200). Subway 1 to 79th Street. **Open** 5-10pm Tue-Thur, Sun; 5-11pm Fri, Sat. **Main course** $14. **No credit cards. Map** p405 C19 ⓫⓬
This casual eaterie serves rustic Hellenic cuisine, and the equally artful yet laid-back dishes includes a variety of memorable meze, and flavourful spreads (tsatsiki, eggplant, fava and top-notch taramasalata). Beverage director Kostas Damianos is vastly knowledgeable about the all-Greek wine list and makes excellent recommendations.

Mexican

Rosa Mexicano

61 Columbus Avenue, at 62nd Street (1-212 977 7700). Subway 1 to 66th Street-Lincoln Center. **Open** noon-3pm, 5-10pm Mon-Fri; 5-10pm Sat; noon-3pm, 4-10pm Sun. **Main course** $23. **Credit** AmEx, DC, Disc, MC, V. **Map** p405 C21 113
The jazzy technicolour journey up vivid terrazzo steps to the cavernous dining room is alone worth the trip uptown. But the famous guacamole is still the main draw, smashed to order at your table. As the waiter unwraps a parchment package of braised lamb shank, the rich aroma of chilli, cumin and clove envelopes the table. Veracruz-style red snapper is stuffed with crab and brightened with a punchy sauce of tomatoes, olives and capers.

Upper East Side

American

Lexington Candy Shop

1226 Lexington Avenue, at 83rd Street (1-212 288 0057). Subway 4, 5, 6 to 86th Street. **Open** 7am-7pm Mon-Sat; 9am-6pm Sun. **Main course** $9. **Credit** AmEx, Disc, MC, V. **Map** p405 E19 114
You won't find much candy for sale at Lexington Candy Shop. Instead, you'll find a preserved retro diner, lined with chatty locals digging into gigantic chocolate malts or peanut butter and bacon sandwiches. The shop was founded in 1925 and has appeared in numerous films, including the Robert Redford classic *Three Days of the Condor*.

Austrian

Café Sabarsky

Neue Galerie, 1048 Fifth Avenue, at 86th Street (1-212 288 0665). Subway 4, 5, 6 to 86th Street. **Open** 9am-6pm Mon, Wed; 9am-9pm Thur-Sun. **Main course** $14. **Credit** AmEx, MC, V. **Map** p406 E18 115
Nearby museum-goers come to this elegant Viennese café on Fifth Avenue for lunch plates such as smoked trout and goulash with spaetzle. But the savoury stuff is little more than a prelude to the real works of art that come after – apple strudel in crackling golden pastry, feather-light quark cheesecake, luscious Sachertorte and magnificent cream-topped (*mit Schlag*) coffee. Breakfast is a particularly serene moment for appreciating the beautifully carved dark-wood restaurant walls and the spectacularly leafy park views.

French

Daniel

60 E 65th Street, between Madison & Park Avenues (1-212 288 0033). Subway F to Lexington Avenue-63rd Street; 6 to 68th Street-Hunter College. **Open** 5.45-11pm Mon-Thur; 5.30-11pm Fri, Sat. **Prix fixe** $85-$160. **Credit** AmEx, DC, MC, V. **Map** p405 E21 116
Some things are guaranteed when you dine at Daniel Boulud's flagship: you will feel like royalty when you enter the room; you will be surrounded by movers and shakers in very nice suits; and you will savour exquisite seasonal dishes, even if you order something as simple as roasted chicken. *See p214* **Gallic in Gotham**.
Other locations: Café Boulud, 20 E 76th Street, between Fifth & Madison Avenues (1-212 772 2600).

Italian

Uva

1486 Second Avenue, at 77th Street (1-212 472 4552). Subway 6 to 77th Street. **Open** noon-1am Mon-Thur, Sun; noon-2am Fri, Sat. **Main course** $15. **Credit** AmEx, MC, V ($30 minimum). **Map** p405 F19 117
Although the Upper East Side has plenty of rustic Italian restaurants, the neighbourhood could still do with a few more wine bars. Thankfully, Luigi Lusardi and his brother Mauro opened Uva to fill the void. A 200-year-old wooden floor and antique couches give the place a warm, worn-in feel, and as per the wine bar formula, you can take your pick of cured meats and cheeses to pair with most Italian wines (30 are available by the glass).

Seafood

Central Park Boathouse Restaurant

Central Park Lake, park entrance on Fifth Avenue, at 72nd Street (1-212 517 2233). Subway 6 to 68th Street-Hunter College. **Open** *Apr-Nov* noon-4pm, 5.30-11pm Mon-Fri; 9.30am-4pm, 6-11pm Sat, Sun. *Dec-Mar* noon-4pm Mon-Fri; 9.30am-4pm Sat, Sun. **Main course** $26. **Credit** AmEx, MC, V. **Map** p405 D20 118
Paying for location is par for the course in New York; here, it's well worth it. The Boathouse salad is a gorgeous sculpture of tomatoes, cucumbers, red onion, olives and large, rectangular chunks of feta cheese. Crab cakes, more crab than cake, are worth every penny. Fish and fowl are fresh and beautifully presented, if sometimes a little bland.

116th Street & above

American

Kitchenette Uptown

1272 Amsterdam Avenue, between 122nd & 123rd Streets (1-212 531 7600). Subway 1 to 125th Street. **Open** 8am-11pm daily. **Main course** $16. **Credit** AmEx, DC, MC, V. **Map** p407 C14 119

Riding the wave of South Harlem gentrification, Kitchenette Uptown brings Tribeca-style country dining to a sunlit space in Morningside Heights. At brunch, order the BLT on challah bread – it does cartwheels around the egg dishes. Cheese grits with own-made turkey sausage also make a great meal, followed by a homely slice of cherry pie. All-day breakfast and weekend brunch attract a lively group of university types, as does the BYOB dinner with chicken potpie and four-cheese macaroni.

Miss Maude's Spoonbread Too

547 Malcolm X Boulevard (Lenox Avenue), between 137th & 138th Streets (1-212 690 3100). Subway B, C to 135th Street. **Open** 11.30am-9.30pm Mon-Sat; 11am-8pm Sun. **Main course** $12. **Credit** AmEx, MC, V. **Map** p407 D11 120

Norma Jean Darden knows that sometimes nothing will do but real home cookin'. The three-year-old offshoot of Darden's original Morningside Heights spot makes everything from scratch. Get a load of fall-off-the-bone short ribs, flaky cornmeal-crusted catfish, or thick-cut pork chops smothered in creamy gravy, and dig into sides like smoky collard greens. Weekend brunch includes nap-inducing favourites like pecan waffles, fried fish and biscuits.

Caribbean

809 Sangria Bar & Grill

112 Dyckman Street, between Nagle & Post Avenues (1-212 304 3800). Subway 1 to Dyckman Street. **Open** 11.45am-11pm Mon-Wed; 11.45am-midnight Thur, Fri; 11.45am-1am Sat; 5-11pm Sun. **Main course** $20. **Credit** MC, V. **Map** p409 C3 121

An upscale Latin restaurant has landed near the top of Manhattan. Patrons can feast on modern updates of classic dishes and take in original oil paintings by famed Dominican artists. This is sangria heaven, and you'd be silly to order any beverage other than the half-dozen varieties on the menu; most pack a sweet, alcoholic punch.

Chinese

Ginger

1400 Fifth Avenue, at 116th Street (1-212 423 1111). Subway 2, 3 to 116th Street-Lenox Avenue; 6 to 116th Street-Lexington Avenue. **Open** 5.30-10.30pm Mon-Thur; 5.30-11.30pm Fri; 11.30am-4.30pm, 5.30-11.30pm Sat; 5.30-10pm Sun. **Credit** AmEx, DC, Disc, MC, V. **Main course** $15. **Map** p407 E14 122

Big-name developers aren't the only people breaking new ground in East Harlem. What's novel about this organic Chinese restaurant – aside from the fact that it's on East 116th Street – is what executive chef James Marshall (Vong, China Grill) won't do to the food: there will be no deep-frying and no excessive use of oil or salt. Instead, fresh vegetables and lean meats are doused in citrusy sauces; and the menu lists pineapple-and-mango-glazed porks chops as well as apricot-glazed chicken. Authentic it ain't; delicious (and healthy) it most certainly is.

Pizza

Patsy's

2287 First Avenue, between 117th & 118th Streets (1-212 534 9783). Subway 6 to 116th Street. **Open** 11am-11pm Mon-Sat; 1-10pm Sun. **Pizza** $12. **No credit cards. Map** p407 F14 123

Megu Midtown. *See p208.*

This is East Harlem's favourite parlour, and with good reason. Sit down for a pie or stand up for a slice at the 71-year-old uptown joint.

Brooklyn

American

Applewood

501 11th Street, at Seventh Avenue, Park Slope (1-718 768 2044). Subway F to Seventh Avenue. **Open** 5-11pm Tue-Sat; 10am-3pm Sun. **Main course** $20. **Credit** AmEx, Disc, MC, V. **Map** p410 T12 124

David and Laura Shea met at the Culinary Institute of America and then returned to New York to open this charming eaterie with country style and organic produce. Tables are adorned with bundles of fresh herbs, there's a working fireplace, and many of the ingredients come from a friend's upstate farm. On the opening menu: ricotta dumplings with braised pork shoulder, roasted chicken with chanterelle-sage gravy, and wild striped bass with roasted corn and curried mussel chowder.

Brooklyn Fish Camp

162 Fifth Avenue, between DeGraw & Douglass Streets, Park Slope (1-718 783 3264). Subway 2, 3 to Bergen Street. **Open** noon-3pm, 6-11pm Mon-Sat. **Main course** $19. **Credit** AmEx, MC, V. **Map** p410 T11 125

Brooklyn Fish Camp is no flop: the cultish lobster roll, rosemary-stuffed whole fish and succulent lobster knuckles are fresh and delicious. Spicy calamari tossed with grape tomatoes and chickpeas are equally satisfying. You'll eat well here, and when the weather's nice you can do so on the outdoor deck.

Schnäck

122 Union Street, at Columbia Street, Carroll Gardens (1-718 855 2879). Subway F, G to Carroll Street. **Open** 11am-1am daily. **Burgers** $6. **No credit cards. Map** p410 S10 126

A greasy spoon with a sense of humour, Schnäck has a knack for burgers. You can order up to five small patties stacked on a single bun, with a full array of toppings (the likes of 'schnäck sauce', spicy onions, chilli and kraut). The $2 quickie – a mini-burger with a 'children's portion' of beer – is easily one of the best deals in Brooklyn. Buttermilk-soaked onion rings fry up flaky-crisp and come sprinkled with salt and parsley seasoning. The award-winning beer milkshake tastes just like a regular milkshake, but has an undeniable buzz to it, offering the best of both worlds at once.

American creative

DuMont

432 Union Avenue, between Devoe Street & Metropolitan Avenue, Williamsburg (1-718 486 7717). Subway G to Metropolitan Avenue; L to Lorimer Street. **Open** 11am-3pm, 6-11pm daily. **Main course** $12. **Credit** MC, V. **Map** p411 V8 127

DuMont is the kind of place where Byron, Shelley and Keats might have gathered for a drink – a gently worn joint with pressed-tin ceilings, a wooden bar, retro brown leather booths and plenty of candles. A private den in the back doubles as a bar and holding pen for those who are waiting to dig into excellent seasonal American dishes such as frothy lobster bisque with a dollop of curry butter, or braised duck leg risotto. Luckily for all of us, the lardon-laced macaroni and cheese never disappears.

Italian

DOC Wine Bar

83 North 7th Street, at Wythe Avenue, Williamsburg (1-718 963 1925). Subway L to Bedford Avenue. **Open** 6pm-midnight Mon-Thur; 6pm-1am Fri-Sun. **Small plate** $7. **No credit cards. Map** p411 U7 128

Gallic in Gotham

Top chef **Daniel Boulud** brings out the informal francophile in New Yorkers.

Despite the steadily dwindling popularity of French fine dining restaurants throughout Manhattan over the past few years, French chefs are still among New York City's most influential foodie figures. Chief among them is enigmatic chef, restaurateur and Lyon native **Daniel Boulud** (of Daniel and Café Boulud). A shining example of a businessman who understands the casual direction that NYC dining is taking, Boulud has used this knowledge to perpetuate his own brand in Gotham. He is one of several French chefs (another is Jean Georges Vongerichten) who have parlayed a traditional culinary background in established restaurants (Boulud spent six career-making years as executive chef at Le Cirque) into a dining empire.

As well as owning both the elegant French eaterie **Daniel** and fantastic **Café Boulud** (for both, *see p211*), a neighbourhood restaurant for wealthy types on the Upper East Side, Boulud also started to explore more informal dining with the opening of **DB Bistro Moderne** (55 W 44th Street, between Fifth & Sixth Avenues, 1-212 391 2400) in 2001. With this clever move, he revealed the extent of his marketing savvy by becoming a leading figure in the famous NYC burger wars with a $69 sirloin patty, stuffed with black truffles, braised short ribs and foie gras. As we went to press, Boulud-the-entrepreneur was poised to continue the relaxed dining theme with the opening of **Bar Boulud** (1900 Broadway, at 64th Street), a French-focused wine bar near Lincoln Center. For this venture he is bringing in Parisian charcutier Gilles Verot to assemble a selection of seriously vino-friendly terrines, pâtés and cured meats.

In 2008, keep an eye out for Boulud's first move downtown with an already buzz-generating burger joint on the Bowery (an initial name for the project, DBGB, which stands for Daniel Boulud Good Burger, attracted threats of litigation from defunct downtown rock club CBGB). If Boulud's trajectory is anything to go by, high-quality French cuisine certainly still thrives in NYC – albeit disguised in denim.

Tucked on a quiet side street, this unpretentious spot pleases with brown-paper-covered tables and menus held together with wooden spoons, exuding an artfully rustic charm that perfectly complements the cuisine on hand. Peruse the list of 70 Italian wines and a menu of small plates: vegetarian carpaccio serves up as a mound of thin, perfectly rolled slices of carrot and courgette topped with parmesan shavings. Pistokku – traditional flatbread from Sardinia – is served pizza-style, warm and crisp with toppings such as bresaola (air-cured beef), goat's cheese and arugula (rocket).

Mexican

Alma

187 Columbia Street, at DeGraw Street, Cobble Hill (1-718 643 5400). Subway F, G to Carroll Street. **Open** 5.30-10pm Mon-Fri; 6-11pm Sat, Sun. **Main course** $15. **Credit** MC, V. **Map** p410 S10 129

From the subway, it's a long walk west (when you get to the far side of the BQE overpass, you're almost there), but if you want to chill with local margarita-lovin' arty types, it's worth heading over to this sexy

Mexi spot. Start by having a drink at the ground-floor bar, B61, then head upstairs to Alma's colourful dining room. In good weather, snag a table on the rooftop deck, which has industrial-chic views of the Brooklyn waterfront and the downtown Manhattan skyline. Citrusy ceviche of shrimp, scallop and bass has a hint of jalapeño; a side of black beans with sticky, luscious sautéed plantains is pure south-of-the-border comfort.

Pizza

Totonno's

1524 Neptune Avenue, between W 15th & W 16th Streets, Coney Island, Brooklyn (1-718 372 8606). Subway F to Neptune Avenue. **Open** noon-7.30pm Wed-Sun. **Pizza** $12. **No credit cards.**
See p206 **The upper crust**.

Di Fara Pizza

1424 Avenue J, at E 15th Street, Midwood (1-718 258 1367). Subway Q to Avenue J. **Open** 11.30am-10pm daily. **Pizza** $12. **No credit cards.**
See p206 **The upper crust**.

Steakhouse

Peter Luger

178 Broadway, at Driggs Avenue, Williamsburg (1-718 387 7400). Subway J, M, Z to Marcy Avenue. **Open** 11.30am-10pm Mon-Thur, Sun; 11.30am-11pm Fri, Sat. **Steak for two** $65. **No credit cards. Map** p411 U8 130

Does this Williamsburg landmark deserve its rep as one of the best steakhouses in America? A four-star experience this isn't, but the quality of the beef may just make you forgive any shortcomings. Established as a German beer hall in 1887, the restaurant serves only one cut: a porterhouse that's char-broiled black on the outside, tender and pink on the inside. Service is sluggish to say the least, provided as it is by waiters who would rather give out wisecracks than water. And remember to stuff your wallet with cash before you start stuffing your face, as Luger's doesn't take credit cards (although it will accept US debit cards).

Thai

SEA Thai Restaurant & Bar

114 North 6th Street, at Berry Street, Williamsburg (1-718 384 8850). Subway L to Bedford Avenue. **Open** 11.30am-12.30am Mon-Thur, Sun; 11.30am-1.30am Fri, Sat. **Main course** $9. **Credit** AmEx, MC, V. **Map** p411 U7 131

SEA could be mistaken for a nightclub, given the reverberating dance music and a mod lounge complete with bubble-chair swing. Get a table by the reflecting pool and flip through the campy postcard menu. For a place so stylish, prices are cheap and the food good. Stuffed with shrimp and real crab, jade seafood dumplings come alongside a nutty Massaman sauce, while the Queen of Siam beef with basil and red chilli is at its most delicious when you ask the kitchen to fire it up.

Queens

French

718

35-01 Ditmars Boulevard, at 35th Street, Astoria (1-718 204 5553). Subway N, W to Astoria-Ditmars Boulevard. **Open** 5.30-10.30pm Mon-Thur; 5.30pm-1am Fri; noon-5pm, 5.30pm-1am Sat; noon-4pm, 5.30-10.30pm Sun. **Main course** $15. **Credit** AmEx, DC, Disc, MC, V. **Map** p412 X3 132

Queens achieved a certain critical mass two and a half years ago when French chef Alain Allaire co-opened 718 on a promising corner of Ditmars Boulevard's restaurant row. The joint has since become a consistent crowd-pleaser. It is at once a bar, a warm-weather café, a brunch hang, a late-night tapas haunt, a weekly belly-dancing-and-salsa club and – most crucially – a dependable kitchen.

Greek

Cavo

42-18 31st Avenue, between 42nd & 43rd Streets, Astoria (1-718 721 1001). Subway G, R, V to Steinway Street. **Open** 5pm-2am Mon-Sat; noon-4am Sun. **Main course** $18. **Credit** AmEx, MC, V. **Map** p412 X4 133

Space-starved New Yorkers love to luxuriate in the immense outdoor garden of this upscale Astoria restaurant, bar and lounge. The menu features Greek classics such as whole-roasted fish, along with modern inspirations like the giant filo-wrapped shrimp drizzled with Cretan honey. Don't miss the keftedakia – crispy beef and pork meatballs oozing with kefalograviera, a goat and cow's milk cheese, and dressed with ladolemono, an olive oil and lemon emulsion.

Malaysian

Sentosa Malaysian Cuisine

39-07 Prince Street, between Roosevelt & 39th Avenues, Unit 1F, Flushing (1-718 886 6331). Subway 7 to Flushing-Main Street. **Open** 11am-11pm Mon-Thur, Sun; 11am-11.30pm Fri, Sat. **Main course** $11. **Credit** MC, V.

Malaysian cuisine is a fusion of Cantonese and Indonesian, so you'll find fried rice and spare ribs on the menu, along with Javanese and Sumatran dishes. Most diners start with roti canai, crêpes you dip in curried chicken soup. Satay tofu, another fine appetiser, covers fried, sprout-stuffed tofu pillows with chopped peanuts. To finish, the intensely flavoured, panna cotta-textured coconut pudding served inside a fresh coconut is a must. *See also p168* **Cheap date**.

Eat, Drink, Shop

Bars

Drink up, down and all over town.

Welcome to boozing paradise. New York has nearly 5,000 bars, pubs and clubs to keep your favourite libation flowing from as early as 8am until 4am – which leaves you with a few hours to catch some shut-eye before starting over.

Our 'average drink' price covers a standard well drink (spirit) plus mixer, or equivalent.

Downtown

Tribeca & South

Another Room

249 West Broadway, between Beach & North Moore Streets (1-212 226 1418). Subway A, C, E to Canal Street. **Open** 5pm-4am daily. **Average drink** $7. **No credit cards**. **Map** p402 E31 ❶

Like its siblings, this sleek and civilised bar doubles as an art gallery. You won't find any hard liquor, but the selection of fine beer and wine is varied and vast, and the crowd – gay, straight, fashionistas, 9-to-5 execs – interesting. If the weather is decent, sit at the picnic table out front.

Other locations: The Other Room, 143 Perry Street, between Greenwich & Washington Streets (1-212 645 9758); The Room, 144 Sullivan Street, between Houston & Prince Streets (1-212 477 2102).

Bin No.220

220 Front Street, between Beekman Street & Peck Slip (1-212 374 9463). Subway A, C to Broadway-Nassau Street; J, M, Z, 2, 3, 4, 5 to Fulton Street. **Open** 4pm-midnight Mon-Sat; 4-11pm Sun. **Average drink** $10. **Credit** MC, V. **Map** p402 F32 ❷

This sleek Italian-style wine bar, where banker types devour cured meats, cheeses and olive oil, offers refuge from the South Street Seaport tourist scene. Located on historic Front Street, this spot boasts a centuries-old brick wall, cast-iron columns, a polished walnut bar and a nifty metal wine rack that stores bottles sideways. Most imbibers come for the selection of 60 wines, but a well-stocked shelf also accommodates those who prefer the hard stuff.

Brandy Library

25 North Moore Street, at Varick Street (1-212 226 5545). Subway 1 to Franklin Street. **Open** 4pm-4am daily. **Average drink** $12. **Credit** AmEx, MC, V. **Map** p402 E31 ❸

> ❶ Pink numbers given in this chapter correspond to the location of each bar as marked on the street maps. *See pp402-412.*

Cocktail connoisseurs and spirit snobs will find themselves at home inside this handsome cognac-coloured liquor lounge. Wood panelling, low-slung couches, a long bar and blue-note jazz create an atmosphere that begs for a smoking jacket (you can smoke cigars on the heated terrace out front).

Bubble Lounge

228 West Broadway, between Franklin & White Streets (1-212 431 3433). Subway 1 to Franklin Street. **Open** 5pm-2am Mon, Tue; 5pm-3am Wed; 5pm-4am Thur; 4.30pm-4am Fri; 6pm-4am Sat. **Average drink** $22. **Credit** AmEx, DC, Disc, MC, V. **Map** p402 E31 ❹

This warm L-shaped and couch-filled champagne and sparkling wine bar doesn't get jammed until late. Feeling in a festive mood? Ask to have your bottle opened in the traditional celebratory way: with the blade of a sabre.

Dekk

134 Reade Street, between Greenwich & Hudson Streets (1-212 941 9401). Subway 1, 2, 3 to Chambers Street. **Open** 11am-4am Mon-Fri; 10am-4am Sat, Sun. **Average drink** $8. **Credit** AmEx, MC, V. **Map** p402 E31 ❺

Decorated with antique Parisian subway seats and French doors, Dekk has a screening room in the back that shows depraved films like *Cecil B Demented* and *Tromeo and Juliet*. A long list of wines by the glass complements a menu of thin-crust pizzas and northern Italian pastas.

Kimono Bar at Megu

62 Thomas Street, between Church Street & West Broadway (1-212 964 7777). Subway A, C, 1, 2, 3 to Chambers Street. **Open** 11.30am-2.30pm, 5.30-11.30pm Mon-Fri; 5.30-11.30pm Sat, Sun. **Average drink** $16. **Credit** AmEx, DC, Disc, MC, V. **Map** p402 E31.

The lounge of this high-end, high-profile Japanese restaurant is show-stopping: white columns are fashioned from porcelain rice bowls, and saké bottles and kimono fabrics abound. Kimono's cocktails are similarly fancy; Autumn Rain, for example, is a refreshing blend of citrus vodka, elderflower syrup, Asian-pear purée and ginger.

Trinity Place

115 Broadway, between Cedar Street & Trinity Place, entrance on Cedar Street (1-212 964 0939). Subway 2, 3, 4, 5, J, M, Z to Wall Street. **Open** 11am-2am daily. **Average drink** $9. **Credit** MC, V. **Map** p402 E33 ❻

Trinity Place is a great place to meet people who make six figures. Indeed, the recently opened spot, recognisable by its 19th-century, 35-ton bank-vault doors, serves stiff drinks and continental fare to a well-heeled crowd of stockbrokers and bond traders.

Chinatown, Little Italy & Nolita

Palais Royale

173 Mott Street, between Broome & Grand Streets (1-212 941 6112). Subway J, M, Z to Bowery; 6 to Spring Street. **Open** 1pm-2am Mon-Wed; 1pm-4am Thur-Sun. **Average drink** $6. **Credit** AmEx, MC, V. **Map** p403 F30 ❼

Palais Royale might be the city's first haute dive bar. The owners, who also run Double Happiness and Orchard Bar, are serious about booze – they serve 30 types of bourbon – but they're having fun with the menu: check out the Hungry Man and Lean Cuisine microwaveable meals. A pool table and televisions above the bar add to the 'dive' quotient.

Xicala Wine & Tapas Bar

151B Elizabeth Street, between Broome & Kenmare Streets (1-212 219 0599). Subway J, M, Z to Bowery. **Open** 5pm-2am daily. **Average drink** $8. **Credit** AmEx, MC, V. **Map** p403 F30 ❽

Everything about this Spanish spot, located on an ungentrified block, is incongruous. A bright neon sign leads to a dark, tiny space. Classic tapas – chorizo, codfish, olives – co-exist with chocolate fondue, and powerhouse wines are properly chilled and generously poured. The full capacity of the place is just 20 people, so in warm weather patrons spill out on to the pavement.

Lower East Side

Barrio Chino

253 Broome Street, between Ludlow & Orchard Streets (1-212 228 6710). Subway F to Delancey Street; J, M, Z to Delancey-Essex Streets. **Open** 6pm-2am Mon-Thur, Sun; 6pm-4am Fri, Sat. **Average drink** $8. **Credit** MC, V. **Map** p403 G30 ❾

Neighbourhood cool kids have taken up positions at Barrio Chino's rough-hewn wooden bar. Owners Patrick Durocher and Dylan Dodd are aiming to 'give tequila credibility as a sipping liquor, like Scotch'. Some 50 tequilas are available ($6 to $25 per shot). Each comes with a slice of mango and a glass of Sangrita, a tomato-citrus palate-cleanser. There's also a list of unusual but delicious margaritas.

The Delancey

168 Delancey Street, at Clinton Street (1-212 254 9920). Subway F to Delancey Street; J, M, Z to Delancey-Essex Streets. **Open** 4pm-4am daily. **Average drink** $6. **Credit** MC, V. **Map** p403 G30 ❿

The tropical-themed rooftop is what keeps luring the cool crowd – a wooden deck lined with potted palms, equipped with a fishpond, a bar and a margarita machine. When the alfresco party ends at midnight, you can head down to the main floor for DJs, or into the basement to catch a live show.

And the winner is...

Every year, *Time Out New York* recognises the best of the city's thousands of bars. The combination of our staff drinkers and the votes of our *Time Out New York* readers result in a list of outstanding bars. Here are some of the winners from the 2007 awards.

Best new bar of the year

reBar (*see p227*).

Best new wine bar

Bin No.220 (*see p216*).

Best new beer bar

The Village Pourhouse (*see p221*).

The Village Pourhouse

East Side Company Bar

49 Essex Street, at Grand Street (1-212 614 7408). Subway F to Delancey Street; J, M, Z to Delancey-Essex Streets. **Open** 8pm-4am daily. **Average drink** $8. **Credit** AmEx, MC, V. **Map** p403 G30 ⑪

If you still can't get into Milk & Honey (the exclusive reservation-only bar owned by Sasha Petraske), you'll fare much better at his new Lower East Side spot. The phone number is listed, and you can also walk in off the street. The snug new space also has a 1940s-era vibe (leather booths, classic cocktails).

Home Sweet Home

131 Chrystie Street, between Broome & Delancey Streets (1-212 226 5708). Subway B, D to Grand Street; J, M, Z to Bowery. **Open** 8pm-4am daily. **Average drink** $9. **Credit** MC, V. **Map** p403 F30 ⑫

It's homey, we suppose, if you keep taxidermy in your living room. Descend the chandelier-lit stairwell to this concrete-floored, signless subterranean den bedecked with stuffed critters – there's a beaver, an eagle, even a jackalope. Bartenders dispense drinks from a bar inlaid with display cases housing icky knick-knacks (we like the dental moulds).

'inoteca

98 Rivington Street, at Ludlow Street (1-212 614 0473). Subway F to Delancey Street; J, M, Z to Delancey-Essex Streets. **Open** noon-3am Mon-Fri; 10am-3am Sat, Sun. **Average drink** $8. **Credit** AmEx, MC, V. **Map** p403 G29 ⑬

Where chefs drink, their partisans follow. So Jason Denton and his partners at the microscopic wine bar 'ino opened a bigger space across town. Same warm atmosphere, same foodie crowd, but there's also a menu of great pan-Italian share-plates and enough space to give your glass a proper swirl. The downstairs wine cellar is more conversation-friendly.

Punch & Judy

26 Clinton Street, between Houston & Stanton Streets (1-212 982 1116). Subway F to Delancey Street; J, M, Z to Delancey-Essex Streets. **Open** 6pm-2am Mon-Wed, Sun; 6pm-4am Thur-Sat. **Average drink** $10. **Credit** AmEx, MC, V. **Map** p403 G29 ⑭

This stylish, modern wine bar and lounge, furnished with 1930s theatre seats and red couches, offers 150 wines that pair beautifully with nibbles like a lobster club sandwich, cheese plates or a Caprese salad, for which the ingredients are rolled up sushi-style.

Schiller's Liquor Bar

For listing, see p188. **Map** p403 G29 ⑮

Keith McNally's downtown bar attracts the hep cats with decidedly unsnobbish wine list categories ('cheap', 'decent' and 'good').

Soho

Fanelli's Café

94 Prince Street, at Mercer Street (1-212 226 9412). Subway N, R, W to Prince Street. **Open** 10am-1.30am Mon-Thur, Sun; 10am-3.30am Fri, Sat. **Average drink** $5. **Credit** AmEx, MC, V. **Map** p403 E29 ⑯

On a lovely cobblestoned corner, this 1847 joint claims to be the second-oldest continuously operating bar and restaurant in the city. Prints of boxing legends and one of the city's best burgers add to the easy feel. The banter of locals and the merry clinking of pint glasses blesses the place with a soundtrack right out of the old days. *See also p189.*

Fiamma Osteria

206 Spring Street, between Sixth Avenue & Sullivan Street (1-212 653 0100). Subway C, E to Spring Street. **Open** noon-2.30pm, 5.30-11pm Mon-Thur, Sun; noon-2.30pm, 5.30pm-midnight Fri; 5.30pm-midnight Sat. **Average drink** $13. **Credit** AmEx, Disc, MC, V. **Map** p403 E30 ⑰

After a short glass-elevator ride up to the second floor, you find a hidden lounge that looks like an upscale building-material showroom: stone walls, hardwood floors, leather banquettes and a brigade of tealights. Regulars get giddy over the smooth cappuccino martini, but wine aficionados come for a sampling of one of the city's best wine lists.

Grand Bar & Lounge

SoHo Grand Hotel, 310 West Broadway, between Canal & Grand Streets (1-212 965 3000). Subway A, C, E, 1 to Canal Street. **Open** noon-1.30am Mon-Wed, Sun; noon-2.30am Thur-Sat. **Average drink** $12. **Credit** AmEx, DC, Disc, MC, V. **Map** p403 E30 ⑱

They've been around for a while, but the second-floor bar and lounge still draw a media-industry crowd. The two spaces – a wood-panelled bar and a

Death & Co.

plush lounge drenched in chocolate hues – are linked by a long corridor. Sip a pricey cocktail or glass of wine while you take in evening sessions of newly released lounge imports. Hungry drinkers can order grilled salmon BLTs or truffled turkey burgers to soak up some of the booze.

MercBar

151 Mercer Street, between Houston & Prince Streets (1-212 966 2727). Subway B, D, F, V to Broadway-Lafayette Street; N, R, W to Prince Street; 6 to Bleecker Street. **Open** 5pm-2am Mon, Tue, Sun; 5pm-2.30am Wed; 5pm-3am Thur; 5pm-4am Fri, Sat. **Average drink** $9. **Credit** AmEx, MC, V. **Map** p403 E29 ⑲

Need a sharp-looking place for a blind date? Head to the MercBar, where the well-coiffed after-work crowd comes to engage in polite conversation and to avoid mingling. The interior – with soft lighting, log-cabin-like walls, landscape paintings and a canoe hanging above the sleek wooden bar – feels like your rich friend's parents' mountain lodge, but the drinks are city-slick. The Concorde blends apple schnapps, Bacardi Limón and grape juice.

East Village

Ace Bar

531 E 5th Street, between Avenues A & B (1-212 979 8476). Subway F, V to Lower East Side-Second Avenue. **Open** 2pm-4am daily. **Average drink** $5. **Credit** AmEx, MC, V. **Map** p403 G28 ⑳

Recreational opportunities abound at roomy bar Ace – there's Big Buck Hunter, two pool tables (the bar even has a league going) and the daily 4-to-7pm happy hour is ideal for the serious afternoon drinker (14 beers on tap let you keep the pints rotating).

Against the Grain

620 E 6th Street, at Avenue B (1-212 358 7065). Subway F, V to Lower East Side-Second Avenue; L to First Avenue. **Open** 6pm-1am Mon, Tue, Sun; 6pm-2am Wed-Sat. **Average drink** $5. **No credit cards. Map** p403 G28.

This closet-size, pretension-free beer emporium, adorned with exposed brick and stamped tin, sits adjacent to the wine-centric Grape & Grain. Join brew aficionados at the communal table (dubbed 'the mingler'), snack on spiced nuts and listen carefully while bartenders explain the globe-spanning suds menu. Then consider pairing Bear Republic Racer 5 India Pale Ale with nibbles like pastry-wrapped chorizo and beer-steamed shrimp.

Baraza

133 Avenue C, between 8th & 9th Streets (1-212 539 0811). Subway L to First Avenue; 6 to Astor Place. **Open** 7.30pm-4am daily. **Average drink** $5. **No credit cards. Map** p403 G28 ㉑

One of the pioneers on Avenue C, this lively Latin spot is famous for its good $5 caipirinhas and mojitos, which draw a sleek boho crowd (the place is always packed). In the candlelit lounge past the bar, patrons puzzle over the Barbie aquarium, in which the plastic diva and Ken enjoy a lovely beach scene.

Death & Co

433 E 6th Street, between First Avenue & Avenue A (1-212 388 0882). Subway F, V to Lower East Side-Second Avenue; L to First Avenue; 6 to Astor Place. **Open** 6pm-1am Sun-Thur; 6pm-2am Fri, Sat. **Average drink** $9. **Credit** AmEx, MC, V. **Map** p403 F28 ㉒

The nattily attired mixologists are deadly serious about drinks at this pseudo speakeasy with Gothic flair. Ravi DeRossi and David Kaplan serve cocktails, wine and small plates at this clandestine lounge with 1920s-style decor.

Detour

349 E 13th Street, between First & Second Avenues (1-212 533 6212). Subway L to First Avenue; N, Q, R, W, 4, 5, to 14th St-Union Square. **Open** 4pm-2am Mon-Thur, Sun; 4pm-4am Fri, Sat. **Average drink** $5. **Credit** AmEx, Disc, MC, V. **Map** p403 F28 ㉓

Basement parties went out of style with Afros and bell-bottoms, right? Well, everything has come back around at Detour, where Christmas lights dangle from the ceiling and '50s college-football-team portraits hang along the brick walls.

In Vino

215 E 4th Street, between Avenues A & B (1-212 539 1011). Subway F, V to Lower East Side-Second Avenue. **Open** 5.30pm-midnight Mon-Thur, Sun; 5.30pm-1am Fri, Sat. **Average drink** $8. **Credit** MC, V. **Map** p403 G29 ㉔

This cave-like space offers hundreds of regional Italian wines along with tasty, rustic appetisers.

Luca Lounge

220 Avenue B, between 13th & 14th Streets (1-212 674 9400). Subway L to First Avenue. **Open** 5pm-1am Mon-Wed, Sun; 5pm-4am Thur-Sat. **Average drink** $4. **No credit cards. Map** p403 G28 ㉕
See below **Craft night**.

Le Souk

47 Avenue B, between 3rd & 4th Streets (1-212 777 5454). Subway F, V to Lower East Side-Second Avenue. **Open** 6pm-4am daily. **Average drink** $9. **Credit** MC, V. **Map** p403 G29 ㉖

In the early evening, the muted lighting and *shishas* (hookas) give this two-room lounge the feel of a North African teahouse; a few hours on, it's a bump-and-grind bar; later still, when the tables and chairs are cleared away, it seems like a private after-hours party. Le Souk is an absolute hit every night, whether for weeknight belly dancing, the weekend's Arabic-infused house beats or Sunday night's legendary progressive house party.

Sutra Lounge

16 First Avenue, between 1st & 2nd Streets (1-212 677 9477). Subway F, V to Second Avenue-Lower East Side. **Open** 9pm-4am Mon-Sat. **Average drink** $8. **Credit** AmEx, MC, V. **Map** p403 F29 ㉗

Craft night

Some local watering holes now offer arty activities as well as beer and pretzels.

Back in 2002, Corinna Mantlo established an informal knitting class at **Luca Lounge** (*see above*; www.boozeandyarn.com) to attract guys and girls from different walks of life. 'A lot of formal classes charge obscene amounts of money, and some were actually banning guys from enrolling,' she says. 'I wanted to keep the community-minded part of knitting alive.' Mantlo, who has also held 'booze and yarn' sessions in New Orleans, says alcohol helps relax newcomers to the weekly Wednesday gathering and facilitates flirting, but that 'some people are so focused on getting the stitch right, they order a drink but don't take a sip all night.' Knitters can bring their own tools or buy a starter kit from Mantlo for just $20.

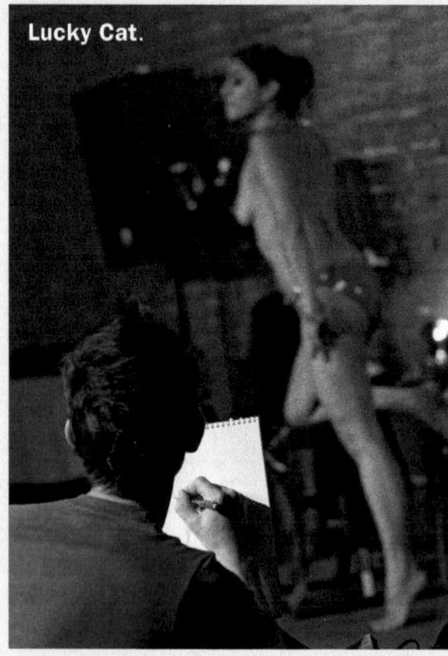
Lucky Cat.

Want to relive the glory days of elementary school but this time with a tequila chaser? On the first Tuesday of every month, participants in **Freddy's** (*see p226*; www.freddysbackroom.com) 'diorama night' plumb their craft kits for foil, Popsicle sticks and other random bits to help nail the evening's theme, with the best display chosen by consensus. Past prizes have included a glue gun and a bottle of vodka.

You won't find boring bowls of fruit at Molly Crabapple's biweekly drawing class at the **Lucky Cat** (*see p227*; www.drsketchy.com); instead you'll see comely burlesque queens pose for amateur Da Vincis. Patrons compete for honours such as the 'Best Left-Handed Drawing', with winners treated to a suitable drink (a shot of Chartreuse, say, for a green-haired model). Ever the trooper, Crabapple has occasionally stepped in when things have gone awry: 'Once a famous model never showed,' she recalls, 'so I had to run home, get a sparkly bikini and pose myself.'

The idea for this weekly crafts night came to Krista Madsen when she first opened **Stain Bar** (*see p227*; www.stainbar.com). 'My friends were coming in to help decorate anyway, so I decided to make it a regular thing.' Like the kitschy Williamsburg club it's held in, PAINTStain is a rather casual affair. Each Monday, Madsen offers free paints, fabrics and other gems from her box of goodies, or patrons bring their own projects.

Sutra wants to put you in the mood, seducing you with incense and warm amber lighting the moment you enter. A downstairs cave is preserved as an old Turkish gentleman's club, and an upstairs bar and billiards room is lined with red velvet banquettes. Delicacies such as chocolate-covered strawberries complement concoctions like the Sutra martini, with vodka, vermouth and crème de cassis.

The Village Pourhouse

64 Third Avenue, at 11th Street (1-212 979 2337). Subway L to Third Avenue; 6 to Astor Place. **Open** 11am-2am Mon-Wed, Sun; 11am-4am Thur-Sat. **Average drink** $4. **Credit** AmEx, Disc, MC, V. **Map** p403 F28 ㉘

Fans of exotic beers – and sports – can sip global finds such as Hong Kong's Macau and Bahamanian brew Kalik, while watching one of no less than 21 high-resolution televisions at this East Village tavern. A hearty menu, with entrees like chicken madeira, helps to soak up the suds.

Greenwich Village & Noho

Centovini

25 W Houston Street, at Greene Street (1-212 219 2113). Subway B, D, F, V to Broadway-Lafayette Street; 6 to Bleecker Street. **Open** 8am-midnight Mon; 8am-2am Tue-Fri; 9am-2am Sat; 9am-midnight Sun. **Average drink** $15. **Credit** AmEx, MC, V. **Map** p403 E29 ㉙

The design snobs at Soho's Moss have partnered with the wine geeks at I Trulli and Vino to open a wine bar with 100 Italian wines available by the glass, bottle and case. Much of the decor can be purchased around the corner at Moss.

Pegu Club

77 W Houston Street, between West Broadway & Wooster Street (1-212 473 7348). Subway 6 to Bleeker Street; B, D, F, V to Broadway-Lafayette Street. **Open** 5pm-2am Mon, Wed-Sun; 5pm-4am Thur-Sat. **Average drink** $12. **Credit** AmEx, Disc, DC, MC, V. **Map** p403 E29 ㉚

Located on an unassuming Soho block, this bar is both hidden and welcoming. Upstairs, an elegant space with a long maple bar greets cocktail connoisseurs. Owner-mixologist Audrey Saunders stubbornly discourages trendy vodkas – gin is the basis for most of the menu.

Von Bar

3 Bleecker Street, between Bowery & Elizabeth Street (1-212 473 3039). Subway B, D, F, V to Broadway-Lafayette Street; 6 to Bleecker Street. **Open** 5pm-2am Mon-Wed, Sun; 5pm-4am Thur-Sat. **Average drink** $7. **Credit** AmEx, MC, V. **Map** p403 F29 ㉛

This low-key two-room lair, all candlelit dark wood and exposed brick, is a perfect first-date spot. A large blackboard trumpets an extensive selection of (mostly French) wines by the glass, but the bar also has a full liquor licence. Pick a full-bodied red, such as the Vacqueyras, take your friend by the hand, and head for one of the benches in the back room.

West Village & Meatpacking District

APT

For listing, see p295. **Map** p403 C27 ㉜

By shifting its focus from door attitude to DJs, APT lives up to India Mahdavi's sleek, polished design.

5 Ninth

For listing, see p197. **Map** p403 C28 ㉝

The bar inside the rustic restaurant, in a charming three-storey 1848 house, vibrates with speakeasy charm; old-school Scotches, cognacs and whiskeys are the main ingredients of the heady cocktails (like the fizzy Floridora), which are all named after Broadway shows. Fireplaces, exposed brick and one of the city's loveliest gardens contribute to the intimacy, which encourages chatting up strangers.

Little Branch

20-22 Seventh Avenue South, at Leroy Street (1-212 929 4360). Subway 1 to Houston Street. **Open** 7pm-3am Mon-Fri; 9pm-3am Sat. **Average drink** $9. **No credit cards**. **Map** p403 D29 ㉞

Milk & Honey owner Sasha Petraske is letting commoners into this candlelit, subterranean spot to sample his legendary cocktails. No reservations needed.

Spice Market

403 W 13th Street, at Ninth Avenue (1-212 675 2322). Subway A, C, E to 14th Street; L to Eighth Avenue. **Open** 6pm-2am daily. **Average drink** $12. **Credit** AmEx, DC, MC, V. **Map** p403 C27 ㉟

Glide down the dramatic staircase and enter a glamorous world where votive candles flicker over a fashionable crowd that comes for the scene, the fruity cocktails and the street market-inspired dishes.

Turks & Frogs

323 W 11th Street, between Greenwich & Washington Streets (1-212 691 8875). Subway A, C, E to 14th Street; L to Eighth Avenue. **Open** 5pm-4am daily. **Average drink** $7. **Credit** AmEx, DC, MC, V. **Map** p403 C28 ㊱

In addition to the Turkish and French pottery doing decoration duty, visitors will find 50 wines (including some from owner Osman Cakir's native Turkey) and a small menu of prepared Mediterranean food (there's no oven on the premises). Cakir has also managed to pack an antique couch, a small bar and a few tables into the 800 sq ft place.

Midtown

Chelsea & Flatiron

Flatiron Lounge

37 W 19th Street, between Fifth & Sixth Avenues (1-212 727 7741). Subway F, N, R, V, W to 23rd Street; 1 to 18th Street. **Open** 5pm-2am Mon-Wed, Sun; 5pm-4am Thur-Sat. **Average drink** $10. **Credit** AmEx, MC, V. **Map** p403 E27 ㊲

To get to the 30ft mahogany bar (built in 1927), follow an arched hallway warmed by the soft glow of candles. You'll find an art deco space with red leather booths, round glass tables, flying-saucer-shaped lamps and an imaginative cocktail menu you'll want to dive straight into. Co-owner Julie Reiner is the mistress of mixology; the Persephone, for instance, is a subtle pomegranate martini named for the queen of Hades.

Park Bar

15 E 15th Street, between Fifth Avenue & Union Square West (1-212 367 9085). Subway L, N, Q, R, W, 4, 5, 6 to 14th Street-Union Square. **Open** 3pm-5am daily. **Average drink** $7. **Credit** AmEx, MC, V. **Map** p403 E27 38

What's small, dark and packed all over? Park Bar's dusky den of a room might be teensier than the average studio apartment, but for all that it has charm to spare. You'll need to arrive early to have any hope of a seat at the bar. Hungry drinkers often order pizza from nearby Giorgio's.

Passerby

436 W 15th Street, between Ninth & Tenth Avenues (1-212 206 7321). Subway A, C, E to 14th Street; L to Eighth Avenue. **Open** 6pm-2am Mon-Sat. **Average drink** $8. **Credit** AmEx, MC, V. **Map** p403 C27 39

The unmarked Passerby is a sort of clubhouse for arty types. Flashing coloured floor panels, created by artist Piotr Uklansky, pulse with the DJ's beats and lend an ambient glow. Early evening, this is a civilised place for a drink; later on, things have been known to get deliciously raucous.

230 Fifth

230 Fifth Avenue, between 26th & 27th Streets (1-212 725 4300). Subway N, R, W to 28th Street. **Open** 4pm-4am daily. **Average drink** $11. **Credit** AmEx, MC, V. **Map** p404 E26 40

The rooftop bar dazzles with truly spectacular views of the Manhattan skyline, but the indoor lounge – with its wraparound sofas and bold lighting – should not be overlooked. Drinks are expensive and unremarkable, but the crowd is too busy bopping to the fantastic '80s music to mind much.

Midtown West

Ava Lounge

Majestic Hotel, 210 W 55th Street, between Seventh Avenue & Broadway (1-212 956 7020). Subway N, Q, R, W to 57th Street. **Open** 5pm-3am Mon, Tue; 5pm-4am Wed-Fri; 6pm-4am Sat; 6pm-3am Sun. **Average drink** $9. **Credit** AmEx, Disc, MC, V. **Map** p405 D22 41

The top of the Majestic Hotel has been transformed into a penthouse lounge and rooftop deck with views of both the twinkling cityscape and the blondes in black who serve key lime martinis and flirtinis. Modern, chic and slick but not overdesigned, the space is often used for private parties, and the outdoor patio is a lure for smokers.

Bamboo 52

344 W 52nd Street, between Eighth & Ninth Avenues (1-212 315 2777). Subway C, E to 50th Street. **Open** 4pm-4am daily. **Average drink** $8. **Credit** AmEx, MC, V. **Map** p404 C23 42

This Hell's Kitchen eaterie has a front porch, a bamboo garden, a sushi bar (sushi sandwiches for those willing to mix it up) and a drinks menu listing saké champagne, Asian microbrews and Japanese single malt whiskies. Things really take off during the popular daily happy hour.

Hudson Bar

The Hudson, 356 W 58th Street, between Eighth & Ninth Avenues (1-212 554 6500). Subway A, B, C, D, 1 to 59th Street-Columbus Circle. **Open** 4pm-2am Mon-Sat; 4pm-1am Sun. *Library bar* noon-2am Mon-Sat; noon-1am Sun. **Average drink** $10. **Credit** AmEx, DC, Disc, MC, V. **Map** p405 C22 43

Like a lime-green stairway to heaven, an escalator leads to the lobby of Ian Schrager's Hudson hotel (*see p67*), where you'll find three separate bars. Most dazzling is the postmodern Hudson Bar, with a backlit glass floor. The Library bar marries class (leather sofas) and kitsch (photos of cows in pillbox hats). If that's too cute, then get some air in the seasonal Private Park (open April to November), the leafy, cigarette-friendly outdoor bar lit by candle chandeliers and perfect for close encounters.

Kemia Bar

630 Ninth Avenue, at 44th Street (1-212 582 3200). Subway A, C, E to 42nd Street-Port Authority. **Open** 6pm-1am Tue-Fri; 8pm-2am Sat. **Average drink** $8. **Credit** AmEx, MC, V. **Map** p404 C24 44

Descending into this lush Middle Eastern oasis is like penetrating the fourth wall of a brilliant stage set. Kemia's former bank building has been entirely

Eat, Drink, Shop

transformed: gossamer fabric billows from the ceiling, ottomans are clustered around low tables, and dark-wood floors are strewn with rose petals. A soulful DJ enhances the ambience, as do the luscious libations on offer.

Single Room Occupancy

360 W 53rd Street, between Eighth & Ninth Avenues (1-212 765 6299). Subway B, D to Seventh Avenue; C, E to 50th Street. **Open** 7.30pm-2am Mon, Tue; 7.30pm-4am Wed-Sat. **Average drink** $8. **Credit** AmEx. **Map** p404 C23 ㊺

It's hard to overstate the importance of feeling like a New York insider during any stay in this most knowing of cities. At this wine and beer speakeasy, where you must ring the doorbell to enter, you'll be deliciously in the know. SRO comfortably fits 20 or so, but more have been known to squeeze into the cave-like medieval-modern space. Locals tend to think of owner Markos as the host of their favourite nightly party, and on one random evening a month, he rewards them with a riotous performance of glamorous go-go dancers.

Sortie

329 W 51st Street, between Eighth & Ninth Avenues (1-212 265 0650). Subway C, E to 50th Street. **Open** 5pm-4am daily. **Average drink** $9. **Credit** AmEx, MC, V. **Map** p404 C23 ㊻

The owners of this sultry bordello-like bar made sure their subterranean space would never be a boring place to drink. To this end, they painted the walls a deep red, and added velvet banquettes and studded black-leather café tables to raise their game aethetically. They also hired flamenco dancers and serious guest DJs to liven up the party vibe, and came up with an extensive menu that specialises in tapas, cocktails and 30 artisanal beers.

Midtown East

Artisanal

2 Park Avenue, at 32nd Street (1-212 725 8585). Subway E, V to Lexington Avenue-53rd Street; 6 to 51st Street. **Open** noon-11pm Mon-Thur; noon-midnight Fri, Sat; 11am-10pm Sun. **Average drink** $11. **Credit** AmEx, DC, Disc, MC, V. **Map** p404 E25 ㊼

Wine and cheese move into the realm of art at this restaurant's boisterous bar. There are 150-plus wines by the glass, and 250 or so cheeses – enough permutations for you to forever swear off chardonnay and brie. Pairing flights of wine can help the uninitiated. The bar area is packed for dinner, when fondue-craving hordes await their tables.

Brasserie

For listing, see p208. **Map** p404 E23 ㊽

A trip to striking Brasserie – located in the basement of Mies van der Rohe's much-lauded Seagram Building and outfitted by Diller + Scofidio – is like taking an architectural tour. It features backlit bottles stored horizontally behind opaque glass, a long granite bar and curved walls made of pear-tree wood. You can spy on new arrivals via stop-motion images on screens mounted above the bar.

Monkey Bar

Hotel Elysée, 60 E 54th Street, between Madison and Park Avenues (1- 212 838 2600). Subway E, V to Lexington Avenue-53rd Street; 6 to 51st Street. **Open** 11am-4am daily. **Average drink** $12. **Credit** AmEx, DC, Disc, MC, V. **Map** p405 E22 ㊾

The Monkey Bar is defined by its past. The mischievous, 71-year-old simian murals that give this Hotel Elysée den its name, and the glamorous icons from

Monkey Bar.

…entury who frequented its stools – Joe …o, Tennessee Williams, Marlon Brando – … multiple layers of lore. These days, the soigné celebs have been replaced by expense-accounting executives during the week and clusters of wide-eyed tourists on the weekend.

Sakagura

211 E 43rd Street, between Second & Third Avenues (1-212 953 7253). Subway 42nd Street S, 4, 5, 6, 7 to 42nd Street-Grand Central. **Open** noon-2.30pm, 6pm-midnight Mon-Thur; noon-2.30pm, 6pm-1am Fri; 6pm-1am Sat; 6-11pm Sun. **Average drink** $7. **Credit** AmEx, DC, Disc, MC, V. **Map** p404 F24 ⑳

At Sakagura, you'll have to do a little work: walk through the unmarked lobby of an office building, down a few stairs and along a basement corridor. Finally, enter a quiet room of bamboo and blond wood, and prepare to learn everything there is to know about saké. The 200 kinds available here, categorised by region, are served in delicate handblown glass vessels. If you can't decide, try a Sakagura Tasting Set, which teams an appetiser, entrée and dessert with three corresponding sakés. Be sure to check out the candlelit restrooms, cleverly fashioned from giant saké casks.

Uptown

Upper West Side

Barcibo Enoteca

2020 Broadway, between 69th & 70th Streets (1-212 595 2805). Subway 1 to 66th Street. **Open** 5pm-midnight daily. **Average drink** $10. **Credit** AmEx, MC, V. **Map** p405 C20 51

The Upper West Side's latest wine bar offers more than just 100 vinos; the menu also features a range of rare spirits and small plates.

Bin 71

237 Columbus Avenue, at 71st Street (1-212 362 5446). Subway B, C to 72nd Street. **Open** 5pm-midnight Mon, Tue; 11am-1am Wed-Sun. **Average drink** $8. **Credit** AmEx, Disc, MC, V. **Map** p405 C20 52

This classy wine bar from father and son Anselmo and Lawrence Bondulich helps fill the neighbourhood's wine bar void. Anselmo is coming out of retirement to create dishes such as pink-snapper sashimi with garlic oil, and meatballs braised in white wine, lemon and bay leaves. Snackers can share antipasto platters or cheese plates, paired with wines from California, Italy, France and Spain. Of course, there's plenty of fine beer on hand for those with less enthusiasm for the grape.

Loft

505 Columbus Avenue, between 84th & 85th Streets (1-212 362 6440). Subway B, C to 86th Street. **Open** 6pm-midnight Mon-Thur, Sun; 6pm-4am Fri, Sat. **Average drink** $10. **Credit** AmEx, DC, Disc, MC, V. **Map** p406 C18 53

Ginger martinis recently became the equivalent of the bindi on Gwen Stefani's forehead: the exotic co-opted as mere fashion. But at this sexy Moroccan-accented lounge and restaurant, the addition of pungent spices makes for some profoundly unusual drinking. The Sirocco, a blast of bourbon and lime juice, gets its sweet and vicious snap from lavender-flower honey. And for its basil mojito, Loft boils down sugarcane. This concoction is also available by the carafe; it's as seriously intoxicating as absinthe and similarly addictive.

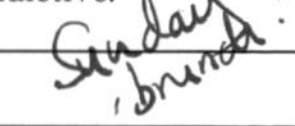

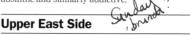

Upper East Side

Central Park Boathouse

Central Park Lake, Park Drive North, at 72nd Street (1-212 517 2233). Subway 6 to 68th Street-Hunter College. **Open** noon-4pm, 5.30-9.30pm Mon-Fri; 9.30am-4pm, 6-9.30pm Sat, Sun. **Average drink** $7. **Credit** AmEx, DC, MC, V. **Map** p405 D20 54

The view from the tree-shaded deck bordering the boat-freckled lake looks like a shot framed by Woody Allen. Step into the film at the outdoor bar after Sunday brunch (the bloody marys are mighty powerful). Plush leather armchairs near the fireplace beckon in winter. A Boathouse Martini (Bacardi Limón, triple sec and a splash each of lime and cranberry juices) will make you smile all year long.

Lexington Bar & Books

1020 Lexington Avenue, at 73rd Street (1-212 717 3902). Subway 6 to 77th Street. **Open** 5pm-3am Mon-Wed, Sun; 5pm-4am Thur-Sat. **Average drink** $10. **Credit** AmEx, DC, MC, V. **Map** p405 E20 55

Order a drink here, and the barman offers you an ashtray. Yes, it's a legal cigar bar – and one with class: walls are lined with books and fine brandies, beer and Martini glasses are frosted, and the selection of single-malt Scotches and cognacs is top-flight. If James Bond was an East Sider, you would find him sipping his trademark tipple here.

Lollipop

27 E 61st Street, between Madison & Park Avenues (1-212 752 8900). Subway 4, 5, 6 to 59th Street. **Open** 5pm-3.30am Mon-Sat. **Average drink** $8. **Credit** AmEx, MC, V. **Map** p405 E22 56

This seductive underground lounge features various sumptuous touches like a see-through bar and red velvet banquettes. Here, expense-account businessmen and high-heeled women sip herb-muddled cocktails, chow down kobe beef and coconut-prawn skewers, and blather beneath a selection of appreciably low-volume house music.

Pudding Stones

1457 Third Avenue, between 82nd & 83rd Streets (1-212 717 5797). Subway 4, 5, 6 to 86th Street. **Open** 5pm-2am daily. **Average drink** $18. **Credit** AmEx, MC, V. **Map** p405 F19 57

Oenophiles know that pudding stones are found in rocky soils and help nurture grapes. They can discuss this and engage in all the terroir talk they want

It's reigning, it's pouring: **reBar**, *Time Out New York*'s best new bar of the year. *See p227.*

while perusing more than 100 options available by the bottle, glass and flight. Bistro fare, artisanal cheeses and a downstairs tasting room are added incentives for a visit.

Subway Inn

143 E 60th Street, between Lexington & Third Avenues (1-212 223 8929). Subway N, R, W to Lexington Avenue-59th Street; 4, 5, 6 to 59th Street. **Open** 8am-4am daily. **Average drink** $3. **No credit cards**. **Map** p405 F22 58

The bar near the Lexington Avenue and 60th Street subway exit is a 74-year-old watering hole that really is a hole. The clientele varies based on the time of day, but you're likely to see a mix of what appears to be Bowery-bum-like boozers, regular guys and confused tourists, seated either in decrepit booths or at the bar. Drinks prices appear to be lost in a time warp too – beer starts at $3.50.

Uva

1486 Second Avenue, at 77th Street (1-212 472 4552). Subway 6 to 77th Street. **Open** noon-2am Mon-Thur, Sun; noon-3am Fri, Sat. **Average drink** $9. **Credit** AmEx, MC, V ($30 minimum). **Map** p405 F19 59

The Upper East Side has plenty of rustic Italian restaurants but it could use a few more wine bars. A 200-year-old wooden floor and antique couches give this one a warm, worn-in feel, with cured meats and cheeses paired with regional Italian wines.

Above 116th Street

Den

2150 Fifth Avenue, between 131st & 132nd Streets (1-212 234 3045). Subway 2, 3 to 135th Street. **Open** 6pm-1am Mon-Thur; 6pm-4am Fri, Sun. **Average drink** $9. **Credit** AmEx, Disc, MC, V. **Map** p407 E12 60

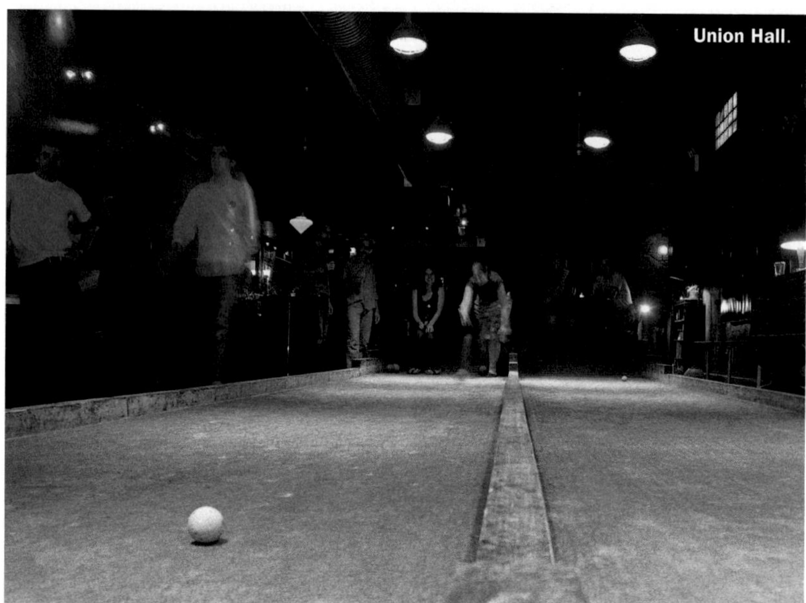
Union Hall.

Under the glow of a classic old streetlamp, a dapper doorman tips his derby and welcomes visitors to a subterranean lounge set in a Harlem brownstone. Designer Carlos Jimenez has cast a lush red haze over the 1920s-era room lined with exposed brick and accented by a copper-topped bar.

Lenox Lounge

288 Malcolm X Boulevard (Lenox Avenue), between 124th & 125th Streets (1-212 427 0253). Subway 2, 3 to 125th Street. **Open** noon-4am daily. **Average drink** $5 (cover varies). **Credit** AmEx, DC, MC, V. **Map** p407 D13 61

This is where a street hustler named Malcolm worked before he found religion and added an X to his name. Now the famous Harlem bar, lounge and jazz club welcomes a mix of old-school cats and unobtrusive booze hounds into its arms. Settle into the refurbished art deco area at the front or take a table in the zebra-papered back room, then tune in to the haunting presence of music from the likes of Billie Holiday and Miles Davis.

Brooklyn

Bembe

81 South 6th Street, at Berry Street, Williamsburg (1-718 387 5389). Subway J, M, Z to Marcy Avenue; L to Bedford Avenue. **Open** 7.30pm-4am Mon-Thur; 7pm-4am Fri-Sun. **Average drink** $5. **No credit cards. Map** p411 U8 62

At an unmarked hideaway under the Williamsburg Bridge, the swinging Bembe clientele dances by candlelight to Latin beats laid down by sexy DJs. Take a breather from the salsa and refuel with tequila shots at the sleek wooden bar. If you really want to blend in, it's worth noting that regulars swear by the unusual post-shot practice of sucking the lime after dipping one side in fresh coffee and the other in sugar.

Brooklyn Social

335 Smith Street, between Carroll & President Streets, Carroll Gardens (1-718 858 7758). Subway F, G to Carroll Street. **Open** 6pm-2am Mon-Thur; 6pm-4am Fri, Sat; 5pm-2am Sun. **Average drink** $6. **No credit cards. Map** p410 S10 63

When Matt Dawson heard that Società Riposto was closing, he thought the old Sicilian social club would make an ideal hipster watering hole. So he gutted the bland card-playing room and installed designer touches, right? Fuhgeddaboudit. He kept every detail he could and even hung photographs of the original members on the walls. The bar remains simple, but there's one major add-on: a backyard with a patio.

Freddy's

485 Dean Street, at Sixth Avenue, Prospect Heights (1-718 622 7035). Subway 2, 3 to Bergen Street. **Open** 11am-4am daily. **Average drink** $4. **No credit cards. Map** p410 T10 64

See p220 **Craft night**.

Galapagos

For listing, see p315. **Map** p411 U7 65

This perennial Williamsburg fave doubles as a performance space for all kinds of art.

Lucky Cat

245 Grand Street, between Driggs Avenue & Roebling Street, Williamsburg (1-718 782 0437). Subway L to Bedford Avenue. **Open** noon-2am Mon-Thur; 10am-4am Fri-Sun. **Average drink** $4. **Credit** AmEx, Disc, MC, V. **Map** p411 U8 ⓺⓺
See p220 **Craft night**.

Moto

394 Broadway, at Hooper Street, Williamsburg (1-718 599 6895). Subway J, M to Hewes Street. **Open** 6pm-2am Mon-Thur, Sun; 6pm-3am Fri, Sat. **Average drink** $6. **No credit cards**. **Map** p411 V8 ⓺⓻
Owners Billy Phelps and John McCormick have somehow created a café-bar evocative of 1930s Paris in a former cheque-cashing store beneath the J and M elevated tracks. The documentary *Eat This New York* captured Moto's rocky transformation on celluloid. However, the menu is Italian, the wines are handpicked and the selection of beers behind the bar includes Belgian Corsendonk. The pan-Euro attitude, easy subway access, and good food and drink in an eminently intimate triangular room make Moto a Williamsburg must-go.

reBar

147 Front Street, between Jay & Pearl Streetss Dumbo (1-718 797 2322). Subway F to York Street. **Open** 11am-2am Mon, Tue; 11am-4am Wed-Sat; 1pm-midnight Sun. **Average drink** $6. **Credit** AmEx, MC, V. **Map** p411 T9 ⓺⓼
Past the handwrought gate and stained-glass windows, the tulip chandeliers' orange glow illuminates 15 taps dispensing potent American microbrews (Bear Republic's Red Rocket, Sixpoint's Bengali Tiger) and rich Belgian beers (Delirium Tremens, Kwak). The quality quaffs extend to by-the-glass organic wines, which paint-flecked artists swig alongside asparagus and smoked salmon bocadillos and fried almonds by the fistful. *Photos p225.*

Stain Bar

766 Grand Street, at Humboldt Street, Williamsburg (1-718 387 7840). Subway L to Grand Street. **Open** 5pm-1am daily. **Average drink** $4. **No credit cards**. **Map** p411 V8
See p220 **Craft night**.

Superfine

126 Front Street, at Pearl Street, Dumbo (1-718 243 9005). Subway A, C to High Street; F to York Street. **Open** 11.30am-3pm, 6pm-1am Tue-Thur; 11.30am-3pm, 6pm-4am Fri; 2pm-4am Sat; 11am-3pm, 6-10pm Sun. **Average drink** $6. **Credit** AmEx, MC, V. **Map** p411 T9 ⓺⓽
Praised for its weekend Southwestern Chili Brunch, this eaterie is also a fine place for drinks any evening of the week (there's even a tiny art gallery that attracts scruffy types in smart-guy glasses). The worn-in mix-and-match furniture is usually occupied by young, suited professionals downing cosmos, or arty locals who hang at the pool table. You might even see regulars from the Federation of Black Cowboys, who hitch their horses at the door before sitting at the bar.

Union Hall

702 Union Street, between Fifth & Sixth Avenues, Park Slope (1-718 638 4400). Subway M, R to Union Street. **Open** 4pm-4am Mon-Fri; noon-4am Sat, Sun. **Average drink** $5. **Credit** AmEx, MC, V. **Map** p410 T11 ⓻⓪
Upstairs at Union Hall couples chomp on miniburgers and nip at microbrews in the gentlemen's club anteroom (decorated with Soviet-era globes, paintings of fez-capped men, fireplaces) – before battling it out on the clay bocce courts. Downstairs, in the taxidermy-filled basement, the stage is packed with blaring bands, comedians and a monthly Mr Wizard-esque science night.

Queens

Bohemian Hall & Beer Garden

29-19 24th Avenue, between 29th & 31st Streets, Astoria (1-718 274 0043). Subway N, W to Astoria Boulevard. **Open** 5pm-2am Mon-Fri; noon-3am Sat, Sun. **Average drink** $4. **Credit** MC, V ($10 minimum). **Map** p412 X3 ⓻⓵
Echt Mitteleuropa in the Greek precinct of Astoria? Czech! This authentic (c1910) beer hall is a throwback to the time when hundreds of such places dotted the town; the vibe manages to combine the ambience of that era with the youthful spirit of a junior year in Prague. Go for the platters of Czech sausage, $4 Stolis, Spaten Oktoberfests and the rockin' juke. In summer, the huge, tree-canopied beer garden beckons al fesco drinker outdoors.

Lighting up

Despite the strict citywide smoking ban of 2003, there are still some venues where you can legally light up. In addition, at press time smoking was still permitted at many outdoor patios and roof decks. If the weather is fine you can light up at **Ava Lounge** (*see p222*), the **Central Park Boathouse** (*see p224*) and **Glass** (287 Tenth Avenue, between 26th & 27th Streets, 1-212 904 1580).

Circa Tabac *32 Watts Street, between Sixth Avenue & Thompson Street (1-212 941 1781).*

Club Macanudo *26 E 63rd Street, between Madison & Park Avenues (1-212 752 8200).*

Karma *51 First Avenue, between 3rd & 4th Streets (1-212 677 3160).*

Velvet Cigar Lounge *80 E 7th Street, between First & Second Avenues (1-212 533 5582).*

Shops & Services

Spree for all.

America's style capital also boasts the nation's most democratic fashion scene. Even the top fashion editors will stride down Fifth Avenue in outfits plucked from cheap-and-chic chains like H&M, Uniqlo and Target, and famously blasé locals won't be fazed if you sport a body stocking to fetch your morning coffee (you might actually earn a few compliments for your sartorial daring).

Not surprisingly, the city that spawned such incongruous trends as East Village punk and Upper East Side chic offers myriad shopping options for virtually every taste and price range. Scan the following pages for an array of depots selling affordable gems, priceless vintage treasures and just about everything in between, including a selection of the latest jewellery boutiques (*see p240* **Treasure hunt**). But before you part with your hard-earned cash, take this tactical spending tip to heart: arrange your retail excursions by neighbourhood; for a guide, *see below* **Where to shop**. And, while all the top designers have shops in the city, be sure to scour independent local stores for items by emerging labels, guaranteeing that someone at home won't be wearing the same thing.

SALE AWAY

Though major markdowns are traditionally held at the end of each season, the best finds can be scored throughout the year from two insider events: Barneys' ever-popular twice-yearly warehouse sale and designers' frequent sample sales make excellent sources for reduced-price clothing by established and cutting-edge labels. To find out where the bargain fests are during any given week, consult the Seek section of *Time Out New York*. **Top Button** (www.topbutton.com) and the **SSS Sample Sales hotline** (1-212 947 8748, www.clothingline.com) also provide excellent discount resources. Sales are usually held in the designers' shops, showrooms or rented loft spaces, and are known to get seriously heated. Typically, most sales lack changing rooms, so

Where to shop

Fifth Avenue

Between 42nd & 59th Streets you'll find palatial department stores from another era. Bergdorf Goodmans, Henri Bendels, to name two, are simply enchanting. The avenue is difficult to beat for posh goods and artful window displays.

Lower East Side

Rumours of an H&M opening up on Delancey Street not withstanding, this is the very same neighbourhood where you'll find tons of mini boutiques loaded with duds by cutting-edge designers. Spend an afternoon strolling Orchard, Allen, Ludlow Streets south of Houston and you won't be disappointed.

Nolita

Another area that champions indie designers, especially along Mott and Mulberry Streets.

Soho

Soho's days for edgy fashions are sadly long gone. Dozens of mall-type chain stores line Broadway, Spring and Prince Streets. Still, there are plenty of hangers-on to be found, especially along Lafayette Street, where urban designers still rule the roost.

West Village & Meatpacking

Over on the west side of the island, the West Village's Bleecker Street has cemented itself as a swank pit stop, touting the likes of James Perse Men (just two blocks south of the LA designer's women's shop), Miguelina, Juicy Couture, along with recently opened: Coach Legacy, Tommy Hilfiger and a fourth Marc Jacobs outpost. Further west, amble along W 14th Street and the streets just south for a look at some seriously pricey shabby-chic offerings.

Williamsburg, Brooklyn

The first stop in Brooklyn on the L train is Bedford Avenue. The street is packed with arty shops and the hip kids who live noisily in the neighbourhood.

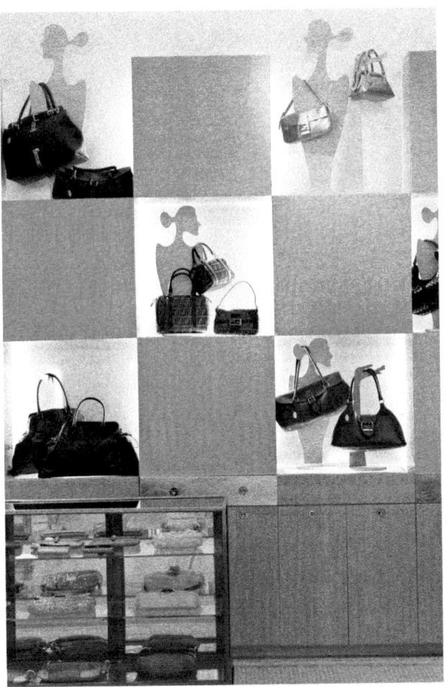

Barneys New York, where one size department store fits all.

bring a courageous spirit with you (and plenty of cash) and remember to wear appropriate undergarments to avoid embarrassment.

RETAIL RECONNAISSANCE

If the weather is disagreeable and you need some retail therapy, head to one of New York's shopping malls. You won't get the best deal or the uniqueness of a boutique, but the **Manhattan Mall** (Sixth Avenue, at 33rd Street), the **Shops at Columbus Circle** (Time Warner Center, 10 Columbus Circle, at 59th Street), and the myriad stores in **Trump Tower** (Fifth Avenue, at 56th Street), **Grand Central Terminal** (42nd Street, at Park Avenue) and South Street Seaport's charming cobblestoned **Pier 17** (Fulton Street, at the East River) are convenient options.

Thursday is the unofficial shop-after-work night; most stores remain open until at least 7pm. Stores downtown generally stay open an hour or so later than those uptown. Some of the shops listed here have more than one location; we have given up to two branches. For bigger chains, check individual websites or get stuck into the business pages in the phone book for further addresses across the city.

To find spanking-new stores and hotspots on New York's design scene, visit www.timeoutnewyork.com, and click on Shopping.

General

Department stores

Barneys New York

660 Madison Avenue, at 61st Street (1-212 826 8900/www.barneys.com). Subway N, R, W to Fifth Avenue-59th Street; 4, 5, 6 to 59th Street. **Open** 10am-8pm Mon-Fri; 10am-7pm Sat; 11am-6pm Sun. **Credit** AmEx, MC, V. **Map** p405 E22.

The top designers are represented at this bastion of New York style. At Christmas time, Barneys has the most provocative windows in town. Its co-op branches carry young designers, as well as secondary lines from heavies like Marc Jacobs and Theory. Every February and August, the Chelsea co-op hosts the Barneys Warehouse Sale, when prices are slashed by 50 to 80 per cent.

Other locations: throughout the city.

Bergdorf Goodman

754 Fifth Avenue, at 57th Street (1-212 753 7300/www.bergdorfgoodman.com). Subway E, V to Fifth Avenue-53rd Street; N, R, W to Fifth Avenue-59th Street. **Open** 10am-8pm Mon-Fri; 10am-7pm Sat; noon-6pm Sun. **Credit** AmEx, DC, MC, V. **Map** p405 E22.

If Barneys aims for a young, trendy crowd, then Bergdorf's is dedicated to an elegant, understated clientele that has plenty of disposable income. Luxury clothes, accessories and even stationery are found here, along with an over-the-top beauty floor. Handily, the famed men's store happens to be just across the street (745 Fifth Avenue).

Bloomingdale's

1000 Third Avenue, at 59th Street (1-212 705 2000/www.bloomingdales.com). Subway N, R, W to Lexington Avenue-59th Street; 4, 5, 6 to 59th Street. **Open** 10am-8.30pm Mon-Fri; 10am-7pm Sat; 11am-7pm Sun. **Credit** AmEx, MC, V. **Map** p405 F22.

Bloomies is a gigantic, glitzy department store offering everything from handbags and cosmetics to furniture and designer duds. Brace yourself for the crowds – this store ranks among the city's most popular tourist attractions, right up there with the Empire State Building. Be sure to check out the cool new sister branch in Soho.

Other locations: 504 Broadway, between Broome & Spring Streets, Soho (1-212 279 5900).

Henri Bendel

712 Fifth Avenue, at 56th Street (1-212 247 1100/ www.henribendel.com). Subway E, V to Fifth Avenue-53rd Street; N, R, W to Fifth Avenue-59th Street. **Open** 10am-8pm Mon-Sat; noon-7pm Sun. **Credit** AmEx, DC, Disc, MC, V. **Map** p405 E22.

Bendel's lavish quarters resemble an opulent townhouse. Naturally, there are elevators – no one expects you to walk, this is Fifth Avenue – but it's nicer to saunter up the elegant, winding staircase. Prices are comparable to those of other upscale stores, but the merchandise somehow seems more desirable here – we guess it must be those darling brown-striped shopping bags.

Jeffrey New York

449 W 14th Street, between Ninth & Tenth Avenues (1-212 206 1272/www.jeffreynewyork.com). Subway A, C, E to 14th Street; L to Eighth Avenue. **Open** 10am-8pm Mon-Wed, Fri; 10am-9pm Thur; 10am-7pm Sat; 12.30-6pm Sun. **Credit** AmEx, MC, V. **Map** p403 C27.

Jeffrey Kalinsky, a former Barneys shoe buyer, was a Meatpacking District pioneer with his namesake shop. Designer clothing abounds here – Helmut Lang, Versace and Yves Saint Laurent among other brands. But the centrepiece is without doubt the shoe salon, which features the work of Manolo Blahnik, Prada and Robert Clergerie.

Macy's

151 W 34th Street, between Broadway & Seventh Avenue (1-212 695 4400/www.macys.com). Subway B, D, F, N, Q, R, V, W to 34th Street-Herald Square; 1, 2, 3 to 34th Street-Penn Station. **Open** 10am-9pm Mon-Sat; 11am-8pm Sun. **Credit** AmEx, MC, V. **Map** p404 D25.

Behold the real miracle on 34th Street. Macy's has everything a shopper could ever want: designer labels and lower-priced knockoffs, a pet supply shop, a restaurant in the Cellar (the homeware section), a Metropolitan Museum of Art gift shop and, would you believe it, a McDonald's on the kids' floor. The store also offers Macy's By Appointment (1-800 343 0121), a free service that allows you to order goods or clothing over the phone and have them shipped anywhere in the world.

Saks Fifth Avenue

611 Fifth Avenue, at 50th Street (1-212 753 4000/ www.saksfifthavenue.com). Subway E, V to Fifth Avenue-53rd Street. **Open** 10am-7pm Mon-Wed, Fri, Sat; 10am-8pm Thur; noon-6pm Sun. **Credit** AmEx, DC, Disc, MC, V. **Map** p404 E23.

Although Saks maintains a presence in 24 states, the Fifth Avenue location is the original, established in 1924 by New York retailers Horace Saks and Bernard Gimbel. The store features all the big names in women's fashion, from Armani to Yves Saint Laurent, plus an excellent menswear department and a children's section. There are also fine household linens, La Prairie skincare and attentive customer service. New management is exploring the possibility of a major overhaul; at the time of writing, Frank Gehry's name had made the rumour mill as the architect to take things to the next level.

National chains

Many New Yorkers regard chain stores as unimaginative places to shop, but that doesn't mean you won't have to stand behind a long line of locals while waiting at the register. Stores such as American Apparel, Anthropologie, Banana Republic, Express, H&M, Old Navy, Target and Urban Outfitters abound across New York. To find the nearest location of your own favourite chain, have a flip through the phone book.

Specialist

Books & magazines

Chain stores

Barnes & Noble has a number of megastores, and several feature readings by authors. The smaller Borders chain also provides under-one-roof browsing. Check the phone book for the location nearest to you, and pick up a copy of the weekly *Time Out New York* magazine for listings of readings at bookstores and other venues. For more on readings, *see pp276-278.*

General

192 Books

192 Tenth Avenue, between 21st & 22nd Streets (1-212 255 4022/www.192books.com). Subway C, E to 23rd Street. **Open** noon-6pm Mon, Sun; 11am-7pm Tue-Sat. **Credit** AmEx, MC, V. **Map** p404 C26.

In an era when many an indie bookshop has closed its doors, this youngster, open since 2003, is proving that quirky boutique booksellers can make it after all. Owned and 'curated' by art dealer Paula Cooper and her husband, editor Jack Macrae, 192 offers a strong selection of art books and literature, as well as sections on gardening, history, politics, design, music and memoirs. Regular readings, signings and discussions, some featuring well-known writers, are further good reasons to drop by, plus its a great place to meet like-minded literary types.

St Mark's Bookshop

31 Third Avenue, between 8th & 9th Streets (1-212 260 7853/www.stmarksbookshop.com). Subway N, R, W to 8th Street-NYU; 6 to Astor Place. **Open** 10am-midnight Mon-Sat; 11am-midnight Sun. **Credit** AmEx, Disc, MC, V. **Map** p403 F28.

Students, academics and art professionals gravitate to this East Village bookseller, which opened in 1977. It maintains strong inventories on cultural theory, graphic design, poetry and film studies, as well as numerous avant-garde journals and 'zines.

Specialist

Books of Wonder

18 W 18th Street, between Fifth & Sixth Avenues (1-212 989 3270/www.booksofwonder.com). Subway F, V to 14th Street; L to Sixth Avenue; 1 to 18th Street. **Open** 10am-7pm Mon-Sat; noon-6pm Sun. **Credit** AmEx, Disc, MC, V. **Map** p403 E27.

It recently moved two doors down and combined forces with the Cupcake Café in late 2004, but the city's only independent children's bookstore still features both the very new (the staff hosted a midnight madness party to celebrate the release of the latest *Harry Potter*) and the very old (rare and out-of-print editions), plus foreign-language and reference titles, and a special collection of Oz books.

East West

78 Fifth Avenue, between 13th & 14th Streets (1-212 243 5994/www.eastwest.com). Subway L, N, Q, R, W, 4, 5, 6 to 14th Street-Union Square. **Open** 10am-9pm Mon-Sat; 11am-6.30pm Sun. **Credit** AmEx, Disc, MC, V. **Map** p403 E27.

This spiritual titles bookshop devotes equal space to Eastern and Western traditions, from alternative health and yoga to philosophy.

Forbidden Planet

840 Broadway, at 13th Street (1-212 475 6161/ www.fpnyc.com). Subway L, N, Q, R, W, 4, 5, 6 to 14th Street-Union Square. **Open** 10am-10pm Mon, Tue, Sun; 10am-midnight Wed-Sat. **Credit** AmEx, Disc, MC, V. **Map** p403 E27.

Embracing both the pop-culture mainstream and the cult underground, the Planet takes comics as seriously as the guys and girls that pack the place out. You'll find graphic novels (Neil Gaiman's *Sandman*, Craig Thompson's *Blankets*), comic serials (*Asterix*, *Batman*), and film and TV tie-ins.

Hue-Man Bookstore & Café

2319 Frederick Douglass Boulevard (Eighth Avenue), between 124th & 125th Streets (1-212 665 7400/ www.huemanbookstore.com). Subway A, B, C, D to 125th Street. **Open** 10am-8pm Mon-Sat; 11am-7pm Sun. **Credit** AmEx, Disc, MC, V. **Map** p407 D13.

Focusing on African-American non-fiction and fiction, this superstore-sized Harlem indie also stocks bestsellers and general-interest books.

Mysterious Bookshop

58 Warren Street, between Church & West Broadway Streets (1-212 5871011/www.mysteriousbookshop.com). Subway A, C, 1, 2 to Chambers Street. **Open** 11am-7pm daily. **Credit** AmEx, DC, Disc, MC, V. **Map** p402 E32.

Devotees of mystery, crime and spy genres will know owner Otto Penzler, both as an editor and from his book recommendations on Amazon.com. His shop holds a wealth of paperbacks, hardbacks and autographed first editions.

Used & antiquarian

Housing Works Used Book Café

126 Crosby Street, between Houston & Prince Streets (1-212 334 3324/www.housingworksubc.com). Subway B, D, F, V to Broadway-Lafayette Street; N, R, W to Prince Street; 6 to Bleecker Street. **Open** 10am-9pm Mon-Fri; noon-9pm Sat; noon-7pm Sun. **Credit** AmEx, MC, V. **Map** p403 E29.

Housing Works is extraordinarily ususual and endearing. The two-level space – which stocks literary fiction, non-fiction, rare books and collectibles – is a peaceful spot for solo relaxation or for meeting friends over coffee or wine. All proceeds from the café go to providing support services for homeless people living with HIV/Aids. The premises also host an interesting array of literary events, such as book readings. *See also p277.*

Labyrinth Books

536 W 112th Street, between Amsterdam Avenue & Broadway (1-212 865 1588/www.labyrinthbooks.com). Subway 1 to 110th Street-Cathedral Parkway. **Open** 9am-10pm Mon-Fri; 10am-8pm Sat; 11am-7pm Sun. **Credit** AmEx, Disc, MC, V. **Map** p406 C15.

The academic crowd thrives in Labyrinth's rarefied air. You may find remaindered copies of *Heidegger, Coping and Cognitive Science* or a coffee-table book entitled *Black Panthers 1968*.

Strand Book Store

828 Broadway, at 12th Street (1-212 473 1452/ www.strandbooks.com). Subway L, N, Q, R, W, 4, 5, 6 to 14th Street-Union Square. **Open** 9.30am-10.30pm Mon-Sat; 11am-10.30pm Sun. **Credit** AmEx, DC, Disc, MC, V. **Map** p403 E28.

Owned by the Bass family since 1927, the legendary Strand – with its '18 miles of books' – offers incredible deals on new releases, loads of used books, plenty of hard-to-finds and New York City's largest rare book collection. Staff are pretty good at pointing you in the right direction if you feel a little at sea.

Green scene

So you're an environmentalist. Most likely that means you like recycling, conserving energy and avoiding nasty chemicals. It also means you're conscious of your carbon footprint – and, considering the jet fuel you most likely burned to get here, maybe you're feeling a little guilty? Fortunately, being green in New York is not as hard as you might think.

Visiting **John Masters**' Soho salon (*see p249*), for example, is just as intoxicating as a trip to a botanical garden. 'No perms, no nails, nothing that reeks of chemicals,' Masters explains while surveying his wonderfully aromatic headquarters, an intimate space that looks and feels like an old-school apothecary. While no permanent hair colour (save the red-redder-reddest-spectrum henna you used in high school) is completely organic, Masters imports ColorHerbe, an ammonia-free brand from Italy, and then mixes it with essential oils and silk protein to effect hues that look and feel as good as anything achieved with synthetic products (which usually contain silicone, a plastic coating intended to make hair look shiny). During summer 2007, Masters debuted his new garden oasis out back, where you can wait for your appointment or hang out while your highlights take. The main feature is an inviting deck constructed with locally acquired black locust tree wood, an alternative to traditional timbered western red cedar or rainforest hardwoods, and the organic garden even helps manage storm water runoff.

Over in Brooklyn, the various treatments at **Greenhouse Holistic** (88 Roebling Street, at N 7th Street, Williamsburg, 1-718 599 3113) – part yoga studio, part spa – are executed with pure organic fruit- and vegetable-based products. Its Gentlemen's Facial involves a fruit-pulp-and-paprika cleanser for blackheads, a menthol-and-rose-hip salve for ingrown hairs and a healing stonecrop mask (made with an aloe-like plant), which minimises sunspots. Expectant moms and compulsive nail-biters venture to **Priti Organic Spa** (35 E 1st Street, at First Avenue, 1-212 254 3628). Here, polishes are free of harmful solvents like formaldehyde and toluene, and their soy-based remover is non-toxic and acetone-free. The geranium sugar scrubs, essential-oil foot soaks and herb-infused lotions (made in-house) are also organic, and the disposable slippers are, of course, biodegradable.

Birdbath.

Visitors to New York can now improve their closet and their eco credentials, thanks to a crop of eco-chic boutiques. To minimise its impact on the Earth, **Project No.8** (138 Division Street, between Ludlow & Orchard Streets, 1-212 925 5599) conducted a sun study before it opened its doors, resulting in energy-saving elements such as concrete radiant floors and a vacuum-sealed storefront. Its collections aren't always organic, but you can pick up eco-conscious labels like Moral Fervor and NatureVsFuture.

'I have worked to keep my store badass,' says owner Anne Bernstein of her cosy four-year-old eco-friendly shop **Gominyc** (443 E 6th Street, between First Avenue & Avenue A, 1-212 979 0388, www.gominyc.com). As the first green clothing spot to grace the East Village, it stays true to her ethos with edgy lines by names such as Brooklyn-based Vanessa Barrantes (who incorporates renewable fibres into her designs) and Species by the Thousands recycled jewellery.

Joining Williamsburg's burgeoning green scene, rustic **Om Sweet Home** (59 Kent Avenue, between N 10th & N 11th Streets, 1-718 963 6986, www.omsweethomenyc.com) covers every aspect of living and dressing stylishly with minimal impact on the planet. The beyond-Birkenstock fashion items include supersoft tanks from Stewart + Brown and organic cotton jumpers from Bahar Shahpar.

Project No.8.

Never mind stoner-style necklaces, hemp can be chic, particularly if the earth-friendly fibre is fashioned into low-slung cigarette pants like the ones featured at studio-size depot **Organic Avenue** (101 Stanton Street, between Ludlow & Orchard Streets, 1-212 334 4593). Owner Denise Mari, a vegan and former model, also offers Tierra Del Forte pesticide-free denim and popular Ahimsa silk scarves, which leave silkworms unharmed.

Naturally, eco-friendly shopping will work up an appetite. Head over to recently opened green café **Birdbath** (145 Seventh Avenue, at Charles Street, 1-646 722 6565), with its countertops that look and feel like slate but are actually made from recycled paper. New treats include the Green Energy Cookie, an organic butter cookie made with chillies.

If you are hungry for a full-on meal then head to Fort Greene, Brooklyn to **Habana Outpost** (757 Fulton Street, at S Portland Avenue, 1-718 858 9500; *see p187*). The eaterie sells all the favourites from the popular Nolita spot (grilled corn, Cuban sandwiches, mango and jicama salad) but with a twist: the indoor/outdoor restaurant is run on solar power and employs various environmentally friendly practices and materials. Designer Atom Cianfarani helped create the multipurpose space, which on weekends hosts an outdoor market selling clothes, accessories and antiques (you can view the events at www.ecoeatery.com). If you down too many fried plantains, you can hop on the stationary bike and mix your own margarita in the human-powered blender.

John Masters Organics.

Other locations: Strand, 95 Fulton Street, between Gold & William Streets, Financial District (1-212 732 6070); Strand Kiosk, Central Park, Fifth Avenue, at 60th Street, Upper East Side (1-646 284 5506).

Children

Fashion

Calypso Enfant

426 Broome Street, between Crosby & Lafayette Streets (1-212 966 3234/www.calypso-celle.com). Subway 6 to Spring Street. **Open** 11am-7pm Mon-Sat; noon-7pm Sun. **Credit** AmEx, MC, V. **Map** p403 E30.

Fans of Calypso Christiane Celle (*see below*) adore this Francophile children's boutique, which blurs the boundaries between cute and couture. The tiny wool coats look as if they could have been lifted straight from the pages of a classic children's book.

Yoya

636 Hudson Street, between Horatio & Jane Streets (1-646 336 6844/www.yoyashop.com). Subway A, C, E to 14th Street; L to Eighth Avenue. **Open** 11am-7pm Mon-Sat; noon-5pm Sun. **Credit** AmEx, Disc, MC, V. **Map** p403 C28.

Various Village sensibilities – European, bohemian and hip – come together in this store, which is aimed at infants to six-year-olds. Labels such as Erica Tanov, Temperley for Little People, and Imps & Elves are available, as well as tiny-size (but not quite so tiny-priced) Diesel Ts.

Toys

Kidding Around

60 W 15th Street, between Fifth & Sixth Avenues (1-212 645 6337). Subway F, V to 14th Street; L to Sixth Avenue. **Open** 10am-7pm Mon-Sat; 11am-6pm Sun. **Credit** AmEx, Disc, MC, V. **Map** p403 E27.

Loyal customers frequent this quaint shop for clothing and toys for the brainy baby, with the emphasis as firmly on educating kids as entertaining them. The play area in the back will keep your little one occupied while you shop.

Toys 'R' Us Times Square

1514 Broadway, between 44th & 45th Streets (1-800 869 7787). Subway N, Q, R, W, 42nd Street S, 1, 2, 3, 7 to 42nd Street-Times Square. **Open** 9am-10pm Mon-Sat; 11am-6pm Sun. **Credit** AmEx, Disc, MC, V. **Map** p404 D24.

The chain's flagship location is the world's largest toy store – big enough for a 60ft-high Ferris wheel inside and an animatronic tyrannosaur to greet you at the door. Kids, needless to say, think it's the centre of the universe. Brands rule here: there's an incredible two floors of Barbie paraphernalia, displayed in a life-sized Barbie house, plus a café with its very own sweetshop – Candy Land – that's designed to look like the board game.

Other locations: throughout the city

Fashion

Boutiques

New York has so many fab little shops it's impossible to visit them all. Here is a selection of our favourites to get you started.

Annie O

105 Rivington Street, between Essex & Ludlow Streets (1-212 475 3490/www.hotelonrivington.com). Subway F to Delancey. **Open** 2pm-11pm Tue-Sat; noon-6pm Sun. **Credit** AmEx, MC, V. **Map** p403 G29.

Party like a rock star? Now you can shop like one too at Annie O, a music-themed boutique, tucked into the Hotel on Rivington (*see p60*) on the Lower East Side. Shop curator Annie Ohayon – a former music publicist for acts such as Pearl Jam, Lou Reed and the Smashing Pumpkins – handpicks goods spiked with a naughty, rock 'n' roll sensibility. The shop has been quick to garner rave reviews from the local press and the public seems to agree.

Bird

430 Seventh Avenue, between 14th & 15th Streets, Park Slope, Brooklyn (1-718 768 4940). Subway F to 15th Street-Prospect Park. **Open** 11.30am-7pm Mon-Sat; noon-6pm Sun. **Credit** AmEx, Disc, MC, V. **Map** p403 D27.

Park Slope's Bird has always been a favourite of neighbourhood girls looking for designer dresses and Ts, but new owner Jennifer Mankins recently made it the spot in Brooklyn for jeans, stocking Chip & Pepper, James Jeans, Wrangler and more.

Bond 07

7 Bond Street, between Broadway & Lafayette Street (1-212 677 8487). Subway B, D, F, V to Broadway-Lafayette Street; 6 to Bleecker Street. **Open** 11am-7pm Mon-Sat; noon-7pm Sun. **Credit** AmEx, MC, V. **Map** p403 E29.

Selima Salaun has branched out from undies and eyewear to embrace an eclectic mix of clothing (Alice Roi, Colette Dinnigan), accessories and French furniture. Vintage eyewear and bags are also available.

Calypso Christiane Celle

654 Hudson Street, between Gansevoort & W 13th Streets (1-646 638 3000/www.calypso-celle.com). Subway A, C, E to 14th Street; L to Eighth Avenue. **Open** 11am-7pm Mon-Sat; noon-7pm Sun. **Credit** AmEx, DC, MC, V. **Map** p403 C28.

Christiane Celle has created a Calypso empire, of which this outpost in the Meatpacking District is the crown jewel. Stop by any of the shops for gorgeous slip dresses, suits, sweaters and scarves, many from little-known French designers.

Other locations: throughout the city.

Cantaloup

1036 Lexington Avenue, at 74th Street (1-212 249 3566). Subway 6 to 77th Street. **Open** 11am-7pm Mon-Sat; noon-6pm Sun. **Credit** AmEx, MC, V. **Map** p405 E20.

Finally, a boutique that gives UES girls a reason to skip the trip down to Nolita. Cantaloup is full of new labels such as James Coviello and Chanpaul, and it's less picked over than the below-Houston boutiques. **Other locations**: 1359 Second Avenue, at 74th Street, Upper East Side (1-212 288 3569).

Comme des Garçons

520 W 22nd Street, between Tenth & Eleventh Avenues (1-212 604 9200). Subway C, E to 23rd Street. **Open** 11am-7pm Tue-Sat; noon-6pm Sun. **Credit** AmEx, DC, Disc, MC, V. **Map** p404 C26.

In this austere store devoted to Rei Kawakubo's architectural designs for men and women, clothing is hung like art in an innovative space that feels like a gallery – well placed in Chelsea.

Elizabeth Charles

639 Hudson Street, between Gansevoort & Horatio Streets (1-212 243 3201/www.elizabeth-charles.com). Subway A, C, E to 14th Street; L to Eighth Avenue. **Open** noon-7.30pm Tue-Sat; noon-6.30pm Sun. **Credit** AmEx, MC, V. **Map** p403 C28.

Oz native Elizabeth Charles transferred her eponymous shop from the West Village to the fashion nexus of the Meatpacking District last year, allowing for an even greater selection of flirty clothes from designers Down Under. Most labels are exclusive to the store, so chances are you won't see your outfit on anyone else – unless you go to Australia.

Kirna Zabete

96 Greene Street, between Prince & Spring Streets (1-212 941 9656/www.kirnazabete.com). Subway C, E to Spring Street; R, W to Prince Street. **Open** 11am-7pm Mon-Sat; noon-6pm Sun. **Credit** AmEx, MC, V. **Map** p403 E30.

The Nick Dine-designed, futuristic-feeling store stocks avant-garde yet wearable women's clothing and shoes from haute designers like Jean Paul Gaultier and Balenciaga, along with a range of fragrances, and the kind of jeans you probably won't want to do the decorating in.

Opening Ceremony

35 Howard Street, between Broadway & Lafayette Street (1-212 219 2688). Subway J, M, N, Q, R, W, Z, 6 to Canal Street. **Open** 11am-8pm Mon-Sat; noon-7pm Sun. **Credit** AmEx, MC, V. **Map** p403 E30.

Opening Ceremony offers a stylish trip around the world, in a warehouse-size space gussied up with grape-coloured walls and crystal chandeliers. The boutique presents fashions by country, with an emphasis on European work. Buyers cull from couture labels, independent designers, mass-market brands and open-air markets.

Patricia Field

302 Bowery, between Bleecker & Houston Streets (1-212 966 4066/www.patriciafield.com). Subway C, E to Spring Street. **Open** noon-8pm Mon-Thur, Sun; noon-9pm Fri, Sat. **Credit** AmEx, Disc, MC, V. **Map** p403 F29.

Some people celebrate their 40th anniversary with diamonds or extravagant parties. Not Patricia Field. She commemorated her 40th year in retail with this boutique. Marking a return to the East Village after closing her seminal 8th Street store over a decade ago in 1996, the two-level Bowery shop is a veritable *This Is Your Life*-style retrospective of the fashion icon's costume-design career. Graffiti by street artist De la Vega, trophies from the sets of *Sex and the City* and *The Devil Wears Prada*, and a neon sign from her now-closed Hotel Venus outpost make some lively set dressings for playful garb.

Pieces

671 Vanderbilt Avenue, at Park Place, Prospect Heights, Brooklyn (1-718 857 7211/www.piecesofbklyn.com). Subway 2, 3 to Grand Army Plaza. **Open** 11am-7pm Tue-Thur; 11am-8pm Fri, Sat; 11am-6pm Sun. **Credit** AmEx, MC, V. **Map** p410 U11.

At this husband-and-wife-owned store, white-washed brick walls are the backdrop for vibrant clothing and accessories along the lines of Pretty Punk miniskirts, Ant pinstriped dress shirts and Anja Flint clutches. A selection of menswear is also stocked in the store.

Other locations: Pieces of Harlem, 228 W 135th Street, between Adam Clayton Powell Jr Boulevard (Seventh Avenue) & Frederick Douglass Boulevard (Eighth Avenue), Harlem (1-212 234 1725).

Rebecca Taylor

260 Mott Street, between Houston & Prince Streets (1-212 966 0406/www.rebeccataylor.com). Subway B, D, F, V to Broadway-Lafayette Street; N, R, W to Prince Street; 6 to Bleecker Street. **Open** noon-6pm daily. **Credit** AmEx, MC, V. **Map** p403 F29.

This New Zealand designer's shop is adorned with murals of fairy worlds and butterflies – perhaps the source of inspiration for her whimsical, kittenish dresses and jackets.

Scoop

861 Washington Street, between 13th & 14th Streets (1-212 691 1905/www.scoopnyc.com). Subway A, C, E to 14th Street; L to Eighth Avenue. **Open** 11am-8pm Mon-Fri; 11am-7pm Sat; noon-6pm Sun. **Credit** AmEx, DC, Disc, MC, V. **Map** p403 C27.

Scoop represents the ultimate fashion editor's closet. Clothing from the likes of Juicy Couture, Diane von Furstenberg, Philosophy and others is arranged by hue, not by label. The newest outposts, in the Meatpacking District, have fab finds for both genders at neighbouring stores; hit the Soho shop for women only, the uptown branch if you're after a more classic look for guys and gals. For the menswear store up the street, *see p240*.

Other locations: 532 Broadway, between Prince & Spring Streets, Soho (1-212 925 2886); 1275 Third Avenue, between 73rd & 74th Streets, Upper East Side (1-212 535 5577).

Steven Alan

103 Franklin Street, between Church Street & West Broadway (1-212 343 0692/www.stevenalan.com). Subway 1 to Franklin Street. **Open** 11.30am-7pm Mon-Wed, Fri, Sat; 11.30am-8pm Thur. **Credit** AmEx, MC, V. **Map** p402 E31.

Trina Turk. *See p238.*

Decorated like an old-school general store, this roomy shop leans slightly in favour of the ladies – the front section is earmarked for hot-chick labels such as Botkier, Christopher Deane and, of course, Steven Alan. The back area does right by the gents, though, with Rogan jeans and items from Filson, an outdoorsmen's line. Don't skip the excellent range of jewellery glittering up front.
Other locations: 465 Amsterdam Avenue, between 82nd & 83rd Streets, Upper West Side (1-212 595 8451).

TG-170

170 Ludlow Street, between Houston & Stanton Streets (1-212 995 8660/www.tg170.com). Subway F to Delancey Street; J, M, Z to Delancey-Essex Streets. **Open** noon-8pm daily. **Credit** AmEx, MC, V. **Map** p403 G29.
Terri Gillis has an eye for emerging designers: she was the first to carry Built by Wendy and Pixie Yates. Nowadays, you'll come across the likes of Jared Gold and Liz Collins pieces hanging in her newly expanded store.

Designer

These big-name designers have huge flagship stores in New York that have clothes horses chomping at the bit for their latest threads.

Alexander McQueen

417 W 14th Street, between Ninth & Tenth Avenues (1-212 645 1797/www.alexandermcqueen.com). Subway A, C, E to 14th Street; L to Eighth Avenue. **Open** 11am-7pm Mon-Sat; 12.30-6pm Sun. **Credit** AmEx, DC, Disc, MC, V. **Map** p403 C27.
A barrel-vaulted ceiling and serene lighting make the rebellious Brit's Meatpacking District store feel like a religious retreat. But the top-stitched denim skirts and leather jeans are far from monastic.

Ben Sherman

96 Spring Street, at Mercer Street (1-212 680 0160/www.benshermanusa.com). Subway C, E to Spring Street; N, R, W to Prince Street. **Open** 10am-9pm Mon-Sat; 11am-7pm Sun. **Credit** AmEx, MC, V. **Map** p403 E30.
Bringing a touch of London's Carnaby Street to Soho, Ben Sherman, the eponymous streetwear brand born of the original swinging '60s mod god, has dropped its first US flagship. As a salute to its English roots, the co-ed emporium is peppered with mannequins and an antique settee covered in a charming Union Jack pattern.

Bottega Veneta

699 Fifth Avenue, between 54th & 55th Streets (1-212 371 5511/www.bottegaveneta.com). Subway E, V to Fifth Avenue-53rd Street; N, R, W to Fifth Avenue-59th Street. **Open** 10am-6.30pm Mon-Wed, Fri, Sat; 10am-7pm Thur; noon-5pm Sun. **Credit** AmEx, DC, Disc, MC, V. **Map** p405 E22.
At this luxe Italian label's largest store worldwide, a dramatic leather-and-steel staircase links the ground floor with a mezzanine. The gargantuan emporium stocks the complete line of shoes and handbags, along with men's and women's apparel that is available only here.

Diane von Furstenberg

874 Washington Street, at W 14th Street, (1-646 486 4800/www.dvf.com). Subway A, C, E to 14th Street; L to Eighth Avenue. **Open** 11am-6pm Mon-Wed, Fri; 11am-8pm Thur; 11am-5pm Sat; noon-5pm Sun. **Credit** AmEx, Disc, MC, V. **Map** p403 C27.
Indefatigable socialite Diane von Furstenberg's new flagship store shows off classic wrap dresses (she sold five million of them in the 1970s) and much more at this enormous space. Whether you go for ultra-feminine dresses or sporty knits, you'll emerge from the changing room feeling like a princess.

Donna Karan New York

819 Madison Avenue, between 68th & 69th Streets (1-212 861 1001/www.donnakaran.com). Subway 6 to 68th Street-Hunter College. **Open** 10am-6pm Mon-Wed, Fri, Sat; 10am-7pm Thur; noon-6pm Sun. **Credit** AmEx, DC, MC, V. **Map** p405 E21.
Created around a central garden with a bamboo forest, Donna Karan's flagship store caters to men, women and the home. Check out the organic café at the nearby DKNY store, as well as Donna-approved reads, clothing, shoes and vintage furniture.
Other locations: DKNY, 655 Madison Avenue, at 60th Street, Upper East Side (1-212 223 3569).

Marc Jacobs

163 Mercer Street, between Houston & Prince Streets (1-212 343 1490/www.marcjacobs.com). Subway B, D, F, V to Broadway-Lafayette Street; N, R, W to Prince Street; 6 to Bleecker Street. **Open** 11am-7pm Mon-Sat; noon-6pm Sun. **Credit** AmEx, DC, Disc, MC, V. **Map** p403 E29.
Men and women get fashion parity at Jacobs's Soho boutique. A separate-but-equal policy rules at his trio of Bleecker Street shops – men's, women's and accessories – keeping the West Village kitted-out.
Other locations: Marc by Marc Jacobs, 403-405 Bleecker Street, at 11th Street, Meatpacking District (1-212 924 0026); Marc Jacobs Accessories, 385 Bleecker Street, at Perry Street, Meatpacking District (1-212 924 6126).

Ralph Lauren

867 Madison Avenue, at 72nd Street (1-212 606 2100/www.polo.com). Subway 6 to 68th Street-Hunter College. **Open** 10am-7pm Mon-Wed, Fri, Sat; 10am-8pm Thur; noon-5pm Sun. **Credit** AmEx, DC, Disc, MC, V. **Map** p405 E20.
Ralph Lauren spent $14 million turning the old Rhinelander mansion into an Ivy League dream of a superstore: it's filled with oriental rugs, paintings, riding whips, leather club chairs and fresh flowers. The skate-happy homeboys who've adopted Ralph's togs head straight to Polo Sport across the street.
Other locations: Ralph Lauren Boutique, 380 Bleecker Street, between Charles & Perry Streets, Meatpacking District (1-212 645 5513); Polo Sport, 381 Bleecker Street, between Charles & Perry Streets, Meatpacking District (1-646 638 0684).

Stella McCartney

429 W 14th Street, between Ninth & Tenth Avenues (1-212 255 1556/www.stellamccartney.com). Subway A, C, E to 14th Street; L to Eighth Avenue. **Open** noon-7pm Mon-Sat; 12.30-6pm Sun. **Credit** AmEx, DC, Disc, MC, V. **Map** p403 C27.

Celeb designer Stella McCartney, who won great acclaim for her rock-star collections for Chloé, now focuses on showcasing pricey lines of glam-sprite womenswear, shoes and accessories at her first stand-alone store in New York.

Tracy Reese

641 Hudson Street, between Gansevoort & Horatio Streets (1-212 807 0505). Subway A, C, E to 14th Street; L to Eighth Avenue. **Open** 11am-7pm Mon-Wed; 11am-8pm Thur-Sat; noon-7pm Sun. **Credit** AmEx, Disc, MC, V. **Map** p403 C28.

With the opening of her eponymous Meatpacking District flagship, apostles of arch-feminine designer Tracy Reese now have a house of worship. The 2,200sq ft of curvaceous walls, twinkly chandeliers and fuchsia cushioned settees pays tribute to all things girly and glamorous.

Trina Turk

67 Gansevoort Street, between Greenwich & Washington Streets (1-212 206 7383/www.trinaturk.com). Subway A, C, E to 14th Street; L to Eighth Avenue. **Open** 11am-7pm Mon-Sat; noon-6pm Sun. **Credit** AmEx, MC, V. **Map** p403 C28.

Fans of Left Coast designer Trina Turk's vintage-inspired pieces are in luck. In collaboration with chipper home-design star Jonathan Adler, the Palm Springs-based couturier has opened her first NYC outpost, a sprawling 2,500-square-foot space that evokes 1970s Big Sur style with lovely white terracotta tiles, chairs styled after coral and a giant wooden tree sculpture. *Photo p236.*

Discount

Century 21

22 Cortlandt Street, between Broadway & Church Street (1-212 227 9092/www.c21stores.com). Subway R, W to Cortlandt Street. **Open** 7.45am-8pm Mon-Wed, Fri; 7.45am-8.30pm Thur; 10am-8pm Sat; 11am-7pm Sun. **Credit** AmEx, MC, V. **Map** p402 E32.

A white Gucci men's suit for $300? A Marc Jacobs cashmere sweater for less than $200? Roberto Cavalli sunglasses for a scant $30? No, you're not dreaming – you're shopping at Century 21. The prized score is admittedly rare but the place is still intoxicating; savings range between a staggering 25% and 75% off regular store prices, making this a mecca for less-minted fashionistas.

Other locations: 472 86th Street, between Fourth & Fifth Avenues, Bay Ridge, Brooklyn (1-718 748 3266).

Find Outlet

229 Mott Street, between Prince & Spring Streets (1-212 226 5167). Subway N, R, W to Prince Street; 6 to Spring Street. **Open** noon-7pm daily. **Credit** MC, V. **Map** p403 F30.

Skip the sample sales and head to Find Outlet instead. High-fashion samples and overstock are sold at drastically reduced prices (with 50% off, on average), so you can dress like a fashion editor on an editorial assistant's budget.

Other locations: 361 W 17th Street, between Eighth & Ninth Avenues, Chelsea (1-212 243 3177).

Market NYC

268 Mulberry Street, between Houston & Prince Streets (1-212 580 8995/www.themarketnyc.com). Subway B, D, F, V to Broadway-Lafayette Street; N, R, W to Prince Street; 6 to Bleecker Street. **Open** 11am-7pm Sat, Sun. **No credit cards. Map** p403 F29.

Yes, it's housed rather modestly in the gymnasium of a church's youth centre, but this place is no small shakes when it comes to clothing. Every weekend, contemporary fashion and accessory designers hawk their (usually unique) wares here.

Menswear

Atelier New York

125 Crosby Street, between Houston & Prince Streets (1-212 941 8435). Subway N, R, W to Prince Street. **Open** 11am-7pm Mon-Fri; noon-7pm Sat; noon-6pm Sun. **Credit** AmEx, DC, MC, V. **Map** p403 E29.

This sophisticated men's-only store distinguishes itself from the high-fashion Soho pack with rarefied labels such as Balenciaga, Cloak and Les Hommes. A genuine score for the boys.

J. Press

380 Madison Avenue, between 46th & 47th Streets (1-212 687 7642/www.jpressonline.com). Subway 4, 5, 6, 7, S at Grand Central-42nd Street. **Open** 9am-7pm Mon-Sat. **Credit** AmEx, MC, V. **Map** p404 E23.

Lovingly embrace your inner preppie at the recently opened flagship store of J. Press. Patchwork Madras perhaps not your thing? Not a problem: these guys will deck you out in classic collegiate clobber faster than you can say Skull & Bones.

Odin

328 E 11th Street, between First & Second Avenues (1-212 475 0666). Subway L to First Avenue. **Open** noon-8pm daily. **Credit** AmEx, MC, V. **Map** p403 F28.

Gentlemen generally prefer one-stop shopping to trawling the town for threads, and so tend to favour this East Village guys' emporium, which tows the line between boys' street-savvy threads and men's tailored attire – all with an edge, of course.

Paul Smith

108 Fifth Avenue, between 15th & 16th Streets (1-212 627 9770/www.paulsmith.co.uk). Subway L, N, Q, R, W, 4, 5, 6 to 14th Street-Union Square. **Open** 11am-7pm Mon-Wed, Fri, Sat; 11am-8pm Thur; noon-6pm Sun. **Credit** AmEx, Disc, MC, V. **Map** p403 E27.

Paul Smith devotees love this store's raffish English gentleman look. They're even more partial to the designs and accessories that combine the elegance, quality and wit that characterises the label's creations – as do the serious price tags.

J. Press.

Treasure hunt

Load up with precious cargo from the city's hottest jewellery shops.

Though Fifth Avenue's illustrious diamond houses such as Cartier and Tiffany possess a posh allure, NYC also offers a whole bevy of highly intimate boutiques for one-of-a-kind adornments, particularly in the West Village. Once home to antique stores, the genteel neighbourhood is quickly becoming the new gold coast, thanks to **Ginette_NY Jewelry Bar** (172 W 4th Street, between Sixth & Seventh Avenues, 1-212 627 3763), the first boutique dedicated to Provençal native Frédérique Dessemond's chic line. Formerly sold at chichi department stores such as Barneys, her signature 14-karat gold flat disks – which can be personalised with custom monograms, words or numbers – are actually based on the traditional adornments worn by women in her hometown of Marseille. Just a stone's throw away is perhaps the city's smallest bauble boutique, **Phoenix Roze** (183 W 10th Street, between Seventh Avenue South & W 4th Street, 1-212 255 2362, www.phoenixroze.com), a nook (formerly an alley) lined with second-generation jewellery maker and owner Guy Rozenstrich's handmade creations, along with Pamela Norris's chunky quartz bracelets. You'll find goods for both sexes, including superfemme moonstone-drop earrings and handsome silver shark's tooth pendants. Rozenstrich will also whip up custom pieces.

For accessories with worldly flair, visit **Jane Eadie** (248 Elizabeth Street, between E Houston & Prince Streets, 1-212 334 7975), the eponymous boutique of a former assistant to the Prince of Wales and the president of Polo Ralph Lauren. Her tiny, shabby-chic spot, which is like the United Nations of baubles, brings together Italian designer Daniela de Marchi's cocktail rings and JMR Fontan's cuffs from Brazil, among other hard-to-find pieces from designers all around the world.

If you're tired of cliché charms, pluck decidedly ungirly creations at **Bittersweets New York** (37 Broadway, between Kent & Wythe Avenues, Williamsburg, Brooklyn, 1-718 218 8595, www.bittersweetsny.com) in trendy Brooklyn neighbourhood Williamsburg. There, artist and co-owner Robin Adams's quirky embellishments, such as 18-karat gold-plate cuffs modelled after earthworms, walk the line between creepy and beautiful in a former gallery bedecked with vintage wallpaper and antique cabinets.

Scoop Men

873 Washington Street, between 13th & 14th Streets (1-212 929 1244/www.scoopnyc.com). Subway A, C, E to 14th Street; L to Eighth Avenue. **Open** 11am-8pm Mon-Fri; 11am-7pm Sat; noon-6pm Sun. **Credit** AmEx, DC, Disc, MC, V. **Map** p403 C27.

Choice cuts for men from a variety of big name designers. For review, *see p235* **Scoop**.

Other locations: 1273 Third Avenue, between 73rd & 74th Streets, Upper East Side (1-212 535 5577).

Seize sur Vingt

243 Elizabeth Street, between Houston & Prince Streets (1-212 343 0476/www.16sur20.com). Subway B, D, F, V to Broadway-Lafayette Street; N, R, W to Prince Street; 6 to Bleecker Street. **Open** 11am-7pm Mon-Sat; noon-6pm Sun. **Credit** AmEx, Disc, MC, V. **Map** p403 F29.

Seize sur Vingt was founded in 1998 with the aim of combining tailored elegance with youthful exuberance. Ready-to-wear men's shirts are available here, but the real draws are the bespoke suits and custom-cut button-downs. Shirts come in Wall Street pinstripes and preppy gingham, with mother-of-pearl buttons and short, square collars. Be sure to check out the fine handkerchiefs too.

Sneakers

Alife Rivington Club

158 Rivington Street, between Clinton & Suffolk Streets (1-212 375 8128/www.rivingtonclub.com). Subway F to Delancey Street; J, M, Z to Delancey-Essex Streets. **Open** noon-7pm daily. **Credit** AmEx, MC, V. **Map** p403 G29.

'Sneakers' equal 'religion' in this tiny, out-of-the-way shop, which is arguably the city's main hub for hard-to-get shoes and so draws a huge number of obsessive sneaker heads. The store, like its wares, has a rather exclusive vibe: there's no sign, no street number, no indication that the joint even exists from the outside. Look closely and ring the bell to check out the rotating selection of 60 or so styles.

Classic Kicks

298 Elizabeth Street, between Houston & E 1st Streets (1-212 979 9514). Subway B, D, F, V to Broadway-Lafayette; 6 to Bleecker Street. **Open** noon-7pm Mon-Sat. **Credit** AmEx, MC, V. **Map** p403 F29.

One of the more female-friendly sneaker shops, Classic Kicks stocks mainstream and rare styles of

Converse, Lacoste, Puma and Vans, to name but a few, for both style-conscious boys and girls, along with a decent selection of clothes.

Clientele

267 Lafayette Street, at Prince Street (1-212 219 0531). Subway N, R, W to Prince Street; 6 to Spring Street. **Open** noon-8pm Mon-Sat; noon-7pm Sun. **Credit** AmEx, MC, V. **Map** p403 E29.

Set up like an art gallery display, the kicks line one wall of the minimalist store, and patrons sit on a long wooden bench to admire them.

Streetwear

A Bathing Ape

91 Greene Street, between Prince & Spring Streets (1-212 925 0222). Subway N, R to Prince Street. **Open** 11am-8pm Mon-Sat; noon-7pm Sun. **Credit** AmEx, MC, V. **Map** p403 E29.

The cult label created by Japanese designer Nigo planted its first US flagship in Soho last spring. Nigo, who has collaborated with Pharrell Williams, among others, devotes most of his shop to BAPE threads, while an upstairs shoe salon housing BAPEsta kicks has made the city's sneaker-hungry masses literally go ape.

Autumn

436 E 9th Street, between First Avenue & Avenue A (1-212 677 6220/www.autumnskateboarding.com). Subway L to First Avenue; 6 to Astor Place. **Open** noon-7pm daily. **Credit** AmEx, Disc, MC, V. **Map** p403 F28.

Proprietor and amateur skateboarder David Mimms and his wife, Kristen Yaccarino, stock DVS, Emerica, Etnies, iPath, Lakai and Vans for your half-pipe pleasure. Ts and jeans, not to mention scores of boards, are available too.

Brooklyn Industries

162 Bedford Avenue, at North 8th Street, Williamsburg, Brooklyn (1-718 486 6464/www.brooklynindustries.com). Subway L to Bedford Avenue. **Open** 11am-9pm Mon-Sat; noon-8pm Sun. **Credit** AmEx, Disc, MC, V. **Map** p411 U7.

Bags sporting the skyline label and zippered sweatshirt hoodies with Brooklyn emblazoned across the chest are just the tip of the iceberg at this store, which seems more popular with every passing year.

Other locations: 286 Lafayette Street, between Prince & Spring Streets, Soho/Little Italy (1-212 219 0862); 206 Fifth Avenue, at Union Street, Park Slope, Brooklyn (1-718 789 2764); 100 Smith Street, at Atlantic Avenue, Boerum Hill, Brooklyn (1-718 596 3986); 184 Broadway, at Driggs, Williamsburg, Brooklyn (1-718 218 9166).

Dave's Quality Meat

7 E 3rd Street, between Bowery & Second Avenue (1-212 505 7551/www.davesqualitymeat.com). Subway F, V to Lower East Side-Second Avenue. **Open** noon-7pm Mon-Sat; noon-6pm Sun. **Credit** AmEx, Disc, MC, V. **Map** p403 F29.

Dave Ortiz – formerly of ghetto urban-threads label Zoo York – and professional skateboarder Chris Keefe stock a range of top-shelf streetwear in their wittily designed shop complete with meat hooks and mannequins sporting butchers' aprons. Homemade graphic-print Ts are wrapped in plastic and then displayed in a deli case.

Phat Farm

129 Prince Street, between West Broadway & Wooster Street (1-212 533 7428/www.phatfarmstore.com). Subway C, E to Spring Street; N, R, W to Prince Street. **Open** 11am-7pm Mon-Sat; noon-6pm Sun. **Credit** AmEx, Disc, MC, V. **Map** p403 E29.

Def Jam impresario Russell Simmons' classy, conservative take on hip hop couture has swept urban culture around the world: phunky-phresh baggy clothing for guys; for gals, the Baby Phat line. Not one for posers, pretenders or part-timers.

Recon

359 Lafayette Street, between Bleecker & Bond Streets (1-212 614 8502/www.reconstore.com). Subway 6 to Bleecker Street. **Open** noon-7pm Mon-Thur, Sun; noon-8pm Fri, Sat. **Credit** AmEx, MC, V. **Map** p403 E29.

The joint venture of one-time graffiti artists Stash and Futura, Recon offers graf junkies a chance to wear the work on clothing and accessories.

Stüssy

140 Wooster Street, between Houston & Prince Streets (1-212 274 8855). Subway N, R, W to Prince Street. **Open** noon-7pm Mon-Fri; 11am-7pm Sat; noon-6pm Sun. **Credit** AmEx, MC, V. **Map** p403 E29.

Tricky isn't the only one who wants to be dressed up in Stüssy. Come here for all the skate and surf wear that made Sean Stüssy famous, as well as utilitarian Japanese bags from Headporter.

Supreme

274 Lafayette Street, between Jersey & Prince Streets (1-212 966 7799). Subway B, D, F, V to Broadway-Lafayette Street; N, R, W to Prince Street; 6 to Spring Street. **Open** 11.30am-7pm Mon-Sat; noon-6pm Sun. **Credit** AmEx, MC, V. **Map** p403 E29.

Filled mostly with East Coast brands such as Chocolate, Independent and Zoo York, this skatewear store also stocks its own line. Look for pieces by snowboard company Burton and DC Shoe, the latter a sponsor of professional skaters like Colin McKay and Danny Way.

Unis

226 Elizabeth Street, between Houston & Prince Streets (1-212 431 5533). Subway B, D, F, V to Broadway-Lafayette Street; N, R, W to Prince Street; 6 to Bleecker Street. **Open** noon-7pm Mon-Wed, Sun; noon-7.30pm Thur-Sat. **Credit** AmEx, Disc, MC, V. **Map** p403 F29.

Korean-American designer Eunice Lee's structured streetwear used to be for boys only, but she let the girls in on the fun in 2003. Both collections are featured in her sleek Nolita boutique, along with Botkier bags and other accessories.

Used & vintage

Goodwill and the Salvation Army are great for vintage finds, but it can take hours of digging to discover a gem. Enter thrift boutiques, where the digging has been done for you. We have listed a wide range here, from the far more extravagant shops that cherry-pick vintage YSL and Fiorucci for their racks, to T-shirt havens, as well as a few that fall in between.

Allan & Suzi

416 Amsterdam Avenue, at 80th Street (1-212 724 7445/www.allanandsuzi.net). Subway 1 to 79th Street. **Open** 12.30-7pm Mon-Sat; noon-6pm Sun. **Credit** AmEx, Disc, MC, V. **Map** p405 C19.
Models and celebs drop off worn-once Gaultiers, Muglers, Pradas and Manolos here. The platform shoe collection is flashback-inducing and incomparable, as is the selection of vintage jewellery.

Beacon's Closet

88 North 11th Street, between Berry Street & Wythe Avenue, Williamsburg, Brooklyn (1-718 486 0816/ www.beaconscloset.com). Subway L to Bedford Avenue. **Open** noon-9pm Mon-Fri; 11am-8pm Sat, Sun. **Credit** AmEx, Disc, MC, V. **Map** p411 U7.
Some vintage boutiques boast prices more akin to major fashion labels. Not so at this bustling Brooklyn favourite, where not only are the prices great, but so is the Williamsburg-appropriate clothing selection – from iconic T-shirts and party dresses to sneakers, leathers and denim, plus second-hand CDs.
Other locations: 220 Fifth Avenue, between President & Union Streets, Park Slope, Brooklyn (1-718 230 1630).

D/L Cerney

13 E 7th Street, between Second & Third Avenues (1-212 673 7033). Subway N, R, W to 8th Street-NYU; 6 to Astor Place. **Open** noon-8pm Tue-Sun. **Credit** AmEx, MC, V. **Map** p403 F28.
Specialising in timeless, original designs for stylish fellows, the store also carries menswear from the 1940s to the '60s. Mint-condition must-haves include hats (including some pristine fedoras), ties and shoes. An adjacent shop carries D/L Cerney's new women's line, which also merits a look.

Edith Machinist

104 Rivington Street, between Essex & Ludlow Streets (1-212 979 9992). Subway F to Delancey Street; J, M, Z to Delancey-Essex Streets. **Open** 1-8pm Mon-Fri; noon-8pm Sat, Sun. **Credit** AmEx, MC, V. **Map** p403 G29.
Check out one of the city's best collections of (mostly) fine leather bags, not to mention an army of shoes, here at this slightly below-street-level shop. There's no trash here – only the cream of the vintage crop. The front rack displays Edith & Daha's own line of designer clothing.

Foley & Corinna

114 Stanton Street, between Essex & Ludlow Streets (1-212 529 2338/www.foleyandcorinna.com). Subway F to Delancey Street; J, M, Z to Delancey-Essex Streets. **Open** noon-8pm Mon-Sat; noon-7pm Sun. **Credit** AmEx, MC, V. **Map** p403 G29.
Vintage-clothing fiends like Liv Tyler and Donna Karan know they can have it both ways: shoppers freely mix old (Anna Corinna's vintage finds) with new (Dana Foley's original creations, including lace tops, leather-belted pants and sheer wool knits) to

Roger Vivier: well heeled in more ways than one. *See p244.*

compose a truly one-of-a-kind look. Encourage the boy in your life to spiff up at the men's store, conveniently located just around the corner.
Other locations: Foley & Corinna Men, 143 Ludlow Street, between Rivington & Stanton Streets, Lower East Side (1-212 529 5043).

INA

101 Thompson Street, between Prince & Spring Streets (1-212 941 4757/www.inanyc.com). Subway C, E to Spring Street. **Open** noon-7pm Mon-Thur, Sun; noon-8pm Fri, Sat. **Credit** AmEx, MC, V. **Map** p403 E29.
For the past 11 years, INA on Thompson Street has reigned over the downtown consignment scene. The Soho location features drastically reduced couture pieces, the shop on Prince Street carries trendier clothing, and the Mott Street shop is for men.
Other locations: 21 Prince Street, between Elizabeth & Mott Streets, Little Italy (1-212 334 9048); 208 E 73rd Street, between Second & Third Avenues, Upper East Side (1-212 249 0014); 262 Mott Street, between Houston & Prince Streets, Soho (1-212 334 2210).

Local Clothing

328 E 9th Street, between First & Second Avenues (1-212 777 3850). Subway L to Third Avenue. **Open** noon-8pm Mon-Thur, Sun; noon-9pm Fri, Sat. **Credit** AmEx, Disc, MC, V. **Map** p403 F28.
It's funny how vintage never gets old. NYC's latest instalment in aged threads is East Village shop Local Clothing, a women's vintage trove that focuses on garb from as far back as the Victorian era up to the first MTV generation.

Marmalade

172 Ludlow Street, between Houston & Stanton Streets (1-212 473 8070/marmaladevintage.com). Subway F, V to Lower East Side-Second Avenue. **Open** noon-9pm daily. **Credit** AmEx, MC, V. **Map** p403 G29.
Marmalade, one of the cutest vintage-clothing stores on the Lower East Side, has some of the hottest 1970s and '80s threads to be found below Houston Street. That slinky cocktail dress or ruffled blouse is tucked amid a selection of well-priced, well-cared-for items including accessories and vintage shoes.

Fashion accessories

Jewellery

For more jewellery, *see p240* **Treasure hunt**.

Alexis Bittar

465 Broome Street, between Greene & Mercer Streets (1-212 625 8340/www.alexisbittar.com). Subway N, R, W to Prince Street; 6 to Spring Street. **Open** 11am-7pm Mon-Sat; noon-6pm Sun. **Credit** AmEx, MC, V. **Map** p403 E30.
A Brooklyn-based designer known for his chunky Lucite and semi-precious stone accessories, Bittar adorned his recently opened boutique with vintage wallpaper and a Victorian lion's-paw table.

Doyle & Doyle

189 Orchard Street, between Houston & Stanton Streets (1-212 677 9991/www.doyledoyle.com). Subway F, V to Lower East Side-Second Avenue. **Open** 1-7pm Tue, Wed, Fri; 1-8pm Thur; noon-7pm Sat, Sun. **Credit** AmEx, Disc, MC, V. **Map** p403 F29.

Whether your taste is art deco or nouveau, Victorian or Edwardian, gemologist sisters Pam and Elizabeth Doyle, who specialise in estate and antique jewellery, will have that one-of-a-kind piece you're looking for, including engagement and eternity rings.

Fragments

116 Prince Street, between Greene & Wooster Streets (1-212 334 9588/www.fragments.com). Subway B, D, F, V to Broadway-Lafayette Street; N, R, W to Prince Street. **Open** 11am-7pm Mon-Sat; noon-6pm Sun. **Credit** AmEx, DC, Disc, MC, V. **Map** p403 E29.

Over two decades, Fragments owner Janet Goldman has assembled a stable of more than 100 pet jewellery designers, who offer their creations to her before selling them to major stores such as Barneys.

Tiffany & Co

727 Fifth Avenue, at 57th Street (1-212 755 8000/ www.tiffany.com). Subway E, V to Fifth Avenue-53rd Street; F to 57th Street; N, R, W to Fifth Avenue-59th Street. **Open** 10am-7pm Mon-Fri; 10am-6pm Sat; noon-5pm Sun. **Credit** AmEx, DC, Disc, MC, V. **Map** p405 E22.

The heyday of Tiffany's was at the turn of the 20th century, when Louis Comfort Tiffany, the son of founder Charles Lewis Tiffany, took the reins and began to create sensational art nouveau jewellery. Today, the design stars are the no-less-august Paloma Picasso and Elsa Peretti. Three floors are stacked with precious jewels, silver, watches, porcelain and the classic Tiffany engagement rings. FYI: breakfast is not served.

Lingerie & underwear

Most department stores have comprehensive lingerie sections, and Victoria's Secret shops abound; but the following spots are special places to go for extra-beautiful bedroom and beachside wear.

Agent Provocateur

133 Mercer Street, between Prince & Spring Streets (1-212 965 0229/www.agentprovocateur.com). Subway B, D, F, V to Broadway-Lafayette Street; N, R, W to Prince Street; 6 to Spring Street. **Open** 11am-7pm Mon-Sat; noon-6pm Sun. **Credit** AmEx, MC, V. **Map** p403 E29.

Looking for something to rev up your sweetie's heartbeat? Then check out this patron saint of provocative panties. Va-va-voomy bras, garters and bustiers are dubbed with Bond-girl names.

Catriona MacKechnie

400 W 14th Street, between Ninth & Tenth Avenues (1-212 242 3200). Subway A, C, E to 14th Street. **Open** 11am-7.30pm Mon-Sat; noon-6pm Sun. **Credit** AmEx, MC, V. **Map** p403 C27.

Glasgow-born Catriona MacKechnie has turned lingerie into haute couture with her dramatically decked out eponymous shop. Along with exclusive UK labels and the proprietor's own line, MacKechnie offers custom knicker fittings.

Mixona

262 Mott Street, between Houston & Prince Streets (1-646 613 0100/www.mixona.com). Subway B, D, F, V to Broadway-Lafayette Street; N, R, W to Prince Street; 6 to Bleecker Street. **Open** 11am-7.30pm Mon-Fri, Sun; 11am-8pm Sat. **Credit** AmEx, MC, V. **Map** p403 F29.

Luxurious under-things by 30 designers are found here, including Christina Stott's leather-trimmed mesh bras and Passion Bait's lace knickers.

Shoes

Camper

125 Prince Street, at Wooster Street (1-212 358 1842/www.camper.es). Subway N, R, W to Prince Street. **Open** 11am-8pm Mon-Sat; noon-6pm Sun. **Credit** AmEx, DC, MC, V. **Map** p403 E29.

Dozens of styles from the Spanish-made line of casual shoes are stocked in this large corner store.

Chuckies

1073 Third Avenue, between 63rd & 64th Streets (1-212 593 9898). Subway F to Lexington Avenue-63rd Street. **Open** 10.45am-7.45pm Mon-Fri; 10.45am-7.30pm Sat; 12.30-7pm Sun. **Credit** AmEx, DC, Disc, MC, V. **Map** p405 E21.

An alternative to department stores, Chuckies carries high-profile labels for men and women. Its stock ranges from old-school Calvin Klein and Jimmy Choo to up-and-coming Ernesto Esposito.

Jimmy Choo

645 Fifth Avenue, at 51st Street (1-212 593 0800/ www.jimmychoo.com). Subway E, V to Fifth Avenue-53rd Street. **Open** 10am-6pm Mon-Wed, Fri, Sat; 10am-7pm Thur; noon-5pm Sun. **Credit** AmEx, MC, V. **Map** p404 E23.

Jimmy Choo, famed for conceiving Princess Diana's custom-shoe collection, has conquered America with his six-year-old emporium, which features chic boots, sexy stilettos, curvaceous pumps and kittenish flats. Prices start at $450.

Otto Tootsi Plohound

137 Fifth Avenue, between 20th & 21st Streets (1-212 460 8650). Subway N, R, W to 23rd Street. **Open** 11.30am-8pm Mon-Fri; 11am-8pm Sat; noon-7pm Sun. **Credit** AmEx, DC, Disc, MC, V. **Map** p403 E27.

One of the best places for the latest shoe styles, Tootsi has a big selection of trendy (and rather ambitiously priced) imports for women and men.

Other locations: throughout the city.

Roger Vivier

750 Madison Avenue, at 65th Street (1-212 861 5371/www.rogervivier.com). Subway 6 to 68th Street. **Open** 10am-6pm Mon-Sat. **Credit** AmEx, MC, V. **Map** p405 E21.

Manhattan's gals got a lift last year with the opening of French shoe label Roger Vivier. Here's where you'll find the iconic, chrome-buckle, squared-toe flats, plus handbags and accessories. *Photo p243.*

Food & drink

There are more than 20 open-air 'greenmarkets', sponsored by the city authorities, in various locations on different days. The largest and best known is at **Union Square**, where small producers of cheese, flowers, herbs, fruits and vegetables hawk their goods on Mondays, Wednesdays, Fridays and Saturdays (8am-6pm). Arrive early, before the prime stuff sells out. For other venues, check with the **Council on the Environment of NYC** (1-212 788 7476, www.cenyc.org).

Bakeries

Amy's Bread

672 Ninth Avenue, between 46th & 47th Streets (1-212 977 2670/www.amysbread.com). Subway C, E to 50th Street; N, R, W to 49th Street. **Open** 7.30am-11pm Mon-Fri; 8am-11pm Sat; 9am-6pm Sun. **No credit cards**. **Map** p404 C23.

Whether you want sweet (chocolate-chubbie cookies) or savoury (semolina-fennel bread, hefty French sourdough boules), Amy's never disappoints.

Other locations: Chelsea Market, 75 Ninth Avenue, between 15th & 16th Streets, Chelsea (1-212 462 4338).

Billy's Bakery

184 Ninth Avenue, between 21st & 22nd Streets (1-212 647 9956/www.billysbakerynyc.com). Subway C, E to 23rd Street. **Open** 9am-11pm Mon-Thur, Sun; 9am-midnight Fri, Sat. **Credit** AmEx, Disc, MC, V. **Map** p404 C26.

Amid super-sweet retro delights such as coconut cream pie, Hello Dollies and Famous Refrigerator Cake, you'll find friendly service in a setting that will remind you of Grandma's kitchen – or, at least, it will if your grandmother was Betty Crocker.

Magnolia Bakery

401 Bleecker Street, at 11th Street (1-212 462 2572). Subway 1 to Christopher Street. **Open** noon-11.30pm Mon; 9am-11.30pm Tue-Thur; 9am-12.30am Fri; 10am-12.30am Sat; 10am-11.30pm Sun. **Credit** AmEx, Disc, MC, V. **Map** p403 D28.

Part sweet market, part meet market, Magnolia skyrocketed to fame after featuring on *Sex and the City*, and it's still oven-hot. The pastel-iced cupcakes are much vaunted, but you can also pick up a cup of custardy, Southern-style banana pudding (Brits: think trifle) or a scoop from the summertime ice-cream cart. Then, sweetmeat in hand, join the other happy eaters clogging nearby apartment stoops. Comfort food doesn't get much more classy.

Sullivan Street Bakery

533 W 47th Street, between Tenth & Eleventh Avenues (1-212 265 5580/www.sullivanstreetbakery.com). Subway C, E at 50th Street. **Open** 7am-7pm Mon-Sat; 8am-4pm Sun **Credit** MC, V. **Map** p404 C23.

Superlative Italian breads and thin-crust pizza to go, as popular with lunch-breakers as it is with local celebrity chefs. *See p206* **The upper crust**.

Chocolatiers

See also p247 **Sweet love**.

Jacques Torres Chocolate Haven

350 Hudson Street, between Charlton & King Streets, entrance on King Street (1-212 414 2462/www.jacquestorres.com). Subway 1 to Houston Street. **Open** 9am-7pm Mon, Wed-Fri; 10am-8pm Sat; 11am-7pm Sun. **Credit** AmEx, MC, V. **Map** p403 D29.

Walk into Jacques Torres's new glass-walled shop and café, and you'll be surrounded by a Willy Wonka-esque chocolate factory that turns raw cocoa beans into luscious goodies before your very eyes. Sweets for sale range from the sublime (deliciously rich hot chocolate, steamed to order) to the ridiculous (chocolate-covered fortune cookies).

Other locations: Jacques Torres Chocolate, 66 Water Street, between Dock & Main Streets, Dumbo, Brooklyn (1-718 875 9772).

La Maison du Chocolat

1018 Madison Avenue, between 78th & 79th Streets (1-212 744 7117/www.lamaisonduchocolat.com). Subway 6 to 77th Street. **Open** 10am-7pm Mon-Sat; noon-6pm Sun. **Credit** AmEx, MC, V. **Map** p405 E19.

This suave cocoa-brown boutique, the creation of Robert Linxe, packages refined (and pricey) examples of edible Parisian perfection as if they were fine jewellery. A small café serves hot and cold chocolate drinks, and a selection of sweets.

Other locations: 30 Rockefeller Plaza, 49th Street, between Fifth & Sixth Avenues (1-212 265 9404).

Richart

7 E 55th Street, between Madison & Fifth Avenues (1-888 742 4278/www.richart-chocolates.com). Subway E, V to Fifth Avenue-53rd Street. **Open** 10am-7pm Mon-Fri; 10am-6pm Sat. **Credit** AmEx, MC, V. **Map** p405 E22.

French master-chocolatier Michel Richart is an intellectual sensualist, one who's as likely to fill a bonbon with green-tea essence or basil ganache as with the more expected coffee or hazelnuts. His precisely geometric squares are topped with cool graphic patterns – swirls, bubbles, even leopard prints – to indicate the fillings within.

Scharffen Berger

473 Amsterdam Avenue, at 83rd Street (1-212 362 9734/www.scharffenberger.com). Subway 1 to 86th Street. **Open** 10am-8pm Mon-Thur; 10am-9pm Fri, Sat; 11am-7pm Sun. **Credit** AmEx, Disc, MC, V. **Map** p405 C19.

At this bite-sized boutique from the artisanal chocolate maker from Berkeley, California, you'll find gift boxes of remarkable dark ganache-filled treats (in unexpected flavours like fresh lemon and sea-salt caramel), plus jars of chocolate sauce and essential oddities like chocolate-mint lip balm.

General

Dean & DeLuca

560 Broadway, at Prince Street (1-212 431 1691/ www.deananddeluca.com). Subway N, R, W to Prince Street. **Open** 10am-8pm Mon-Sat; 10am-7pm Sun. **Credit** AmEx, Disc, MC, V. **Map** p403 E29.

Dean & DeLuca's flagship store (one of only two that offer more than just a fancy coffee bar) provides the most sophisticated (and highly pricey) selection of speciality food items in the city.

Other locations: throughout the city.

Whole Foods

Concourse level, Time Warner Center, 10 Columbus Circle, at Broadway (1-212 823 9600/www.whole foods.com). Subway A, B, C, D, 1 to 59th Street-Columbus Circle. **Open** 8am-10pm daily. **Credit** AmEx, Disc, MC, V. **Map** p405 D22.

You'll feel healthier just walking around looking at this veritable cornucopia of fresh food. Gorgeous as well as good for you, Whole Foods is the city's best bet for organic offerings. Take advantage of the well-stocked wine store seven days a week.

Other locations: 4 Union Square South, between Broadway & University Place, Greenwich Village (1-212 673 5388); 250 Seventh Avenue, at 24th Street, Flatiron District (1-212 924 5969).

Zabar's

2245 Broadway, at 80th Street (1-212 787 2000/ www.zabars.com). Subway 1 to 79th Street. **Open** 8am-7.30pm Mon-Fri; 8am-8pm Sat; 9am-6pm Sun. **Credit** AmEx, MC, V. **Map** p405 C19.

Zabar's is more than just a market – it's a genuine New York City landmark. Sure, you might leave the place feeling a little light in the wallet, but you can't beat the top-flight prepared foods. Besides the famous smoked fish and rafts of Jewish delicacies, Zabar's has fabulous selections of bread, cheese and coffee – and an entire floor dedicated to well-priced gadgets and housewares.

Specialist

Guss' Pickles

85-87 Orchard Street, between Broome & Grand Streets (www.gusspickle.com). Subway F to Delancey Street; J, M, Z to Delancey-Essex Streets. **Open** 9.30am-6.30pm Mon-Thur; 9.30am-4pm Fri; 10am-6pm Sun. **Credit** AmEx, MC, V. **Map** p403 G30.

After moving twice in recent years, the Pickle King has settled down, and the complete, delicious array of sours and half-sours, pickled peppers, watermelon rinds and sauerkraut is now available to enormously grateful New Yorkers once again.

Russ & Daughters

179 E Houston Street, between Allen & Orchard Streets (1-212 475 4880/www.russanddaughters. com). Subway F, V to Lower East Side-Second Avenue. **Open** 9am-7pm Mon-Sat; 8am-5.30pm Sun. **Credit** AmEx, Disc, MC, V. **Map** p403 F29.

Russ & Daughters, which has been open for nigh on a century (since 1914, to be precise), sells eight kinds of smoked salmon and many Jewish-inflected Eastern European delectables, along with dried fruits, chocolates and caviar.

Gifts & souvenirs

Love Saves the Day

119 Second Avenue, at 7th Street (1-212 228 3802). Subway 6 to Astor Place. **Open** noon-9pm daily. **Credit** AmEx, MC, V. **Map** p403 F28.

Kitsch reigns here, with Yoda dolls, Elvis lamps, ant farms, lurid machine-made tapestries of the Madonna, glow-in-the-dark crucifixes, collectable toys and Mexican Day of the Dead statues. Vintage clothing is peppered throughout the store.

Matter

405 Broome Street, between Centre & Lafayette Streets (1-212 343 2600/www.mattermatters.com) Subway 6 to Spring Street. **Open** noon-7pm Mon-Fri; 11am-7pm Sat; 11am-6pm Sun. **Credit** AmEx, MC, V. **Map** p403 F30.

The Soho spin-off of Brooklyn design store Matter offers a similarly excellent selection of housewares, like Loyal Loot Collective log bowls and Iraqi-Brit architect Zaha Hadid's Milanese stools. *Photo p250.*

Metropolitan Opera Shop

136 W 65th Street, at Broadway (1-212 580 4090/ www.metguild.com/shop). Subway 1 to 66th Street-Lincoln Center. **Open** 10am-10pm Mon-Sat; noon-6pm Sun. **Credit** AmEx, Disc, MC, V. **Map** p405 C21.

This shop, in the Metropolitan Opera House at Lincoln Center, sells CDs and cassettes, opera books and DVDs, plus educational CDs for kids.

Pearl River Mart

477 Broadway, between Broome & Grand Streets (1-212 431 4770/www.pearlriver.com). Subway J, M, N, Q, R, W, Z to Canal Street; 6 to Spring Street. **Open** 10am-7.20pm daily. **Credit** AmEx, Disc, MC, V. **Map** p403 E30.

This browse-worthy downtown emporium is filled with all things Chinese: slippers, clothing, gongs, groceries, medicinal herbs, stationery, teapots and all sorts of fun trinkets and gift items.

Health & beauty

Beauty & cosmetics

Face Stockholm

110 Prince Street, at Greene Street (1-212 966 9110/ www.facestockholm.com). Subway N, R, W to Prince Street. **Open** 11am-7pm Mon-Sat; noon-6pm Sun. **Credit** AmEx, MC, V. **Map** p403 E29.

In addition to a full line of eyeshadows, lipsticks, blushers and tools, Face offers make-up application lessons to help improve your technique.

Other locations: 226 Columbus Avenue, between 70th & 71st Streets, Upper West Side (1-212 769 1420).

Sweet love

A wave of new premium chocolate shops has provided ample choice for chocoholic Manhattanites looking for a fix. Legendary chocolatier Jacques Torres has unveiled his most irresistible creation yet: **Chocolate Haven** (*see p245*), an 8,000-square-foot factory that serves as the Manhattan hub for the pastry chef's growing chocolate empire. The space features a cocoa-pod-shaped café overlooking the candy-making facilities, so visitors can indulge in chocolate treats and watch as cocoa beans are transformed into exquisite chocolate bars.

West Village sweet boutique **Chocolate Bar** (48 Eighth Avenue, between Horatio & Jane Streets, 1-212 366 1541) carries only candies, cookies and brownies from local makers of the highest calibre. This is also, as the name suggests, the place to score an updated version of the candy bar. Chocolate Bar has created some worthy options, such as hefty dark-chocolate bars that are flavoured liberally with mint or orange. For something bite-size, check out the shop's mojito truffle, flavoured with rum, lime and mint, or lemon-hazelnut or peanut-butter caramel. If that's not enough, then simply stroll down to No.80 Eighth Avenue, at West 14th Street, and load up on more dark stuff at **Li-Lac Chocolates** (1-212 274 7374, www.li-lacchocolates.com). This neighbourhood institution has been sweetly pushing sweets on locals since 1923, but in 2005 they upped and moved into this cute corner shop, painted lilac of course.

Boozehounds on the other hand will fall head over heels for **Chocolat Michel Cluizel** (www.chocolatmichelcluizel.com). The fine French chocolatier opened his first stateside shop inside the Flatiron's ABC Carpet & Home (888 Broadway, at 19th Street, 1-212 473 3000), and even managed to score a liquor license. His 'adult' bonbons contain premium hooch and are wrapped in foil. Smooth, top-quality chocolate, is spiked with tipples such as rum, cognac, calvados, vodka or whisky.

If you like chocolate on your candies, check out **Divalicious** (365 Broome Street, between Elizabeth & Mott Streets, 1-212 343 1243). Here, you'll find chocolate-covered everything – fortune cookies, graham crackers and pretzels – as well as chocolate lollipops and charming chocolate hearts.

Li-Lac Chocolates.

John Masters Organics

77 Sullivan Street, between Spring & Broome Streets (1-212 343 9590/www.johnmasters.com). Subway C, E to Spring Street; N, R, W to Prince Street. **Open** 11am-7pm Mon-Sat. **Credit** AmEx, MC, V. **Map** p403 E30.

Organic doesn't get more orgasmic than in John Masters's supremely chic apothecary line. Blood orange and vanilla body wash, and lavender and avocado intensive conditioner are just two of the good-enough-to-eat products that you can get to go. *See also p232* **Green scene**.

Kiehl's

109 Third Avenue, between 13th & 14th Streets (1-212 677 3171/www.kiehls.com). Subway L to Third Avenue; N, Q, R, W, 4, 5, 6 to 14th Street-Union Square. **Open** 10am-7pm Mon-Sat; noon-6pm Sun. **Credit** AmEx, DC, MC, V. **Map** p403 F27.

Although it is 154 years old and has recently expanded, this New York institution is still a mob scene. Check out the Motorcycle Room, full of vintage Harleys (the owner's obsession). Try a dab of Kiehl's moisturiser, lip balm or body lotion from the plentiful free samples, and you'll be hooked.

Other locations: 150 Columbus Avenue, between 66th & 67th Streets, Upper West Side (1-212 799 3438).

MAC

113 Spring Street, between Greene & Mercer Streets (1-212 334 4641/www.maccosmetics.com). Subway C, E to Spring Street. **Open** 11am-7pm Mon-Wed; 11am-8pm Thur-Sat; noon-7pm Sun. **Credit** AmEx, DC, Disc, MC, V. **Map** p403 E30.

Make-up Art Cosmetics is increasingly famous for lipsticks and eyeshadows in must-have colours and for its raft of always offbeat celebrity spokesmodels like RuPaul and k.d. lang.

Other locations: throughout the city.

Ricky's

509 Fifth Avenue, between 42nd & 43rd Streets (1-212 949 7230/www.rickys-nyc.com). Subway B, D, F, V to 42nd Street-Bryant Park; 7 to Fifth Avenue. **Open** 8am-9pm Mon-Fri; 10am-8pm Sat; 10am-7pm Sun. **Credit** AmEx, Disc, MC, V. **Map** p404 E24.

Stock up on stylish tweezers and make-up cases that look like souped-up fishing tackle boxes at this mecca for make-up. Ricky's own line, Mattése, is also well worth a look.

Other locations: throughout the city.

Perfumeries

Bond No.9

9 Bond Street, between Broadway & Lafayette Street (1-212 228 1940). Subway B, D, F, V to Broadway-Lafayette Street; 6 to Bleecker Street. **Open** 11am-8pm Mon-Sat; noon-6pm Sun. **Credit** AmEx, MC, V. **Map** p403 E29.

Custom-blended bottles of bliss, and scents that pay olfactory homage to New York City – Wall Street, Nouveau Bowery, New Harlem – are available here. Don't worry, there's no Chinatown Sidewalk.

Other locations: 680 Madison Avenue, at 61st Street, Upper East Side (1-212 838 2780); 897 Madison Avenue, at 73rd Street, Upper East Side (1-212 794 4480).

CB I Hate Perfume

93 Wythe Avenue, between North 10th & 11th Streets, Williamsburg, Brooklyn (1-718 384 6890/www.cbihateperfume.com). Subway L to Bedford. **Open** noon-6pm Tue-Sat. **Credit** MC, V. **Map** p411 U7.

Contrary to his shop's name, Christopher Brosius doesn't actually hate what he sells, he just despises the concept, if that makes any sense. Collaborate with the olfactory genius on a signature scent of your own, or pick up a ready-made splash of quirky scents like Crayon and Rubber Cement; home fragrances include Gathering Apples.

Jo Malone

949 Broadway, at 22nd Street (1-212 673 2220/www.jomalone.com). Subway N, R, W to 23rd Street. **Open** 10am-8pm Mon-Sat; noon-6pm Sun. **Credit** AmEx, DC, Disc, MC, V. **Map** p404 E26.

British perfumer Jo Malone champions the 'layering' of scents as a way of creating a personalised aroma. Along with perfumes and colognes, her Flatiron District boutique offers candles, skincare products and super-pampering facials. Both treatments and products hit the mark.

Other locations: 946 Madison Avenue, between 74th & 75th Streets (1-212 472 0074).

Spas & salons

New York is the city of fresh starts; and what better way to begin anew than with your hair? Whether you want a full-out makeover, a rock 'n' roll do, or just a trim, there's a salon for you. The styling superstars at **Frédéric Fekkai Beauté de Provence** (1-212 753 9500) and **Louis Licari** (1-212 758 2090) are top-notch, but they do tend to charge hair-raising prices. The following salons offer specialised services – budget, rocker, ethno-friendly – and unique settings for your special NYC cut.

Astor Place Hair Stylists

2 Astor Place, at Broadway (1-212 475 9854). Subway N, R, W to 8th Street-NYU; 6 to Astor Place. **Open** 8am-8pm Mon-Sat; 9am-6pm Sun. **No credit cards. Map** p403 E28.

An army of barbers does everything from neat trims to more complicated and creative shaved designs. You can't make an appointment; just take a number and wait outside with the crowd. Sunday mornings are usually more quiet. Cuts start at $12; blow-drys, $20; dreads, $75.

Blow Styling Salon

342 W 14th Street, between Eighth & Ninth Avenues (1-212 989 6282). Subway A, C, E to 14th Street. **Open** 8am-8pm Mon-Fri; 10am-8pm Sat; noon-6pm Sun. **Credit** AmEx, Disc, MC, V. **Map** p403 C27.

Matter. *See p246.*

Jennifer Denton and Vigdis Boulton's own award-winning Meatpacking District spot is scissor-free, focusing instead on pampering head massages and expertly executed blow-outs (from around $40).

John Masters Organics

For listing, see p249.

A trip to John Masters is like visiting an intoxicating botanical garden: the organic scalp treatment will send you into relaxed oblivion, and ammonia-free, herbal-based colour treatments will appeal to your inner purist. Cuts or colouring treatments start at $90. *See also p232* **Green scene**.

Juvenex

5th Floor, 25 W 32nd Street, between Broadway & Fifth Avenue (1-646 733 1330/www.juvenexspa.com). Subway B, D, F, N, Q, R, V, W to 34th Street-Herald Square. **Open** 24hrs daily. **Credit** AmEx, Disc, MC, V. **Map** p404 E25.

This formerly girls-only 24-hour spa gained a cult following among post-partiers seeking communal detox in its jade igloo sauna. But boys can finally join the fun every night after 9pm. Treatments (unlike the sauna) are private; specialist facials include the Oxygen ($130 for 75 minutes) and the Energizing Ginseng ($105 for 60 minutes). The price of a massage starts from $95.

Laicale

129 Grand Street, between Broadway & Crosby Street (1-212 219 2424). Subway J, M, N, Q, R, W, Z, 6 to Canal Street. **Open** 11am-8pm Mon-Fri; 10am-6pm Sat; noon-6pm Sun. **Credit** AmEx, MC, V. **Map** p403 E30.

Get your locks chopped at this industrial chrome-and-glass hair mecca while the shop's own DJ spins the tunes. Most of the stylists here also work for magazines and runway shows. Cuts start at $75; highlights can be had from $145.

Miwa/Alex Salon

24 E 22nd Street, between Broadway & Park Avenue South (1-212 228 4422/www.miwaalex.com). Subway N, R, W, 6 to 23rd Street. **Open** 8.30am-5.30pm Mon; 8.30am-7pm Tue-Fri. **Credit** MC, V. **Map** p404 E26.

Tucked inside a posh, friendly space in the Flatiron District, Miwa/Alex delivers the sort of smart and unique cut you expect in New York. Cuts start at $65 for women; $50 for men.

Mudhoney

148 Sullivan Street, between Houston & Prince Streets (1-212 533 1160). Subway C, E to Spring Street. **Open** noon-8pm Tue-Fri; noon-6pm Sat. **No credit cards**. **Map** p403 E29.

Don't be surprised if the stylist never removes his orange-tinted sunglasses; you're in the city's premier rock 'n' roll salon. The decor alone – a torture chair, lascivious stained-glass – will make the time in this tiny, attitude-packed place fly by. Cuts start at $75, and attract just as much attention as you want.

Other locations: 7 Bond Street, between Broadway & Lafayette Street, East Village (1-212 228 8128).

Nickel

77 Eighth Avenue, at 14th Street (1-212 242 3203/www.nickelformen.com). Subway A, C, E to 14th Street; L to Eighth Avenue. **Open** 1-9pm Mon, Sun; 11am-9pm Tue-Fri; 10am-9pm Sat. **Credit** AmEx, Disc, MC, V. **Map** p403 D27.

New York's official temple of male grooming offers facials, waxing, massages, manicures and pedicures. The product line includes Washing Machine shower gel and Fire Insurance aftershave, as well as Self-Absorbed suntan oil – for the Narcissus in all of us.

Oasis Day Spa

2nd Floor, 108 E 16th Street, between Union Square East & Irving Place (1-212 254 7722/www.oasisdayspanyc.com). Subway L, N, Q, R, W, 4, 5, 6 to 14th Street-Union Square. **Open** 10am-10pm Mon-Fri; 9am-9pm Sat, Sun. **Credit** AmEx, Disc, MC, V. **Map** p403 E27.

The flagship location of this posh wellness sanctuary features everything from hair styling and detoxifying mud wraps to acupuncture. Stressed-out travellers can stop at the JFK branch (Jet Blue Terminal 6, 1-212 254 7722) for manicures, hot shaves or even full-body massages.

Other locations: throughout the city.

Tattoos & piercing

Tattooing was made legal in New York back in 1997; piercing remains relatively unregulated.

New York Adorned

47 Second Avenue, between 2nd & 3rd Streets (1-212 473 0007/www.nyadorned.com). Subway F, V to Lower East Side-Second Avenue. **Open** 1-9pm Mon-Thur, Sun; 1-10pm Fri, Sat. **Credit** AmEx, MC, V. **Map** p403 F29.

Proprietor Lori Leven hires world-class tattoo artists to wield needles at her eight-year-old gothic-elegant establishment. Those with low pain thresholds can try gentler decorations such as henna tattoos, weirldy ethereal white-gold cluster earrings, crafted by Leven, or pieces by emerging body-jewellery designers.

Venus Modern Body Arts

199 E 4th Street, between Avenues A & B (1-212 473 1954). Subway F, V to Lower East Side-Second Avenue. **Open** 1-9pm Mon-Thur, Sun; 1-10pm Fri, Sat. **Credit** AmEx, Disc, MC, V. **Map** p403 G29.

Venus has been tattooing and piercing New Yorkers since 1992 – before body art became de rigueur. It also offers a positively enormous selection of jewellery, so you can put diamonds in your navel and platinum in your tongue.

House & home

Antiques

Among bargain-hungry New Yorkers, flea market rummaging is pursued with religious devotion. What better way to walk off that overstuffed omelette from brunch than to explore aisles of old vinyl records, unusual trinkets, vintage linens and funky furniture?

The Garage

112 W 25th Street, between Sixth & Seventh Avenues (no phone). Subway F, V to 23rd Street. **Open** sunrise-sunset Sat, Sun. **No credit cards. Map** p404 D26.

Designers (and the occasional dolled-down celebrity) hunt regularly – and early – at this flea market inside an emptied parking garage. This spot specialises in old prints, vintage clothing, silver and linens; there's lots of household paraphernalia too.

Greenflea

Intermediate School 44, Columbus Avenue, at 76th Street. Subway B, C to 72nd Street; 1 to 79th Street. **Open** 10am-5.30pm Sun. **No credit cards. Map** p405 C20.

Greenflea is an extensive market that offers rare books, African art, antiques, handmade jewellery, crafts and eatables like vegetables and spiced cider (hot or cold, depending on the season). Visit both the labyrinthine interior and the schoolyard.

Hell's Kitchen Flea Market

39th Street, between Ninth & Tenth Avenues. Subway A, C, E to 34th Street-Penn Station. **Open** sunrise-sunset Sat, Sun. **No credit cards. Map** p404 C24.

The huge Annex Antiques Fair & Flea Market on 26th Street lost its lease to a property developer, so many of the vendors packed up and moved to this stretch of road in Hell's Kitchen. Anyone familiar with the mind-boggling array of goods on offer at the former site may likely feel a bit cheated in the new space, but there are treasures to be found and momentum is growing.

General

ABC Carpet & Home

888 Broadway, at 19th Street (1-212 473 3000/ www.abchome.com). Subway L, N, Q, R, W, 4, 5, 6 to 14th Street-Union Square. **Open** 10am-8pm Mon-Thur; 10am-6.30pm Fri, Sat; noon-6pm Sun. **Credit** AmEx, Disc, MC, V. **Map** p403 E27.

At this shopping landmark, the selection of accessories, linens, rugs and reproduction and antique furniture (Western and Asian) is unbelievable; so are the (mostly steep) prices. For bargains, head to ABC's warehouse outlet in the Bronx.

Other locations: 20 Jay Street, at Plymouth Street, Dumbo, Brooklyn (1-718 643 7400); ABC Carpet & Home Warehouse, 1055 Bronx River Avenue, between Bruckner Boulevard & Westchester Avenue, Bronx (1-718 842 8772).

Charlotte Moss

20 E 63rd Street, between Madison & Fifth Avenues (1-212 308 3888/www.charlottemoss.com). Subway 4, 5, 6 at 59th Street. **Open** 10am-6pm Mon-Sat. **Credit** AmEx, DC, Disc, MC, V. **Map** p405 E21.

If your idea of fun is snooping around a rich person's fancy townhouse – and you're not friends with Donald Trump – we have got just the store for you. The luxuriously appointed digs at Charlotte Moss are set up like a real and highly desirable residence, so not only can you walk away with a prize purchase but you'll also learn a thing or two about how to put a room together in the process.

Las Venus

163 Ludlow Street, between Houston & Stanton Streets (1-212 982 0608). Subway F, V to Second Avenue. **Open** noon-8pm Mon-Sat; noon-7pm Sun. **Credit** AmEx, Disc, MC, V. **Map** p403 G29.

Local hipsters all head to this epicentre of 20th-century pop culture to feed their kitsch furniture fixes. Vintage pieces by the greats – Miller, McCobb, Kagan, among others – are flanked by reproductions and the overall collection creates an artfully cluttered reservoir of affordable finds.

Other locations: Las Venus at ABC, 888 Broadway, at 19th Street, Flatiron District (1-212 473 3000 ext 519).

Eat, Drink, Shop

MoMA Design Store

44 W 53rd Street, between Fifth & Sixth Avenues (1-212 767 1050/www.momastore.org). Subway E, V to Fifth Avenue-53rd Street. **Open** 10am-6.30pm Mon-Thur, Sat, Sun; 10am-8pm Fri. **Credit** AmEx, MC, V. **Map** p405 E22.

A must for contemporary art fans of all inclinations, this store is as wide-ranging and wonderful as the museum's collection itself. State-of-the-art home items on display include casseroles, coffee tables, high-design chairs, lighting, office workstations, kids' furniture, jewellery, calendars and lots of very stylish Christmas ornaments.

Other locations: 81 Spring Street, at Crosby Street, Soho (1-646 613 1367).

Moss

146 Greene Street, between Houston & Prince Streets (1-212 204 7100). Subway B, D, F, V to Broadway-Lafayette Street; N, R, W to Prince Street; 6 to Bleecker Street. **Open** 11am-7pm Mon-Sat; noon-6pm Sun. **Credit** AmEx, Disc, MC, V. **Map** p403 E29.

Proprietor Murray Moss has curated perhaps the most impressive collection of high-design items in the city. Many of the streamlined clocks, curvy sofas and funky household items are kept protected under glass at this temple of contemporary home design. For creativity on a larger scale, stop by his newly opened 'museum' adjacent to the store.

Music

Classical

Westsider Records

233 W 72nd Street, between Broadway & West End Avenue (1-212 874 1588). Subway 1, 2, 3 to 72nd Street. **Open** 11am-8pm daily. **Credit** MC, V. **Map** p405 C20.

This solidly classical store has traditionally stocked only vinyl, but the 21st century has swept in a wave of CDs. It also carries a sprinkling of jazz records, and drama and film books.

Charlotte Moss.

Electronica

Dance Tracks

91 E 3rd Street, at First Avenue (1-212 260 8729/ www.dancetracks.com). Subway F, V to Lower East Side-Second Avenue. **Open** noon-8pm Mon-Fri; noon-8pm Sat; noon-7pm Sun. **Credit** AmEx, Disc, MC, V. **Map** p403 F29.

European imports hot off the plane make this store a must. But it also has racks of domestic house, enticing bins of Loft/Paradise Garage classics and private decks on which to sample them.

Hip hop & R&B

Beat Street Records

494 Fulton Street, between Bond Street & Elm Place, Brooklyn (1-718 624 6400/www.beatst.com). Subway A, C, G to Hoyt-Schermerhorn; 2, 3, 4, 5 to Nevins Street. **Open** 10am-7pm Mon-Sat; 10am-6pm Sun. **Credit** AmEx, Disc, MC, V. **Map** p410 T10.

In a block-long basement with two DJ booths, Beat Street proffers the latest vinyl. CDs run from dancehall to gospel, but the 12in singles and new hip hop albums make this the first stop for local DJs.

Fat Beats

2nd Floor, 406 Sixth Avenue, between 8th & 9th Streets (1-212 673 3883/www.fatbeats.com). Subway A, B, C, D, E, F, V to W 4th Street. **Open** noon-9pm Mon-Sat; noon-6pm Sun. **Credit** MC, V. **Map** p403 D28.

Everyone – Beck, DJ Evil Dee, DJ Premier, Mike D, Q-Tip – shops at this tiny Greenwich Village shrine to vinyl for treasured hip hop, jazz, funk and reggae releases, underground magazines (like *Wax Poetics*), and cult flicks (such as *Wild Style*).

Jazz

Jazz Record Center

Room 804, 236 W 26th Street, between Seventh & Eighth Avenues (1-212 675 4480/www.jazzrecord center.com). Subway C, E to 23rd Street; 1 to 28th Street. **Open** 10am-6pm Mon-Sat. **Credit** Disc, MC, V. **Map** p404 D26.

The city's best jazz store stocks current and out-of-print records, books, videos and other jazz-related merchandise. Worldwide shipping is available for those not lucky enough to be local.

Multigenre

Bleecker Bob's

118 W 3rd Street, between MacDougal Street & Sixth Avenue (1-212 475 9677/www.bleeckerbobs.com). Subway A, B, C, D, E, F, V to W 4th Street. **Open** 11am-1am Mon-Thur, Sun; 11am-3am Fri, Sat. **Credit** AmEx, MC, V. **Map** p403 E29.

Come to Bleecker Bob's for hard-to-find new and used music, especially on vinyl. An online ordering service is due imminently.

Etherea

66 Avenue A, between 4th & 5th Streets (1-212 358 1126/www.ethereaonline.com). Subway F, V to Lower East Side-Second Avenue. **Open** noon-10pm Mon-Thur, Sun; noon-11pm Fri, Sat. **Credit** AmEx, Disc, MC, V. **Map** p403 G29.

Etherea stocks mostly electronic, experimental, house, indie and rock CDs.

Mondo Kim's

6 St Marks Place, between Second & Third Avenues (1-212 598 9985/www.kimsvideo.com). Subway 6 to Astor Place. **Open** 9am-midnight daily. **Credit** AmEx, MC, V. **Map** p403 F28.

Each branch of this movie and music mini-chain has a slightly different name but all offer a great selection for collector geeks: electronic, indie, krautrock, prog, reggae, soul, soundtracks and used CDs.

Other locations: throughout the city.

Other Music

15 E 4th Street, between Broadway & Lafayette Street (1-212 477 8150/www.othermusic.com). Subway N, R, W to 8th Street-NYU; 6 to Astor Place. **Open** noon-9pm Mon-Fri; noon-8pm Sat; noon-7pm Sun. **Credit** AmEx, MC, V. **Map** p403 E29.

This wee audio temple is dedicated to small-label, often imported new and used CDs and LPs. It organises music by arcane categories (for instance, 'La Decadanse' includes lounge, Moog and slow-core soundtracks) and sends out a free weekly email with staffers' reviews of their favourite new releases.

St Marks Sounds

20 St Marks Place, between Second & Third Avenues (1-212 677 3444). Subway 6 to Astor Place. **Open** noon-9pm Mon-Thur, Sun; noon-10pm Fri, Sat. **No credit cards. Map** p403 F28.

Housed in two neighbouring storefronts, Sounds is the best bargain on the block for new and used music. The shop specialises in all kinds of jazz and international recordings both obscure and less so.

Subterranean Records

5 Cornelia Street, between Bleecker & W 4th Streets (1-212 463 8900). Subway A, B, C, D, E, F, V to W 4th Street. **Open** noon-8pm Mon-Wed; noon-10pm Thur-Sat; noon-7pm Sun. **Credit** MC, V. **Map** p403 D29.

Just off Bleecker Street, this shop carries new, used and live recordings, as well as a large selection of imports. Vinyl LPs and 45s fill the basement.

Musical instruments

Sam Ash Music

160 W 48th Street, between Sixth & Seventh Avenues (1-212 719 2299/www.samashmusic.com). Subway B, D, F, V to 47th-50th Streets-Rockefeller Center; N, R, W to 49th Street. **Open** 10am-8pm Mon-Sat; noon-6pm Sun. **Credit** AmEx, MC, V. **Map** p404 D23.

This octogenarian musical-instrument emporium dominates its midtown block with four contiguous

Holiday helpers

Regular department stores and malls can make for wildly unimaginative presents and even duller shopping sessions – which is where the city's holiday bazaars come in. These sprawling temporary shops are filled with offbeat toys, handmade crafts, more soap and candles than you ever thought existed, and no shortage of warming hot chocolates or cappuccinos. Look for them from Thanksgiving through New Year's Day.

Holiday Market at Union Square

The goods Festive red and white booths sell pretty candles and soaps, plus toys, ties, clocks and crèche sets. Most items are reasonably priced, though some jewellery and imported goods can push the budget.
The vibe The labyrinth of tents is fun to wander, and the festive energy runs high even when you're shopping elbow to elbow. Competition for customers is fierce, and vendors are fairly aggressive.

Grand Central Terminal Holiday Fair

The goods You'll find lots of jewellery incorporating silver and/or turquoise at this indoor fair, as well as booths housing unusual (and pricey) gifts from Our Name is Mud, the Czechoslovak-American Marionette Theatre and the American Folk Art Museum. But the biggest draw is a huge selection of Christmas tree ornaments.
The vibe Interesting gifts, musicians playing over-the-top Christmas tunes and a low-key crowd make it well worth a visit.

Holiday Market at Columbus Circle

The goods This one's from the same people who put on the Union Square Market, but it seems to have more diverse merchandise – though the air still hangs thick with soap and candles. Plenty of food stalls.
The vibe No-nonsense shopping.

shops. New, vintage and custom guitars of all varieties are available, along with amps, DJ equipment, drums, keyboards, recording equipment, turntables and an array of sheet music.
Other locations: throughout the city.

World music

World Music Institute

Suite 903, 49 W 27th Street, between Broadway & Sixth Avenue (1-212 545 7536/www.worldmusicinstitute.org). Subway N, R, W to 28th Street. **Open** 10am-6pm Mon-Fri. **Credit** AmEx, MC, V. **Map** p404 E26.
The shop is small, but if you can't find what you're looking for, then WMI's expert, helpful employees can order sounds from the remotest corners of the planet and have them shipped to you, usually within two to four weeks.

Sex shops

Leather Man

111 Christopher Street, between Bleecker & Hudson Streets (1-212 243 5339/www.theleatherman.com). Subway 1 to Christopher Street. **Open** noon-10pm Mon-Sat; noon-8pm Sun. **Credit** AmEx, Disc, MC, V. **Map** p403 D28.
Cock rings, padlocks and sturdy handcuffs beckon from wall-mounted cabinets on the first floor, while the basement (of course) is where serious bondage apparel is hung. There are also fake penises aplenty.

Myla

20 E 69th Street, between Fifth & Madison Avenues (1-212 570 1590). Subway 6 to 68th Street-Hunter College. **Open** 10am-6pm Mon-Fri. **Credit** AmEx, Disc, MC, V. **Map** p405 E20.
London-based naughty-nighties emporium Myla sells elegant boudoir accessories, including tasteful (yet nipple-exposing) 'peephole' bras, silk wrist-ties and blindfolds, plus a few sculptural vibrators.

Toys in Babeland

94 Rivington Street, between Ludlow & Orchard Streets (1-212 375 1701/www.babeland.com). Subway F, V to Lower East Side-Second Avenue. **Open** noon-10pm Mon-Thur, Sun; noon-11pm Fri, Sat. **Credit** AmEx, MC, V. **Map** p403 G29.
At this friendly sex-toy boutique – run by women and skewed towards women – browsers are encouraged to handle all manner of buzzing, wriggling and bendable playthings. The ladies also host frank sex-ed classes on a variety of subjects.
Other locations: 43 Mercer Street, between Broome & Grand Streets, Soho (1-212 966 2120).

Speciality

Brooklyn Superhero Supply Company

372 Fifth Avenue, between 5th & 6th Streets, Park Slope, Brooklyn (1-718 499 9884/www.superherosupplies.com). Subway F, R to 4th Avenue-9th Street. **Open** 11am-5pm daily. **Credit** AmEx, Disc, MC, V. **Map** p410 T11.

BAKER
BAKER
DUSTIN DOLLIN
TERRY KENNEDY
CHOCOLATE
RICK McCRANK

D
K
K

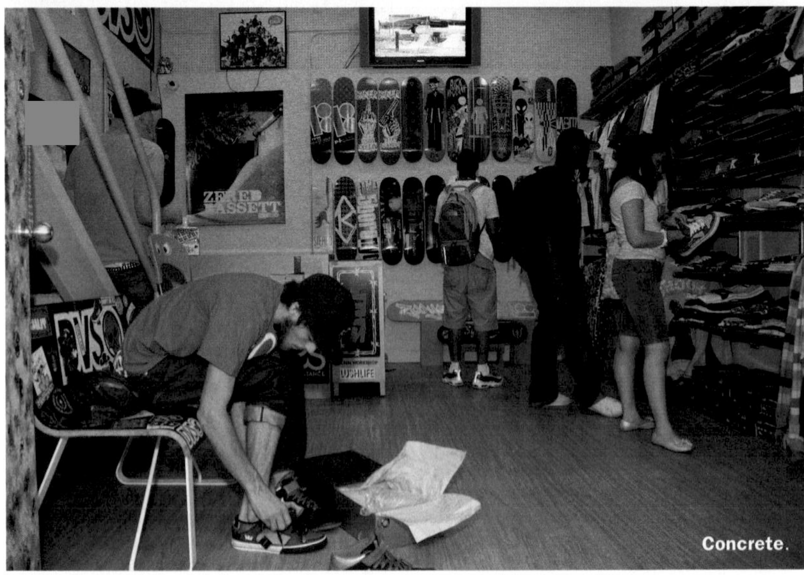

Concrete.

When he's not busy writing books or publishing his literary journal *McSweeney's*, Dave Eggers defends truth and virtue at this kitschy costume shop where you can buy powerful anti-matter by the can. But beware: you must take the superhero pledge with every purchase.

Kate's Paperie

72 Spring Street, between Crosby & Lafayette Streets (1-212 941 9816/www.katespaperie.com). Subway N, R, W to Prince Street; 6 to Spring Street. **Open** 10am-8pm daily. **Credit** AmEx, Disc, MC, V. **Map** p403 E30.

Kate's is the ultimate paper mill. Choose from more than 5,000 kinds of paper by mining the rich vein of stationery, custom-printing services, journals, photo albums and creative, amazingly beautiful gift wrap.

Other locations: throughout the city.

Nat Sherman

489 Fifth Avenue, between Fifth & Madison Avenues, entrance on 42nd Street (1-212 764 5000/www.natsherman.com). Subway B, D, F, V to 42nd Street-Bryant Park; 7 to Fifth Avenue. **Open** 8.30am-8pm Mon-Fri; 10am-7pm Sat; 11am-5pm Sun. **Credit** AmEx, DC, MC, V. **Map** p404 E24.

Nat Sherman, recently moved into a new premises just across the road, offers its own brand of slow-burning cigarettes, as well as cigars and related accoutrements, for your smoking pleasure. Flick your Bic in the upstairs smoking room.

Pearl Paint

308 Canal Street, between Broadway & Church Street (1-212 431 7932/www.pearlpaint.com). Subway J, M, N, Q, R, W, Z, 6 to Canal Street. **Open** 9am-7pm Mon-Fri; 10am-6.30pm Sat; 10am-6pm Sun. **Credit** AmEx, Disc, MC, V. **Map** p403 E30.

This huge art and drafting supplies commissary sells everything you could possibly need to create your own masterpiece.

Other locations: 207 E 23rd Street, between Second & Third Avenues, Gramercy Park (1-212 592 2179).

Q Security

240 E 29th Street, between Second & Third Avenues (1-212 889 1808). Subway 6 to 33rd Street. **Open** 10am-6.30pm Mon-Fri; noon-5pm Sat. **Credit** AmEx, DC, Disc, MC, V. **Map** p404 F25.

Spy wannabes and budding paranoids can buy body armour or high-powered bugs here. The store will also custom-bulletproof your favourite jacket.

Sports

Blades, Board & Skate

659 Broadway, between Bleecker & Bond Streets (1-212 477 7350/www.blades.com). Subway B, D, F, V to Broadway-Lafayette Street; 6 to Bleecker Street. **Open** 10am-9pm Mon-Sat; 11am-7pm Sun. **Credit** MC, V. **Map** p403 E29.

The requisite clothing and accessories is sold alongside in-line skates, skateboards and snowboards.

Other locations: throughout the city.

Concrete

37 W 13th Street, between Fifth & Sixth Avenues (1-212 242 5770). Subway L, N, Q, R, W, 4, 5, 6 to 14th Street-Union Square. **Open** noon-6pm Mon-Fri. **Credit** AmEx, DC, MC, V. **Map** p403 E27.

Seek and ye shall find: through an unmarked door and down a hallway lies this eensy skate gear paradise, where boarders can watch videos of serious tricks and wince-inducing slams while scoping out decks from Shut NYC ($50).

Gerry Cosby & Co

3 Pennsylvania Plaza, Madison Square Garden, Seventh Avenue, at 32nd Street (1-212 563 6464/ 1-877 563 6464/www.cosbysports.com). Subway A, C, E, 1, 2, 3 to 34th Street-Penn Station. **Open** 9.30am-7.30pm daily. **Credit** AmEx, Disc, MC, V. **Map** p404 D25.

Cosby has a huge selection of official team wear and other sporting necessities for sports nuts of all ages and inclinations. The store is open during – and until 30 minutes after – evening Knicks and Rangers games, in case you feel like celebrating.

Paragon Sporting Goods

867 Broadway, at 18th Street (1-212 255 8036/www.paragonsports.com). Subway L, N, Q, R, W, 4, 5, 6 to 14th Street-Union Square. **Open** 10am-8pm Mon-Sat; 11.30am-7pm Sun. **Credit** AmEx, DC, Disc, MC, V. **Map** p403 E27.

Three floors of equipment and clothing for almost every activity (at every level of expertise) make this New York's sports gear mecca.

Travellers' needs

For shipping packages to your home, *see p371.*

Coach

595 Madison Avenue, at 57th Street (1-212 989 0001/www.coach.com). Subway N, R, W to Fifth Avenue-59th Street. **Open** 10am-8pm Mon-Sat; 11am-6pm Sun. **Credit** AmEx, DC, Disc, MC, V. **Map** p405 E22.

Coach's butter-soft leather briefcases, wallets and handbags have always been exceptional, but the Manhattan Coach stores also stock the label's luxurious outerwear collection.

Other locations: throughout the city.

Flight 001

96 Greenwich Avenue, between Jane & W 12th Streets (1-212 691 1001/www.flight001.com). Subway A, C, E to 14th Street; L to Eighth Avenue. **Open** 11am-8.30pm Mon-Fri; 11am-8pm Sat; noon-6pm Sun. **Credit** AmEx, DC, Disc, MC, V. **Map** p403 D28.

Forgotten something? Or taken greater advantage of New York's shopping than your bags can handle? This one-stop West Village shop carries guidebooks and chic luggage, along with fun travel products such as pocket-size aromatherapy kits. Flight 001's 'essentials' wall features packets of Woolite, mini-dominoes and everything in between.

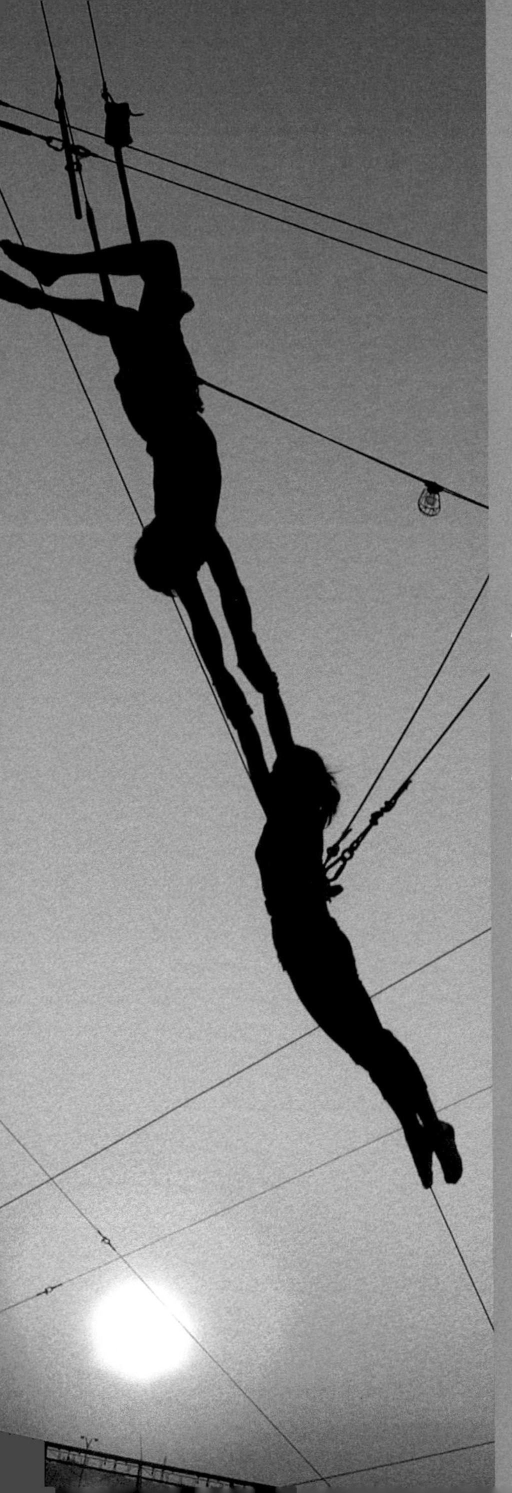

Arts & Entertainment

Festivals & Events	**260**
Art Galleries	**267**
Books & Poetry	**276**
Cabaret & Comedy	**279**
Children	**284**
Clubs	**291**
Film & TV	**298**
Gay & Lesbian	**301**
Music	**312**
Sport & Fitness	**333**
Theatre & Dance	**340**

Features

Cheap date	271
The clubbing commandments	293
DJ profile: Justine D	295
Oh, gay corral!	304
Cheap date	315
Live from New York	324

Trapeze School New York. *See p339.*

Festivals & Events

Come together.

Despite their hard-edged reputation, New Yorkers are a highly sociable bunch – and there are eight million of them, so you can bet that on any day of the week a few hundred are throwing some sort of get-together. Be it a parade, a concert or an art fair, flowers, films or fireworks, NYC has a happening for every taste. For more events, check out the other chapters in the Arts & Entertainment section or have a look at the Around Town section of *Time Out New York* magazine. Keep in mind that before you set out or plan a trip around an event, it's always wise to call and make sure that the fling is still set to swing.

Spring

St Patrick's Day Parade

Fifth Avenue, from 44th to 86th Streets (www.saintpatricksdayparade.com). **Dates** 17 Mar. **Map** *Start* p404 E24. *Finish* p406 E18.

This massive march is one of the city's longest running annual traditions – it dates from 1762. If you feel like braving huge crowds and potentially nasty weather, you'll see thousands of green-clad merrymakers strutting to the sounds of pipe bands. Celebrations continue late into the night as the city's Irish bars teem with suds-swigging revellers.

Ringling Bros and Barnum & Bailey Circus Animal Parade

34th Street, from the Queens Midtown Tunnel to Madison Square Garden, Seventh Avenue, between 31st & 33rd Streets (1-212 307 7171/www.ringling.com). **Dates** Mar. **Map** *Start* p412 U5. *Finish* p404 D25.

Elephants, horses and zebras march through the tunnel and on to the streets of Manhattan in this unmissable spectacle. Midnight parades open and close the circus's Manhattan run.

Easter Parade

Fifth Avenue, from 49th to 57th Streets (1-212 484 1222). Subway E, V to Fifth Avenue-53rd Street. **Dates** 23 Mar. **Map** *Start* p404 E23. *Finish* p405 E22.

Parade is a misnomer for this little festival of creative hat making. Starting at 11am on Easter Sunday, Fifth Avenue becomes a car-free promenade of gussied-up crowds milling and showing off extravagant bonnets. Arrive early to secure a prime viewing spot near St Patrick's Cathedral, at 50th Street. After the parade, head to Tavern on the Green (Central Park West, at 67th Street) for the Mad Hatter's Easter Bonnet Contest, where you'll see even more head-covers.

New York International Auto Show

Jacob K Javits Convention Center, Eleventh Avenue, between 34th & 39th Streets (1-800 282 3336/www.autoshowny.com). Subway A, C, E to 34th Street-Penn Station. **Dates** 21-30 Mar. **Map** p404 B25.

This gearheads' paradise has more than 1,000 autos and futuristic concept cars on display.

Armory Show

Piers 90 & 92, Twelfth Avenue, between 50th & 52nd Streets (1-212 645 6440/www.thearmoryshow.com). Subway C, E to 50th Street. **Dates** 27-30 Mar. **Map** p404 B23.

The show that, in 1913, heralded the arrival of modern art in the US is now a contemporary art mart.

New York Antiquarian Book Fair

Park Avenue Armory, Park Avenue, between 66th & 67th Streets (1-212 777 5218/www.sanfordsmith.com). Subway 6 to 68th Street-Hunter College. **Dates** 4-6 Apr. **Map** p405 E21.

Book dealers from around the globe showcase first editions, illuminated manuscripts and all manner of rare and antique tomes; you'll even find original screenplays and shooting scripts.

Tribeca Film Festival

Various Tribeca locations (1-212 941 2400/www.tribecafilmfestival.org). Subway A, C, 1, 2, 3 to Chambers Street. **Dates** 23 Apr-4 May.

Organised by neighbourhood resident Robert De Niro, this festival is packed with hundreds of screenings of independent and international films; it's attended by more than 300,000 film fans.

Cherry Blossom Festival

For listing, see p164 Brooklyn Botanic Garden. **Dates** late Apr/early May.

Nature's springtime blooms adorn the garden's 200-plus cherry trees at this annual festival, which features performances, demonstrations and workshops.

Global Marijuana March

March starts Broadway, at Houston Street, and proceeds to Battery Park (1-212 677 7180). **Dates** 3 May. **Map** *Start* p403 E29. *Finish* p402 E34.

A good place to meet local stoners, this annual march (which takes place simultaneously in cities around the world) is mainly a rally for legalisation.

Bike New York: The Great Five Boro Bike Tour

Battery Park to Staten Island (1-212 932 2453/www.bikenewyork.org). Subway A, C, J, M, Z, 1, 2, 3 to Chambers Street; R, W to City Hall; 4, 5, 6 to Brooklyn Bridge-City Hall, then bike to Battery Park. **Dates** 4 May. **Map** p402 E34.

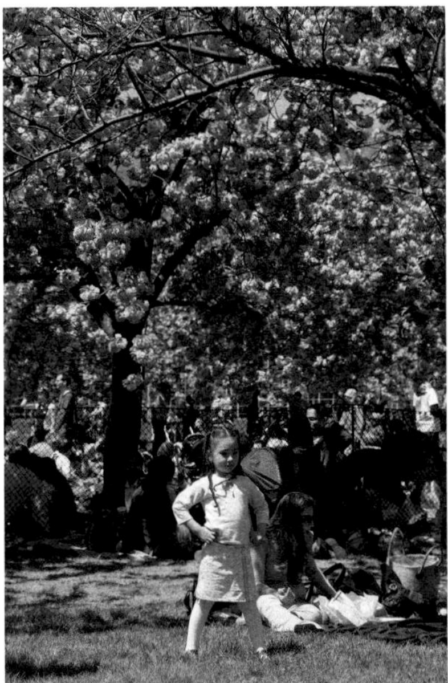

The **Cherry Blossom Festival** springs eternal.

Thousands of cyclists take over the city for a 42-mile Tour de New York. (Pedestrians and motorists should plan on extra getting-around time.) Advance registration is required. Event organisers suggest the trains listed above, as some subway exits below Chambers Street may be closed to bike-toting cyclists for safety reasons, and bikes are not allowed at the South Ferry (1 train), Whitehall Street (R, W) and Bowling Green (4, 5) stations.

High Line Festival

Various locations in Chelsea (www.highlinefestival.com). Subway A, C, E , L to 14th Street; C, E to 23rd Street. **Dates** mid May.

In 2007, David Bowie curated the first annual High Line Festival. The event celebrates the much-anticipated High Line Park (*see p118* **Walking the line**), an elevated train track (stretching from Gansevoort to 34th Street along Tenth Avenue in Chelsea) that is being refurbished as a verdant pedestrian walkway. The ten-day music and arts extravaganza is set to become the next big arts fest.

Bryant Park Free Summer Season

Bryant Park, Sixth Avenue, at 42nd Street (1-212 768 4242/www.bryantpark.org). Subway B, D, F, V to 42nd Street-Bryant Park; 7 to Fifth Avenue. **Dates** May-Aug. **Map** p404 E24.

One of the highlights of the park's free entertainment season is the ever-popular Monday night alfresco movie series, but there's plenty of fun in the daylight hours as well. You can catch Broadway musical numbers as part of the Broadway in Bryant Park series; *Good Morning America* mini-concerts featuring big-name acts; and a variety of readings, classes and public art projects.

Lower East Side Festival of the Arts

Theater for the New City, 155 First Avenue, between 9th & 10th Streets (1-212 254 1109/www.theaterforthenewcity.net). Subway L to First Avenue; 6 to Astor Place. **Dates** 23-25 May. **Map** p403 F28.

This celebration of artistic diversity features performances by dozens of theatrical troupes, poetry readings, films and family-friendly programming.

Red Hook Waterfront Arts Festival

Various locations in Red Hook, Brooklyn (1-718 596 2507/www.bwac.org). Subway A, C, F to Jay Street-Borough Hall, then B61 bus to Van Brunt Street; F, G to Smith-9th Streets, then B77 bus to Van Brunt Street. **Dates** late May/early June.

This rapidly evolving neighbourhood cultural bash includes dance and music performances, along with the Brooklyn Waterfront Artists' Pier Show.

Washington Square Outdoor Art Exhibit

Various streets surrounding Washington Square Park (1-212 982 6255). Subway A, B, C, D, E, F, V to W 4th Street; R, W to 8th Street-NYU. **Dates** 24-26, 30, 31 May; 1 June; 30, 31 Aug; 1, 5-7 Sept (2008).

Exhibitors here show off photography, sculpture, paintings and one-of-a-kind crafts. It's a great way for browsers and buyers to spend an afternoon.

SOFA New York

Seventh Regiment Armory, 643 Park Avenue, at 67th Street (1-800 563 7632/www.sofaexpo.com). Subway 6 to 68th Street-Hunter College. **Dates** 29 May-1 June. **Map** p405 E21.

Browse this giant show of Sculptural Objects and Functional Art, and you might find that perfect conversation piece for your home.

Summer

Met in the Parks

Various locations (1-212 362 6000/www.metopera.org). **Dates** June.

The Metropolitan Opera (*see p327*) stages free opera performances in Central Park and other NYC parks in June every year. Grab a blanket, pack a picnic (no alcohol or glass bottles) and show up in the afternoon to nab a good spot.

Central Park SummerStage

Rumsey Playfield, Central Park, entrance on Fifth Avenue, at 72nd Street (1-212 360 2777/www.summerstage.org). Subway 6 to 68th Street-Hunter College. **Dates** June-Aug. **Map** p405 E20.

A festival that breaks down the boundaries between artistic mediums. Rockers, symphonies, authors and dance companies take over the stage at this very popular, mostly free annual series. Show up early or plan to listen from outside the gates (not a bad option if you bring a blanket and snacks). Benefit shows and special events carry ticket prices.

Shakespeare in the Park at the Delacorte Theater

For listing, see p349. **Dates** June-Aug.

One of Manhattan's best summer events – at the Delacorte Theater in Central Park – gets stars to pull on tights and take a whack at the Bard. *Photo p265.*

River to River Festival

Various venues along the West Side & southern waterfronts of Manhattan (www.rivertorivernyc.org). **Dates** June-Sept.

Lower Manhattan organisations and venues come together to present more than 500 free events in some of the city's coolest waterfront locations. Musical performers last year ranged from Arlo Guthrie to Yo La Tengo. The Hudson River Festival (1-212 528 2733, www.hudsonriverfestival.com) augments the affair with visual arts shows, walking tours, theatre, dance and family events, and additional concert programming is produced in conjunction with the always popular Seaport Music Festival (www.seaportmusicfestival.com, June-Aug).

Museum Mile Festival

Fifth Avenue, from 82nd to 105th Streets (1-212 606 2296/www.museummilefestival.org). **Dates** 10 June. **Map** *Start* p405 E19. *Finish* p406 E16.

For one day each year, nine of the city's major museums open their doors free of charge to the public. You can also catch live music, street performers and other arty happenings along Fifth Avenue.

National Puerto Rican Day Parade

Fifth Avenue, from 44th to 86th Streets (1-718 401 0404). **Dates** 14 June. **Map** *Start* p404 E24. *Finish* p406 E18.

Salsa music blares, and scantily clad revellers dance along the route and ride colourful floats at this freewheeling party celebrating the city's single largest Hispanic community.

Broadway Bares

Roseland Ballroom, 239 W 52nd Street, between Broadway & Eighth Avenue (1-212 840 0770/www.broadwaycares.org). Subway 1 to 50th Street. **Dates** mid June. **Map** p404 D23.

Equal parts ingenius and unusual, this new annual fundraiser for Broadway Cares/Equity Fights AIDS is your chance to see some of the Great White Way's hottest bodies sans costumes. Broadway Cares also hosts an annual auction of star-autographed teddy bears ('Broadway Bears') in February, and a show-tune-filled Easter Bonnet Competition in April, as well as several other fun theatre-themed events throughout the year.

JVC Jazz Festival

Various locations (1-212 501 1390/www.festivalproductions.net). **Dates** last 2wks June.

A direct descendant of the Newport Jazz Festival, this jazz bash is a New York City institution. The festival not only fills Carnegie and Avery Fisher Halls with big draws, but also sponsors gigs in Harlem and downtown clubs.

Mermaid Parade

Coney Island, Brooklyn (1-718 372 5159/www.coneyisland.com). Subway D, F, N, Q to Coney Island-Stillwell Avenue. **Date** 22 June.

Decked-out mermaids and mermen of all shapes, sizes and ages share the parade route with elaborate, kitschy floats, come rain or shine. It's the wackiest summer solstice event you'll likely ever witness, and draws a suitably diverse crowd as a direct result. Check the website for details, as the parade location varies from year to year.

Central Park SummerStage. *See p261.*

Gay & Lesbian Pride March

From Fifth Avenue, at 52nd Street to Christopher Street (1-212 807 7433/www.hopinc.org). **Dates** 23 June. **Map** *Start* p404 E23. *Finish* p403 D29.

Downtown Manhattan becomes a sea of rainbow flags as gays and lesbians from the city and beyond parade down Fifth Avenue in commemoration of the 1969 Stonewall Riots. After the march, there's a massive street fair and a dance on the West Side piers.

Summer Restaurant Week

Various locations (www.nycvisit.com/restaurantweek). **Date** late June/early July.

Gastronomes take note: twice a year, for two weeks at a stretch, some of the city's finest restaurants dish out three-course prix-fixe lunches for $20.07; some places also offer dinner for $30.07 (the lunch price reflects the year). For the full list of participating restaurants, visit the website. The whole thing is understandably popular and you are advised to make reservations well in advance.

Midsummer Night Swing

Lincoln Center Plaza, Columbus Avenue, between 64th & 65th Streets (1-212 875 5766/www.lincoln center.org). Subway 1 to 66th Street-Lincoln Center. **Dates** late June-mid July. **Map** p405 C21.

Lincoln Center's plaza is turned into a giant dance-floor as bands play salsa, Cajun, swing and other music. Each night is devoted to a different dance style; parties are preceded by lessons.

Celebrate Brooklyn! Performing Arts Festival

Prospect Park Bandshell, Prospect Park West, at 9th Street, Park Slope, Brooklyn (1-718 855 7882/www. celebratebrooklyn.org). Subway F to Seventh Avenue. **Dates** late June-late Aug. **Map** p410 T12.

A series of major outdoor events that includes music, dance, film and spoken-word acts. Huge crowds flock to the park's bandshell to hear artists such as They Might Be Giants and Los Lobos. A token $3 donation is requested, and admission is charged for a few benefit shows.

Nathan's Famous Fourth of July Hot Dog Eating Contest

Outside Nathan's Famous, corner of Surf & Stillwell Avenues, Coney Island, Brooklyn (www.nathans famous.com). Subway D, F, N, Q to Coney Island-Stillwell Avenue. **Dates** 4 July.

Liable to amuse and appal in equal meaure, there's no denying the bizarre fascination of Nathan's. Competitive eaters gather from all over the world to pig out at this, the granddaddy of pig-out contests, which has been happening annually in Coney Island for more than a decade.

Macy's Fireworks Display

East River, location varies (1-212 494 4495). **Dates** 4 July at around 9pm.

This world-famous annual fireworks display is the city's star attraction on Independence Day. The pyrotechnics are launched from barges on the East River, so look for outdoor vantage points along the lower FDR Drive (closed to traffic), the Brooklyn and Long Island City waterfronts, or on Roosevelt Island. Keep in mind, however, that spectators are packed like sardines at prime public spots, so many choose to view the display from a distance. *Photo p266.*

Spiegeltent

South Street Seaport, Pier 17, Fulton Street, at South Street (1-212 279 4200/www.spiegelworld. com). Subway A, C to Broadway-Nassau Street; J, M, Z, 2, 3, 4, 5 to Fulton Street. **Dates** Aug. **Map** p402 F33.

The grand European tradition known as the Spiegeltent – complete with a line-up of stellar performers and a beer garden – arrives in Manhattan for two (to three) months of rousing entertainment. The schedule is always action packed with a diverse array of performers, such as burlesque, drag, family-friendly fare, artistic activism and all kinds of music. Performance Space 122 (*see p351*) also presents a varied roster of artists.

New York Philharmonic Concerts in the Parks

Various locations (1-212 875 5900/www.newyork philharmonic.org). **Dates** July-Aug.

The New York Philharmonic has presented a varied classical music programme in many of New York's larger parks for more than 40 years.

Seaside Summer & Martin Luther King Jr Concert Series

Various locations (1-718 469 1912/www.brooklyn concerts.com). **Dates** July-Aug.

Pack a picnic, grab a lawn chair and listen to free pop, funk, soul and gospel at these highly popular outdoor concerts in Brooklyn.

P.S.1 Warm Up

For listing, see p297 P.S.1 Contemporary Art Center. **Dates** *July-Sept* 3-9pm Sat.

For years, this weekly Saturday afternoon bash in the museum's courtyard has drawn fashionable types from all over the city to dance, drink beer and relax in a beach-like environment. Local and international DJs and bands provide the soundtrack, which is as diverse as can be.

Mostly Mozart

Lincoln Center, Columbus Avenue, between 64th & 65th Streets (1-212 875 5766/www.lincolncenter. org). Subway 1 to 66th Street-Lincoln Center. **Dates** late July-Aug. **Map** p405 C21.

For more than 35 years, this four-week-long festival has been mounting a packed schedule of works by Mozart and his contemporaries.

Lincoln Center Out of Doors Festival

For listing, see p328 Lincoln Center. **Dates** Aug.

Free dance, music, theatre, opera and more make up this ambitious and family-friendly festival of classic and contemporary works.

New York International Fringe Festival

Various locations (1-212 279 4488/www.fringenyc.org). **Dates** Aug.

Wacky, weird and sometimes great, Downtown's Fringe Festival shoehorns hundreds of performances into 16 theatre-crammed days.

Harlem Week

Various Harlem locations (1-212 862 8477/www.harlemdiscover.com). Subway B, C, 2, 3 to 135th Street. **Dates** Aug.

Get into the groove at this massive street fair, which serves up live music, art and food along 135th Street. Concerts, film, dance, fashion and sports events are on tap all week.

Central Park Zoo Chillout! Weekend

Central Park, entrance on Fifth Avenue, at 65th Street (1-212 439 6500/www.wcs.org). Subway N, R, W to Fifth Avenue-59th Street; 4, 5, 6 to 59th Street. **Dates** early Aug. **Map** p405 E21.

If you're roaming the city's streets during the dog days of August, this two-day party offers the perfect chilly treat. The weekend freeze-fest features penguin and polar-bear talent shows, games, zookeeper challenges and other frosty fun.

Autumn

West Indian-American Day Carnival

Eastern Parkway, from Utica Avenue to Grand Army Plaza, Brooklyn (1-718 467 1797/www.wiadca.org). Subway 2, 3 to Grand Army Plaza; 3, 4 to Crown Heights-Utica Avenue. **Dates** 2 Sept. **Map** *Start* off map. *Finish* p410 U11.

The streets come alive with the jubilant clangour of steel-drum bands and the steady throb of calypso and soca music at this colourful cultural celebration. Mas bands – elaborately costumed marchers – dance along the parade route, thousands move to the beat on sidewalks, and vendors sell Caribbean crafts, clothing, souvenirs and food.

Howl!

Various East Village locations (1-212 505 2225/www.howlfestival.com). **Dates** 4-7 Sept.

Taking its name from the seminal poem by longtime neighbourhood resident Allen Ginsberg, this all-things-East Village fest is a grab bag of art events, films, performance art, readings and much more. The event is an excellent way to dip into local life, not to mention a buzzing hub for beatniks and Bohemians of all ages and inclinations.

Broadway on Broadway

43rd Street, at Broadway (1-212 768 1560/www.broadwayonbroadway.com). Subway N, Q, R, W to 42nd Street; S, 1, 2, 3, 7 to 42nd Street-Times Square. **Dates** early-mid Sept. **Map** p404 D24.

Broadway's biggest stars convene in the middle of Times Square to belt out show-stopping numbers. The season's new productions mount sneak previews, and it's all free.

Atlantic Antic

Atlantic Avenue, from Fourth Avenue to Hicks Street, Brooklyn (1-718 875 8993/www.atlanticave.org). Subway B, Q, 2, 3, 4, 5 to Atlantic Avenue; D, M, N, R to Pacific Street. **Dates** mid Sept. **Map** *Start* p410 T10. *Finish* p410 S10.

Entertainment, ethnic foods, kids' activities and the inimitable World Cheesecake-Eating Contest pack the avenue with wide-eyed punters at this monumental Brooklyn festival.

CMJ Music Marathon & FilmFest

Various locations (1-917 606 1908/www.cmj.com). **Dates** mid Sept.

The annual *College Music Journal* schmooze-fest draws thousands of young fans and music-industry types to one of the best showcases for new rock, indie rock, hip hop and electronica acts. The FilmFest, which runs in tandem with the music blow-out, includes a wide range of feature and short films, many music-related, and pulls in a crowd that's suitably hip and happening.

Feast of San Gennaro

Mulberry Street, from Canal to Houston Streets (1-212 768 9320/www.sangennaro.org). Subway B, D, F, V to Broadway-Lafayette Street; J, M, N, Q, R, W, Z, 6 to Canal Street. **Dates** mid Sept. **Map** p404 F30.

This massive street fair stretches along the main drag of what's left of Little Italy. Come on opening and closing days to see the marching band of old-timers, or after dark, when sparkling lights arch over Mulberry Street and the smells of frying *zeppole* and sausages hang in the sultry air.

Next Wave Festival

For listing, see p327 Brooklyn Academy of Music. **Dates** 1 Oct-15 Dec.

The best of the best in the city's avant-garde music, dance, theatre and opera scenes are performed at this lengthy annual affair.

New York Film Festival

Alice Tully Hall, Avery Fisher Hall & Walter Reade Theater at Lincoln Center, Broadway, at 65th Street (1-212 875 5050/www.filmlinc.com). Subway 1 to 66th Street-Lincoln Center. **Dates** 26 Sept-12 Oct. **Map** p405 C21.

This uptown institution, founded in 1962, is still a worthy cinematic showcase, packed with premières, features and short flicks from around the globe, plus a stellar list of cinematic celebrities for the various red-carpet events.

Open House New York

Various locations (1-917 583 2398/www.ohny.org). **Dates** 4 & 5 Oct.

Get an insider's view – literally – of the city that even most locals haven't seen. More than 100 sites of architectural interest that are normally off-limits to visitors throw open their doors and welcome the curious during a weekend of urban exploration. A range of lectures and an educational programme are also on offer all week.

Bard for life: **Shakespeare in the Park at the Delacorte Theater**. *See p262.*

d.u.m.b.o. art under the bridge

Various locations in Dumbo, Brooklyn (1-718 694 0831/www.dumboartscenter.org). Subway A, C to High Street; F to York Street. **Dates** mid Oct.

Dumbo has become something of a Brooklyn art destination, and this weekend of art appreciation is a hugely popular event among local creative types. The progamme features concerts, forums, a short-film series and in-studio visits.

Village Halloween Parade

Sixth Avenue, from Spring to 22nd Streets (www.halloween-nyc.com). **Dates** 8pm 31 Oct. **Map** *Start* p403 E30. *Finish* p404 D26.

The sidewalks at this iconic Village shindig are always packed beyond belief. For the best vantage point, put on a colourful costume and watch from inside the parade (line-up starts at 6.30pm on Sixth Avenue, at Spring Street).

New York City Marathon

Staten Island side of the Verrazano-Narrows Bridge, to Tavern on the Green, in Central Park (1-212 423 2249/www.nycmarathon.org). **Dates** 2 Nov.

The sight of 35,000 marathoners hotfooting it through all five boroughs over a 26.2-mile course is an impressive one. Scope out a spot somewhere in the middle (the starting and finish lines are mobbed) to get a good view of the herd.

Macy's Thanksgiving Day Parade & Eve Balloon Blowup

Central Park West, at 77th Street to Macy's, Broadway, at 34th Street (1-212 494 4495/www.macysparade.com). **Dates** 9am 27 Nov. **Map** *Start* p405 D19. *Finish* p404 D25.

The stars of this nationally televised parade are the gigantic balloons, the elaborate floats and good ol' Santa Claus. New Yorkers brave the cold night air to watch the rubbery colossi take their shape at the inflation area on the night before Thanksgiving (from 77th to 81st Streets, between Central Park West & Columbus Avenue).

Winter

Radio City Christmas Spectacular

For listing, see p319 Radio City Music Hall. **Dates** Nov-early Jan.

The high-kicking Rockettes and an onstage nativity scene with live animals are the attractions at this (pricey) annual homage to the Yuletide season.

The Nutcracker

New York State Theater, Lincoln Center, Columbus Avenue, at 63rd Street (1-212 870 5570/www.nycballet.com). Subway 1 to 66th Street-Lincoln Center. **Dates** 29 Nov-1st wk in Jan. **Map** p405 C21.

Performed by the New York City Ballet, George Balanchine's fantasy world of fairies, princes and toy soldiers is a family-friendly holiday diversion.

Christmas Tree-Lighting Ceremony

Rockefeller Center, Fifth Avenue, between 49th & 50th Streets (1-212 332 6868/www.rockefellercenter.com). Subway B, D, F, V to 47th-50th Streets-Rockefeller Center. **Dates** late Nov/early Dec. **Map** p404 E23.

The crowds can be overwhelming here, even if you stake out a place early. Those who brace them will witness celebrity appearances and pop-star performances. But there's plenty of time during the holiday season to marvel at the giant evergreen.

The National Chorale Messiah Sing-In

Avery Fisher Hall, Lincoln Center, Columbus Avenue, at 65th Street (1-212 333 5333/www.lincolncenter.org/www.nationalchorale.org). Subway 1 to 66th Street-Lincoln Center. **Dates** 16 Dec. **Map** p405 C21.

Hallelujah! Chase those holiday blues away by joining with the National Chorale and hundreds of your fellow audience members in a rehearsal and performance of Handel's *Messiah*. No previous singing experience is necessary to take part, and you can buy the score on site, though picking one up early for advance perusal would certainly help novices.

Macy's Fireworks Display. *See p263.*

New Year's Eve Ball Drop

Times Square (1-212 768 1560/www.timessquare bid.org). Subway N, Q, R, W, 42nd Street S, 1, 2, 3, 7 to 42nd Street-Times Square. **Dates** 31 Dec. **Map** p404 D24.

Meet up with half a million others and watch the giant illuminated ball descend amid a blizzard of confetti and cheering. Expect freezing temperatures, densely packed crowds, absolutely no bathrooms – and very tight security.

New Year's Eve Fireworks

Naumburg Bandshell, middle of Central Park, at 72nd Street (www.centralparknyc.org). Subway B, C to 72nd Street; 6 to 68th Street-Hunter College. **Dates** 31 Dec. **Map** p405 E20.

The fireworks explode at midnight, and there's a variety of evening festivities, including dancing and a costume contest. The best views are from Tavern on the Green (at 67th Street), Central Park West (at 72nd Street) and Fifth Avenue (at 90th Street).

New Year's Eve Midnight Run

Naumburg Bandshell, middle of Central Park, at 72nd Street (1-212 860 4455/www.nyrrc.org). Subway B, C to 72nd Street; 6 to 68th Street-Hunter College. **Dates** 31 Dec. **Map** p405 E20.

Start the new year with a four-mile jog through the park. There's also a masquerade parade, fireworks, prizes and a booze-free toast at the halfway mark.

New Year's Day Marathon Poetry Reading

For listing, see p278 Poetry Project. **Dates** 1 Jan.

Big-name Bohemians (Patti Smith, Richard Hell, Jim Carroll) step up to the mic during this free, all-day spoken-word spectacle.

Winter Antiques Show

Seventh Regiment Armory, 643 Park Avenue, between 66th & 67th Streets (1-718 292 7392/www.winterantiquesshow.com). Subway 6 to 68th Street-Hunter College. **Dates** 18-27 Jan. **Map** p405 E21.

One of the world's most prestigious antiques shows, this event brings together more than 70 American and international dealers.

Winter Restaurant Week

For listing, see p263 Summer Restaurant Week. **Date** late Jan/early Feb.

The Winter Restaurant Week provides yet another opportunity to sample delicious gourmet food at soup-kitchen prices (well, almost).

Chinese New Year

Around Mott Street, Chinatown (1-212 966 0100). Subway J, M, N, Q, R, W, Z, 6 to Canal Street. **Dates** 7 Feb.

Gung hay fat choy!, the greeting goes. Chinatown bustles with colour and is charged with energy during the two weeks of the Lunar New Year. Festivities on hand include a staged fireworks display, a vivid dragon parade (which snakes in and out of several Chinese restaurants), various performances and a predictable wealth of delicious Chinese food. 2008 is the year of the Rat.

Art Show

Seventh Regiment Armory, 643 Park Avenue, between 66th & 67th Streets (1-212 940 8590/www.art dealers.org). Subway 6 to 68th Street-Hunter College. **Dates** 21-25 Feb. **Map** p405 E21.

Whether you're a serious collector or just a casual art fan, this vast fair is a great chance to peruse some of the world's most impressive for-sale pieces dating from the 17th century to the present.

Galleries

Canvas city.

Looking for visual stimulation? Boy, have you come to the right place. The art scene is booming in New York right now, not only in the 300-plus galleries in Chelsea and the freshly opened venues in newly thriving clusters throughout the boroughs, but also in shop windows, office building lobbies and even on the dividing median in the middle of Park Avenue. These days it seems like you couldn't avoid seeing art if you tried. The recent swell of commercial interest in the scene, which has pushed prices for art through the roof, has given the whole industry a boost (*see pp45-48* **Art Goes Boom**). Blue chip giants sit cheek-by-jowl with small but influential not-for-profit spaces in West Chelsea, which is (for now) the centre of the contemporary art frenzy. In the sleek white cubes of this area, you'll find group shows of up-and-comers, blockbuster exhibits of art world celebrities and a slew of seriously provocative, cutting-edge work in between.

Those with more traditional tastes will find what they're looking for Uptown, where the **Museum Mile** galleries are filled with works by the old masters, while the old-guard 57th Street crew turns out a continuous series of blue-chip shows. **Soho**, the Chelsea of the 1980s, still lays claim to some top-quality galleries and not-for-profit spaces, while the nearby **Lower East Side** rumbles with new activity. As we went to press, two newcomers were poised to open in the neighbourhood: Eleven Rivington (11 Rivington Street), helmed by artist and curator Augusto Arbizo, a 700-square-foot space from the sophisticated Uptown gallery Greenberg Van Doren; and an offshoot of Chelsea mainstay Lehmann Maupin (201 Chrystie Street) will open with a show from Korean artist Do-Ho Suh in November 2007.

The ever-gentrifying **Williamsburg** is spawning contemporary galleries at breakneck speed, while the **Cobble Hill** area shows more leisurely signs of expansion. Even **Dumbo**, with a handful of interesting art venues along its waterfront, is worth a gander. Queens' own artistic hotbed lies in **Long Island City**, where MoMA's scrappier younger sibling **P.S.1 Contemporary Art Center** (*see p171*) never fails to gratify the art pilgrims who venture there. In short, art is taking over the city, infiltrating the far reaches of our boroughs, and no one is sorry to hear it.

Before you hit the pavement, be sure to consult *Time Out New York* magazine for reliable and up-to-date listings and reviews, or the Friday and Sunday editions of the *New York Times*. For unopinionated (yet extensive) listings, pick up the monthly *Gallery Guide* (www.galleryguide.org). It's usually available in galleries for free, or alternatively for around $3 at newsstands across the city.

Note that galleries are generally closed on Mondays and holidays (*see p376* **Holidays**), and many are open only on weekdays from May or June to early September – some close for the entire month of August. Summer hours are listed for most venues, but it's always wise to call first before heading out.

Lower East Side

The Lower East Side is without a doubt the new 'it' art neighbourhood. Established Uptown galleries are getting in on the action by opening outposts in the area, while newer names – and the **New Museum of Contemporary Art** (*see p113*) – are setting up shop here too.

Subway *F to East Broadway or Delancey Street; F, V to Lower East Side-Second Avenue; J, M, Z to Delancey-Essex Streets.*

Miguel Abreu Gallery

36 Orchard Street, between Canal & Hester Streets (1-212 995 1774/www.miguelabreugallery.com). **Open** *Sept-July* 11am-6.30pm Wed-Sun. Phone for summer hours. **Map** p403 G30.

In March 2006, acutely intellectual filmmaker Abreu opened his space with an exhibition juxtaposing two films by Jean-Marie Straub and Daniele Huillet with a series of paintings by Blake Rayne. The gallery represents such inspired artists as Hans Bellmer, Liz Deschenes and Eileen Quinlan.

Orchard

47 Orchard Street, between Grand & Hester Streets (1-212 219 1061/www.orchard47.org). **Open** *Sept-July* 1-6pm Thur-Sun. **Map** p403 G30.

Orchard is a 12-person collaboration of artists, film-makers, critics and curators (the cohort includes Andrea Fraser, Rebecca Quaytman and Gareth

▶ For more information on the current boom taking the New York art world by storm, *see pp45-48* **Art Goes Boom**.

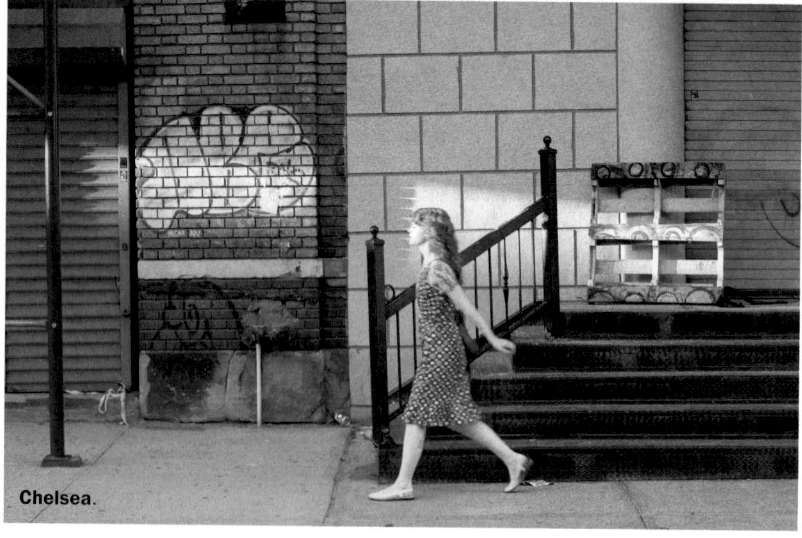

Chelsea.

James). While most art galleries focus on developing artists' careers, Orchard's mission is stewardship – both of art history (screening a Michael Asher film unseen since the 1970s, for instance) and also political consciousness.

Reena Spaulings Fine Art

165 East Broadway, at Rutgers Sreet (1-212 477 5006/www.reenaspaulings.com). **Open** *Sept-July* noon-6pm Thur-Sun. **Map** p402 G31.

What started as artist Emily Sundblad's storefront studio has become – with help from critic and gallery co-founder John Kelsey – Reena Spaulings Fine Art. Since 2004, the establishment has housed conceptual collaborative exhibitions, as well as solo shows by up-and-coming artists from the US and Europe. Seth Price, Jutta Koether and Josh Smith are among the artists who have exhibited here.

Rivington Arms

4 E 2nd Street, at Bowery (1-646 654 3213/www.rivingtonarms.com). **Open** *Sept-July* 11am-6pm Tue-Fri; noon-6pm Sat, Sun. *Aug* noon-6pm Mon-Fri. **Map** p403 F29.

This intimate storefront space, run by Melissa Bent and Mirabelle Marden (painter Brice Marden's daughter), has attracted both a fashionable crowd of followers and enviable critical kudos.

Soho

The main concentration of Manhattan galleries may have shifted to the western blocks of Chelsea, but a few worthwhile additions have opened up here in recent years and a number of the city's most important not-for-profit venues continue to make the area a vital stop for more creatively minded culture vultures.

Subway *A, C, E, J, M, N, Q, R, W, Z, 1, 6 to Canal Street; B, D, F, V to Broadway-Lafayette Street; N, R, W to Prince Street; 6 to Spring Street.*

Deitch Projects

18 Wooster Street, between Canal & Grand Streets (1-212 343 7300/www.deitch.com). **Open** noon-6pm Tue-Sat. **Map** p403 E30.

Jeffrey Deitch is an art-world impresario whose gallery features live spectacles, as well as large-scale, sometimes overly ambitious efforts by artists working in virtually all media. (By comparison, Deitch's original Grand Street site seems small and sedate, but it's the one of his two Soho spaces that we most confidently recommend.) Solo shows, by the likes of Yoko Ono and, more recently, Michel Gondr aim to be both complex and accessible.

Other locations: 6 Grand Street, at Wooster Street (1-212 343 7300).

Gavin Brown

620 Greenwich Street, at Leroy Street (1-212 627 5258/www.gavinbrown.biz). **Open** *Sept-July* 10am-6pm Tue-Sat. *Aug* 10am-6pm Mon-Fri. **Map** p403 D29.

London hotshot Brown made a splash in Chelsea by debuting such art stars as Elizabeth Peyton and Chris Ofili. Recently, after opening popular bar Passerby adjoining the 15th Street space, he turned his attention to Soho, where this informal gallery showcases the creative output of Rob Pruitt and Peter Doig, among others.

Guild and Greyshkul

28 Wooster Street, between Canal & Grand Streets (1-212 625-9224/www.guildgreyshkul.com). **Open** *Sept-July* 11am-6pm Tue-Sat. *Aug* 11am-6pm Mon-Fri. **Map** p403 E30.

Three up-and-coming artists, Sara and Johannes VanDerBeek (children of the late filmmaker Stan VanDerBeek) and their friend Anya Kielar, opened this studio and exhibition space in 2003 with the aim of fostering intellectual exchange among their peers. The gallery met with great success almost immediately and expanded in 2005.

Maccarone

630 Greenwich Street, at Morton Street (1-212 431 4977/www.maccarone.net). **Open** *Sept-July* 10am-6pm Tue-Sat. *Aug* 10am-6pm Mon-Fri. **Map** p403 D29.

The flighty Michele Maccarone, whom Jerry Saltz once called 'our own Calamity Jane/Peggy Guggenheim', recently relocated to this 8,000 sq ft space, where she dedicates herself to representing Nate Lowman, Corey McCorkle and Christian Jankowski, among others.

Peter Blum

99 Wooster Street, between Prince & Spring Streets (1-212 343 0441/www.peterblumgallery.com). **Open** *Sept-June* 10am-6pm Tue-Fri; 11am-6pm Sat. Closed Aug. **Map** p403 E30

This elegant space is manned by a dealer with an impeccable eye and wide tastes. Past exhibitions have run the gamut from drawings by art stars Robert Ryman and Alex Katz to terracotta funerary figures from West Africa and colourful quilts from the hands of noted African-American folk artist Rosie Lee Tompkins.

Chelsea

Chelsea has the city's highest concentration of galleries; just be advised that it can be hard to see even half the neighbourhood in one day. The subway takes you only as far as Eighth Avenue, so you'll have to walk at least one long block westward to get to the galleries. You can also take the M23 crosstown bus.

Subway *A, C, E to 14th Street; C, E to 23rd Street; L to Eighth Avenue.*

Alexander & Bonin

132 Tenth Avenue, between 18th & 19th Streets (1-212 367 7474/www.alexanderandbonin.com). **Open** *Sept-June* 10am-6pm Tue-Sat. *July* 10am-6pm Tue-Fri. *Aug* by appointment only. **Map** p403 C27.

This long, cool drink of an exhibition space features contemporary painting, sculpture and photography by artists such as Willie Doherty, Mona Hatoum, Rita McBride, Doris Salcedo and Paul Thek.

Andrea Rosen Gallery

525 W 24th Street, between Tenth & Eleventh Avenues (1-212 627 6000/www.andrearosen gallery.com). **Open** *Sept-June* 10am-6pm Tue-Sat. *July, Aug* 10am-6pm Mon-Fri. **Map** p404 C26.

During the past 17 years, Andrea Rosen has established several major careers: the late Felix Gonzalez-Torres got his start here (the gallery now handles the artist's estate), as did Wolfgang Tillmans, Andrea Zittel and John Currin (who left for the Gagosian Gallery in 2003). Recent additions to the gallery's roster, such as the much-touted young sculptor David Altmejd, promise great things.

Andrew Kreps Gallery

525 W 22nd Street, between Tenth & Eleventh Avenues (1-212 741 8849/www.andrewkreps.com). **Open** *Sept-June* 10am-6pm Tue-Sat. *July, Aug* 10am-6pm Mon-Fri. **Map** p404 C26.

The radicals in Andrew Kreps's adventurous stable of artists include Ricci Albenda, Roe Ethridge, Robert Melee and Ruth Root.

Anton Kern Gallery

532 W 20th Street, between Tenth & Eleventh Avenues (1-212 367 9663/www.antonkerngallery.com). **Open** *Sept-June* 10am-6pm Tue-Sat. *July, Aug* 10am-6pm Mon-Fri. **Map** p403 C27.

The son of artist Georg Baselitz, Kern presents young American and European artists whose installations have provided the New York art scene with some of its most visionary shows. The likes of Kai Althoff, Sarah Jones and Jim Lambie show here.

Barbara Gladstone

515 W 24th Street, between Tenth & Eleventh Avenues (1-212 206 9300/www.gladstonegallery.com). **Open** *Sept-July* 10am-6pm Tue-Sat. *Aug* 10am-6pm Mon-Fri. **Map** p404 C26.

Gladstone is strictly blue-chip, focusing on the conceptualist and the daring. Matthew Barney, Sarah Lucas and Anish Kapoor exhibit. *Photos pp272-273.*

Bellwether

134 Tenth Avenue, between 18th & 19th Streets (1-212 929 5959/www.bellwethergallery.com). **Open** *Sept-June* 10am-6pm Tue-Sat. *July, Aug* 11am-6pm Mon-Fri. **Map** p403 C27.

The hot-pink luminous neon sign in the window heralds the arrival of this former Brooklyn stalwart over the river at its street-level digs in Chelsea. Setting trends within the art world since 1999, Bellwether represents such promising talents as Ellen Altfest, Adam Cvijanovic and Amy Wilson.

Daniel Reich Gallery

537A W 23rd Street, between Tenth & Eleventh Avenues (1-212 924 4949/www.danielreich gallery.com). **Open** *Sept-June* 11am-6pm Tue-Sat. *July, Aug* 11am-6pm Mon-Fri. **Map** p404 C26.

Young gallerist Daniel Reich exhibited works out of his tiny apartment before settling into this current ground-floor space. Despite its white-cube setting, it continues to host a group of artists thinking out of the box, like Christian Holstad, Hernan Bas, Anya Kielar and Futoshi Miyagi.

David Zwirner

525 W 19th Street, between Tenth & Eleventh Avenues (1-212 727 2070/www.davidzwirner.com). **Open** *Sept-June* 10am-6pm Tue-Sat. *July, Aug* 10am-6pm Mon-Fri. **Map** p403 C27.

German expatriate David Zwirner has assembled a genuinely head-turning roster of international contemporary artists on his books that includes such luminaries as Marcel Dzama, Luc Tuymans, Chris Ofili, Neo Rauch and Lisa Yuskavage.

Other locations: 519 W 19th Street, between Tenth & Eleventh Avenues (1-212 727 2070); 533 W 19th Street, between Tenth & Eleventh Avenues (1-212 727 2070).

Friedrich Petzel Gallery

535 W 22nd Street, between Tenth & Eleventh Avenues (1-212 680 9467/www.petzel.com). **Open** *Sept-June* 10am-6pm Tue-Sat. *July, Aug* 10am-6pm Mon-Fri. **Map** p404 C26.

The Friedrich Petzel Gallery represents some of the brightest young stars on the international scene, so you can count on intriguing shows. Sculptor Keith Edmier, photographer Dana Hoey, painter and filmmaker Sarah Morris, and installation artists Jorge Pardo and Philippe Parenno all show here.

Other locations: 537 W 22nd Street, between Tenth & Eleventh Avenues (1-212 680 9467).

Gagosian Gallery

555 W 24th Street, between Tenth & Eleventh Avenues (1-212 741 1111/www.gagosian.com). **Open** *Sept-June* 10am-6pm Tue-Sat. *July-Aug* 10am-6pm Mon-Fri. **Map** p404 C26.

Larry Gagosian's mammoth (20,000 sq ft) contribution to 24th Street's top-level galleries was launched in 1999 with an exhilarating show of Richard Serra sculptures. There's been no slackening of the reins since then, with follow-up exhibitions featuring works by Douglas Gordon, Ellen Gallagher, Damien Hirst, Ed Ruscha, Julian Schnabel and Andy Warhol. There's also another Gagosian Gallery located over in Uptown (*see p274*).

Greene Naftali Gallery

8th Floor, 526 W 26th Street, between Tenth & Eleventh Avenues (1-212 463 7770/www.greene naftaligallery.com). **Open** *Sept-June* 10am-6pm Tue-Sat. *July, Aug* 10am-6pm Mon-Fri. **Map** p404 C26.

You don't have to be an art boffin to enjoy dropping in at Greene Naftali, a gallery that's well worth visiting purely for its wonderful light and spectacular panorama. That said, the always keen vision of Carol Greene outdoes even the eighth-floor view. Mavericks like sculptor Rachel Harrison and video artist Paul Chan continue to put smiles on the faces of both critics and punters alike.

John Connelly Presents

625 W 27th Street, between Eleventh & Twelfth Avenues (1-212 337 9563/www.johnconnelly presents.com). **Open** *Sept-June* 10am-6pm Tue-Sat. *July, Aug* 10am-6pm Mon-Fri. **Map** p404 B26.

Connelly, long-time director of the Andrea Rosen Gallery, quickly earned a reputation as one of the most exciting young dealers around after he struck out on his own. In 2006, he and six other Chelsea gallerists moved their enterprises into a string of old loading dock bays along 27th Street, creating one of the hottest gallery-hopping blocks in the 'hood. Expect provocative works by emerging young artists, with an emphasis on installation.

The Kitchen

512 W 19th Street, between Tenth & Eleventh Avenues (1-212 255 5793/www.thekitchen.org). **Open** noon-6pm Tue-Fri; 11am-6pm Sat. Phone for summer hours. **Map** p403 C27.

In its infancy in the early 1970s, the Kitchen (originally located in Soho) provided a safe haven for artists to take risks in the fields of experimental video art and music. Under the direction of Deb Singer since 2004, this not-for-profit centre for video, music, dance, performance, film and literature continues to house exhilarating avant-garde performances and bold, unpredictable art exhibitions.

Lehmann Maupin

540 W 26th Street, between Tenth & Eleventh Avenues (1-212 255 2923/www.lehmannmaupin.com). **Open** *Sept-June* 10am-6pm Tue-Sat. *July, Aug* 10am-6pm Mon-Fri. **Map** p404 C26.

This gallery left its Rem Koolhaas-designed loft in Soho but kept Koolhaas on board when it came to designing its new Chelsea digs, located in a former garage. Epic exhibitions feature hip international artists – the likes of Tracey Emin, Gilbert & George, Teresita Fernandez, Do-Ho Suh and Juergen Teller.

Leo Koenig Inc

545 W 23rd Street, between Tenth & Eleventh Avenues (1-212 334 9255/www.leokoenig.com). **Open** *Sept-July* 10am-6pm Tue-Sat. **Map** p404 C26.

Leo Koenig's father is Kasper Koenig, the internationally known curator and museum director, but Leo has been making a name for himself independently by showcasing cutting-edge American and German talent – Meg Cranston, Torben Giehler and Lisa Ruyter are among those he has exhibited here.

Luhring Augustine Gallery

531 W 24th Street, between Tenth & Eleventh Avenues (1-212 206 9100/www.luhringaugustine.com). **Open** *Sept-June* 10am-6pm Tue-Sat. *July, Aug* 10am-5.30pm Mon-Fri. **Map** p404 C26.

Designed by Richard Gluckman, the area's architect of choice, the Luhring Augustine Gallery features work from an impressive index of contemporary artists, such as British sculptor Rachel Whiteread, Swiss video star Pipilotti Rist, Japanese photographic artist Yasumasa Morimura, and Americans Janine Antoni, Larry Clark and Gregory Crewdson.

Cheap date

For a quick hit of avant-garde up-and-coming artists, spend your Saturday afternoon strolling down **20th Street** between Tenth and Eleventh Avenues, where you can puzzle over photos, canvases and sculpture – sans admission fees. Biting into a forbidden apple might have been Adam and Eve's downfall, but at American joint **Cookshop** (*see p198*) – a few steps away – sinful comfort food won't cost you your soul or pay check. Chef Marc Meyer's gallery-like setting is a fitting showcase for his opulent dishes, all made with seasonable, sustainable ingredients. Espresso martinis and warm jelly-filled doughnuts offer an elegant riff on a classic morning coupling, while banana-topped cornmeal pancakes and sunny-side-up eggs with Berkshire bacon are equally enticing acts of performance art.

Mary Boone Gallery

541 W 24th Street, between Tenth & Eleventh Avenues (1-212 752 2929/www.maryboone gallery.com). **Open** *Sept-June* 10am-6pm Tue-Sat. *July, Aug* by appointment only. **Map** p404 C26.

Mary Boone made her name in the 1980s representing Julian Schnabel, Jean-Michel Basquiat and Francesco Clemente at her renowned Soho gallery. She later moved to Midtown and, in 2000, added this sweeping space in a former garage in Chelsea, showing established artists like David Salle, Barbara Kruger and Eric Fischl alongside up-and-comers like Brian Alfred and Hilary Harkness.

Matthew Marks Gallery

523 W 24th Street, between Tenth & Eleventh Avenues (1-212 243 0200/www.matthewmarks.com). **Open** *Sept-June* 11am-6pm Tue-Sat. *July* 11am-6pm Mon-Fri. **Map** p404 C26.

The Matthew Marks Gallery was a driving force behind Chelsea's transformation into one of the city's top art destinations and, with three outposts to its name, it remains one of the neighbourhood's powerhouses. The gallery showcases such international talent as Robert Gober, Nan Goldin, Andreas Gursky, Ellsworth Kelly and Brice Marden.

Other locations: 521 W 21st Street, between Tenth & Eleventh Avenues (1-212 243 0200); 523 W 24th Street, between Tenth & Eleventh Avenues (1-212 243 0200).

Metro Pictures

519 W 24th Street, between Tenth & Eleventh Avenues (1-212 206 7100/www.metropictures gallery.com). **Open** *Sept- June* 10am-6pm Tue-Sat. *July* 10am-6pm Mon-Fri. **Map** p404 C26.

The gallery is best known for representing the art-world superstar Cindy Sherman, along with such big contemporary names as multi-media artist Mike Kelley, Robert Longo (known for his works produced using photography and charcoal) and the late German artist Martin Kippenberger.

PaceWildenstein Gallery

534 W 25th Street, between Tenth & Eleventh Avenues (1-212 929 7000/www.pacewildenstein.com). **Open** *Sept-June* 10am-6pm Tue-Sat. *July, Aug* 10am-6pm Mon-Thur; 10am-4pm Fri. **Map** p404 C26.

In a space designed by the renowned artist Robert Irwin, this welcoming Chelsea branch of the famous 57th Street gallery stages rather grand-scale shows by major contemporary talents such as Chuck Close, Alex Katz, Sol LeWitt, Robert Rauschenberg, Elizabeth Murray and Kiki Smith.

Other locations: 545 W 22nd Street, between Tenth & Eleventh Avenues (1-212 989 4258).

Paula Cooper Gallery

534 W 21st Street, between Tenth & Eleventh Avenues (1-212 255 1105/www.paulacoopergallery.com). **Open** *Sept-June* 10am-6pm Tue-Sat. *Aug* 10am-6pm Mon-Fri. **Map** p404 C26.

First in Soho and thence to Chelsea, Paula Cooper has built up an impressive art temple for worshippers of contemporary work. She has also opened a second space, located across the street. The gallery is best known for minimalist and conceptualist work, including pieces by photographer Andres Serrano and sculptors such as Carl Andre, Donald Judd and Sherrie Levine. You'll also see younger artists like Kelley Walker and John Tremblay.

Other locations: 521 W 21st Street, between Tenth & Eleventh Avenues (1-212 255 5247); 465 W 23rd Street, between Ninth & Tenth Avenues (1-212 255 1105).

Postmasters Gallery

459 W 19th Street, between Ninth & Tenth Avenues (1-212 727 3323/www.postmastersart.com). **Open** *Sept-July* 11am-6pm Tue-Sat. *Aug* 10am-6pm Mon-Fri. **Map** p403 C27.

Postmasters Gallery, run by the savvy duo of Magdalena Sawon and Tamas Banovich, emphasises technologically inflected art (most of which leans towards the conceptualist) in the form of sculpture, painting, new media and installations from the likes of Diana Cooper and Christian Schumann.

Sonnabend

536 W 22nd Street, between Tenth & Eleventh Avenues (1-212 627 1018/www.sonnabendgallery.com). **Open** *Sept-July* 10am-6pm Tue-Sat. **Map** p404 C26.

Sonnabend is a well-established standby with a museum-like space that shows new work by Ashley Bickerton, Gilbert & George, Candida Höfer, Jeff Koons, Haim Steinbach and Matthew Weinstein.

303 Gallery

525 W 22nd Street, between Tenth & Eleventh Avenues (1-212 255 1121/www.303gallery.com). **Open** *Sept-July* 10am-6pm Tue-Sat. *Aug* 10am-6pm Mon-Fri. **Map** p404 C26.

Rirkrit Tiravanija made his well-known Thai cooking sculpture debut at this gallery's original Soho location. It currently represents Doug Aitken, Stephen Shore, Thomas Demand and various other artists in the middle of their careers.

Tracy Williams

313 W 4th Street, between Bank & W 12th Streets (1-212 229 2757/www.tracywilliamsltd.com). **Open** *Sept-July* 11am-6pm Tue-Sat. **Map** p403 D28.

Once senior vice president of contemporary art at both Sotheby's and Christie's, Williams opened a place of her own (in her very own 1840s townhouse)

Barbara Gladstone. See p270.

in 2004. Visit the gallery on any opening night and you'll be rewarded in turn with an al fresco jaunt in its charming back garden.

57th Street

The home of Carnegie Hall, Tiffany & Co, Bergdorf Goodman and a number of art galleries, the area surrounding 57th Street is a hive of commercial activity that's lively, cultivated, chic and very expensive.

Subway *E, V to Fifth Avenue-53rd Street; F to 57th Street; N, R, W to Fifth Avenue-59th Street.*

Greenberg Van Doren Gallery

7th Floor, 730 Fifth Avenue, at 57th Street (1-212 445 0444/www.gvdgallery.com). **Open** *Sept-June* 10am-6pm Tue-Sat. *July, Aug* 10am-5pm Mon-Fri. **Map** p405 E22.

This elegant gallery represents established artists James Brooks and Richard Diebenkorn, as well as younger talent like painters Benjamin Edwards and Cameron Martin plus photographers Tim Davis and Jessica Craig-Martin. Nor does the creative pedigree end there: the gallery is also due to open a brand new space on the Lower East Side called Eleven Rivington (11 Rivington Street) in late 2007, to be curated by Augusto Arbizo.

McKee Gallery

4th Floor, 745 Fifth Avenue, between 57th & 58th Streets (1-212 688 5951/www.mckeegallery.com). **Open** *Sept-July* 10am-5pm Tue-Fri. *Aug* by appointment only. **Map** p405 E22.

McKee's major claim to fame is the estate of art legend Philip Guston. Need another reason to visit? You'll also find the work of Martin Puryear, Vija Celmins and the playful Jeanne Silverthorne in this extremely airy midtown space.

Marian Goodman Gallery

4th Floor, 24 W 57th Street, between Fifth & Sixth Avenues (1-212 977 7160/www.mariangoodman.com). **Open** *Sept-June* 10am-6pm Tue-Sat. *July, Aug* 10am-6pm Mon-Fri. **Map** p405 E22.

This well-known space offers a host of renowned names on its roster of exhibiting artists. Look out for John Baldessari, Christian Boltanski, Maurizio Cattelan, Gabriel Orozco, Gerhard Richter, Thomas Struth and Jeff Wall, among others.

PaceWildenstein Gallery

2nd Floor, 32 E 57th Street, between Madison & Park Avenues (1-212 421 3292/www.pacewildenstein.com). **Open** *Sept-May* 9.30am-6pm Tue-Sat. *June-Aug* 9.30am-6pm Mon-Fri. **Map** p405 E22.

To view shows by a few of the 20th century's most significant artists, head to this institution on 57th Street. Here you'll find pieces by such notables as Chuck Close, Agnes Martin, Pablo Picasso, Ad Reinhardt, Mark Rothko, Lucas Samaras, Elizabeth Murray and Kiki Smith. The Pace Prints division at this location exhibits works on paper by everyone from old masters to notable contemporaries. And if you're not content with that, the gallery also deals in fine ethnic and world art.

The Project

3rd Floor, 37 W 57th Street, between Fifth & Sixth Avenues (1-212 688 1585/www.elproyecto.com). **Open** *Sept-June* 10am-6pm Mon-Sat. *July, Aug* 10am-5pm Mon-Fri. **Map** p405 E22.

This gallery has been the darling of European critics and curators ever since it opened to a flurry of excitement in 1998, and its move from Harlem to Midtown has only increased its keen following among press and public alike. Expect work by acclaimed young artists along the lines of Julie Mehretu, Peter Rostovsky and Stephen Vitiello).

Upper East Side

Many of the galleries on the Upper East Side specialise in selling masterpieces to billionaires. Still, anyone can look at the exhibited works for free, and some pieces are treasures that will vanish from public view for years if sold to private collectors, so don't pass up the chance.

Subway *6 to 68th Street-Hunter College or 77th Street.*

Gagosian Gallery

980 Madison Avenue, at 76th Street (1-212 744 2313/www.gagosian.com). **Open** *Sept-June* 10am-6pm Tue-Sat. *July, Aug* 10am-6pm Mon-Fri. **Map** p405 E20.

Long a force to be reckoned with in the world of contemporary art, Larry Gagosian runs pristine temples Uptown and in Chelsea (*see p270*). Featured artists include Francesco Clemente and Richard Serra, plus younger creative starlets like Cecily Brown and British badboy Damien Hirst.

Knoedler & Co

19 E 70th Street, between Fifth & Madison Avenues (1-212 794 0550/www.knoedlergallery.com). **Open** *Sept-May* 9.30am-5.30pm Tue-Sat. *June-Aug* 9.30am-5pm Mon-Fri. **Map** p405 E20.

Opened in 1846, this is the oldest gallery in New York and continues to uphold its formidable reputation by exhibiting museum-quality post-war work and excellent contemporary art from the like Lee Bontecou and John Walker.

L&M Arts

45 E 78th Street, at Madison Avenue (1-212 861 0020/www.lmgallery.com). **Open** *Sept-June* 10am-5.30pm Tue-Sat. *July* 10am-5pm Mon-Fri. **Map** p405 E19.

Here lies Yves Klein's US headquarters, the estate of Joseph Cornell and a stable of artists (Sol LeWitt, Agnes Martin, Louise Bourgeois) that reads like a best-of list for the 20th century.

Zwirner & Wirth

32 E 69th Street, between Madison & Park Avenues (1-212 517 8677/www.zwirnerandwirth.com). **Open** *Sept-June* 10am-6pm Tue-Sat. *July-Labor Day* 10am-6pm Mon-Fri. **Map** p405 E20.

Z&W, located in a stylishly renovated townhouse space, exhibits a wide range of modern and contemporary masters along the lines of Dan Flavin, Martin Kippenberger and Bruce Nauman.

Harlem

Triple Candie

461 W 126th Street, between Morningside & Amsterdam Avenues (1-212 865 0783/www.triplecandie.org). Subway A, B, C, D, 1 to 125th Street. **Open** noon-5pm Thur-Sun. **Map** p407 C13.

This thriving multicultural arts centre brings exhibitions and an excellent educational programme to Harlem's highly creative west side.

Brooklyn

Artists who live and work in Brooklyn have created a thriving art scene, with **Williamsburg** its uncontested hub. For a printable map of the area's venues, visit www.williamsburggalleryassociation.com. While many galleries have migrated to Chelsea after blossoming in the borough, plenty of exceptional spaces have stayed put. Most are open on Sundays and Mondays, when the majority of galleries in Manhattan are closed.

Black & White Gallery

483 Driggs Avenue, between North 9th & 10th Streets, Williamsburg, Brooklyn (1-718 599 8775/www.blackandwhiteartgallery.com). Subway L to Bedford Avenue. **Open** *Sept-July* noon-6pm Mon, Fri-Sun & by appointment. *Aug* 10am-6pm Mon-Fri. **Map** p411 U7.

Gallery founder and director Tatyana Okshteyn is good at finding new talent. At a typical show opening, you can expect to see large-scale installations in the outdoor courtyard, sculpture or paintings throughout the gallery and enthusiastic gallery-goers spilling on to the sidewalk.

Other locations: 636 W 28th Street, between Eleventh & Twelfth Avenues (1-212 244 3007).

Jack the Pelican Presents

487 Driggs Avenue, between North 9th & 10th Streets, Williamsburg, Brooklyn (1-718 782 0183/www.jackthepelicanpresents.com). Subway L to Bedford Avenue. **Open** noon-6pm Mon, Thur-Sun. **Map** p411 U7.

Jack the Pelican joined the newest wave of Williamsburg galleries in 2003 when partners Don Carroll and Matt Zalla opened this space dedicated to offbeat and edgy art.

Pierogi

177 North 9th Street, between Bedford & Driggs Avenues, Williamsburg, Brooklyn (1-718 599 2144/www.pierogi2000.com). Subway L to Bedford Avenue. **Open** *Sept-July* 11am-6pm Mon, Thur-Sun and by appointment. **Map** p411 U7.

Pierogi, one of Williamsburg's established galleries, presents the Flat Files, a series of drawers containing works on paper by some 800 artists. Don't pass up the chance to don the special white gloves and handle the archived artwork yourself.

Not-for-profit spaces

apexart

291 Church Street, between Walker & White Streets (1-212 431 5270/www.apexart.org). Subway J, M, N, Q, R, W, Z, 6 to Canal Street; 1 to Franklin Street. **Open** *Sept-July* 11am-6pm Tue-Sat. **Map** p402 E31.

Founded in 1994 by artist Steven Rand, apexart's inspiration comes from the independent critics, curators and artists selected for its curatorial programme, which tends to dictate rather than follow prevailing fashions in the art world.

Artists Space
Third floor, 28 Greene Street, at Grand Street (1-212 226 3970/www.artistsspace.org). Subway A, C, E to Canal Street. **Open** *Sept-June* 11am-6pm Tue-Sat. *July* 11am-5pm Tue-Fri. **Map** p403 E30.
Open since 1972, this three-floor space exhibits a diverse crew of young artists working in all media. The organisation also plays host to one of the largest artist registries in the country.

Drawing Center
35 Wooster Street, between Broome & Grand Streets (1-212 219 2166/www.drawingcenter.org). Subway A, C, E, J, M, N, Q, R, W, Z, 6 to Canal Street. **Open** *Sept-July* 10am-6pm Tue-Fri; 11am-6pm Sat. **Map** p403 E30.
This 30-year-old Soho standout, a stronghold of works on paper, assembles critically acclaimed programmes that feature not only soon-to-be art stars but also museum-calibre legends such as James Ensor, Ellsworth Kelly and even the works of Old Masters like Rembrandt.

Momenta Art
72 Berry Street, between N 9th & 10th Streets, Williamsburg, Brooklyn (1-718 218 8058/www.momentaart.org). Subway L to Bedford Avenue. **Open** *Sept-June* noon-6pm Mon, Thur-Sun. **Map** p411 U7.
Momenta is housed in a tiny Brooklyn space, yet it conveys the importance of a serious Chelsea gallery. You'll find solo and group exhibitions from a cross-section of emerging artists – most of them will be conceptualists, all of them will be challenging the norms in one way or another.

SculptureCenter
44-19 Purves Street, at Jackson Avenue, Long Island City, Queens (1-718 361 1750/www.sculpture-center.org). Subway E, V to 23rd Street-Ely Avenue; G to Long Island City-Court Square; 7 to 45th Road-Court House Square. **Open** 11am-6pm Mon, Thur-Sun. **Map** p412 V5.
One of the best places to see work by blossoming and mid-career artists, this gallery is known for its very broad definition of sculpture. The impressive steel-and-brick digs, designed by architect Maya Lin, opened in late 2002.

Smack Mellon Gallery
92 Plymouth Street, between Washington & Main Streets, Dumbo, Brooklyn (1-718 834 8761/www.smackmellon.org). Subway A, C to High Street; F to York Street. **Open** noon-6pm Wed-Sun. **Map** p411 T9.
Avant-garde group shows fill this gallery's new waterfront digs. The recently renovated 12,000sq ft space has ample room for emerging and mid-career artists to exhibit work in all media.

White Columns
320 W 13th Street, between Hudson & W 4th Streets, entrance on Horatio Street (1-212 924 4212). Subway A, C, E, 1, 2, 3 to 14th Street; L to Eighth Avenue. **Open** noon-6pm Tue-Sat. **Map** p403 D28.
British-born Matthew Higgs – artist, writer, 2006 Turner Prize judge and now director and chief curator here at New York's oldest alternative art space – has been getting high marks for shaking things up. He has kept White Columns committed to under-represented artists, while also expanding the curatorial focus far beyond New York.

Photography

New York is photo country, no doubt about it. For a comprehensive overview of local exhibitions, keep an eye out for the bimonthly directory *Photograph* ($8 at galleries or online at www.photography-guide.com).

Bonni Benrubi
13th Floor, 41 E 57th Street, at Madison Avenue (1-212 888 6007/www.bonnibenrubi.com). **Open** *Sept-June* 10am-6pm Mon-Fri, 11am-6pm Sat. *July, Aug* 10am-6pm Mon-Fri. **Map** p405 E22.
You'll find a wealth of both 20th-century American photography (like Lewis Hine and Walker Evans) and contemporary photography from emerging artists (such as Abe Morell and Matthew Pillsbury) at this gallery, which turned 20 in 2007.

Edwynn Houk Gallery
4th Floor, 745 Fifth Avenue, between 57th & 58th Streets (1-212 750 7070/www.houkgallery.com). Subway N, R, W to Fifth Avenue-59th Street. **Open** *Sept-June* 11am-6pm Tue-Sat. *July* 9.30am-5pm Mon-Fri. **Map** p405 E22.
The Edwynn Houk Gallery is a respected specialist in vintage and contemporary photography. Among the artists exhibited are Brassaï, Lynn Davis, Dorothea Lange, Annie Leibovitz, Man Ray and Alfred Stieglitz, each commanding, as you'd expect for talent of this calibre, the very top-dollar prices.

Howard Greenberg Gallery
41 E 57th Street, at Madison Avenue (1-212 334 0010/www.howardgreenberg.com). **Open** *Sept-June* 10am-6pm Tue-Sat. *July, Aug* 10am-6pm Mon-Thur; 10am-5pm Fri. **Map** p405 E22.
Named Photofind at its inception in 1981, the Howard Greenberg Gallery was one of the first spaces to exhibit photojournalism and street photography. The gallery's collection includes countless images snapped by Berenice Abbot, Edward Steichen and Henri Cartier-Bresson.

Pace/MacGill
9th Floor, 32 E 57th Street, between Madison & Park Avenues (1-212 759 7999/www.pacemacgill.com). Subway N, R, W to Lexington Avenue-59th Street; 4, 5, 6 to 59th Street. **Open** *Sept-late June* 9.30am-5.30pm Tue-Fri; 10am-6pm Sat. *Late June-Aug* 9.30am-5.30pm Mon-Thur; 9.30am-4pm Fri. **Map** p405 E22.
Pace/MacGill shows work by such well-known names as Walker Evans, Robert Frank and Irving Penn, in addition to groundbreaking contemporaries like Chuck Close and Kiki Smith.

Books & Poetry

Rewriting the art of reading.

One evening recently, New York writers Ben Marcus, Wayne Koestenbaum and Dale Peck gathered at the KGB Bar to read fiction – unusually, though, not their own. Instead they paid homage to the late, great and highly acerbic Austrian author Thomas Bernhard. Over in Brooklyn, the Littoral Reading Series, part of an arts organisation called Issue Project Room, has been pairing highly innovative authors such as Joe Wenderoth (*Letters to Wendy's*) with like-minded musicians – in Wenderoth's case, Gibby Haynes of the band Butthole Surfers. Meanwhile, 826NYC, the McSweeney's programme dedicated to helping city teens learn to write, just threw a benefit that featured live performances by singer-songwriter Sufjan Stevens and author and social commentator Sarah Vowell.

In case you hadn't inferred it from all that name-dropping, we'll spell it out: literary events are changing. People who curate New York City's own events have long been rethinking the concept of the book reading. No longer content with the now standard formula of an author stepping up to a podium and reading from his or her own most recent book, organisers are inviting musicians along, and asking readers to do something a little different. Often these events are one-offs, so you have to be on the lookout, but some reading series are consistently surprising. Take the Upstairs at the Square series at Barnes & Noble at Union Square, for example, where Dana Spiotta recently talked about her excellent novel *Eat the Document* and then turned the stage over to Badly Drawn Boy. And the Happy Ending Series, run by novelist and raconteur Amanda Stern, continues to be dynamic by showcasing excellent authors *and* requiring them to take 'at least one risk' onstage.

Of course, there are still plenty of excellent good old-fashioned book readings too. Some of the best events can be found at class act **92nd Street Y**, where you can see the likes of Don DeLillo and Lydia Davis; the elegant **New York Public Library**, which recently hosted an event with legendary novelists Günter Grass and Norman Mailer; and the cosier independent bookstore **192 Books**, where you can catch authors such as John Ashbery and Miranda July. It's also a good idea to watch out for festivals organised by the Brooklyn Literary Council (www.visitbrooklyn.org), *The New Yorker* (www.newyorker.com) and PEN World Voices (www.pen.org), all of which bring authors together in surprising ways.

Whatever the type of event, readings are like the rock shows of the book world, providing you with a chance to see your favourite writers in the flesh. Even better, they're a chance to interact with literature in a different way from being alone with a book, since authors tend to add dimension to their work with their tone and through the Q&A sessions that usually follow. To find out who's reading and where, check out the weekly listings in *Time Out New York*.

For more on local literature, *see p230-234*.

Author appearances

Barnes & Noble

33 E 17th Street, between Broadway & Park Avenue South (1-212 253 0810/www.barnesandnoble.com). Subway L, N, Q, R, W, 4, 5, 6 to 14th Street-Union Square. **Admission** free. **Map** p403 E27.

Many an author touches down at a Barnes & Noble. This Union Square branch offers an especially varied schedule. Recent names include William Gibson, Al Gore, David Lynch and Dana Spiotta.

Bluestockings

172 Allen Street, between Rivington & Stanton Streets (1-212 777 6028/www.bluestockings.com). Subway F, V to Lower East Side-Second Avenue. **Admission** free; suggested donation $10. **Credit** AmEx, MC, V. **Map** p403 F29.

This progressive bookstore and café hosts frequent readings and discussions, often on feminist and lesbian themes. Past readers have included graphic novelist Alison Bechdel, novelist Aoibheann Sweeney and political writer Michelle Goldberg.

Half King

505 W 23rd Street, between Tenth & Eleventh Avenues (1-212 462 4300/www.thehalfking.com). Subway C, E to 23rd Street. **Admission** free. **Map** p404 C26.

Co-owned by Sebastian Junger, the author of *The Perfect Storm*, the Half King holds Monday night readings by authors including Ishmael Beah, Elizabeth Gilbert and Junger himself.

Happy Ending Series

Happy Ending, 302 Broome Street, between Eldridge & Forsyth Streets (1-212 334 9676). Subway F, V to Delancey Street; J, M, Z to Delancey-Essex Streets. **Admission** free. **Map** p403 F30.

Hosted by Amanda Stern, these reading events (which also include musical interludes) take place in a massage parlour turned popular watering hole. The bar setting lends the series an eminently laid-back, convivial vibe. Recent readers have included Jean Thompson, Alison Bechdel, Joshua Furst, Tao Lin and Rebecca Curtis.

Housing Works Used Book Café

126 Crosby Street, between Houston & Prince Streets (1-212 334 3324/www.housingworks.org/usedbookcafe). Subway 6 to Bleecker Street; B, D, F to Broadway-Lafayette; W, R to Prince Street. **Admission** free; book donations encouraged. **Map** p403 E29.

Both the emerging and the illustrious mingle at the microphone (and in the audience) at this Soho bookstore and café, which has one of the best reading series in the city. What's more, all of the profits from events go towards providing shelter and support services to homeless people living with HIV and AIDS. Visiting authors run the gamut, and have recently included Gary Shteyngart, Lynne Tillman, Sam Lipsyte and Jonathan Lethem.

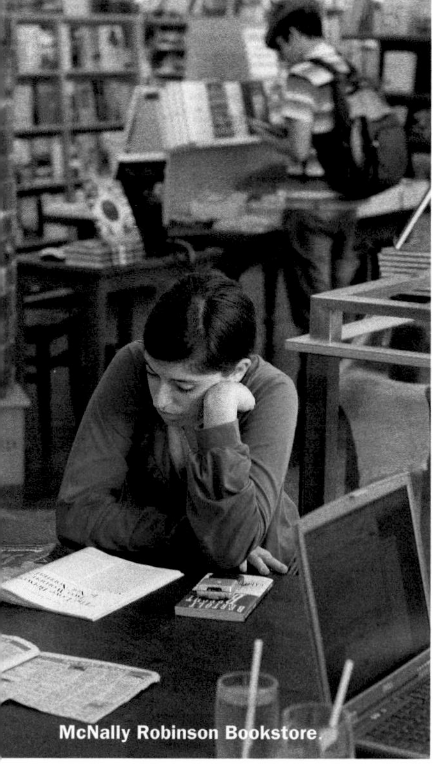

McNally Robinson Bookstore.

Hue-Man Bookstore

2319 Frederick Douglass Boulevard (Eighth Avenue), between 124th & 125th Streets (1-212 665 7400/www.huemanbookstore.com). Subway A, B, C, D to 125th Street. **Admission** free. **Map** p407 D13.

This spacious Harlem bookstore holds frequent readings, as well as in-store appearances by authors such as Chris Abani, with an emphasis on African-American writers and topics.

KGB Bar

2nd Floor, 85 E 4th Street, between Second & Third Avenues (1-212 505 3360/www.kgbbar.com). Subway F, V to Lower East Side-Second Avenue; 6 to Astor Place. **Admission** free. **Map** p403 F29.

This dark and formerly smoky East Village hang-out with an old-school communist theme runs several top-notch weekly series, featuring NYC writers, poets, fantasy authors and more.

Littoral

Issue Project Room, The Can Factory, 232 3rd Street, at Third Avenue, Brooklyn (1-718 330 0313/www.issueprojectroom.org). Subway F, G to Carroll Street. **Admission** $5-$15. **No credit cards**. **Map** p410 T11.

This series likes to mix boundary-pushing literature and avant-garde music. Recent readers include Lynne Tillman, Gary Lutz and Tao Lin.

McNally Robinson Bookstore

50 Prince Street, between Lafayette & Mulberry Streets (1-212 274 1160/www.mcnallyrobinson.com). Subway N, R to Prince Street; 6 to Spring Street. **Admission** free. **Map** p403 F29.

McNally Robinson is an excellent newish independent bookstore. To cement its reputation, it is inviting a wide range of non-fiction writers and novelists – Rupert Thompson, Kate Christensen, Edward P Jones and Darcey Steinke, among others – to read in its comfortable café space.

New School University

66 W 12th Street, between Fifth & Sixth Avenues (1-212 229 5353/tickets 1-212 229 5488/www.newschool.edu). Subway F, V to 14th Street; L to Sixth Avenue. **Admission** free-$15; free students. **Credit** AmEx, MC, V. **Map** p403 E28.

Christian Hawkey, Anne Carson and Eileen Myles are a few of the writers who have participated in the New School University's wide-ranging readings and literary forums. It's also worth looking out for political discussions and poetry nights.

New York Public Library

Humanities & Social Sciences Library, Celeste Bartos Forum, 42nd Street, at Fifth Avenue (1-212 930 0571/www.nypl.org/events). Subway F, V to 42th Street. **Admission** free-$10. **No credit cards**. **Map** p404 E24.

This elegant large space invites leading authors to discuss books and engage in lively literary debates with punters. Recent guests include genocide historian Samantha Power, novelist Colm Toibin and legendary writer Norman Mailer.

92nd Street Y

1395 Lexington Avenue, at 92nd Street (1-212 415 5500/www.92y.org). Subway 6 to 96th Street. **Admission** $16-$35. **Credit** AmEx, MC, V. **Map** p406 F17.

Big-name novelists, journalists and poets preside over some grand intellectual feasts here, with talks by critic James Wood, as well as a reading series featuring writers along the lines of Don DeLillo, Derek Walcott and Claire Messud. The Biographers/Critics and Brunch events are also popular.

192 Books

192 Tenth Avenue, at 21st Street (1-212 255 4022). Subway C, E to 23rd Street. **Admission** free. **Map** p404 C26.

This independent bookstore offers a wide variety of books, focusing on literary titles and art history. Its reading series is phenomenal, bringing in top authors such as Tom Bissell and Miranda July.

Poetry Project

St Mark's Church in-the-Bowery, 131 E 10th Street, at Second Avenue (1-212 674 0910/www.poetryproject.com). Subway L to First Avenue; 6 to Astor Place. **Admission** $8; $7 seniors, students. **No credit cards**. **Map** p403 F28.

The Project, housed in a beautiful old church, has hosted an amazing roster of poets since its inception in 1966, including creative luminaries like the late Ted Berrigan, Patti Smith and Eileen Myles. It also offers workshops, lectures, book parties and an open poetry reading on the first Monday of each month.

Printed Matter

195 Tenth Avenue, at 21st Street (1-212 925 0325/www.printedmatter.org). Subway C, E to 23rd Street. **Admission** free. **Credit** MC, V. **Map** p404 C26.

Located across the street from 192 Books, this treasure trove of a bookshop doesn't host many readings, but it does have a great selection of art books.

Sunny's Bar

253 Conover Street, between Beard & Reed Streets, Red Hook, Brooklyn (1-718 625 8211/www.sunnysredhook.com). Subway F, G to Smith-9th Streets, then bus B77 to Conover Street. **Admission** $3. **No credit cards**. **Map** p410 R11.

Red Hook is becoming a popular neighbourhood, but it still offers a taste of old Brooklyn, as this onetime dockers' bar goes to show. One Sunday a month, the watering hole invites authors such as Phillip Lopate, Meg Wolitzer and Peter Blauner to share their work.

Spoken word

Most spoken-word events begin with a featured poet or two, before moving on to an open mic. If you'd like to participate, show up a little early and ask for the sign-up sheet. Feel free to express approval out loud, but keep criticism to yourself. For an up-to-date schedule of events throughout the city, check the **Ultimate NYC Poetry Calendar** (www.poetz.com/calendar).

Winging it at the **Moth StorySLAM**.

Bowery Poetry Club

308 Bowery, between Bleecker & Houston Streets (1-212 614 0505/www.bowerypoetry.com). Subway B, D, F, V to Broadway-Lafayette Street; 6 to Bleecker Street. **Admission** free-$15. **No credit cards**. **Map** p403 F29.

Celebrating the grand oral traditions and cyberific future of poetry, the funky BPC features spoken-word events nightly, with readings and performances in the afternoon. The Urbana National Slam team leads an open mic on Thursdays. The venue also hosts diverse music acts (*see p314*).

Moth StorySLAM

1-212 742 0551/www.themoth.org.

Better at talking than at writing? The Moth, known for its big-name monthly storytelling shows, also sponsors open slams in various venues. Ten raconteurs get five minutes each to tell a favourite story (no notes allowed!) to a panel of judges.

Nuyorican Poets Café

236 E 3rd Street, between Avenues B & C (1-212 505 8183/www.nuyorican.org). Subway F, V to Lower East Side-Second Avenue. **Admission** $5-$15. **No credit cards**. **Map** p403 G29.

This 30-plus-year-old East Village community arts centre is known for its long history of raucous slams, jam sessions and anything-goes open mics.

SOS: Sunday Open Series

ABC No Rio, 156 Rivington Street, between Clinton & Suffolk Streets (1-212 254 3697/www.abcnorio.org). Subway F to Delancey Street; J, M, Z to Delancey-Essex Streets. **Show** 3pm Sun. **Admission** $3. **No credit cards**. **Map** p403 G29.

Community-based art centre ABC No Rio's long-running Sunday afternoon open mic promises a welcoming vibe, no time limits and 'no BS'.

Cabaret & Comedy

Let NY make you laugh and cry.

Cabaret

When many people hear 'cabaret', they think of the fast-and-louche, hyper-sexed decadence depicted in Bob Fosse's classic 1972 movie musical *Cabaret*. But these days, cabaret usually means something quite different. If you're looking to see nubile young women shaking their tassles, you can find them at one of New York's many burlesque extravaganzas. But, in a cabaret show, it's just the music that gets stripped down: reduced to its bare essence in the form of a vocalist in a cosy nightclub, singing into a standing microphone, backed by a piano and perhaps a double bass. A cabaret act is a thing of intense intimacy, and the best performers around can make each person in the audience feel personally serenaded.

Perhaps no other genre offers quite so diverse an array of performers. Hip jazz types, grand old broads, bright young musical-theatre belters, semi-classical recitalists, female impersonators, neo-lounge singers – all share the same crowded rooms. Cabaret today is a confluence of opposites: the heights of polish and the depths of amateurism; intense honesty and airy pretense; earnestness and camp.

Manhattan's three toniest cabarets are located in fancy hotels: the **Oak Room** (at the Algonquin), **Feinstein's** (at the Loews Regency) and the **Café Carlyle** (at, yes, the Carlyle). These rooms are throwbacks to a more elegant era of New York nightlife, where well-heeled daters can take in dinner and a show in one swank package; the men wear jackets, the women are often tastefully bejewelled. Neighbourhood clubs such as **Don't Tell Mama** and the **Duplex** are casual, fun and a lot less pricey, but the talent is often entry-level. If the hotel venues recall scenes from an old Woody Allen movie, these joints often bring to mind the campy one-man show 'Just Jack!' from *Will & Grace*. The **Laurie Beechman Theater** falls somewhere between the two poles, as does the city's most hopping new venue: the **Metropolitan Room**, whose programming strikes a lively balance between beloved veterans and bright young newcomers.

Cabaret music tends to draw from what is known as the 'Great American Songbook', a vast repertoire of classic tunes by the likes of Cole Porter and the Gershwins, supplemented with songs by such contemporary composers as Joni Mitchell and Rufus Wainwright. The emphasis tends to be on storytelling and lyrical interpretation, with a special affinity for the ins and outs of romance. Torch singing is best experienced up close and personal, where you can really feel its intense heat. The Great American Songbook may be old-fashioned, but until people stop falling in and out of love, it will never be out of date.

A **Metropolitan Room** moment. *See p281.*

Classic nightspots

Café Carlyle

The Carlyle, 35 E 76th Street, at Madison Avenue (1-212 744 1600/reservations 1-800 227 5737/www.thecarlyle.com). Subway 6 to 77th Street. **Shows** 8.45pm Mon-Thur; 8.45pm, 10.45pm Fri, Sat. **Cover** varies, usually $50-$125 (sometimes with compulsory dinner). **Credit** AmEx, DC, Disc, MC, V. **Map** p405 E20.

This elegant boîte in the Carlyle hotel, with its airy murals by Marcel Vertes, is the epitome of sophisticated New York chic, attracting such top-level singers as Eartha Kitt, Barbara Cook and Judy Collins. Woody Allen often plays clarinet with Eddie Davis and his New Orleans Jazz Band on Monday nights (call ahead to confirm). Don't dress casually – embrace the high life. To drink in some atmosphere without the high price, try Bemelmans Bar across the hall, which always features an excellent pianist (5.30pm-12.30am Mon-Sat, $20-$25 cover).

Feinstein's at the Loews Regency

Loews Regency Hotel, 540 Park Avenue, at 61st Street (1-212 339 4095/www.feinsteinsatthe regency.com). Subway N, R, W to Lexington Avenue-59th Street; 4, 5, 6 to 59th Street. **Shows** 8.30pm Tue-Thur; 8.30pm, 11pm Fri, Sat. **Cover** $60-$75, $40 food/drink minimum. **Credit** AmEx, DC, Disc, MC, V. **Map** p405 E22.

Cabaret's crown prince, Michael Feinstein, draws A-list talent to this swank room in the Regency. It's pricey, but you usually get what you pay for. Recent performers have included top names such as Chita Rivera, Diahann Carroll and Ben Vereen.

Oak Room

Algonquin Hotel, 59 W 44th Street, between Fifth & Sixth Avenues (1-212 840 6800/reservations 1-212 419 9331/www.algonquinhotel.com). Subway B, D, F, V to 42nd Street-Bryant Park; 7 to Fifth Avenue. **Shows** 9pm Tue-Thur; 9pm, 11.30pm Fri, Sat. **Cover** $50-$65, $25 drink minimum; $60 dinner compulsory at 9pm Fri & Sat shows. **Credit** AmEx, DC, Disc, MC, V. **Map** p404 E24.

This banquette-lined room is the place to enjoy cabaret luminaries such as Karen Akers and Andrea Marcovicci, plus rising stars like Maude Maggart and the formidable jazz singer Paula West. And yes, all you Dorothy Parker fans, it's *that* Algonquin.

Standards

Don't Tell Mama

343 W 46th Street, between Eighth & Ninth Avenues (1-212 757 0788/www.donttellmama.com). Subway A, C, E to 42nd Street-Port Authority. **Shows** times vary; 2-3 shows per night. *Piano bar* 9pm-4am daily. **Cover** $5-$20 plus 2-drink minimum. *Piano bar* no cover, but 2-drink minimum. **Credit** AmEx, DC, Disc, MC, V. **Map** p404 C23.

Showbiz pros and piano-bar buffs adore this dank but homey Theater District stalwart, where acts range from the strictly amateur to potential stars of tomorrow. The nightly lineup may include pop, jazz and musical-theatre singers, as well as female impersonators, comedians and musical revues.

Duplex

61 Christopher Street, at Seventh Avenue South (1-212 255 5438). Subway 1 to Christopher Street-Sheridan Square. **Shows** 7pm, 9pm daily. *Piano bar* 9pm-4am daily. **Cover** $5-$20 plus 2-drink minimum. **Credit** AmEx, MC, V. **Map** p403 D28.

This cosy, brick-lined room – located upstairs from a piano bar in the heart of the West Village – is a good-natured testing ground for new talent. The eclectic offerings often come served with a generous dollop of good, old-fashioned camp.

Laurie Beechman Theatre

407 W 42nd Street, at Ninth Avenue (1-212 695 6909/www.theduplex.com). Subway A, C, E to 42nd Street-Port Authority. **Shows** 7pm, 9.30pm Mon, Fri, Sun. *Open mic* 10.30pm-2am Fri. **Cover** $15-$25 plus $15 minimum. **Credit** AmEx, MC, V. **Map** p404 C24.

Tucked away beneath the West Bank Café, the city's newest cabaret joint is home to many local favourites, such as Lisa Asher and the irrepressible Brandon Cutrell (who also hosts the After Party, a racy and raucous open mic show tune showcase pulling in the crowds on Friday nights).

Metropolitan Room

34 W 22nd Street, between Fifth & Sixth Avenues (1-212 206 0440/www.metropolitanroom.com). Subway F, R, V, W to 23rd Street. **Shows** times vary. **Cover** $15-$35 plus 2-drink minimum. **Credit** AmEx, MC, V. **Map** p404 E26.

The Met Room has quickly established itself as the must-go venue for high-level nightclub singing that won't bust your wallet. Regular performers range from rising musical-theatre stars to established cabaret aces (including the leonine Baby Jane Dexter and the lacerating English songstress Barb Jungr), plus bona fide legends such as Tammy Grimes, Julie Wilson and Annie Ross. *Photo p279.*

Comedy

In this city, where dozens of shows happen every night, it's easy for jaded locals to take the comedy scene for granted. But the unspoilt audience member notices instantly that New York City has the most exciting, happening comedy scene in the country. In addition to the plethora of small stand-up clubs showcasing tomorrow's stars, the city has not one, but three headliner clubs. The sketch and improv communities continue to grow as the theatres pump out students who move on to start DIY variety shows of their own. And no matter where you are, the well-worn teaser 'You never know who might stop by!' continues to deliver, with marquee names such as Dave Chappelle, Louis CK or Demetri Martin known to drop in unannounced to try new material in a laid-back setting. Of course, the jaded locals are the first to brag to their friends, 'Guess who *I* just saw?'.

Ars Nova

511 W 54th Street, between Tenth & Eleventh Avenues (1-212 977 1700/www.arsnovanyc.com). Subway C, E to 50th Street. **Shows** times vary. **Cover** free-$20. **Average drink** $5. **Credit** AmEx, Disc, MC, V (website only). **Map** p405 C22.

Thoughtful, professional productions are nurtured in the impeccably curated programme at Ars Nova. The space isn't bad either: rather than dusty bar glasses or dripping basement fixtures, crowds are treated to comfortable cabaret seating and a professional light and sound artist. Schedules are erratic, but the Thursdays at Ten series is always a good bet.

Carolines on Broadway

1626 Broadway, between 49th & 50th Streets (1-212 757 4100/www.carolines.com). Subway N, R, to 49th Street; 1 to 50th Street. **Shows** times vary. **Cover** $15-$45 plus 2-drink minimum. **Average drink** $7. **Credit** AmEx, DC, MC, V. **Map** p404 D23.

Carolines is a New York City institution. The club's long-term relationships with national headliners, sitcom stars and cable-special pros ensure that the stage, whose style harks back to the '80s boom days, always features marquee names. You probably won't see anything especially edgy or underground, but you'll never see anything less than professional.

Chicago City Limits

Ground floor of the Improv, 318 W 53rd Street, between Eighth & Ninth Avenues (1-212 888 5233/www.chicagocitylimits.com). Subway C, E to 50th Street. **Shows** 8pm Wed-Fri; 8pm, 10pm Sat. **Cover** $15 plus 2-drink minimum. **Credit** AmEx, Disc, MC, V.

CCL moved its sketch- and improv-comedy revues here from Chicago in 1979. The group's topical sketches, songs and audience-inspired improv is more closely related to the classic Second City format than to the kind of long-form shows taking place in the rest of the city's improv theaters. As such, it sometimes feels a bit outdated. Still, the venerable institution manages to hold on to some of the city's longest-running performers.

Comedy Cellar

117 MacDougal Street, between Bleecker & W 3rd Streets (1-212 254 3480/www.comedycellar.com). Subway A, B, C, D, E, F, V to W 4th Street. **Shows** 9pm, 10.45pm Mon-Thur, Sun; 9pm, 10.45pm, 12.30am Fri; 7.30pm, 9.15pm, 11pm, 12.45am Sat. **Cover** $15 (2-drink minimum). **Average drink** $6. **Credit** AmEx, MC, V. **Map** p403 E29.

Even after being dubbed one of the best stand-up clubs in the city year after year, the Comedy Cellar has somehow maintained a hip, underground feel. It gets incredibly crowded in the cosy Village basement. But the superb bookings, which typically include Colin Quinn, Jim Norton and Marina Franklin, are more than enough to distract you from your bachelorette-party neighbours.

Comedy Village

82 W 3rd Street, between Sullivan & Thompson Streets (1-212 477 0130/www.comedyvillage.com). Subway A, B, C, D, E, F, V to W 4th Street. **Shows** 9.30pm, 11.30pm Mon-Thur, Sun; 8.30pm, 10pm, 12.30am Fri, Sat. **Cover** $20 plus 2-drink minimum Mon-Thur; $25 plus 2-drink minimum Fri, Sat. **Map** p403 E29.

PJ Landers is building an army of no-nonsense stand-ups in his intimate, bare-boned venue. Look out for regular Mike DeStefano whose gruff candour is winning over both shock-craving crowds and audiences after a bit of vulnerability.

Dangerfield's

1118 First Avenue, between 61st Street & 62nd Streets (1-212 593 1650/www.dangerfields.com). Subway N, R, W to Lexington Avenue-59th Street; 4, 5, 6 to 59th Street. **Shows** 8.45pm Mon-Thur, Sun; 8.30pm, 10.30pm Fri; 8pm, 10.30pm, 12.30am Sat. **Cover** $12.50-$20. **Average drink** $7. **Credit** AmEx, DC, Disc, MC, V. **Map** p405 F22.

Walking into New York's oldest comedy club feels a bit like you've just come through a time warp. The decor and gentility are both throwbacks to the era of its namesake, who founded it as a cabaret back in 1969. Best thing about the club? Instead of putting eight to ten comics in a showcase, Dangerfield's gives three or four stand-ups the chance to settle into longer acts. And it's still the only club to abstain from drink minimums.

Gotham Comedy Club

208 W 23rd Street, between Seventh & Eighth Avenues (1-212 367 9000/www.gothamcomedyclub.com). Subway F, N, R, V to 23rd Street. **Shows** 8.30pm Mon-Thur, Sun; 8.30pm, 10.30pm Fri; 7.30pm, 9.30pm, 11.30pm Sat. **Cover** $12-$20 (2-drink minimum). **Average drink** $7. **Credit** AmEx, MC, V. **Map** p404 D26.

Audience members and national headliners are both drawn to Chris Mazzilli's vision for his club: elegant surroundings, professional behaviour and mutual respect. That's why the talents he fosters, such as Jim Gaffigan and Tom Papa, keep coming back to his club long after they've found on-screen fame. It's also why crowds keep returning to see who he's championing – and who might just 'drop by'.

Laugh Factory

669 Eighth Avenue, between 42nd & 43rd Streets (1-212 586 7829/www.laughfactory.com). Subway A, C, E to 42nd Street-Port Authority. **Shows** 8.30pm Mon-Thur, Sun; 8.30pm, 11.30pm Fri; 8.30pm, 10.30pm, 12.30am Sat. **Cover** $15-$40 plus 2-drink minimum. **Average drink** $7. **Credit** AmEx, Disc, MC, V. **Map** p404 D24.

The New York outpost of Jamie Masada's famed LA club fills its multiple stages with loads of on-the-cusp local talent. On any given night, you might catch Laurie Kilmartin, Christian Finnegan or Judah Friedlander. While inside, scan the walls for traces of the space's former strip-club days.

Laugh Lounge NYC

151 Essex Street, between Rivington & Stanton Streets (1-212 614 2500/www.laughloungenyc.com). Subway F to Delancey Street; J, M, Z to Delancey-Essex Streets. **Shows** 8.30pm and/or 10.30pm Mon-Thur, Sun; 8.30pm, 10.30pm Fri, Sat. **Cover** $10 (2-drink minimum); phone for student discounts. **Average drink** $8. **Credit** AmEx, MC, V. **Map** p403 G29.

Expect a mix of fresh faces and circuit regulars behind the mic at this bar and stand-up club. As a mainstream space, it feels a bit out of place on the Lower East Side, where most rooms feature edgier talent, but the Lounge is a good spot for tourists looking for something more staid in the area.

Magnet Theater

254 W 29th Street, between Seventh & Eighth Avenues (1-212 244 8824/www.magnettheater.com). Subway A, C, E to 34th Street-Penn Station; 1 to 28th Street. **Shows** times vary. **Cover** free-$7. **Average drink** $4. **No credit cards. Map** p404 D25.

In the past year, the community of house teams and solo performers at Armando Diaz's upstart black-box has grown strong, cementing the Magnet as one of the best places to watch improv in the city. You won't see faces from VH1 onstage, but you will see thoughtful, patient improv.

Rififi.

People's Improv Theater

2nd Floor, 154 W 29th Street, between Sixth & Seventh Avenues (1-212 563 7488/www.improvcentral.com). Subway 1 to 28th Street. **Shows** times vary. **Cover** $5-$12; free Wed. **Average drink** $3 (no alcohol). **No credit cards. Map** p404 D25.

While talented young sketch groups make a name for themselves on the weekends and improv teams pack audiences on Wednesday nights (which are always free), it's the teaching programme that really put the PIT on the creative map. Teachers from *Saturday Night Live* and *The Daily Show,* as well as accomplished stand-ups and writers, offer a rolling programme of classes in various media.

Rififi

Cinema Classics, 332 E 11th Street, between First & Second Avenues (1-212 677 1027/www.rififinyc.com). Subway L to First Avenue. **Shows** times vary. **Cover** free-$5. **No credit cards. Map** p403 F28.

Although burlesque and music still regularly pop up onstage in the back room of this lovably shabby bar, the enormous success of Eugene Mirman's long-running stand-up show *Invite Them Up* (Wed) has kept the seven-nights-a-week programming almost exclusively comedic. Established alt-scene stars such as Michael Showalter and Demetri Martin perform alongside future indie stars like John Mulaney and Rob Lathan.

Stand-Up New York

236 W 78th Street, at Broadway (1-212 595 0850/www.standupny.com). Subway 1 to 79th Street. **Shows** 9pm Mon-Thur, Sun; 8pm, 10pm, midnight Fri, Sat. **Cover** $15-$20 plus 2-drink minimum. **Average drink** $6. **Credit** AmEx, MC, V. **Map** p405 C19.

Under new management, the lineups at this musty uptown club – the only in its nabe – have started garnering attention for the first time in years. Jay Oakerson and Patrice Oneal have both frequented the small space (with an even smaller stage) in the past year, and plans to expand programming beyond stand-up also look promising.

Upright Citizens Brigade Theatre

307 W 26th Street, between Eighth & Ninth Avenues (1-212 366 9176/www.ucbtheatre.com). Subway C, E to 23rd Street; 1 to 28th Street. **Shows** times vary. **Cover** $5-$20. **Average drink** $3. **No credit cards. Map** p404 D26.

In a growing sea of improv troupes and sketch groups, the ones anchored at UCBT are the best. Competitive booking practices, paired with a massive and dedicated following of students, have kept UCBT at the top of its game since the theatre first opened its door almost a decade ago. Stars of *Saturday Night Live*, VH1 and writers for late-night talk shows gather on Sunday nights to wow relentless crowds in the long-running improv show *ASSSSCAT 3000.* Other improv teams that are certain never to let you down include Mother (Sat), the Stepfathers (Fri) and Reuben Williams (Sat).

Children

New York is one big playground (and it's not *all* for grown-ups).

Are you sitting comfortably? **Storytelling at the Hans Christian Andersen Statue.**

The excitement among visitors to New York is palpable. The streets are teeming with people, jammed with museums and all sorts of goodies, and the nights glitter with a billion flashing bulbs. It's the perfect environment for short attention spans (young and old), so even the most hard-to-please kid will find something to smile about. Just be forewarned: all this stimulation can overload the circuits of the very young. So take in the sights, but, in between the Empire State Building and the Statue of Liberty, put away the map and have a wander, or park yourself in one of the dozens of playgrounds for a breather.

To keep up with the child-friendly events happening during your stay, pick up a copy of *Time Out New York Kids*.

Where to stay

Most hotels, especially the big chain hotels, will move a crib or an extra bed into your room in order to accommodate your tot. Ask if this service is available when you book, and check on the size of the room; it is often the case that the hipper the hotel, the smaller the rooms, since most of the trendy places assume that their guests will be out on the town all night.

A few places that are especially child-friendly are listed below. For more on hotels across the city, *see pp54-80*.

Beacon Hotel

2130 Broadway, between 74th & 75th Streets (1-212 787 1100/1-800 572 4969/www.beaconhotel.com).
For review, *see p79*.

Holiday Inn Midtown

440 W 57th Street, between Ninth & Tenth Avenues (1-212 581 8100/1-800 465 4329/www.hi57.com).
The Hell's Kitchen branch of the international chain.

Inn on 23rd Street

131 W 23rd Street, between Sixth & Seventh Avenues (1-212 463 0330/www.innon23rd.com).
For review, *see p69*.

Roger Smith

501 Lexington Avenue, between 47th & 48th Streets (1-212 755 1400/1-800 445 0277/ www.rogersmith.com).
For review, *see p71*.

Babysitting

Baby Sitters' Guild

1-212 682 0227/www.babysittersguild.com. **Bookings** 9am-9pm daily. **No credit cards.**

Long- or short-term multilingual sitters cost from $20 per hour and up (four-hour minimum), plus cab fare. Babysitters are available around the clock.

Pinch Sitters

1-212 260 6005. **Bookings** 8am-5pm Mon-Fri. **No credit cards.**

Charges are $17 per hour (with a four-hour minimum), plus the babysitter's cab fare after 9pm ($10 maximum). You can also email your babysitter requests to pinchsitters@yahoo.com.

Classic kids' New York

Astroland Amusement Park

1000 Surf Avenue, at West 10th Street, Coney Island, Brooklyn (1-718 372 0275/www.astroland.com). Subway D, F, Q to Coney Island-Stillwell Avenue. **Open** *Mid Apr-mid June* noon-6pm Sat, Sun, weather permitting (plus weekdays during public-school spring break). *Mid June-Labor Day* noon-midnight daily. *Early Sept-early Oct* opens at noon Sat, Sun; closing time depends on weather. **Admission** $2.50-$6 per ride; $24 per 6hr unlimited rides session (Mon-Thur & Fri mornings). **Credit** MC, V.

At press time, the fate of this well-aged, iconic Coney Island amusement park was unknown. What we can tell you is that developers have been in a buying frenzy, snapping up parcels of land all along the beach and boardwalk, and even Astroland. The amusement park was fated to close at the end of 2007, but construction delays have allowed opening in 2008 – surely its last season. Call before heading out. If you're lucky you can ride the world-famous Cyclone rollercoaster; young ones will prefer the Tilt-a-Whirl or the carousel.

Dinosaurs at the American Museum of Natural History

For listing, see p148 American Museum of Natural History.

Children of all ages request repeat visits to this old-fashioned, exhibit-based museum – especially to see the infamous dinosaur skeletons, the enormous blue whale and, in the colder months, the free-flying butterflies. During the holiday season, look for the Christmas tree decorated with origami ornaments (they include dinosaur shapes, naturally). Paper-folders are on hand to help visitors make their own.

The Nutcracker

For listing, see p353 New York State Theater.

Generations of New York kids have counted on the New York City Ballet to provide this Balanchine holiday treat. The pretty two-act production features an on-stage snowstorm, a flying sleigh, a one-ton Christmas tree and child dancers.

Storytelling at the Hans Christian Andersen Statue

Central Park, entrance on Fifth Avenue, at 72nd Street (www.centralparknyc.org). Subway 6 to 68th Street-Hunter College. **Dates** *June-Sept* 11am-noon Sat. **Admission** free. **Map** p405 E20.

Storytelling is one tradition that suits New York down to the ground, and children five and older have gathered for decades at the foot of this climbable statue to hear master storytellers from all over the country weave their tales.

Temple of Dendur at the Met

For listing, see p143 Metropolitan Museum of Art.

The Met can be overwhelming unless you make a beeline for one or two specific galleries. The impressive Temple of Dendur, a real multi-roomed ancient temple with carvings and reliefs (and graffiti), was brought here from Egypt stone by stone, and it's a perennial hit. Also check out the mummies in the Egyptian Room, and the medieval arms and armour collection. Pick up a few of the Met's printed *Family Guides* (free at the museum's information desks and available for online download), which give kids the inside scoop on what they're seeing. Note that the Met now opens on most Monday holidays – and provides special children's programming – when many other museums are closed.

Circuses

Each spring, **Ringling Bros and Barnum & Bailey**'s three-ring circus (*see p260*) comes to Madison Square Garden, and so do animal-rights picketers declaiming their treatment of the show's real stars. You can't beat the world-famous circus for spectacle, but the one-ring alternatives listed below are more fun.

Big Apple Circus

Damrosch Park, Lincoln Center, 62nd Street, between Columbus & Amsterdam Avenues (1-212 268 2500/www.bigapplecircus.org). Subway 1 to 66th Street-Lincoln Center. **Dates** Oct-Jan. Phone or visit website for schedule & prices. **Credit** AmEx, Disc, MC, V. **Map** p405 C21.

New York's travelling circus was founded 29 years ago as an intimate answer to the Ringling Bros extravaganza. The clowns in this not-for-profit show are among the most creative in the country. The circus performs a special late show on New Year's Eve, at the end of which the entire audience joins the performers in the ring.

UniverSoul Circus

1-800 316 7439/www.universoulcircus.com. **Dates** early Apr-late May. Phone or visit website for venue, schedule & prices. **Credit** AmEx, DC, Disc, MC, V.

This one-ring 'circus of colour' has the requisite clowns and animals with a twist: instead of familiar circus music, you get hip hop, R&B, salsa – and a morality-tale finale. The group usually appears in Brooklyn's Prospect Park in the spring.

Film

New York International Children's Film Festival

Various venues (1-212 349 0330/www.gkids.com). **Dates** Feb-Mar. Phone or visit website for schedule & prices. **Credit** AmEx, MC, V.

This three-week fest is a hot ticket both for movie-going kids and their cinema-mad parents. An exciting mix of shorts and full-length features is presented to everyone from tots to teens. Many of the films are by international indie filmmakers – and not just those who make kids' flicks. Children determine the winners, which are then screened at an awards ceremony.

Tribeca Film Festival

Various Tribeca venues (www.tribecafilmfestival.org). **Dates** late Apr-early May. Visit website for schedule & prices. **Credit** AmEx, MC, V.

Robert De Niro's affair may be primarily aimed at adults, but it also includes two weeks of screenings for kids, both commercial premières and shorts programmes, plus an outdoor street festival.

Museums & exhibitions

Museums usually offer a series of weekend and school-break workshops, as well as interactive exhibitions. Even very young children will love exploring the **American Museum of Natural History**; its **Rose Center for Earth and Space** (*see p148*) features exhibits and a multimedia space show within the largest suspended glass cube in the US. Children of all ages will be fascinated by the amazing scale-model *Panorama of the City of New York* at the **Queens Museum of Art** (*see p171*) and by the toy collection at the **Museum of the City of New York** (*see p145*), with teddy bears, games and dolls' houses. At the **Museum of the Moving Image** (*see p299*), kids mess with *Jurassic Park* sound effects and play with moving-image technology. The **Intrepid Sea-Air-Space Museum** (*see p127*), which reopens in autumn 2008, houses interactive war-related exhibits on an aircraft carrier, something understandably popular with boys fascinated by battle.

Many art museums offer family tours and workshops that may include sketching in the galleries, notably the **Brooklyn Museum** (*see p164*), the **Metropolitan Museum of Art** (*see p143*) and the **Whitney Museum of American Art** (*see p145*). The **Museum of Modern Art** (*see p131*) also caters to families in its expanded midtown home, with a large variety of programmes, including the Ford Family Programs and Family Art Workshops; MoMA family programmes include admission to the museum – which saves you a bundle.

Brooklyn Children's Museum

145 Brooklyn Avenue, at St Marks Avenue, Crown Heights, Brooklyn (1-718 735 4400/www.brooklynkids.org). Subway A to Nostrand Avenue; C to Kingston-Throop Avenue; 3 to Kingston Avenue. **Open** *July, Aug* 1-6pm Tue-Fri; 11am-6pm Sat, Sun. *Sept-June* 1-6pm Wed-Fri; 11am-6pm Sat, Sun. Phone or visit website for holiday hrs. **Admission** $5; free under-1s. **Credit** AmEx, Disc, MC, V. **Map** p410 V11.

Founded in 1899, BCM is the world's first museum designed for kids. It has more than 27,000 artefacts in its main collection, including prehistoric fossils and present-day toys from around the world. Hands-on exhibits and live small animals rule the Animal Outpost, and the People Tube (a huge sewer pipe) connects four exhibit floors. On weekends, a free shuttle bus makes a circuit from the Grand Army Plaza subway station to the Brooklyn Museum and this museum.

Children's Museum of Manhattan

212 W 83rd Street, between Amsterdam Avenue & Broadway (1-212 721 1234/www.cmom.org). Subway 1 to 86th Street. **Open** 10am-5pm Wed-Sun. Phone for summer & holiday hrs. **Admission** $9; $6 seniors; free under-1s. **Credit** AmEx, MC, V. **Map** p405 C19.

This children's museum promotes several types of literacy, and encourages creativity through its interactive exhibitions and programmes. In the Inventor Center, computer-savvy kids can take any idea they dream up – a flying bike, a talking robot – and design it on-screen using digital imaging.

Children's Museum of the Arts

182 Lafayette Street, between Broome & Grand Streets (1-212 274 0986/www.cmany.org). Subway 6 to Spring Street. **Open** noon-5pm Wed, Fri-Sun; noon-6pm Thur. **Admission** $9. Voluntary donation 4-6pm Thur. **Credit** AmEx, MC, V ($35 minimum). **Map** p403 E30.

While most museums aspire to being as highbrow as possible, this one encourages and exhibits works by children. As such, kids under seven love the floor-to-ceiling blackboards, art computers and vast store of art supplies to help bring their visions to life.

New York Hall of Science

For listing, see p171.

Known for the 1964 World's Fair pavilion in which it is housed and the rockets from the US space programme that flank it, this museum has always been worth a trek for its discovery-based exhibits. Since its massive expansion in 2005, it's become a must for curious kids. The new building houses permanent hands-on exhibits that deal with 21st-century concepts such as networks, the science of sports and, in a massive pre-school-science area, the urban world. From March to December, the 30,000sq ft outdoor Science Playground teaches children the principles of balance, gravity and energy. Other standouts at the New York Hall of Science include the first interactive exhibit devoted to maths (designed by Charles and Ray Eames).

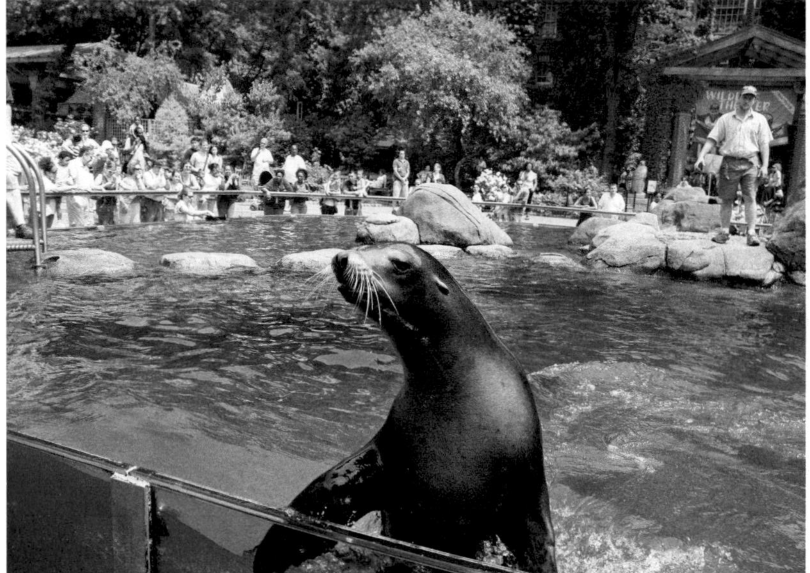

Walk with the animals, talk with the animals at the **Central Park Zoo**. *See p288.*

Arts & Entertainment

Central Park.

Sony Wonder Technology Lab

Sony Plaza, 56th Street, between Fifth & Madison Avenues (1-212 833 8100/www.sonywondertechlab.com). Subway E, V to Fifth Avenue-53rd Street; N, R, W to Fifth Avenue-59th Street. **Open** 10am-5pm Tue-Sat; noon-5pm Sun; reservations recommended. **Admission** free. **Map** p405 E22.

This digital wonderland lets visitors use state-of-the-art technology to play at designing video games, editing TV shows and operating robots. A new interactive exhibit even lets visitors rock out in a band.

Outdoor places

Battery Park City Parks

Battery Park City, Hudson River, between Chambers Street & Battery Place (1-212 267 9700/www.bpcparks.org). Subway A, C, 1, 2, 3 to Chambers Street; 1 to Rector Street. **Open** 6am-1am daily. **Admission** free. **Map** p402 D32.

Besides watching the boats along the Hudson, kids can enjoy one of New York's best playgrounds, an open field for ball games, Frisbee and lazing, and a park house that has balls, board games and toys for borrowing. Kids' events are held from May to October (visit the website for a schedule). Don't miss the picnic garden near the Chambers Street entrance, where kids love to interpret (and climb on) sculptor Tom Otterness's *Real World* installation.

Riverbank State Park

Hudson River, at 145th Street (1-212 694 3600). Subway 1 to 145th Street. **Open** 6am-11pm daily. *Ice skating* Nov-Jan varies. **Admission** free. Rink $1; skate rental $4. **Map** p408 B10.

This 28-acre park features a skating rink and other athletic facilities, along with the popular Totally Kid Carousel (June-Aug), designed by children.

Central Park

Most New Yorkers don't have their own garden – instead, they let off steam in public parks. The most popular of all is Central Park, with places and programmes just for kids. Visit www.centralparknyc.org for a calendar. Don't miss the beautiful antique carousel (Apr-Nov 10am-6pm daily; Dec-Apr 10am-4.30pm Sat & Sun; $1.50 per ride). The Heckscher Playground (one of 20) boasts an up-to-date adventure area.

Central Park Zoo

For listing, see p137.

The stars of this refurbished wildlife centre are the penguins and the polar bear, which live in glass habitats so that visitors can watch their underwater antics. The zoo also runs breeding programmes for some endangered species. *Photos p287.*

Conservatory Water

Central Park, entrance on Fifth Avenue, at 72nd Street. Subway 6 to 68th Street-Hunter College. **Open** *July, Aug* 11am-7pm Mon-Fri, Sun; 2-7pm Sat, weather permitting. **Admission** free. **Map** p405 E20.

Stuart Little Pond, named after EB White's storybook mouse, is a mecca for model-yacht racers. When the boat master is around, you can rent a remote-controlled vessel ($10 per hr).

Henry Luce Nature Observatory

For listing, see p137.

Inside the Gothic Belvedere Castle, telescopes, microscopes and hands-on exhibits teach kids about the plants and animals living in the park. With ID, you can borrow a Discovery Kit: binoculars, a bird-watching guide and other cool tools to explore nature in all its glory.

North Meadow Recreation Center

Central Park, Midpark, at 97th Street (1-212 348 4867/www.centralparknyc.org). Subway B, C, 6 to 96th Street. **Open** check website for hrs. **Admission** free. **Map** p406 E17.

Park visitors with photo ID can check out the Field Day Kit, which includes a Frisbee, Hula-Hoop, jump rope, kickball, and a Wiffle ball and bat.

Victorian Gardens

Central Park, Wollman Rink (1-212 982 2229/www.victoriangardensnyc.com). Subway N, R, W to Fifth Avenue-59th Street. **Open** *Mid May-early Sept* 11am-7pm Mon-Fri; 10am-8pm Sat, Sun. **Admission** $1 per game/ride. $6.50 general admission, $12 unlimited rides weekdays; $7.50 general admission, $14 unlimited rides weekends, holidays. Free admission for children under 36in tall. **No credit cards. Map** p405 D21.

Central Park's first Disneyesque kids feature is this nostalgia-themed amusement park geared to younger children. It's hardly white-knuckle stuff, but the mini-teacup carousel and Rio Grande train are bound to be hits with little kids.

Wollman Rink

For listing, see p338.

Skating in Central Park amid snowy trees, with grand apartment buildings towering in the distance, is a New York tradition, and a classic image of the city that never seems to tarnish with passing years. This popular (read: crowded) rink offers lessons and skate rentals, plus a snack bar where you can warm up with hot chocolate.

Performing arts

Carnegie Hall Family Concerts

For listing, see p328. **Tickets** $8.

Even kids who profess to hate classical music are usually impressed by a visit to Carnegie Hall. The Family Concert series features first-rate classical, world-music and jazz performers, along with pre-concert workshops and storytelling. Concerts run from autumn to spring and are recommended for kids aged five to 12.

Family Matters

For listing, see p353 Dance Theater Workshop. **Tickets** $20; $10 children.

Curated by a pair of choreographer parents and geared for children aged three and up (some shows are also performed for pre-teens and teens), Family Matters is a quirky variety show blending art, dance, music and theatre. Call or check the website for a schedule.

Jazz for Young People

For listing, see p321 Jazz at Lincoln Center.

This series of participatory concerts, held at Jazz at Lincoln Center's smart new digs and modelled on the New York Philharmonic Young People's Concerts, are led by the trumpeter and all-round jazz great Wynton Marsalis.

Kids'n Comedy

Gotham Comedy Club, 208 W 23rd Street, between Seventh & Eighth Avenues (1-212 877 6115/www.kidsncomedy.com). Subway F, N, R, V, W to 23rd Street. **Shows** Phone or visit website for schedule; reservations required. **Tickets** $15 plus 1-drink minimum. **Credit** AmEx, MC, V. **Map** p404 D26.

Kids'n Comedy has a stable of funny kids, aged nine to 17, who deliver their own stand-up material, much of it mined from the homework-sucks vein (although some lines have clearly been culled from Daddy's last cocktail party).

Little Orchestra Society

Various venues (1-212 971 9500/www.littleorchestra.org). **Tickets** $12-$50. **Credit** MC, V.

Since 1947 this orchestra has presented classical concerts for kids, including the popular interactive *Peter and the Wolf* for pre-schoolers and December's spectacular *Amahl and the Night Visitors*.

New Victory Theater

For listing, see p347. **Tickets** $10-$50.

As New York's only full-scale young people's theatre, the New Victory presents international theatre and dance companies at junior prices. Shows often sell out well in advance, so reserve seats early.

New York Theatre Ballet

Florence Gould Hall, 55 E 59th Street, between Madison & Park Avenues (1-212 355 6160/www.nytb.org). Subway N, R, W to Lexington Avenue-59th Street; 4, 5, 6 to 59th Street. **Tickets** $30; $25 under-12s; also available through Ticketmaster. **Credit** AmEx, MC, V. **Map** p405 E22.

Enjoy one-hour adaptations of classic ballets such as *The Nutcracker*. The interactive *Carnival of the Animals* teaches the audience basic dance moves, and *Alice in Wonderland* is a vaudeville-style romp. *See also p351.*

Swedish Cottage Marionette Theater

Central Park West, at 81st Street (1-212 988 9093). Subway B, C to 81st Street-Museum of Natural History. **Shows** *Oct-June* 10.30am, noon Tue-Fri; 1pm Sat. *July, Aug* 10.30am, noon Mon-Fri. **Tickets** $6; $5 children. **No credit cards. Map** p405 D19.

Reservations are essential at this intimate theatre, located in an old Swedish schoolhouse run by the City Parks Foundation.

Theatreworks/NYC

Lucille Lortel Theatre, 121 Christopher Street, between Bleecker & Hudson Streets (1-212 647 1100/www.theatreworksusa.org). Subway 1 to Christopher Street. **Shows** Nov, Dec, Mar, Apr, July, Aug. **Tickets** $35. **Credit** AmEx, MC, V. **Map** p403 D28.

Over 45 years, the respected travelling company Theatreworks/USA has developed a reputation for producing dependable, if somewhat bland, mostly musical adaptations of kid-lit classics. The company finally formed a New York arm in 2005.

Urban Word NYC

Various venues (www.urbanwordnyc.org).

A DJ hosts poetry slams and open mics for 'the next generation'. Teens bring their own (uncensored) poems and freestyle rhymes or give props to other kids performing theirs.

Sports & activities

For cycling, horseback riding and ice skating, *see pp333-339.*

Chelsea Piers

Piers 59-62, W 17th through 23rd Streets, at Eleventh Avenue (1-212 336 6666/www.chelseapiers.com). Subway C, E to 23rd Street. **Map** p404 B26.

A roller rink, gym, pool, toddler gym, extreme-skating park, ice skating rinks, batting cages and rock-climbing walls are all found in this vast and hugely energetic complex. The Flip 'n' Flick programme (occasional Saturdays, 7pm to 11pm) allows parents a night off while the kids enjoy athletic activities and a movie.

Downtown Boathouse

Riverside Park South Pier, at 72nd Street & Hudson River (1-646 613 0740/www.downtownboathouse.org). Subway 1, 2, 3 to 72nd Street. **Open** *15 May-15 Oct* 10am-5pm daily. **Map** p405 B20.

From 15 May to 15 October, weather permitting, this volunteer-run organisation offers free kayaking on weekends for outdoorsy kids and their families. All trips are offered on a first-come, first-served basis, and you must be able to swim.

Other location: Pier 96, at 56th Street & Hudson River, Midtown.

Sydney's Playground

66 White Street, between Broadway & Church Street (1-212 431 9125/www.sydneysplayground.com). Subway J, M, N, Q, R, W, Z, 6 to Canal Street. **Open** *Sept-May* 10am-6pm daily. *Memorial Day-Labor Day* 10am-6pm Mon-Fri. **Admission** $13 for 1st child with adult; $6 each additional child/adult. **Credit** AmEx, Disc, MC, V. **Map** p402 E31.

For kids aged five and under, this huge indoor play space resembles a streetscape, complete with a multi-level 'climbing city', a 'roadway' for ride-on toys and a cheerful café.

Trapeze School New York

For listing, see p339.

Kids over six can fly through the air with the greatest of ease. (You can also just stop along the esplanade and watch.) Under-12s must be accompanied by an adult.

Willy Bee's Family Lounge

302 Metropolitan Avenue, between Driggs Avenue & Roebling Street, Williamsburg, Brooklyn (1-718 599 3499/www.willybees.com). Subway L to Bedford Avenue. **Open** 9am-7pm Mon-Thur; 9am-8pm Fri; 10am-8pm Sat; 10am-6pm Sun. **Credit** MC, V. **Map** p411 U8.

NYC's hippest neighbourhood, across the river from the Lower East Side, has started turning into baby-central as its artsy residents couple and procreate. Visit for a blast of alternakid culture and a pit stop at Willy Bee's café and play space, a favourite hang-out for local parents. Sip wine while the children check out the toys or mess around in the backyard with their new found friends.

Tours

ARTime

1-718 797 1573. **Open** *Oct-June* 11am-12.30pm 1st Sat of mth. **Admission** $25 per parent-child pair, $5 each additional child. **No credit cards**.

Since 1994 art historians with backgrounds in education have led monthly contemporary-art tours of Chelsea galleries for groups of kids aged five to ten (and their parents).

Confino Family Apartment Tour

For listing, see p109 Lower East Side Tenement Museum.

A weekly interactive tour teaches children aged five to 14 the facts about immigrant life in early 20th-century New York. To help get the message across and bring the story to life, kids play games and handle knick-knacks from the era.

Zoos

Bronx Zoo

Bronx River Parkway, at Fordham Road (1-718 367 1010/www.bronxzoo.org). Subway 2, 5 to West Farms Square-East Tremont Avenue. **Open** *Apr-Oct* 10am-5pm Mon-Fri; 10am-5.30pm Sat, Sun, holidays. *Nov-Mar* 10am-4.30pm daily. **Admission** $14; $12 seniors, $10 3-12s; free under-2s. Voluntary donation Wed. (Some rides and exhibitions cost extra.) **Credit** AmEx, DC, Disc, MC, V.

Inside the Bronx Zoo is the Bronx Children's Zoo, with lots of domesticated critters to pet, plus exhibits that show the world from an animal's point of view. Beyond the Children's Zoo, camel rides (Apr-Oct) and sea-lion feedings (11am and 3pm) are other can't-miss attractions for visitors with kids. *See also p176.*

New York Aquarium

610 Surf Avenue, at West 8th Street, Coney Island, Brooklyn (1-718 265 3474/www.nyaquarium.com). Subway D to Coney Island-Stillwell Avenue; F, Q to W 8th Street-NY Aquarium. **Open** Visit website for hrs. **Admission** $12; $8 seniors, 2-12s; free under-2s. **Credit** AmEx, Disc, MC, V.

Like the rest of Coney Island, this aquarium is admittedly a little on the shabby side, but kids always enjoy seeing the famous beluga whale family, the scary sharks and the entertaining sea-lion show, or giggling at the unintentional hilarity of the walruses before taking a stroll on the Coney Island boardwalk. The aquarium has a respected conservation arm that organises educational events for kids.

Clubs

It'll take more than noise codes and rocketing rents to break up the NY party.

Get cosy at attitude-free **Cielo**. *See p292.*

The Loft, the Paradise Garage, Studio 54, Danceteria, Area, Jackie 60, Twilo and Body & Soul are just a few of the storied venues that have made New York City synonymous with world-class, forward-thinking clubbing. To many, Gotham was at one time the clubbing capital of the world, with people from all over flocking to NYC in search of the perfect beat. Nowadays, seekers of clubland nirvana would be more likely to make a sojourn to Berlin, London or Ibiza in that quest.

NYC's declined clubbing status is due, at least in part, to the attitude that the city fathers have towards nightlife. The Giuliani administration was quite explicit and rabid in its dislike for after-dark fun; deputy mayor Rudy Washington famously derided dance clubs as 'little buckets of blood', and it was Giuliani who sited the archaic, Prohibition-era cabaret laws in his zeal to shut them down. Though the current Bloomberg government is a little less public in its anti-clubbing quest, it's certainly more businesslike. For example, it has just enacted a noise code that stipulates a bar or club can be fined if music is 'plainly audible' 15 feet from the entrance, a requirement that, if enforced as written, would apply to pretty much every venue with music loud enough to dance to.

But the problems run far deeper than official interference. The demographics of the city have changed drastically since clubland's halcyon days, largely due to spiralling rents. The artist who was paying $300 a month in 1990 for an East Village studio apartment, for instance, was probably more interested in a vibrant club scene than the financial advisor who's now paying $3,000 for the same space. The shortsightedness of many of the industry's entrepreneurs doesn't help either. A few years back, franchised nightlife became all the rage, with chain clubs Avalon, Crobar, Spirit and Pacha all opening in a one-year span. This, in the city that led the world in the field of creative nightlife. Rather predictably, the first three have already closed down, with Pacha surviving largely because of a progressive, boundary-pushing musical policy.

Still, this is New York, and you can't stop people from going out dancing – and happily, there are still plenty of great places to do just that. The Meatpacking District's **APT** (*see p296*) regularly scores some of the world's best spinners to play at what's essentially nothing more than a bar with a sound system, albeit a killer sound system. Just around the corner, **Cielo** – a lovely, intimate jewelbox of a boîte – regularly features spinners on the level of Louie Vega and François K, along with visiting DJ royalty from around the world. There's the rollicking rock 'n' roll circus **Motherfucker** (*see p297*), a roving party that is regularly touted as the world's best – why not decide for yourself? **P.S.1 Warm Up** (*see p297*), a weekly summertime soirée held in a courtyard at a Queens museum, attracts thousands of kids who like nothing better than to get down to some pretty twisted DJs. The newish **Studio B** (*see p295*), tucked away in an isolated corner of Brooklyn, has become the centre of NYC's electro-rock scene. And if you're really lucky, you might even hear about an illegal warehouse party hidden away in the outer boroughs – though you'd better hope that the cops don't hear about it too.

Bear in mind that most clubs take cash only on the door and operate a credit card minimum (typically $20) at the bar.

Clubs

The Bunker

Galapagos Art Space (back room), 70 North 6th Street, between Kent & Wythe Avenues, Williamsburg, Brooklyn (1-718 782 5188/www.beyondbooking.com/thebunker). Subway L to Bedford Avenue. **Open** 11pm-4am Fri. **Cover** $10-$15. **Average drink** $10. **Map** p411 U7.

Gotham's electronic music fans were in a tizzy when Tonic, the long-time home of the Bunker, closed down in 2007, but the shindig is now happily ensconced in Williamsburg's Galapagos. And, as befits the party that helped to kick off the current craze for all things minimal and techno in NYC, residents DJ Spinoza and Derek Plaslaiko are still scoring top stars of the scene, with big guns from labels like Spectral Sound and Kompakt regularly packing the bunker-like room.

Cielo

18 Little W 12th Street, between Ninth Avenue & Washington Street (1-212 645 5700/www.cieloclub.com). Subway A, C, E to 14th Street; L to Eighth Avenue. **Open** 10pm-4am daily. **Cover** $5-$20. **Average drink** $10. **Map** p403 C28.

You'd never guess from the Paris Hilton wannabes in the neighbourhood that the attitude inside this exclusive club is close to zero. Grab a cocktail from the bar, then move to the sunken dancefloor where hip-to-hip crowds gyrate to deep beats from top DJs, including NYC old-schoolers François K, Tedd Patterson and Louis Vega, as well as international spinners ranging from Ellen Allien to Dimitri from Paris. Cielo, which features a crystal-clear sound system, has won a bevy of 'best club' awards in its four years of existence – and in our opinion it deserves them all. *Photo p291.*

Club Shelter

150 Varick Street, at Vandam Street (1-646 862 6117/www.clubshelter.com). Subway 1 to Houston Street. **Open** 11pm-noon Sat. **Cover** $15-$20. **Average drink** $6. **Map** p403 D30.

This address has been home to a variety of nightspots over the years. The current beloved incarnation is Shelter (and before Shelter, it was Club Standard), the city's longest-running house 'n'

Element.

The clubbing commandments

NYC bouncers' tips on how to stay on their good side.

Don't smoke

Don't spark up in front of security, whether you're smoking tobacco or anything else.

Curtail the bathroom antics

Squeezing more than one body into a bathroom stall is a big no-no. 'I don't care what you're doing in there,' one bouncer tells us. 'I'm gonna pound on that door until you're not doing it any more.'

Don't try to score off the bouncer

For some reason, a lot of people assume that bouncers double as drug vendors. You may not get kicked out for asking a bouncer for illicit substances, but you'll surely go on his shit list.

The bribes won't work

Don't assume that cosying up to the security staff will grant you any special status. To avoid waiting in line, for instance, 'women promise to flash their tits and men offer cash,' a Meatpacking District bouncer says. 'Unfortunately, I can't do anything for them. So no tits and no tips.'

Men, respect the ladies

Bouncers tend to be protective of their female co-workers, often taking on a big brotherly role. A patron's drunken, slobbering pick-up attempt just might result in an early exit.

No name-dropping

Never allow the phrase 'Don't you know who I am?' to leave your lips. Name-droppers are the security professional's pet peeve.

Follow instructions

When the night is over and the bouncer bellows that it's time to leave, that's not just a suggestion – consider it an order. 'Everyone who works at the club is tired and wants to go home,' says a particularly hulking bouncer. 'Don't they realise that we're people too?'

classics party. The Saturday-night no-attitude dance marathon is a New York institution that's been around in one form or another for some 15 years, and which continues to draw a wild-looking agglomeration of people to the dark, sweaty dancefloor. Timmy Regisford, the resident DJ for the Shelter shindig, hypnotises dancefloor denizens week after week – many disciples stay until the music stops sometime on Sunday afternoon.

Element

225 E Houston Street, at Essex Street (1-212 254 2200/www.elementny.com). Subway F, V to Lower East Side-Second Avenue. **Open** 10pm-4am Fri, Sat. Phone for events on other nights. **Cover** $10-$20 (cash only). **Average drink** $9. **Map** p403 G29.

A former bank, goth hotspot and studio of Jasper Johns, this hulking space offers a massive dancefloor encircled by a perfect-view balcony, a mellow VIP area and a cool underground vault. Look out for nights dedicated to soul, house and new-wave sounds, plus the Saturday night queer-party action. Be sure to check out the downstairs lounge, Vault (accessible via a separate entrance), which features underground sounds of all sorts.

Lotus

409 W 14th Street, between Ninth Avenue & Washington Street (1-212 243 4420/www.lotusnewyork.com). Subway A, C, E to 14th Street; L to Eighth Avenue. **Open** 10pm-4am Tue-Sun. **Cover** $20. **Average drink** $8. **Map** p403 C27.

Though a few years past its pioneer days, this chichi model-infested club is still a central hotspot. The triple-tiered, Asian-accented space, with an overlooking balcony, allows for prime people-watching opportunities. Sample delicate hors d'oeuvres and fresh watermelon martinis at the bar, or turn up late with your best-dressed buddies and throw down a few hundred bucks on a few bottles. A contingent of downtown hipsters comes for the Friday night GBH affair; the rest of the week, expect tall girls, guys with thinning hair and plenty of Eurotrash.

Love

40 W 8th Street, at MacDougal Street (1-212 477 5683/www.musicislove.net). Subway A, B, C, D, E, F, V to W 4th Street; R, W (weekdays only) to 8th Street-NYU. **Open** 10pm-4am Wed-Sat; 5pm-1am Sun. **Cover** $10-$15. **Average drink** $6. **Map** p403 E28.

The focus here is squarely on the music and building a scene. It's hardly a revolutionary concept, but in today's nightlife world of going for the quick buck, Love stands out from the crowd. The main room is a sparsely furnished box, but the DJ line-up is pretty impressive – the likes of the Greenskeepers' James Curd, Dubtribe's Sunshine Jones and Body & Soul's Joe Claussell have all graced the decks here. Lately, the boîte has been branching out beyond house music by hosting nights devoted to drum 'n' bass and dubstep; played over Love's stunning sound system, it all sounds great.

Pacha.

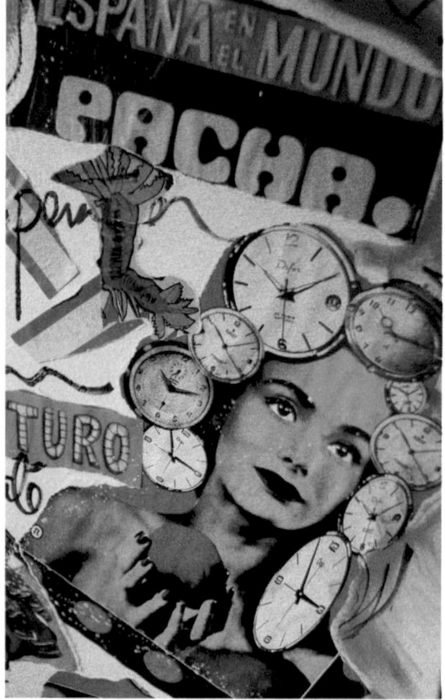

Marquee

289 Tenth Avenue, between 26th & 27th Streets (1-646 473 0202). Subway C, E to 23rd Street. **Open** 10pm-4am Tue-Sat. **Cover** $20. **Average drink** $9. **Map** p404 C26.

The owners tore the roof off a former garage, and custom-made everything here: the vaulted ceiling, the glass-beaded chandelier, even the champagne buckets. The centrepiece is a spectacular double-sided staircase that leads to a mezzanine level, where a glass wall overlooks the action below. The club accommodates up to 600 people, but despite having been around for a couple of years, this spot is still so hot (the bartenders too) that you'll have trouble getting past the velvet rope. Don't expect much musically, though – as with many places where the scene trumps the tunes, it's largely middle-of-the-road fare. Christina Aguilera and Paris Hilton both had their album release parties here.

Pacha

618 W 46th Street, between Eleventh & Twelfth Avenues (1-212 209 7500/www.pachanyc.com). **Open** 5pm-4am Thur; 10pm-6am Fri, Sat. **Cover** $20-$25. **Average drink** $9. **Map** p404 B23.

The worldwide glam clubbing chain Pacha, with outposts in nightlife hotspots such as Ibiza, London and Buenos Aires, recently hit the US market with its swanky NYC outpost helmed by superstar spinner Erick Morillo. The spot attracts heavyweights ranging from local hero Danny Tenaglia to big-time visiting jocks such as Jeff Mills and Josh Wink, but like most big clubs, it pays to check the line-up ahead if you're into underground beats: it's been known in the past to book overtly commercial spinners.

Pyramid

101 Avenue A, between 6th & 7th Streets (1-212 228 4888). Subway F, V to Lower East Side-Second Avenue; L to First Avenue; 6 to Astor Place. **Open** 10pm-4am daily. **Cover** free-$15. **Average drink** $7. **Map** p403 G28.

In a clubbing era that's long gone, the Pyramid was a cornerstone of forward-thinking queer club culture. In what could be considered a sign of the times, the venue's sole remaining gay soirée is Friday night's non-progressive '80s dance-fest, 1984. Otherwise, the charmingly decrepit space features the long-running drum 'n' bass bash Konkrete Jungle, as well as an interesting rotating roster of goth and new-wave affairs.

Sapphire

249 Eldridge Street, between Houston & Stanton Streets (1-212 777 5153/www.sapphirenyc.com). Subway F, V to Lower East Side-Second Avenue. **Open** 7pm-4am daily. **Cover** $5. **Average drink** $5. **Map** p403 F29.

The bare walls and minimal decorations are as raw as it gets – and not particularly appealing – yet the energetic, unpretentious clientele is oblivious to the aesthetic. A dance crowd packs the place every night of the week. Various nights feature house, hip hop, reggae and disco.

Arts & Entertainment

Sullivan Room

218 Sullivan Street, between Bleecker & W 3rd Streets (1-212 252 2151/www.sullivanroom.com). Subway A, B, C, D, E, F, V to W 4th Street. **Open** 10pm-4am Mon, Tue, Thur-Sat. **Cover** $5-$15. **Average drink** $8. **Map** p403 E29.

Where's the party? It's right here in this unmarked subterranean space, which hosts some of the best deep-house, tech-house and breaks bashes the city has to offer. It's an utterly unpretentious club, with little of the glitz of bigger clubs – but hell, all you really need are some thumpin' beats and a place to move your feet, right? Keep a special lookout for the nights hosted by local stalwarts Sleepy and Boo.

Studio B

259 Banker Street, between Calyer Street & Mesearole Avenue, Greenpoint, Brooklyn (1-718 389 1680/www.clubstudiob.com). Subway A, B, C, D, E, F, V to W 4th Street. **Open** 10pm-4am Thur-Sat. **Cover** $5-$15. **Average drink** $7. **Map** p411 U7.

It's way off the beaten track – the dark outskirts of Brooklyn's Greenpoint neighborhood, to be precise – but since opening at the end of 2006, the one-time Polish disco Studio B has been regularly packing in hundreds of cool kids on to its ample dance floor. The secret to the club's success is simple: no attitude, an ace sound system and a forward-thinking booking policy. The list of DJs and bands

DJ profile: Justine D

For the iPod school of DJs – staples at New York hipster parties – a song can often seem little more than a cheap bauble, a disposable divertissement. Enter vinyl junkie-turned-pro DJ Justine D, who flies the flag for eclectic sounds and old-school spinning.

A native New Yorker, Justine was born and raised in Chinatown and used to sneak out to clubs with her brother in the early 1990s. All the early exposure clearly paid off as, in 2000, Justine launched the popular roving rock 'n' roll soirée **Motherfucker** (*see p297*) with a small group of like-minded friends. The messy, sprawling party has been held at clubs throughout downtown Manhattan on holiday weekends ever since, attracting up to 900 people of all stripes and sexual persuasions. Justine and her clan feel the event remains a necessary response to the way the city's nightlife has been heading. What started as an anti-Giuliani party has gathered steam as the city continues to crack down on the clubbing scene. 'What's funny is that the worse things get, the more people want to escape,' says Justine. 'And escape is certainly what we provide.'

Justine is also now the creative force behind **Studio B** (*see above*), the music-driven club on an out-of-the-way block in Greenpoint, Brooklyn. The newish venue, which holds about 1,000 revellers, has made its home in a former Polish disco and boasts a superb sound system, crazy lighting and a smoke machine left over from its disco days. 'The club hired me knowing what I had already done. I took the ball and ran with it, booking DJs and bands based on my own tastes, which aren't really mainstream,' says Justine. Studio B hosts both live and DJ events, and veers mostly towards electro-rock, but its DJ parties can vary from straight-up funk and hip hop to techno.

To sample some of Justine D's tunes, seek out 'Rvng Presents MX5', her 2007 techno-electro mix CD. An impressive salmagundi of sounds, it has a cool downtown vibe and plenty of spine-tingling moments.

who have played at Studio B is a sterling one, with techno deity Carl Craig, electro-house duo Booka Shade, neo-disco band Escort and the nu-ravey Klaxons just a small sampling of those who have braved the G train to rock the house. *See also p295* **DJ profile: Justine D**.

Webster Hall

125 E 11th Street, between Third & Fourth Avenues (1-212 353 1600/www.webster-hall.com). Subway L, N, Q, R, W, 4, 5, 6 to 14th Street-Union Square. **Open** 10pm-5am Thur-Sat. **Cover** free-$30. **Average drink** $6. **Map** p403 F28.

Should you crave the sight of big hair, muscle shirts and gold chains, Webster Hall offers all that and, well, not much more. The grand four-level space, built in the 1800s as a dance hall, is nice enough, and the DJs aren't bad (spinning disco, hip hop, soul, Latin, trance, progressive house or pop hits), but it's hard to forget who you're sharing the dancefloor with. Wet T-shirt and striptease contests also feature.

Lounges & DJ bars

APT

419 W 13th Street, between Ninth Avenue & Washington Street (1-212 414 4245/www.aptwebsite.com). Subway A, C, E to 14th Street; L to Eighth Avenue. **Open** 7pm-4am daily. **Cover** varies. **Average drink** $9. **Map** p403 C27.

Kicking back in APT's formerly exclusive street-level space (the neat design is by architect and designer India Mahdavi) is like being at an impromptu party in some trust-fund babe's Upper East Side townhouse. Down below, people looking for the perfect beat gather in a minimalist, faux-wood-panelled rectangular room. The space features an amazing array of DJs; top spinners, such as locals DJ Spun and the Negroclash crew, and superstars like cosmic-disco dons the Idjut Boys and house-music hero Tony Humphries, regularly regale the tipplers with a wide range of underground sounds.

Slipper Room

167 Orchard Street, at Stanton Street (1-212 253 7246/www.slipperroom.com). Subway F, V to Lower East Side-Second Avenue. **Open** 8pm-4am Tue-Sat. **Cover** free. **Average drink** $8. **Map** p403 F29.

New York City has a healthy neo-burlesque scene, and the petite Slipper Room is, if not at its nexus, then pretty darn close, offering a weekly roster of events. Many of the Victorian-looking venue's happenings, notably Friday's Hot Box hoedown, feature plenty of bump-and-grind action, with DJs spinning the appropriate beats; the occasional live band completes the picture.

Le Souk

47 Avenue B, between 3rd & 4th Streets (1-212 777 5454/www.lesoukny.com). Subway F V to Lower East Side-Second Avenue. **Open** 6pm-4am Mon-Sat; 1pm-4am Sun. **Cover** free. **Average drink** $9. **Map** p403 G29.

You might not suspect a Middle Eastern eaterie and hookah bar to be one of the mainstays of New York's clubbing scene, but if you're at all into straight-up house music, make sure you stop by Le Souk on a Sunday any time between mid afternoon and, say, mid Monday morning. That's when you'll find local vets Astro&Glyde and Swamy manning the decks, along with top guests. And when we say top, we mean it: folks on the level of Sasha and Paul Oakenfold have been known to tickle the Technics here. There are DJs on other nights too, but really, it's all about Sundays here.

Triple Crown

108 Bedford Avenue, at North 11th Street, Williamsburg, Brooklyn (1-718 388 8883/www.triplecrownpage.com). Subway L to Bedford Avenue. **Open** 6pm-4am daily. **Cover** free. **Average drink** $8. **Map** p411 U7.

Since its autumn 2004 opening, sleek Williamsburg lounge Triple Crown has managed to rise to the top of the city's hip hop venues. Granted, the competition for that status isn't exactly fierce, but when you regularly score spinners on the level of Rob

A-list sounds at **Studio B**. *See p295.*

Swift from the X-Ecutioners, A Tribe Called Quest's Ali Shaheed Muhammad and old-school legend Schoolly D, you're obviously doing something right.

Roving & seasonal parties

New York has a number of peripatetic and season-specific shindigs. Nights, locations and prices vary, so call, email or hit the websites for the latest updates.

Cooper-Hewitt Summer Sessions: Summer Sessions

2 E 91st Street, at Fifth Avenue, Uptown (1-212 849 8400/www.cooperhewitt.org). Subway 4, 5, 6 to 86th Street. **Open** *July, Aug* 6-9pm Fri. **Cover** $10 (incl museum admission). **Average drink** $8. **Map** p406 E18

In the warmer months, the city's premier design museum hosts after-work outdoor revelry, but these aren't garden parties in the traditional sense. DJs ranging from local funksters to international superstars work the crowd with all manner of underground beats. Still, the vibe is a lot more genteel than the similar P.S.1 Warm Up party (*see below*).

Giant Step

www.giantstep.net.

Giant Step parties have been among the best of the nu-soul scene since the early '90s – back before there was a nu-soul scene. Sadly, the gang doesn't throw as many fêtes as it once did, now preferring to concentrate on live shows and record promotions. But on the rare occasion that Giant Step does decide to pack a dancefloor, you'd be a fool to miss it: the music is always great, and the multicultural crowd always gorgeous beyond belief.

Motherfucker

www.motherfuckernyc.com.

This roaming, polysexual trash fest, helmed by veteran NYC scenesters Justine D, Michael T, Georgie Seville and Johnny T, is generally considered the best bash going on in town right now. Held on the eves of major holidays at an array of the city's biggest nightspots, it features Justine, Michael and guests spinning an anarchic mix of sleazed-out electro, new wave and disco, plus the most utterly deviant menagerie of club freaks that you're likely to come across nowadays. In many ways, it's a throwback to the glory days of New York's once-decadent clubbing scene.

P.S.1 Warm Up

P.S.1 Contemporary Art Center, 22-25 Jackson Avenue, at 45th Road, Jackson Heights, Queens (1-718 784 2084/www.ps1.org). Subway E, V to 23rd Street-Ely Avenue; G to 21st Street-Jackson Avenue; 7 to 45th Road-Court House Square. **Open** *July-Sept* 2-9pm Sat. **Cover** $8 (incl museum admission). **Average drink** $6. **Map** p412 V5.

Back in 1997, who could have guessed that the courtyard of the MoMA-affiliated P.S.1 Contemporary Art Center would play host to some of the most anticipated, resolutely underground clubbing events in the city? Since the Warm Up series kicked off that year, summer Saturdays truly haven't been the same. Thousands of dance-music fanatics make the pilgrimage to Queens to pack the space, swig beer, dance and generally make a mockery of the soirée's arty setting. The sounds range from spiritually inclined soul to full-bore techno, spun by local and international stars.

Turntables on the Hudson

1-212 560 5593/www.turntablesonthehudson.com.

This ultra-funky affair lost its longtime home at the Lightship Frying Pan when the city put the kibosh on the vessel's parties (no surprise there), but they still pop up all over the place – sometimes on the Hudson, sometimes not. DJs Nickodemus, Mariano and their guests do the dub-funky, world-beat thing, and live percussionists add to the flavour. As good as it gets.

Film & TV

Step into the screen.

Hollywood might hog all the attention but New Yorkers know better: their city is a movie 24-7. Seeking a little ape-on-building action à la King Kong? Visit the iconic Empire State Building. Or maybe it's Woody Allen who's got you in the mood for some fast-paced gab over nosh; try the Carnegie Deli (*Broadway Danny Rose*) or chummy Elaine's (*Manhattan*). Cinephiles won't be disappointed no matter where they go; New York is the ultimate scene. And let's not forget the small screen either: you can still line up for *Saturday Night Live* or *The Daily Show*, and the TV crews are everywhere these days. Stroll by (act natural!) and you might just make the cut.

Film

It's no exaggeration to call New York a film lover's paradise. Of course, you can check out Hollywood's latest blockbusters at the swanky multiplexes on 42nd Street. But Gotham's real gems are its dozens of smaller art houses and museums, contributing immeasurably to the daily bill of fare with everything from Korean thrillers and African comedies to silent classics. Annual festivals and retrospectives ensure that New Yorkers stay seasoned and at the cutting edge. For current listings, pick up a copy of *Time Out New York.*

Art & revival houses

Angelika Film Center

18 W Houston Street, at Mercer Street (1-212 995 2000/www.angelikafilmcenter.com). Subway B, D, F, V to Broadway-Lafayette Street; N, R, W to Prince Street; 6 to Bleecker Street. **Tickets** $10.75; $7 seniors, under-12s. **Credit** AmEx, MC, V. **Map** p403 E29.

The six-screen Angelika puts the emphasis on independent fare, both American and foreign. The complex is a zoo on weekends, so come extra early or visit the website to buy advance tickets.

BAM Rose Cinemas

Brooklyn Academy of Music, 30 Lafayette Avenue, between Ashland Place & St Felix Street, Fort Greene, Brooklyn (1-718 636 4100/www.bam.org). Subway B, Q, 2, 3, 4, 5 to Atlantic Avenue; C to Lafayette Street; D, M, N, R to Pacific Street; G to Fulton Street. **Tickets** $11; $7.50 students (Mon-Thur only); seniors, children. **Credit** AmEx, MC, V. **Map** p403 E27.

Brooklyn's premier art-film venue does double duty as a repertory house for well-programmed classics and a first-run multiplex for independent films.

Cinema Village

22 E 12th Street, between Fifth Avenue & University Place (1-212 924 3363/www.cinemavillage.com). Subway L, N, Q, R, W, 4, 5, 6 to 14th Street-Union Square. **Tickets** $10; $7.50 students; $5.50 seniors, under-13s. **Credit** MC, V. **Map** p403 E27.

This three-screen cinema specialises in American indie flicks and foreign movies. Check out the subway turnstile that admits ticket holders to the lobby.

Film Forum

209 W Houston Street, between Sixth Avenue & Varick Street (1-212 727 8110/www.filmforum.com). Subway 1 to Houston Street. **Tickets** $10.50; $5.50 seniors, under-12s (senior discount before 5pm Mon-Fri). **Credit** *Box office* cash only. *Website* AmEx, MC, V. **Map** p403 D29.

Though its seats and sight lines leave something to be desired, this three-screen art theatre presents documentaries, new and repertory films, and a cute crowd of budding NYU auteurs and film geeks.

IFC Center

323 Sixth Avenue, at 3rd Street (1-212 924 7771/ www.ifccenter.com). Subway A, B, C, D, E, F, V to W 4th Street. **Tickets** $10.75; $7 seniors, under-12s. **Credit** AmEx, MC, V. **Map** p403 D29.

The long-darkened Waverly has risen again as a modernised three-screen art house, showing the latest indie hits, choice midnight cult items and the occasional foreign classic. A high-toned café provides sweets, lattes and substantials; and you might rub elbows with the talent on screen, since many come to introduce their work on opening night.

The ImaginAsian

239 E 59th Street, between Second & Third Avenues (1-212 371 6682/www.theimaginasian.com). Subway N, R, W to Lexington Avenue-59th Street; 4, 5, 6 to 59th Street. **Tickets** $10; $7 seniors, students, under-12s. **Credit** MC, V. **Map** p405 F22.

Since its 2004 rechristening, this 300-seat movie palace has faithfully devoted itself to all things Asian or Asian-American. Typical fare includes jolting J-horror freak-outs, cutting-edge Korean dramas and the latest dance moves bustin' outta Bollywood.

Landmark's Sunshine Cinema

143 E Houston Street, between First & Second Avenues (1-212 330 8182/777 3456). Subway F, V to Lower East Side-Second Avenue. **Tickets** $10.75; $7 seniors. **Credit** AmEx, Disc, MC, V. **Map** p403 F29.

Screenings with meaning at the **Film Forum**.

This beautifully restored 1898 Yiddish theatre has become one of New York's snazziest art houses, airing independent cinema in a luxurious atmosphere.

Leonard Nimoy Thalia

Symphony Space, 2537 Broadway, at 95th Street, entrance on 95th Street (1-212 864 5400/www.symphonyspace.org). Subway 1, 2, 3 to 96th Street. **Tickets** $10; $8 seniors, students. **Credit** AmEx, MC, V. **Map** p406 B17.

The famed Thalia art house – featured in *Annie Hall* – was recently reworked. It's more comfortable now, and still offers retrospectives of foreign classics, but with more cutting-edge stuff thrown into the mix.

Quad Cinema

34 W 13th Street, between Fifth & Sixth Avenues (1-212 255 8800/www.quadcinema.com). Subway F, V to 14th Street; L to Sixth Avenue. **Tickets** $10; $7 5-12s, seniors. **Credit** *Box office* cash only. *Website* AmEx, MC, V. **Map** p403 E27.

Four small screens (in Downtown's first multiplex) show a range of foreign and American independents, as well as documentaries, many covering gay sexuality and politics. Under-fives are not admitted.

Two Boots Pioneer Theater

155 E 3rd Street, between Avenues A & B (1-212 591 0434/www.twoboots.com). Subway F, V to Lower East Side-Second Avenue. **Tickets** $9; $6.50 seniors, students, children. **Credit** AmEx, Disc, MC, V. **Map** p403 G29.

Phil Hartman, founder of the Two Boots pizza chain, also runs this East Village alternative film centre, which shows an assortment of newish indies, horror revivals and themed festivals.

Museums & societies

Anthology Film Archives

32 Second Avenue, at 2nd Street (1-212 505 5181/www.anthologyfilmarchives.org). Subway F, V to Lower East Side-Second Avenue. **Tickets** $8; $5 seniors, students. **No credit cards**. **Map** p403 F29.

Set in a crumbling landmark building, Anthology is a fiercely independent cinema showcasing foreign and experimental film and video. Its first offering, in 1970, was a typewritten manifesto.

Brooklyn Museum

For listing, see p164.

The eclectic roster at Brooklyn's stately palace of fine arts concentrates on offbeat foreign films and smart documentaries.

Film Society of Lincoln Center

Walter Reade Theater, Lincoln Center, 165 W 65th Street, between Broadway & Amsterdam Avenue, plaza level above Alice Tully Hall (1-212 875 5601/www.filmlinc.com). Subway 1, 9 to 66th Street-Lincoln Center. **Tickets** $10; $7 students; $5 seniors (before 6pm Mon-Fri), 6-12s. **Credit** *Box office* cash only. *Website* MC, V. **Map** p405 C21.

The FSLC was founded in 1969 to support filmmakers and promote contemporary film and video. It operates the Walter Reade Theater, a state-of-the-art venue in Lincoln Center with the city's most comfortable cinema seats and best sight lines. Programmes are usually thematic with an international perspective. In autumn, the Society hosts the New York Film Festival (*see p264*).

IMAX Theater

For listing, see p148 American Museum of Natural History.

The IMAX screen is an eye-popping four storeys high and its child-friendly movies explore the myriad wonders of the natural world.

Metropolitan Museum of Art

For listing, see p142.

The Met offers a programme of documentaries on art – many relating to current museum exhibitions – that are screened in the Uris Center Auditorium (near the 81st Street entrance).

Museum of Modern Art

For listing, see p131.

The city's smartest destination for superb programming of art films and experimental work, drawing from a vast vault that's second to none.

Museum of the Moving Image

For listing, see p168.

Moving Image, the first American film museum, puts on an impressive schedule of more than 700 films a year, many of which are organised into some of the most creatively curated series in the city.

Paley Center for Media (formerly the Museum of Television & Radio)

For listing, see p133.
A multimedia collection including thousands of TV programmes that can be viewed at private consoles.

Foreign-language films

Many of the institutions listed above also screen films in languages other than English.

Asia Society & Museum

For listing, see p138.
See works from China, India and other Asian countries, as well as Asian-American productions.

French Institute Alliance Française

For listing, see p328 Florence Gould Hall.
FIAF shows French and francophone movies.

Goethe-Institut New York

For listing, see p143.
Screens German films in various locations around the city, as well as in its own opulent auditorium.

Film festivals

Each spring, MoMA and the Film Society of Lincoln Center (FSLC) sponsor the highly regarded **New Directors/New Films** series, presenting works by on-the-cusp filmmakers from around the world. The FSLC, together with Lincoln Center's *Film Comment* magazine, also puts on the popular **Film Comment Selects** series, which allows the magazine's editors to showcase their favourite movies that have yet to be distributed in the US. Plus, every September and October, the FSLC hosts the prestigious **New York Film Festival** (*see p264*). The **New York Independent Film & Video Festival** (www.nyfilmvideo.com) lures cinéastes twice yearly, in April and November. Every April, Robert De Niro rolls out his own **Tribeca Film Festival** (*see p260*), a big hit with film lovers. The **New York Lesbian & Gay Film Festival** (1-212 571 2170, www.newfestival.org) takes place in early June. January brings the annual **New York Jewish Film Festival** (1-212 875 5600) to Lincoln Center's Walter Reade Theater.

TV

Studio tapings

The Daily Show with Jon Stewart

513 W 54th Street, between Tenth & Eleventh Avenues (1-212 586 2477/www.comedycentral.com). Subway C, E to 50th Street. **Tapings** 5.30pm Mon-Thur. **Map** p405 C22.
Reserve tickets at least three months ahead online, or call at 11.30am on the Friday before you'd like to attend and see if there's a cancellation. You must be at least 18 and have a photo ID.

Late Night with Conan O'Brien

30 Rockefeller Plaza, Sixth Avenue, between 49th & 50th Streets (1-212 664 3056/www.nbc.com/conan). Subway B, D, F, V to 47th-50th Streets-Rockefeller Center. **Tapings** 5.30pm Tue-Fri. **Map** p404 E23.
Call at least three months in advance for tickets. A small number of same-day standby tickets are distributed at 9am (49th Street entrance); one ticket per person. You must be at least 16 and have a photo ID.

Late Show with David Letterman

1697 Broadway, between 53rd & 54th Streets (1-212 975 1003/www.lateshowaudience.com). Subway B, D, E to Seventh Avenue. **Tapings** 5.30pm Mon-Wed; 5.30pm, 8pm Thur. **Map** p405 D22.
Seats can be hard to come by. Try requesting tickets for a specific date by filling out a form on the show's website. You may also be able to get a standby ticket by calling 1-212 247 6497 at 11am on the day of taping. You must be 18 and have a photo ID.

Saturday Night Live

30 Rockefeller Plaza, Sixth Avenue, between 49th & 50th Streets (1-212 664 3056/www.nbc.com/snl). Subway B, D, F, V to 47th-50th Streets-Rockefeller Center. **Tapings** dress rehearsal at 8pm; live show at 11.30pm. **Map** p404 E23.
Tickets are notoriously difficult to snag, so don't get your hopes up. The season is assigned by lottery every autumn. Email snltickets@nbc.com in August, or try the standby ticket lottery on the day of the show. Line up by 7am under the NBC Studio marquee (50th Street, between Fifth & Sixth Avenues). You must be at least 16 and have a photo ID.

Tours

Both of the following tours are very popular, so be sure to call in advance.

Sex and the City Tour

Meet at Pulitzer Fountain, near the Plaza Hotel, Fifth Avenue, between 58th & 59th Streets (1-212 209 3370/www.sceneontv.com). Subway N, R, W to Fifth Avenue-59th Street. **Tours** 11am Mon-Fri; 10am, 11am, 3pm Sat; 10am, 11am, 3pm Sun. **Tickets** $37. **Credit** MC, V. **Map** p405 E22.
The show has long since wrapped, but it lives on in syndication and, apparently, on this tour, which takes you to more than two dozen sites.

The Sopranos Tour

Meet at the giant button sculpture, Seventh Avenue, at 39th Street (1-212 209 3370/www.sceneontv.com). Subway N, Q, R, W to 42nd Street; S, 1, 2, 3, 7, 9 to 42nd Street-Times Square. **Tours** 9am, 2pm Sat, Sun. **Tickets** $40. **Credit** MC, V. **Map** 404 D24.
A bus takes you to New Jersey to check out Tony's haunts, from the Bada Bing! to Pizzaland.

Gay & Lesbian

You're here, you're queer – they're used to it!

Feeling liberated as a lesbian, gay, bisexual or transgender person while visiting NYC is natural. It's the proud birthplace of gay rights, after all – home to the Stonewall Inn (*see p308*), the place where, on a summer night in 1969, homo tipplers decided they were fed up with a series of harassing police raids, fighting back when cops crashed their party. It was a moment of moxie that led to days of resistance now known as the famous Stonewall Riots, which in turn sparked decades of powerful gay activism.

Since that historic moment, progress has continued at breakneck speed in New York, with the constant formation and dissolution of organisations from ACT UP to the Lesbian Avengers, and storied nightclubs from the Saint to the Roxy. New Yorkers have also had no shortage of queer role models, including artists (Ross Bleckner, Annie Leibowitz), performers (Bill T Jones, Alan Cumming), designers (Marc Jacobs, Patricia Field), wordsmiths (Michael Cunningham, Sarah Schulman), activists (Larry Kramer, Leslie Feinberg) and politicians (including the second most influential legislator in the city after the mayor, City Council Speaker Christine Quinn, a very out lesbian).

New York laws foster a healthy gay existence, criminalising anti-gay violence, forbidding discrimination in the workplace and affording same-sex couples comprehensive domestic partnership rights. Though the state's highest court declared gay marriage illegal in July 2006 after a lengthy court battle, Governor Spitzer has vowed repeatedly to turn that around. Still, for the moment, the city continues to fall short when it comes to the thorny subject of equal marriage rights for gay couples.

That's not for you to worry over, though, as your gay time in New York will most likely consist of cruising around from bar to club to restaurant, and taking stock of all the lovely eye candy on the street in between. You'll find your place in the sun no matter what scene you desire – whether it's of muscle queens or punkish baby dykes, handsome transmen or skinny glam-rock boys. There's a community for everyone, every day of the week, in all five boroughs, whether at a park or in a nightclub or on the TV or radio.

As an out-of-towner who's short on time but who wants to get a taste of the gay scene that's right for you, make an instant beeline for the **Lesbian, Gay, Bisexual & Transgender Community Center** (*see p303*). It's a great first-stop, as the information desk attendant will be more than happy to supply you with an informative visitor's packet, as well as a schedule listing the gatherings of more than 300 groups that use the facility, from the Armenian Gay & Lesbian Organization (a social group) to Zappalorti Society (providing support for LGBT people with mental illness). Its racks of flyers and various publications upstairs contain details of practically every single queer group, venue and event in the entire city.

The biggest queer event, the annual **Gay Pride Week**, takes place in June, bringing a swirl of parties and performances. Though some jaded New Yorkers find the celebration a little passé, there are still a half-million or so spectators and participants at the **Pride March** (*see p263* and *photo p302*), which takes five hours to wind down Fifth Avenue, from midtown to the West Village. August, meanwhile, brings **Pride in the City** (www.prideinthecity.com), the official black LGBT pride event that delivers picnics, dance soirées, concerts, queer health forums and a massive party on the beach out in the Rockaways of Queens. But don't despair if you miss the big-time gatherings – gay pride, in this city, is never in short supply.

Books & media

Because of the explosion of bookstore chains that sell everything (but don't necessarily know their Sedaris from their Sappho), the number of gay bookstores has dropped significantly in recent years. In fact, after the recent demise of Creative Visions in the West Village, there is but one left – **Oscar Wilde**. **Bluestockings**, though, has a good stock of LGBT titles.

Bluestockings

172 Allen Street, between Rivington & Stanton Streets (1-212 777 6028/www.bluestockings.com). Subway F, V to Lower East Side-Second Avenue. **Open** noon-10pm Mon-Fri; 10am-10pm Sat, Sun. **Credit** AmEx, MC, V. **Map** p403 F29.

This radical bookstore, Fairtrade café and activist resource centre carries a nice load of LGBT writings and erotica, and regularly hosts queer (often dyke-feminist) events, including dyke knitting circles and women's open mic nights.

Pride March. *See p301.*

Oscar Wilde Bookshop

15 Christopher Street, between Sixth & Seventh Avenues (1-212 255 8097/www.oscarwildebooks.com). Subway 1 to Christopher Street-Sheridan Square. **Open** 11am-7pm daily. **Credit** AmEx, Disc, MC, V. **Map** p403 D28.

The world's first gay bookstore, Wilde opened in 1967 and has gone through many changes of hands. Its current owner, Kim Brinster, is passionate about stocking all manner of queer titles.

Publications

Time Out New York's Gay & Lesbian section offers its own weekly guide to happenings all around the city. Both of New York's weekly gay entertainment magazines – *HX* and *Next* – include extensive boycentric information on bars, clubs, restaurants, events, group meetings and sex parties. The monthly *Go NYC* – 'a cultural road map for the city girl' – gives the lowdown on the lesbian nightlife and travel scene. The newspaper *Gay City News* provides feisty political coverage with an activist slant; its thin rival, the *New York Blade* (published by *HX*), has mostly pickup stories about gay news in the city and around the world. All are free and widely available in street boxes or at gay and lesbian bars and bookstores. *MetroSource* ($4.95) is a bi-monthly glossy with a fashion victim slant and tons of listings.

Television & radio

The two gay-only channels are Logo, from MTV, and the on-demand Here! TV, both of which offer original programming of films, talk shows and documentaries and can be seen via local Time Warner Cable provider. The local Manhattan Neighborhood Network (MNN) is a public-access station that allows any ol' New Yorker to have a programme, and the many homegrown queer shows include *Gay USA* (a news programme) and the long-running *Dyke TV* (be aware that you may not be able to watch these shows on a hotel TV because cable carriers vary). *HX* and *Next* magazines provide the most current gay-TV listings. You can also catch frequent reruns of *Will & Grace*, late at night, on channel 11 or *The L Word* on Showtime. And Bravo channel has various gayish shows – *Life on the D-List, Project Runway* – thanks to boasting its own gay head of programming.

Over in the radio, NYC's community-activist station, WBAI-FM 99.5, features the progressive gay talk show *Out-FM* on Mondays at 11am. Sirius satellite radio, meanwhile, offers the 24/7 *OutQ* on channel 106, with programming from various noted New York personalities.

Centres & helplines

Gay & Lesbian Switchboard of New York

1-212 989 0999/www.glnh.org. **Open** 4pm-midnight Mon-Fri; noon-5pm Sat.

This phone service offers excellent peer counselling, legal referrals, details on gay and lesbian organisations, and information on bars, restaurants and hotels. Outside New York (but within the US), callers can contact the toll-free Gay & Lesbian National Hotline (1-888 843 4564).

Gay Men of African Descent

103 E 125th Street, at Park Avenue (1-212 828 1697/www.gmad.org). Subway 4, 5, 6 to 125th Street. **Open** hrs vary; events usually begin at 6pm. Check website for schedule. **Map** p407 E13.

This is a vibrant community centre, located in Harlem, for same-gender-loving men of colour. It's a great resource for health information, and hosts daily meetings and events, from HIV support-group gatherings to queer-youth celebrations.

Gay Men's Health Crisis

119 W 24th Street, between Sixth & Seventh Avenues (1-212 367 1000/AIDS advice hotline 1-212 807 6655/www.gmhc.org). Subway F, V, 1 to 23rd Street. **Open** *Hotline* 10am-6pm Mon-Fri; noon-3pm Sat; recorded information in English & Spanish at other times. *Office* 10am-6pm Mon-Fri. **Map** p404 D26.

GMHC was the world's first organisation dedicated to helping people with AIDS. Its threefold mission is to push for better public policies; to educate the public to prevent the further spread of HIV; and to provide services and counselling to people living with HIV. Local support groups usually hold their meetings here in the evening.

Lesbian, Gay, Bisexual & Transgender Community Center

208 W 13th Street, between Seventh & Eighth Avenues (1-212 620 7310/www.gaycenter.org). Subway A, C, E, 1, 2, 3 to 14th Street; L to Eighth Avenue. **Open** 9am-11pm daily. **Map** p403 D27.

This is a place to get information, find support and just hang out with other queer folks. It's a friendly resource that provides guidance to gay tourists, plus meeting space for 300-odd groups, including 12-step and other support meetings. The National Museum & Archive of Lesbian & Gay History and the Pat Parker/Vito Russo Library are housed here, as is an art gallery and small computer center.

Lesbian Herstory Archives

484 14th Street, between Eighth Avenue & Prospect Park West, Park Slope, Brooklyn (1-718 768 3953/www.lesbianherstoryarchives.org). Subway F to 15th Street-Prospect Park. **Open** times vary; phone or visit website for more information. **Map** p410 T12.

Located in Brooklyn's Park Slope neighbourhood, the Herstory Archives contain more than 20,000 books (cultural theory, fiction, poetry, plays), 1,600

Oh, gay corral!

Forget *Brokeback Mountain*. Against the odds – which is to say in a town without so much as a country music radio station – country and western has managed to find a devoted audience within Gotham's gay and lesbian community. Always curious, *Time Out* just had to get the lowdown, and discovered that there are performance groups, weekly parties, one-off events, even provisioners of high-end duds, all with a gay-targeted country bent.

Big Apple Ranch

Why saddle up? This is your chance to don your chaps and show some skin. This dance venue offers public lessons and a party every Saturday from 8pm to 1am.
The roadhouse Fifth floor, 39 W 19th Street, at Fifth Avenue (1-212 358 5752/www.bigappleranch.com). **Time** lesson starts 8pm. **Admission** $10. **Map** p403 E27.

delaCav

Why saddle up? This boutique boot-seller is quickly being branded as *the* place for queer cowpokes to find individually customised, handcrafted Western boots. Folks can pick from an array of skins, including eel, alligator, lizard, python, stingray and even vegan boots, and can even add personal touches. A pair of delaCav boots will set you back around $375.
Where to buy Space Downtown Studio, 276 W 25th Street, between 7th & 8th Avenue (1-631 614 3699/www.delacav.com). **Map** p404 D26.

The Manhattan Prairie Dogs

Why saddle up? To see a group of sexy men in cowboy boots and skirts whip up a combination of country and western and high-camp dance moves. The New York-based travelling dance troupe performs nationwide and is known to pull off seamless costume changes in the middle of a routine.
The roadhouse Big Apple Ranch (*see above*). **Time** 11pm; call for performance days. **Admission** $10.

ShitKickers!

Why saddle up? This one has the ladies in mind. Two cowgirls, Splenda and DJ Sancho, serve up old and new country from Dolly to the Dixie Chicks. ShitKickers! offers dance lessons and a heaving party every Thursday night from 8pm onwards.
The roadhouse Cattyshack (*see p309*). **Time** 8pm-3am Thur. **Admission** free before 9pm; $5 after 9pm.

Times Squares

Why saddle up? It's one of the few square dances where you can show up without a partner – anyone who knows the steps is welcome. Times Squares also allows participants to dance either gender role. Classes run from October through April.
The roadhouse LGBT Center, 208 W 13th Street, at 7th Avenue (1-212 749 4291/www.timessquares.org). **Time** 5pm; see website for dates. **Admission** free.

periodicals and assorted memorabilia. The cosy brownstone also hosts occasional film screenings, readings and social gatherings, plus an annual open house held in early June, to coincide with the annual Brooklyn Gay Pride celebration.

NYC Gay & Lesbian Anti-Violence Project

Suite 200, 240 W 35th Street, between Seventh & Eighth Avenues (24hr bilingual hotline 1-212 714 1141/1184/www.avp.org). Subway A, C, E, 1, 2, 3 to 34th Street-Penn Station. **Open** 10am-8pm Mon-Thur; 10am-6pm Fri. **Map** p404 D25.

The Project works with local police to provide support to victims of anti-gay crime, plus volunteers who offer advice on seeking help from police. Long- and short-term counselling services are available. The Project is also the place to call (in addition to the police) to report any sort of gay bias attack, which is sadly as possible a problem in New York as anywhere else in the world.

Sylvia Rivera Law Project

1-212 337 8550/www.srlp.org.

Call for information on special training and workshops provided by SRLP, named after civil rights pioneer and Stonewall uprising veteran Sylvia Rivera. The project provides free legal services to transgender, intersex and gender-nonconforming people of colour with low incomes.

Trevor Project

24hr hotline 1-866 488 7386/www.thetrevorproject.org.

Basing their operation upon the belief that 98% of teen suicides are preventable, the Trevor Project runs a hotline for LGBT youth who are desperately seeking a reason to live. Gay teens are three times more likely to attempt suicide than their heterosexual peers. The folks on the other end of this phone line want to put an end to that statistic. The call centre is based in Los Angeles, but plans for a New York office are currently in the works.

Queer New York

Though it's hard to get consensus about anything among New Yorkers, most would probably agree that the hottest 'gaybourhood' at this point is **Hell's Kitchen** (also known by its more staid name, Clinton). It's a western swath of Midtown that is located, perhaps not coincidentally, alongside the Theater District. It's a place where slick new bars, eateries and boutiques catering to gay men have been opening at a fast and furious rate. Until very recently, it was also still possible to find a cool apartment at a reasonable price, something that appealed to the pioneering, gentrifying tendencies of many queer lads. Ninth Avenue in the stretches of the 40s and 50s is where you'll notice most of the drinking, dining and strutting action taking place.

Not to be completely outdone, of course, is **Chelsea**, which borders Hell's Kitchen to the south (with a little break in between, in the 30s). This has been Manhattan's gay top dog for more than a decade – and some would argue it still is – though, as inevitably happens in gay ghettos, its cool factor has more recently dissipated, showing both its maturity, through growing numbers of male couples pushing their baby strollers, and its mainstreaming, with new throngs of straight folks who want in on the fun. Still, there are a slew of boy bars and clubs, from Barracuda to Splash, plus eateries, gyms, roving parties, the drag-queen-hosted Chelsea Classics campy film series (held at Clearview Cinemas, 260 W 23rd Street, between Seventh & Eighth Avenues, Thur 7pm) and muscled characters cruising up and down Eighth Avenue. This is, after all, the neighbourhood that inspired the spot-on comic-strip series, *Chelsea Boys*, penned by New Yorkers Glen Hanson and Allan Neuwirth.

Just south of here you'll find the original gay bohemia: the **West Village**. It's home to the famed Christopher Street – where you'll find both the Stonewall Inn and Oscar Wilde Books, plus plenty of other gay watering holes and a string of shops selling rainbow-flag-coloured souvenirs – as well as the deep, still-palpable roots of gay liberation. It's also the end point of the annual Gay Pride March (*see p263*), which wends its way past the lovely brick townhouses of Christopher Street and over to the Hudson River, where Pier 45 attracts mighty scores of whooping Latino and African-American gay and transgender youths, who descend upon the place nightly to flirt, cruise and find supportive, kindred spirits. Across town, in the East Village, is a steadfast network of nightspots that cater to dykes and gays on the creative, edgy side; it's the type of place where you might rub elbows with latex-clad club kids, none-too-polished drag queens, and skinny, electronica-lovin', twentysomething boys.

There are several neighbourhoods beyond Manhattan worth exploring, too. In Brooklyn, the leafy **Park Slope** is a long-time enclave for lesbians and gay men of all types – not only the settled-down types with kids and careers who have long escaped Manhattan's bustle, but more adventurous queers as well, as the monthly SPAM (*see below*) will attest to. During the first weekend in June, the Slope hosts the borough's annual Brooklyn Pride March, a (very) scaled-down version of the main NYC event (*see p263*).

Brooklyn's extremely hip **Williamsburg** neighbourhood is also home to a large queer population, reminiscent of the tattooed masses of the East Village. And in Queens, the racially diverse neighbourhood of **Jackson Heights** is home to several LGBT bars and clubs and a large South American queer population. Chueca (69-04 Woodside Avenue, at 69th Street, 1-718 424 1171) is a hopping spot for salsa-dancing lesbian couples. And the **Queens Pride March**, held in Jackson Heights in mid June, is a less corporate, more soulful version of the main Pride event in Manhattan.

Sex parties are, of course, part of any gay scene, and New York is no exception. Men of all ages, shapes and sizes frequent private sex and fetish soirées (see *HX* magazine for thorough listings), including Brooklyn's **SPAM** (1-718 789 4053, www.submitparty.com). **Gay Male S/M Activists** (www.gmsma.org) holds frequent parties and workshops on kinky play, with its central star attraction being the annual Folsom Street East festival held in June in the Meatpacking District. A popular post-nightclub hook-up spot is the sleazy underground (and frequently shuttered) **Bijou** (82 E 4th Street, behind the red door), where porn on a big screen is just a warm-up for the private play booths. Libidinous lesbians should head over to one of the friendly, dyke-owned **Toys in Babeland** (*see p255*) boutiques, which hold occasional workshops on topics from female ejaculation to anal pleasure, or to the perpetually wild women's sex party **Submit** (1-718 789 4053, www.submitparty.com), where a den of slings, shower rooms and handcuffs awaits more adventurous punters on a monthly basis.

Where to stay

Chelsea Mews Guest House

344 W 15th Street, between Eighth & Ninth Avenues (1-212 255 9174). Subway A, C, E to 14th Street; L to Eighth Avenue. **Rates** $100-$200 double. **No credit cards**. **Map** p403 C27.

Built in 1840, this guesthouse caters to gay men. Rooms are comfortable and well furnished and, in most cases, have semi-private bathrooms. A laundry service and bicycles are complimentary. The charming Anne Frank Suite (room 110) has two twin beds and a private bathroom.

Chelsea Pines Inn

317 W 14th Street, between Eighth & Ninth Avenues (1-212 929 1023/1-888 546 2700/ www.chelseapinesinn.com). Subway A, C, E to 14th Street; L to Eighth Avenue. **Rates** (incl breakfast) $175-$275. **Credit** AmEx, DC, Disc, MC, V. **Map** p403 C27.

On the border of Chelsea and the West Village, Chelsea Pines welcomes gay guests of all persuasions. The 25 recently renovated rooms are clean and comfortable and have classic-film themes; most have private bathrooms, and all have a radio, TV, free Wi-Fi and a refrigerator.

Colonial House Inn

318 W 22nd Street, between Eighth & Ninth Avenues (1-212 243 9669/1-800 689 3779/ www.colonialhouseinn.com). Subway C, E to 23rd Street. **Rates** (incl breakfast) $130 double with shared bath; $95-$145 double with private bath (higher on weekends). **Credit** MC, V. **Map** p404 C26.

This beautifully renovated 1850s townhouse sits on a quiet street in Chelsea. Run by, and primarily for, gay men, it's a great place to stay, even if some of the less expensive rooms are a bit snug. Bonuses: a fireplace in three of the deluxe rooms, a rooftop deck for all (nude sunbathing allowed) and an owner, Mel Cheren, who is famous in the dance-music world as the CEO of West End Records and financial backer of the legendary Paradise Garage.

East Village B&B

244 E 7th Street, between Avenues C & D (1-212 260 1865). Subway F, V to Lower East Side-Second Avenue. **Rates** (incl breakfast) $120 double. **No credit cards**. **Map** p403 G28.

This lesbian-owned gem is tucked into a turn-of-the-20th-century apartment building on a quiet East Village block. The space has gleaming wood floors and exposed brick, plus an eclectic art collection. The bedrooms are done up in bold colours, one of the bathrooms has a small tub, and the living room has a TV and CD player.

Incentra Village House

32 Eighth Avenue, between Jane & W 12th Streets (1-212 206 0007/www.incentravillage.com). Subway A, C, E to 14th Street; L to Eighth Avenue. **Rates** $199 double. **Credit** AmEx, MC, V. **Map** p403 D28.

Two cute 1841 townhouses in the West Village make up this nicely restored guesthouse run in style by gay men and offering a suitably laidback atmosphere for similarly orientated guests. The spacious rooms have private bathrooms and kitchenettes; some also have fireplaces to boot. A 1939 Steinway baby grand piano graces the parlour and sets a tone of easy sophistication.

Ivy Terrace

230 E 58th Street, between Second & Third Avenues (1-516 662 6862/www.ivyterrace.com). Subway N, R, W to Lexington Avenue-59th Street; 4, 5, 6 to 59th Street. **Rates** (incl breakfast) $200-$300 double. **Credit** AmEx, MC, V. **Map** p405 F22.

This lovely lesbian-run B&B has three cosy rooms that feature wood floors and lacy bedspreads on old-fashioned sleigh beds. The owners serve breakfast each morning. You're also free to create your own meals: each room has a gas stove and a full-size fridge for those essential midnight feasts.

Bars

Whatever your nightlife pleasure – sleek martini lounge, old-school neighbourhood kitsch den, leathery kink cave, dive bar with cheap cans of Pabst Blue Ribbon – you'll find a queer watering hole that caters to you. Most offer plenty of happy hours, drink specials, live performances, go-go dancers and rotating theme nights, like bingo parties or 'talent' contests. Though trendy bars come and go each year, there are several handfuls that you can always count on, no matter what your pleasure.

Lower East Side & East Village

The Cock

29 Second Avenue, at 2nd Street (no phone). Subway F, V to Lower East Side-Second Avenue. **Open** 9pm-4am daily. **Cover** $5-$10. **Average drink** $7. **No credit cards**. **Map** p403 F29.

This wonderfully dark and sleazy fag-rock spot has nightly soirées featuring lots of cruising, cocktail

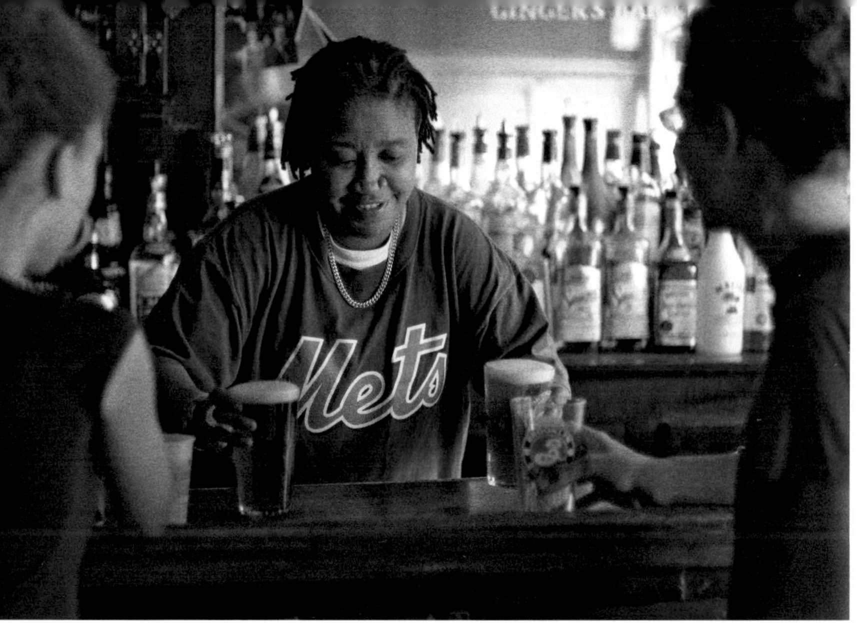

Women on the pull at **Ginger's Bar**. *See p309.*

guzzling and heavy petting among the rail-thin, messy-haired young boys. Frequent drag performers and holiday-pegged theme nights rock the house.

Eastern Bloc

505 E 6th Street, between Avenues A & B (1-212 777 2555/www.easternblocnyc.com). Subway F, V to Lower East Side-Second Avenue. **Open** 7pm-4am daily. **Cover** free-$5. **Average drink** $7. **No credit cards**. **Map** p403 G28.

This cool little space has a red-scare Commie feel – in the sexiest of ways, with TV screens that show Bettie Page films, and Soviet-era posters. Bartenders are cuties, and there are nightly themes and happy hours to get the ball rolling.

Nowhere

322 E 14th Street, at First Avenue (1-212 477 4744). Subway L to First Avenue. **Open** 3pm-4am daily. **Average drink** $5. **No credit cards**. **Map** p403 F27.

A friendly, spacious bar from the same folks who run the nearby Phoenix (447 E 13th Street, between First Avenue & Avenue A, 1-212 477 9979). Nowhere attracts attitude-free crowds filled with everyone from dykes to bears, thanks to a fun line-up of theme nights. Its pool table's a big draw too.

The Urge

33 Second Avenue, at 2nd Street (1-212 533 5757). Subway F, V to Lower East Side-Second Avenue. **Open** 4pm-4am daily. **Average drink** $7. **No credit cards**. **Map** p403 F29.

A mellow neighbourhood spot with lots of space and great drink specials, the Urge looks like a sleek lounge at first, but feels more like a cosy dive once you're settled in. It gets frequently festive thanks to its regular fun theme nights – like Monday night games hosted by Gusty Winds, Zany Thursdays with DJ Guto and a hot Saturday-night go-go boys.

West Village

Chi Chiz

135 Christopher Street, at Hudson Street (1-212 462 0027). Subway 1 to Christopher Street-Sheridan Square. **Open** 3pm-4am daily. **Average drink** $5. **No credit cards**. **Map** p403 D29.

One of a string of eight neighbourhood gay pubs along Christopher Street, this is a cruisy spot for men of colour, just steps from the way-gay Pier 45. Popular nights include Monday bingo and Tuesday karaoke, plus frequent pool tournaments.

Cubbyhole

281 W 12th Street, at 4th Street (1-212 243 9041). Subway A, C, E to 14th Street; L to Eighth Avenue. **Open** 4pm-2am Mon-Wed; 4pm-4am Thur, Fri; 2pm-4am Sat, Sun. **Average drink** $6. **No credit cards**. **Map** p403 E28.

This friendly lesbian spot is always chock-full of flirtatious girls (and their dyke-friendly boy friends), with the standard set of Melissa Etheridge or KD Lang blaring in the background. Chinese paper lanterns, tissue-paper fish and old holiday decorations emphasise the festive, homemade charm.

Henrietta Hudson

438 Hudson Street, at Morton Street (1-212 924 3347/www.henriettahudson.com). Subway 1 to Christopher Street-Sheridan Square. **Open** 4pm-4am Mon-Fri; 1pm-4am Sat, Sun. **Average drink** $6. **Credit** AmEx, MC, V. **Map** p409 D29.

A long-time, beloved lesbian bar, Henrietta Hudson is a glammy lounge that attracts young hottie girls from all over the New York area, especially the nearby 'burbs. Every night's a different party, with hip hop, pop, rock and live-music shows among the musical pulls. Super-cool native New Yorker Lisa Cannistraci is the lady in charge.

Monster

80 Grove Street, at Sheridan Square (1-212 924 3558). Subway 1 to Christopher Street-Sheridan Square. **Open** 4pm-4am Mon-Fri; 2pm-4am Sat, Sun. **Average drink** $5. **No credit cards**. **Map** p403 D28.

Upstairs, locals gather to sing show tunes in the piano lounge, adorned with strings of lights and rainbow paraphernalia. And, honey, you haven't lived till you've witnessed a bunch of tipsy queers belting out the best of Broadway. The downstairs disco caters to a young, fun outer-borough crowd with ants in their pants.

Stonewall Inn

53 Christopher Street, between Seventh Avenue South & Waverly Place (1-212 463 0950). Subway 1 to Christopher Street-Sheridan Square. **Open** 4pm-4am daily. **Average drink** $6. **No credit cards**. **Map** p403 D28.

This is the gay landmark next door to the actual location of the 1969 gay rebellion against police harassment. After a long closure following a serious lull in patronage, the spot has been remodelled in a way that both preserves its historic dignity and strives to attract a new generation of revellers. Special party nights range from dance soirées to the ubiquitous bingo gathering.

Chelsea

Barracuda

275 W 22nd Street, between Seventh & Eighth Avenues (1-212 645 8613). Subway C, E to 23rd Street. **Open** 4pm-4am daily. **Average drink** $6. **No credit cards**. **Map** p404 D26.

This long-time staple has much less attitude than a great deal of the neighbourhood competition. It's got a traditional low-lit bar up front and a frequently redecorated lounge in the back. A host of local drag-queen celebrities perform throughout the week, and there's never a cover charge, which is good news for those hoping to pop in for a quick drink.

The Eagle

554 W 28th Street, between Tenth & Eleventh Avenues (1-646 473 1866/www.eaglenyc.com). Subway C, E to 23rd Street. **Open** 10pm-4am Mon-Sat; 5pm-4am Sun. **Average drink** $5. **No credit cards**. **Map** p404 C26.

A must for kink fans, the Eagle is a fetish bar that hosts beer blasts, foot-worship fêtes, leather soirées, and simple nights of pool playing and cruising. Summer brings popular rooftop barbecues for pleasing punters with al fresco aspirations.

G Lounge

225 W 19th Street, between Seventh & Eighth Avenues (1-212 929 1085). Subway 1 to 18th Street. **Open** 10pm-4am Mon-Sat; 5pm-4am Sun. **Average drink** $9. **Credit** AmEx, MC, V. **Map** p403 D27.

The 'hood's original slick boy lounge is this rather moodily lit cave with a cool brick and glass arched entrance. It's a favourite after-work cocktail spot, where an excellent roster of DJs stay on top of the mood. A recent remodelling has turned it into a design marvel that resembles a sophisticated Ian Schrager boutique hotel lounge.

Gym

167 Eighth Avenue, at 18th Street (1-212 337 2439/www.gymsportsbar.com). Subway A, C, E to 14th Street; L to Eighth Avenue. **Open** 4pm-4am daily. **Average drink** $7. **No credit cards**. **Map** p403 D27.

This popular spot is all about games – of the actual sporting variety, that is. Catch theme parties that revolve around gay sports leagues, plus pool tables, video games and pro events from rodeo competitions to figure skating (everyone's favourite) shown on various big-screen TVs.

Midtown

HK Lounge

523 Ninth Avenue, at 39th Street (1-212 947 4208/www.hkhellskitchen.com). Subway A, C, E to 34th Street-Penn Station. **Open** 5pm-4am daily. **Average drink** $9. **Credit** AmEx, Disc, MC, V. **Map** p404 C24.

The newest spot on the scene is this Hell's Kitchen beauty, attached to the equally atmospheric HK eaterie. It's an intimate, cool cave of couches, gargantuan potted plants, low tables and dim lighting, and the site of occasional performances and special DJ evenings. Perfect for a post-theatre cosmo.

Therapy

348 W 52nd Street, between Eighth & Ninth Avenues (1-212 397 1700/www.therapy-nyc.com). Subway C, E to 50th Street. **Open** 5pm-2am Mon-Wed, Sun; 5pm-4am Thur-Sat. **Average drink** $7. **Credit** AmEx, MC, V. **Map** p404 C23.

Therapy is just what the analyst ordered: the minimalist, dramatic two-level space offers comedy and musical performances, clever cocktails (including the Freudian Sip) and, of course, a crowd of beautiful boys. You'll find good food and a cosy fireplace.

Vlada

331 W 51st Street, between Eighth & Ninth Avenues (1-212 974 8030/www.vladabar.com). Subway C, E to 50th Street. **Open** 4pm-4am Tue-Sun. **Average drink** $6. **Credit** AmEx, MC, V. **Map** p404 C23.

This Hell's Kitchen favourite is a narrow, modern and hyper-stylish lounge that attracts scores of handsome men for homemade infused-vodka cocktails, nibbly bits like paninis and cheese plates, and entertainment from drag shows to stand-up.

Uptown

Candle Bar

309 Amsterdam Avenue, at 74th Street (1-212 874 9155). Subway 1, 2, 3 to 72nd Street. **Open** 2pm-4am daily. **Average drink** $5. **No credit cards.** **Map** p406 C15.
An Upper West Side mainstay, Candle Bar is a dank, cruisy neighbourhood kind of place, with regulars and a well-used pool table. Catch nightly drink specials, from Buds to potent margaritas.

No Parking

4168 Broadway, between 177th Street & 178th Streets (1-212 923 8700). Subway 1, 2, 3 to 168th Street. **Open** 7pm-4am daily. **Average drink** $6. **No credit cards.** **Map** p409 B6.
If you're feeling frisky, head straight to No Parking in Washington Heights, where a beefy doorman frisks you before entering. Don't be scared, though: the only pistols these cute locals are packing are the fun kind. The bar also boasts a crew of awesome R&B, disco and hip hop video-DJs.

Suite

992 Amsterdam Avenue, at 109th Street (1-212 222 4600/www.suitenyc.com). Subway 1, 2, 3 to 110th Street. **Open** 4pm-4am daily. **Average drink** $5. **No credit cards.** **Map** p406 C15.
Suite offers a relaxed and comfortable Uptown atmosphere for local gay resident and Columbia students alike. Nightly drag performances have a fun, let's-put-on-a-show feel.

Brooklyn

Cattyshack

249 Fourth Avenue, between Carroll & President Streets, Park Slope (1-718 230 5740/www.cattyshackbklyn.com). Subway M, R to Union Street. **Open** 2pm-4am Mon-Fri; noon-4am Sat, Sun. **Average drink** $7. **No credit cards.** **Map** p410 T11.
This hoppin', bi-level space is all industrial-chic, spare-design charm. It's a full-time lesbian joint, courtesy of former Meow Mix cat Brooke Webster, and its theme nights, excellent DJs and breezy roof deck brings in crowds from all over.

Excelsior

390 Fifth Avenue, between 6th & 7th Streets, Park Slope (1-718 832 1599). Subway M, R to Union Street. **Open** 6pm-4am Mon-Fri; 2pm-4am Sat, Sun. **Average drink** $7. **No credit cards.** **Map** p410 T11.
Homey Excelsior has a spacious deck and garden out back, and inside, an eclectic jukebox and an excellent selection of beers on tap.

Ginger's Bar

363 Fifth Avenue, between 5th & 6th Streets, Park Slope (1-718 788 0924). Subway M, R to Union Street. **Open** 5pm-4am Mon-Fri; 2pm-4am Sat, Sun. **Average drink** $6. **No credit cards.** **Map** p410 T11.
The front room of Ginger's, with its dark-wood bar, looks out on to a bustling street. The back, which has an always-busy pool table, evokes a rec room. while the patio feels like a friend's yard. This local hang is full of all sorts of dykes, many with their dogs or favourite gay boys – in tow. *Photo p307.*

Metropolitan

559 Lorimer Street, at Metropolitan Avenue, Williamsburg (1-718 599 4444). Subway G to Metropolitan Avenue, L to Lorimer Street. **Open** 3pm-4am daily. **Average drink** $5. **No credit cards.** **Map** p411 V8.
The hipster enclave of Williamsburg has its fair share of queers, and this is its sole gay standby. Stop in to refresh with an icy brew while you're tooling around the neighbourhood; you'll find an eminently mellow crowd (featuring lots of beards – of the facial hair variety), a host of video games, a patio and drinks specials galore.

Clubs

In addition to the full-time staples, a number of non-gay-specific New York clubs have weekly or monthly queer nights. For more clubs, plus additional information about some of those listed below, *see pp291-297.*

Acid Disko

Lucky Cheng's, 24 First Avenue, between 1st & 2nd Streets (1-212 995 5500/www.aciddisko.com). Subway F, V to Lower East Side-Second Avenue. **Open** 10pm-4am Fri. **Cover** $10. **Average drink** $8. **Credit** AmEx, DC, Disc, MC, V. **Map** p403 F29.
Acid Betty, Anarexia, Tom Coppola and the rest of the wacky drag-prone crowd take over this Asian-theme eaterie every Friday for a night of debauched glamour, including go-go boys, fancy cocktails and plenty of colourful performances.

Alegria

Studio Mezmor, 530 W 28th Street, between Tenth & Eleventh Avenues (1-212 629 9000/www.alegriaevents.com). Subway C, E to 23rd Street. **Open** 11pm-4am Mon, Thur-Sun. **Cover** $50-$70. **Average drink** $9. **Credit** AmEx, DC, Disc, MC, V. **Map** p404 B26.
Ric Sena's occasional special event, landing in Studio Mezmor about eight times a year, has grown into one of the most popular dance parties on the circuit. Go for the awe-inspiring space, sea of shirtless muscle boys and top-notch music from DJs like Tony Moran and Abel.

GirlNation

Nation, 12 W 45th Street, between Fifth & Sixth Avenues (1-212 391 8053). Subway B, D, F, V to 47-50 Street-Rockefeller Center. **Open** 10pm-4am Sat. **Cover** $5. **Average drink** $7. **No credit cards.** **Map** p404 E24.
This weekly lesbian bash is the place to be on Saturday nights. The two-level space, on a quiet, business-minded block of Midtown, gets rowdy and

Mr Black.

super-fun with its diverse and very cute crowd of girls, who flock here to dance, drink and flirt themselves senseless from all over the city.

Motherfucker

www.motherfuckernyc.com.

If rock 'n' roll is your thing, you'll want to check out Motherfucker, the wildly popular polysexual dance party that takes place about seven times a year, rarely at the same venue. Its Independence Day and Labor Day blowouts are particularly popular with the punters. *See also p297.*

Mr Black

643 Broadway, at Bleecker Street (1-212 253 2560/www.mrblacknyc.com). Subway B, D, F, V to Broadway-Lafayette Street. **Open** 9pm-4am daily. **Cover** $5-$10. **Average drink** $6. **No credit cards. Map** p403 E29.

A friendly, alternative dance den that sits on the edge of the East Village, West Village and Soho, this space created a quick buzz when it opened with its varied party nights. Catch Rocket Queen Wednesdays, Fridays with DJ Sammy Jo (who toured with the Scissor Sisters) and Jonny McGovern's Boys Gone Wild on Saturdays. Its vibe is wacky, edgy, young and creative.

Saint at Large

1-212 674 8541/www.saintatlarge.com.

The now-mythical Saint was one of the first venues where New York's gay men could enjoy dancefloor freedom. The club closed, but the clientele keeps the memory alive with occasional special events and one huge and *très* important annual circuit party: the fetishy Black Party in March, with mind-blowing themes that revolve around kink and sex shows. The White Party, its angelic answer, has been on hiatus for a few years, but check the website for updates on its buzzed-about reappearance.

Snapshot

Bar 13, 35 E 13th Street, at University Place (1-212 979 6677/www.snapshotnyc.com). Subway L, N, Q, R, W, 4, 5, 6 to 14th Street-Union Square. **Open** 9pm-4am Tue. **Cover** $8. **Average drink** $7. **No credit cards. Map** p403 E28.

This party for hip young dykes and their pals has been injecting a sense of excitement into Tuesday evenings for a few years. Its second-floor space features plenty of space for lounging and dancing (to fresh-faced DJs), and the outdoor roof deck is an atmospheric place for a smoke. Watch for its cool annual Pride party, Proud as Fuck.

Splash

50 W 17th Street, between Fifth & Sixth Avenues (1-212 691 0073/www.splashbar.com). Subway F, V to 14th Street; L to Sixth Avenue. **Open** 4pm-4am Mon-Thur, Sun; 4pm-5am Fri, Sat. **Cover** $5-$20. **Average drink** $7. **No credit cards. Map** p403 E27.

This Chelsea institution offers 10,000 square feet of dance and lounge space, as well as the famous onstage showers, where hunky go-go boys get wet and wild. The supermuscular bartenders here seem bigger than ever. Nationally known DJs rock the house, local drag celebs give good face, and in-house VJs flash eclectic hypnotice snippets of classic musicals spliced with video visuals.

Restaurants & cafés

Same-sex couples holding hands across a candlelit table are pretty commonplace in New York. But if you'd like to be certain you'll be in the gay majority when you dine, then check out the following places where it's the straight folks who get the second glances. Note that the prices given here are averages.

Better Burger NYC

178 Eighth Avenue, at 19th Street (1-212 989 6688). Subway C, E to 23rd Street; 1 to 18th Street. **Open** 11am-midnight Mon-Thur, Sun; 11am-1am Fri, Sat. **Burger** $6. **Credit** AmEx, MC, V. **Map** p403 D28.

Gayest burger joint ever! It's also the healthiest. But don't worry, the menu – which includes lean patties of beef, turkey or soya – is as delicious as the hunky clientele. And although it is a fast-food joint, it's a classy one, listing organic beers and wines to go with your burger, as well as air-baked fries and their own house-made ketchup.

Counter

105 First Avenue, between 6th & 7th Streets (1-212 982 5870). Subway F, V to Lower East Side-Second Avenue. **Open** 5pm-midnight Mon-Fri; 11am-1am Sat, Sun. **Average main course** $15. **Credit** AmEx, MC, V. **Map** p403 F28.

This hip, lesbian-owned East Village spot takes vegetarian cuisine to a whole new level, adding a wine bar with a dozen organic offerings (and serving a well-mixed crowd). Pair a glass or two with one of the lip-smackin' vegan tapas, or try bigger eats, such as portobello au poivre or curried plantain dumplings drizzled in coconut sauce. There's also a popular brunch served on weekends.

Elmo

156 Seventh Avenue, between 19th & 20th Streets (1-212 337 8000/www.elmorestaurant.com). Subway 1 to 18th Street. **Open** 11am-midnight Mon-Thur; 11am-2am Fri, Sat; 10am-midnight Sun. **Average main course** $14. **Credit** AmEx, Disc, MC, V. **Map** p403 D27.

This spacious, brightly decorated eaterie has good, reasonably priced food and a bar that offers a view of the dining room that is jammed with guys in clingy tank tops – regardless of the weather. And then there's the fun basement lounge, which hosts frequent readings, comedy and drag shows, plus the occasional chic-lesbian soirée.

44 & X Hell's Kitchen

622 Tenth Avenue, at 44th Street (1-212 977 1170). Subway A, C, E to 42nd Street-Port Authority. **Open** 5.30pm-midnight Mon-Wed; 5.30pm-12.30am Thur, Fri; 11.30am-12.30am Sat, Sun. **Average main course** $20. **Credit** AmEx, MC, V. **Map** p404 C24.

Fabulous queens pack out the sleek dining space that was one of the first bright spots on quickly gentrifying Tenth Avenue. It's situated alongside the Theater District and the Manhattan Plaza high-rises, home to thousands of artistes. The food's great too – classics like creamy mac 'n' cheese, and American specialities like filet mignon feature.

HK

523 Ninth Avenue, at 39th Street (1-212 947 4208/www.hkhellskitchen.com). Subway A, C, E to 34th Street-Penn Station. **Open** 5pm-4am daily. **Main course** $13. **Credit** AmEx, Disc, MC. **Map** p404 C24.

Located on a gritty Hell's Kitchen corner, HK is a swankily-lit hotspot that opens its glass sides in warm months and lets tables spill out onto the sidewalk. Enjoy an extensive list of strong cocktails and cuisine that ranges from creative salads and pasta dishes to burgers, soups, fish dishes and more. The new HK Lounge is right next door, offering a modish venue for violently hip (if rather overpriced) drinking experiences – pumping tunes, artfully pouting punters and all.

Lips

2 Bank Street, at Greenwich Avenue (1-212 675 7710). Subway 1, 2, 3 to 14th Street. **Open** 5.30pm-midnight Mon-Thur; 5.30pm-1am Fri, Sat; 11.30am-4pm, 5.30-11pm Sun. **Average main course** $18. **Credit** AmEx, DC, MC, V. **Map** p403 D28.

This festive restaurant generates an enjoyable, jovial atmosphere: the drag-queen waitstaff serve tasty meals and perform for very enthusiastic patrons. Midweek events tend to be a lot gayer than the weekends, when scores of shrieking straight chicks descend on the place for their bachelorette parties. The Sunday brunch is quite a show.

Lucky Cheng's

24 First Avenue, between 1st & 2nd Streets (1-212 995 5500/www.planetluckychengs.com). Subway F, V to Lower East Side-Second Avenue. **Open** 6pm-2am Mon-Thur, Sun; 6pm-4am Fri, Sat. **Average main course** $32 per person dinner/show. **Credit** AmEx, DC, Disc, MC, V. **Map** p403 F29.

This Asian drag-queen theme palace is a popular dinner-and-show kind of place that attracts straight and queer folks alike. Sassy ladies serve pan-Asian fare, put on a show and lead post-meal karaoke. On Fridays, the gay night Acid Disko (*see p309*) takes over the space with glamorous gusto.

Rubyfruit Bar & Grill

531 Hudson Street, between Charles & Washington Streets (1-212 929 3343). Subway 1 to Christopher Street-Sheridan Square. **Open** 2pm-4am Mon-Thur; 3pm-4am Fri, Sat; 11.30am-2am Sun. **Average main course** $20. **Credit** AmEx, DC, Disc, MC, V. **Map** p403 D28.

The food is good, but it's not the main selling point at this dedicated lesbian restaurant and bar. An eclectic mix of music and congenial customers make Rubyfruit a hit with fun-loving, old-school dykes.

Superfine

126 Front Street, between Jay & Pearl Streets, Dumbo, Brooklyn (1-718 243 9005). Subway F to York Street. **Open** 11.30am-3pm, 6-11pm Tue-Thur; 11.30am-3pm, 6pm-4am Fri; 2.30pm-4am Sat; 11.30am-2am Sun. **Average main course** $15. **Credit** AmEx, MC, V. **Map** p411 T9.

Owned by a couple of super-cool lesbians, this spacious eaterie, bar and art gallery serves seasonal Mediterranean cuisine in its massive, hip space. The mellow vibe and pool table draw a mixed, local crowd. The south-western themed brunches are delicious and justifiably popular.

Music

New York hits all the right notes, from sophisticated symphonies to raucous rock.

If music be the food of love then **Cake Shop** is baking on a daily basis. *See p314.*

Popular

At a glance, the music industry is locked in a disheartening free fall. CD sales are sluggish, big-label layoffs are rampant and once-mighty record stores have been run out of town altogether. The world of live music, however, tells an entirely different story, as more and more musicians take to the road to chase the profits that have otherwise dissipated. Even as beloved clubs like Tonic and CBGB close their doors, New York's live music scene thrives, with venues new and old scattered across Manhattan and Brooklyn. Plan accordingly and you could catch more than one world-class show in a single night.

Keep in mind that bigger is not always better. While no sweeping American tour is complete without a Manhattan stop – whether that means Beyoncé filling **Madison Square Garden** or bluegrass family act Cherryholmes cutting a rug at **Joe's Pub** – what makes New York concert-going so unique is the never-ending supply of upstarts, hopefuls and local weirdos. These performances can be more exciting, intimate and, yes, affordable. Nellie McKay and Regina Spektor, for instance, were both discovered playing for tip money at the tiny **Sidewalk Café**, an East Village spot that's free (with a modest drink minimum).

For larger seated shows, the iconic theatres uptown can't be beaten. The palatial art deco totem **Radio City Music Hall**, Harlem's decaying benchmark the **Apollo Theater** and **Carnegie Hall** all lend historic import to even the more tedious performances. For smaller gigs, the best bets lie across Downtown Manhattan and select neighbourhoods in Brooklyn. Rock music dominates the Lower East Side and Williamsburg, while a smattering of cosy jazz clubs thrive in Greenwich Village. And you don't have to look far for hip hop, soul, blues, folk, world music and everything in between.

To help you navigate the music scene, we've organised the city's most active and notable venues by genre. Note to the musically anal: these categories are loose. Many spots will feature scraggly rock one night and jazz the next, or skip from Brazilian music to folk in a single evening. And be prepared to linger: if a listing says a favourite band is going on at 11pm, you might wait till midnight or later. A valid photo ID proving that you're 21 or over is essential, not only to drink but often just to get in (a passport or a driver's license are best). NYC bouncers have heard it all, and they're impervious to excuses (*see p293* **The clubbing commandments**); grey hair does not always prove one's adulthood (wrinkles and a cane might do the trick, though).

Tickets are usually available from clubs in advance and at the door. A few small and medium-size venues also sell advance tickets through local record stores. For larger events, it's wise to buy through **Ticketmaster** (*see p383*) on the web, over the phone or at one of the outlets located throughout the city. Tickets for some events are available from **Ticket Web** (www.ticketweb.com). You can also buy them online from websites of specific venues (URLs are included in venue listings where available). And remember to phone ahead for information and show times, which often change without notice.

Arenas

Continental Airlines Arena

For listing, see p333 Meadowlands Sports Complex.
New Jersey's answer to Madison Square Garden has recently played host to the likes of the Police, Beyoncé, Genesis and Keith Urban. Oldies showcases and radio-sponsored pop and hip hop extravaganzas also take place here, pulling in predictably enormous crowds on a regular basis.

Madison Square Garden

For listing, see p333.
Madison Square Garden, one of the world's most famous arenas, is where the biggest acts – Justin Timberlake, the White Stripes, Muse, for example – come out to play. Whether you'll actually be able to see them well depends a lot on your seat or the quality of your binoculars.

Nassau Veterans Memorial Coliseum

For listing, see p333.
Long Island's arena hosts mainstream acts such as Bon Jovi and Aerosmith, punctuated by occasional teen-pop sock hops (*American Idol* Live!) and garish Bollywood showcases.

Rock, pop & soul

Apollo Theater

253 W 125th Street, between Adam Clayton Powell Jr Boulevard (Seventh Avenue) & Frederick Douglass Boulevard (Eighth Avenue) (1-212 531 5305/ www.apollotheater.com). Subway A, B, C, D, 1 to 125th Street. **Box office** 10am-6pm Mon, Tue, Thur, Fri; 10am-8.30pm Wed; noon-6pm Sat. **Tickets** $20-$100. **Credit** AmEx, DC, Disc, MC, V. **Map** p407 D13.

Visitors might think they know Harlem's venerable Apollo from TV's *Showtime at the Apollo*, but as the saying goes, the small screen adds about 10lb. Inside, the elegant yet lived-in theatre – still the city's home of R&B and soul music – is actually quite cosy. Known for launching the careers of Ella Fitzgerald, Michael Jackson and D'Angelo, to name just a few, the Apollo continues to bring in veteran talent like Dionne Warwick, as well as special performances by younger artists – when Gorillaz took its live *Demon Days* spectacle from Manchester to the States, this is the theatre Mr Albarn selected.

BB King Blues Club & Grill

237 W 42nd Street, between Seventh & Eighth Avenues (1-212 997 4144/www.bbkingblues.com). Subway A, C, E to 42nd Street-Port Authority; N, Q, R, W to 42nd Street; S, 1, 2, 3, 7 to 42nd Street-Times Square. **Box office** 11am-midnight daily. **Tickets** $12-$150. **Credit** AmEx, DC, Disc, MC, V. **Map** p404 D24.

The location and appearance might suggest that this place is geared to tourists, but BB's joint in Times Square stages one of the most varied music programmes in town: cover bands and soul tributes fill the gaps between big-name bookings such as Ralph Stanley and Little Richard. Lately, the club has also proved a viable space for extreme metal bands (Napalm Death, Obituary, Hate Eternal) and neo-soul and hip hop acts (such as Angie Stone, the Clipse and even Kool Keith). For many shows, the best seats are at the dinner tables at the front, but the menu prices are steep (and watch out for drink minimums). The Harlem Gospel Choir buffet brunch, on Sundays, raises the roof, while live classic rock, jazz and blues groups play for free most nights at Lucille's Bar & Grill, the restaurant named after King's cherished guitar.

Beacon Theatre

2124 Broadway, at 74th Street (1-212 496 7070). Subway 1, 2, 3 to 72nd Street. **Box office** 11am-7pm Mon-Fri; noon-6pm Sat. **Tickets** $15-$175. **No credit cards**. **Map** p405 C20.

This spacious Upper West Side theatre hosts a variety of popular acts, from Kaiser Chiefs to ZZ Top, and once a year the Allman Brothers take over the place for a lengthy residency. While the theatre's sound and vastness can be daunting to performers and audience alike, the gaudy, gilded interior and uptown location make you feel like you're having a real night out on the town.

Blender Theater at Gramercy

127 E 23rd Street, between Park & Lexington Avenues (1-212 777 6800). Subway R, W, 6 to 23rd Street. **Box office** noon-6.30pm Mon-Fri; 1-4pm Sat. **Tickets** $15-$30. **Credit** AmEx, MC, V. **Map** p404 E26.

One of a handful of new mid-size venues, the Blender Theater looks exactly like what it is: a run-down former movie theatre. Live Nation, which runs the joint, didn't exactly go the extra mile when retooling the space, but it has a decent sound system and good sightlines. Concert-goers can lounge in raised movie theatre seats on the top level or get closer to the stage. Bookings have included indie stalwarts (the mighty Mekons, Califone), hot up-and-comers (New Zealand comic duo Flight of the Conchords) and long runs by established stars (Rufus Wainwright, whose huge gay audience got to stroll over from nearby Chelsea). *See also p324* **Live from New York**.

Bowery Ballroom

6 Delancey Street, between Bowery & Chrystie Street (1-212 533 2111/www.boweryballroom.com). Subway J, M, Z to Bowery; 6 to Spring Street. **Box office** at the Mercury Lounge, *see p317*. **Tickets** $13-$40. **Credit** AmEx, MC, V (bar only). **Map** p403 F30.

Probably the best venue in the city for seeing indie bands (either on the way up or holding their own), the Bowery nonetheless manages to bring in a diverse range of artists from in town and around the world, as well as offering a clear view and loud, bright sound from just about any spot. Past bookings have included the Black Lips, Sons and Daughters and Lyrics Born. Not into an opening band? The spacious downstairs lounge is a great place to relax and socialise between (or during) sets.

Bowery Poetry Club

308 Bowery, at Bleecker Street (1-212 614 0505/ www.bowerypoetry.com). Subway B, D, F, V to Broadway-Lafayette Street; 6 to Bleecker Street. **Shows** check website for schedule. **Tickets** $3-$10. **Credit** AmEx, MC, V (bar only). **Map** p403 F29.

The name of this colourful joint on the Bowery reveals its roots in the poetry slam scene, but it's also the truest current iteration of the East Village's legendary arts scene: all kinds of jazz, folk, hip hop and improv theatre acts can be found here routinely. If you have a taste for the bizarre and aren't easily offended, keep your eyes peeled for anything from the Jollyship to the Whiz-Bang musical-puppet crew. The BPC offers a range of sandwiches, and hot and cold drinks – and there are generally seats available to rest one's weary feet. *See also p278.*

The Box

189 Chrystie Street, between Rivington & Stanton Streets (1-212 982 9301/www.theboxnyc.com). Subway F, V to Lower East Side-Second Avenue. **Shows** check website for schedule. **Tickets** $20-$150. **Credit** AmEx, MC, V. **Map** p403 F29.

Simon Hammerstein (grandson of Oscar) recently opened this elegantly decrepit room on the Lower East Side, with ambitious vaudeville dreams for the opulent little space. So far, it's mostly been reserved for private parties and industry showcases, but promises to host bands, cabaret acts and more. The drinks prices seem geared more towards Hollywood celebrities than young New Yorkers, and the shape of the room can make it hard to see the stage, but the Box is gorgeous and makes any show into a special evening. *See also p324* **Live from New York**.

Cake Shop

152 Ludlow Street, between Rivington & Stanton Streets (1-212 253 0036/www.cake-shop.com). Subway F, V to Lower East Side-Second Avenue. **Shows** doors open at 8pm. **Tickets** $6-$8. **No credit cards**. **Map** p403 G29.

It can be difficult to see the stage in this narrow, stuffy basement space – but it gets big points for its keen indie rock bookings, among the best and most adventurous in Manhattan. It's located in the heart of the Lower East Side, scrunched between Pianos (*see p319*) and the Living Room (*see p317*) on Ludlow Street. Cake Shop lives up to its name, selling vegan pastries and coffee upstairs. The brightly lit back room on street level sells used vinyl and CDs, as well as a smattering of new releases, DVDs, 'zines and other record-store ephemera. *Photos p312.*

Canal Room

285 W Broadway, at Canal Street (1-212 941 8100/ www.canalroomlive.com). Subway A, C, E, 1 to Canal Street. **Box office** 10am-6pm Mon-Fri; noon-6pm Sat. **Tickets** $7-$25. **Credit** AmEx, DC, MC, V. **Map** p403 E30.

A medium-sized club at the northern tip of Tribeca, the Canal Room hosts DJ nights as well as concerts. Performers include songwriters on the way up (Todd Snider), *Billboard* veterans with cult followings (Glenn Tilbrook, Colin Hay) and tribute bands paying homage to classic rock stars. And every Sunday, the club hosts a reggae party, Reminisce Reggae Sundays. When shows are packed, things can get uncomfortable and the door people tend to be a bit uptight.

Club Europa

98-104 Meserole Avenue, at Manhattan Avenue, Greenpoint, Brooklyn (1-718 383 5723/www.europa club.com). Subway G to Nassau Avenue. **Tickets** from www.ticketweb.com. **Credit** AmEx, Disc, MC, V. **Map** p411 V7.

You'll hear anything from cutting-edge metal to Polish bubblegum pop in this Polish nightclub in Brooklyn. It's a bit cheesy but has occasionally solid bookings (the reunited Sebadoh, for instance) and dancetastic light shows. At the bar, Eastern-Euro beauties sling cheap drinks. *See also p324* **Live from New York**.

Fillmore New York at Irving Plaza

17 Irving Place, at 15th Street (1-212 777 6800/ www.irvingplaza.com). Subway L, N, Q, R, W, 4, 5, 6 to 14th Street-Union Square. **Box office** noon-630pm Mon-Fri; 1-4pm Sat. **Tickets** $10-$60. **Credit** AmEx. **Map** p403 E27.

With the rise of clubs like Webster Hall and Gramercy Theater, Irving Plaza has lost its monopoly on concerts by mid-size touring bands. What to do? Rename itself! Nobody actually *calls* the club 'Fillmore New York', and the renovations that came with the name are largely cosmetic, yet it's still a great place to see big stars slumming (the White Stripes playing a late-night gig) and medium heavies like Lily Allen, on their way up to larger spaces. And from the parlour-lit lounge downstairs to the glamorous photos of old music scenes, this pleasantly worn old ballroom whispers of New York's rock past.

Galapagos Art Space

70 N 6th Street, between Kent & Wythe Avenues, Williamsburg, Brooklyn (1-718 782 5188/www.galapagosartspace.com). Subway L to Bedford Avenue. **Shows** times vary. **Cover** free-$7. **No credit cards. Map** p411 U7.

A roomy Williamsburg art and performance space, famed for the dark pool in the entrance, focuses on Brooklyn artists, but its mix of music, performance art, readings and film screenings doesn't discriminate. Burlesque and vaudeville nights are weekly staples, while the Mekons have stopped by for readings and art events. In June 2008, Galapagos – which established itself in Williamsburg years before the neighbourhood's renaissance – is set to move to a much larger space at No.16 Main Street in Dumbo, Brooklyn. Call or consult website for information before visiting.

Hammerstein Ballroom

Manhattan Center, 311 W 34th Street, between Eighth & Ninth Avenues (1-212 279 7740/www.mcstudios.com). Subway A, C, E to 34th Street-Penn Station. **Box office** noon-5pm Mon-Sat. **Tickets** $10-$50. **Credit** AmEx, MC, V. **Map** p404 C25.

Patrons can at times be treated like cattle here, the drinks prices are among the most outlandish in town – upwards of ten bucks for a cheap cocktail in a plastic cup – and if you're seated in the far reaches of the balcony, bring binoculars. Still, this cavernous space regularly draws big performers in the limbo between club and arena shows. The once-poor sound quality has been rectified, but unless you land tickets on the floor, it takes quite an amazing act to make a night special.

Highline Ballroom

431 W 16th Street, between Ninth & Tenth Avenues (1-212 414 5994/www.highlineballroom.com). Subway A, C, E to 14th Street; L to Eighth Avenue. **Cover** $15-$50. **Box office** 11am-10pm Mon-Sat; 11am-6pm Sun. **Credit** AmEx, MC, V. **Map** p403 C27.

This new club, tucked on the rock-deprived west side across the street from Chelsea Market, is perfect on paper: the sound is top-of-the-heap, sightlines are pretty good and it's even relatively clean. The bookings are also impressive, ranging from the experimental (Negativland) to dance fun (Junior Senior) and from old-guard stars (Lou Reed) to indie favourites (Bill Callahan). The overall vibe, however, can feel more LA than New York. *See also p324* **Live from New York**.

Hiro Ballroom at Maritime Hotel

371 Ninth Avenue, at 16th Street (1-212 625 8553/www.themaritimehotel.com/hiroballroom). Subway A, C, E to 14th Street; L to Eighth Avenue. **Open** 10pm-4am Thur-Sun. **Cover** $10-$35. **Credit** AmEx, MC, V. **Map** p403 C27.

Hiro Ballroom reeks of Manhattan chic, with a flamboyant sushi-bar-of-tomorrow atmosphere – a place in which James Bond might feel comfortable checking out a band. The hotel space is a glamorous setting to see an act, be it Tegan and Sara or the Fall. The room feels much fancier than the price of admission suggests – but beware the velvet rope. Most shows here are part of larger dance nights, which can bring tacky crowds and snooty door guys.

Joe's Pub

The Public Theater, 425 Lafayette Street, between Astor Place & E 4th Street (1-212 539 8770/www.joespub.com). Subway N, R, W to 8th Street-NYU; 6 to Astor Place. **Box office** 1-6pm Mon, Sun; 1-7pm Tue-Sat. **Tickets** $12-$30. **Credit** AmEx, MC, V. **Map** p403 E28.

Probably the city's premier small spot for sit-down audiences, Joe's Pub brings in impeccable talent of all genres and national origins. It often gets artists ahead of the curve, playing the room months before taking their act to much larger venues. While some well-established names such as Sinéad O'Connor, Suzanne Vega and They Might Be Giants have played here recently, Joe's also provides a stage for up-and-coming singers (Bat for Lashes, Christina Courtin). It's one of the only clubs in town where something interesting is likely to be happening at some point on any night. A small but solid menu and deep bar selections seal the deal – just keep an eye on the drink prices.

Cheap date

Elegant 40-seat sake bar **Satsko** (245 Eldridge Street, between E Houston & Stanton Streets, 1-212 358 7773) offers a three-course prix fixe ($40 for two) that's both affordable and desirable. Sink into one of the red brocade banquettes, sip a glass of rice wine and graze on refined Pan-Asian fare, such as sirloin steak with wasabi-mashed potatoes. Afterwards, bypass the earplug-requiring indie-rock bands at **Pianos** (*see p319*) – three streets away – and duck into its (free) quiet upstairs haunt. The low-key tunes within won't cause a shouting match this early in your relationship.

Clean water. It's the most basic human necessity. Yet one third of all poverty related deaths are caused by drinking dirty water. Saying *I'm in* means you're part of a growing movement that's fighting the injustice of poverty. Your £8 a month can help bring safe water to some of the world's poorest people. We can do this. We *can* end poverty. Are you in?

shouldn't everyone get clean water? I don't think that's too much to ask for

Let's end poverty together.
Text 'WATER' and your name to 87099 to give £8 a month.

Standard text rates apply. Registered charity No.202918

oxfam.org.uk

I'm in

Oxfam

Sarite Morales, Greenwich

Knitting Factory

74 Leonard Street, between Broadway & Church Street (1-212 219 3132/www.knittingfactory.com). Subway A, C, E to Canal Street; 1 to Franklin Street. **Box office** 4-11pm Mon-Sat; 2-11pm Sun. **Tickets** $5-$20. **Credit** AmEx, MC, V. **Map** p402 E31.

This three-floor circus was once known as NYC's downtown home of avant-garde jazz, but a couple of ownership changes later and jazz is scarce. Great artists still pop in on occasion – Jonathan Richman, Art Brut – but these are becoming rare. The smaller Tap Bar and claustrophobic Old Office, both under the main room (and with separate admissions), often have good DJs in among the busy flow of bands taking part.

Lakeside Lounge

162 Avenue B, between 10th & 11th Streets (1-212 529 8463/www.lakesidelounge.com). Subway L to First Avenue; N, Q, R, W, 4, 5, 6 to 14th Street-Union Square. **Shows** 9.30pm or 10pm. **Tickets** admission free. **Credit** AmEx, MC, V (bar only). **Map** p403 G28.

Because this comfortable East Village joint is co-owned by guitarist and producer Eric Ambel, the roadhouse and roots acts that come through tend to be fun. Local country-tinged talents appear often – and bigger names like Amy Rigby stop by on occasion. The bar, the jukebox and the photo booth are all attractions in their own right – and there's never a cover charge.

Living Room

154 Ludlow Street, between Rivington & Stanton Streets (1-212 533 7235/www.livingroomny.com). Subway F to Lower East Side-Second Avenue; J, M, Z to Delancey-Essex Streets. **Open** 6pm-2am Mon-Thur, Sun; 3pm-4am Fri, Sat. **Cover** free; 1-drink minimum. **No credit cards. Map** p403 G29.

Many local clubs try to lay claim to being the place where Norah Jones got her start, but the Living Room is the real McCoy (she even donated a piano as a way of saying thanks). Still, that was in the venue's old (and drab) location; since moving to the Lower East Side's version of Main Street, the stream of singer-songwriters that fill the schedule here has taken on a bit more gleam, and the warmly lit environs seem to be always bustling. In recent years, performers like Fionn Regan and Ane Brun have stopped here before moving on to larger local spaces.

Luna Lounge

361 Metropolitan Avenue, at Havermeyer Street, Williamsburg, Brooklyn (1-718 384 7112/www.lunalounge.com). Subway L to Lorimer Street; G to Metropolitan. **Cover** $8-$15. **Box office** tickets from www.ticketweb.com. **Credit** AmEx, MC, V. **Map** p411 U8.

Originally, Luna Lounge was a tiny Lower East Side space for singer-songwriters and small local bands. After being closed for a couple of years, it reopened as a larger (400-capacity) room in Williamsburg. The new Luna Lounge is friendly, cavernous and somewhat flavourless. Bigger shows (sometimes booked by Live Nation) include mid-size bands both local (Northern State) and touring (Meat Puppets); most nights, however, feature an assortment of rock up-and-comers. *See also p324* **Live from New York**.

Maxwell's

1039 Washington Street, at 11th Street, Hoboken, NJ (1-201 798 0406/www.maxwellsnj.com). PATH train to Hoboken, then taxi, Red Apple bus or NJ Transit 126 bus to 12th Street. **Box office** varies. **Tickets** $7-$20. **Credit** AmEx, Disc, MC, V. **Map** p403 C28.

The trip out to Maxwell's can be a hassle, but the 15-minute walk from the PATH train (which is not unpleasant if the weather's on your side) can make you feel like you're in small-town America. The restaurant in front is big and friendly, and for dessert you can feast on indie-rock fare from such popular artists as the Thermals and Peter Bjorn and John, as well as a slew of garage acts (Holly Golightly, the Black Lips). Hometown heroes Yo La Tengo stage their more or less annual Hanukkah shows at this local institution.

Mercury Lounge

217 E Houston Street, between Essex & Ludlow Streets (1-212 260 4700/www.mercuryloungenyc.com). Subway F, V to Lower East Side-Second Avenue. **Shows** daily; times vary. **Box office** noon-7pm Mon-Sat. **Tickets** $8-$15; some shows require advance tickets. **Credit** AmEx, DC, Disc, MC, V (bar only). **Map** p403 G29.

The unassuming, boxy Mercury Lounge is both an old standby and pretty much the No.1 indie rock club in town, with solid sound and sightlines (and a cramped bar in the front room). With four-band bills almost every night, you can catch plenty of locals (Cause Co-Motion, Takka Takka) and touring bands (the Howling Hex, 1990s) in the course of just one week. Only two caveats: bills can seem stylistically haphazard, and the set times are regularly later than advertised. Note that some of the spot's bigger shows sell out in advance, mainly through online sales. *Photo p318.*

Mo Pitkin's House of Satisfaction

34 Avenue A, between 2nd & 3rd Streets (1-212 777 5660/www.mopitkins.com). Subway F, V to Lower East Side-Second Avenue. **Shows** daily; times vary. **Box office** tickets from www.ticketweb.com. **Cover** $8-$15 (most shows with 1-drink minimum). **Credit** AmEx, MC, V. **Map** p403 G29.

Opened in 2005 by brothers Phil and Jesse Hartman (the former co-owns local pizza institution Two Boots; the latter is a musician known for his work as Laptop), Mo Pitkin's is an only-in-Manhattan type of joint. On the first floor lies a great Jewish-Latino restaurant and bar. Above is a cabaret space featuring all sorts of comedy and music, including up-and-coming singer-songwriters, roots artists, comedians, burlesque acts and more. The bookings increasingly tilt toward unknown singer-songwriters, and pesky drink minimums are annoying, but the latkes (Jewish pancakes) are among the best in town.

Mercury Lounge. See p317.

Music Hall of Williamsburg

66 N 6th Street, between Kent & Wythe Avenues, Williamsburg, Brooklyn (1-718 599 5103/ www.williamsburgmusichall.com). Subway L to Bedford Avenue. **Shows** vary. **Box office** noon-7pm Mon-Sat (advance online purchase recommended). **Tickets** $12-$35. **No credit cards. Map** p411 U7.

The somewhat ostentatiously named Music Hall of Williamsburg was formerly Northsix, the first well-sized rock club to open in the fabled 'hood. (This was way back in 2001 – roughly a century ago in trend-culture terms.) In the autumn of 2007, the expanding Bowery Presents (an independent concert promoter) found itself in great need of a Williamsburg outpost, gave the club a face-lift and took over bookings. Now it's basically a Bowery Ballroom in Brooklyn, with bands such as Black Lips and Apples in Stereo headlining, often a day after playing Bowery.

New Jersey Performing Arts Center

1 Center Street, at the waterfront, Newark, NJ (1-888 466 5722/www.njpac.org). PATH train to Newark, then Loop shuttle bus to NJPAC. **Box office** noon-6pm Mon-Sat; 10am-3pm Sun. **Tickets** $12-$100. **Credit** AmEx, Disc, MC, V.

Visible from Manhattan (and quite easy to get to, too), New Jersey Performing Arts Center offers up legends of disco (Donna Summer), Broadway stars such as Brian Stokes Mitchell in cabaret performances, plus crowd-pleasing swing and soul music. The summer programme is chock-full of outdoor entertainment geared to families.

Nokia Theatre Times Square

1515 Broadway, at 44th Street (1-212 307 7171). Subway N, Q, R, W to 42nd Street; S, 1, 2, 3, 7 to 42nd Street-Times Square. **Box office** 4-11pm daily (advance online purchase recommended). **Tickets** $20-$40. **Credit** AmEx, MC, V. **Map** p404 D24.

This large Times Square corporate club begs for character – its a cookie-cutter aura would befit a suburban mega-mall – but finds redemption in its creature comforts. The sound and sightlines are both good and well planned, and there's even edible food. Those who wish to look into a musician's eyes can stand in the ample front section, while foot-weary fans can sit in the cinema-like section at the back. It's a comfortable place to see a well-known band that hasn't (yet) reached stadium-filling fame. Belle & Sebastian, Morcheeba, Anthrax and Damian 'Jr Gong' Marley have all played here.

Pete's Candy Store

709 Lorimer Street, between Frost & Richardson Streets, Williamsburg, Brooklyn (1-718 302 3770/ www.petescandystore.com). Subway L to Lorimer Street. **Open** 5pm-2am Mon-Wed, Sun; 5pm-4am Thur-Sat. **Cover** free. **No credit cards. Map** p411 V7.

An overlooked gem of a venue, tucked away in an old candy shop situated in an obscure corner of Williamsburg. Pete's is gorgeous, tiny and always free. The performers are generally unknown and the crowds sometimes thin, but it can be a romantic, comfortable place to catch a singer-songwriter. And at times, terrific local underdogs – Jeffrey Lewis, Hannah Marcus – stop by for casual sets.

Pianos

158 Ludlow Street, between Rivington & Stanton Streets (1-212 505 3733/www.pianosnyc.com). Subway F to Delancey Street; J, M, Z to Delancey-Essex Streets. **Shows** vary. **Box office** 3pm-4am daily. **Tickets** free-$12. **Credit** AmEx, DC, MC, V. **Map** p403 G29.

When it opened a few years ago, this small club seemed like ground zero for all things New York hip. That's no longer the case, as a lot of the cooler bookings have moved either to Brooklyn or down the block (to venues such as Cake Shop; *see p314*). Still, while sound is often lousy and the room can become uncomfortably mobbed, there are always good reasons to go back. And the emerging talent booked in the charming, free upstairs lounge is often a good bet.

Radio City Music Hall

1260 Sixth Avenue, at 50th Street (1-212 247 4777/ www.radiocity.com). Subway B, D, F, V to 47th-50th Streets-Rockefeller Center. **Box office** 10am-8pm Mon-Sat; 11am-8pm Sun. **Tickets** $25-$125. **Credit** AmEx, MC, V. **Map** p404 D23.

Few rooms scream 'New York City!' more than this gilded hall, which has recently drawn Björk, Lyle Lovett and James Blunt as headliners. The greatest challenge for any performer is not to get upstaged by the awe-inspiring art deco surroundings – but these same surroundings lend historic heft to even the flimsiest showing.

Roseland

239 W 52nd Street, between Broadway & Eighth Avenue (1-212 247 0200/www.roselandballroom.com). Subway B, D, E to Seventh Avenue; C to 50th Street. **Box office** at Fillmore New York at Irving Plaza (*see p314*). **Tickets** $17-$75. **No credit cards**. **Map** p404 D23.

Roseland is a slightly depressing Times Square club that's bigger than Irving Plaza and smaller than the Hammerstein Ballroom. As at any large club, you'll find any artist who can fill the room performing here, with past acts including My Morning Jacket, Massive Attack and the Fratellis.

Sidewalk Café

94 Avenue A, at 6th Street (1-212 473 7373). Subway F, V to Lower East Side-Second Avenue; 6 to Astor Place. **Shows** around 7.30pm. **Cover** free; 2-drink minimum. **Credit** AmEx, MC, V (bar only). **Map** p403 G28.

Despite its cramped and awkward layout, the Sidewalk café is the undisputed focal point of the city's anti-folk scene – though that category means just about anything from piano pop to wry folk. Nellie McKay, Regina Spektor and the Moldy Peaches all started here; Monday's Antihootenanny with anti-folk host Lach is an institution.

S.O.B.'s

204 Varick Street, at Houston Street (1-212 243 4940/www.sobs.com). Subway 1 to Houston Street. **Box office** 11am-6pm Mon-Sat. **Tickets** $10-$25. **Credit** AmEx, DC, Disc, MC, V (food & bar only). **Map** p403 D29.

The titular sounds of Brazil are just some of many global genres that keep this Tribeca spot hopping. Hip hop, soul, reggae and Latin beats figure in the musical mix, with Seu Jorge, Zap Mama, Vivian Green and Hugh Masekela each appearing of late. Be careful at the bar, however, as the drinks are very highly priced. That said, the sharp-looking clientele doesn't seem to mind.

Southpaw

125 Fifth Avenue, between Sterling & St Johns Places, Park Slope, Brooklyn (1-718 230 0236/ www.spsounds.com). Subway B, Q, 2, 3, 4, 5 to Atlantic Avenue; D, M, N, R to Pacific Street. **Shows** times vary. **Tickets** $7-$20. **No credit cards**. **Map** p410 T11.

Another cool space that's far enough out of Manhattan to ensure you'll never come just to chill out, but only to see someone specific – which is hardly a problem, since the calendar welcomes prime outfits that would play in slightly larger Manhattan rooms, including Heartless Bastards, KRS-One and the Dirtbombs. Like its Park Slope neighbourhood, Southpaw tends to draw cool, mellow audiences, and with all this elbow room, getting to the (huge!) bar is hardly an issue.

Studio B

259 Banker Street, between Calyer Street & Meserole Avenue, Greenpoint, Brooklyn (1-718 389 1880/ www.clubstudiob.com). Subway L to Bedford Avenue; G to Nassau Avenue. **Shows** times vary. **Tickets** $10-$20. **No credit cards**. **Map** p411 U7.

A newish club in now trendoid Greenpoint, Studio B has a colossal, muscular sound system and hip bookings. Tasteful local bands such as Fiery Furnaces and Oneida have played the joint, as have cool out-of-towners like Gravy Train!!!! and Mountain Goats – not to mention loud DJs. Just ignore the '80s disco decor and lighting. *See also p324* **Live from New York**.

Terminal 5

610 W 56th Street, between 11th & 12th Avenues (1-212 260 4700/www.terminal5nyc.com). Subway A, B, C, D, 1 to 59th Street-Columbus Circle. **Tickets** $20-$40. **Box office** noon-7pm Mon-Sat. **No credit cards**. **Map** p405 C22.

Terminal 5 is a massive club on the far west side opened by Bowery Presents at the end of 2007. With three floors and room for 3,000 fans, it's the largest midtown venue to set up shop in more than a decade. Acts include bands that not long ago were playing smaller Bowery confines – the Shins and the National, for example – as well as big stars (M.I.A.) and scruffy veterans with considerable loyal fanbases (Ween).

Town Hall

123 W 43rd Street, between Sixth & Seventh Avenues (1-212 997 1003/www.the-townhallnyc.org). Subway B, D, F, V to 42nd Street-Bryant Park; N, Q, R, W to 42nd Street; S, 1, 2, 3, 7 to 42nd Street-Times Square. **Box office** noon-6pm Mon-Sat. **Tickets** $15-$85. **Credit** AmEx, MC, V. **Map** p404 D24.

Acoustics at the 'people's auditorium' are superb, and there's no doubting the gravitas of Town Hall's surroundings. Lindsey Buckingham, Jenny Lewis and Sufjan Stevens have each put on shows here in recent times – and Bright Eyes frontman Conor Oberst likes the theatre so much, he famously played a seven-night stand here.

Union Hall

702 Union Street, at Fifth Avenue, Park Slope, Brooklyn (1-718 638 4400/www.unionhallny.com). Subway M, R to Union Street. **Open** 4pm-4am Mon-Fri; noon-4am Sat, Sun. **Tickets** $5-$20. **Credit** AmEx, MC, V. **Map** p410 T11.

The spacious main floor of this Brooklyn bar has a garden, food service and, its raison d'être, a bocce ball court. Tucked into the basement is a comfortable performance space dominated by the more delicate side of indie rock – with occasional sets by indie comics such as Eugene Mirman and Michael Showalter thrown in for good measure. And if a show drags – there's always bocce.

WaMu Theater at Madison Square Garden

Seventh Avenue, between 31st & 33rd Streets (1-212 465 6741/www.thegarden.com). Subway A, C, E, 1, 2, 3 to 34th Street-Penn Station. **Box office** noon-6pm Mon-Sat. **Tickets** vary. **Credit** AmEx, DC, Disc, MC, V. **Map** p404 D25.

This smaller space within the Garden has better sound than the arena. The WaMu Theater has hosted world-music celebrations, as well as mainstream hip hop and the annual music festival known as the Jammys.

Warsaw at the Polish National Home

261 Driggs Avenue, at Eckford Street, Greenpoint, Brooklyn (1-718 387 0505/www.warsawconcerts.com). Subway G to Nassau Avenue; L to Bedford Avenue, then 15-min walk. **Box office** tickets for sale at bar 6pm-midnight Tue-Sun. **Tickets** from $15. **Credit** AmEx, MC, V. **Map** p411 V7.

Warsaw is a nice mid-size venue in Greenpoint. The sound isn't fantastic and getting here from Manhattan can be a bit of a chore (the best bet is to take the L train to Bedford Avenue and then walk). For Brooklynites, however, the club offers a good chance to see bands like the Walkmen or Liars without leaving the borough.

Webster Hall

125 E 11th Street, between Third & Fourth Avenues (1-212 353 1600/www.websterhall.com). Subway L to Third Avenue; N, Q, R, W, 4, 5, 6 to 14th Street-Union Square. **Shows** see website for schedule. **Tickets** free-$30. **Credit** AmEx, DC, MC, V. **Map** p403 F28.

The recent addition of Webster Hall to the local scene provides a great-sounding alternative for bands (not to mention fans) who might have had their fill of comparably sized Irving Plaza. Bowery Presents, the folks who run Bowery Ballroom and Mercury Lounge, provide the bookings here, which is why the schedule features bands that have grown out of those rooms (Hot Chip, Mastodon, Brian Jonestown Massacre). As indie rock grows in popularity, its performance spaces are booming – which is all well and good, but be sure to show up early if you want to see much.

Jazz & experimental

Barbès

376 9th Street, at Sixth Avenue, Park Slope, Brooklyn (1-718 965 9177/www.barbesbrooklyn.com). Subway F to Seventh Avenue. **Tickets** free-$8. **Credit** (bar only) Disc, MC, V. **Map** p410 T11.

Show up early if you want to get into Park Slope's global-bohemian club (and believe us you do) – it's tiny. This boîte, run by musically inclined French expats, brings in jazz of the traditional swing and more daring stripes, plus world-music-derived hybrids (Las Rubias del Norte) and acts that often defy categorisation (One Ring Zero).

Birdland

315 W 44th Street, between Eighth & Ninth Avenues (1-212 581 3080/www.birdlandjazz.com). Subway A, C, E to 42nd Street-Port Authority. **Box office** phone for details. **Tickets** $20-$50, plus $10 food/drink minimum. **Credit** AmEx, DC, Disc, MC, V. **Map** p404 C24.

The name means jazz, but, perhaps in deference to its Theater District digs, Birdland is also a prime destination for cabaret. The jazz names that pass through are unimpeachable (Kurt Elling, Jim Hall, Paquito D'Rivera) and the cabaret stars glowing (Christine Andreas, Christine Ebersole). Residencies are among the better ones in town (the Chico O'Farrill Afro-Cuban Jazz Orchestra owns Sundays and David Ostwald's Louis Armstrong Centennial Band hits on Tuesdays; Mondays find cabaret's waggish Jim Caruso and his Cast Party).

Blue Note

131 W 3rd Street, between MacDougal Street & Sixth Avenue (1-212 475 8592/www.bluenote.net). Subway A, B, C, D, E, F, V to W 4th Street. **Box office** phone or visit website for reservations. **Tickets** $10-$65, plus $5 food/drink minimum. **Credit** AmEx, DC, MC, V. **Map** p403 E29.

On a bustling, slightly seedy Greenwich Village block sits the Blue Note, which prides itself on being

Carnegie Hall.

'the jazz capital of the world'. Bona fide musical titans (Cecil Taylor, Abbey Lincoln) rub against hot young talents (Matthew Shipp, Jason Lindner) on the calendar, while the close tables in the club get patrons rubbing up against each other. The Late Night Groove series and the Sunday brunches are the best bargain bets.

Carnegie Hall

For listing, see p328.
Carnegie Hall means the big time. In recent years Zankel Hall – a state-of-the-art 599-seat subterranean theatre – has greatly augmented Carnegie's pop, jazz and world music offerings. Between them both, the complex has welcomed Dave Brubeck, Wayne Shorter, Bobby McFerrin, Brad Mehldau and Fred Hersch of late, among many other high-wattage musical names.

Cornelia Street Café

29 Cornelia Street, between Bleecker & W 4th Streets (1-212 989 9319/www.corneliastreetcafe.com). Subway A, B, C, D, E, F, V to W 4th Street. **Open** from 9pm. **Tickets** $8-$12, plus $6 drink minimum. **Credit** AmEx, DC, MC, V. **Map** p403 D29.
Upstairs is a cosy little Greenwich Village eaterie. Go downstairs and you'll find an even cosier music space that hosts adventurous jazz, poetry, world music and folk. Regular mini-festivals spotlight blues, songwriters and new concert-theatre works.

Iridium Jazz Club

1650 Broadway, at 51st Street (1-212 582 2121/ www.iridiumjazzclub.com). Subway 1 to 50th Street. **Box office** phone for details. **Tickets** $25-$35, plus $10 food/drink minimum. **Credit** AmEx, DC, Disc, MC, V. **Map** p404 D23.
One of the nicer places to dine while being hit with top-shelf jazz (both from household names and cats who are more for insiders), Iridium is located smack bang in the middle of Broadway's bright lights. Recent guests include Art Ensemble of Chicago, Mose Allison, and Archie Shepp and Roswell Rudd. Monday nights belong to wise-cracking guitar legend Les Paul; Tuesdays mean the Mingus Big Band. Advance bookings recommended.

55 Bar

55 Christopher Street, between Seventh Avenue South & Waverly Place (1-212 929 9883/www.55bar.com). Subway 1 to Christopher Street-Sheridan Square. **Shows** doors open 5.30pm Fri, Sat; 9.30pm Sun. **Tickets** free-$15. **No credit cards**. **Map** p403 D28.
Though tiny (oh, call it intimate), this Prohibition-era dive is now one of New York's most artist-friendly rooms, thanks to its knowledgeable, appreciative audience. You can catch emerging talent almost every night at the free-of-charge early shows, while late sets regularly feature established artists, including Chris Potter and Mike Stern.

Jazz at Lincoln Center

Broadway, at 60th Street (1-212 258 9595/www.jazzatlincolncenter.org). Subway A, B, C, D, 1 to 59th Street-Columbus Circle. **Shows** 7.30pm, 9.30pm. **Box office** phone for reservations. **Tickets** $10-$30, plus food/drink minimums; phone for details. **Credit** AmEx, MC, V. **Map** p405 D22.
Seductively lit, decorated with elegant photography and blessed with clear sightlines and a gorgeous view of 59th Street and Central Park South, Dizzy's Club Coca-Cola at Jazz at Lincoln Center might be a Hollywood cinematographer's ideal vision of what a Manhattan jazz club ought to be. The swanky, intimate club – a regular hang for some of the most outstanding players in the business – is a class act in all but its clunky, commercialised name.

Jazz Gallery

290 Hudson Street, between Dominick & Spring Streets (1-212 242 1063/www.jazzgallery.org). Subway C, E to Spring Street. **Shows** 9pm, 10.30pm. **Box office** phone for reservations. **Tickets** $12-$15. **No credit cards**. **Map** p403 D30.
The fact that there's no bar here should be a tip-off: the Jazz Gallery is a place to witness true works of art, from the sometimes obscure but always interesting jazzers who play the club (Henry Threadgill

Uptown Jazz Lounge at Minton's Playhouse.

and Steve Coleman to name a couple), to the photos and artefacts displayed on the walls. The tiny room's acoustics are sublime.

Jazz Standard

116 E 27th Street, between Park Avenue South & Lexington Avenue (1-212 576 2232/www.jazz standard.com). Subway 6 to 28th Street. **Box office** phone for reservations. **Tickets** $15-$30. **Credit** AmEx, DC, Disc, MC, V. **Map** p404 E26.

The room's airy, multi-tiered floor plan makes for splendid sightlines to match the sterling sound quality, and in keeping with the rib-sticking chow offered upstairs (at restaurateur Danny Meyer's Blue Smoke barbecue joint), the jazz is often of the groovy, hard-swinging variety, with musicians such as pianist Vijay Iyer and tenorist David Murray. Pianist Fred Hersch's annual series of duets is a delight.

Lenox Lounge

288 Malcolm X Boulevard (Lenox Avenue), between 124th & 125th Streets (1-212 427 0253/www. lenoxlounge.com). Subway 2, 3 to 125th Street. **Shows** 9pm, 10.30pm, midnight (subject to change). **Cover** $5-$20, plus 2-drink minimum. **Credit** Disc, MC, V. **Map** p407 D13.

This classy art deco lounge in Harlem once hosted Billie Holiday and has drawn stars since the late 1930s. Saxist Patience Higgins's Sugar Hill Jazz Quartet jams into the wee hours on Monday nights. *See also p226.*

Merkin Concert Hall

For listing, see p328.

Just north of Lincoln Center is this home for classical and jazz composers. Merkin's polished digs also provide an intimate setting for chamber music and jazz, folk, cabaret and experimental performers. The New York Guitar Festival mounts elaborate multi-artist tribute concerts that feature the cream of the six-string crop; other series include the New York Festival of Song, WNYC's New Sounds Live and Broadway Close Up.

Uptown Jazz Lounge at Minton's Playhouse

20 W 118th Street, between St Nicholas Avenue & Adam Clayton Powell Jr Boulevard (1-212 864 8346/www.uptownatmintons.com). Subway B, C to 116th Street. **Open** 2pm-4am daily. **Shows** 10pm, 11.30pm, 1am Fri, Sat (earlier on week nights). **Cover** $10, 2-drink minimum (Fri, Sat only). **Credit** AmEx, MC, V. **Map** p407 D14.

One of the true jewels in Harlem's crown, Minton's Playhouse reopened recently after being boarded up for more than 30 years. Few clubs in the city can boast as rich a history as Minton's, which Miles Davis once dubbed 'the black jazz capital of the world'. During the 1940s, when Thelonious Monk was the resident pianist, late-night jams brought such luminaries as Dizzy Gillespie and Charlie Parker to the club, giving birth to bebop. Minton's presents five house bands from Sunday through Thursday. On weekends – when it gets more crowded – you can see guest acts, which have included the likes of percussionist Joe Chambers and his Outlaw Band.

92nd Street Y

1395 Lexington Avenue, at 92nd Street (1-212 415 5500/www.92y.org). Subway 6 to 92nd Street. **Box office** 9am-9pm Mon-Thur; 9am-5pm Fri; 6-9pm Sat. **Tickets** from $20. **Credit** AmEx, MC, V. **Map** p406 F17.

Best known for the series Jazz in July (now directed by pianist Bill Charlap) and Lyrics & Lyricists, the uptown Y's schedule extends to gospel, mainstream jazz and singer-songwriters. The small, handsome theatre provides a fine setting for the sophisticated fare that's offered here.

Smoke

2751 Broadway, between 105th & 106th Streets (1-212 864 6662/www.smokejazz.com). Subway 1 to 103rd Street. **Shows** 9pm, 11pm, 12.30am Mon-Sat; 6pm Sun. **Cover** free, $10 drink minimum Mon-Thur, Sun; $15-$25 Fri, Sat. **Credit** Disc, MC, V. **Map** p406 C16.

Not unlike a swanky living room, Smoke is a classy little joint that acts as a haven for local jazz legends and touring artists looking to play an intimate space. Early in the week, evenings are themed: on Sunday, it's Latin jazz; Tuesday, organ jazz. On weekends, internationally renowned jazzers (Hilton Ruiz, Tom Harrell, Eddie Henderson) hit the stage, relishing the opportunity to play informal gigs uptown.

The Stone

Avenue C, at 2nd Street (no phone/www.thestone nyc.com). Subway F, V to Lower East Side-Second Avenue. **Shows** doors from 8pm; Tue-Sun. **Cover** $10. **No credit cards**. **Map** p403 G29.

Don't call sax star John Zorn's not-for-profit venture a 'club'. You'll find no food or drinks here, and no nonsense, either – the Stone is an art space dedicated to 'the experimental and the avant-garde'. If you're down for some rigorously adventurous sounds (think Anthony Coleman, Okkyung Lee, Tony Conrad, and the ever-shifting constellation of sterling players that live here and pass through) – Zorn has made it easy: no advance ticket sales; all ages are admitted (kids 19 and under get discounts); and the bookings are left to a different artist-cum-curator each month.

Sweet Rhythm

88 Seventh Avenue South, between Bleecker & Grove Streets (1-212 255 3626/www.sweetrhythm ny.com). Subway 1 to Christopher Street-Sheridan Square. **Shows** 8pm, 10pm Mon-Thur, Sun; 8pm, 10pm, midnight Fri, Sat. **Cover** $10-$25 ($10 minimum per person per set). **Credit** AmEx, DC, MC, V. **Map** p403 D28.

In the same location as the legendary Sweet Basil you'll now find Sweet Rhythm, which is more of a destination to see a particular artist than a general hangout (due to the uninviting seating plan). While a variety of jazz sounds does dominate (swing, standards, bop), and big names such as Sonny Fortune and Rashied Ali still drop in occasionally (not to mention Jane Ira Bloom and Carl Allen), blues and world music are also to hand. Tuesday nights are devoted to vocalists.

Swing 46

349 W 46th Street, between Eighth & Ninth Avenues (1-212 262 9554/www.swing46.com). Subway A, C, E to 42nd Street-Port Authority. **Shows** vary. **Cover** $5-$12. **Credit** AmEx, DC, Disc, MC, V. **Map** p404 C23.

Swing isn't merely a trend at this supper club – whether peppy or sappy, these cats really mean it. Bands (with names like the Flying Neutrinos and the Flipped Fedoras) that jump, jive and wail await you, so be sure to wear your dancin' shoes. If you need to brush up on your technique, dance lessons are available for the inexperienced.

Village Vanguard

178 Seventh Avenue South, at Perry Street (1-212 255 4037/www.villagevanguard.com). Subway A, C, E, 1, 2, 3 to 14th Street; L to Eighth Avenue. **Shows** 9pm, 11pm Mon-Thur, Sun; 9pm, 11pm, 12.30am Fri, Sat. **Tickets** $20, plus $10 drink minimum; phone or visit website for reservations. **Credit** AmEx, MC, V (online purchases only; cash on door). **Map** p403 D28.

Over 70 years old and still going strong, the Village Vanguard is one of New York's real jazz meccas. History surrounds you here: John Coltrane, Miles Davis and Bill Evans have all grooved in this

Live from New York

We grade six of the city's newest live music venues, scrutinising the stage, the bathroom and everything in between.

Blender Theater at Gramercy

Capacity 600
Sound quality Adequate, if not awesome.
Sightlines They're good, whether you're close to the stage or lounging in slanted seats.
Programming Mid-size touring acts such as Bebel Gilberto and Pretty Girls Make Graves.
Input/output The drinks, like everything else, are standard. The toilets are functional, but don't bring a newspaper.
Final grade The Blender is basically a run-down movie theatre with a stage and a soundboard – we're docking a grade for drabness. **C+**
For listings see p314.

The Box

Capacity 200
Sound quality It's ideal in every inch of this small, plush room.
Sightlines Get in early if you want a good view, whether you're on the first floor by the stage or on the small balcony.
Programming A wide range of musicians and unconventional entertainment.
Input/output Top-shelf drinks run at more than $15. The restrooms are equally opulent.
Final grade You feel cool just entering this jewel in an old sign factory. **B**
For listings see p314.

Club Europa

Capacity 550
Sound quality It's more pro than you'd expect of a cheesy Polish nightclub.
Sightlines There's a low stage, so you get a waist-up view if you're standing in back.
Programming You can expect to hear anything from cutting-edge metal to Polish bubblegum pop.
Input/output Eastern European beauties sling cheap drinks. The bathrooms never get too crowded.
Final grade Disco light shows and occasional miniskirt nights are enough to make us forgive all the gold chains. **B**
For listings see p314.

Highline Ballroom

Capacity 700
Sound quality Top-of-the-heap sound gear is very easy on the ears.
Sightlines The wide-angle layout means there's hardly a bad spot to be had.
Programming You'll find more jazz, jam bands and world acts than in most rooms this size.
Input/output Servers roam the floor, so you can stay put. The toilet facilities are too new to be offensive.
Final grade The room is comfortable, but it lacks character. The industrial-chic vibe feels more warehouse than ballroom. **B+**
For listings see p315.

Luna Lounge

Capacity 400
Sound quality It's solid and functional, if unmemorable.
Sightlines The high stage is unobstructed from all directions.

hallowed hall, and the walls are lined with photos and artefacts. The big names, old and new, continue to fill the Vanguard's lineup, and the 16-piece Vanguard Jazz Orchestra has been the Monday night regular for almost 40 years. Reservations are strongly recommended, and note that the Vanguard takes only cash or travellers' cheques at the door.

Zebulon

258 Wythe Avenue, between Metropolitan Avenue & North Third Street, Williamsburg, Brooklyn (1-718 218 6934/www.zebuloncafeconcert.com). Subway L to Bedford Avenue. **Shows** doors from 4pm daily. **Cover** free. **Credit** AmEx. **Map** p411 U7.

For years now, people have been talking about Williamsburg as NYC's leading hipster enclave. But how hip could it have been before killer jazz spot Zebulon came along? Emphasising young firebrands (like Gold Sparkle Band and Tyshawn Sorey) over the establishment, Zebulon also welcomes the daring wing of the local rock scene (such as the great singer-songwriter Hannah Marcus). While the café opens in the afternoon, don't expect live music till closer to 10pm.

Blues, country & folk

See also p313 **BB King Blues Club & Grill**.

Paddy Reilly's Music Bar

519 Second Avenue, at 29th Street (1-212 686 1210/www.paddyreillys.com). Subway 6 to 28th

Highline Ballroom.

Programming Local and touring alternative pop and rock, such as the Giraffes.
Input/output Average drinks. Clean toilets.
Final grade This friendly, unadorned, cavernous room has little in common with its smaller Lower East Side precursor. **B**
For listings see p317.

Studio B

Capacity 500
Sound quality Sound geeks, get your kicks here – the system is powerful and clear.
Sightlines Good from the floor, and even better from the back and the raised side.
Programming It's diverse, but you'll mainly find cool names from the scene, like Oneida, LCD Soundsystem or the Fucking Champs.
Input/output Drinks are a buck more than you'd expect. The bathrooms are spacious, unskeevy and dimly lit.
Final grade The '80s disco decor and lighting can be disorienting at first, but this is an all-round great addition to the club circuit. **A**
For listings see p319.

Street. **Shows** 9.30pm Mon-Thur; 10.30pm Fri, Sat; 4-8pm Sun. **Cover** $5-$7. **Credit** AmEx, Disc, MC, V. **Map** p404 F29.

Patrons flock to this Gramercy institution for the silky Guinness – the house's only draft – but they stay for the lively Irish folk and rock acts that bring the room to life. Popular pub-rockers the Prodigals are regulars on Friday nights, while the rest of the weekend features Irish rock as well as more traditional jam sessions.

Rodeo Bar & Grill

375 Third Avenue, at 27th Street (1-212 683 6500/ www.rodeobar.com). Subway 6 to 28th Street. **Shows** 10pm Mon-Sat; 9pm Sun. **Tickets** free. **Credit** AmEx, DC, Disc, MC, V (bar only). **Map** p404 F26.

The unpretentious crowd and roadhouse atmosphere, not to mention the lack of a cover charge, make the Rodeo the city's best roots club, with a steady stream of rockabilly, country and related sounds. Rockabilly filly Rosie Flores is a regular, and bluegrass scion Chris Scruggs has visited from Nashville to play his '50s-style rock. Watch out for the peanut shells spread across the floor, and the frat boys from the (dreaded) Murray Hill 'hood.

Latin, reggae & world

See also p319 **S.O.B.'s**.

BAMcafé at Brooklyn Academy of Music

For listing, see p327 Brooklyn Academy of Music.

Among the cornucopia of live-entertainment programmes found at BAM is the BAMcafé above the lobby, which comes to life on weekend nights with country, spoken word, hip hop, world music and more, by performers such as Son de Madre and Manze. The NextNext series, which began in 2002, focuses on performers in their 20s.

Nublu

62 Avenue C, between 4th & 5th Streets (no phone/ www.nublu.net). Subway F, V to Lower East Side-Second Avenue. **Shows** doors from 8pm daily. **Cover** $5-$10. **No credit cards**. **Map** p403 G29.

Nublu's prominence on the local globalist club scene has been inversely proportional to its size – not to mention its seemingly out-of-the-way location deep in Alphabet City. A pressure cooker of creativity, Nublu gave rise to the Brazilian Girls, who started jamming at one late-night session and haven't stopped yet, as well as starting NYC's romance with the northern Brazilian style *forró*. Even on weeknights, events usually start no earlier than 10pm and can run into the wee hours – but if you show up early (and find the unmarked door), the bar is well stocked with wine selections, among other beverages, and the staff as warm as the music.

Zinc Bar

90 W Houston Street, between La Guardia Place & Thompson Street (1-212 477 8337/www.zincbar.com). Subway A, B, C, D, E, F, V to W 4th Street. **Open** 6pm-3.30am daily. **Cover** $5. **Credit** AmEx, DC, Disc, MC, V (bar only). **Map** p403 E29.

Located where Greenwich Village meets Soho, the Zinc Bar is the place to hoot and holler with diehard night owls. The after-hours atmosphere is enhanced by music from a cool mix of African, flamenco, jazz and samba bands.

Summer venues

Castle Clinton

Battery Park, Battery Place, at State Street (1-212 835 2789). Subway R, W to Rector Street; 1 to South Ferry; 4, 5 to Bowling Green. **Tickets** free. **Map** p402 E34.

One of the nicest views in all of Manhattan is found at its bottom tip, in the heart of Battery Park. This historic fort welcomes established stars whenever the weather is warm, with special events often found on 4 and 14 July. Lyle Lovett, the Flatlanders, Laura Cantrell and the Dave Holland Quartet have all performed for free in the evening air here, but note: tickets do have to be picked up in person on the day of a show, and they always go fast.

Central Park SummerStage

For listing, see p261.

Now in its 22nd year, the City Parks Foundation fills summers in the park with just about every sound under the sun. This New York institution has an ear for world music of all types – MIA, Television and Amadou and Mariam have all played in recent years, as have Zap Mama, Nortec Collective and Neko Case. Many of the shows are free, with a handful of benefits (Beastie Boys, Black Crowes) covering for them.

Giants Stadium

For listing, see p333 Meadowlands Sports Complex.

At New Jersey's Giants Stadium you can catch Hot97's annual Summer Jam, one of the biggest hip hop shows in the country, as well as other biggies like the Rolling Stones and Bruce Springsteen.

Lincoln Center Plaza

For listing, see p328 Lincoln Center.

Lincoln Center's multi-tiered floor plan allows for several outdoor stages in one sprawling facility, but the most popular venues are the North Plaza, which houses the well-loved Midsummer Night Swing dance concerts (*see p263*), and the Damrosch Park Bandshell, which rolls out the red carpet for the likes of sax icon Sonny Rollins. When the weather's hot, a wide variety of music from around the world creates a rich global feast.

Nikon at Jones Beach Theatre

Jones Beach, Long Island (1-516 221 1000/www.tommyhilfigerjonesbeach.com). LIRR from Penn Station, Seventh Avenue at 32nd Street, to Freeport, then Jones Beach bus. **Box office** 10am-9pm Mon (show days); 10am-6pm Tue-Sat; noon-6pm Sun; open till 9pm show days. **Tickets** $30-$135. **Credit** AmEx, MC, V.

It's a long haul, especially if you don't have your own wheels, and the sound is generally indifferent. Still, you can't beat the open-air setting at this beachside amphitheatre (which before switching sponsors was known as Tommy Hilfiger at Jones Beach Theater). From July to September, the biggest tours stop here, including package shows, as well as veterans such as Tom Petty, younger singers like Fiona Apple and soul stars both current (Erykah Badu) and classic (Anita Baker).

Prospect Park Bandshell

For listing, see p263 Celebrate Brooklyn! Performing Arts Festival.

Prospect Park Bandshell is to Brooklynites what Central Park SummerStage is to Manhattanites: the place to hear cool tunes in the great outdoors. Adventurous programming for the summer's Celebrate Brooklyn! Performing Arts Festival (*see p263*) runs the global gamut, from exotic (Africa Day) to less so (Canada Day). Of course, everything from blues titans (Bettye LaVette and Charlie Musselwhite) and Latin sounds (Eddie Palmieri, Milly Quezada) to classic movie-and-music pairings round out the calendar. Even Prince has stopped by.

Classical

Given all the buzz being generated by Peter Gelb's populist revolution at the Metropolitan Opera for the 2006/7 season, **Lincoln Center**'s other two major musical residents – the **New York City Opera** and the **New York Philharmonic** – needed to take drastic steps in order to not be completely overshadowed. Remarkably, both actually surpassed public expectations: City Opera announced the hiring of the radical Belgian provocateur Gerard Mortier, responsible for visionary new compositions, as well as widely reviled productions of standard works, as its next general director. And the Philharmonic, for its part, appointed Alan Gilbert, a young, inquisitive American-born conductor (and thus the antithesis of his two predecessors, Kurt Masur and Lorin Maazel), as its next music director. Since Mortier and Gilbert begin their tenures in 2009, breathless anticipation remains the name of the game in New York City once again.

Clive Gillinson has begun to put his own stamp on **Carnegie Hall**'s 2007/8 season with the ambitious 'Berlin in Lights' series. And young, hip New Yorkers not normally drawn to classical music will surely welcome the return of the **Wordless Music Series**, independent impresario Ronen Givony's nomadic, wildly successful series that pairs serious chamber music performances with leading indie, post-rock and electronica artists (see www.wordlessmusic.org for lineups and locations).

The standard New York concert season lasts from September to June, but there are plenty of off-season events and performances. In summer, box office hours may change so phone ahead or check websites for times.

BUYING TICKETS

You can buy tickets directly from most venues, whether by phone, online or at the box office. However, a surcharge is generally added to tickets not bought in person. For more ticket information, *see p383.*

CarnegieCharge

1-212 247 7800/www.carnegiehall.org. **Box office** (by phone) 8am-8pm daily. **Fee** $6 surcharge per ticket. **Credit** AmEx, DC, Disc, MC, V.

Centercharge

1-212 721 6500. **Box office** (by phone) 10am-8pm Mon-Sat; noon-8pm Sun. **Fee** $5.50 surcharge per ticket. **Credit** AmEx, Disc, MC, V.

Centercharge sells tickets for events at Alice Tully Hall, Avery Fisher Hall and the Juilliard School, as well as for the Lincoln Center Out of Doors Festival.

Metropolitan Opera

1-212 362 6000/www.metoperafamily.org/metopera. **Box office** (by phone) 10am-8pm Mon-Sat; noon-6pm Sun. **Fee** $5.50 surcharge per ticket. **Credit** AmEx, Disc, MC, V.

The Met sells tickets for performances held in its opera house (*see p329*), including those of the resident American Ballet Theatre.

BACKSTAGE PASSES

Curious music lovers can go behind the scenes at several of the city's major concert venues. **Backstage at the Met** (1-212 769 7020, www.metoperafamily.org/education) shows you around the famous house during the opera season, which runs from September to May; **Lincoln Center Tours** (1-212 875 5350) escorts you inside Avery Fisher and Alice Tully Halls, as well as the New York State Theater; **Carnegie Hall** (1-212 247 7800) guides you through what is perhaps the world's most famous concert hall. For a $16 fee, you may also sit in on rehearsals of the **New York Philharmonic** (1-212 875 5656), usually held on the Thursday before a concert.

Major concert halls

Brooklyn Academy of Music

30 Lafayette Avenue, between Ashland Place & St Felix Street, Fort Greene, Brooklyn (1-718 636 4100/www.bam.org). Subway B, Q, 2, 3, 4, 5 to Atlantic Avenue; C to Lafayette Street; D, M, N, R to Pacific Street; G to Fulton Street. **Box office** noon-6pm Mon-Sat; noon-4pm Sun (show days). **Admission** varies. **Credit** AmEx, MC, V. **Map** p410 T10.

America's oldest academy for the performing arts continues to present some of the freshest programming in the city. Every autumn and winter, the Next Wave Festival provides an overview of avant-garde music, dance and theatre, while spring brings lauded European opera productions. The nearby BAM Harvey Theater offers a smaller, more atmospheric setting for new creations by composers such as Tan Dun and Meredith Monk, as well as innovative stagings of baroque opera. Meanwhile, the resident Brooklyn Philharmonic Orchestra continues to provide innovative programming under the direction of its ambitious young conductor, Michael Christie.

Carnegie Hall

154 W 57th Street, at Seventh Avenue (1-212 247 7800/www.carnegiehall.org). Subway N, Q, R, W to 57th Street. **Box office** 11am-6pm Mon-Sat; noon-6pm Sun. **Admission** varies. **Credit** AmEx, DC, Disc, MC, V. **Map** p405 D22.

The stars – both soloists and orchestras – in the classical music firmament continue to shine most brightly in the Isaac Stern Auditorium, inside this renowned concert hall. Still, it's the spunky upstart Zankel Hall that has generated the most buzz; the below-street-level space offers an eclectic mix of classical, contemporary, jazz, pop and world music. Next door, Weill Recital Hall hosts intimate concerts and chamber music programmes.

Florence Gould Hall

French Institute Alliance Française, 55 E 59th Street, between Madison & Park Avenues (1-212 355 6160/ www.fiaf.org). Subway N, R, W to Fifth Avenue-59th Street; 4, 5, 6 to 59th Street. **Box office** 11am-7pm Tue-Fri; 11am-3pm Sat. **Admission** $10-$35. **Credit** AmEx, MC, V. **Map** p405 E22.

Programming in this small, comfortable hall has a decidedly French tone, in both artists and repertoire.

Merkin Concert Hall

Kaufman Center, 129 W 67th Street, between Broadway & Amsterdam Avenue (1-212 501 3330/www.kaufman-center.org). Subway 1 to 66th Street-Lincoln Center. **Box office** noon-7pm Mon-Thur, Sun; noon-4pm Fri. **Admission** $10-$50. **Credit** AmEx, MC, V (advance purchases only). **Map** p405 C21.

Tucked on a side street in the shadow of Lincoln Center, this unimposing gem of a concert hall offers a robust mix of early music and avant-garde programming, plus an increasing amount of jazz, folk and some more eclectic fare. The hall is undergoing extensive renovation this season, and will reopen to the public in January 2008.

New Jersey Performing Arts Center

For listing, see p318.

It only takes around 20 minutes to reach Newark's sumptuous performing arts complex from Midtown, and it's well worth the trip. Tickets for big-name acts that are sold out at Manhattan venues can often be found here, and performances may be slightly different to those in concurrent Gotham gigs.

92nd Street Y

For listing, see p323.

The Y has always stood for solidly traditional orchestral, solo and chamber masterpieces. But the organisation also fosters the careers of young musicians and explores European and Jewish-American music traditions, with innovative and far-reaching results.

Lincoln Center

Columbus Avenue, at 65th Street (1-212 546 2656/ www.lincolncenter.org). Subway 1 to 66th Street-Lincoln Center. **Map** p405 C21.

Built in the 1960s, this massive complex is the nexus of Manhattan's performing arts scene. Lincoln Center hosts lectures and symposia in the **Rose Building**, in addition to events in the main halls: **Alice Tully Hall**, **Avery Fisher Hall**, **Metropolitan Opera House**, **New York State Theater**, and the **Vivian Beaumont** and **Mitzi E Newhouse Theaters**. Also situated here are the **Juilliard School** (*see p332*) and the **Fiorello H La Guardia High School of Music & Art and Performing Arts** (108 Amsterdam Avenue, between 64th & 65th Streets, www.laguardiahs.org), which frequently hosts professional performances.

Big stars like Valery Gergiev, Sir Colin Davis and the Emerson Quartet are Lincoln Center's meat and potatoes, but lately the great divide between the flagship Great Performers season and the relatively audacious, multidisciplinary **Lincoln Center Out of Doors Festival** (*see p263*) has begun to narrow, thanks to fresher programming. Arguably freshest of all is the **Mostly Mozart** festival (*see p263*), a formerly moribund summer staple that has been thoroughly reinvented with progressive bookings and innovative juxtapositions.

The main entry point for Lincoln Center is at Columbus Avenue, at 65th Street but the venues that follow are spread out across the square of blocks from 62nd to 66th Streets, between Amsterdam and Columbus Avenues.

Alice Tully Hall

1-212 875 5050. **Box office** 11am-6pm Mon-Sat; noon-6pm Sun. **Admission** free-$75. **Credit** AmEx, Disc, MC, V.

Home to the Chamber Music Society of Lincoln Center (1-212 875 5788, www.chambermusicsociety.org), Alice Tully Hall somehow manages to make its auditorium of 1,096 seats feel cosy. Right now, however, the hall is closed for extensive remodelling, and won't reopen until winter 2008; in the meantime, the Chamber Music Society has moved to Jazz at Lincoln Center's Columbus Circle headquarters (*see p321*) and other temporary new homes around town.

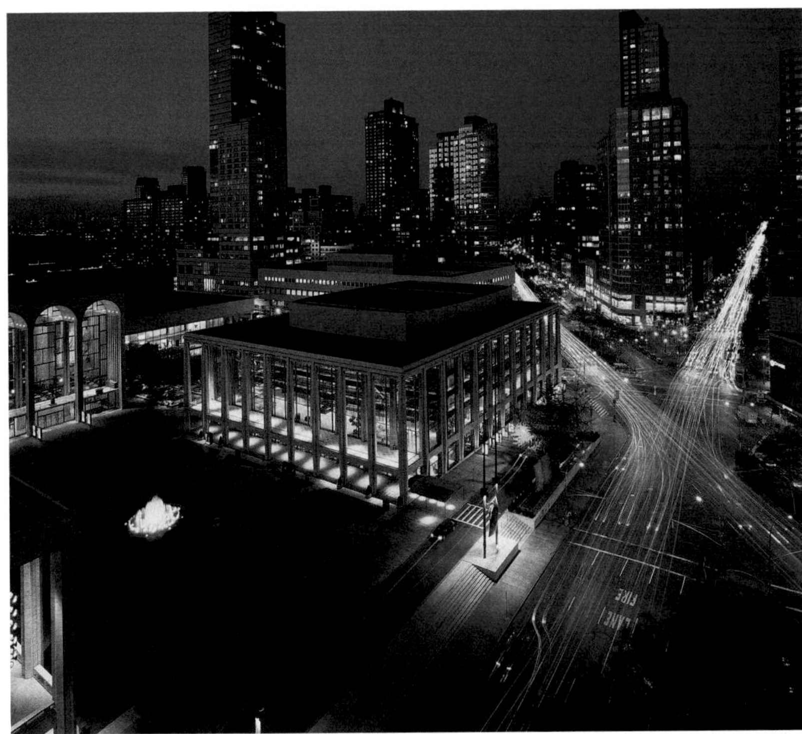

Bright lights, big stars at **Lincoln Center**.

Avery Fisher Hall

1-212 875 5030. **Box office** 10am-6pm Mon-Sat; noon-6pm Sun. **Admission** $20-$114. **Credit** AmEx, Disc, MC, V.

This handsome, comfortable 2,700-seat hall is the headquarters of the New York Philharmonic (1-212 875 5656, www.nyphilharmonic.org), the country's oldest symphony orchestra (founded in 1842) and one of its finest. The sound, which ranges from good to atrocious depending on who you ask, stands to be improved. Inexpensive early-evening 'rush hour' concerts and open rehearsals are presented on a regular basis. The Great Performers series features top international soloists and ensembles.

Metropolitan Opera House

1-212 362 6000/www.metopera.org. **Box office** 10am-8pm Mon-Sat; noon-6pm Sun. **Admission** $25-$320. **Credit** AmEx, Disc, MC, V.

The Met is the grandest of the Lincoln Center buildings, so it's a spectacular place to see and hear opera. It hosts the Metropolitan Opera from September to May, and major visiting companies during the summer. Opera's biggest stars (think Domingo, Fleming and Gheorghiu) appear here regularly, and artistic director James Levine has turned the orchestra into a true symphonic force. Audiences are knowledgeable and fiercely partisan, with subscriptions remaining in families for generations. Still, the Met had already started to become more inclusive even before current impresario Peter Gelb took the reins last year. Now, the company is placing a priority on creating novel theatrical experiences (and often hiring Broadway directors in the effort), while assembling a new company of physically graceful, telegenic stars (Anna Netrebko, Rolando Villazón and Juan Diego Floréz among them) for an ever-increasing programme of high-definition movie-theatre broadcasts. Most tickets will be rather expensive for those not used to forking out for the arts, but 200 prime seats for all Monday through Thursday performances are held until the last hour, then sold for a mere $20 apiece. In 2008, look out for productions of *Otello*, *Carmen* and *La Bohéme*.

New York State Theater

1-212 870 5570. **Box office** 10am-7.30pm Mon; 10am-8.30pm Tue-Sat; 11.30am-7.30pm Sun. **Admission** $16-$120. **Credit** AmEx, DC, Disc, MC, V.

NYST houses the New York City Ballet (www.nycballet.com), as well as the New York City Opera (www.nycopera.com). The opera company has tried to overcome its second-best reputation by being both ambitious and defiantly populist. Rising young American singers often take their first bows at City Opera (many of them eventually make the trek across the plaza to the Met), where casts and productions have long tended to be younger and sexier than those of its more patrician counterpart. Although it still enjoys a reputation for fierce commitment to the unconventional – from modern American works and musical theatre productions to intriguing Handel stagings and forgotten *bel canto* gems – City Opera lost considerable ground to the Met's populist revolution last year. The 2007/8 season has some interesting offerings, but it's the following season, and Gerard Mortier's arrival, that will really be exciting.

Walter Reade Theater

1-212 875 5600/tickets 1-212 496 3809/www.filmlinc.com. **Box office** noon-6pm Mon-Fri; 30mins before shows Sat, Sun. **Admission** $10; $7 students; $6 members; $5 6-12s. **No credit cards.**

This theatre's acoustics are less than fabulous; still, the Great Performers series offers Sunday morning events fuelled by pastries and hot beverages sold in the lobby, and composer-lecturer Robert Kapilow's 'What Makes It Great?' series provides an entertaining introduction to major classical works.

Opera

The Metropolitan Opera and the New York City Opera may be the leaders of the pack, but they're hardly the only game in town. Feisty upstarts and long-standing grass-roots companies ensure that Manhattan's operaphiles are among the best served in the world. Call the organisations or visit their websites for information on ticket prices, schedules and venue. Music schools (*see p332*) also have regular opera programmes.

Amato Opera Theater

319 Bowery, at 2nd Street (1-212 228 8200/www.amato.org). Subway B, D, F, V to Broadway-Lafayette Street; 6 to Bleecker Street. **Admission** $30; $25 seniors, students, children. **Credit** AmEx, Disc, MC, V. **Map** p403 F29.

New York's beloved mom-and-pop opera shop offers charming, fully staged productions in a theatre that's only 20ft wide – it's almost like watching opera in your living room. The casting can be inconsistent, but many well-established singers have performed here.

American Opera Projects

South Oxford Space, 138 South Oxford Street, between Atlantic Avenue & Hanson Place, Fort Greene, Brooklyn (1-718 398 4024/www.operaprojects.org). Subway B, Q, 2, 3, 4, 5 to Atlantic Avenue; C to Lafayette Avenue; D, M, N, R to Pacific Street; G to Fulton Street. **Admission** varies. **No credit cards. Map** p410 T10.

American Opera Projects is not so much an opera company as a living, breathing workshop that allows you the opportunity to follow a new work from gestation to completion.

Dicapo Opera Theatre

184 E 76th Street, between Lexington & Third Avenues (1-212 288 9438/www.dicapo.com). Subway 6 to 77th Street. **Admission** $47.50. **Credit** MC, V. **Map** p405 F20.

This top-notch chamber-opera troupe benefits from City Opera-quality singers performing in a delightfully intimate setting in the basement of St Jean Baptiste Church.

Gotham Chamber Opera

Harry de Jur Playhouse, 466 Grand Street, at Pitt Street (1-212 598 0400/www.gothamchamberopera.org). Subway B, D to Grand Street; F to East Broadway. **Admission** $30-$65. **Credit** AmEx, MC, V. **Map** p403 G30.

The newest addition to NYC's lyrical firmament, this fine young company specialises in chamber opera: not scaled-down versions of big-stage classics, but rather those rarely staged shows specifically designed for smaller forces in intimate settings.

New York Gilbert & Sullivan Players

www.nygasp.org.

Is Victorian camp your vice? This troupe presents a rotating schedule of the Big Three (*HMS Pinafore, The Mikado* and *The Pirates of Penzance*), plus lesser-known works by Gilbert and Sullivan. The annual New Year's Eve Champagne Gala is at Symphony Space (*see p331*).

Other venues

Bargemusic

Fulton Ferry Landing, between Old Fulton & Water Streets, Dumbo, Brooklyn (1-718 624 2083/www.bargemusic.org). Subway A, C to High Street; F to York Street. **Admission** $25-$40. **Credit** MC, V. **Map** p411 S9.

This former coffee-bean barge presents four chamber concerts a week (plus one jazz programme), set against a panoramic view of lower Manhattan. It's a magical experience, but wrap up in winter. When the weather warms, you can enjoy a drink on the upper deck during the concert's intermission.

Frick Collection

For listing, see p139.

Concerts in the Frick Collection's elegantly appointed concert hall are a rare treat, generally featuring lesser-known but nonetheless world-class performers. After holding the line for free concerts far longer than expected, the Frick finally imposed a $20 ticket charge in 2005; ironically, however, this might make it easier to get tickets, which were routinely snatched up by members before the public even had a chance. Concerts are also broadcast live in the Garden Court, where tickets are not required.

Kaye Playhouse

Hunter College, 68th Street, between Park & Lexington Avenues (1-212 772 4448/http://kaye playhouse.hunter.cuny.edu). Subway 6 to 68th Street-Hunter College. **Box office** noon-6pm Mon-Sat. **Admission** $10-$70. **Credit** AmEx, MC, V. **Map** p405 E21.

Named after its benefactors – comedian Danny Kaye and his wife Sylvia – this refurbished theatre offers an eclectic programme of music and dance.

Kitchen

For listing, see p354.

A meeting place for the avant-garde in music, dance and theatre for more than 30 years, the Kitchen has played a less prominent role in the local scene during recent seasons. Still, edgy art can be found here, and prices range from free to $25.

Kosciuszko Foundation

15 E 65th Street, at Fifth Avenue (1-212 734 2130/www.thekf.org). Subway F to Lexington Avenue-63rd Street; 6 to 68th Street-Hunter College. **Admission** $15-$30. **Credit** MC, V. **Map** p405 E21.

This East Side townhouse hosts a chamber music series with a mission: each programme usually features at least one work by a Polish composer. You're less likely to get choked up with Chopin than to hear something novel by Paderewski or Szymanowski.

Gilder Lehrman Hall

Morgan Library & Museum, 225 Madison Avenue, at 36th Street (1-212 685 0008/www.themorgan.org). Subway 6 to 33rd Street. **Admission** varies. **Credit** MC, V. **Map** p404 E25.

The latest arrival on the New York concert music scene, this elegant little gem of a concert hall seats between 236 and 295 people: perfect for song recitals and chamber groups. The St Luke's Chamber Ensemble and Glimmerglass Opera were among the first groups to establish a presence here.

Metropolitan Museum of Art

For listing, see p143.

When it comes to established virtuosos and revered chamber ensembles, the Met's programming is consistently rich and full (and ticket prices are correspondingly high). The museum has also established a youthful resident ensemble, Metropolitan Museum Artists in Concert. Seasonally inspired early music concerts are held uptown in the truly stunning Fuentidueña Chapel at the Cloisters (*see p155*).

Miller Theatre at Columbia University

Broadway, at 116th Street (1-212 854 7799/www.millertheatre.com). Subway 1 to 116th Street-Columbia University. **Box office** noon-6pm Mon-Fri (plus 2hrs before performance on show days). **Admission** $20; $12 students. **Credit** AmEx, MC, V. **Map** p407 C14.

Columbia's Miller Theatre has single-handedly made contemporary classical music sexy in New York City. The credit belongs to executive director George Steel, who proved that presenting challenging fare by composers such as Ligeti, Birtwistle and Zorn in a casual, unaffected setting could attract a young audience – and hang on to it. Miller's early music offerings, many of which are conducted by Steel, are also exemplary.

New York Public Library for the Performing Arts

For listing, see p148.

The library's Bruno Walter Auditorium regularly hosts free recitals, solo performances and lectures.

Symphony Space

2537 Broadway, at 95th Street (1-212 864 5400/www.symphonyspace.org). Subway 1, 2, 3 to 96th Street. **Box office** noon-6pm Tue-Sat. **Admission** varies ($2 surcharge per order). **Credit** AmEx, MC, V. **Map** p406 C17.

Despite its name, Symphony Space provides programming that is anything but symphony-centric: recent seasons have featured saxophone quartets, Indian classical music and politically astute performances of Purcell's *Dido and Aeneas*. The annual Wall to Wall marathons serve up a full day of music – free of charge – focusing on a particular composer, from Bach to Sondheim.

Tenri Cultural Institute

43A W 13th Street, between Fifth & Sixth Avenues (1-212 645 2800/www.tenri.org). Subway F, V to 14th Street; L to Sixth Avenue; L, N, Q, R, W, 4, 5, 6 to 14th Street-Union Square. **Admission** varies. **No credit cards. Map** p403 E27.

A not-for-profit organisation devoted to promoting the Japanese language and appreciation of international art, Tenri also regularly hosts concerts by New York's leading contemporary music ensembles, such as the American Modern Ensemble, in its clean, effortlessly cosy gallery space.

Tishman Auditorium

New School University, 66 W 12th Street, at Sixth Avenue (1-212 243 9937/box office 1-212 229 5488). Subway F, V to 14th Street; L to Sixth Avenue. **Admission** free-$15. **No credit cards. Map** p403 D28.

The New School's modestly priced Schneider Concerts chamber series features up-and-coming musicians. Established artists also play here – for a fraction of the prices charged elsewhere.

Churches

From sacred to secular, a thrilling variety of music is performed in New York's churches. Superb acoustics, out-of-this-world choirs and serene surroundings make these houses of worship particularly attractive venues. A bonus is that some concerts are free or very cheap.

Cathedral Church of St John the Divine

1047 Amsterdam Avenue, at 112th Street (1-212 316 7540/www.stjohndivine.org). Subway B, C, 1 to 110th Street-Cathedral Parkway. **Tickets** phone or visit website for details **Admission** varies. **Credit** AmEx, Disc, MC, V. **Map** p406 C15.

The stunning neo-Gothic, 3,000-seat sanctuary is a heavenly atmosphere for the church's own choir and visiting ensembles. Acoustics, however, are murky.

Christ & St Stephen's Church

120 W 69th Street, between Columbus Avenue & Broadway (1-212 787 2755/www.csschurch.org). Subway 1, 2, 3 to 72nd Street. **Admission** varies. **No credit cards**. **Map** p405 C21.

This small, pleasant West Side church offers one of the most diverse concert rosters in the city.

Church of St Ignatius Loyola

980 Park Avenue, at 84th Street (1-212 288 2520/ www.saintignatiusloyola.org). Subway 4, 5, 6 to 86th Street. **Admission** $10-$40. **Credit** AmEx, Disc, MC, V. **Map** p406 E18.

The Sacred Music in a Sacred Space series is a high point of Upper East Side music culture. Lincoln Center also holds concerts here, capitalising on the church's fine acoustics and prime location.

Church of the Ascension

12 W 11th Street, between Fifth & Sixth Avenues (1-212 358 1469/www.voicesofascension.org). Subway N, R, W to 8th Street-NYU. **Admission** $10-$50. **Credit** MC, V (advance purchases only). **Map** p403 E28.

There's a first-rate professional choir, the Voices of Ascension, at this little Village church. You can catch the choir at Lincoln Center on occasion, but home turf is the best place to hear it.

Corpus Christi Church

529 W 121st Street, between Amsterdam Avenue & Broadway (1-212 666 9266/www.mb1800.org). Subway 1 to 116th Street-Columbia University. **Admission** varies. **Credit** MC, V. **Map** p407 C14.

Fans of early music can get their fix from Music Before 1800, a series that regularly imports the world's leading antiquarian artists and ensembles.

St Bartholomew's Church

109 E 50th Street, between Park & Lexington Avenues (1-212 378 0248/www.stbarts.org). Subway E, V to Lexington Avenue-53rd Street; 6 to 51st Street. **Admission** varies. **Credit** AmEx, MC, V. **Map** p403 E23.

This magnificent church hosts the Summer Festival of Sacred Music – one of the city's most ambitious choral music series – and fills the rest of the year with performances by resident ensembles and guests.

St Thomas Church Fifth Avenue

1 W 53rd Street, at Fifth Avenue (1-212 757 7013/ www.saintthomaschurch.org). Subway E, V to Fifth Avenue-53rd Street. **Admission** $15-$70. **Credit** AmEx, MC, V. **Map** p405 E22.

The country's only fully accredited choir school for boys keeps the great Anglican choral tradition alive and well in New York. St Thomas's annual performance of Handel's *Messiah* is a must-hear that's well worth the rather steep ticket price.

Trinity Church/St Paul's Chapel

Trinity Church, Broadway, at Wall Street; St Paul's Chapel, Broadway, at Fulton Street (1-212 602 0747/www.trinitywallstreet.org). Subway R, W to Rector Street; 4, 5 to Wall Street. **Admission** Concerts at One series $2 donation. **No credit cards**. **Map** p402 E33.

Historic Trinity, situated in the heart of the Financial District, plays host to the inexpensive Concerts at One series. Performances are held (at 1pm) on Mondays at St Paul's Chapel, and on Thursdays at Trinity Church.

Schools

The **Juilliard School** and the **Manhattan School of Music** are renowned for their talented students, faculty and artists in residence, all of whom regularly perform for free or at low cost. Lately, **Mannes College of Music** has made great strides to rise to the same level. Noteworthy music and innovative programming can also be found at several other colleges and schools in the city.

Juilliard School

60 Lincoln Center Plaza, Broadway, at 65th Street (1-212 769 7406/www.juilliard.edu). Subway 1 to 66th Street-Lincoln Center. **Admission** usually free. **Map** p405 C21.

NYC's premier conservatory stages weekly concerts by student soloists, orchestras and chamber ensembles, as well as elaborate opera productions that can often rival many professional presentations.

Manhattan School of Music

120 Claremont Avenue, at 122nd Street (1-212 749 2802 ext 4428/www.msmnyc.edu). Subway 1 to 125th Street. **Admission** usually free. **Map** p407 B14.

The Manhattan School of Music offers masterclasses, recitals and off-site concerts by its students and faculty as well as visiting professionals. The American String Quartet, which has been in residence here since 1984, gives concerts regularly, while the Augustine Guitar Series includes recitals by top soloists.

Mannes College of Music

150 W 85th Street, between Columbus & Amsterdam Avenues (1-212 580 0210/www.mannes.edu). Subway B, C, 1 to 86th Street. **Admission** usually free. **Map** p406 C18.

In addition to student concerts and faculty recitals, Mannes also mounts its own ambitious, historically themed concert series; the summer is given over to festivals and workshops for instrumentalists. Most of these events provide affordable performances by some of the world's leading musicians.

Sport & Fitness

Gotham means game time.

Couch potatoes (yes, you know who you are), welcome to spectator sport bliss. New York has two pro football teams, three pro hockey teams and three pro basketball teams, plus two major league and two minor league baseball teams, all just waiting to be cheered on. More of a show-off, are you? Well, no bench-warming for you. New York City is packed to the gills with a huge variety of ways to get your muscles burning: kayak on the Hudson, go ice skating at Rockefeller Center, swing a golf club at Chelsea Piers, or pedal a bike along park trails in any of the five boroughs. Looking for something a little more Zen? Then check out one of the dozens of yoga studios.

Spectator sports

Major venues

All advance tickets for events at these venues are sold through **Ticketmaster** (*see p382*).

Madison Square Garden

Seventh Avenue, between 31st & 33rd Streets (1-212 465 6741/www.thegarden.com). Subway A, C, E, 1, 2, 3 to 34th Street-Penn Station. **Open** *Box office* 9am-6pm Mon-Fri; 10am-6pm Sat; noon-1hr after event begins Sun. **Tickets** $25-$350. **Credit** AmEx, DC, Disc, MC, V. **Map** p404 D25.

The New York Rangers (hockey) and New York Knicks (basketball) call this home. Four-legged athletes take over the arena every February for the Westminster Kennel Club Dog Show (*see p335*).

Meadowlands Sports Complex

East Rutherford, NJ (1-201 935 3900/www.meadowlands.com). NJ Transit Meadowlands Sports Complex bus from Port Authority Bus Terminal. **Open** *Box office* 11am-6pm Mon-Sat; 2hrs prior to event Sun. **Tickets** from $25. **Credit** *Giants & Jets games & Meadowlands Racetrack* No credit cards. *All other events* AmEx, DC, Disc, MC, V.

Continental Airlines Arena (*see p334*), Giants Stadium and the Meadowlands Racetrack are part of this massive multi-venue complex across the river. All are serviced by the same bus.

Nassau Veterans Memorial Coliseum

1255 Hempstead Turnpike, Uniondale, Long Island (1-516 794 9303/www.nassaucoliseum.com). LIRR (www.lirr.org) train from Penn Station to Hempstead, then N70, N71 or N72 bus. **Tickets** from $25. **Credit** AmEx, Disc, MC, V.

This is where the New York Islanders hockey team wows spectators, and you can also catch a variety of cute ice skating shows alongside a roster of sell-out gigs by major rock and pop stars.

Baseball

New York City is home to two major league teams – the Yankees and the Mets – and each one has a distinct personality (and fan base). The American League's Yankees are the team with the rich history (think Babe Ruth, Mickey Mantle), the long list of championships and a payroll that would bankrupt a small country. At press time, the Bronx was burning with the Yankees putting in one of their worst seasons in 2007 – and whether or not coaxing Roger Clemens out of retirement for a hefty multi-million dollar contract was worth it remains to be seen. The National League's Mets are the relatively new kids on the block: they came along in 1961 to fill the gap that was created after the working-class favourite Brooklyn Dodgers moved to Los Angeles in 1958. The club's scruffy underdog personality keeps many fans rooting for it (fruitlessly, on the whole) year after year. But, 2007 may be the turning point fans have been praying for. For the past few seasons, the souvenir jersey of David Wright, Mets' third baseman, has even outsold that of Yankees' golden boy Derek Jeter. Could this possibly be a sign of things to come? Only time will tell.

Minor league excitement returned in 2001, when the Staten Island Yankees and the Brooklyn Cyclones (the Mets' minor league team) opened new ballparks with wonderful cityscape settings.

Brooklyn Cyclones

KeySpan Park, 1904 Surf Avenue, between West 17th & 19th Streets, Coney Island, Brooklyn (1-718 449 8497/www.brooklyncyclones.com). Subway D, F, Q to Coney Island-Stillwell Avenue. **Open** *Box office* 10am-4pm Mon-Sat. **Tickets** $6-$13. **Credit** AmEx, Disc, MC, V.

New York Mets

Shea Stadium, 123-01 Roosevelt Avenue, at 126th Street, Flushing, Queens (1-718 507 8499/www.mets.com). Subway 7 to Willets Point-Shea Stadium. **Open** *Box office* 9am-5.30pm Mon-Fri; 9am-2pm Sat, Sun. **Tickets** $20-$72. **Credit** AmEx, Disc, MC, V.

New York Rangers.

New York Yankees

Yankee Stadium, River Avenue, at 161st Street, Bronx (1-718 293 6000/www.yankees.com). Subway B, D, 4 to 161st Street-Yankee Stadium. **Open** *Box office* 9am-5pm Mon-Sat; 10am-4pm Sun; during games. **Tickets** $12-$110. **Credit** AmEx, Disc, MC, V. **Map** p408 B8.

Staten Island Yankees

Richmond County Bank Ballpark, 75 Richmond Terrace, at Bay Street, Staten Island (1-718 720 9200/www.siyanks.com). Staten Island Ferry to St George Terminal. **Open** *Box office* 9am-6pm Mon-Fri; 10am-6pm Sat; during games. **Tickets** $5-$13. **Credit** AmEx, Disc, MC, V.

Basketball

Both of the area's NBA teams – the New York Knicks and the New Jersey Nets – are in what could tactfully be described as 'rebuilding phases'. After a few years near the top of the Eastern Conference, the Nets are hoping to make the finals again. The Knicks, the true New York home team, continue to stumble and 2007's scandals surely won't help matters. Watching either squad in its home arena can be an exciting way to spend a night, and tickets are easier to come by these days. The Knicks play at Madison Square Garden; many seats are filled with basketball diehards (like Spike Lee), while Nets games (at the Continental Airlines Arena in New Jersey) are more family-friendly. For real excitement, check out college teams in the Big East Tournament or the National Invitation Tournament – both take place in March 2008 at Madison Square Garden. The ladies of the WNBA's New York Liberty hold court at MSG in the summer.

New York Knicks

Madison Square Garden (for listing, see p333). www.nyknicks.com. **Tickets** $34-$115.

New York Liberty

Madison Square Garden (for listing, see p333). www.nyliberty.com. **Tickets** $10-$65.

New Jersey Nets

Continental Airlines Arena (for listing, see p333 Meadowlands Sports Complex). *1-800 765 6387/ www.njnets.com.* **Tickets** $15-$150.

Boxing

Church Street Boxing Gym

25 Park Place, between Broadway & Church Street (1-212 571 1333/www.nyboxinggym.com). Subway 2, 3 to Park Place; 4, 5, 6 to Brooklyn Bridge-City Hall. **Open** Phone or visit website for schedule. **Tickets** $20-$30. **No credit cards. Map** p402 E32.

Church Street is a workout gym and an amateur boxing venue located in an atmospheric cellar downtown. Evander Holyfield, Mike Tyson and other heavy-hitters have trained here before Garden matches. About ten times a year, on Fridays, the gym hosts white-collar bouts.

Gleason's Gym

83 Front Street, between Main & Washington Streets, Dumbo, Brooklyn (1-718 797 2872/www.gleasonsgym.net). Subway F to York Street. **Open** Phone or visit website for schedule. **Tickets** $20. **Credit** DC, Disc, MC, V. **Map** p411 T11.

Although it occupies an undistinguished second-floor warehouse space in a now-groovy neighbourhood, Gleason's is *the* professional boxer's address in New York. The 'sweet scientists' who have trained at the city's most storied gym include Muhammad Ali and Jake (Raging Bull) La Motta. Monthly white-collar fights draw doctors, lawyers and stockbrokers – in and out of the ring.

Madison Square Garden

For listing, see p333. **Tickets** $30-$305.
Once the country's premier boxing venue, the Garden still hosts some pro fights plus the city's annual Golden Gloves amateur championships.

Dog show

Westminster Kennel Club Dog Show

Madison Square Garden (for listing, see p333). www.westminsterkennelclub.org. **Tickets** $40-$95. **Dates** Feb.
America's most prestigious dog show prances into Madison Square Garden each February. One of the oldest 'sporting' events in the country, it's your chance to see some of the most beautiful, well-trained pooches on the planet compete for the coveted Best in Show trophy – and tasty dog treats.

Football

Every Sunday from September to January, New Yorkers get religious… about football. The city, uniquely, lays claim to two NFL teams, and the Giants and the Jets have equally rabid followings – so rabid that every home game for both squads is officially sold out. But the teams sometimes release a few seats (generally, those that weren't claimed by the visiting team) on the day of the game. Call for availability on the Friday before kick-off. You can also try your luck on eBay or with a scalper (risky; tickets may be counterfeit). Fans of the fast-paced, high-scoring Arena Football League should head out to Nassau Coliseum to witness the inimitable New York Dragons, who play from February through to May.

New York Dragons

Nassau Veterans Memorial Coliseum (for listing, see p333). 1-866 235 8499/www.newyorkdragons.com. **Tickets** $15-$110.

New York Giants

Giants Stadium (for listing, see p333 Meadowlands Sports Complex). *1-201 935 8222/www.giants.com.* **Tickets** $65-$85.

New York Jets

Giants Stadium (for listing, see p333 Meadowlands Sports Complex*). 1-516 560 8100/www.newyorkjets.com.* **Tickets** $60-$80.

Hockey

Failed contract negotiations in 2005 cancelled a whole season, but the National Hockey League is now gathering momentum again. Check newspapers for the schedule. The formerly powerful New York Rangers have repeatedly failed to make the play-offs for an increasingly uncomfortable number of seasons. The upstart New Jersey Devils have captured three Stanley Cups in the last 13 seasons and always play an exciting, hard-nosed brand of hockey. The New York Islanders skate at the suburban Nassau Coliseum on Long Island. Tickets for all three teams are on sale throughout the season, which runs from October to April.

New Jersey Devils

Continental Airlines Arena (for listing, see p333 Meadowlands Sports Complex*). www.newjerseydevils.com.* **Tickets** $20-$90.

New York Islanders

Nassau Veterans Memorial Coliseum (for listing, see p333). www.newyorkislanders.com. **Tickets** $25-$175.

New York Rangers

Madison Square Garden (for listing, see p333). www.newyorkrangers.com. **Tickets** $25-$630.

Horse racing

There are three major racetracks situated near Manhattan: thoroughbreds run at Aqueduct, Belmont and the Meadowlands. If you don't want to trek all the way to Long Island or New Jersey, then catch the action (and the seedy atmosphere) at any off-track betting (OTB) parlour (check the Yellow Pages for locations). And yes, betting is legal at all New York tracks.

Aqueduct Racetrack

110-00 Rockaway Boulevard, at 110th Street, Jamaica, Queens (1-718 641 4700/www.nyra.com/aqueduct). Subway A to Aqueduct Racetrack. **Races** *Thoroughbred* Oct-May Wed-Sun. **Admission** *Clubhouse* $2. *Grandstand* $1. Free 2 Jan-7 Mar. **No credit cards**.
The Wood Memorial, a test run for promising three-year-olds, is held each spring.

Belmont Park

2150 Hempstead Turnpike, Elmont, Long Island (1-516 488 6000/www.nyra.com/belmont). From Penn Station, Seventh Avenue at 32nd Street, take LIRR (www.lirr.org) to Belmont Park. **Races** *Thoroughbred* May-July, Sept, Oct Wed-Sun. **Admission** *Clubhouse* $5. *Grandstand* $2. **No credit cards**.
This big beauty of an oval is home to the third and longest leg of US horse racing's Triple Crown, the infamous mile-and-a-half Belmont Stakes, which will be held in June in 2008.

Meadowlands Racetrack

For listing, see p333 Meadowlands Sports Complex. *1-201 843 2446/www.thebigm.com.* **Races** *Thoroughbred* Oct, Nov. *Harness* Nov-Aug. Check website for schedule. **Admission** *Clubhouse* $3. *Grandstand* $1. **No credit cards**.

Meadowlands Racetrack offers an established programme of both harness (trotting) and thoroughbred racing. Top harness racers compete for more than $1 million in the prestigious Hambletonian, which is held on the first Saturday of August.

Soccer

The Brits call it football; many Americans call it boring. Still, in a city that's home to such a large immigrant population, footy commands a huge number of fans, even if it often plays second fiddle to more obviously American sports when it comes to media coverage. You'll find pick-up games in many city parks, and the pro RedBulls play across the river at Giants Stadium, which also occasionally hosts top European teams (such as Manchester United) for exhibition games in front of crowds of tens of thousands of crazed fans. Check www.meadowlands.com for the schedule.

RedBulls

Giants Stadium (for listing, see p333 Meadowlands Sports Complex). *1-201 583 7000/www.metrostars.com.* **Tickets** $18-$38.

Tennis

US Open

USTA National Tennis Center, Flushing Meadows-Corona Park, Queens (1-866 673 6849/www.usopen.org). Subway 7 to Willets Point-Shea Stadium. **Tickets** $22-$120. **Credit** AmEx, MC, V.

Tickets go on sale late in the spring for this late-summer grand-slam thriller, which the USTA says is the highest-attended annual sporting event in the world. Check the website for match schedules.

Active sports

A visit to New York means a lot of watching: watching plays, watching concerts, watching that weird cowboy guy who plays guitar in his underwear in Times Square. But if you get a hankering to do something yourself, then the city won't let you down.

All-in-one sports centre

Chelsea Piers

Piers 59-62, W 17th through to 23rd Streets, at Eleventh Avenue (1-212 336 6666/www.chelseapiers.com). Subway C, E to 23rd Street. **Open** times vary; phone or visit website. **Map** p403 C27.

This massive sports complex, which occupies a six-block stretch of riverfront real estate, offers just about every popular recreational activity in a bright, clean, well-maintained facility. Would-be Tigers can practise their swings at the Golf Club (Pier 59, 1-212 336 6400); bowlers can set up their pins at the AMF Lanes (between Piers 59 and 60, 1-212 835 2695). Ice skaters spin and glide at the Sky Rink (Pier 61, 1-212 336 6100). Rather skate on wheels? Hit the Roller Rink and Skate Park (Pier 62, 1-212 336 6200). The Field House (Pier 62, 1-212 336 6500) has a toddler adventure centre, a rock-climbing wall, a gymnastics training centre, batting cages, basketball courts, indoor playing fields and more. At the Sports Center gym (Pier 60, 1-212 336 6000), you'll find classes in everything from triathlon training to hip hop dance. Hours and fees vary; call or consult the website for more information.

Bowling

Bowlmor Lanes

110 University Place, between 12th & 13th Streets (1-212 255 8188/www.bowlmor.com). Subway L, N, Q, R, W, 4, 5, 6 to 14th Street-Union Square. **Open** 11am-3am Mon; 11am-2am Tue-Thur; 11am-4am Fri, Sat; 11am-1am Sun. **Fees** $8.95-$9.45 per person per game; $5.50 shoe rental. Under-21s not admitted after 5pm Tue-Sun. **Credit** AmEx, MC, V. **Map** p403 E28.

Renovation turned a seedy but historic Greenwich Village alley (Richard Nixon bowled here) into a hip downtown nightclub. Monday evening's Night Strike features glow-in-the-dark pins and a techno-spinning DJ in addition to unlimited bowling from 10pm to 3am ($22 per scenester; includes shoes).

Harlem Lanes

3rd Floor, 2116 Adam Clayton Powell Jr Boulevard (Seventh Avenue), at 126th Street (1-212 678 2695/www.harlemlanes.com). Subway 2, 3, A, B, C, D to 125th Street. **Open** 11am-11pm Mon-Thur; 11am-2am Fri, Sat; 11am-9pm Sun. **Cost** from $5.50 per game. **Credit** AmEx, MC, V. **Map** p407 D13.

Harlem Lanes offers 24 lanes in stylish surroundings and at reasonable prices.

Cycling

Hundreds of miles of paths make it easy for the recreational biker to get pretty much anywhere in New York. Construction continues on the paths that run alongside the East and Hudson Rivers, and it will soon be possible for riders to completely circumnavigate the island of Manhattan. Visitors can either take a DIY trip using rental bikes and path maps or go on organised rides. A word of caution: cycling in the city is a serious business. Riders must stay alert and abide by traffic laws, especially because drivers and pedestrians often don't. If you keep your ears and eyes open – and wear a helmet – you'll enjoy an adrenaline-pumping ride. Or skip the traffic and just take a spin through one of the city's many parks, including Central and Prospect Parks.

Bike hire

Gotham Bike Shop *112 West Broadway, between Duane & Reade Streets (1-212 732 2453/www.gothambikes.com). Subway A, C, 1, 2, 3 to Chambers Street.* **Open** 10am-6.30pm Mon-Wed, Fri, Sat; 10am-7.30pm Thur; 10.30am-5pm Sun. **Fees** $10/hr; $30/24hrs (includes helmet). **Credit** AmEx, MC, V (credit card and ID required for rental). **Map** p402 E31.
Rent a sturdy set of wheels from this shop and ride the short distance to the Hudson River esplanade.

Loeb Boathouse *Central Park, entrance on Fifth Avenue, at 72nd Street (1-212 517 2233/www.centralparknyc.org). Subway 6 to 68th Street-Hunter College.* **Open** 10am-6pm daily, weather permitting. **Fees** $6-$21/hr (includes helmet). **Credit** AmEx, MC, V (credit card & ID required for rental). **Map** p405 E20.
If you want to cruise through Central Park, this is your place, with more than 100 bikes available.

Metro Bicycles *1311 Lexington Avenue, at 88th Street (1-212 427 4450/www.metrobicycles.com). Subway 4, 5, 6 to 86th Street.* **Open** 9.30am-6.30pm daily. **Fees** $7/hr; $35/day. **Credit** AmEx, Disc, MC, V. **Map** p406 E18.
Trek and Fisher bikes are here available to hire by the day; check Metro's website or call for additional locations across Manhattan.

Bike-path maps

Department of City Planning Bookstore
22 Reade Street, between Broadway & Elk Street, Manhattan (1-212 720 3667). Subway J, M, Z to Chambers Street; R, W to City Hall; 4, 5, 6 to Brooklyn Bridge-City Hall. **Open** 10am-4pm Mon-Fri. **Map** p402 E31.
The city's Bicycle Master Plan includes nearly 1,000 miles of cycling lanes. Free annual updates are available at this shop or at www.nyc.gov.

Transportation Alternatives *Suite 127, 10th Floor, W 26th Street, between Sixth & Seventh Avenues (1-212 629 8080/www.transalt.org). Subway B, D, F, N, Q, R, V, W to 34th Street-Herald Square; 1, 2, 3 to 34th Street-Penn Station.* **Open** 9.30am-6pm Mon-Fri. **Map** p404 D26.
Transportation Alternatives (TA) is a not-for-profit citizens' group that lobbies for more bike-friendly streets. You can pop into the office to get free maps, or download them from the website.

Organised bike rides

Bike the Big Apple
1-201 837 1133/www.bikethebigapple.com.
Trips include a Lower East Side and Brooklyn ride that makes stops at chocolate and beer factories.

Fast & Fabulous
1-212 567 7160/www.fastnfab.org.
This 'queer and queer-friendly' riding group leads tours throughout the year, usually meeting in Central Park and heading out of the city.

Five Borough Bicycle Club
1-212 932 2300 ext 115/www.5bbc.org.
This local club always offers a full slate of leisurely rides around the city, as well as jaunts that head further afield. Best of all, most trips are free.

Time's Up!
1-212 802 8222/www.times-up.org.
An alternative-transportation advocacy group, Time's Up! sponsors rides year-round, including Critical Mass, in which hundreds of cyclists and skaters meet at Union Square Park (7pm on the last Friday of every month) and go tearing through the city, often ending up in Greenwich Village and lending the streets a vibrant party atmosphere.

Gyms

Many gyms offer single-day membership. If you can schedule a workout during off-peak hours (instead of just before or after the workday), you likely won't have to compete for time on the machines. Call for class details.

Crunch

623 Broadway, between Bleecker & Houston Streets (1-212 420 0507/1-888 227 8624/www.crunch.com). Subway B, D, F, V to Broadway-Lafayette Street; 6 to Bleecker Street. **Open** 6am-10pm Mon-Fri; 9am-7pm Sat, Sun. **Fees** $24 day pass. **Credit** AmEx, DC, Disc, MC, V. **Map** p403 E29.
For a downtown feel without the downtown attitude, Crunch wins hands down. Most of the ten New York locations feature NetPulse cardio equipment, which lets you surf the web or watch a personal TV while you exercise. Visit Crunch's website for a comprehensive list of locations across the city.

New York Sports Club

151 E 86th Street, between Lexington & Third Avenues (1-800 301 1231/www.nysc.com). Subway 4, 5, 6 to 86th Street. **Open** 5.30am-11pm Mon-Thur; 5.30am-10pm Fri; 8am-9pm Sat, Sun. **Fees** $25 day pass. **Credit** AmEx, MC, V. **Map** p406 F18.
A day membership at New York Sports Club includes aerobics classes and access to the weights room, cardio machines, steam room and sauna. The 62nd and 86th Street branches feature squash courts. Visit the website for a full list of New York Sports Club locations across the city.

Horseback riding

Kensington Stables

51 Caton Place, at East 8th Street, Kensington, Brooklyn (1-718 972 4588/www.kensingtonstables.com). Subway F to Fort Hamilton Parkway. **Open** 10am-sunset daily. **Fees** *Guided trail ride* $25/hr. *Private lessons* $45/hr. Reservations suggested. **Credit** AmEx, Disc, MC, V. **Map** p410 U13.
The paddock is small, but miles of lovely riding trails wind through Prospect Park (*see p163*), particularly in the Ravine, which was designed to be seen from horseback.

Ice skating

The Pond at Bryant Park

Bryant Park, Sixth Avenue, between 40th & 42nd Streets (1-212 382 2953). Subway B, D, F, V to 42nd Street-Bryant Park; 7 to Fifth Avenue. **Open** 8am-10pm Mon-Thur, Sun; 8am-midnight Fri, Sat. **Fees** free. **Skate rental** $8.75. **Map** p404 D24.

Head over to Bryant Park for some skating on a 17,000 sq ft rink. It'll probably be packed, especially as Christmas starts approaching, but you can't beat the price – it's free if you bring your own skates (or you can rent them).

Rockefeller Center Ice Rink

1 Rockefeller Plaza, from 49th to 50th Streets, between Fifth & Sixth Avenues (1-212 332 7654/www.therinkatrockcenter.com). Subway B, D, F, V to 47-50th Streets-Rockefeller Center. **Open** Oct-Apr; phone or visit website for hours. **Fees** $14-$17; $7-$12 under-12s. **Skate rental** $8-$10. **Credit** AmEx, Disc, MC, V. **Map** p404 E23.

Easily among the city's most recognisable tourist attractions, Rockefeller Center's rink, under the giant statue of Prometheus, is spot-on for atmosphere – but pretty bad for elbow room. The rink opens with an energetic ice show in mid October but attracts the most visitors when the towering Christmas tree is lit and looming over the skating crowds.

Wollman Rink

Central Park, midpark at 62nd Street (1-212 439 6900/www.wollmanskatingrink.com). Subway N, R, W to Fifth Avenue-59th Street. **Open** *Late Oct-Mar* 10am-2.30pm Mon, Tue; 10am-9pm Wed, Thur, Sun; 10am-11pm Fri, Sat. **Fees** *Mon-Thur* $8.50; $4.25 children. *Fri-Sun* $11; $4.50 children. **Skate rental** $4.75. **No credit cards. Map** p405 E21.

Less crowded – especially after the holidays – than Rock Center, the rink offers a lovely setting beneath the trees of Central Park.

In-line skating

In-line skating is very popular in New York: the choking traffic makes it practical, and the landscape makes it pleasurable (a beautiful paved loop circumnavigates Central Park; bike paths run along the Hudson River). Join a group skate, or go it alone. The gear shop **Blades, Board & Skate** (120 W 72nd Street, between Columbus & Amsterdam Avenues, 1-212 787 3911) rents by the day ($20).

Empire Skate Club of New York

PO Box 20070, London Terrace Station, New York, NY 10011 (1-212 774 1774/www.empireskate.org).

This club organises in-line and roller skating events throughout the city, including island-hopping tours and night-time rides such as the Thursday Evening Roll: skaters meet from May to October at Columbus Circle (Broadway, at 59th Street, south-west corner of Central Park) at 6.45pm.

Kayaking

Kayaking is a great way to explore New York Harbor and the Hudson River. Given the tricky currents, the tidal shifts and the hairy river traffic, it's best to go on an organised excursion.

Downtown Boathouse

Pier 96, Clinton Cove Park, 56th Street & Westside Highway (1-646 613 0375/www.downtown boathouse.org). Subway A, C, E, 1 to Columbus Circle. **Open** *June-Aug* 5-7pm Mon-Fri; 10am-5pm Sat, Sun, holidays. **Classes** 6-8pm Wed. **Fee** free. **Map** p405 B22.

Weather permitting, this volunteer-run organisation offers free kayaking (no appointment necessary) in front of the boathouses, at two locations. It also offers free Wednesday evening classes and three-hour guided kayak trips on weekend mornings. All trips are offered on a first-come, first-served basis; you must be able to swim.

Other locations: Riverside Park promenade, 72nd Street.

Manhattan Kayak Company

Pier 63 Maritime, Twelfth Avenue, at 23rd Street (1-212 924 1788/www.manhattankayak.com). Subway C, E to 23rd Street. **Open** phone or visit website for schedule and prices. **Credit** AmEx, Disc, MC, V. **Map** p404 B26.

Run by veteran kayaker Eric Stiller, who once paddled halfway around Australia, Manhattan Kayak offers beginner to advanced classes and tours. Adventures include the Sushi Tour ($100 per person), in which the group paddles to Edgewater, New Jersey, to dine at a sushi restaurant.

Running

The path ringing the Central Park reservoir is probably the most popular jogging trail in the entire city, but dozens of parks and paths are waiting to be explored. Just tie on a cushy pair of sneakers and go where your feet lead you.

New York Road Runners

9 E 89th Street, between Fifth & Madison Avenues (1-212 860 4455/www.nyrrc.org). Subway 4, 5, 6 to 86th Street. **Open** 10am-8pm Mon-Fri; 10am-5pm Sat; 10am-3pm Sun. **Fees** vary. **Credit** AmEx, MC, V. **Map** p406 E18.

Hardly a weekend passes without some sort of run or race sponsored by the NYRR, which is responsible for the New York City Marathon. Most races take place in Central Park and are open to the public. The club also offers classes and clinics.

NYC Hash House Harriers

1-212 427 4692/www.hashnyc.com. **Fees** $15 (covers food and beer after the run).

This energetic, slightly wacky group has been running in the Big Apple for more than 20 years and always welcomes newcomers. A 'hash' is part training run, part scavenger hunt, part keg party. The

High times at the **Trapeze School New York**.

participants follow a three- to five-mile trail that a member (called 'the hare') marks with chalk or other visual clues. After the exercise, the group retires to a local watering hole for drinks and grub.

Swimming

The Harlem, Vanderbilt and West Side YMCAs (www.ymcanyc.org) have decent-sized pools (plus day passes), as do some private gyms. Many hotel pools provide day-pass access as well. The city of New York maintains several Olympic-sized (and plenty of smaller) facilities. Its outdoor pools are free of charge and open from late June to Labor Day: Hamilton Fish (Pitt Street, between Houston & Stanton Streets, 1-212 387 7687); Asser Levy Pool (23rd Street, between First Avenue & FDR Drive, 1-212 447 2020); Tony Dapolito Recreation Center (Clarkson Street, at Seventh Avenue South, 1-212 242 5228). Recreation Center 54 (348 54th Street, between First & Second Avenues, 1-212 754 5411) has an indoor pool. For information, call **New York Parks & Recreation** (1-212 639 9675, www.nycgovparks.org).

Tennis

From April through to November, the city authorities maintain excellent municipal courts throughout the five boroughs. Single-play (one-hour) tickets cost $8. For a list of city courts, visit www.nycgovparks.org.

Trapeze

Trapeze School New York

Hudson River Park, between Canal & Vestry Streets (1-917 797 1872/www.trapezeschool.com). Subway 1 to Canal Street. **Open** May-Nov, weather permitting. **Fees** $47-$75 2hr class, plus $22 one-time application fee. **Credit** AmEx, Disc, MC, V. **Map** p403 D30.

Sarah Jessica Parker did it on an episode of *Sex and the City* several years ago, so it must be cool. Set in a large, cage-like construction on the bank of the Hudson River (a tent for year-round operation is in the works at Pier 40), the school teaches those aged six and upwards to fly through the air with the greatest of ease. You can also watch on while a loved one has a fling, if that floats your boat.

Yoga

Laughing Lotus Yoga Center

3rd Floor, 59 W 19th Street, between Fifth & Sixth Avenues (1-212 414 2903/www.laughinglotus.com). Subway F, N, R, V, W to 23rd Street. **Open** phone or check website for schedule. **Fees** $11-$16 single class. **Credit** AmEx, Disc, MC, V. **Map** p403 E27.

These roomy Chelsea digs accommodate a kind of yogic community centre that has weekly holistic workshops, classes, and an in-house tarot reader and astrologist. Among the regular offerings: midnight yoga, reflexology and absolute-beginner classes.

Levitate Yoga

3rd Floor, 780 Eighth Avenue, between 47th & 48th Streets (1-212 974 2288/www.levitateyoga.com). Subway C, E to 50th Street. **Open** phone or visit website for schedule. **Fees** $18 single class; $12 students. **Credit** AmEx, MC, V. **Map** p404 D23.

This highly popular, modern-looking studio caters to beginners, tourists from nearby hotels, and casts and crews performing at nearby theatres. In the warmer months, special al fresco classes are held on the 2,000sq ft rooftop terrace.

Om Yoga Center

6th Floor, 826 Broadway (above Strand Bookstore), between 12th & 13th Streets (1-212 254 9642/www.omyoga.com). Subway L, N, Q, R, W, 4, 5, 6 to 14th Street-Union Square. **Open** phone or visit website for schedule. **Fees** $18 single class. **Credit** AmEx, Disc, MC, V. **Map** p403 E28.

Cyndi Lee's famed yoga spot offers all-level, flowing-style vinyasa yoga classes with a focus on alignment, popular with celebrities and mortals alike.

Theatre & Dance

New York is kicking – and singing and acting and dancing…

Theatre

Something odd has happened on Broadway. The usual line is that the Great White Way, as it is nicknamed, is a crass commercial wasteland pandering only to tourists, and all the true art is to be found Off and Off-Off. However, recent seasons seem to have turned that conventional wisdom topsy turvy. Most of 2006 and 2007's best plays and musicals – *The Coast of Utopia*, *The Drowsy Chaperone* and *Spring Awakening*, to name three – either opened on Broadway or subsequently moved there. And non-musical plays, that most truly endangered species in the Broadway ecology, persist in popping up as well, through a combination of transfers from the not-for-profit sector and English imports that carry a classy imprimatur.

It continues to be a fertile period for the American musical comedy. Fast, irreverent and, dare we say, hip tuners such as *Avenue Q* and *The 25th Annual Putnam County Spelling Bee* are not just for Broadway fanatics, but are now enjoying broader appeal. And those who want a little more heart with their show-stoppers have made an astounding success of *Wicked*, the girl-power musical 'prequel' to *The Wizard of Oz*.

For all the advance sales and lucre, however, the question remains: is Broadway really the place to see the best theatre in New York? The answer is rather complicated. To be sure, producers and creative teams shy away from material perceived as either too controversial or 'New Yorky'. But there is an impressive amount of diversity right now. There are perennial family-friendly draws such as *The Lion King* and *Mary Poppins*; delirious musical comedies like *Young Frankenstein* and *Hairspray*; and top-drawer dramas and revivals from Manhattan Theatre Club and the Roundabout Theatre Company.

That said, the savvy and intrepid theatre-goer will know to look past the glittering lights of Broadway and seek out the best new theatrical offerings that take place further downtown. From Midtown's landmark palaces to Downtown's funky Off Broadway and Off-Off Broadway spaces, there is a place – and a show – to suit every taste.

BUYING TICKETS

If you have a major credit card, then buying Broadway tickets is simply a matter of picking up the phone. Nearly all Broadway and Off Broadway shows are served by one of the city's 24-hour ticketing agencies, which are listed in the shows' print advertisements or in the capsule reviews that run each week in *Time Out New York*. The venues' information lines can also refer you to ticket agents, sometimes by merely transferring your call (for additional ticketing info, *see p383*). Theatre box offices usually charge a small fee for phone orders.

Some of the cheapest tickets on Broadway are 'rush' tickets (tickets purchased the day of a show at the theatre's box office), which cost an average of $25 – but not all theatres offer these, and some reserve them for students. A few distribute rush tickets through a lottery, usually held two hours before the performance. If a show is sold out, it's worth waiting for standby tickets just before curtain time. Tickets are slightly cheaper for matinées (typically on Wednesdays, Saturdays and Sundays) and previews, and for students or groups of 20 or more. For discount seats, your best bet is **TKTS** (*see p383*), where you can get tickets on the day of the performance for as much as 75 per cent off the face value. Arrive early as lines can be long. TKTS also sells matinée tickets the day before a show. Beware of scam artists trying to sell tickets to those waiting in line: they're often fake. Consider purchasing a set of vouchers from the Theatre Development Fund if you're interested in seeing more than one Off-Off Broadway show or dance event.

Theatre Development Fund

1501 Broadway, between 43rd & 44th Streets (1-212 221 0885/www.tdf.org). Subway N, Q, R, W to 42nd Street; S, 1, 2, 3, 7 to 42nd Street-Times Square. **Open** 10am-6pm Mon-Fri. **No credit cards. Map** p404 D24.

For $36, TDF offers a book of four vouchers that can be purchased only at its office by visitors who bring their passport or out-of-state driver's licence, or by students and residents on the TDF mailing list. Each voucher is good for one admission to an Off-Off Broadway theatre, dance or music event at venues such as the Atlantic Theater Company, the Joyce, the Kitchen, Performance Space 122 and many more. TDF's NYC/Onstage service (1-212 768 1818) provides information by phone on all events in town.

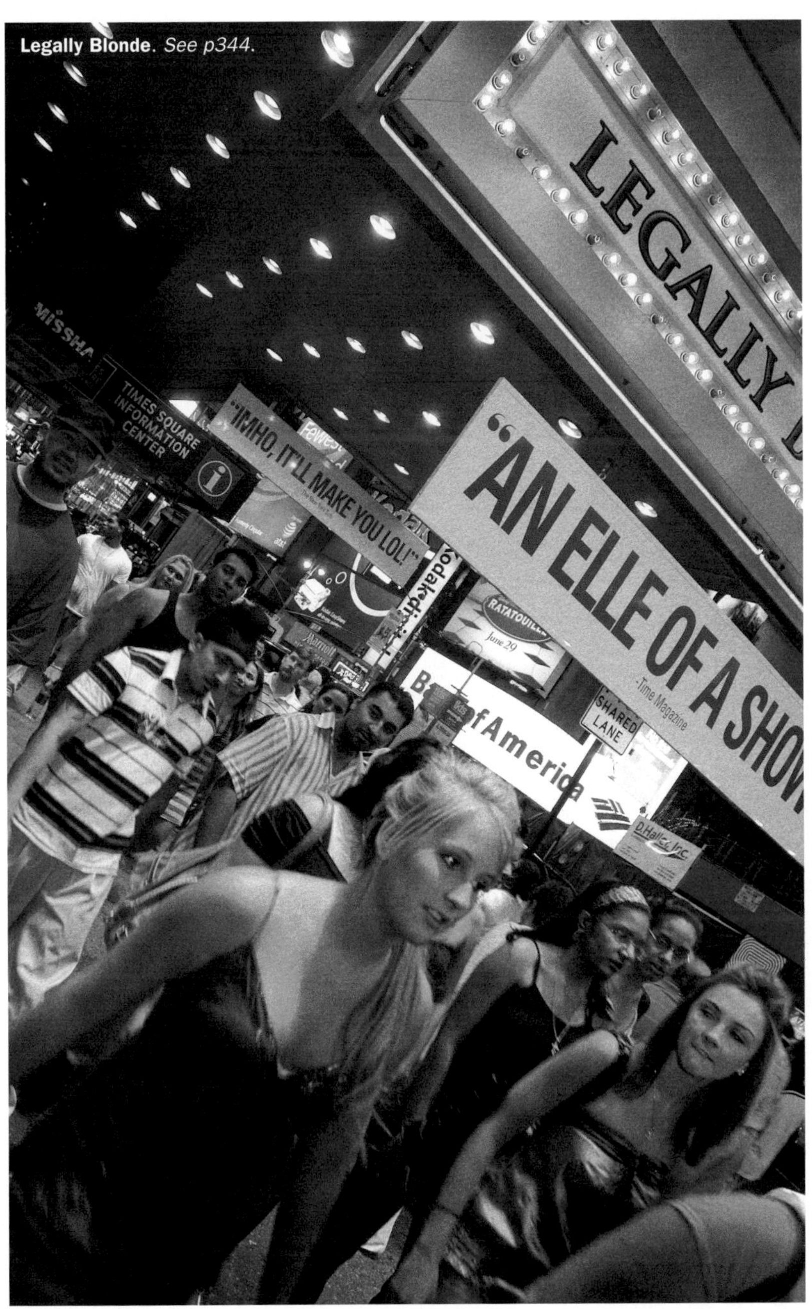

Legally Blonde. *See p344.*

THE NEW
MEL BROOKS
MUSICAL
YOUNG FRANKENSTEIN
Book by MEL BROOKS & THOMAS MEEHAN Music & Lyrics by MEL BROOKS
Starring
ROGER BART MEGAN MULLALLY
SUTTON FOSTER SHULER HENSLEY ANDREA MARTIN
FRED APPLEGATE CHRISTOPHER FITZGERALD
Direction & Choreography by SUSAN STROMAN
Tickets at YoungFrankensteinTheMusical.com,
Broadway.Yahoo.com or Ticketmaster.com 212-307-4100
Hilton Theatre 42nd Street at 7th Avenue
PROUDLY SPONSORED BY
Fidelity INVESTMENTS

Broadway

Subways *C, E, 1 to 50th Street; N, Q, R, W to 42nd Street; S, 2, 3, 7 to 42nd Street-Times Square.*

Technically speaking, 'Broadway' is the Theater District that surrounds Times Square on either side of Broadway (the actual avenue), mainly between 41st and 53rd Streets. This is where you'll find the grand theatres that were built largely between 1900 and 1930. Officially, 38 of them are designated as being part of Broadway – and full-price tickets at one of these venues can set you back more than $100. The big shows are hard to ignore; high-profile revivals and new blockbusters announce themselves from giant billboards and drench the airwaves with radio advertisements.

Still, there's more to Broadway than splashy musicals and flashy pop spectacles. In recent years, provocative dramas like The Coast of Utopia and jukebox musicals such as Jersey Boys and Mamma Mia! have had remarkable success, as have revivals of American classic plays and musicals.

The **Roundabout Theatre Company** (American Airlines Theatre, 227 W 42nd Street, between Seventh & Eighth Avenues, 1-212 719 1300; Studio 54, 254 W 54th Street, between Broadway & Eighth Avenue) usually pairs beloved chestnuts with celebrity casts; it was the force behind the recent revivals of *Sunday in the Park with George* by Stephen Sondheim and James Lapine, and George Bernard Shaw's *Pygmalion.* You can either subscribe to the Roundabout's full season or buy single tickets.

Long-running shows

Straight (non-musical) plays can provide some of Broadway's most stirring experiences, but they're less likely than musicals to enjoy long runs. If you aren't in search of song, check *Time Out New York* for current listings and reviews of new or revived dramatic plays.

Avenue Q

Golden Theater, 252 W 45th Street, between Broadway & Eighth Avenue (1-212 239 6200/ www.avenueq.com). Subway A, C, E to 42nd Street-Port Authority. **Box office** 10am-8pm Mon-Sat; noon-7pm Sun. **Tickets** $46.25-$101.25. **Shows** 8pm Tue-Fri; 2pm, 8pm Sat; 2pm, 7pm Sun. **Length** 2hrs 15mins; 1 intermission. **Credit** AmEx, DC, Disc, MC, V. **Map** p404 D24.

Mixing puppets and live actors with irreverent jokes and snappy songs, this clever, good-hearted musical comedy, which opened off-broadway, was a surprise hit. It garnered several 2004 Tonys, including Best Musical, and has travelled across the country and beyond, to London's West End.

Chicago

Ambassador Theatre, 219 W 49th Street, between Broadway & Eighth Avenue (1-212 239 6200). Subway N, R, W to 49th Street; 1 to 50th Street. **Tickets** $58-$111. **Box office** 10am-8pm Mon-Sat; noon-6pm Sun. **Shows** 7pm Tue; 2pm, 8pm Wed, Thur, Fri; 8pm Sat; 6.30pm Sun. **Length** 2hrs 30mins; 1 intermission. **Credit** AmEx, MC, V. **Map** p404 D23.

This snappy 1975 John Kander-Fred Ebb-Bob Fosse show tells the dark saga of chorus girl Roxie Hart, who murders her lover, avoids prison and, with the help of a huckster lawyer, becomes a musical star. Director Walter Bobbie and choreographer Ann Reinking's minimalist strip-club aesthetic panders to some abstract lust, but the story is wicked fun and the brassy score infectious.

The Color Purple

Broadway Theatre, 1681 Broadway, at 53rd Street (1-212 239 6200). Subway N, R, W to 49th Street; 1 to 50th Street. **Tickets** $26.25-$101.25. **Box office** 10am-8pm Mon-Sat; noon-6pm Sun. **Shows** 2pm, 8pm Wed, Sat; 8pm Thur, Fri; 2pm, 7.30pm Sun. **Length** 2hrs 40mins; 1 intermission. **Credit** AmEx, MC, V. **Map** p404 D23.

Marsha Norman's musical adaptation of Alice Walker's hard-hitting 1982 bestseller retains as much of the novel as could reasonably be expected; the nearly sung-through score, crafted by a trio of seasoned pop songwriters, bobs along in a pleasant, mildly funky R&B groove.

Hairspray

Neil Simon Theatre, 250 W 52nd Street, between Broadway & Eighth Avenue (1-212 307 4100/ www.hairsprayonbroadway.com). Subway C, E, 1 to 50th Street. **Box office** 10am-8pm Mon-Sat; noon-6pm Sun. **Tickets** $75-$110. **Shows** 7pm Tue; 2pm, 8pm Wed, Sat; 8pm Thur, Fri; 3pm Sun. **Length** 2hrs 35mins; 1 intermission. **Credit** AmEx, DC, Disc, MC, V. **Map** p404 D23.

John Waters's classic kitsch film about a big girl with big hair and an ambition to dance has become an eye-popping song-and-dance stage extravaganza (with an original score by Marc Shaiman) that is bigger, brighter, more satirical and much funnier than the original version. If you loved the recent movie remake, then you have to see the musical that inspired it. *Photo p354.*

Jersey Boys

August Wilson Theatre, 245 W 52nd Street, between Broadway & Eighth Avenues (1-212 239 6200). Subway C, E, 1 to 50th Street. **Tickets** $96.25-$121.50. **Box office** 10am-8pm Mon-Sat; noon-6pm Sun. **Shows** 7pm Tue; 2pm, 8pm Wed, Thur, Sat; 8pm Fri; 3pm Sun. **Length** 2hrs 15mins; 1 intermission. **Credit** AmEx, Disc, MC, V. **Map** p404 D23.

The Broadway musical finally does right by the jukebox with this nostalgic behind-the-music tale, presenting the Four Seasons' infectiously energetic 1960s tunes (including 'Walk Like a Man' and 'Big

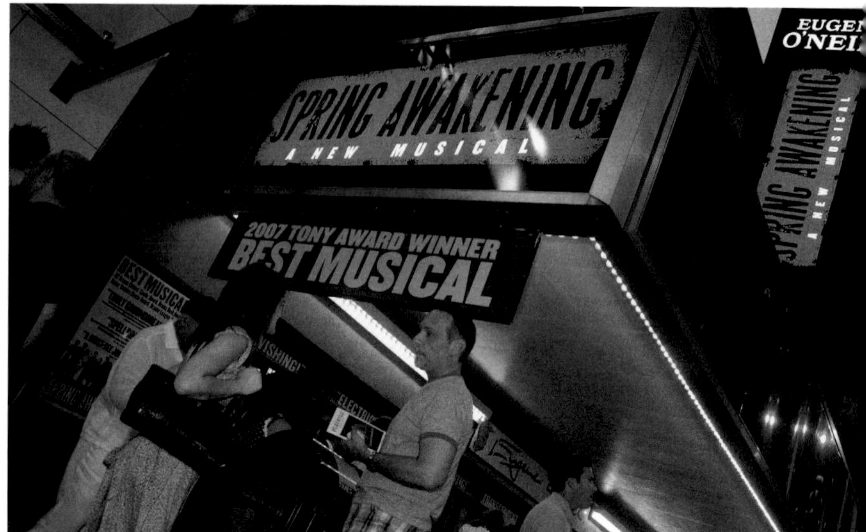

Girls Don't Cry') as they were intended to be performed. A dynamic cast under the sleek direction of Des McAnuff (*700 Sundays*) ensures that Marshall Brickman and Rick Elice's script feels canny instead of canned.

Legally Blonde

Palace Theatre, 1564 Broadway, at 47th Street (1-212 307 4100/www.legallyblondethemusical.com). Subway N, R, W to 49th Street; 1 to 50th Street. **Tickets** $65-$110. **Box office** 10am-8pm Mon-Sat; noon-6pm Sun. **Shows** 2pm, 8pm Wed, Sat; Thur, Fri 8pm; 2pm, 7pm Sun. **Length** 2hrs 30mins; 1 intermission. **Credit** AmEx, DC, Disc, MC, V. **Map** p404 D23.

If only director-choreographer Jerry Mitchell and his creative partners had found as many gradations of romantic comedy as pink for this movie-to-musical spectacle. Laura Bell Bundy, Christian Borle and Orfeh help to distract from the weak book, the synthetic tweener-pop score and Mitchell's busy, incessant dances. Still, teenage girls line up for blocks to see the antics of this upstart goldilocks. *Photo p341.*

Spring Awakening

Eugene O'Neill Theatre, 230 W 49th Street, between Broadway & Eighth Avenue (1-212 239 6200/ www.springawakening.com). Subway N, Q, R, W to 42nd Street; S, 1, 2, 3, 7 to 42nd Street-Times Square. **Box office** 10am-8pm Mon-Sat; noon-6pm Sun. **Tickets** $31.25-$111.25. **Shows** 8pm Mon; 7pm Tue; 2pm, 8pm Wed, Sat; 8pm Thur, Fri. **Length** 2hrs 20mins; 1 intermission. **Credit** AmEx, DC, Disc, MC, V. **Map** p404 D23.

Singer-songwriter Duncan Sheik and playwright Steven Sater have taken Frank Wedekind's controversial 1891 play about confused German teens stumbling toward a tragic adolescence, and created the most exciting rock musical in a generation. High in concept – actors in 19th-century period costumes whip microphones out of their jackets and launch into foot-stomping rock numbers – this show is a major leap forward for the Broadway musical.

Wicked

Gershwin Theatre, 222 W 51st Street, between Broadway & Eighth Avenue (1-212 307 4100). Subway C, E, 1 to 50th Street. **Box office** 10am-8pm Mon-Sat; noon-6pm Sun. **Tickets** $51-$121. **Shows** 7pm Tue; 2pm, 8pm Wed, Sat; 8pm Thur, Fri; 3pm Sun. **Length** 2hrs 45mins; 1 intermission. **Credit** AmEx, DC, Disc, MC, V. **Map** p404 D23.

Based on novelist Gregory Maguire's 1995 riff on *The Wizard of Oz* mythology, *Wicked* provides a witty prequel to both the classic children's book and legendary movie. At the time of writing, Joe Mantello's sumptuous production starred Kate Reinders and Edin Espinosa as young versions of Glinda the Good Witch and the Wicked Witch of the West respectively.

Off Broadway

As the cost of mounting a show on Broadway continues to soar, many serious playwrights are opening their productions in the more adventurous (and less financially demanding) Off Broadway houses. Off Broadway theatres have between 200 and 500 seats, and tickets usually run from $20 to $70. Here, we've listed some of our favourite long-running shows, followed by a few of the best theatres and repertory companies.

Adolescent angst rocks in **Spring Awakening**.

Long-running shows

Altar Boyz

New World Stages, 340 W 50th Street, between Eighth & Ninth Avenues (1-212 239 6200). Subway C, E, 1 to 50th Street. **Box office** 1-6pm Mon, Sun; 1-7.30pm Tue-Sat. **Tickets** $25-$75. **Shows** 8pm Mon, Tue, Thur, Fri; 2pm, 8pm Sat; 3pm, 7pm Sun. **Length** 1hr 30mins; no intermission. **Credit** AmEx, MC, V. **Map** p404 D23.

The Altar Boyz sing about Jesus in the unlikely idiom of boy-band pop, complete with five-part harmony, synchronised steps and prefab streetwise posturing. Mad props where mad props are due: the show's young stars really work their crosses off.

Blue Man Group

Astor Place Theater, 434 Lafayette Street, between Astor Place & E 4th Street (1-212 254 4370/ www.blueman.com). Subway N, R, W to 8th Street-NYU; 6 to Astor Place. **Box office** noon-7.45pm daily. **Tickets** $69-$79. **Shows** 8pm Tue-Thur; 7pm, 10pm Fri; 4pm, 7pm, 10pm Sat; 2pm, 5pm, 8pm Sun. **Length** 2hrs; no intermission. **Credit** AmEx, DC, Disc, MC, V. **Map** p403 F28.

Three men with extraterrestrial imaginations (and head-to-toe blue body paint) carry this long-time multimedia, musical favourite – a show that is as smart as it is ridiculous.

Stomp

Orpheum Theater, 126 Second Avenue, between St Marks Place & E 7th Street (1-212 477 2477). Subway N, R, W to 8th Street-NYU; 6 to Astor Place. **Box office** 1-7pm Tue-Fri. **Tickets** $37-$65. **Shows** 8pm Tue-Fri; 7pm, 10.30pm Sat; 3pm, 7pm Sun. **Length** 1hr 30mins; no intermission. **Credit** AmEx, MC, V. **Map** p403 F28.

This show is billed as a 'percussion sensation' because there's no other way to describe it. Using garbage-can lids, buckets, brooms, sticks and just about anything they can get their hands on, these aerobicised dancer-musicians make a lovely racket.

Repertory companies & venues

Atlantic Theater Company

336 W 20th Street, between Eighth & Ninth Avenues (Telecharge 1-212 239 6200/www.atlantictheater.org). Subway C, E to 23rd Street. **Box office** 6-8pm Tue-Fri; noon-2pm, 6-8pm Sat; 1-3pm Sun. **Credit** AmEx, Disc, MC, V. **Map** p403 D27.

Created in 1985 as an offshoot of acting workshops taught by playwright David Mamet and film star William H Macy, this dynamic theatre has presented nearly 100 plays, including Martin McDonagh's *The Lieutenant of Inishmore* and Duncan Sheik and Steven Sater's *Spring Awakening*. Both productions transferred to Broadway.

Brooklyn Academy of Music

For listing, see p237.

Brooklyn's grand old opera house (along with the Harvey Theater, two blocks away on Fulton Street) stages the multidisciplinary Next Wave Festival (*see p264*); in 2007, it hosted British thespian legend Ian McKellen in *King Lear* and *The Seagull*, as well as Anne Bogart and Charles Mee's experimental *Hotel Cassiopeia*.

Arts & Entertainment

Classic Stage Company

136 E 13th Street, between Third & Fourth Avenues (Ticket Central 1-212 677 4210/www.classicstage.org). Subway L, N, Q, R, W, 4, 5, 6 to 14th Street-Union Square. **Box office** noon-5pm Mon-Fri. **Credit** AmEx, MC, V. **Map** p403 F27.

From Greek tragedies to medieval mystery plays, the Classic Stage Company (under the tutelage of artistic director Brian Kulick) makes the old new again with open rehearsals, staged readings and full-blown productions.

59E59

59 E 59th Street, between Madison & Park Avenues (1-212 279 4200/www.59e59.org). Subway N, R, W to Lexington Avenue-59th Street; 4, 5, 6 to 59th Street. **Box office** noon-7pm daily. **Credit** AmEx, MC, V. **Map** p405 E22.

This chic new state-of-the-art East Side venue, which comprises an Off Broadway space and two smaller theatres, made a splash in its first year with the Brits Off Broadway festival. The Off Broadway company Primary Stages now makes its home here. The three theatres are used for not-for-profit productions.

Irish Repertory Theatre

132 W 22nd Street, between Sixth & Seventh Avenues (1-212 727 2737/www.irishrepertorytheatre.com). Subway F, V, 1 to 23rd Street. **Box office** 10am-6pm Mon-Fri; 11am-6pm Sat, Sun. **Credit** AmEx, MC, V. **Map** p404 D26.

This Chelsea company puts on compelling shows by Irish playwrights. Past productions include fine revivals of George Bernard Shaw classics.

Lincoln Center Theater

For listing, see p328.

The always majestic Lincoln Center Theater complex includes two amphitheatre-style drama venues: the 1,138-seat Vivian Beaumont Theater (the Broadway house) and the 338-seat Mitzi E Newhouse Theater (Off Broadway). Expect polished, often star-studded productions of dense plays and new musicals (for example, Adam Guettel's *The Light in the Piazza*). The organisation also commanded the considerable resources necessary to mount Tom Stoppard's epic, three-play study of Russian history, *The Coast of Utopia*, which ran during the 2006/7 season to huge critical acclaim. LCT's founding policy ensures that ticket prices are kept reasonable, averaging $50. In spring 2008, look out for a new staging of the famous Rodgers and Hammerstein musical *South Pacific* (28 Feb-15 June).

Manhattan Theatre Club

City Center, 131 W 55th Street, between Sixth & Seventh Avenues (1-212 581 1212/Telecharge 1-212 239 6200/www.mtc-nyc.org). Subway B, D, E to Seventh Avenue. **Box office** 11am-5pm Mon, Sun; noon-7pm Tue-Sat. **Credit** AmEx, DC, Disc, MC, V. **Map** p405 D22.

Manhattan Theatre Club has a history of sending plays to Broadway, as seen with successes like John Patrick Shanley's *Doubt*. The club's two theatres are located in the basement of City Center. The 275-seat Stage I Theater features four plays a year; the Stage II Theater offers works in progress, workshops and staged readings, as well as full-length productions. MTC also has a Broadway home in the renovated Biltmore Theatre (261 W 47th Street, between Broadway & Eighth Avenue; tickets from Telecharge on 1-212 239 6200).

New Victory Theater

209 W 42nd Street, between Seventh & Eighth Avenues (1-646 223 3020/Telecharge 1-212 239 6200/www.newvictory.org). Subway N, Q, R, W to 42nd Street; S, 1, 2, 3, 7 to 42nd Street-Times Square. **Box office** 11am-5pm Mon, Sun; noon-7pm Tue-Sat. **Credit** AmEx, MC, V. **Map** p404 D24.

The New Victory is a perfect symbol for the transformation of Times Square. Built in 1900 by Oscar Hammerstein II, Manhattan's oldest theatre became a strip club and adult cinema in the 1970s and '80s. Renovated by the city in 1995, the building now features a full season of family-friendly plays.

New World Stages

340 W 50th Street, between Eighth & Ninth Avenues (1-646 871 1730/www.newworldstages.com). Subway C, E, 1 to 50th Street. **Box office** 1-6pm Mon, Sun; 1-7.30pm Tue-Sat. **Credit** AmEx, MC, V. **Map** p404 C23.

Formerly a movie multiplex, this relatively new centre boasts a shiny, space-age interior and five gorgeous, fully renovated theatres presenting everything from campy revues such as *Naked Boys Singing* to world premières of new musicals, such as *Altar Boyz* (*see p345*).

New York Theatre Workshop

79 E 4th Street, between Bowery & Second Avenue (1-212 460 5475/www.nytw.org). Subway F, V to Lower East Side-Second Avenue; 6 to Astor Place. **Box office** 1-6pm Tue-Sun. **Credit** AmEx, MC, V. **Map** p403 F29.

Founded in 1979, the New York Theatre Workshop works with emerging directors eager to take on challenging pieces. Besides plays by the likes of Caryl Churchill (*Far Away, A Number*) and Tony Kushner (*Homebody/Kabul*), this company also premièred *Rent*, Jonathan Larson's Pulitzer Prize-winning musical, which still packs 'em in on Broadway more than a decade later.

Playwrights Horizons

416 W 42nd Street, between Ninth & Tenth Avenues (Ticket Central 1-212 279 4200/www.playwrightshorizons.org). Subway A, C, E to 42nd Street-Port Authority. **Box office** noon-8pm daily. **Credit** AmEx, MC, V. **Map** p404 C24.

More than 300 important contemporary plays have premièred here, including dramas such as *Driving Miss Daisy* and *The Heidi Chronicles*. Recent seasons have included works by Adam Rapp (*Essential Self-Defense*) and an acclaimed musical version of *Grey Gardens*.

Eternally Yours
TM
The longest-running musical ever.
TELECHARGE.COM: (212) 239-6200/(800) 432-7250
日本語 : (212) 239-2959 • ESPAÑOL: (212) 239-6240 • SEATS AVAILABLE FROM $26.50
ShowTrans: Commentaire audio en français disponible, 日本語のオーディオコメンタリあります。
Comentários em audio disponíveis em português, Comentario de audio en español disponible.
MAJESTIC THEATRE 247 West 44th St. www.thephantomoftheopera.com

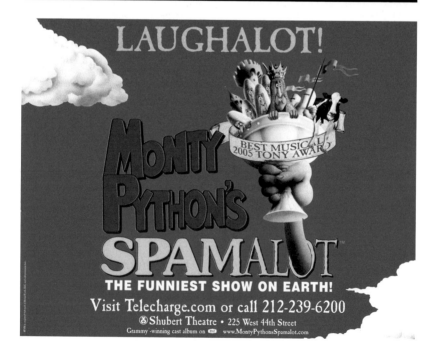

Public Theater

425 Lafayette Street, between Astor Place & E 4th Street (1-212 539 8500/Telecharge 1-212 239 6200/ www.publictheater.org). Subway N, R, W to 8th Street-NYU; 6 to Astor Place. **Box office** 1-6pm Mon, Sun; 1-7.30pm Tue-Sat. **Credit** AmEx, MC, V. **Map** p403 F28.

Founded by the late Joseph Papp and dedicated to the work of new American playwrights and performers, this Astor Place landmark is also known for its Shakespeare productions (*see below* Shakespeare in the Park). The building houses five stages and the cabaret space Joe's Pub (*see p315*). The Public recently recruited Oskar Eustis (formerly of the Trinity Repertory Company in Providence, Rhode Island) to serve as the new artistic director.

Second Stage Theatre

307 W 43rd Street, at Eighth Avenue (1-212 246 4422/www.secondstagetheatre.com). Subway A, C, E to 42nd Street-Port Authority. **Box office** noon-6pm Tue-Sun. **Credit** AmEx, MC, V. **Map** p404 D24.

Now located in a beautiful Rem Koolhaas-designed space near Times Square, Second Stage produces the works of new American playwrights, including the New York premières of Mary Zimmerman's *Metamorphoses* and Lisa Loomer's *Living Out*.

Shakespeare in the Park at the Delacorte Theater

Park entrance on Central Park West, at 81st Street, then follow the signs (1-212 539 8750/www.public theater.org). Subway B, C to 81st Street-Museum of Natural History. **Map** p405 D19.

The Delacorte Theater in Central Park is the fair-weather sister of the Public Theater (*see above*). When not producing Shakespeare in the East Village, the Public offers the best of the Bard outdoors during the New York Shakespeare Festival (June-Sept). Tickets are free (two per person); they're distributed at both theatres at 1pm on the day of the performance. Around 9am is normally a good time to begin waiting, although the line can start forming as early as 6am when big-name stars are on the bill.

Soho Rep

46 Walker Street, between Broadway & Church Street (1-212 868 4444/box office 1-212 941 8632/ www.sohorep.org). Subway A, C, E, N, R, 6 to Canal St; 1 to Franklin Street. **Box office** 9am-8pm Mon-Fri; 10am-8pm Sat; 10am-6pm Sun. **Credit** AmEx, MC, V. **Map** p402 E31.

This Off-Off mainstay recently moved to an Off-Broadway contract, meaning that tickets will be $25 to most shows (still fairly inexpensive for Off Broadway). Under artistic director Sarah Benson, the programming is wonderfully diverse and adventurous. The 2007/8 lineup includes a six-hour performance installation by the Nature Theater of Oklahoma, and the New York première of Sarah Kane's brutal, controversial 1995 play *Blasted*. The Soho Rep is definitely worth a trip down to trendy Tribeca.

Vineyard Theatre

108 E 15th Street, at Union Square East (1-212 353 0303/box office 1-212 353 0303/www.vineyard theatre.org). Subway L, N, Q, R, W, 4, 5, 6 to 14th Street-Union Square. **Box office** 10am-6pm Mon-Fri. **Credit** AmEx, MC, V. **Map** p403 E27.

This theatre near Union Square produces excellent new plays and musicals, including the downtown cult hit *[title of show]* (yes, that's its actual name) and the Tony Award-winning Broadway hit *Avenue Q* (*see p343*).

Off-Off Broadway

Technically, 'Off-Off Broadway' denotes a show that is presented at a theatre with fewer than 100 seats and created by artists who aren't necessarily card-carrying union professionals. It's where some of the most daring writers and performers create their edgiest work. The **New York International Fringe Festival** (1-212 279 4488, www.fringenyc.org), held every August, offers a great opportunity to experience the wacky side of theatre. The cheekily named **National Theater of the United States of America** (www.ntusa.org), **Radiohole** (www.radiohole.com) and the **International WOW Company** (www.internationalwow.org) are both troupes that consistently offer inspired, envelope-pushing work. But Off-Off Broadway – where tickets run from $10 up to $25 – is not restricted to experimental or solo shows. You can also see classical works and more traditional plays staged by companies such as the **Mint Theater** (3rd Floor, 311 W 43rd Street, between Eighth & Ninth Avenues, 1-212 315 0231, www.mintheater.org) and at venues like **HERE** and **Performance Space 122** (for both, *see p351*).

Repertory companies & venues

The Brick

575 Metropolitan Avenue, between Lorimer Street & Union Avenue, Williamsburg, Brooklyn (1-718 907 3457/www.bricktheater.com). Subway G to Metropolitan Avenue; L to Lorimer Street. **Box office** opens 15mins prior to curtain. **No credit cards**. **Map** p411 V8.

This chic, brick-lined venue in Williamsburg presents a variety of experimental work. Its themed summer festivals have covered such tongue-in-cheek categories as 'moral values' in 2005 and 2007's 'pretentious festival'.

Flea Theater

41 White Street, between Broadway & Church Street (1-212 226 2407/www.theflea.org). Subway A, C, E, J, M, N, Q, R, W, Z, 1, 6 to Canal Street. **Box office** noon-6pm Mon-Sat. **Credit** AmEx, MC, V. **Map** p402 E31.

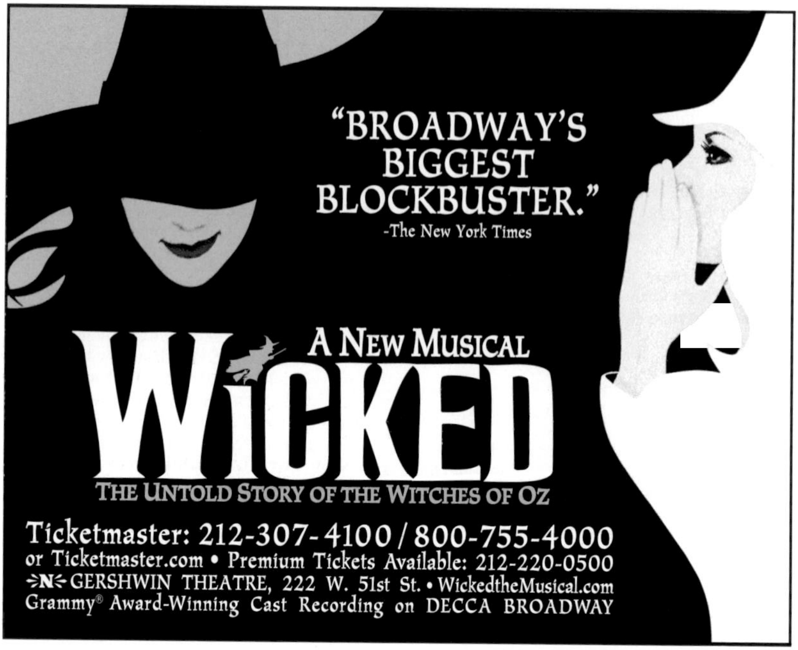
"BROADWAY'S BIGGEST BLOCKBUSTER."
-The New York Times
A NEW MUSICAL
WICKED
THE UNTOLD STORY OF THE WITCHES OF OZ
Ticketmaster: 212-307-4100 / 800-755-4000
or Ticketmaster.com • Premium Tickets Available: 212-220-0500
N GERSHWIN THEATRE, 222 W. 51st St. • WickedtheMusical.com
Grammy® Award-Winning Cast Recording on DECCA BROADWAY

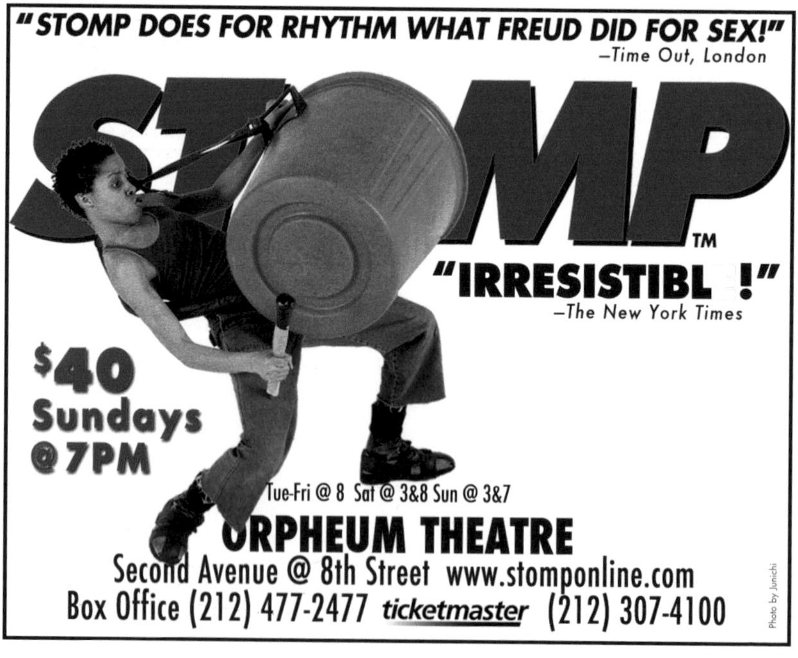
"STOMP DOES FOR RHYTHM WHAT FREUD DID FOR SEX!"
–Time Out, London
STOMP™
"IRRESISTIBL !"
–The New York Times
$40 Sundays @7PM
Tue-Fri @ 8 Sat @ 3&8 Sun @ 3&7
ORPHEUM THEATRE
Second Avenue @ 8th Street www.stomponline.com
Box Office (212) 477-2477 ticketmaster (212) 307-4100
Photo by Junichi

First founded in fashionable Tribeca in 1997, Jim Simpson's cosy, well-appointed venue has presented both avant-garde experimentation (such as the work of Mac Wellman) and politically provocative satires (mostly by AR Gurney).

HERE

145 Sixth Avenue, at Broome Street (1-212 647 0202/Smarttix 1-212 868 4444/www.here.org). Subway C, E to Spring Street. **Box office** 4-10pm daily. **Credit** AmEx, MC, V. **Map** p403 E30.
Containing three intimate performance spaces, an art gallery and a chic café, this lovely Tribeca arts complex, dedicated to not-for-profit arts enterprises, has hosted a number of exciting companies. It was the launching pad for such well-known shows as Eve Ensler's *The Vagina Monologues*.

Performance Space 122

150 First Avenue, at 9th Street (1-212 477 5288/ www.ps122.org). Subway L to First Avenue; 6 to Astor Place. **Box office** 11am-6pm daily. **Credit** AmEx, MC, V. **Map** p403 F28.
One of New York's most interesting venues, this not-for-profit arts centre presents experimental dance, performance art, music, film and video. Eric Bogosian, Whoopi Goldberg, John Leguizamo and others have developed projects here. Australian trendsetter Vallejo Gantner recently took over as artistic director of this downtown institution, promising to make its programming more international in flavour. The dance programming is also worthy of note; *see p354*.

Dance

Simply put, New York is the centre of the dance universe. Not only do the world's foremost ballet and modern dance companies call the city home, but so do untold numbers of independent, innovative choreographers. Along with this home-grown talent, national and international touring companies are continually passing through. This mix means that on virtually any given day, you can witness some amazing talent in action.

For the classically minded, the **New York City Ballet** (NYCB) offers the unparalleled repertory of George Balanchine, who established the prestigious School of American Ballet in 1934, and whose choreography transformed ballet in the 20th century. In 2007, the city's ballet world got a real shot in the arm when Christopher Wheeldon, NYCB's then-resident choreographer, launched his own company, Morphoses, to extend ballet's appeal to a wider audience – by experimenting with movement, music and visual art.

New York's modern-dance scene is as eclectic and vast as the city itself. The companies of modern-dance icons Martha Graham, Alvin Ailey, Merce Cunningham and Trisha Brown are based here, while exceptional artists like Stephen Petronio, Neil Greenberg, Aszure Barton and RoseAnne Spradlin keep finding new ways to explore the human body and spirit. And in a city where the Judson Dance Theater spawned the 'postmodern' dance movement in the 1960s, there remains a host of smaller venues that serve as incubators for emerging companies.

Of course, dance is more than the two camps of ballet and modern, especially in a city as diverse as New York. The World Music Institute presents a variety of ethnic dance at venues like **Symphony Space** and **City Center**, while the **Japan Society** (333 E 47th Street, 1-212 832 1155, www.japansociety.org) is a fine place for discovering both avant-garde voices and the purity of traditional dance.

There are two major dance seasons – March to June, and October to December. Spring is particularly busy: start with Paul Taylor's consistently brilliant company at City Center in March, then secure your seats for the programmes of the American Ballet Theatre (ABT) and NYCB. That's not to say that dance is dead from July to September; summer is a great time to catch smaller modern-dance troupes and outdoor performances at the open-air **Central Park SummerStage** (*see p353*), the Lincoln Center **Out of Doors Festival** (*see p263*) and the **River to River Festival** (*see p262*) in lower Manhattan. In the early autumn, two dance festivals – DancenOw/ NYC, at Dance Theater Workshop, and Fall for Dance, at City Center – get audiences back into the groove after the summer repose.

If you too yearn to get your move on, there are dozens of dance schools that offer classes in everything from ballet to hip hop. You'll find information about classes and workshops in *Time Out New York* magazine. Walk-ins are welcome at most spaces.

Traditional venues

Brooklyn Academy of Music

For listing, see p237.
BAM, which showcases superb local and out of town companies, is one of New York's most prominent cultural institutions. The 2,100-seat Howard Gilman Opera House, with its Federal-style columns and carved marble, is a stunning dance venue. The Mark Morris Dance Group generally performs here in the spring. The 1904 Harvey Theater (651 Fulton Street, between Ashland & Rockwell Places, Fort Greene, Brooklyn), formerly the Majestic, has hosted modern dance choreographers such as John Jasperse and Sarah Michelson. Yearly events include the DanceAfrica Festival, which is held every Memorial

A CHORUS LINE
THE BEST MUSICAL. EVER.
Photo: Paul Kolnik
Schoenfeld Theatre, 236 West 45th St.
www.AChorusLine.com

ITS TIME TO VISIT SOHO!
The Smash Hit
Flanagan's Wake
12yrs+
The Hilarious Irish interactive Wake
"Sheer Energy!" IrishEcho "A Hoot!" BostonGlobe
Thur Fri Sat & Sun
BOOK YOUR GROUP PARTY NOW!
Discounts available (Groups 10+)
ALSO PLAYING EVERY SAT NIGHT
IN IT'S 3RD YEAR!
Simon Lovell's
18yrs+
"Strange and Unusual Hobbies"
"A dazzling show!" WSJ "Mindblowing" NYC Daily News
CALL FOR SHOWTIMES OR VISIT
WWW.SOHOPLAYHOUSE.COM
Use disc code TONY for $5 off either show
SOHO PLAYHOUSE
15 Vandam Street (btwn Varick&6th)
Box Office: (212)691-1555

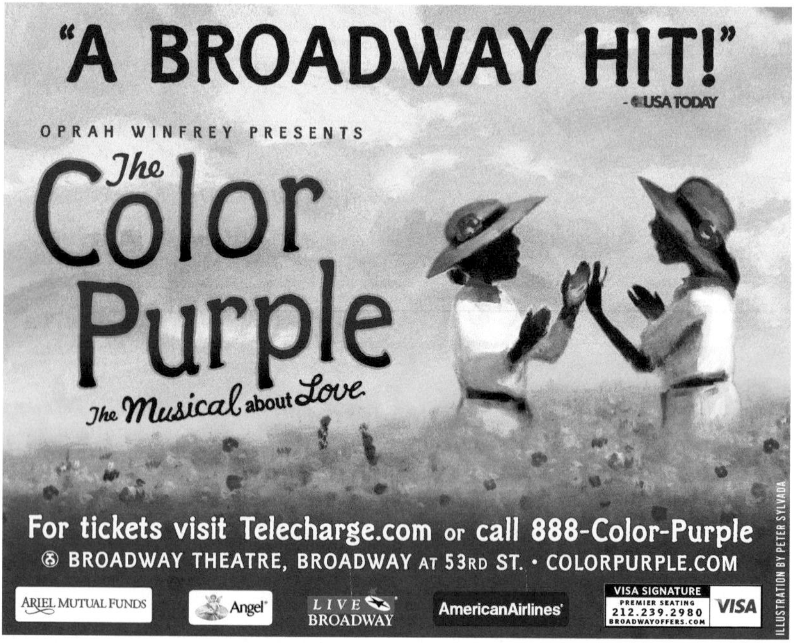

Day weekend; each October, BAM's Next Wave Festival highlights established and lesser-known experimental dance groups. *See also p345.*

City Center

131 W 55th Street, between Sixth & Seventh Avenues (1-212 581 7907/www.nycitycenter.org). Subway B, D, E to Seventh Avenue; F, N, Q, R, W to 57th Street. **Tickets** $15-$125. **Credit** AmEx, MC, V ($4.75 per-ticket surcharge). **Map** p405 D22.

Before the creation of Lincoln Center changed the cultural geography of New York, this was the home of the American Ballet Theatre, the Joffrey Ballet and the New York City Ballet. City Center's lavish decor is golden – as are the companies that pass through here. The ABT graces the stage every autumn, while the Alvin Ailey American Dance Theater, the Paul Taylor Dance Company and Morphoses/The Wheeldon Company offer superb performances throughout the year.

Joyce Theater

175 Eighth Avenue, at 19th Street (1-212 242 0800/ www.joyce.org). Subway A, C, E to 14th Street; 1 to 18th Street; L to Eighth Avenue. **Tickets** $30-$45. **Credit** AmEx, DC, Disc, MC, V. **Map** p403 D27.

This intimate space, formerly a cinema, is one of the finest theatres in town. Of the 472 seats at the Joyce, there's not a single bad one. Companies and choreographers who present work here, including the Ballet Hispanico, Pilobolus Dance Theater and Doug Varone, tend to be more traditional than experimental. In 2008, look for the Trisha Brown Dance Company in February, and Momix and the Stephen Petronio Company in the spring. During the summer, when many theatres are dark, the Joyce continues its programming. At the Joyce Soho, emerging companies present work nearly every weekend.

Other locations: Joyce Soho, 155 Mercer Street, between Houston & Prince Streets, Downtown (1-212 334 7479).

Metropolitan Opera House

For listing, see p329.

A range of international companies, from the Paris Opera Ballet to the Kirov Ballet, perform at the Met. In the spring, this majestic space is home to the American Ballet Theatre, which presents full-length traditional story ballets, as well as contemporary classics by Frederick Ashton and Antony Tudor. The acoustics are wonderful, but the theatre is immense: get as close to the stage as you can afford.

New York State Theater

Lincoln Center, 64th Street, at Columbus Avenue (1-212 870 5570/www.nycballet.com). Subway 1 to 66th Street-Lincoln Center. **Tickets** $30-$110. **Credit** AmEx, DC, Disc, MC, V. **Map** p405 C21.

The neo-classical New York City Ballet headlines at this opulent theatre, which Philip Johnson designed to resemble a jewellery box. NYCB has two seasons: winter begins just before Thanksgiving and features more than a month of performances of George Balanchine's magical *The Nutcracker*, and the season continues until the end of February with repertory performances. The nine-week spring season usually begins in April. The best seats are in the first ring, where the music comes through loud and clear and, even better, you can enjoy the dazzling patterns of the dancers. The works are by Balanchine (the 89ft-by-58ft stage was built to his specifications); Jerome Robbins; Peter Martins, the company's ballet master in chief; and former resident choreographer Christopher Wheeldon. Weekly cast lists are available online or at the theatre.

Alternative venues

Brooklyn Arts Exchange

421 Fifth Avenue, at 8th Street, Park Slope, Brooklyn (1-718 832 0018/www.bax.org). Subway F, M, R to Fourth Avenue-9th Street. **Tickets** $8-$15. **No credit cards**. **Map** p403 E28.

This multi-arts, not-for-profit organisation presents dance concerts by emerging choreographers. There are also performances just for children.

Central Park SummerStage

For listing, see p261.

This outdoor dance series runs during the heat of summer. Temperatures can get steamy, but at least you're outside. Count on seeing traditional and contemporary dance; arrive early to secure a spot close to the stage.

Dance New Amsterdam (DNA)

280 Broadway, at Chambers Street (1-212 625 8369/ www.dnadance.org). Subway R, W to City Hall. **Tickets** $10-$25. **Credit** MC, V. **Map** p402 E31.

Housed in the historic Sun Building, DNA (the former Dance Space Center) has a 135-seat theatre that hosts about 50 performances a year, by groups like the Sean Curran Company and Liz Lerman Dance Exchange.

Dance Theater Workshop

Bessie Schönberg Theater, 219 W 19th Street, between Seventh & Eighth Avenues (1-212 924 0077/www.dtw.org). Subway 1 to 18th Street. **Tickets** $12-$25. **Credit** AmEx, Disc, MC, V. **Map** p403 D27.

Dance Theater Workshop hosts work by contemporary choreographers, both local and foreign. This space features a 194-seat theatre, two dance studios and an artists' media lab.

Danspace Project

St Mark's Church in-the-Bowery, 131 E 10th Street, at Second Avenue (1-212 674 8194/www. danspaceproject.org). Subway L to Third Avenue; 6 to Astor Place. **Tickets** $12-$20. **No credit cards**. **Map** p403 F28.

This gorgeous, high-ceilinged sanctuary for downtown dance is at its most sublime when the music is live. The choreographers who take on the four-sided performance space tend towards pure movement rather than technological experimentation. The venue also hosts a free series of works-in-progress.

The crowds for cult classic **Hairspray** are as big as the bouffants. *See p343.*

Harlem Stage/Aaron Davis Hall
City College, Convent Avenue, at W 135th Street (1-212 650 7100/www.harlemstage.org). Subway 1 to 137th Street-City College. **Tickets** $10-$45. **Credit** AmEx, MC, V. **Map** p407 C12.
Performances at this Harlem centre celebrate African-American life and culture. Companies that have graced the modern, spacious theatre include the Bill T Jones/Arnie Zane Dance Company and the Alvin Ailey junior company, Ailey II.

The Kitchen
512 W 19th Street, between Tenth & Eleventh Avenues (1-212 255 5793/www.thekitchen.org). Subway A, C, E to 14th Street; L to Eighth Avenue. **Tickets** $5-$15. **Credit** AmEx, MC, V. **Map** p403 C27.
Although best known as an avant-garde theatre space, the Kitchen also offers experimental dance by inventive, often provocative artists. Famous choreographers such as Dean Moss and Elizabeth Streb have presented work here.

LaMaMa Etc
74A E 4th Street, between Second Avenue & Bowery (1-212-475-7710/www.lamama.org). Subway F to Second Avenue. **Tickets** $15-$20. **Credit** MC, V. **Map** p403 F29.
This East Village experimental theatre hosts the 'LaMaMa Moves' dance festival every spring, featuring up-and-coming companies.

Merce Cunningham Studio
11th Floor, 55 Bethune Street, between Washington & West Streets (1-212 691 9751/www.merce.org). Subway A, C, E to 14th Street; L to Eighth Avenue. **Tickets** $10-$30. **No credit cards**. **Map** p403 C28.
Located in the Westbeth complex on the edge of the West Village, the space is rented to independent choreographers, so performance quality varies. The stage and seating area are in a large dance studio, so be prepared to take off your shoes.

Movement Research
Judson Church, 55 Washington Square South, at Thompson Street (1-212 539 2611/www.movementresearch.org). Subway A, B, C, D, E, F, V to W 4th Street. **Tickets** free.
This free performance series is a great place to check out up-and-coming artists and experimental works. Held every Monday, from September to May.

Performance Space 122
For listing, see p351.
Up-and-coming choreographers present new works at what was once an abandoned public school. Ron Brown and Doug Varone started out here.

Symphony Space
For listing, see p331.
The World Music Institute hosts traditional dancers from around the globe, while the regular season features contemporary choreographers.

Trips Out of Town

Day Trips **356**

Features

Retreats by rail 359

Sandy Hook. *See p358.*

Day Trips

Take a break from pavement-pounding and neck-craning on an easy escape.

Paradise regained: well-being in full bloom at the **Mayflower Inn & Spa**.

Naturally, you'll want to soak up every last watt of bright lights the big city has to offer. But even New Yorkers crave a little downtime – how else do you think they recharge their batteries for life in the rat race? For many people (especially first-time visitors), the attractions of New York City far outshine those in the surrounding area. Still, it is fun to get out of town and see what the hinterland has to offer you. Whether you prefer hiking, sunbathing on the beach, or losing your lunch on a rollercoaster, you'll find plenty of options within just a few hours (or even less) of NYC. Many getaway spots are accessible by public transport; avoid the high car-rental rates (and nightmare traffic in and out of town) by relaxing on a bus, train or ferry.

GENERAL INFORMATION

NYC & Company, the New York visitors and convention bureau (www.nycvisit.com), has many brochures on out-of-town excursions. Look for special packages if you're planning to spend a few days away. The *New York Times*' Sunday travel section carries some excellent advertised deals for both transport and accommodation. *Time Out New York* magazine's annual 'Summer Getaways' issue will also point you in the right direction.

TRANSPORT

We've included information on how to reach all listed destinations from New York City. Metro-North and the Long Island Rail Road, or LIRR (*see p369*), are the two main commuter-rail systems. Both offer theme tours during the summer. Call the Port Authority Bus Terminal (*see p367*) for more detailed information on all bus transport from the city.

For a more scenic route altogether, you can always travel by water: NY Waterway (*see p89*) offers services to areas outside Manhattan. For more information on airports, buses, car rental and trains, *see pp366-370*.

Chill out

Mayflower Inn & Spa

It didn't surprise us to find a copy of John Milton's *Paradise Lost* in the poetry section of the library at Adriana and Robert Mnuchin's Mayflower Inn in Washington, Connecticut: nearly everything about the ritzy property's 20,000-square-foot destination spa is Edenic. In between treatments, exercise classes and wellness seminars, guests tend to knock about the gorgeously landscaped grounds, wear matching nude-looking tan sweat suits and, of course, eat divine organic produce. The closing ceremony to each five-day session even features a banishing of personal demons by way of writing them on paper slips, which are then tossed into a roaring fire.

Of course, there are differences between this paradise and the one inhabited by Adam and Eve. For one, the Sunday-to-Friday session is exclusively for women (weekend stays are co-ed). The original wasn't within two hours of New York City, and God didn't charge hefty sums per person to frolic in the garden. Then again, God also didn't offer unlimited spa treatments. Yes, you're welcome to as many massages, facials, body scrubs and energy therapies as your muscles, face, epidermis and chakras can pack into five days. The other two aspects of the Mayflower's triangle of wellness experiences – fitness classes and mind-spirit seminars – are also offered, smörgåsbord-style. Each daily schedule features two exercise options, which may include Mayflower Yoga for Flexibility, Cardio Circuit, Aquatic Ballet and Pilates, among others. The afternoon schedule is similar, but lists workshop titles such as Dream Interpretation, the Zen of Archery and Hypnotherapy. Hiking excursions, canoeing, tennis and golf are also available. And when you tire of appointments, you can lounge in the whirlpool, read in the library, wander through the waist-high maze of hedges or meditate your way through a granite and grass labyrinth.

Guests choose at the start of their stay whether they want to bond with others or stray from the pack. Itineraries are tailored to personal goals such as getting fit, sleeping better, losing weight or alleviating nutritional concerns. But all of those things should happen no matter what your focus is. The property exudes serenity and the experience, unlike nearby Canyon Ranch, is intimate; capacity is only 28 people. The staff are accommodating, the instructors are knowledgeable, and both Adriana Mnuchin and daughter Lisa Hedley are involved and gracious hosts. The rooms, housing elevated four-poster beds, showers and bathtubs, are the epitome of comfort. The all-inclusive health-conscious cuisine manages to be satiating and delicious.

The only unattractive aspect, in fact, is the steepness of the price tag. But to the clientele, about half of whom are New Yorkers, money isn't a roadblock to well-being. And if they are chastising themselves – for that or anything else – five days at the destination spa should correct it. It's about shedding original guilt and 'giving yourself permission to enjoy the experience,' Hedley says, in the welcoming Stretch and Release class. In other words, you'll never leave the garden full of shame.

Mayflower Inn & Spa

118 Woodbury Road, route 47, Washington, CT (860 868 9466/www.mayflowerinn.com). Call for rates and special package deals.

Getting there: For this trip, it's best to rent a car. Check online at www.mayflowerinn.com for driving directions.

Art star

Dia:Beacon

Take a model example of early 20th-century industrial architecture. Combine it with some of the most ambitious and uncompromising art of the past 50 years. What do you get? One of the finest, most luxuriant aesthetic experiences on earth. Indeed, for the 24 artists whose work is on view, and for the visiting public, Dia:Beacon (*photo p358*), Dia Art Foundation's outpost in the Hudson Valley, is a blessing indeed.

Despite the cavernous galleries it had in Chelsea (which now serve only as office space while Dia searches for new Manhattan digs), Dia has never had adequate space to put its hugely scaled collection on permanent display. Its founders, Heiner Friedrich and his wife, Philippa de Menil, an heir to the Schlumberger oil fortune, acquired many of their holdings in the 1960s and '70s. They had a taste for the minimal, the conceptual and the monumental, and supported artists with radical ideas about what art was, what it could do and where it should happen. Together with others of their generation, the Dia circle (Robert Smithson, Michael Heizer, Walter De Maria, Donald Judd and Dan Flavin) made it difficult to consider a work of art apart from its context – be it visual, philosophical or historical – ever again. Thanks to the institution's current director Jeffrey Weiss, curator Lynne Cooke and its board chairman Nathalie de Gunzburg, that context is now the biggest contemporary art museum in the world.

An 80-minute train ride from Grand Central, Dia:Beacon sits on a 31-acre tract overlooking the Hudson River. The 300,000-square-foot complex of three brick buildings was erected in 1929 as a box-printing factory for snack-manufacturing giant Nabisco (National Biscuit Company). No less than 34,000 square feet of north-facing skylights provide almost all of the illumination within. Nowhere does that light serve the art here better than in the immense gallery where 72 of the 102 canvases that make up Andy Warhol's rarely exhibited *Shadows* (1978-9) hang end to end like a strangely mesmerising series of solar flares.

What really sets the Dia:Beacon experience apart, however, is its confounding intimacy. The design of the galleries and gardens by California light-and-space artist Robert Irwin, in collaboration with the Manhattan architectural collective OpenOffice, seems close to genius. Not only does it make this enormous museum feel more like a private house, it also allows Cooke to draw correspondences between artworks into an elegant and intriguing narrative of connoisseurship.

Dia:Beacon

Reggio Galleries, 3 Beekman Street, Beacon, NY (1-845 440 0100/www.diabeacon.org). **Open** *Mid Apr-mid Oct* 11am-6pm Mon, Thur-Sun. *Mid Oct-mid Apr* 11am-4pm Mon, Fri-Sun. **Admission** $10; $7 seniors, students; free under-12s. **Credit** AmEx, MC, V. **Getting there**: Metro-North trains service the Beacon station, and discount rail and admission packages are available (www.mta.info).

Beach day

Sandy Hook

One thing you should know about Sandy Hook (*photos pp360-361*): there's a nude beach at its north end (Gunnison Beach, located at parking lot G, in case you're curious). Sure, the swingers there compel boaters with binoculars to anchor close to shore, and it's also home to a cruisy gay scene – but there's much more to this 1,665-acre natural wonderland than sunbathers in the buff. Along with seven miles of dune-backed ocean beach, the **Gateway National Recreation Area** is home to the nation's oldest lighthouse (the only one remaining from colonial times), as well as extensive fortifications from the days when Sandy Hook formed the outer line of defence for New York Harbor. Natural areas like the Maritime Holly Forest attract an astounding variety of birds. In fact, large stretches of beach are closed in summer to allow the endangered piping plover a quiet place to mate. The park really does offer a bit of everything – including surfers catching waves within sight of the Manhattan skyline.

With all that the expansive Hook has to offer, it's a bit like having an island getaway at NYC's doorstep. There's even a cool way to get there: rather than take to the roads and their awful

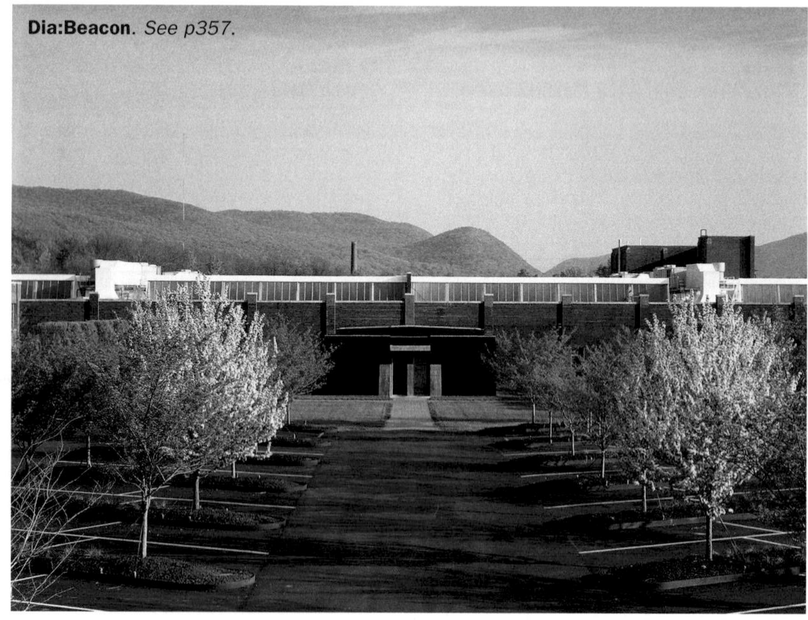

Dia:Beacon. *See p357.*

Trips Out of Town

Retreats by rail

Take a train along the Hudson River to a string of opulent historic mansions.

Kykuit.

Neatly perched atop a tall hill in Westchester County, **Kykuit**, the Rockefeller family's stately manor, with its elaborately landscaped grounds, resembles a miniature Versailles. The estate had actually been fully off-limits to the public for almost 80 years, but today a train travelling from Manhattan is met with taxis that take you to Kykuit; tours are held in conjunction with historic Philipsburg Manor in nearby Sleepy Hollow. (You'll be familiar with the village's name from Tim Burton's 1999 eponymous film, itself based on a story about a headless horseman by Washington Irving.)

Kykuit, the Rockefeller family's primary home dwelling until the 1980s, first opened to the public in 1992. The two-hour tour of the house and galleries snakes through eight of the boxy Italianate mansion's 40 rooms. Art on display includes stunning Ming vases, sculptures by Rodin and Giacometti, and a dozen or so Picasso tapestries. At midpoint, the tour spills into the Beaux Arts garden abutting the house; from the back terrace, verdant hills unfurl towards the Hudson like an Asher B Durand landscape. After descending into a basement-chamber-turned-art-gallery, tour groups head to the coach house – a shrine of sorts for about 30 vintage carriages and automobiles, which have been accumulated by the family over the years. Motorised vehicles on display include a Ford Model S Roadster from 1907, a 1924 Model T and Nelson Rockefeller's spectacular bulletproof black limousine.

Several other magnificent historic homes (and their sprawling estates) dot the hills overlooking the Hudson River. Several notable figures have called Gothic Revival **Lyndhurst Castle** home, including former New York City mayor William Paulding and Jay Gould. The interior is sumptuously decorated and lovingly maintained. Nearby **Sunnyside** was home to author Washington Irving (1783-1859), who became an American literary icon with classics like *The Legend of Sleepy Hollow* and *Rip Van Winkle*. He renovated and expanded his 18th-century Dutch colonial cottage in Tarrytown, adding a stepped-gable entrance and a Spanish-style tower.

Kykuit

Pocantico Hills, Tarrytown (1-914 631 9491/ www.hudsonvalley.org). **Open** *May-early Nov* 9am-3pm Mon, Wed-Sun. **Admission** varies; phone or check website. **Credit** AmEx, MC, V.
Getting there: Take the train from Grand Central; the estate is a scenic 40-minute trip by Metro-North (Hudson line) to Tarrytown and a five-minute taxi ride from the train station (www.mta.info).

Lyndhurst Castle

635 South Broadway, Tarrytown, NY (1-914 631 4481/www.lyndhurst.org). **Open** *Mid Apr-Oct* 10am-5pm Tue-Sun, Mon holidays. *Nov-mid Apr* 10am-4.15pm Sat, Sun, Mon holidays. **Admission** $10; $9 seniors; $4 12-17s; free under-12s. *Grounds only* $4. **Credit** AmEx, MC, V.
Getting there: directions for Kykuit (*see above*).

Sunnyside

West Sunnyside Lane, off Route 9, Tarrytown, NY (1-914 591 8763/www.hudsonvalley.org). **Open** *Mar* 10am-3pm Sat, Sun. *Apr-Oct* 10am-5pm Mon, Wed-Sun. *Nov, Dec* 10am-4pm Mon, Wed-Sun. **Admission** $12; $10 seniors; $6 5-17s; free under-5s. **Credit** AmEx, MC, V.
Getting there: directions for Kykuit (*see above*).

traffic only to find at the end of the drive that the parking lots are full, hop the ferry boat from Manhattan, and turn an excursion to the beach into a scenic mini-cruise. Once you dock at Fort Hancock after the one-hour crossing, it's a short walk to most of the beaches; and if you've still got energy for more, shuttle buses will transport you to any one of the other six strands along the peninsula.

As you'd expect, typical waterside snacks like hot dogs are available at concession stands, which can be found at each of the beach areas. But for more ambitious grub, like Caesar salad with grilled tuna, head to the **Seagull's Nest** (1-732 872 0025), the park's one restaurant; it's located at Area D, about three miles south of the ferry dock. Blanket picnics in the sand are permitted, so a great tip is to bring along goodies for dining alfresco. There are tables and grills for barbecues at Guardian Park at the south end of Fort Hancock.

If baking and eating in the sun all day doesn't appeal to you, there are plenty of historic sites worth exploring other than the lighthouse. The **Fort Hancock Museum** is located in one of the elegant century-old officer's houses that form an arc facing Sandy Hook Bay, and the abandoned forts make for an interesting day of cultural sightseeing.

Sandy Hook Gateway National Recreation Area

1-732 872 5970/www.nps.gov/gate.

Getting there: Take the ferry. Board weekdays and weekends (June to Labor Day) from E 34th Street at East River or at Pier 11 in the Financial District (at the eastern end of Wall Street). Contact Sea Streak (1-800 262 8743, www.seastreak.com) for reservations, fares and departure times. **Travel time** 55mins.

Hit the trail

The city's parks are great places for hanging out, but if you are hankering for a real fresh-air escape, you need to be more than a few blocks away from Times Square. These three nearby day hikes will satisfy your desire for nature. When heading out, be sure to take bottled water and energy-producing snacks.

Breakneck Ridge

The trek at Breakneck Ridge is a favourite of many local hikers for its accessibility, variety of trails and awe-inspiring views of the Hudson Valley. The head is roughly a two-mile walk along the highway from the Cold Spring stop on Metro-North's Hudson line (on weekends the train stops closer to the trail at the Breakneck Ridge stop). You'll find the start of the trail on the river's eastern bank, atop a tunnel that was drilled out for Route 9D; it's marked with small white paint splotches (called blazes in hiking parlance) on nearby trees. Be advised, though: Breakneck got its name for a reason. The initial trail ascends 500 feet in a mile and a half and gains another 500 feet by a series of dips and rises over the next few miles. The hike is not recommended if you're not in good shape. If you do choose this path, there are plenty of dramatic overlooks where you can rest, refuel with water and a snack, and stretch out on a rock. After the difficult initial climb, Breakneck Ridge offers options for all levels of hikers. Several crossings in the first few miles provide alternative routes down. Trail information and maps of all the paths (strongly advised), which are clearly marked with differently coloured blazes along the way, are available from the **New York-New Jersey Trail Conference** (1-201 512 9348, www.nynjtc.org). Depending on your trail choices, you can spend anywhere from two hours to a full day hiking Breakneck, so make sure you plan your route in advance.

Getting there: Take the Metro-North Hudson train from Grand Central to the Cold Spring stop. You can get closer to the start of the trail by catching the line's early train to the Breakneck Ridge stop, Sat & Sun only. **Fares** Contact the MTA for fares and schedules (www.mta.info).

Sandy Hook. *See p358.*

Harriman State Park

Just across the Hudson and south-west of the sprawling campus of West Point is Harriman State Park. You can access its more than 200 miles of trails and 31 lakes – many of which you can swim in – from stops on the Metro-North Port Jervis line. Of the trail options, our favourite is the **Triangle Trail**, an eight-mile jaunt beginning just past the parking lot at Tuxedo station – about an hour from Penn Station. Triangle leads up steadily more than 1,000 feet towards the summit of Parker Cabin Mountain before turning south to offer views of lakes Skenonto and Sebago. From there, it heads down steadily, steeply at times, and ends, after roughly five miles, at a path marked with red dashes on white. It's a long distance to cover, but the terrain is varied and there are shortcuts. On a hot day, however, the best detour is a dip in one of the lakes and a nap in the sun.
Getting there: Take the Metro-North/NJ Transit Port Jervis train, Penn Station to Tuxedo line (with a train switch in Secaucus, NJ). **Fares** Contact the MTA for fares and schedules (www.mta.info). For park information and maps of all the trails in Harriman State Park, contact the New York-New Jersey Trail Conference (1-201 512 9348, www.nynjtc.org); or Harriman State Park (1-845 786 2701, www.nysparks.state.ny.us).

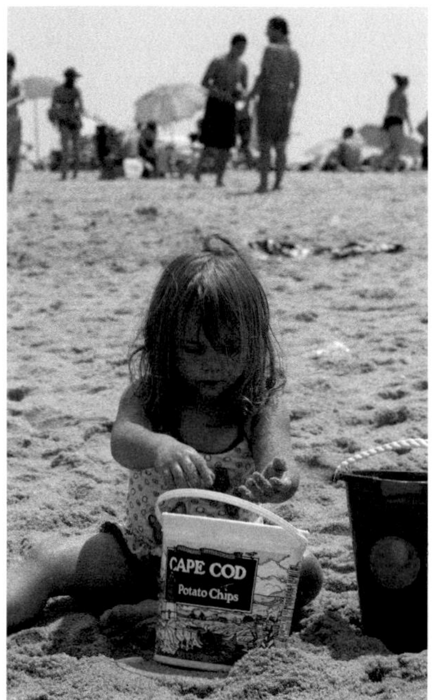

Otis Pike Wilderness

If you're looking for ocean views and a less aggressive hike, Fire Island's Otis Pike Wilderness Area is the trek for you. Though it's an hour and a half on the LIRR from Penn Station to Patchogue, followed by a 30-minute ferry ride to the Watch Hill Visitor Center, Otis Pike's pristine beaches and wildlife are worth the journey. The stretch of preserved wilderness from Watch Hill to Smith Point is home to deer, rabbits, foxes and numerous types of seabirds, including the piping plover, which nests during the summer. Just be sure you stay out of the plovers' nesting grounds, which are marked with signs, and don't feed any wildlife you see along the way.

Fire Island is completely flat, apart from a few sand dunes, though trolling the beaches and sandy paths can be slow going. After traversing the boardwalk leading from the Watch Hill Center, hike along Burma Road, a path that runs across the entire island, and in seven miles you'll arrive at the Wilderness Visitor Center at Smith Point.
Getting there: LIRR Montauk Line, Penn Station to Patchogue. **Fares** call for fares and schedules: LIRR 1-718 217 5477. For the Davis Park Ferry from Patchogue to Watch Hill; call 1-631 475 1665. For Otis Pike information, contact Fire Island National Seashore (1-631 289 4810, www.nps.gov/fiis).

New England in New York

City Island

Out here, you've got your clam diggers and you've got your mussel suckers. Clam diggers are those folks who were born on City Island – the 1.5-by-1-mile spit of land that lies off the north-east coast of the Bronx on Long Island Sound. Mussel suckers are everybody else.

Today, the number of clam diggers is dwindling. But the small-town feel on City Island – like a tiny New England fishing village in New York City – survives. This is despite the legions of off-islanders who cross the bridge from Pelham Bay Park each weekend to inhale fried clams at one of the restaurants lining City Island Avenue before dashing back to the city. Buffered from the rest of New York by the expanse of Pelham Bay Park, this community of 4,500 feels preserved in amber. There's even a City Island accent: a unique blend of Bronx squonk and New England bray.

The **City Island Nautical Museum** (190 Fordham Street, between Minnieford & King Avenues, 1-718 885 0008, open 1-5pm Sun only), housed in a quaint former schoolhouse, is stocked with model ships, Revolutionary War artefacts and tributes to such local heroes as Ruby Price Dill, the island's first kindergarten teacher. It also has a room that's devoted to the island's past as a centre of maritime activity. In its heyday, around World War II, City Island was home to no fewer than 17 shipyards. Seven America's Cup-winning yachts were built on the island (and, residents inevitably add, the Cup was lost in 1983 – the very same year they stopped building the boats here).

There are still a handful of yacht clubs in operation on these shores and a few sailmakers in the phone book, but City Islanders are far more likely to head into Manhattan for work nowadays. Few commercial fishermen are left, though you'd hardly guess it walking into the **Boat Livery** (663 City Island Avenue, at Sutherland Street, 1-718 885 1843) – a bait-and-tackle shop and bar that's changed so little over the past decades that the 'updated' boat-rental prices painted next to the door still read '$2 per day'. The bar, full of fishing paraphernalia and old Christmas lights, is known as the Worm Hole; it serves beer in plastic cups that you can take to the dock and drink while you watch the rented boats as they return to shore at sunset.

In the summer, City Island is also worth an evening trip. With crab shanties on every corner and boats bobbing in the background, the maritime community exudes a striking Nantucket charm. Over on Belden Point are **Johnny's Reef** (2 City Island Avenue, 1-718 885 2086) and **Tony's Pier Restaurant** (1 City Island Avenue, 1-718 885 1424); both have outdoor seating areas, and Johnny's Reef has telescopes too. Grab a couple of beers and a basket of fried clams, sit at one of the picnic benches and watch the boats sail by. On Wednesday evenings from mid May to mid September the island offers yacht races: the Eastchester Bay Wednesday Series.

Getting there: Take the 6 train to Pelham Bay Park and transfer to the Bx29 bus to City Island.

Theme-park larks

Six Flags Great Adventure

If you like adrenaline-pumping rides and deep-fried junk food, with a lot of shirt-soaking water rides thrown in for good measure, then we have the theme park for you – **Six Flags Great Adventure**. In 2005, Great Adventure heralded the grand opening of the 'fastest and tallest rollercoaster on Earth', Kingda Ka. Not for the faint of heart, this monster hurls riders 456 feet into the sky at speeds up to 128 miles per hour. (Psst! We hear that the best way to experience this thrilling ride is to eat a few burgers right before you go on and sit in the very front car.)

Whatever rides you choose, it's best to start slowly. You'll need to build courage (and stomach) for the more turbulent attractions to come. A good place to begin is on the huge Ferris wheel, which affords a bird's-eye view of all the main attractions. Swinging from a basket 150 feet in the air, you can scope out the goods on offer: 12 rollercoasters lie in wait for you, not to mention the various spin and puke rides, like Spinmeister and Taz Twister. Follow up the Ferris wheel with a jaunt on Skull Mountain, an in-the-dark rollercoaster (think Disney World's Space Mountain, only smaller). Runaway Train is another coaster with training wheels. Or if you're feeling wimpy, stick to the carousel.

Food is central to Great Adventure, so you should indulge in a corn dog and some cheese fries during a break from the rides. Post-digestion, it's time for the biggies. On the less scary side, there's Rolling Thunder, a wooden coaster that reminds New Yorkers of Coney Island's Cyclone; it's fun but bumpy. Next up, try the Great American Scream Machine, which has more loops than a Slinky toy. Medusa, a 61mph 'floorless' coaster (the seats are designed so that you're strapped in, but your feet dangle in the air) that plunges from a full 13 storeys in the sky is a hoot. There's also the Chiller, a terrifying-looking coaster that goes both forward and back. Afterwards, you can opt for a hot funnel cake, a sweet way to refuel after a full eight hours of adrenaline surge and burn.

Six Flags Great Adventure
Route 537, Jackson, NJ (1-732 928 1821).
Getting there: NJ Transit buses service to Great Adventure daily from Port Authority. Call 1-800 772 2222 for fares and schedules. Ask about a round-trip ticket and park admission package.

A mood for food

Culinary Institute of America

If you're the type of person who rips the recipes out of glossy food magazines but hardly ever so much as cracks an egg, you might well need a stint at the Culinary Institute of America. Of course, no one's suggesting that you actually change your ways by enrolling in a cooking school. But if you're a food lover, a great place to spend a day is on the CIA campus in Hyde Park, where just one afternoon can fulfil all sorts of epicurean fantasies.

Sprawled over 150 hilly and beautiful acres that overlook the Hudson River, this is the country's oldest culinary college, and also a monument to the romance of the cooking life. The academy once housed a seminary, and as a result the lush campus retains a wonderful sense of calm and serenity.

Family fun unfurled at **Six Flags Great Adventure**.

Although the 2,500 full-time students here pay up to $20,000 a year for the privilege, you can get in on the action for just $5 – not much more than an issue of *Saveur*. The price buys you a tour through Roth Hall, which contains the majority of the campus's 38 kitchens and three of its four restaurants. On Mondays (10am and 4pm), Wednesdays and Thursdays (4pm), enthusiastic student guides take you past the fragrant kitchens, where aspiring chefs work on buttery sauces, vegetable sautées, roast meats and chocolate sculptures. Roth Hall was clearly designed with the voyeur firmly in mind, with windows to the instructional kitchens facing the hallways.

And if this isn't enough, diehard foodies can enroll in a Saturday class. You can choose from a wide range of topics listed on the CIA website. These six-hour classes will set you back about $180 or more – but just think of all the money you'll save when you start cooking at home instead of eating out!

When you call to sign up for a tour, it's a good idea to book a table at one of the school's four public restaurants: St Andrews Café (serving up grilled meats and fish; vegetarian entrées), Caterina de Medici (perfect for Italian food), American Bounty (for a more upscale American menu) or the Escoffier Restaurant (elegant classical French cuisine). The food alone makes a meal here almost worth the trip – with the walking tour as an added bonus. The school also has a no-reservation-required café: the Apple Pie Bakery – perfect for a sweet treat. If you are visiting between January and March, or September and early December, ask about the CIA Dining Series – a selection of lectures and tastings that are sure to inspire.

The restaurants stay open for dinner, but by the time the evening rolls around, you'll be ready to board the train back home to get a headstart filling out that CIA application form you picked up on your tour.

Culinary Institute of America

1946 Campus Drive, Hyde Park, NY (1-845 471 6608/www.ciachef.edu).

Getting there: Take a Metro-North train from Grand Central to Poughkeepsie. A cab ride from Poughkeepsie station to the CIA costs about $7. (There's almost always a cab or two waiting at the station's taxi stand.) **Fares** Contact the MTA for fares and schedules (www.mta.info).

Directory

Getting to & from NYC	366
Getting Around	368
Resources A-Z	371
Further Reference	384
Index	386
Advertisers' Index	395

Features

Travel advice	371
Holidays	376
Passport update	377
Size charts	380
Public loo lowdown	385

Directory

Getting to & from NYC

By air

Airlines

Air Canada *1-800 361 5373/ www.aircanada.ca.*
American Airlines *1-800 433 7300/www.aa.com.*
British Airways *1-800 247 9297/ www.britishairways.com.*
Delta Air Lines *1-800 221 1212/ www.delta.com.*
JetBlue Airways *1-800 538 2583/ www.jetblue.com.*
Northwest/KLM *1-800 225 2525/ www.nwa.com.*
United Airlines *1-800 241 6522/ www.united.com.*
US Airways *1-800 428 4322/ www.usairways.com.*
Virgin Atlantic *1-800 862 8621/ www.virgin-atlantic.com.*

To & from the airport

For a list of transport services between New York City and its major airports, call 1-800 247 7433. Public transport is the cheapest method, but it can be both frustrating and time-consuming. None of the local airports are particularly close or convenient. Private bus or van services are usually the best bargains. Medallion (city-licensed) yellow cabs, which can be flagged on the street or picked up at designated locations at airports, are more expensive but take you all the way to your destination for a fixed, zoned price, with any tolls on top. (Not so in reverse.) You may also reserve a car service in advance to pick you up or drop you off (*see p369* **Taxis & car services**). Although it is illegal, many of the car-service drivers and unlicensed 'gypsy cabs' solicit riders around the baggage-claim areas. Avoid them.

Bus services

Coach USA
1-212 964 6233/1-877 894 9155/ www.coachusa.com. Call or visit website for schedule.
Coach USA operates between Newark Airport and Manhattan, stopping outside Grand Central Station (41st Street, between Park & Lexington Avenues), and inside Port Authority. The fare is $14 one way (round trip $23); buses leave every 15-30mins, day and night.

New York Airport Service
1-212 875 8200/www.nyairport service.com. Call or visit website for schedule.
Buses operate frequently between Manhattan and both JFK (one way $15/round trip $27) and La Guardia ($12/$21), from early morning to late at night, with stops near Grand Central Terminal (Park Avenue, between 41st & 42nd Streets), near Penn Station (33rd Street, at Seventh Avenue), inside the Port Authority Bus Terminal (*see p367*) and outside a number of midtown hotels (for an extra charge). Buses also operate from JFK to La Guardia (one way $13).

SuperShuttle
1-212 209 7000/www.supershuttle.com. 24hrs daily.
Blue SuperShuttle vans offer door-to-door service between NYC and the three major airports. Allow extra time to catch your flight, as vans will be picking up other passengers. The fare varies from $13 to $22, depending on pick-up location and destination. Always call to confirm.

Airports

Three major airports service the New York City area, plus the smaller MacArthur Airport on Long Island, which is served by domestic flights only.

John F Kennedy International Airport
1-718 244 4444/www.panynj.gov.
At $2, the bus and subway link from JFK is dirt cheap but it can take up to two hours to get to Manhattan. At the airport, look for the yellow shuttle bus to the Howard Beach station (free), then take the A train to Manhattan. Thankfully, JFK's AirTrain now offers faster service between all eight airport terminals and the A, E, J and Z subway lines, as well as the Long Island Rail Road, for $5. Visit www.airtrainjfk.com for more information. Private bus and van services are a good compromise between value and convenience (*see above* **Bus services**). A medallion yellow cab from JFK to Manhattan will charge a flat $45 fare, plus toll (varies by route, but usually $4) and tip (if service is fine, give at least $5). Although metered, the fare to JFK from Manhattan will be about the same cost. Check out www.nyc.gov/taxi for the latest cab rates.

La Guardia Airport
1-718 533 3400/www.panynj.gov.
Seasoned New Yorkers take the M60 bus ($2), which runs between the airport and 106th Street, at Broadway. The ride takes 40mins to an hour (depending on traffic) and runs from 4.30am to 1.30am daily. The route crosses Manhattan at 125th Street in Harlem. Get off at Lexington Avenue for the 4, 5 and 6 trains; at Malcolm X Boulevard (Lenox Avenue) for the 2 and 3; or at St Nicholas Avenue for the A, B, C and D trains. You can also disembark on Broadway at 116th or 110th Street for the 1 and 9 trains. Less time-consuming options: private bus services cost around $14; taxis and car services charge about $28, plus toll and tip.

MacArthur Airport
1-631 467 3210/www.macarthur airport.com.
Some flights into this airport in Islip, Long Island, may be cheaper than flights into those above. Getting to Manhattan, of course, 50 miles away, will take longer and be more expensive, unless you take the LIRR. Fares are generally $13 and a shuttle from the airport to the train station is $5. For cars, Colonial Transportation (1-631-589 3500) will take up to four to Manhattan for $143, including tolls and tip.

Newark Liberty International Airport

1-973 961 6000/www.newarkairport.com.
Even though it's in next-door New Jersey, Newark still has good mass transit access to NYC. The best bet is a 40min, $11.55 trip by the New Jersey Transit to or from Penn Station. The airport's monorail, AirTrain Newark (www.airtrainnewark.com), is now linked to the NJ Transit and Amtrak train systems. For cheap buses, see bus services below. A car or taxi will run at about $45, plus toll and tip.

By bus

Buses are an inexpensive means of getting to and from New York City, though the ride takes longer and is sometimes uncomfortable. Buses are particularly useful if you want to leave in a hurry; many don't require reservations. Most out-of-town buses come and go from the **Port Authority Bus Terminal**.

Bus stations

George Washington Bridge Bus Station

4211 Broadway, between 178th & 179th Streets (1-212 564 8484/www.panynj.gov). Subway A, 1 to 181st Street. **Map** p409 B6.
A few bus lines that serve New Jersey and Rockland County, New York, use this station.

Port Authority Bus Terminal

625 Eighth Avenue, between 40th & 42nd Streets (1-212 564 8484/www.panynj.gov). Subway A, C, E to 42nd St-Port Authority. **Map** p410 S13.
This somewhat unlovely terminus is the hub for many transportation companies offering commuter and long-distance bus services to and from New York City. If you have an early departure, bring your own breakfast, as the concessions don't open until around 7am. As with any transport terminal, watch out for petty criminals, especially at night.

Long-distance lines

Greyhound Trailways

1-800 229 9424/www.greyhound.com. **Open** 24hrs daily. **Credit** AmEx, DC, Disc, MC, V.
Greyhound offers a programme of long-distance bus travel to destinations across North America.

New Jersey Transit

1-800 772 2222/www.njtransit.com. Call or visit website for schedules. **Credit** MC, V.
NJT provides bus service to nearly everywhere in the Garden State and some destinations in New York State; most of the buses run right around the clock.

Peter Pan

1-800 343 9999/www.peterpanbus.com. **Open** 24hrs daily. **Credit** MC, V.
Peter Pan runs extensive services to cities across the North-east; its tickets are also valid on Greyhound.

By car

If you drive to the city, you may encounter delays at bridge and tunnel crossings (check www.nyc.gov and www.panynj.gov before driving in). Tune your car radio to **WINS** (1010 on the AM dial) for up-to-the-minute traffic reports. Delays can run anywhere from 15 minutes to two hours – plenty of time to get your money out for the toll ($4 is average). It makes sense, of course, to time your arrival and departure against the commuter flow.

For more information on driving in the city, *see p370.*

Parking

We recommend that if you drive to NYC, you should head for a garage, park your car and leave it there. Parking on the street is problematic and car theft is not unheard of. Garages are plentiful but expensive. If you want to park for less than $15 a day, try a garage outside Manhattan and take public transport into the city. Listed below you'll find Manhattan's better deals. For other options, see the Yellow Pages.

Central Kinney System

www.centralparking.com. **Open** 24hrs daily, most locations. **Credit** AmEx, MC, V.
One of the city's largest parking companies, Kinney is accessible and reliable, though not exactly the cheapest in town.

GMC Park Plaza

1-212 888 7400. **Open** 24hrs daily, most locations. **Credit** AmEx, MC, V.
GMC has more than 70 locations in the city. At $30 overnight, including tax, the one at 407 E 61st Street, between First and York Avenues (1-212 838 4158) is one of the least expensive options.

Icon Parking

www.iconparking.com. **Open** 24hrs daily, most locations. **Credit** AmEx, MC, V.
Choose from over 160 locations via the website to guarantee a spot and price ahead of time.

Standard Parking

Pier 40, West Street, at W Houston Street (1-800 494 7007). **Open** 24hrs daily. **Rates** $22/12hrs. **Credit** AmEx, MC, V. **Map** p412 U6.
Mayor Parking, another of the city's large chains, offers both indoor and outdoor parking. Call for info and for other locations.

By train

America's national rail service is run by Amtrak. Nationwide routes are slow, infrequent and unreliable (if characterful), but there are some good fast services linking the eastern seaboard cities. For commuter rail services, *see p369.*

Train stations

Grand Central Terminal

From 42nd to 44th Streets, between Vanderbilt & Lexington Avenues. Subway 42nd Street S, 4, 5, 6, 7 to 42nd Street-Grand Central. **Map** p404 E24.
Grand Central is home to Metro-North, which runs trains to more than 100 stations throughout New York State and Connecticut. Schedules are available at the terminal. It's also a big retail centre with some excellent eating and drinking venues.

Penn Station

31st to 33rd Streets, between Seventh & Eighth Avenues. Subway A, C, E, 1, 2, 3 to 34th Street-Penn Station. **Map** p404 D25.
Amtrak, Long Island Rail Road and New Jersey Transit trains depart from this terminal, which has printed schedules available.

Getting Around

Orientation

Manhattan is divided into three sections: **Downtown**, which includes neighbourhoods south of 14th Street; **Midtown**, roughly the area between 14th and 59th Streets; and **Uptown**, north of 59th Street.

Generally, avenues run north-south along the entire length of Manhattan. They are always parallel to one another and are logically numbered, with a few exceptions, such as Broadway, Columbus and Lexington Avenues. Manhattan's centre is **Fifth Avenue**, so all buildings located east of it will have 'East' addresses, with numbers getting higher towards the East River, and those west of it will have 'West' numbers that get higher towards the Hudson River. Streets are also parallel to one another, but they run east to west, or crosstown, and are numbered, from 1st Street up to 220th Street.

The neighbourhoods of lower Manhattan – including the Financial District, Tribeca, Chinatown and Greenwich Village – were settled prior to urban planning and can be confusing to walk through. Their charming lack of logic makes frequent reference to a map essential.

Public transport

Changes to subway and bus schedules can occur at the last minute, so pay attention to the posters on subway station walls and any announcements you may hear in trains and on subway platforms.

Metropolitan Transportation Authority (MTA)
Travel info 1-718 330 1234/updates 1-718 243 7777/www.mta.info.
The MTA runs the subway and bus lines, as well as a number of alternative commuter services to points outside Manhattan. You can get news of service interruptions and download the most current MTA maps from the website. Be warned: backpacks and handbags may be subject to random searches.

City buses

MTA buses are fine… if you're not in a hurry, or just using them for sightseeing. They are white and blue, and display a digital destination sign on the front, along with a route number preceded by a letter (M for Manhattan). The $2 fare is payable with a **MetroCard** (*see below*) or exact change (coins only; no pennies). MTA's express buses usually head to the outer boroughs for a $5 fare.

MetroCards allow for an automatic transfers from bus to bus, and between buses and subways. If you pay cash, and you're travelling uptown or downtown and want to go crosstown (or vice versa), ask the driver for a transfer when you get on – you'll be given a ticket for use on the second leg of your journey, valid for two hours. Maps are posted on most buses and at all subway stations; they're also available from **NYC & Company** (*see p383*). The Manhattan bus map is reprinted in this guide; *see p413*. All local buses are equipped with wheelchair lifts. Contact the MTA for further information.

Subways

The subway is the fastest way to get around town during the day, and it's far cleaner and safer than it was 20 years ago. The city's system is one of the world's largest and cheapest: $2 will get you from the depths of Brooklyn to the furthest reaches of the Bronx and anywhere in between (though the subway doesn't service Staten Island). Trains run around the clock, but with sparse service and fewer riders at night, it's advisable to take a cab after 10pm.

Ongoing improvements have resulted in several big changes. This guide provides the most current subway map at press time (*see pp414-415*); you can also ask MTA workers in service booths for a free copy.

To ensure safety, don't stand near the edge of the platform. Late at night and early in the morning, board the train from the designated off-peak waiting area, usually located near the middle of the platform; this area is more secure than the ends of the platforms or the outermost cars, which are often less populated at night. Standard urban advice: hold your bag with the opening facing you, keep your wallet in a front pocket and don't wear flashy jewellery. Remember that petty crime levels increase during the holidays.

METROCARDS

To enter the subway system, you need a **MetroCard** (it also works on buses), which you can buy from a booth in the station or from one of the brightly coloured MetroCard vending machines, which accept cash, debit and credit cards (AmEx, Disc, MC, V), as well as from the NY Convention & Visitors Bureau, the New York Transit Museum in Brooklyn, and many hotels. Free transfers between buses and subways are available only with a MetroCard.

There are two types of metro card: **pay-per-use** and **unlimited ride**. Up to four people can use a pay-per-use card, which is sold in denominations from $4 (two trips) to $80. A $20 card offers 12 trips for the price of ten. If you're planning to use the subway or buses often, an unlimited-ride MetroCard is great value. These cards are offered in three amounts: a single-day Fun Pass ($7, available at station vending machines but not at booths), a seven-day pass ($24) and a 30-day pass ($76). These are good for unlimited rides, but you can't share a card with your travel companions, since you can only swipe it once every 18 minutes at a given subway station or on a bus.

SUBWAY LINES

Trains are identified by letters or numbers and are colour-coded according to the line on which they run. Stations are most often named after the street on which they're located. Entrances are marked with a green globe (open 24 hours) or a red globe (limited hours). Many stations have separate entrances for the uptown and downtown platforms – look before you pay.

Local trains stop at every station on the line; express at major-station stops only.

Train

The following commuter trains service NY's hinterland.

Long Island Rail Road

1-718 217 5477/www.lirr.org.
LIRR provides rail services from Penn Station, Brooklyn and Queens.

Metro-North

1-212 532 4900/1-800 638 7646/ www.mnr.org.
Commuter trains service towns north of Manhattan and leave from Grand Central Terminal.

New Jersey Transit

1-973 762 5100/1-800 772 2222/ www.njtransit.com.
Service from Penn Station reaches most of New Jersey, some points in New York State and Philadelphia.

PATH Trains

1-800 234 7284/www.pathrail.com.
PATH (Port Authority Trans-Hudson) trains run from six stations in Manhattan to various places across the Hudson River in New Jersey, including Hoboken, Jersey City and Newark. The system is fully automated, and entry costs $1.50. You need to have either change or crisp bills for the ticket machines, and trains run 24 hours a day. Manhattan PATH stations are marked on the subway map (*see p416*).

Taxis & car services

Taxicabs

Yellow cabs are hardly ever in short supply – except, of course, at rush hour and in nasty weather. Use only yellow medallion (licensed) cabs; avoid unregulated gypsy cabs. If the centre light on top of the taxi is lit, that means the cab is available and should stop if you flag it down. Jump in and then tell the driver where you're going. (New Yorkers generally give cross-streets rather than addresses.)

Taxis will carry up to four passengers for the same price: $2.50 plus 40¢ per fifth of a mile, with an extra 50¢ charge from 8pm to 6am and a $1 surcharge during rush hour (weekdays from 4pm to 8pm). The average fare for a three-mile ride is $9-$11, depending on the time of day and on the traffic (the meter adds another 20¢ per minute while the car is idling). Cabbies rarely allow more than four passengers in a cab (it's illegal, unless the fifth person is a child under seven), though it may be worth asking in advance.

Not all drivers know their way around the city, so it helps if you know where you're going – and speak up. By law, taxis cannot refuse to take you anywhere inside the five boroughs or to New York airports, so don't be duped by a reluctant cabbie. If you have a problem, take down the medallion and driver's numbers, posted on the partition. Always ask for a receipt – there's a meter number on it. To complain or to trace lost property, call the **Taxi & Limousine Commission** (1-212 227 0700, 8am-4pm Mon-Fri) or visit www.nyc.gov/taxi. Tip 15-20 per cent, as in a restaurant.

Late at night, cabs stick to fast-flowing routes. Try the avenues and key streets (Canal, Houston, 14th, 23rd, 34th, 42nd, 57th, 72nd and 86th). Bridge and tunnel exits are good for a steady flow of taxis returning from airports, and cabbies will usually head for nightclubs and big hotels. Otherwise, try the following:

Chinatown

Chatham Square, where Mott Street meets the Bowery, is an unofficial taxi stand. You can also try hailing a cab exiting the Manhattan Bridge at Bowery and Canal Street.

Lincoln Center

The crowd heads to Columbus Circle for a cab; those in the know go west to Amsterdam Avenue.

Lower East Side

Katz's Deli (Houston Street, at Ludlow Street) is a cabbies' hangout; also try Delancey Street, where cabs come in over the Williamsburg Bridge.

Midtown

Penn Station, Grand Central Terminal and the Port Authority Bus Terminal attract cabs all night.

Soho

If you're on the west side, try Sixth Avenue; east side, the intersection of Houston Street and Broadway.

Times Square

This busy area has 30 taxi stands. Look for the yellow globes on poles.

Tribeca

Cabs head up Hudson Street. The Tribeca Grand (2 Sixth Avenue, between Walker & White Streets) is another good bet.

Car services

Car services are also regulated by the **Taxi & Limousine Commission** (*see above*).

Unlike cabs, they aren't yellow and drivers can make only pre-arranged pickups. If you see a black Lincoln Town Car, it most likely belongs to a car service. Don't try to hail one, and be wary of those that offer you a ride; they may not be licensed or insured, and you could get ripped off.

The following companies will pick you up anywhere in the city, at any time of day or night, for a set fare.

Carmel
1-212 666 6666.

Dial 7
1-212 777 7777.

Limores
1-212 777 7171.

Driving

Manhattan drivers (especially cabbies) are fearless; so taking to the streets is not for the faint of heart. It's best to try to restrict your driving to evening hours, when traffic is lighter and there's more street parking available.

Car rental

Car rental is much cheaper in the city's outskirts and in New Jersey and Connecticut than in Manhattan; reserve ahead for weekends. Another way to save money is to rent from an independent agency, such as Aamcar (*see below*). Log on to www.carrentalexpress.com for more independent companies.

Companies located outside New York State do not include LDW (loss/damage waiver) insurance in their rate, which means you will need to pay for any damage to the car unless you are covered under another policy or by your credit card. Rental companies in New York State are required by law to insure their own cars, though the renter pays for the first $100 in damage to the rental vehicle. Personal liability insurance is advised wherever you rent (unless your travel insurance or home policy covers it). UK residents may find cheaper rental insurance on www.insurance4carhire.com.

You will need a credit card (or a large cash deposit) to rent a car, and you usually have to be at least 25 years old. All car-rental companies listed below add sales tax (8.625 per cent). If you know you want to rent a car before you travel, ask your travel agent or airline to check for special deals and discounts, or look online.

Aamcar
315 W 96th Street, between West End Avenue & Riverside Drive (1-800 722 6923/1-212 222 8500/www.aamcar.com). Subway 1, 2, 3 to 96th Street. **Open** 7.30am-7.30pm Mon-Fri; 9am-3pm Sat; 9am-7pm Sun. **Credit** AmEx, DC, Disc, MC, V. **Map** p406 B17.
Compact rates from $49.95 per day, unlimited mileage; $39.95 with 100 free miles.

Car rental chains
Alamo *US: 1-800 462 5266/ www.alamo.com. UK: 0870 400 562/www.alamo.co.uk.*

Avis *US: 1-800 230 4898/www.avis.com. UK: 0870 606 0100/ www.avis.co.uk.*

Budget *US: 1-800 527 0700/ www.budget.com. UK: 0870 153 170/www.budget.co.uk.*

Dollar *US: 1-800 800 3665/ www.dollar.com. UK: 0800 085 578/www.dollar.co.uk.*

Enterprise *US: 1-800 261 7331/www.enterprise.com. UK: 0870 350 3000/www.enterprise.com/uk.*

Hertz *US: 1-800 654 3131/ www.hertz.com. UK: 0870 844 8844/www.hertz.co.uk.*

National *US: 1-800 227 7368. UK: 0116 217 3884.* Both: *www.nationalcar.com.*

Thrifty *US: 1-800 847 4389/ www.thrifty.com. UK: 01494 51600/www.thrifty.co.uk.*

Street parking

Make sure you read parking and meter signs and never park within 15 feet of a fire hydrant (to avoid a $115 ticket and/or having your car towed). Parking is off-limits on most streets for at least a few hours every day. The **Department of Transportation** (dial 311) provides information on daily changes to parking regulations. If precautions fail, call 1-718 935 0096 for towing and impoundment information.

Emergency towing

City Wide Towing
514 W39 Street, at Eleventh Avenue (1-212-244-4420/ www.citywideautotowing.com). **Open** 24hrs daily. *Repairs* 9am-5pm daily. **Credit** MC, V. **Map** p404 C24.
All types of repairs are carried out on domestic and foreign vehicles.

24-hour gas stations

Exxon
24 Second Avenue, at 1st Street (1-212 979 7000). **Credit** AmEx, MC, V. **Map** p403 F29.
Repairs.

Hess
502 W 45th Street, at Tenth Avenue (1-212 245 6594). **Credit** AmEx, DC, Disc, MC, V. **Map** p404 C24.
No repairs.

Cycling

Aside from the immensely pleasurable cycling in Central Park, and along the wide bike paths around the perimeter of Manhattan (now virtually circumnavigated by paths), biking in the city streets is no picnic and is not recommended for urban beginners. Still, zipping through bumper-to-bumper traffic holds allure for those with the requisite skills and gear. For bike rentals and citywide bike paths, *see p336.*

Walking

One of the best ways to take in NYC is on foot. Most of the streets are laid out in a grid pattern and are relatively easy to navigate. Our full set of street maps (*see pp402-412*) makes it even easier.

Resources A-Z

Age restrictions

In NYC, you must be 18 to buy tobacco products and 21 to buy or to be served alcohol. Some bars and clubs admit patrons between 18 and 21, but you'll be ejected if you're caught drinking alcohol. Always carry picture ID as even those well over 21 can be asked to show proof of age and identity.

Business

Consumer information

Better Business Bureau
1-212 533 6200/www.newyork.bbb.org.
The BBB offers advice on consumer-related complaints (shopping, services, etc). Each phone enquiry costs $5 (plus New York City tax) and must be charged to a credit card; the online service is free.

New York City Department of Consumer Affairs
42 Broadway, between Beaver Street & Exchange Place (311 local, 1-212 639 9675 out of state/www.nyc.gov/consumer). Subway 4, 5 to Bowling Green. **Open** 9am-5pm Mon-Fri. **Map** p402 E33.
File complaints on consumer-related matters here.

New York City 311 Call Center
311.
This non-emergency three-digit number was established in 2004 as a means for residents to get answers and register complaints about city issues ranging from parking regulations and small claims court up to real-estate auctions and consumer tips.

International couriers

DHL Worldwide Express
Call to find the office nearest you or to arrange a pick-up at your door (1-800 225 5345/www.dhl.com). **Credit** AmEx, DC, Disc, MC, V.
DHL will send a courier to pick up packages at any NYC address, or you can deliver packages in person to one of its offices or drop-off points. Cash is not accepted.

FedEx
Call to find the office nearest you or to arrange a pick-up at your door (1-800 247 4747/www.fedex.com). **Credit** AmEx, DC, Disc, MC, V.
Packages heading overseas should be dropped off before 6pm for International Priority delivery (depending on destination), and by 9pm to most destinations in the US (some locations have a later cut-off time; call to check).

UPS
Various locations throughout the city; free pickup at your door (1-800 742 5877/www.ups.com). **Open** hours vary by office; call for locations and times. **Credit** AmEx, MC, V.
Like DHL and FedEx, UPS will send a courier to pick up parcels at any address in the five boroughs. The city's 30 retail locations (formerly Mail Boxes Etc) also offer mailbox rental, mail forwarding, packaging, phone-message service, copying and faxing. UPS provides domestic and international services.

Messenger services

A to Z Couriers
106 Ridge Street, between Rivington & Stanton Streets (1-212 253 6500/www.atozcouriers.com). Subway F to Delancey Street; J, M, Z to Delancey-Essex Streets. **Open** 8am-8pm Mon-Fri. **Credit** AmEx, MC, V. **Map** p403 G29.
These cheerful couriers will deliver inside the city (also both national and international).

Breakaway
335 W 35th Street, between Eighth & Ninth Avenues (1-212 947 4455/www.breakawaycourier.com). Subway A, C, E to 34th Street-Penn Station. **Open** 7am-9pm Mon-Fri; 9am-5pm Sat; noon-5pm Sun. **Credit** AmEx, MC, V. **Map** p404 C25.
Breakaway is a recommended local delivery service that promises to pick up and deliver within just 90 minutes.

Jefron
55 Walker Street, between Church Street & West Broadway (1-212 431 6610/www.jefron.com). Subway 1, 2, 3 to Chambers Street. **Open** 4am-8pm Mon-Fri. **No credit cards. Map** p402 E31.
Jefron specialises in transporting import and export documents.

Photocopying & printing

The Copy Specialist
44 E 21st Street, at Park Avenue South (1-212 533 7560). Subway N, R, W to 23rd Street. **Open** 8.30am-7pm Mon-Fri; 10am-4pm Sat. **Credit** AmEx, MC, V. **Map** p404 E26.
Provides offset, laser and also colour printing; fax; large-format photocopies; binding and more. **Other locations**: 71 W 23rd Street, between Fifth & Sixth Avenues (1-646 336 6999).

Travel advice

For current information on travel to a specific country – including the latest news on health issues, safety and security, local laws and customs – contact your home country's government department of foreign affairs. Most have websites with useful advice for would-be travellers.

Australia
www.smartraveller.gov.au

Canada
www.voyage.gc.ca

New Zealand
www.safetravel.govt.nz

Republic of Ireland
http://foreignaffairs.gov.ie

UK
www.fco.gov.uk/travel

USA
http://travel.state.gov

Servco

1150 Sixth Avenue, between 44th & 45th Streets (1-212 575 0991). Subway B, D, F, V to 47th-50th Streets-Rockefeller Center; 7 to Fifth Avenue. **Open** 8.30am-8pm Mon-Fri. **No credit cards. Map** p404 D24.

Photocopying, offset printing, blueprints and binding services are available.

Translation & language services

All Language Services

77 W 55th Street, between Fifth & Sixth Avenues (1-212 986 1688/ fax 1-212 265 1662). Subway 42nd Street S, 4, 5, 6, 7 to 42nd Street-Grand Central. **Open** 24hrs daily. **Credit** AmEx, MC, V. **Map** p405 E22.

ALS will type or translate documents in any of 59 languages and provide interpreters if needed.

Consulates

Check the phone book for a complete list of consulates and embassies. *See also p371* **Travel advice**.

Australia

1-212 351 6500.

Canada

1-212 596 1628.

Great Britain

1-212 745 0200.

Ireland

1-212 319 2555.

New Zealand

1-212 832 4038.

Customs

US Customs allows foreigners to bring in $100 worth of gifts (the limit is $800 for returning Americans) without paying duty. One carton of 200 cigarettes (or 50 cigars) and one litre of liquor (spirits) are allowed. Plants, meat and fresh produce of any kind cannot be brought into the country – not even a sandwich. You will have to fill out a form if you carry more than $10,000 in currency. You will be handed a white form on your inbound flight to fill in, confirming you have not exceeded any of these allowances.

If it is essential for you to bring prescription drugs into the US, make sure the container is clearly marked, and bring your doctor's statement or a prescription. Marijuana, cocaine and most opiate derivatives, along with a number of other drugs and chemicals, are not permitted: the possession of them is punishable by a stiff fine and/or imprisonment. Check in with the **US Customs Service** (www.customs.gov) before you arrive if you have any questions about what you can bring.

New York might be one of the world's great shopping destinations, but bear in mind that UK Customs still allows returning visitors to bring only £145 worth of 'gifts, souvenirs and other goods' into the country duty-free, along with the usual duty-free goods.

Disabled access

Under New York City law, all facilities constructed after 1987 must provide complete access for the disabled – restrooms, entrances and exits included. In 1990, the Americans with Disabilities Act made the same requirement federal law. In the wake of this legislation, many older buildings have added disabled-access features. There has been widespread (though imperfect) compliance with the law, but call and check ahead.

New York City can still be very challenging for disabled visitors. One useful resource is *Access for All*, a guide to New York's cultural institutions that is published by **Hospital Audiences Inc** (1-212 575 7660, www.hospaud.org). The online guide tells how accessible each location really is and includes information on the height of telephones and water fountains; hearing and visual aids; and passenger-loading zones and alternative entrances. HAI's service for the visually impaired provides recordings of commentaries of theatre performances.

All Broadway theatres are equipped with devices for the hearing-impaired; call **Sound Associates** (1-212 582 7678, 1-888 772 7686) for more information. There are a number of other stage-related resources for the disabled. **Telecharge** (1-212 239 6200) reserves tickets for wheelchair seating in Broadway and Off Broadway venues while Theatre Development Fund's **Theater Access Project** (1-212 221 1103, www.tdf.org) arranges sign-language interpretation and captioning in American Sign Language for both Broadway and Off Broadway shows. **Hands On** (1-212 740 3087, www.handson.org) does the same.

Lighthouse International

111 E 59th Street, between Park & Lexington Avenues (1-212 821 9200/www.lighthouse.org). Subway N, R, W to Lexington Avenue-59th Street; 4, 5, 6 to 59th Street. **Open** 10am-6pm Mon-Fri; 10am-5pm Sat. **Map** p405 E29.

In addition to running a store that sells handy items for the vision-impaired, this organisation also provides helpful information for blind residents of and visitors to New York City.

Mayor's Office for People with Disabilities

2nd Floor, 100 Gold Street, between Frankfort & Spruce Streets (1-212 788 2830). Subway J, M, Z to Chambers Street; 4, 5, 6 to Brooklyn Bridge-City Hall. **Open** 9am-5pm Mon-Fri. **Map** p402 F32.

This city office provides a broad range of services for the disabled.

New York Society for the Deaf

315 Hudson Street, between Vandam & Spring Streets (1-212 366 0066/www.fegs.org). Subway C, E to Spring Street; 1 to Houston Street. **Open** 9am-5pm Mon-Thur; 9am-4.30pm Fri. **Map** p403 D30.

The deaf and hearing-impaired come here for information and a range of services.

Society for Accessible Travel & Hospitality

Suite 610, 347 Fifth Avenue, between 33rd & 34th Streets (1-212 447 7284/www.sath.org). **Map** 404 E25.
This not-for-profit group was founded in 1976 to educate the public about travel facilities for people with disabilities and to promote travel for the disabled worldwide. Membership is $45 a year ($30 for seniors and students) and includes access to an information service and a quarterly travel magazine. No drop-ins; membership by mail only.

Electricity

The US uses 110-120V, 60-cycle alternating current rather than the 220-240V, 50-cycle AC used in Europe and elsewhere. The transformers that power or recharge many newer electronic devices such as laptop computers are designed to handle either current and may need nothing more than an adaptor for the wall outlet. However, most electrical appliances, including most hairdryers, will require a power converter as well. Adaptors and converters of various sorts can be purchased at airport shops, at several pharmacies and department stores, and at Radio Shack branches around the city (consult the phone book for locations), and they can often be borrowed at better hotels.

Emergencies

Ambulance

In an emergency only, dial 911 for an ambulance or call the operator (dial 0). To complain about slow emergency service or poor public treatment, call the Fire Department Complaint Hotline (1-718 999 2646).

Fire

In an emergency only, dial 911.

Police

In an emergency only, dial 911. For the location of the nearest police precinct or for information about police services, call 1-646 610 5000.

Gay & lesbian

For gay/lesbian resources, *see pp301-311.*

Health & medical facilities

The public health-care system is virtually non-existent in the United States, and private health care is prohibitively expensive. If possible, make sure you have comprehensive medical insurance when you travel to New York.

Clinics

Walk-in clinics offer treatment for minor ailments. Most clinics will require immediate payment for treatments and consultations, though some will send their bill directly to your insurance company if you're a US resident. You will have to file a claim to recover the cost of any prescription medication.

D•O•C•S

55 E 34th Street, between Madison & Park Avenues (1-212 252 6000). Subway 6 to 33rd Street. **Open** *Walk-in* 8am-8pm Mon-Thur; 8am-7pm Fri; 9am-3pm Sat; 9am-2pm Sun. Extended hours by appointment. **Base fee** $80 and up. **Credit** AmEx, Disc, MC, V. **Map** p.404 E25.
These excellent primary-care facilities, affiliated with Beth Israel Medical Center, offer by-appointment and walk-in services. If you need X-rays or lab tests, go as early as possible (no later than 6pm) Monday to Friday. **Other locations**: 202 W 23rd Street, at Seventh Avenue (1-212 352 2600).

Dentists

NYU College of Dentistry

345 E 24th Street, between First & Second Avenues (1-212 998 9872/after-hours emergency care 1-212 998 9800). Subway 6 to 23rd Street. **Open** 8.30am-7pm Mon-Thur; 8.30am-3pm Fri. **Base fee** $90. **Credit** Disc, MC, V. **Map** p404 F26.
If you need your teeth fixed on a budget, the final-year students here are slow but proficient, and an experienced dentist is always on hand to supervise.

Emergency rooms

You will be billed for any emergency treatment. Do call your travel insurance company's emergency number before seeking treatment to find out which hospitals accept your insurance. Emergency rooms are always open at:

Cabrini Medical Center

227 E 19th Street, between Second & Third Avenues (1-212 995 6000). Subway L to Third Avenue; N, Q, R, W, 4, 5, 6 to 14th Street-Union Square. **Map** p403 F27.

Mount Sinai Hospital

Madison Avenue, at 100th Street (1-212 241 7171). Subway 6 to 103rd Street. **Map** p406 E16.

New York – Presbyterian Hospital/Weill Cornell Medical Center

525 E 68th Street, at York Avenue (1-212 746 5454). Subway 6 to 68th Street. **Map** p405 G21.

St Luke's – Roosevelt Hospital

1000 Tenth Avenue, at 59th Street (1-212 523 6800). Subway A, B, C, D, 1 to 59th Street-Columbus Circle. **Map** p405 C22.

St Vincent's Hospital

153 W 11th Street, at Seventh Avenue (1-212 604 7998). Subway F, V, 1, 2, 3 to 14th Street; L to Sixth Avenue. **Map** p403 D28.

Gay & lesbian health

See p374 **Helplines**.

House calls

NY Urgent Medical Services

Suite 1D, 952 Fifth Avenue, between 76th & 77th Streets (1-212 737 1212/www.travelmd.com). Subway 6 to 77th Street. **Open** 24hrs daily; appointments required. **Fees** *Weekday hotel visit* $300. *Weekday office visit* $175 (higher for nights and weekends). **Credit** MC, V. **Map** p405 E19.

Dr Ronald Primas and his partners provide their specialist medical attention right in your Manhattan hotel room or private residence, from a simple prescription to urgent medical care.

Pharmacies

Be aware that pharmacies in New York will not refill foreign prescriptions and may not sell the same over-the-counter products as you'll be used to at home.

Duane Reade

224 W 57th Street, at Broadway (1-212 541 9708/www.duanereade.com). Subway N, Q, R, W to 57th Street. **Open** 24hrs daily. **Credit** AmEx, MC, V. **Map** p405 D22.
This chain operates all over the city, and some stores are open 24 hours. Check the website for additional branches.
Other 24-hour locations: 24 E 14th Street, at University Place (1-212 989 3632); 155 E 34th Street, at Third Avenue (1-212 683 3042); 1279 Third Avenue, at 74th Street (1-212 744 2668); 2465 Broadway, at 91st Street (1-212 799 3172).

Rite Aid

303 W 50th Street, at Eighth Avenue (1-212 247 8736/www.riteaid.com). Subway C, E to 50th Street. **Open** 24hrs daily. **Credit** AmEx, Disc, MC, V. **Map** p404 D23.
Selected Rite Aid stores have 24-hour pharmacies. Call 1-800 748 3243 or check the Rite Aid website for a listing of all branches across the capital.
Other 24-hour locations: 408 Grand Street, at Clinton Street (1-212 529 7115); 301 W 50th Street, at Eighth Avenue (1-212 247 8384); 146 E 86th Street, between Lexington & Third Avenues (1-212 876 0600); 2833 Broadway at 110th Street (1-212 663 3135).

STDs, HIV & AIDS

Chelsea Clinic

303 Ninth Avenue, at 28th Street (1-212 720 7128). Subway C, E to 23rd Street. **Open** 8.30am-4.30pm Mon-Fri; 9am-2pm Sat. **Map** p404 B26.
Hours of local walk-in clinics may change at short notice, so be sure to call ahead before visiting. Arrive early, because day-to-day testing is offered on a first-come, first-served basis. (Check the phone book or see www.nyc.gov for other free clinics.)

Women's health

Liberty Women's Health Care of Queens

37-01 Main Street, at 37th Avenue, Flushing, Queens (1-718 888 0018/www.libertywomenshealth.com). Subway 7 to Flushing-Main Street. **Open** by appointment only. **Credit** MC, V. **Map** p412 W4.
This facility provides surgical and non-surgical abortions until the 24th week of pregnancy. Unlike many other clinics, Liberty uses abdominal ultrasound before, during and after the abortion to ensure safety.

Parkmed Eastern Women's Center

7th Floor, 800 Second Avenue, between 42nd & 43rd Streets (1-212 686 6066/www.easternwomenscenter.com). Subway 6 to 28th Street. **Open** by appointment only. **Credit** AmEx, Disc, MC, V. **Map** p404 F24.
Urine pregnancy tests are free. Counselling, contraception services and non-surgical abortions are also available at the centre.

Planned Parenthood of New York City

Margaret Sanger Center, 26 Bleecker Street, at Mott Street (1-212 965 7000/1-800 230 7526/www.ppnyc.org). Subway B, D, F, V to Broadway-Lafayette Street; N, R, W to Prince Street; 6 to Bleecker Street. **Open** 8am-4.30pm Mon, Tue; 8am-6.30pm Wed-Fri; 7.30am-4.30pm Sat. **Credit** AmEx, MC, V. **Map** p403 F29.
This is the best-known, most reasonably priced network of family-planning clinics in the US. Counselling and treatment are available for a full range of needs, including abortion, contraception, HIV testing and treatment of STDs. Call for more information on other services or to make an appointment at any of the centres. Walk-in clients are welcome for both emergency contraception and free pregnancy tests.
Other locations: 44 Court Street, between Joralemon & Remsen Streets, Brooklyn Heights, Brooklyn (appointments 1-212 965 7000).

Helplines

Alcohol & drug abuse

Alcoholics Anonymous

1-212 647 1680. **Open** 9am-10pm daily.

Cocaine Anonymous

24-hour recorded information 1-212 262 2463.

Drug Abuse Information Line

1-800 522 5353. **Open** 8am-10pm daily.
This hotline refers callers to recovery programmes around the state as well as to similar programmes in the rest of the US.

Pills Anonymous

24-hour recorded information 1-212 874 0700.
This helpline offers recorded information on drug-recovery programmes for users of marijuana, cocaine, alcohol and other addictive substances, as well as referrals to Narcotics Anonymous meetings. You can also leave a message.

Child abuse

Childhelp USA's National Child Abuse Hotline

1-800 422 4453. **Open** 24hrs daily.
Counsellors provide general crisis consultation and can help in an emergency. Callers include abused children, runaways and parents having problems with children.

Gay & lesbian

See p303.

Health

Visit the website of the **Centers for Disease Control and Prevention** (CDC) (www.cdc.gov) for up-to-date national health information, or call one of the toll-free hotlines below.

National STD & AIDS Hotline

1-800 342 2437. **Open** 24hrs daily.

Travelers' Health

1-877 394 8747 or visit CDC website. **Open** 24hrs daily.
Provides alerts on disease outbreaks and other information.

Psychological services

Samaritans

1-212 673 3000. **Open** 24hrs daily.

People who may be thinking of committing suicide or are suffering from depression, grief, sexual anxiety or alcoholism can call this volunteer organisation for advice.

Rape & sex crimes

Safe Horizon Crisis Hotline

1-212 577 7777/www.safehorizon.org. **Open** 24hrs daily.
Safe Horizon offers telephone and in-person counselling for any victim of domestic violence, rape or other crime, as well as providing practical help with any court procedures, compensation claims and legal aid.

Special Victims Liaison Unit of the New York Police Department

Rape hotline 1-212 267 7273. **Open** 24hrs daily.
Reports of sex crimes are fielded by a female detective from the Special Victims Liaison Unit. She will inform the appropriate precinct, send an ambulance if requested, and provide counselling and medical referrals. Other issues handled: violence against gays and lesbians, child victimisation, and referrals for the families and friends of crime victims.

St Luke's – Roosevelt Hospital Crime Victims Treatment Center

1-212 523 4728. **Open** 9am-5pm Mon-Fri.
The Rape Crisis Center provides a trained volunteer who will accompany you through all aspects of reporting a rape and getting emergency treatment.

Holidays

See p376 **Holidays**.

Insurance

If you are not an American, it's advisable to take out comprehensive insurance before arriving here; insurance for foreigners is almost impossible to arrange in the US. Make sure you have adequate health coverage; medical costs are high. For a list of New York urgent-care facilities, *see p373* **Emergency rooms**.

Internet

Internet access

Cyber Café

250 W 49th Street, between Broadway & Eighth Avenue (1-212 333 4109). Subway C, E, 1, 9 to 50th Street; N, R, W to 49th Street. **Open** 8am-11pm Mon-Fri; 11am-11pm Sat, Sun. **Cost** $6.40/30mins; 50¢/printed page. **Credit** AmEx, MC, V. **Map** p404 D23.
This is a standard internet access café that also happens to serve great coffee and snacks.

FedEx Kinko's

1-800 463 3339/www.fedex.com.
Outposts of this ubiquitous and very efficient computer and copy centre can be found peppered throughout the city.

New York Public Library

www.nypl.org.
The branch libraries throughout the five boroughs are great places to email and surf the web for free. However, the scarcity of computer stations may make for a long wait, and user time is limited. The Science, Industry and Business Library, 188 Madison Avenue, at 34th Street, has more than 40 workstations that you can use for up to an hour per day.

Wi-Fi

NYCWireless

www.nycwireless.net.
This group has established dozens of hot spots in the city for free wireless access. (For example, most parks below 59th Street are covered.) Visit the website for more information and a map.

Starbucks

www.starbucks.com. **Credit** AmEx, MC, V.
Many branches offer wireless access through T-Mobile (10¢/min).

Legal assistance

If you're arrested for a minor violation (disorderly conduct, harassment, loitering, rowdy partying, etc) and you are very polite to the officer during the arrest (and carry proper ID), then you'll probably get fingerprinted and also photographed at the station and be handed over a desk-appearance ticket with a date to show up at criminal court. After that, you'll most likely get to go home.

Arguing with a police officer or engaging in more serious criminal activity (such as possession of a weapon, drunken driving, illegal gambling or prostitution, for example) might get you 'processed', which means a 24- to 30-hour journey through the system. If the courts are backed up (and they usually are), you'll be held temporarily at a precinct pen. You can make a phone call after you've been fingerprinted. When you get through central booking, you'll arrive at 100 Centre Street for arraignment. A judge will decide whether you should be released on bail and will set a court date. If you can't post bail, then you'll be held at Rikers Island. The bottom line is simple: try not to get arrested, and if you are, don't act foolishly.

Legal Aid Society

1-212 577 3300/www.legal-aid.org. **Open** 9am-5pm Mon-Fri.
Legal Aid gives general information and referrals on a wide range of legal matters.

Sandback, Birnbaum & Michelen Criminal Law

1-800 640 2000. **Open** 24hrs daily.
You might want to carry these numbers with you, in case you find the cops reading you your rights in the middle of the night. If no one at this firm can help you, then you'll be directed to lawyers who can.

Libraries

See above **New York Public Library**.

Locksmiths

The emergency locksmiths listed below are open 24 hours for emergency jobs at short notice. Both require ID and proof of car ownership or residency (driving licence, car registration, utility bill).

Champion Locksmiths

30 locations in Manhattan (1-212 362 7000). **Cost** $20 service charge; $45 minimum to replace the lock. **Credit** AmEx, Disc, MC, V.

Elite Locksmiths

152 E 33rd Street, between Third & Lexington Avenues (1-212 685 1472). Subway 6 to 33rd Street. **Cost** fees vary, call for estimate. **No credit cards. Map** p404 F26.

Lost property

For property lost in the street, contact the police. For lost credit cards or travellers' cheques, *see p379*.

Buses & subways

New York City Metropolitan Transit Authority, 34th Street-Penn Station, near the A-train platform (1-212 712 4500). **Open** 8am-noon Mon-Wed, Fri; 11am-6.30pm Thur. **Map** p404 D25.

Call if you've left something on a subway train or a bus.

Grand Central Terminal

1-212 340 2555. **Open** 7am-6pm Mon-Fri; 8.45am-5pm Sat. Call if you've left something on a Metro-North train.

JFK Airport

1-718 244 4444, or contact your airline.

La Guardia Airport

1-718 533 3400, or contact your airline.

Newark Liberty International Airport

1-973 961 6230, or contact your airline.

Penn Station

1-212 630 7389. **Open** 7.30am-4pm Mon-Fri.
Call for items left on Amtrak, New Jersey Transit or the Long Island Rail Road.

Taxis

1-212 692 8294/www.nyc.gov/taxi.
Call for items left in a cab.

Holidays

New Year's Day
1 January

Martin Luther King Day
Third Monday in January

Presidents' Day
Third Monday in February

Memorial Day
Last Monday in May

Independence Day
4 July

Labor Day
First Monday in September

Columbus Day
Second Monday in October

Veterans Day
11 November

Thanksgiving Day
Fourth Thursday in November

Christmas Day
25 December

Media

Daily newspapers

Daily News

The *News* has drifted politically from the Neanderthal right to a more moderate but always tough-minded stance under the ownership of noted real-estate mogul Mort Zuckerman.

New York Post

Founded in 1801 by Alexander Hamilton, the *Post* is the nation's oldest continuously published daily newspaper. It has swerved sharply to the right under current owner Rupert Murdoch. The *Post* includes more gossip than any other local paper, and its headlines are often sassy and sensational.

The New York Times

As Olympian as ever after more than 150 years, the *Times* remains the city's, and the nation's, paper of record. It has the broadest and deepest coverage of world and national events and, as the masthead proclaims, it delivers 'All the News That's Fit to Print'. The mammoth *Sunday Times* can weigh a full 5lb and typically contains hundreds of pages, including a very well-regarded magazine, as well as book review, travel, real-estate and various other sections.

Other dailies

The *Amsterdam News*, one of the nation's oldest black newspapers, offers its own trenchant African-American viewpoint. New York also supports three Spanish-language dailies: *El Diario*, *Hoy* and *Noticias del Mundo*. *Newsday* is a Long Island-based daily with a tabloid format but a sober tone (it also has a city edition). *USA Today* keeps weary travellers abreast of national news. You may even find your own local paper at a Universal News shop (check the phone book for locations).

Weekly newspapers

Downtown journalism is a battlefield, pitting the *New York Press* against the *Village Voice*. The *Press* consists largely of opinion columns; it's full of youthful energy and irreverence, as well as cynicism and self-absorption. The *Voice* is sometimes passionate and ironic but just as often strident and predictable. Both papers are free. In contrast, the *New York Observer* focuses on the doings of the upper echelons of business, finance, media and politics. *Our Town*, *Chelsea Clinton News*, the *West Sider* and *Manhattan Spirit* are on the sidelines; these free sister publications feature neighbourhood news and local political gossip, and they can be found in street-corner dispensers around town. In a class all of its own is the hilarious, satirical national weekly *The Onion*.

Magazines

New York

This mag is part newsweekly, part lifestyle reporting and part listings.

The New Yorker

Since the 1920s the *New Yorker* has been known for its fine wit, elegant prose and sophisticated cartoons. Today, it's a forum for serious long-form journalism. It usually makes for a lively, intelligent read, in both paper form and on the well-made website.

Time Out New York

Of course, the best place to discover what's going on in town is *Time Out New York*. Based on the tried and trusted format of its London parent magazine, TONY is an indispensable guide to absolutely everything that is going on in the life of the city (if we do say so ourselves). Its Hot 100 restaurants is essential reading.

Passport update

People of all ages (children included) who enter the US on the Visa Waiver Progam (VWP; *see p383*) are now required to carry their own machine-readable passport, or MRP. MRPs are recognisable by the double row of characters along the foot of the data page. All burgundy EU and EU-lookalike passports issued in the UK since 1991 (that is, all that are still valid) should be machine readable. Some of those issued outside the country may not be, however; in this case, holders should apply for a replacement even if the passport has not expired. Check at your local passport-issuing post office if in any doubt at all.

The US's basic requirement for passports to contain a 'biometric' chip applies only to those issued from 26 October 2006. By then, all new and replacement UK passports should be compliant, following a gradual phase-in. The biometric chip contains a facial scan and detailed biographical data.

Though it is being considered for 2008 (when ID cards may be introduced), there is no current requirement for UK passports to contain fingerprint or iris data. The application process remains as it was, except for some new guidelines that ensure that the photograph you submit can be used to generate the facial scan in the chip.

Further information for UK citizens is available from www.passport.gov.uk. Nationals of other countries should check well in advance of their journey whether their current passport meets the requirements for the time of their trip, at http://travel.state.gov/visa and with the issuing authorities of their home country.

Other magazines

Since its launch back in 1996, the bimonthly *Black Book Magazine* has covered New York's high fashion and culture with intelligent bravado. *Gotham*, a monthly from the publisher of the glossy gab-rags *Hamptons* and *Aspen Peak*, unveiled its larger-than-life celeb-filled pages in 2001. And for two decades now, *Paper* has reported monthly on the city's trend-conscious, offering plenty of insider buzz on bars, clubs, downtown boutiques – and the people you'll find in them.

Radio

Nearly 100 stations serve the New York area. On the AM dial, you can find talk radio and phone-in shows that attract everyone from priests to sports nuts. Flip to FM for free jazz, the latest Franz Ferdinand single or any other auditory craving. Radio highlights are printed weekly in *Time Out New York*, and daily in the *Daily News*.

College radio

College radio is innovative and free of commercials. However, smaller transmitters mean that reception is often compromised by Manhattan's high-rise topography.

WNYU-FM 89.1 and **WKCR-FM 89.9** are, respectively, the stations of New York University and Columbia; programming spans the musical spectrum. **WFUV-FM 90.7**, Fordham University's station, plays mostly folk and Irish music but also airs a variety of shows, including *Beale Street Caravan*, easily the most widely distributed blues programme in the world.

Dance & pop

American commercial radio is rigidly formatted, which makes most pop stations extremely tedious and repetitive during the day. Tune in on evenings and weekends for more interesting programming. Always popular, **WQHT-FM 97.1**, 'Hot 97,' is a commercial hip hop station with all-day rap and R&B. **WKTU-FM 103.5** is the premier dance music station. **WWPR-FM 105.1**, 'Power 105,' plays top hip hop, and a few old-school hits. **WBLS-FM 107.5** showcases classic and new funk, soul and R&B.

Jazz

WBGO-FM 88.3 is strictly jazz. Dee Dee Bridgewater's weekly *JazzSet* programme features many legendary artists. **WKCR-FM 89.9**, the student-run radio station of Columbia University, is where you'll hear the sounds of legendary jazz DJ Phil Schaap.

Rock

WSOU-FM 89.5, the station of Seton Hall University, a Catholic college, focuses primarily on hard rock and heavy metal. **WAXQ-FM 104.3** offers classic rock. **WXRK-FM 92.3**'s alternative music format attracts and appals morning listeners with its 6-10am weekday sleaze-fest.

Other music

WQEW-AM 1560, 'Radio Disney', has kids' programming. **WNYC-FM 93.9** and **WQXR-FM 96.3** serve up a range of classical music; WNYC tends towards the progressive end of the classical spectrum. **WCAA-FM 105.9** and **WZAA-FM 92.7** spin Spanish and Latin.

News & talk

WABC-AM 770, **WCBS-AM 880**, **WINS-AM 1010** and **WBBR-AM 1130** (*see also below* **Sports**) offer news throughout the day, plus traffic and weather reports. WABC hosts a morning show featuring the street-accented demagoguery of Guardian Angels founder Curtis Sliwa along with civil-rights attorney Ron Kuby (weekdays 5-10am). Right-winger Rush Limbaugh also airs his views here (noon-3pm).

WNYC-AM 820/FM 93.9, a commercial-free, public radio station, provides news and current-affairs commentary. **WBAI-FM 99.5** is a left-leaning community radio station. **WLIB-AM 1190** is the flagship station of Air America, a far more liberal answer to right-wing talk radio.

Sports

WFAN-AM 660 airs Giants, Nets, Mets and Devils games. Talk-radio fixture Don Imus offers his opinion on… everything (5.30-10am Mon-Fri). **WCBS-AM 880** covers the Yankees, New York's pride and joy.

WEPN-AM 1050 is devoted to news and sports talk and is the home of the Jets, Knicks and Rangers. **WBBR-AM 1130** broadcasts Islanders games. **WADO-AM 1280** provides Spanish-language coverage of many sports events.

Television

A visit to New York often includes some TV time, which can cause often culture shock, particularly for British and European visitors.

Time Out New York offers a rundown of TV highlights. For full schedules, save the *Sunday New York Times* TV section or buy a daily paper.

Networks

Six major networks broadcast nationwide. All offer ratings-driven variations on a theme.

CBS (Channel 2 in NYC) has the top investigative show, *60 Minutes*, on Sundays at 7pm; overall, programming is geared to a middle-aged demographic, but CBS also screens reality shows like *Survivor*. **NBC** (4) is the home of *Law & Order*, the long-running sketch-comedy series *Saturday Night Live* (11.30pm Sat), and popular primetime shows including *The Apprentice*, *Fear Factor*, *ER*, *Scrubs*, *The Office* and *My Name is Earl*. **Fox-WNYW** (5) is popular with younger audiences for shows like *The Simpsons* and *American Idol*. **ABC** (7) is the king of daytime soaps and family-friendly sitcoms. ABC continues to score with its hits: *Desperate Housewives* and *Lost*.

WXTV and **WNJU** are Spanish-language channels that offer game shows and racy Mexican dramas. They're also your best non-cable bets for soccer.

Public TV

Public TV is on channels 13, 21 and 25. Documentaries, arts shows and science series alternate with *Masterpiece Theatre* and reruns of British shows like *Inspector Morse*. Channel 21 broadcasts BBC World News daily at 6am and at 7pm and 11pm.

Cable

For channel numbers for Time Warner Cable or for systems such as Cablevision or RCN, check a local newspaper's TV listings.

Nickelodeon presents shows suitable for kids and adults nostalgic for shows like *The Brady Bunch* and *Happy Days*. **NY1** focuses on local news. The **History Channel**, **Sci Fi** and the **Weather Channel** are self-explanatory. **Discovery Channel** and the **Learning Channel** feature educational nature and science programmes.

VH1, MTV's mature sibling, features programmes that delve into the lives of artists such as Eminem, LL Cool J, Beyoncé Knowles and Nick Lachey. You can also catch *Surreal Life* and *Best Week Ever*. MTV increasingly offers fewer music videos and more of its original programming (*Laguna Beach*, *My Super Sixteen* and *The Real World*). **FUSE**, a new music-video channel, aims for early MTV style.

FSN (Fox Sports Network), **MSG** (Madison Square Garden), **ESPN** and **ESPN2** are all-sports stations.

Bravo shows arts programming, such as *Inside the Actors Studio*, art-house films and *Queer Eye for the Straight Guy*.

Comedy Central is all comedy, airing *South Park* and *The Daily Show* with Jon Stewart.

Cinemax, the **Disney Channel**, **HBO**, the **Movie Channel** and **Showtime** are premium channels often available in hotels. They show uninterrupted feature films, exclusive specials and acclaimed series like *The Sopranos*, *Entourage* and *Curb Your Enthusiasm*.

Money

Over the past few years, much of American currency has undergone a subtle facelift, partly to deter increasingly adept counterfeiters. However, 'old' money still remains in circulation. All denominations except for the $1 bill have recently been updated by the US Treasury. One US dollar ($) equals 100 cents (¢). Coins include copper pennies (1¢) and silver-coloured nickels (5¢), dimes (10¢) and quarters (25¢). Half-dollar coins (50¢) and the gold-coloured dollar coins are less commonly seen, except as change from vending machines.

All paper money is the same size, so make sure you fork over the right bill. It comes in denominations of $1, $2, $5, $10, $20, $50 and $100 (and higher, but you'll never see those bills). The $2 bills are quite rare and make a smart souvenir. Small shops will seldom break a $50 or $100 bill, and cab drivers aren't required to change bills larger than $20, so it's best to carry smaller denominations just to be on the safe side.

ATMs

The city is full of automated teller machines (ATMs), located in bank branches, delis and many small shops. Most accept American Express, MasterCard, Visa and major bank cards, if they have been registered with a personal identification number (PIN). Commonly, there's a usage fee of $1.50 to $2, though the superior exchange rate often makes ATMs worth the extra charge. Holders of accounts at out-of-country banks can also use ATMs but the fees can be high. Though you don't always pay the local charge, some UK banks charge up to £4 per transaction plus a variable payment to cover themselves against any exchange rate fluctuations. Yes, it sounds as dodgy to us as it probably does to you.

US bank account holders who have lost their PIN or whose card is damaged can usually get cash from branches of their bank with proper ID.

Most ATM cards now double as charge cards, if they bear Maestro or Cirrus logos. You can get cashback on this at supermarkets, British customers included (theoretically, and for a percentage charge), though in practice it seems only to work at certain outlets.

Banks & currency exchange

Banks are generally open from 9am to 3pm Monday to Friday, though some stay open longer and on Saturdays. You need a photo ID, such as a passport, to cash travellers' cheques. Many banks will not exchange foreign currency, and the bureaux de change, limited to tourist-trap areas, close between 6pm and 7pm. It's best to arrive in the city with a few dollars in cash and to pay mostly with credit cards or travellers' cheques (accepted in most restaurants and larger stores – but do ask first, and be prepared to show ID). In emergencies, most large hotels will offer 24-hour exchange facilities; the catch is that they charge high commissions and don't give good rates.

Chase Bank

1-212 935 9935/www.chase.com.
Chase's website gives information on foreign currency exchange, banking locations and credit cards. For foreign currency delivered in a hurry, call the number listed above.

Commerce Bank

1-888 751 9000/www.commerce online.com.
All of Commerce Bank's 17 separate Manhattan locations are open seven days a week.

People's Foreign Exchange

3rd Floor, 575 Fifth Avenue, at 47th Street (1-212 883 0550). Subway E, V to Fifth Avenue-53rd Street; 7 to Fifth Avenue. **Open** 9am-6pm Mon-Fri; 10am-3pm Sat, Sun. **Map** p404 E23.
People's provides foreign exchange on bank notes and also travellers' cheques of any denomination for a $2 fee.

Travelex

29 Broadway, at Morris Street (1-800 815 1795). Subway 4, 5 to Bowling Green. **Open** 9am-5pm Mon-Fri. **Map** p402 E33.
A complete range of foreign-exchange services is offered.
Other locations: 510 Madison Avenue, at 53rd Street (1-212 753 0117).

Credit cards

Bring plastic if you have it, or be prepared for a logistical nightmare. Credit cards are essential for renting cars and booking hotels, and handy for buying tickets over the phone and the internet. The five major cards accepted in the US are American Express, Diners Club, Discover, MasterCard and Visa. If cards are lost or stolen, contact:

American Express

1-800 528 2122.

Diners Club

1-800 234 6377.

Discover

1-800 347 2683.

MasterCard/Maestro

1-800 826 2181.

Visa/Cirrus

1-800 336 8472.

Travellers' cheques

Like credit cards, travellers' cheques are also routinely accepted at banks, stores and restaurants throughout the city. Bring your driver's licence or passport for identification. If cheques are lost or stolen, contact:

American Express

1-800 221 7282.

Thomas Cook

1-800 223 7373.

Visa

1-800 336 8472.

Wire services

If you run out of cash, don't expect the folks at your consulate to lend you money. In case of an emergency, you can have money wired to you from your home.

MoneyGram

1-800 666 3947/www.money gram.com.

Western Union

1-800 325 6000/www.westernunion.com.

Postal services

Stamps are available at all US post offices and from drugstore vending machines and at most newsstands. It costs 41¢ to send a 1oz letter within the US. Each additional ounce costs 26¢. Postcards mailed within the US cost 26¢; for international postcards, it's 90¢. Airmailed letters to anywhere overseas cost 80¢ for the first ounce and 90¢ for each additional ounce.

For faster Express Mail, you must fill out a form, either at a post office or by arranging a pickup; 24-hour delivery to major US cities is guaranteed. International delivery takes two to three days, with no guarantee. Call 1-800 275 8777 for more information.

General Post Office

421 Eighth Avenue, between 31st & 33rd Streets (24hr information 1-800 275 8777/www.usps.com). Subway A, C, E to 34th Street-Penn Station. **Open** 24hrs daily. **Credit** MC, V. **Map** p404 D25.
This is the city's main post office; call for the branch nearest you. Queues are long, but stamps are available from vending machines. Branches are usually open 9am-5pm Mon-Fri; hours vary Sat.

General Delivery

390 Ninth Avenue, between 31st & 33rd Streets (1-212 330 3099). Subway A, C, E to 34th Street-Penn Station. **Open** 10am-1pm Mon-Sat. **Map** p404 C25.
US residents without local addresses can receive their mail here; it should be addressed to the recipient, General Delivery, 390 Ninth Avenue, New York, NY 10001. You will need to show a passport or ID card when picking up letters.

Poste Restante

Window 29, 421 Eighth Avenue, between 31st & 33rd Streets (1-212 330 2912). Subway A, C, E to 34th Street-Penn Station. **Open** 8am-6pm Mon-Sat. **Map** p404 D25.
Foreign visitors can receive mail here; mail should be addressed to the recipient, General Post Office, Poste Restante, 421 Eighth Avenue, attn: Window 29, New York, NY 10001. Be sure to bring ID.

Religion

Here are just a few of New York's many places of worship. Check the phone book for more listings.

Baptist

Abyssinian Baptist Church
For listing, *see p152*.

Buddhist

New York Buddhist Church
331-332 Riverside Drive, between 105th & 106th Streets (1-212 678 0305/www.newyorkbuddhistchurch.org). Subway 1 to 103rd Street. **Map** p406 B16.

Catholic

St Patrick's Cathedral
For listing, *see p133*.

Episcopal

Cathedral Church of St John the Divine
For listing, *see p149*.

Jewish

UJA–Federation of New York Resource Line
1-212 753 2288/www.ujafedny.org. **Open** 9am-5pm Mon-Thur; 9am-4pm Fri.
This hotline provides referrals to other organisations, groups, temples, philanthropic activities and synagogues.

Methodist

Church of St Paul & St Andrew, United Methodist
263 W 86th Street, between Broadway & West End Avenue (1-212 362 3179/www.spsanyc.org). Subway 1 to 86th Street. **Map** p406 C18.

Muslim

Islamic Cultural Center of New York
1711 Third Avenue, between 96th & 97th Streets (1-212 722 5234). Subway 6 to 96th Street. **Map** p406 F17.

Presbyterian

Madison Avenue Presbyterian Church
921 Madison Avenue, at 73rd Street (1-212 288 8920/www.mapc.com). Subway 6 to 72nd Street. **Map** p405 E20.

Restrooms

See p385 **Loo lowdown**.

Size charts

Women's clothing

UK	Europe	US
4	32	2
6	34	4
8	36	6
10	38	8
12	40	10
14	42	12
16	44	14

Women's shoes

UK	Europe	US
33	36	5
4	37	6
5	38	7
6	39	8
7	40	9
8	41	10
9	42	11

Men's suits

UK	Europe	US
34	44	34
36	46	36
38	48	38
40	50	40
42	52	42
44	54	44
46	56	46

Men's shoes

UK	Europe	US
36	39	7
71/2	40	71/2
8	41	8
8	42	81/2
9	43	91/2
10	44	101/2
11	45	11

Safety

New York's crime rate, particularly for violent crime, has waned during the past decade. Most crime occurs late at night in low-income neighbourhoods. Don't arrive thinking your safety is at risk wherever you go; it is unlikely that you will ever be bothered.

Still, a bit of common sense won't hurt. Don't flaunt your money and valuables, and try not to look obviously lost. Avoid deserted and poorly lit streets; walk facing oncoming traffic so no one can drive up alongside you undetected, and close to or on the street; muggers prefer to hang back in doorways and shadows. If you are threatened, hand over your valuables at once (your attacker will likely be as anxious to get it over with as you), then dial 911 as soon as you can (it's a free call).

Be extra alert to pickpockets and street hustlers – especially in crowded tourist areas like Times Square – and be wary of diversionary jostles.

Smoking

New Yorkers live under some of the strictest anti-smoking laws on the planet. The 1995 NYC Smoke-Free Air Act makes it illegal to smoke in virtually all indoor public places, including the subway and cinemas. More recent legislation went even further, banning smoking in nearly all restaurants and bars; for a list of exceptions, *see p224* **Lighting up**. Do be sure to ask before you light up.

Students

Student life in NYC is unlike it is anywhere else in the world. An endless extracurricular education exists right outside the dorm room – the city is both teacher and playground. For further guidance, check the

Time Out New York Student Guide, available in August for free on campuses, and $2.95 at Hudson News outlets (consult the phone book for locations).

Student identification

Foreign students should get hold of an International Student Identity Card (ISIC) as proof of student status and in order to secure discounts. These can be bought from your local student-travel agent (ask at your student union or *see below* **STA Travel**). If you buy the card in New York, then you will also get basic accident insurance thrown in – a bargain.

Student travel

Most agents offer discount fares for those under 26. For specialists in student travel deals, visit:

STA Travel

205 E 42nd Street, between Second & Third Avenues (1-212 822 2700/ for other locations 1-800 777 0112/ www.statravel.com). Subway 42nd Street S, 4, 5, 6, 7 to 42nd Street-Grand Central. **Open** 10am-6pm Mon-Sat. **Map** p404 F24.

Tax & tipping

In restaurants, it is customary to tip at least 15 per cent, and since NYC tax is 8.625 per cent, a quick method for calculating the tip is to double the tax. In many restaurants, when you are with a group of six or more, the tip will be included in the bill. For tipping on taxi fares, *see p369*.

Telephones

New York, like most of the world's busy cities, is overrun with telephones, cellular phones, pagers and faxes. (Check with your network operator that the service will be available here.) This increasing dependence on a dial tone accounts for the city's abundance of area codes. As a rule, you must dial 1 + the area code before a number, even if the place you are calling is in the same area code. The area codes for Manhattan are 212 and 646; Brooklyn, Queens, Staten Island and the Bronx are 718 and 347; 917 is now reserved mostly for mobile phones and pagers. Long Island area codes are 516 and 631; codes for New Jersey are 201, 551, 848, 862, 609, 732, 856, 908 and 973. Numbers preceded by 800, 877 and 888 are free of charge when dialled from anywhere in the US.

General information

The Yellow Pages and the White Pages phone books contain a wealth of useful information in the front, including theatre-seating diagrams and maps; the blue pages in the centre of the White Pages directory list all government numbers and addresses. Hotels will have copies; otherwise, check the shelves of local libraries.

Collect calls & credit card calls

Collect calls are also known as reverse-charge calls. To make one, dial 0 followed by the number, or dial AT&T's 1-800 225 5288, MCI's 1-800 265 5328 or Sprint's 1-800 663 3463.

Directory assistance

Dial 411 or 1 + area code + 555 1212. Doing so may cost nothing, depending on the payphone you are using; carrier fees may apply. Long-distance directory assistance may also incur long-distance charges. For a directory of toll-free numbers, dial 1-800 555 1212.

Emergency

Dial 911. All calls are free (including those from pay- and mobile phones).

International calls

Dial 011 + country code (Australia 61; New Zealand 64; UK 44), then the number.

Operator assistance

Dial 0.

Pagers & mobiles

Most US mobile phones will work in NY but since the US doesn't have a standard national network, visitors should check with their provider that their phone will work here, and whether they need to unlock a roaming option. Visitors from other countries will need a tri-band handset and a roaming agreement, and may find charges so high that rental, or, depending on the length of their stay, purchase of a US phone (or SIM card) will make better economic sense.

If you carry a mobile phone, make sure you turn it off on trains and buses and at restaurants, plays, movies, concerts and museums. New Yorkers are quick to show their annoyance at an ill-timed ring. Some establishments now even post signs designating 'cellular-free zones'.

InTouch USA

1-800 872 7626. **Open** 8am-5.30pm Mon-Fri. **Credit** AmEx, DC, Disc, MC, V.

InTouch, the city's largest mobile-phone rental company, leases equipment by the day, week or month.

Public payphones & phonecards

Public payphones are easy to find. Some of them even work (non-Verizon phones tend to be poorly maintained). Phones take any combination of silver coins: local calls usually cost 25¢ for three minutes; a few payphones require 50¢ but allow unlimited time on the call. If you're not used to US phones, then note that the ringing tone is long; the 'engaged' tone, or busy signal, is much shorter and higher pitched.

To call long-distance or to make an international call from a payphone, you need to go through a **long-distance**

company. Most of the payphones in New York automatically use AT&T, but phones in and around transportation hubs usually contract other long-distance carriers, and charges can be outrageous. MCI and Sprint are respected brand names (*see above* **Collect calls & credit-card calls**). Make the call by either dialling 0 for an operator or dialling direct, which is cheaper. To find out how much it will cost, dial the number, and a computerised voice will tell you how much money to deposit. You can pay for calls with your credit card.

The best way to make long-distance calls is with a phonecard, available from any post-office branch or from chain stores like Duane Reade or Rite Aid (*see p374* **Pharmacies**). Both delis and newspaper kiosks sell phonecards, including the New York Exclusive, which has favourable international rates.

Telephone answering service

Messages Plus Inc

1317 Third Avenue, between 75th & 76th Streets (1-212 879 4144). Subway 6 to 77th Street. **Open** 24hrs daily. **Credit** AmEx, DC, Disc, MC, V. **Map** p405 F20.
Messages Plus provides an answering service with specialised (medical, bilingual, etc) receptionists, if required, and plenty of ways to deliver your messages.

Tickets

It's always show time somewhere in New York. And depending on what you're after – music, sports, theatre – scoring tickets can be a real hassle. Smaller venues often have their own box offices. Large arenas like Madison Square Garden have ticket agencies – and many devoted spectators. You may have to try more than one tactic to get into a popular show.

Box-office tickets

Fandango

1-800 326 3264/www.fandango.com. **Open** 24hrs daily. **Surcharge** $1.50 per ticket. **Credit** AmEx, Disc, MC, V.
Fandango is one of the newer services to offer advance credit card purchase of movie tickets online or over the phone. Tickets can be picked up at an automated kiosk in the theatre lobby (but this is not available in all theatres).

Moviefone

1-212 777 FILM/www.moviefone.com. **Open** 24hrs daily. **Surcharge** $1.50 ($1 if purchased online) per ticket. **Credit** AmEx, Disc, MC, V.
Purchase advance film tickets by credit card over the phone or online; pick them up at an automated kiosk in the theatre lobby. This service is not available for every theatre.

Telecharge

1-212 239 6200/www.telecharge.com. **Open** 24hrs daily. **Average surcharge** $6 per ticket. **Credit** AmEx, DC, Disc, MC, V.
A good range of tickets both for Broadway and Off Broadway shows are on offer here.

Ticket Central

416 W 42nd Street, between Ninth & Tenth Avenues (1-212 279 4200/www.ticketcentral.com). Subway N, Q, R, W, 42nd Street S, 1, 2, 3, 7 to 42nd Street-Times Square. **Open** *Box office & phone orders* noon-8pm daily. **Surcharge** varies with ticket price. **Credit** AmEx, MC, V. **Map** p404 C24.
Both Off and Off-Off Broadway tickets are available at the office or by phone.

Ticketmaster

1-212 307 4100/www.ticketmaster.com. **Surcharge** $3-$10 per ticket. **Credit** AmEx, DC, Disc, MC, V.
This reliable service sells tickets to rock concerts, Broadway shows, sports events and more. You can buy the tickets by phone, online or at outlets throughout the city, of which there are many.

TKTS

Duffy Square, 47th Street, at Broadway (1-212 221 0013/www.tdf.org). Subway N, Q, R, W, 42nd Street S, 1, 2, 3, 7 to 42nd Street-Times Square. **Open** 3-8pm Mon-Sat; 11am-7pm Sun. *Matinée tickets* 10am-2pm Wed, Sat; 11am-2pm Sun. **Surcharge** $3 per ticket. **No credit cards. Map** p404 D23.
TKTS has become a New York tradition. Broadway and Off Broadway tickets are sold at discounts of 25%, 35% and even 50% for same-day performances. **Other locations**: 199 Water Street; booth is at the corner of Front and John Streets.

Scalpers & standby tickets

When a show sells out, there's always the illegal scalper option, though the risk that you might end up with a forged ticket does exist. Before you part with cash, make sure that the ticket has all of the correct details, and be warned: the police have been cracking down on such trade of late.

Some venues also offer standby tickets right before show time, while other places give reduced rates for tickets purchased on the same day as the performance for which they're for.

Ticket brokers

Ticket brokers function like scalpers but are legal because they operate from out of state. They can almost guarantee tickets, however costly, for sold-out events and tend to deal only in better seats. On top of this, they also tend to be a great deal less seedy and more regularly patronised than their UK equivalents. For a list of local brokers, look under Ticket Sales in the Yellow Pages.

Apex Tours

1-800 248 9849/www.tixx.com. **Open** 9am-5pm Mon-Fri. **Credit** AmEx, Disc, MC, V.

Prestige Entertainment

1-800 243 8849/www.prestigeentertainment.com. **Open** 8am-6pm Mon-Fri; 8am-5pm Sat; 11am-3pm Sun. **Credit** AmEx, MC, V.

TicketCity

1-800 765 3688/www.ticketcity.com. **Open** 8.30am-8pm Mon-Fri; 10am-6pm Sat; 11am-4pm Sun. **Credit** AmEx, Disc, MC, V.

Time & date

New York is on Eastern Standard Time, which extends from the Atlantic coast to the eastern shore of Lake Michigan and south to the Gulf of Mexico. This is five hours behind Greenwich Mean Time. Clocks are set forward one hour in early March for Daylight Savings Time and back one hour at the beginning of November. Going from east to west, Eastern Time is one hour ahead of Central Time, two hours ahead of Mountain Time and three hours ahead of Pacific Time. In the United States, the date is written as month, day and year; so 2/8/08 is 8 February 2008. Forms that foreigners may need to fill in, however, are often the other way round.

Toilets

See p385 **Loo lowdown**.

Tourist information

NYC & Company

810 Seventh Avenue, between 52nd & 53rd Streets (1-800 NYC VISIT/www.nycvisit.com). Subway B, D, E to Seventh Avenue. **Open** 8.30am-6pm Mon-Fri; 9am-5pm Sat, Sun. **Map** p404 D23.

The city's official (private, non-profit) visitors' and information centre doles out maps, leaflets, coupons and advice, and provides information on tour operators and travel agents.

Other locations: 33-34 Carnaby Street, London W1V 1CA, England (020 7437 8300).

Times Square Visitors Center

1560 Broadway, between 46th & 47th Streets (1-212 869 1890). Subway N, Q, R, W, 42nd Street S, 1, 2, 3, 7 to 42nd Street-Times Square. **Open** 8am-8pm daily. **Map** p404 D24.

This centre offers discount coupons for Broadway tickets, internet access, MetroCards, free maps and other useful goods and services, predominantly for Theatreland.

Visas & immigration

Visas

Some 27 countries currently participate in the **Visa Waiver Program** (VWP). Citizens of Andorra, Australia, Austria, Belgium, Brunei, Denmark, Finland, France, Germany, Iceland, Ireland, Italy, Japan, Liechtenstein, Luxembourg, Monaco, the Netherlands, New Zealand, Norway, Portugal, San Marino, Singapore, Slovenia, Spain, Sweden, Switzerland and the UK do not need a visa for stays in the US shorter than 90 days (business or pleasure) as long as they have a machine-readable passport valid for the full 90-day period and a return ticket. *See also p377* **Passport update**.

If you do not qualify for entry under the VWP, that is if you are not from one of the eligible countries or are visiting for any purpose other than pleasure or business, you will need a visa. Media workers and students note: this includes you. If you are in even the slightest doubt, check ahead. You can obtain the application forms from your nearest US embassy or consulate or from its website. Enquire several months ahead of travel to ask how long the application process is currently taking.

Canadians travelling to the US need visas only in special circumstances.

Whether or not you have a visa, it is not advisable to travel on a passport with six months or less to run.

If you lose your passport inside the US, contact your consulate (*see p372*).

Immigration

Your airline will give all visitors an immigration form to be presented to an official when you land. Fill it in clearly and be prepared to give an address at which you are staying (a hotel is fine).

Upon arrival, you may have to wait an hour or, if you're unlucky, considerably longer, in Immigration, where owing to tightened security you can expect slow-moving queues. You may be expected to explain your visit; be polite and prepared. Note that all visitors to the US are now photographed and fingerprinted on arrival on every trip. You will usually be granted an entry permit.

US Embassy Visa Information

In the US, 1-202 663 1225/in the UK, 09055 444546, 60p per minute/http://travel.state.gov/visa.

When to go

There is no bad time to visit New York, and visitor numbers are fairly steady year-round. The weather can be unpleasantly hot in summer and charmingly, then tediously, snowy in the winter months.

Working in NY

Non-nationals cannot work in the United States without the appropriate visa; these are hard to get and generally require you to prove that your job could not be done by a US citizen. Contact your local embassy for further details. Some student visas allow part-time work after the first academic year.

UK students who want to spend a summer vacation working in the States should contact the British Universities North America Club (BUNAC) for help in securing themselves a temporary job and also the requisite visa (16 Bowling Green Lane, London, EC1R 0QH, England; 020 7251 3472, www.bunac.org/uk).

Further Reference

Books

See also pp276-278.

Edward F Bergman *The Spiritual Traveler: New York City* A guide to sacred and peaceful spaces in the city.

Eleanor Berman *Away for the Weekend: New York* Trips within a 200-mile radius of New York City. *New York Neighborhoods* Foodie guide focusing on ethnic enclaves.

William Corbett *New York Literary Lights* A compendium of detailed information about NYC's literary past.

Dave Frattini *The Underground Guide to New York City Subways*

Gerri Gallagher and Jill Fairchild *Where to Wear* A staple for shopaholics.

Suzanne Gerber *Vegetarian New York City* Going meat free in and around Manhattan.

Alfred Gingold and Helen Rogan *Cool Parent's Guide to All of New York.*

Hagstrom *New York City 5 Borough Pocket Atlas* You won't get lost so long as you carry this thorough street map.

Colleen Kane (ed) *Sexy New York City* Discover erotica in the Naked City.

Chuck Katz *Manhattan on Film 2*

Lyn Skreczko and Virginia Bell *The Manhattan Health Pages*

Earl Steinbicker (ed) *Daytrips New York*

Linda Tarrant-Reid *Discovering Black New York* Local museums, landmarks and more.

Time Out *New York Eating & Drinking 2008* The annual comprehensive critics' guide to thousands of places to eat and drink in the five boroughs.

Architecture

Richard Berenholtz *New York, New York* Mini panoramic images of the city through the seasons.

Stanley Greenberg *Invisible New York* Photographic account of hidden architectural triumphs.

Landmarks Preservation Commission *New York City Landmarks Preservation Guide*

Karl Sabbagh *Skyscraper* How the tall ones are built.

Robert AM Stern et al *New York 1930* A massive coffee-table slab with stunning pictures.

Norval White & Elliot Willensky *AIA Guide to New York City* A comprehensive directory of important buildings.

Gerard R Wolfe *New York: A Guide to the Metropolis* Historical and architectural walking tours.

Culture & recollections

Irving Lewis Allen *The City in Slang* How NY has spawned new words and phrases.

Candace Bushnell *Sex & the City; Trading Up* Smart women, superficial New York.

George Chauncey *Gay New York* The evolution of gay culture from 1890 to 1940.

Martha Cooper and Henry Chalfant *Subway Art.*

Josh Alan Friedman *Tales of Times Square* Sleaze and decay in the old Times Square.

Nelson George *Hip Hop America* The real history of hip hop, from Grandmaster Flash to Puff Daddy.

Robert Hendrickson *New Yawk Tawk* Dictionary of NYC slang.

Jane Jacobs *The Death and Life of Great American Cities.*

AJ Liebling *Back Where I Came From* Personal recollections from the New Yorker columnist.

Gillian McCain and Legs McNeil *Please Kill Me* Oral history of the '70s punk scene.

Frank O'Hara *The Collected Poems of Frank O'Hara* The great NYC poet found inspiration in his hometown.

Andrés Torres *Between Melting Pot and Mosaic* African-American and Puerto Rican life in the city.

Heather Holland Wheaton *Eight Million Stories in a New York Minute.*

EB White *Here Is New York* A clear-eyed love letter to Gotham.

Fiction

Kurt Andersen *Turn of the Century* Millennial Manhattan seen through the eyes of media players.

Paul Auster *The New York Trilogy: City of Glass, Ghosts, and the Locked Room* A search for the madness behind the method of Manhattan's grid.

Kevin Baker *Dreamland* A poetic novel about Coney Island's glory days.

James A Baldwin *Another Country* Racism under the bohemian veneer of the 1960s.

Michael Chabon *The Amazing Adventures of Kavalier and Clay* Pulitzer Prize-winning account of Jewish comic-book artists struggling with crises of identity in the 1940s.

Bret Easton Ellis *Glamorama* A satirical view of dazzling New York City nightlife.

Jack Finney *Time and Again* An illustrator travels back to 19th-century NY.

Larry Kramer *Faggots* Devastating satire of gay NY.

Phillip Lopate (ed) *Writing New York* An excellent anthology of short stories, essays and poems.

Tim McLoughlin (ed) *Brooklyn Noir* An anthology of crime tales set in Brooklyn.

Time Out *Book of New York Short Stories* Naturally, we like these original short stories by 23 US and British authors.

Toni Morrison *Jazz* 1920s Harlem.

David Schickler *Kissing in Manhattan* Explores the lives of quirky tenants in a teeming Manhattan block.

Hubert Selby Jr *Last Exit to Brooklyn* Dockland degradation, circa 1950s.

Edith Wharton *Old New York* Four novellas of 19th-century New York.

Colson Whitehead *The Colossus of New York: A City in 13 Parts* A lyrical tribute to city life.

Tom Wolfe *The Bonfire of the Vanities* Rich/poor, black/white. An unmatched slice of 1980s New York.

History

See p30 **Further reading**.

Films

Annie Hall (1977) Woody Allen co-stars with Diane Keaton in this appealingly neurotic valentine to living and loving in Manhattan.

Breakfast at Tiffany's (1961) Blake Edwards gave Audrey Hepburn her signature role as the cash-poor, time-rich socialite Holly Golightly.

Dog Day Afternoon (1975) Al Pacino makes for a great antihero as a Brooklyn bank robber in Sidney Lumet's uproarious classic.

Do the Right Thing (1989) The hottest day of the summer leads to racial strife in Bedford-Stuyvesant in Spike Lee's incisive drama.

The French Connection (1971) As detective Jimmy 'Popeye' Doyle, Gene Hackman ignores all traffic lights to chase down drug traffickers in William Friedkin's much-imitated thriller.

Public loo lowdown

Where to go when you've simply got to go.

Downtown

Battery Park *Castle Clinton. Subway 1 to South Ferry; 4, 5 to Bowling Green.*

Tompkins Square Park *Avenue A, at 9th Street. Subway L to First Avenue; 6 to Astor Place*

Washington Square Park *Thompson Street, at Washington Square South. Subway A, B, C, D, E, F, V to W 4th Street.*

Midtown

Bryant Park *42nd Street, between Fifth and Sixth Avenues. Subway B, D, F, V to 42nd St-Bryant Park; 7 to Fifth Avenue.*

Grand Central Terminal *42nd Street, at Park Avenue, Lower Concourse. Subway 42nd St reet S, 4, 5, 6, 7 to 42nd Street-Grand Central.*

Penn Station *Seventh Avenue, between 31st & 33rd Streets. Subway A, C, E, 1, 2, 3 to 34th Street-Penn Station.*

Uptown

Avery Fisher Hall *Broadway, at 65th Street. Subway: 1 to 66th Street-Lincoln Center.*

Charles A Dana Discovery Center *Central Park, north side of Harlem Meer, 110th Street, at Malcolm X Blvd (Lenox Avenue). Subway 2, 3 to 110th Street-Central Park North.*

Delacorte Theater *Central Park, midpark, at 81st Street. Subway: B, C to 81st Street-Museum of Natural History.*

The Godfather (1972) and **The Godfather: Part II** (1974) Francis Ford Coppola's brilliant commentary about capitalism in America is told through the violent saga of Italian gangsters.
Mean Streets (1973) Robert De Niro and Harvey Keitel shine as small-time Little Italy hoods in Martin Scorsese's breakthrough film, which still shocks today.
Midnight Cowboy (1969) Street creatures 'Ratso' Rizzo and Joe Buck face an unforgiving Times Square in John Schlesinger's darkly-amusing classic.
Spider-Man (2002) The comic-book web-slinger from Forest Hills comes to life in Sam Raimi's pitch-perfect crowd pleaser.
Taxi Driver (1976) Robert De Niro is a crazed cabbie who sees all of New York as a den of iniquity in Martin Scorsese's bold drama.

Music

For more on New York greatest musicians, *see pp49-52* **New York Rocks**.

Beastie Boys 'No Sleep Till Brooklyn' These now middle-aged hip hoppers began showing their love for their fave borough two decades ago.
Leonard Cohen 'Chelsea Hotel #2' Of all the songs inspired by the Chelsea, this bleak vision of doomed love is on a level of its own.
Billy Joel 'New York State of Mind' This heartfelt ballad exemplifies the city's effect on the souls of its visitors and residents.
Charles Mingus 'Mingus Ah Um' Mingus brought the gospel to jazz and created a NY masterpiece.
Public Enemy 'It Takes a Nation of Millions to Hold Us Back' A ferociously political tour de force from the Long Island hip hop group whose own Chuck D once called rap 'the CNN for black America'.
The Ramones 'Ramones' Four Queens roughnecks, a few buzzsaw chords, and clipped musings on turning tricks and sniffing glue – it transformed rock 'n' roll.
Frank Sinatra 'Theme song from New York, New York' Trite and true, Frank's bombastic love letter melts those little-town blues.
Bruce Springsteen 'My City of Ruins' The Boss praises the city's resilience post-September 11 with this track from 'The Rising'.
The Strokes 'Is This It' The effortlessly hip debut of this hometown band garnered praise and worldwide attention.
The Velvet Underground 'The Velvet Underground & Nico' Lou Reed and company's first album is still the gold standard of downtown cool.
Wu Tang Clan Few artists embodied 90s hip hop like the Wu, its members – RZA, GZA and the late ODB among them – coining a cinematic rap aesthetic that influences artists to this day.

Websites

www.timeoutny.com The *Time Out New York* website covers all the city has to offer. When planning your trip, check out the New York City Guide section for a variety of itineraries that you can use in conjunction with this guide.
eatdrink.timeoutny.com Subscribe to the TONY Eating & Drinking online guide and instantly search thousands of reviews written by our critics.
www.nycvisit.com The site of NYC & Company, the local convention and visitors' bureau.
www.mta.info Subway and bus service changes are always posted here.
www.nyc.gov City Hall's official New York City website has lots of useful links.
www.nytimes.com 'All the News That's Fit to Print' from the New York Times.
www.clubplanet.com Follow the city's nocturnal scene and buy advance tickets to big events.
www.livebroadway.com 'The Official Website of Broadway' is the source for theatres, tickets and tours.
www.hipguide.com A very short 'n' sweet site for those looking for what's considered hip.
www.forgotten-ny.com Remember old New York here.
www.manhattanusersguide.com An insiders' guide to what's going on around town.

Index

Note Page numbers in **bold** indicate section(s) giving key information on a topic; *italics* indicate photographs.

ABC Carpet & Home 120
ABC Television Studios 126
Abyssinian Baptist Church 152
accommodation
apartments rentals 57
bed & breakfasts 57
best hotels, the 54
hostels 63, 76, 80
by price:
budget 63, 75-76, 79-80
expensive 59-60, 65-72, 78
luxury 57-59, 63-65
moderate 60-63, 72-75, 79, 80
for children 284
gay & lesbian 305-306
reservation agencies 54
see also p393 Accommodation index
Adirondack 88
African Burial Ground 103
age restrictions 371
AIA Center for Architecture 44, 114
AIDS 374
airlines 366
airports 366-367
Alexander Hamilton Custom House *see* National Museum of the American Indian
Algonquin, the **65**, 129
Alice Austen House 178
American Folk Art Museum **129**, **130**
American football 335
American Museum of Natural History **147**, **148**, *149*, 285
amusement parks *see* theme parks
Andrew Freedman Home 173
Ansonia Hotel 147
antiques 251-252
apartment rentals *see* accommodation
Apollo Theater 150, *153*, **313**
aquarium 166
architecture 36-44
America's favourite 37
reference books 384
Armory Show 121, **260**
art 45-48
see also galleries; museums
Art Lab 179
Art Show 266
Asia Society & Museum 138
Astor Place 42, 110
Astoria 168-169
Astroland Amusement Park 166, 285
Atlantic Antic 264
Atlantic Avenue 159
Atlantic Yards 42, 156
ATMs 378

B&Bs *see* accommodation
babysitting 285
Bacon, Francis 45
bakeries 245
Balanchine, George 351
ballet *see* dance
Bambaataa, Afrika 51
Bank of New York 21
banks 378-379
Barneys New York 138, **229**, *229*
bars 216-227
award-winning 217
gay & lesbian 306-309
hotel bars in skyscrapers 72
smoking 227
with art activities 220
see also p394 Bars index
Bartholdi, Frédéric-Auguste 24, 95
Bartow-Pell Mansion Museum **174**, **175**
Baruch College Academic Complex 41
baseball 333-334
basketball 334
Battery Maritime Building 94
Battery Park 93
Battery Park City 98-99
parks 288
Battle for New York 21, 32
Bayard-Condict Building 38
beaches
Orchard Beach 174
Sandy Hook 358-360, *360*
Watertaxi Beach 167, *169*
Beacon Theatre 147, **313**
bed & breakfasts *see* accommodation
Belmont Park 335
Belvedere Castle 136
Bergdorf Goodman 130, **229**
Berkowitz, David 'Son of Sam' 32
Bethesda Fountain & Terrace 136, **137**, *137*, 141
bicycles *see* cycling
Bike New York: The Great Five Boro Bike Tour 260
Billopp House *see* Conference House
Bleecker Street 113
Blondie 51
Bloomberg, Michael 31, *31*, 32, 34, 35, 146
Bloomingdale's 230
boat tours 88-89
Boerum Hill 159
book shops 230-234
books 276-278
about New York **31**, **384**
author appearances 276-278
gay & lesbian 301-303
spoken-word events 278
Borough Hall 157, 177
Boulud, Daniel 214, *214*
Bowery Ballroom 107, **314**
Bowery Poetry Club 111, **278**
bowling 336
Harlem Lanes 151
Bowling Green 94
box offices 382
boxing 334-335
Breakneck Ridge 360
Brill Building 124
British Memorial Garden 94
Broadway 83, **124-128**, 340, **343**
Broadway Bares 262
Broadway on Broadway 264
Bronck, Jonas 32, 172
Bronx, the 172-176
Little Italy 173, **175**
Walk of Fame 173
Bronx Academy of Arts & Dance (BAAD) **172**, **176**
Bronx Culture Trolley **172**, **176**
Bronx Museum of the Arts 43, **173**, **176**
Bronx Terminal Market 173
Bronx Zoo/Wildlife Conservation Society **174**, **176**
Brooklyn 156-166
accommodation 80
bars 226-227
galleries 274
restaurants & cafés 213-215
Brooklyn Academy of Music 164, **327**, 345, 351
Brooklyn Botanic Garden 85, **164**
Brooklyn Bridge 23, *23*, 32, 101, **157**, **158**, *158*
Brooklyn Children's Museum 286
Brooklyn Heights 83, **156-159**
Brooklyn Heights Promenade 157
Brooklyn Historical Society **157**, **158**
Brooklyn Museum **164**, 299
Brooklyn Public Library 164
Brooklyn Tourism & Visitor Center 156
Bryant Park *128-129*, 129
Free Summer Season 261
Bryant Park Hotel **65**, 129
bus services **366-367**, **368**
stations 367
tours 90
business services 371-372

c

cabaret 279-281
cabs *see* taxis
cafés *see* restaurants & cafés
Cake Shop 111, *312*, **314**
Calatrava, Santiago 44
Carl Schurz Park 138, 146
Carnegie Hall 32, 126, 321, *321*, **328**
Carnegie Hall Family Concerts 289
Carroll Gardens 159
cars & driving 367
  parking 367, 370
  rental 370
  services 369-370
cash machines *see* ATMs
Castle Clinton 93
Cathedral Church of St John the Divine 149, *150*
Celebrate Brooklyn! Performing Arts Festival 263
Central Park 32, **135-137**, *136*
  carousel *see* Friedsam Memorial Carousel
  for children 288-289
  self-guided walk 140-141
  zoo **136**, **137**, *287*
Central Park SummerStage series 136, **261**, *262*, 353
Central Park Zoo Chillout! Weekend 264
Chapman Catt, Carrie 25
Charles A Dana Discovery Center 137
Chelsea 83, **117-119**
  bars 221-222
  galleries *268*, 269-273
  restaurants & cafés 198-201
Chelsea Hotel **73**, 117
Chelsea Market 119
Chelsea Piers 290, **336**
Cherry Blossom Festival 260, *261*
Chic 49
Childhelp USA's National Child Abuse Hotline 374
children 284-290
  accommodation 284
  babysitting 285
  circuses 260, **285**
  clothes shops 234
  film 286
  museums & exhibitions 286-288
  outdoor activities 288-289
  performing arts 289-290
  sports & activities 290
  tours 290
  toyshops 234
  zoos 290
Children's Museum of Manhattan 286
Children's Museum of the Arts 286
Childs, David 31, 44
China Institute 138
Chinatown 83, *83*, **106-107**, **108-109**, *108-109*
  bars 217
  restaurants & cafés 184-187
Chinatown Fair 106
Chinese New Year 106, **266**
chocolate shops 245, **247**
Christie's **129**, **130**
Christmas Tree-Lighting Ceremony 265
Chrysler Building *38*, 39, **134**
cinemas *see* film
Circle Line Cruises *88*, 89, *91*
circuses 260, **285**
Citicorp Center 41
City Hall **101**, *102*, **103**
City Island 174, **361-362**
CityPass 87
Civic Center 101-103
clinics 373
Clinton, DeWitt 22, 32
Clinton, Hillary Rodham 35
Cloisters 85, **155**
clothes shops 234-240
clothing size charts 380
clubs 291-297
  gay & lesbian 309-310
  lounges & DJ bars 296-297
  roving & seasonal parties 297
CMJ Music Marathon & FilmFest 264
Cobble Hill 159
Coleman, Ornette 51
Columbia University 32, 38, 146, 149
Columbus Circle 146
comedy 281-283
Coney Island 83, **166**
Conference House (Billopp House) 178
Confucius Plaza 106
Conservatory Garden 21
Conservatory Water 288
consulates 372
consumer information 371
Cooper Union building 38, 110
Cooper-Hewitt, National Design Museum 138
cosmetics shops 246-249
Cotton Club 27, **151**
couriers 371
credit cards 379
Criminal Courts Building & Manhattan Detention Complex 102
Culinary Institute of America 362-363
currency exchange 378-379
Cushman Row 119
customs 372
cycling **336-337**, 370
  Bike New York: The Great Five Boro Bike Tour 260
  tours 88

d

da Verrazano, Giovanni *see* Verrazano, Giovanni da
Daily News Building 134
Dairy 137
Dakota apartment building 141, 147
dance 351-354
Dance Theater Workshop 118, **353**
Davis, Miles **49**, 174
day trips 356-363
De Niro, Robert 103, 300
dentists 373
department stores 229-230
designer clothes 237-238
discount shops 238
Dia:Beacon 357-358, *358*
Dia:Chelsea 117
Dinkins, David N 30, 32
dinosaurs 285
disabled access 372-373
dog show 335
Doig, Peter 45
Downtown 93-15
  accommodation 57-63
  bars 216-221
  restaurants & cafés 183-198
Draft Riots of 1863 22
driving *see* cars & driving
Dumbo 157-159
d.u.m.b.o. art under the bridge 158, **265**
Dutch West India Company 19
Dyckman Farmhouse Museum 36

e

East Harlem 154
East Village 83, **110**
  bars 219-221
  restaurants & cafés 190-195
Easter Parade 260
Eastern States Buddhist Temple of America 106, 108
Edgar Allan Poe Cottage **173**, **176**
Edison, Thomas Alva 24
888 Grand Concourse 173
Eldridge Street Synagogue 107
electricity 373
Ellington, Duke **49**, 174
Ellis Island 24, *28*, 32, **93**
Ellis Island Immigration Museum 95, *95*
emergency rooms 373
emergency services 373
Empire State Building 32, 39, **129**, **130**, *131*
  lighting 131
Empire-Fulton Ferry State Park 157
Equitable Building 100
Erie Canal 22, 32
ESPN Zone 126
Essex Street Markets 108
Evening Post 21
events *see* festivals & events
Eyebeam 41

f

fashion 234-244
  accessories 243-244
  boutiques 234-237
Fashion Institute of Technology (FIT) 119
FDR Boardwalk 178
Feast of San Gennaro 105, **264**
Federal Hall National Memorial 32, 36, **100**
Federal Reserve Bank 100
festivals & events 260-266
  film 300
Fifth Avenue 83, **129-133**
55 Central Park West 147
59th Street Bridge 168
57th Street galleries 273
Fig, Joe 47
Fillmore New York at Irving Plaza 121, **314**

film 298-300
art & revival houses 298
festivals 300
for children 286
foreign-language 300
museums & societies 299
set in New York 384-385
Finch, Spencer 47
First Shearith Israel Graveyard 107
fitness *see* sport & fitness
Fitzgerald, Ella 51
Five Points neighbourhood 22
5 Pointz 168
Flatiron 119-120
bars 221-222
restaurants & cafés 201-202
Flatiron Building 25, 32, 39, 120
flea markets 117, **251-252**
Flushing 170-171
Flushing Meadows-Corona Park **170**, **171**
Flushing Town Hall **170**, **171**
food & drink shops 245-246
football 336
American 335
Forest Hills Gardens 171
Fort Greene 164-165, *165*
Fort Greene Park 164
Fort Wadsworth 178
Fraunces Tavern 21
museum 94
Freedom Tower 31, 44
Fresh Kills Park 178
Frick Collection **138**, **139**, 330
Friedsam Memorial Carousel 135, 140, *288*
Fuller Building *see* Flatiron Building
Fulton Ferry Landing 157
Fulton Fish Market 172
Fulton Market 101

g

Galapagos Art Space 165, **315**
galleries 267-275
not-for-profit spaces 274-275
photography 275
Gantry Plaza State Park 168
Garment District 123
gay & lesbian 301-311, 373
accommodation 304-305
bars 305-309
books & media 301-303
centres & helplines 303-304
clubs 309-310
country & western 304
restaurants & cafés 310-311
Gay & Lesbian Pride March **263**, *301*, *302*
Gehry, Frank 41, 103, 119
General Electric Building 129
General Grant National Memorial 148
General Post Office 44, 124
General Theological Seminary of the Episcopal Church 119
George Washington Bridge 32, 154
George Washington Bridge Bus Station 367
German Cultural Center *see* Goethe-Institut New York
Giants, New York *see* New York Giants
Giants Stadium *see* Meadowlands Sports Complex
gift shops 246
Gilbert, Cass 36
Gillespie, Dizzy 51
Giuliani, Rudy 30, 33, 35
Global Marijuana March 260
global warming 34
Goethe-Institut New York **138**, **143**
Governors Island **26-27**, *27*, 94
ferry 27
Gracie Mansion 146
graffiti 43, *43*
Graffiti Hall of Fame 154
Gramercy
park 121-122
restaurants & cafés 201-202
Grand Army Plaza 130
Grand Central Terminal *36*, 38, **133**, **134**, **367**
Grandmaster Flash 51
Great Depression 28
Great Lawn 136
Greeley Square 123
Green-Wood Cemetery *160*, 161, **163**, **164**
Greenwich Village 83, **113-114**
bars 221
restaurants & cafés 195-197
Greyhound Trailways 367
Ground Zero 31, 43, 96, **98**
Guggenheim Museum *see* Solomon R Guggenheim Museum
gyms 337

h

Hamilton, Alexander 21, 32
Hamilton Heights 154
Hanover Square 94
Hans Christian Andersen Statue 285
Harlem 83, **150-154**, *152*
galleries 274
Harlem Renaissance 27
Harlem USA Mall 151
Harlem Week 264
Harriman State Park 361
Haughwout Store 38
Hayden Planetarium 147
health & beauty shops 246-251
health & medical facilities 373-374
Hearst Magazine Building 42, *44*
helicopter tours 90
Hell Gate Bridge 169
Hell's Kitchen 126
Henderson Place Historic District 146
Henry Luce Nature Observatory **136**, **137**, 288
Herald Square 123-124
High Line 41, 117, **118**, *118*
High Line Festival 118, **261**
High Rock Park 178
hiking 360-361
Hindu Temple Society **170**, **171**
Hirst, Damien 45
Hispanic Society of America **154**, **155**
Historic Richmond Town **178**, **179**
history 18-32
key events 32
HIV 374
hockey 335
Holiday, Billie 50
holidays 376
home shops 251-253
horse racing 335-336
horse riding 337
hostels *see* accommodation
hotels *see* accommodation
Howl! 110, **264**
Hudson, Henry 18, 177
Hudson Heights 154
Hunters Point Historic District 168
Hunts Point 172

ice hockey *see* hockey
ice skating 338
IFC Center 114, **298**
Iglesia Pentecostal Camino Damasco 111
IMAX theatre 147
immigration 24, **383**
in-line skating 338
insurance 375
InterActiveCorp *39*, 41, 119
International Center of Photography **129**, **130**
internet
access 375
useful websites 385
Intrepid Sea-Air-Space Museum 127
Inwood 154-155
Inwood Hill Park 155
Irish Hunger Memorial 98
Irving Place 121
Islamic Cultural Center 146

Jackson Heights 169-170
Jacob K Javits Convention Center 127
Jacobs, Jane 29
Jacques Marchais Museum of Tibetan Art **178**, **179**
Jazz at Lincoln Center 146, **321**
Jefferson Market Library 114
Jets, New York *see* New York Jets
jewellery shops **240**, 243-244
Jewish Museum **138**, **143**
Joe's Pub 111, **315**
John F Kennedy International Airport 366
Johnson, Philip 40, 41
Jolson, Al 51
Joyce Theater 118, **353**
Juilliard School 332
JVC Jazz Festival 262

kayaking 338
King's College *see* Columbia University
Kips Bay 122
Kitchen, the 118, **354**
Knicks, New York *see* New York Knickerbockers
Koch, Ed 29, 30
Koh, Terence 46
Koreatown 123
Kykuit 359, *359*

La Guardia, Fiorello 28, 32
La Guardia Airport 366
language services 372
Lefferts Homestead 36
legal assistance 375
Lenape tribe 18, 19
Lennon, John 135, 141
Lenox Lounge 151, **323**
lesbian *see* gay & lesbian
Lesbian Herstory Archives 163, **303**
Lever House 39, 133
Levys' Unique New York, the **89**, *89*, 91
Libeskind, Daniel 31
libraries 375
limousines 369-370
Lincoln Center 32, **147**, **321**, 326, **328-330**, *329*
Lincoln Center Out of Doors Festival 263
lingerie shops 244
Little Italy 105-106
  bars 217
  restaurants & cafés 184-187
Little Italy (Bronx) 173, **175**
locksmiths 375-376
Loeb Boathouse 136, 141, 337
Loew's Paradise Theater 173
London Terrace 118
Long Island City 167-168
lost property 376
Louis Armstrong House **170**, **171**
Low Memorial Building 149
Lower East Side 83, **107-110**
  bars 217-218
  galleries 267-269
  restaurants & cafés 187-189
Lower East Side Festival of the Arts 261
Lower East Side Tenement Museum **107**, **109**
luggage shops 257

Macy's 32, 123, **230**
Macy's Fireworks Display 263, *266*
Macy's Thanksgiving Day Parade & Eve Balloon Blowup 32, 265
Madame Tussaud's New York **126**, **127**
Madison Square 119
Madison Square Garden 123, 313, **333**, 334
Madison Square Park 120
magazines 376-377
Makor/Steinhardt Center 147
Malcolm Shabazz Harlem Market 153
Malcolm X Boulevard 153
Manhattan *see* Downtown; Midtown; Uptown
Marcus Garvey Park 152
MarketSite Tower 126
Masjid Malcolm Shabazz 153
Mayflower Inn & Spa *356*, 357
McCarren Park Pool 165, *166*
McKim, Charles Follen 38
McKim, Mead & White 38, 123, 124
Meadowlands Sports Complex 333
Meatpacking District 83, **114-115**
  bars 221
  restaurants & cafés 197-198
media 376-378
medical facilities 373-374
Meier, Richard 43
menswear shops 238-240
Merchants' Exchange 100
Merchant's House Museum **110**, **113**
Mercury Lounge 111, **317**, *318*
Mermaid Parade 262
messenger services 371
Met in the Parks 261
MetLife Building 25, 39, 133
MetroCards 368
MetroNaps 128
Metropolitan Life Tower 39
Metropolitan Museum of Art 32, **138**, **143**, *143*, 285, 299, 331
Greek & Roman collections 144, *144*
Metropolitan Transportation Authority (MTA) 368
Mets, New York *see* New York Mets
Midsummer Night Swing 147, **263**
Midtown 117-134
  accommodation 63-76
  bars 221-224
  restaurants & cafés 198-208
Midtown East 83, **133-134**
  bars 223-224
  restaurants & cafés 207-208
Midtown West
  bars 222-223
  restaurants & cafés 203-207
Minuit, Peter *18*, 19, 32
money 378-379
Monk, Thelonious 51
Morgan, JP 24
Morgan Library & Museum **38**, **122**, *122-123*
Morningside Heights 148-150
Morningside Park 149
Morris-Jumel Mansion **154**, **155**
Moses, Robert 28, 32, 173, 174
Mostly Mozart festival 263
Mount Morris 153
Mount Morris Park *see* Marcus Garvey Park
Municipal Building 102
Murray Hill 122-123
Museo del Barrio, El **138**, **139**
Museum Mile 138 festival 262
Museum at FIT 119
Museum of American Finance 100
Museum of Arts & Design **146**, **148**
Museum of Bronx History **174**, **176**
Museum of Chinese in the Americas **106**, **107**
Museum of Jewish Heritage 99
Museum of Modern Art (MoMA) 32, **129**, **131**, 299
Museum of Sex 119
Museum of Television & Radio *see* Paley Center for Media
Museum of the City of New York 21, **138**, **145**
Museum of the Moving Image **168**, 299
museums 85-87
  art: American Folk Art Museum **129**, **130**; Asia Society & Museum 138; Bronx Museum of the Arts 43, **173**, **176**; Brooklyn Museum **164**, 299; Cloisters 85, **155**; Dia:Beacon 357-358, *358*; Frick Collection **138**, **139**, 330; Goethe-Institut New York **138**, **143**; Jacques Marchais Museum of Tibetan Art **178**, **179**; Metropolitan Museum of Art 32, **138**, **143**, *143*, 285, 299, 331; Morgan Library & Museum **38**, **122**, *122-123*; Museo del Barrio, El **138**, **139**; Museum of Arts & Design **146**, **148**; Museum of Modern Art (MoMA) 32, **129**, **131**, 299; Neue Galerie 138, **145**; New Museum of Contemporary Art 42, **107**, **110**; Queens Museum of Art **170**, **171**; Solomon R Guggenheim Museum **138**, **145**; Studio Museum in Harlem **151**, **152**, *154*, *155*; Whitney Museum of American Art 32, 118, **138**, **145**
  children: Brooklyn Children's Museum 286; Children's Museum of Manhattan 286; Children's Museum of the Arts 286; Staten Island Children's Museum **178**, **179**
  design: National Design Museum 138; Noguchi Museum 169

fashion: Museum at FIT 119
film: Museum of the Moving Image **168**, 299
finance: Museum of American Finance 100
firefighting: New York City Fire Museum **104**, **105**
general interest: Staten Island Museum 177
history: Bartow-Pell Mansion Museum **174**, **175**; Dyckman Farmhouse Museum 36; Ellis Island Immigration Museum 95, *95*; Fraunces Tavern Museum 94; Historic Richmond Town **178**, **179**; Lower East Side Tenement Museum **107**, **109**; Merchant's House Museum **110**, **113**; Museum of Bronx History **174**, **176**; Museum of Chinese in the Americas **106**, **107**; National Museum of the American Indian 36, **94**, **95**; New-York Historical Society 32, 141, **147**, **148**; Pieter Claesen Wyckoff House Museum 36; South Street Seaport Museum 101; Trinity Church Museum 100; Van Cortlandt House Museum **174**, **176**; World Trade Center Memorial & Museum 98
Judaism: Jewish Museum **138**, **143**; Museum of Jewish Heritage 99
natural history: American Museum of Natural History **147**, **148**, *149*, 285
policing: New York City Police Museum 100
science: New York Hall of Science **170**, **171**, 286; Rose Center for Earth & Space **147**, **148**
sex: Museum of Sex 119
skyscrapers: Skyscraper Museum 99
television & radio: Paley Center for Media **129**, **133**, 300
transport: Intrepid Sea-Air-Space Museum 127; New York Transit Museum **157**, **158**
music 312-332
arenas 313
blues, country & folk 325-326
classical 327-330
in churches 331-332
jazz & experimental 320-325
latin, reggae & world 326
local artists **49-51**, 385
local genres 50
new live music venues 324-325
opera 330
rock, pop & soul 313-320
schools 332
shops 253-255
summer venues 326-327
Music Hall of Williamsburg 165, **318**
musical instruments shops 254-255
musicals *see* theatre
Mutu, Wangechi 47

n

Nathan's Famous Fourth of July Hot Dog Eating Contest 166, **263**
National Arts Club 121
National Chorale Messiah Sing-In, the 265
National Design Museum 138
National Museum of the American Indian 36, **94**, **95**
National Puerto Rican Day Parade 262
NBC Studio Tour 133
Neue Galerie 138, **145**
New Amsterdam 19
New Jersey Nets 334
New Museum of Contemporary Art 42, **107**, **110**
New Year's Day Marathon Poetry Reading 266
New Year's Eve Ball Drop 266
New Year's Eve Fireworks 266
New Year's Eve Midnight Run 266
New York Antiquarian Book Fair 260
New York Aquarium 166
New York Botanical Garden *84*, **174**, **176**
New York Bridge Company 23
New York City Fire Museum **104**, **105**
New York City Marathon 32, 265
New York City Police Museum 100
New York County Courthouse 102
New York Film Festival **264**, 299
New York Giants 32, 335
New York Hall of Science **170**, **171**, 286
New-York Historical Society 32, 141, **147**, **148**
New York International Auto Show 260
New York International Fringe Festival 264
New York Islanders 335
New York Jets 335
New York Knickerbockers 32, 334
New York Mets 32, 333
New York Pass 87
New York Philharmonic Concerts in the Parks 263
New York Post 21
New York Public Library 38, 121, **130**, **133**, *134*, 375
New York Public Library for the Performing Arts **147**, **148**
New York Rangers *334*, 335
New York State Pavilion **40**, *40*, 171
New York State Supreme Court 157
New York Stock Exchange 32, **100**
New York Table Tennis Foundation 109
New York Times 26
New York Transit Museum **157**, **158**
New York University 113
New York Vietnam Veterans Memorial 94
New York Water Taxi 157
New York Yankees 333, **334**
New Yorker, The 27
Newark Liberty International Airport 367
Newhouse Center for Contemporary Art 179
newspapers 376
Next Wave Festival 264, **327**
nightlife *see* clubs
9/11 30, 32
Noguchi Museum 169
Noho
bars 221
restaurants & cafés 195-197
Nolita 105-106
bars 217
restaurants & cafés 184-187
North Lawn 98
North Meadow Recreation Center 289
Nutcracker, The **265**, 285, 353
Nuyorican Poets Café 111, **278**

Olmsted, Frederick Law 135, 137, 140, 147, 163
One Prospect Park 43
Open House New York 264
Orchard Beach 174
Orchard Street Bargain District 108
Otis Pike Wilderness 361

P.S.1 Contemporary Art Center 46, **168**
P.S.1 Warm Up 263, **297**
Paley Center for Media **129**, **133**, 300
Panorama of the City of New York 168, 170
Park Row 102
Park Row Building 39
Park Slope 162-163, *162-163*
parking 367
passports 377, 383
payphones 381-382
Pelham Bay Park 174
Penn Station 123, **367**

perfumeries 249
Pete's Candy Store 165, **318**
pharmacies 374
phonecards 381-382
Piano, Renzo 44
Pier 17 101
Pieter Claesen Wyckoff House Museum 36
planetarium *see* Hayden Planetarium
Plaza Hotel, the 64, *64*, **65**
Poe, Edgar Allan 173, 176
poetry 276-278
  New Year's Day Marathon Poetry Reading 266
Point Community Development Corporation 172
Police Memorial 94
Port Authority Bus Terminal 367
postal services 379
postmodernism (architecture) 41
Pride March 301, *302*
printing services 371-372
Prospect Heights 163-164
Prospect Park 163
Prospect Park Audubon Center at the Boathouse 163
Prospect Park Bandshell 327
Prospect Park Zoo 163
Public Enemy 50
Public Theater 111, **349**
public transgressions 85
public transport 368-369
Puente, Tito 50
Pulitzer, Joseph 24, 26

Queens 167-171
  bars 227
  restaurants & cafés 215
Queens Botanical Garden 170
Queens Jazz Trail **170**, **171**
Queens Museum of Art **170**, **171**
Queens Theatre in the Park 170
Queens Zoo 170

radio 377-378
gay & lesbian 303
Radio City Christmas Spectacular 265
Radio City Music Hall 129, 312, **319**
Ramones, the 51
rape & sex crimes helplines 375
Ravine District 163
Red Hook 159-162
Red Hook Waterfront Arts Festival 261
religion 379-380
restaurants & cafés 182-215
  American 183, 184, 187, 189, 195, 197, 198, 203, 208, 209, 211, 212, 213
  American creative 187, 196, 201, 204, 213
  Austrian 211
  award-winning 185
  best, the 182
  cafés 184, 188, 190, 196, 197, 205, 208, 209
  Caribbean 212
  Chinese 184, 188, 199, 212
  Cuban 184, 190
  desserts 192-193
  eclectic 187, 188, 197, 205, 209
  French 184, 190, 202, 205, 208, 209, 211, 215
  French chefs 214
  gay & lesbian 310-311
  Greek 211, 215
  in museums 85
  Indian 190, 202, 208
  Italian 184, 189, 192, 196, 197, 199, 202, 207, 211, 213
  Japanese 189, 198, 201, 207, 208
  Korean 193, 207
  Malaysian 215
  Mexican 187, 193, 207, 211, 214
  pan-Asian 187, 196, 198, 201, 208
  pizza 187, 195, 198, **206**, 212, 215
  Russian 207
  seafood 195, 198, 211
  Spanish 189, 198, 201, 202
  steakhouse 201, 215
  Thai 195, 197, 215
  Turkish 190
  vegetarian 195, 198, 201, 202
  Venezuelan 195
  Vietnamese 187
  see also p393 Restaurants & cafés index
restrooms 385
Richmond County Savings Bank Ballpark 177
Riis, Jacob A 25, 32
Ringling Bros and Barnum & Bailey Circus Animal Parade 260
River to River Festival 93, **262**
Riverdale 174
Riverside Church 148
Riverside Park 147, **288**
Robert F Wagner Jr Park 98
Rockefeller Center **129**, **133**, *134*
Rockefeller family 359
Rockefeller Jr, John D 85, 129
Rodeo Bar & Grill 122, **326**
Rodham Clinton, Hillary 35
Roosevelt, Theodore 123, 131
Rose Center for Earth & Space **147**, **148**
Run-DMC 50
running 338-339
  New York City Marathon 265
Ruth, Babe 27, 173, 333

safety 380
St Anthony of Padua Roman Catholic Church 105
St George Theater 177
St George-New Brighton Historic District 177
St George's Church 170
St Mark's Church-in-the-Bowery 110
St Marks Place 110
St Nicholas Historic District *see* Strivers' Row
St Patrick's Cathedral **129**, **133**
St Patrick's Day Parade 260
St Patrick's Old Cathedral 105
St Paul's Chapel 36, **100**
Saks Fifth Avenue 130
Salmagundi Club **113**, **114**
salons 249-251
Samaritans 374
San Remo Apartments 147
Sandy Hook 358-360, *360*
Sanger, Margaret 26
Scandinavia House: the Nordic Center in America **122**, **123**
Schomburg Center for Research in Black Culture 152
Science Barge 34, *34*
Seagram Building 39
Seaside Summer & Martin Luther King Jr Concert Series 263
second-hand shops 242-243
sex crimes helplines 375
sex shops 255
Shakespeare in the Park 110, 136, 261, *262*, **349**
Shea Stadium 170
Sheep Meadow 136, 140
Shishkin, Dasha *45*, 47
shoe shops 244
shoe size charts 380
shops & services 228-257
  key areas 228
  department stores 229-230
  eco-friendly 232
  national chains 230
  see also specific products
Show World 124
Showman's Bar 151
Shrine of St Elizabeth Ann Seton 94
Sillman, Amy 46
Silvercup Studios 44, 168
Singer Building 39
Siren Music Festival 166
Six Flags Great Adventure 362, *363*
69th Regiment Armory 121
skating *see* in-line skating
Skyscraper Museum 99
skyscrapers 38
sleep stations 128, *128*
smoking 380
  ban 31
  bars 227
Sniffen Court 122
Snug Harbor Cultural Center **177**, **179**
soccer 336
Socrates Sculpture Park 169
SOFA New York 261
Soho 83, **103-105**
  bars 218-219
  galleries 269
  restaurants & cafés 189-190
Soldiers' and Sailors' Monument 147
Solomon R Guggenheim Museum **138**, **145**

Son of Sam 30, 32
Sonic Youth 51
Sony Wonder Technology Lab 134, **288**
SOS: Sunday Open Series 108
Sotheby's 146
South Bronx Initiative 172
South Street Seaport 100-101
South Street Seaport Museum 101
souvenir shops 246
spas 249-251
Spiegeltent 263
sport & fitness 333-339
active sports 336-339
centres 336
for children 290
shops 257
spectator sports 333-336
Stanton Blatch, Harriet 25
Staten Island 177-179
ferry **90**, 93, 177, *179*
Staten Island Botanical Garden **178**, **179**
Staten Island Children's Museum **178**, **179**
Staten Island Museum 177
Staten Island Yankees 334
Staten Island Zoo **178**, **179**
Statue of Liberty 24, 32, **93**, *94*, **95**
STDs 374
Steinway & Sons 169
stock market crash 28, 32
Stone Street Historic District 94
Stonewall Inn 29, 115, 301, **308**
Stonewall riots 29
Strawberry Fields 135, 140
streetwear shops 240-241
Streisand, Barbara 51
Strivers' Row 153
students 380-381
Studio Museum in Harlem **151**, **152**, *154*, *155*
Stuyvesant, Peter 46, 110
subway 32, **368-369**
Sullivan, Louis 38
Summer Restaurant Week 263
Sunset Park 161
swimming 339
Symphony Space 147

table tennis 109
Talking Heads 51
Taller Latino Americano, El 147
Tammany Hall 23, 102
tattoos & piercings 251
tax 381
in restaurants 189
taxis 369
Teardrop Park 98
telephones 381-382
television 300, 378
gay & lesbian 303
studio tapings 300
tours 300
Temple of Dendur at the Met 285
tennis 336, 339
theatre 340-351
Broadway 340, **343-344**
for children 289-290
off Broadway 344-349
off-off Broadway 349-351
seat sizes 124
Shakespeare in the Park 110, 136
theatre district 124
theme parks
Astroland Amusement Park 166, 285
Six Flags Great Adventure 362, *363*
Theodore Roosevelt Birthplace **121**, **123**
tickets 382
time & date 383
Time Warner Center *142*, 146
Times Square 32, 41, 83, **124-128**, *125*
tipping 189, 381
Titanic Memorial Lighthouse 101
toilets 385
Tompkins Square Park 111, *112*
tourist information 383
tours 89-91
by bicycle 88
by boat 88-90
by bus 90
by helicopter 90
for children 290
television shows 300
walking 90-91
toyshops 234
train services **367**, **369**
stations 367
translation services 372
Trapeze School New York 339
travel advice 371
travel & luggage shops 257
travellers' cheques 379
Triangle Shirtwaist Company fire 25, 32
Tribeca 83, **103**, *105*
bars 216-217
restaurants & cafés 183-184
Tribeca Cinemas 103
Tribeca Film Center 103
Tribeca Film Festival 103, **260**, 286, 300
Triborough Bridge 169
Trinity Church 36, **100**
museum 100
Trump International Hotel & Tower 146
Tudor City 134
Tweed, William 'Boss' 23, 102
Tweed Courthouse 102
twin towers *see* World Trade Center

underground transit system 25
underwear shops 244
Union Square 120-121, *121*
Union Square Greenmarket **120**, **121**
United Nations Headquarters 32, 39, **134**
United States Courthouse 102
Upper East Side 83, **138-146**
bars 224-225
galleries 274
restaurants & cafés 211
Upper West Side 83, **146-148**
bars 224
restaurants & cafés 209-211
Uptown 135-155
accommodation 78-80
bars 224-226
restaurants & cafés 209-215
Urban Glass House 41, *42*

Van Cortlandt House Museum **174**, **176**
Vanderbilt, Cornelius 22
Vaux, Calvert 135, 137, 140, 163
Velvet Underground, the 49
Verrazano, Giovanni da 18, *19*, 32, 177
Verrazano-Narrows Bridge 28, 32
Victorian Gardens 289
Village Halloween Parade 265
Village Vanguard 115, **324**
vintage shops 242-243
visas & immigration 383

w

Waldorf-Astoria 71, 133
Walker, James J 27
walking 370
tours 90-91
walks (self-guided)
Brooklyn's Fifth Avenue 160-161
Central Park 140-141
Downtown after dark 96-97
Wall Street *30*, 83, **99-100**
Warhol, Andy 29, 117, 131
Warsaw at the Polish National Home 165, **320**
Washington, George 21, 32, 36, 94, 95, 97, 100, 113
Washington Heights 154-155
Washington Square Outdoor Art Exhibit 261
Washington Square Park 113, *115*
Watertaxi Beach 167, *169*
Wave Hill House **174**, **176**
weather 383
West Harlem 151-152
West Indian-American Day Carnival 264
West Village 83, **114-115**
bars 221
restaurants & cafés 197-198
White, Stanford 38, 120, 138, 153
Whitman, Walt 158, 164
Whitney Museum of American Art 32, 118, **138**, **145**
Williamsburg 83, **165-166**
Williamsburg Art & Historical Center 165
Williamsburg Savings Bank 164
Wing Fat Shopping 106
Winter Antiques Show 266
Winter Garden 99

Winter Restaurant Week 266
wire services 379
Wolfe's Pond Park 178
Wollman Rink 135, 289, **338**
women's health 374
Woodlawn Cemetery 174
Woolworth Building 25, 39, 102
working visas 383
World Financial Center & Winter Garden **98**, **99**, *99*
World Trade Center 29, 30, 32
memorial & museum 98
Wright, Frank Lloyd 138

Yankee Stadium 32, 173, **334**
Yankees, New York *see* New York Yankees
yoga 339
Yorkville 146

zoos
Bronx **174**, **176**
Central Park **136**, **137**, *287*
Prospect Park 163
Queens 170
Staten Island **178**, **179**

Accommodation

Abingdon Guest House 60
Akwaaba Mansion 80
Algonquin, the 65
Americana Inn 75
Amsterdam Inn 79
Awesome Bed & Breakfast 80
Beacon Hotel 79
Bed & Breakfast on the Park 80
Bentley Hotel 78
Big Apple Hostel 76
Blue Moon 59, *60-61*
Bowery Hotel, the 59, *63*
Bowery's Whitehouse Hotel of New York 63
Broadway Inn 72
Bryant Park Hotel 65
Carlton Arms Hotel 75
Casablanca Hotel 66
Central Park Hostel 80
Chelsea Center 76
Chelsea Hotel 73
Chelsea Lodge 75
Chelsea Mews Guest House 305
Chelsea Pines Inn 306
Chelsea Star Hotel 76
Colonial House Inn 306
Cosmopolitan 61
Country Inn the City 79
Dream Hotel 66
East Village B&B 306
East Village Bed & Coffee 63
Efuru Guest House 79
Flatotel 66
414 Hotel 73
Four Seasons 63
Gershwin Hotel 76
Hampton Inn Manhattan-Seaport 60, *67*
Harlem Flophouse 79
Hostelling International New York 80
Hotel Belleclaire 79
Hotel Chandler 66
Hotel Edison 73
Hotel Elysée 66
Hotel 41 66
Hotel Gansevoort *55*, 57
Hotel Metro 73
Hotel on Rivington 60
Hotel Pennsylvania 73
Hotel QT 74
Hotel 17 76
Hotel Thirty Thirty 74
Hotel 31 76
Hudson 66
Incentra Village House 306
Inn at Irving Place 64
Inn on 23rd Street 67
International House 80
Ivy Terrace 306
Jazz on the Park Hostel 80
Larchmont Hotel 63
Library Hotel 69
London NYC, the 69, *71*
Marcel 74
Maritime Hotel 69
Marrakech *77*, 79
Mayflower Inn & Spa *356*, 357
Mercer 58, *58-59*
Murray Hill Inn 76
New York Palace Hotel 65
Night Hotel 69, *73-74*
Off-Soho Suites Hotel 61
On the Ave Hotel 79
102Brownstone *78*, 79
Park South Hotel 69
Pierre, the 65, *68*
Pioneer of SoHotel 61
Plaza Hotel, the *64*, 65
Pod Hotel, the 75, *75*
Roger Smith 69
St Mark's Hotel 61
60 Thompson 58
SoHo Grand Hotel 59
Time 71
Union Square Inn 63
W New York-Times Square 71
Waldorf-Astoria 71
Wall Street District Hotel 60
Wall Street Inn 60
Warwick New York Hotel 72
Washington Square Hotel 61

Restaurants & Cafés

Abboccato 207
Adrienne's Pizza Bar 184
Agnanti 169
Alice's Tea Cup 209
Alma 214
Almondine 158
Amy Ruth's 153
Antique Garage 190
Applewood 213
Aroma 192
Balthazar 190
Baobab, Le 153
Bar Americain 204
Bar Room at the Modern 204
Bar Tabac 159
Barbuto 197
Barmarché 184
Better Burger NYC 311
Birdbath 233
Bleu Evolution 155
Blossom 201, *203*
BLT Burger *194*, 195
Blue Hill 196
Blue Ribbon 189
Bohemian Hall 169
Bottega, La 199
Bouchon Bakery 209
Bouley Bakery & Market 183
Brasserie 208
Bread 106
BRGR 198
Bridge Café 96, *96*
Brooklyn Fish Camp 213
Brooklyn Ice Cream Factory 157
Brown 188
Bubby's 158
Buco, Il 196
Buddakan 199
Buddha Bar 198
Café Habana 184
Café Sabarsky 211
Cafecito 190
Caracas Arepa Bar 195
Caravan of Dreams 195
Carnegie Deli 126
Casa Mono/Bar Jamón 202
Cavo 215
Cedar Tavern, the 113
Central Park Boathouse Restaurant 211
Centro, El 207
Chestnut 159
Chez Oskar 165
ChikaLicious 190
Chinatown Brasserie 196
Cinco Estrellas 161
Clinton Street Baking Company 187
Cocoa Bar 188, *193*
Congee Village 188
Cookshop 198
Corner Bistro 197
Cortile, Il 106
Counter 311
Country 201
Craftbar 202
Craftsteak *200*, 201
Cube 63 189
Daniel 211
Danny Meyer's Shake Shack 120
Dave & Busters 203
Dévi 202
Ditch Plains 198
DOC Wine Bar 213
Dojo West 196
Dosa Diner 169
Doyers Vietnamese Restaurant 187
DuMont 213
Edigio's 175
809 Sangria Bar & Grill 212
Elmo 311
Empire Diner 199
Employees Only 197
EN Japanese Brasserie 198
Esquina, La 187
Express, Le 202
Falai 189
Fanelli's Café 189
Fara Pizza, Di 215
Five Front 158
5 Ninth 197
Figaro Café, Le 113
Florent 114
44 & X Hell's Kitchen 311
Freemans 188
Fusta, La 170
Ginger 212
Golden Bridge 184
Gordon Ramsay at the London 205
Gran Rancho Jubilee 170
Grand Central Oyster Bar & Restaurant 134
Gray's Papaya 209
Grimaldi's Pizza 158
Grocery, the 159
Habana Outpost 233
Han Bat 207
Happy Ending 106
Heidelberg 146

HK 311
Hungarian Pastry Shop 149
Jack's Stir Brew Coffee 184
Jing Fong 106
Joe at Alessi *185*, 190
Joe's Pizza 198
Joe's Shanghai 106
Johnny's Famous Reef Restaurant 175
Johnny's Reef 362
Junior's Restaurant 165
Katz's Delicatessen 109
Kefi 211
Kitchen Club 187
Kitchenette Uptown 212
Kobe Club 203, *210*
Koi 207
Kyotofu *192*, 205
Landmarc 184
Lanterna di Vittorio, La 196
Lazzara's Pizza Café 207
Lexington Candy Shop 211
Lips 311
Lombardi's 187
Londel's Supper Club 153
Lovely Day 187
Lucky Cheng's 311
Lupa 196
Mario's 174
Market Café 204
Marseille 205
Megu Midtown 208, *212*
Mela, La 106
Mercadito 193
Mermaid Inn 195
Mike's Deli 173
Mint 208
Miss Maude's Spoonbread Too 212
Momofuku Ssäm Bar *191*, 193
Morimoto 201
Naka Naka 201
New Bo Ky Restaurant 109
New Leaf Café 155
New York City Hot Dog Company *183*, 184
Nice Matin 209
Nick's Pizza 171
Nobu 57 207
Odeon 103
Oliva 189
P*Ong 197
Pastis 114
Patsy's 212
Peanut Butter & Co 196
Penelope 208
Per Se 209
Peter Luger 215
Pizza Napoletana, Una 195, *206*
Porter House New York 209
Posto, Del 199
Pre:Post 199
Prem-On Thai 197
PS 450 208
Public 187
Pukk 195
Pure Food & Wine 202
Ramblas, Las 198
Rapture Café & Books 190
Relish 165
Rickshaw Dumpling Bar 201
River Café 157
Robertis, De 111
Roberto's 174
Robin des Bois 159
Rosa Mexicano 211
Rubyfruit Bar & Grill 311
Russ & Daughters 109
Russian Tea Room 207
Sago 170
Schiller's Liquor Bar 188
Schnäck 213
SEA Thai Restaurant & Bar 215
Seagull's Nest 360
Sentosa Malaysian Cuisine 215
Seppi's 205
718 215
'sNice 198, *199*
Spice Cove 190
Spice Market 114
Spotted Pig 197
Stanton Social 188
Suba 189
Superfine 311
Sylvia's 152
Tao 208
Tavern on the Green 136
Taverna Kyclades 169
Telepan 209
Ten Ren 170
Tia Pol 201
Tom's Restaurant 149
Tony's Pier Restaurant 362
Totonno's 215
Tribeca Treats 184
'21' Club 130
Uva 211
Vegetarian Dim Sum House 109
Veniero's Pasticceria and Caffè 111
Verb Café 165
Voce, A 202, *204*
Waterfront Crabhouse 168

Pubs & Bars

Ace Bar 219
Against the Grain 219
Another Room 216
Apropos 160
Artisanal 223
Ava Lounge 222
Bamboo 52 222
Baraza 219
Barcibo Enoteca 224
Barracuda 308
Barrio Chino 217
Bembe 226
Bin 71 224
Bin No.220 216
Bohemian Hall & Beer Garden 227
Brandy Library 216
Brasserie 223
Brooklyn Brewery 166
Brooklyn Social 226
Bubble Lounge 216
Candle Bar 309
Cattyshack 309
Centovini 221
Central Park Boathouse 224
Chi Chiz 307
Chumley's 115
Cock, the 306
Cubbyhole 307
Death & Co 219, *219*
Dekk 216
Delancey, the 217
Den 225
Detour 219
Eagle, the 308
East Side Company Bar 218
Eastern Bloc 307
Excelsior 309
Fanelli's Café 218
Fiamma Osteria 218
5 Ninth 221
Flatiron Lounge 221
Freddy's 226
G Lounge 308
Galapagos 226
Ginger's Bar *306*, *307*, 309
Grand Bar & Lounge 218
Gym 308
Henrietta Hudson 307
HK Lounge 308
Home Sweet Home 218
Hudson Bar 222
In Vino 219
'inoteca 218
Kemia Bar 222
Kimono Bar at Megu 216
Lenox Lounge 226
Lexington Bar & Books 224
Little Branch 221
Loft 224
Lollipop 224
Luca Lounge 220
Lucky Cat 220, *227*
Metropolitan 309
Monkey Bar 223, *223*
Monster 308
Moto 227
No Parking 309
Nowhere 307
O'Connor's 160
169 Bar 96
Palais Royale 217
Park Bar 222
Passerby 222
Pegu Club 221
Pudding Stones 224
Punch & Judy 218
reBar *225*, 227
St Nick's Pub 153
Sakagura 224
Schiller's Liquor Bar 218
Single Room Occupancy 223
Sortie 223
Souk, Le 220
Spice Market 221
Stain Bar 227
Stonewall Inn 308
Subway Inn 225
Suite 309
Superfine 227
Sutra Lounge 220
Therapy 308
Trinity Place 216
Turks & Frogs 221
230 Fifth 222
Union Hall *226*, 227
Urge, the 307
Uva 225
Village Pourhouse, the *217*, 221
Vlada 308 219
Von Bar 221
White Horse Tavern 115
Winnie's 96
Xicala Wine & Tapas Bar 217

Advertisers' Index

Please refer to the relevant pages for contact details

Blue Man Group **IFC**

Contents

Hotel Wolcott **4**

Intro

Top of the Rocks **8**

In Context

Brooklyn Tourism **20**

Where To Stay

Alamo **52**
Jazz Hostel **56**
Marmara Manhattan Hotel **62**

Sightseeing

American Musuem of Natural History **86**
City Pass **92**
Empire State Building Observatory **116**

Eat, Drink, Shop

Hard Rock Café **180**
St. Andrews Pub & Restaurant **186**

Arts & Entertainment

Theatremania.com **258**
Young Frankenstein **342**
Hairspray **346**
Chicago **346**
Phantom of the Opera **348**
Spamalot **348**
Wicked **350**
Stomp **350**
SoHo Playhouse **352**
The Color Purple **352**
A Chorus Line **352**

Directory

Zoom Airlines **364**

Map

MTA/Metrocard **396**
SilverJet **IBC**

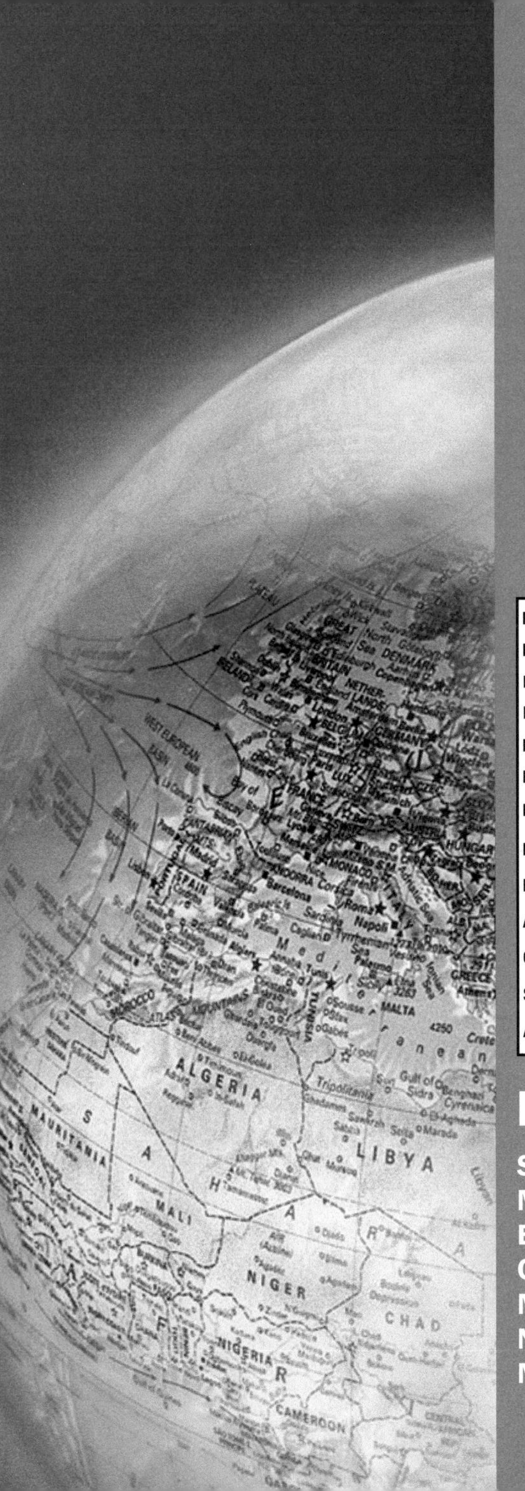

Major sight or landmark	
Hospital or college	
Railway station	
Parks	
River	
Freeway	478
Main road	
Main road tunnel	
Pedestrian road	
Airport	
Church	
Subway station	M
Area name	SOHO

Maps

Street Index 398
Manhattan 402
Brooklyn 410
Queens 412
Manhattan Bus Map 413
New York City Subway 414
Manhattan Subway 416

Street Index

Manhattan

65th St Transverse Rd - p405 D21
79th St Transverse Rd - p405 D19/E19
86th St Transverse Rd - p406 D18/E18
97th St Transverse Rd - p406 D17/E17
145th St Bridge - p408 E10
196th St - p409 B4

Abraham A Kazan St - p403 H30
Academy St - p409 B3/C3
Adam Clayton Powell Jr Blvd - p406 D15, p407 D11-15, p408 D9-11
Albany St - p402 D33/E33
Alex Rose Pl - p409 B5
Alexander Hamilton Bridge - p409 C6
Allen St - p403 F29/30
Amsterdam Ave - p405 C19-22, p406 C15-18, p407 C11-15, p408 C7-11, p409 C4-7
Ann St - p402 E32/F32
Arden St - p409 B3/4
Asser Levy Pl - p404 G26
Astor Pl - p403 E28/F28
Attorney St - p403 G29/30
Audubon Ave - p409 C4-7
Audubon Terr - p408 B9
Ave of the Finest - p402 F31/32
Avenue A - p403 G28/29
Avenue B - p403 G28/29
Avenue C - p403 G28/29
Avenue D - p403 G28/29

Bank St - p403 C28/D28
Barclay St - p402 E32
Barrow St - p403 D29
Battery Pl - p402 E33
Baxter St - p403 F30
Bayard St - p402 F31
Beach St - p402 D31
Beak St - p409 B3
Beaver St - p402 E33
Bedford St - p403 D29
Beekman Pl - p404 F23
Beekman St - p402 E32/F32
Bennett Ave - p409 B4/5/6
Bethune St - p403 C28
Bialystoker Pl - p403 G30
Bleecker St - p403 D28/E29/F29
Bogardus St - p409 B4
Bond St - p403 F29
Bridge St - p402 E33
Broad St - p402 E33
Broadhurst Ave - p408 C9/10
Broadway - p402 E31/32, p403 E27/E29/30, p404 D23/24/25/ E25/26, p405 C19-22, p406 C16-18, p408 B8-11, p409 B3-7/ C1/2
Broadway Terr - p409 B4
Brooklyn Bridge
Brooklyn-Battery Tunnel - p402 E34
Broome St - p403 E30/F30/G30

Cabrini Blvd - p409 B5/6
Canal St - p403 D30/E30
Cardinal Hayes Pl - p402 F31
Carlisle St - p402 E33
Carmine St - p403 D29
Cathedral Parkway - p406 B15/C15/D15
Catherine St - p402 F31
Cedar St - p402 E33
Central Park North - p406 D15/E15
Central Park West - p405 D19-22, p406 D15-18
Centre Market Pl - p403 F30
Centre St - p402 E32/F31
Chambers St - p402 D31/E31
Charles St - p403 C29/D28
Charlton St - p403 D29/30
Cherry St - p402 G31, p403 H30
Chisum Pl - p407 E11
Chittenden Ave - p409 B5
Christopher St - p403 C29/D29
Chrystie St - p403 F29/30
Church St - p402 E31/32
Claremont Ave - p407 B13/14
Clarkson St - p403 D29
Cleveland Pl - p403 E30/F30
Clinton St - p402 G31, p403 G29/30
Coenties Slip –P402 F33
Collister St - p402 D31, p403 D30
Columbia St - p403 H29
Columbus Ave - p405 C19-22, p406 C15-18
Commerce St - p403 D29
Convent Ave - p407 C11/12/13, p408 C10
Cooper St - p409 B2/3
Cornelia St - p403 D29
Cortlandt St - p402 E32
Cotlandt Alley - p402 E31
Crosby St - p403 E29/30
Cumming St - p409 B3
Cuyler's Slip - p402 F33

Delancey St North - p403 G29/30/H29
Delancey St South - p403 F30/G30
Depeyster St - p402 F33
Desbrosses St - p403 D30/E30
Dey St - p402 E32
Division St - p402 F31
Dominick St - p403 D30/E30
Dongan St - p409 B3
Dover St - p402 F32
Downing St - p403 D29
Duane St - p402 E31
Duke Ellington Blvd - p406 B16/C16/D16
Dyckman St - p409 B3/C3/4

E 2nd St - p403 F29/G29
E 3rd St - p403 F29/G29
E 4th St - p403 F29/G29
E 5th St - p403 F28/G28
E 6th St - p403 F28/G28
E 7th St - p403 F28/G28
E 8th St - p403 F28/G28
E 9th St - p403 F28/G28
E 10th St - p403 F28/G28
E 11th St - p403 F28/G28
E 12th St - p403 F28/G28
E 13th St - p403 E27/ F27/G27
E 14th St - p403 E27/ F27/G27
E 15th St - p403 E27/ F27/G27
E 16th St - p403 E27/ F27/G27
E 18th St - p403 E27/F27
E 20th St - p403 E27/ F27/G27
E 22nd St - p404 E26/F26
E 23rd St - p404 E26/F26
E 24th St - p404 E26/F26
E 26th St - p404 E26/F26
E 28th St - p404 E26/F26
E 28th St - p404 F26
E 30th St - p404 E25/ F25/G25
E 32nd St - p404 E25/ F25/G25
E 34th St - p404 E25/ F25/G25
E 36th St - p404 E25/ F25/G25
E 38th St - p404 E24/ F24/G24
E 40th St - p404 E24/ F24/G24
E 42nd St - p404 E24/ F24/G24
E 44th St - p404 E24/ F24/G24
E 46th St - p404 E23/ F23/G23
E 48th St - p404 E23/ F23/G23
E 50th St - p404 E23/ F23/G23
E 52nd St - p404 E23/ F23/G23
E 54th St - p404 E22/ F22/G22
E 56th St - p404 E22/ F22/G22
E 57th St - p404 E22/ F22/G22
E 58th St - p404 E22/ F22/G22
E 60th St - p404 E22/ F22/G22
E 62nd St - p404 E21/ F21/G21
E 64th St - p404 E21/ F21/G21
E 66th St - p404 E21/ F21/G21
E 68th St - p404 E21/ F21/G21
E 70th St - p404 E20/ F20/G20
E 72nd St - p405 E20/ F20/G20
E 74th St - p404 E20/ F20/G20
E 76th St - p404 E20/ F20/G20
E 78th St - p404 E19/ F19/G19
E 79th St - p404 E19/ F19/G19
E 80th St - p404 E19/ F19/G19
E 82nd St - p404 E19/ F19/G19
E 84th St - p406 E18/ F18/G18
E 86th St - p406 E18/ F18/G18
E 88th St - p406 E18/ F18/G18
E 90th St - p406 E18/ F18/G18
E 92nd St - p406 E17/ F17/G17
E 94th St - p406 E17/F17
E 96th St - p406 E17/F17
E 98th St - p406 E17/F17
E 100th St - p406 E16/ F16/G16
E 102nd St - p406 E16/ F16/G16
E 103rd St - p406 E16/ F16/G16
E 105th St - p406 E16/ F16/G16
E 107th St - p406 E16/ F16/G16
E 109th St - p406 E15/ F15/G15
E 111th St - p406 E15/ F15/G15
E 113th St - p406 F15
E 115th St - p407 E15/15
E 117th St - p407 E14/ 14
E 119th St - p407 E14/ 14
E 121st St - p407 E14/ 14
E 123rd St - p407 E13/ 13
E 127th St - p407 E13/ 13
E 129th St - p407 E13/ 13
E 131st St - p407 E12
E 135th St - p407 E12
E Houston St - p403 F29/ G29
East Broadway - p403 G30
East Drive - p405 E21, p406 E16/17/18
East End Ave - p405 G19, p406 G18
Edgecombe Ave - p407 C11, p408 C8/9/10
Eighth Ave - p403 D27/28, p404 D23-26
Eldridge St - p403 F29/30
Eleventh Ave - p404 C23-26, p405 B19-22
Elizabeth St - p403 F29/ 30
Ellwood St - p409 B4
Erickson Pl - p402 D32
Essex St - p403g29/30
Exchange Pl - p402 E33
Exterior St - p409 C3

Fairview Ave - p409 B4/5
Fifth Ave - p403 E27/28, p404 E23-26, p405 E19-22, p406 E15-18, p407 E11-15
First Ave - p403 F27/28, p404 F23-26, p405 F19-22, p406 F15-18, p407 F11-15
First Pl - p402 E33
Fletcher St - p402 F33
Foley Sq - p402 E31/F31
Forsyth St - p402 F31, p403 F29/30
Fort Washington Ave - p408 B7/8, p409 B5/6/7
Fourth Ave - p403 E28/28/29
Frankfort St - p402 E32/F32
Franklin D Roosevelt Dr - p402 F32/33/G31, p403 G27/H27/28/ 29/30, p404 G23-26, p405 G19-22, p406 G15-18
Franklin St - p402 D31/E31
Frederick Douglass Blvd - p407 D11-15, p408 D9-11
Freedom Pl - p404 B21
Freeman Alley - p403 F29/30
Front St - p402 F32/33
Ft. George Hill - p409 C4
Fulton St - p402 E32/F32

Gansevoort St - p403 C28
George Washington Bridge - p409 A6/7
Gold St - p402 F32
Gouverneur Lane - p402 F33
Gouverneur St - p403 H30
Grand St - p403 E30/F30/G30
Great Jones St - p403 F29
Greene St - p403 E28/29/30
Greenwich Ave - p403 D28
Greenwich St - p402 D31/E31/31/E33, p403 D28/29/30
Grove St - p403 D28/29

Hamill Pl - p402 F31
Hamilton Place - p407 C11
Hanover Sq - p402 F33
Hanover St - p402 F33
Harlem River Dr - p408 C7/8/D9/10/E10/11
Harrison St - p402 D31
Haven Ave - p408 B7
Henry Hudson Bridge - p409 B1
Henry Hudson Pkwy - p405 B19-22, p408 B7-11, p409 B1-7
Henry J Browne Blvd - p406 B18/C18/D18
Henry St - p402 F31/G31, p403 G30/H30
Henshaw St - p409 B3
Herald Square - p404 D25
Hester St - p403 E30/F30
Hillside Ave - p409 B4/C4
Holland Tunnel - p403 C30/D30
Horatio St - p403 C28/D28
Howard St - p403 E30
Hubert St - p402 D31
Hudson St - p402 E32, p403 D28/29/30

Indian Rd - p409 B1
Irving Pl - p403e27
Isham St - p409 C2

Jackson St - p403h30
Jane St - p403 C28/D28
Jay St - p402e32
Jefferson St - p402 G31, p403 G30
John St - p402 E32/F32
Jones St - p403 D28/29

Kenmare St - p403 F30
King St - p403 D29

La Guardia Pl - p403 E29
La Salle St - p407 C13
Lafayette St - p402 E31, p403 E29/30
Laight St - p402 D31, p403 D30/E30
Laurel Hill Terr - p409 C5/6
Leonard St - p402 E31
Leroy St - p403 D29
Lewis St - p403 H30
Lexington Ave - p404 E23-26, p405 E19-22, p406 E15-18, p407 E11-15
Liberty St - p402 E32
Lincoln Tunnel - p404 B24
Lispenard St - p403 E30
Little W 12th St - p403 C28
Ludlow St - p403 G29/30

Macdougal St - p403 E29
Madison Ave - p405 E19-22
Madison Ave - p404 E23-26, p406 E15-18, p407 E11-15
Madison St - p402 F31/ G31, p403 G30/H30
Madison Sq - p404 E26
Mahr Circle - p408 C9
Maiden Lane - p402 E32/F33
Malcolm X Blvd - p406 D15, p407 D11-15
Manhattan Ave - p406 C15/16, p407 C11-15
Manhattan Bridge - p402 G31/32

Margaret Corbin Dr - p409 B4
Market St - p402 F31/G31
Marketfield St - p402 E33
Martin Luther King Jr Blvd - p407 B13/C13
Mercer St - p403 E29/30
Mitchell Pl - p404 F23
Monroe St - p402 F31/G31
Montgomery St - p402 H31, p403 G30
Moore St - p402e34
Morningside Dr - p406 C15, p407 C14/15
Morris St - p402 E33
Morton St - p403 D29
Mosco St - p402 F31
Mott St - p403 F29/30
Mt Carmel Pl - p404 F26
Mulberry St - p403 F29/30
Murray St - p402 D32/E32

Nagle Ave - p409 B4/C3/4
Nassau St - p402 E32/33
Nathan D Perlman Pl - p403 F27
New St - p402 E33
Ninth Ave - p404 C23-26, p405 C19-22, p409 C1/2/3
Norfolk St - p403 G29/30
North End Ave - p402 D32
North Moore St - p402 D31/E31

Old Broadway - p407 C13
Old Slip - p402 F33
Oliver St - p402 F31
Orchard St - p403g29/30
Overlook Terr - p409 B5

Park Ave - p405 E19-22, p406 E15-18, p407 E11-15
Park Ave South - p403 E27, p404 E24-26
Park Pl W - p402 D32
Park Row - p402 F31/32
Park Terr E - p409 C1/2
Park Terr W - p409 C1/2
Parkpl - p402 E32
Payson Ave - p409 B2/3
Pearl St - p402 F31/32/33
Peck Slip - p402 F32
Pell St - p402 F31
Perry St - p403 C28/D28
Pike St - p402 G31
Pine St - p402 E33/F33
Pitt St - p403 G29/30
Platt St - p402 F32/33
Prince St - p403 E29
Public Pl - p402 D32

Queens-Midtown Tunnel - p404 G24

Reade St - p402 E31
Rector Pl - p402 D33/E33
Rector St - p402 E33
Reinhold Niebuhr Pl - p407 B14
Renwick St - p403 D30
Ridge St - p403 G29/30
River Terr - p402 D32
Riverside Blvd - p405 C19-22
Riverside Dr - p404 B19/20, p408 B7-11, p409 B3-7
Riverside Dr East - p407 B13, p408 B8/9
Riverside Dr West - p407 B13/14
Rivington St - p403 F29/F29
Rutgers St - p402 G31
Rutherford Pl - p403 F27

S End Ave - p402 D33
S William St - p402 E33
Seaman Ave - p409 B2/C2
Second Ave - p403 F27/28, p404 F23-26, p405 F19-22, p406 F15-18, p407 F11-15
Second Pl - p402 E33
Seventh Ave - p403 D27/28, p404 D23-26, p405 D22
Seventh Ave South - p403 D28/29
Sherman Ave - p409 B3/C2/3
Sickles St - p409 B4
Sixth Ave - p403 D27/28/29, p404 D23-26, p405 D22
South St - p402 G31/32
Spring St - p403 D30/E30/F30/G30
Spruce St - p402 E32/F32
St Andrews Pl - p402 E32
St Clair Pl - p407 B13
St James Pl - p402 F31/32
St John's Ln - p403 E30
St Lukes Pl - p403 D29
St Marks Place - p403 F28
St Nicholas Ave - p406 D15, p407 D14/15, p408 C7-11, p409 C4-7
St Nicholas Pl - p408 C9
St Nicholas Terr - p407 C12/13
Staff St - p409 B3
Stanton St - p403 F29/G29
Staple St - p402e32
Stone St - p402 E33
Stuyvesant St - p403 F28
Suffolk St - p403 G29/30
Sullivan St - p403 E29/30
Sutton Pl - p404 G22
Sutton Pl South - p404 G22
Szold Pl - p403 G28

Tenth Ave - p403 C27, p404 C23-26, p405 C19-22, p409 C2/3
Thames St - p402 E33
Thayer St - p409 B3
The Bowery - p403 F29/30
Third Ave - p403 F27/28, p404 F23-26, p405 F19-22, p406 F15-18, p407 F11-15
Third Ave Bridge - p407 F12/13
Third Pl - p402 E33
Thomas St - p402 E31
Thompson St - p403 E29/30
Tiemann Pl - p407 B13
Times Sq - p404 D24
Trans Manhattan Expwy - p409 B6/C6
Triborough Bridge - p407 G13
Tudor City Pl - p404 F24
Twelfth Ave - p404 B23-26, p407 B11/12

Union Sq - p403 E27
University Pl - p403 E28

Vandam St - p403 D30
Varick St - p402 E32, p403 D29/30/E30
Verdi Square - p405 C20
Vesey Pl - p402 D32
Vesey St - p402 D32/E32
Vestry St - p403 D30/E30

W 3rd St - p403 E29
W 4th St - p403 D28/E28/29
W 8th St - p403 D28/E28
W 9th St - p403 D28/E28
W 10th St - p403 C29/D28/E28
W 11th St - p403 C28/D28/E28
W 12th St - p403 C28/D28/E28
W 13th St - p403 C27/D27/E27
W 14th St - p403 C27/D27/E27
W 16th St - p403 C27/D27/E27
W 18th St - p403 C27/D27/E27
W 20th St - p403 C27/D27/E27
W 22nd St - p404 B26/C26/D26
W 23rd St - p404 B26/C26/D26
W 26th St - p404 B26/C26/D26
W 28th St - p404 B26/C26/D26
W 30th St - p404 B25/C25/D25
W 34th St - p404 B25/C25/D25
W 36th St - p404 B25/C25/D25
W 38th St - p404 B24/C24/D24
W 40th St - p404 B24/C24/D24
W 42nd St - p404 B24/C24/D24
W 44th St - p404 B24/C24/D24
W 46th St - p404 B23/C23/D23
W 48th St - p404 B23/C23/D23
W 50th St - p404 B23/C23/D23
W 52nd St - p404 B23/C23/D23
W 54th St - p404 B22/C22
W 56th St - p404 B22/C22
W 57th St - p404 B22/C22
W 58th St - p404 B22/C22
W 60th St - p404 B22/22
W 62nd St - p404 B21/C21
W 64th St - p404 B21/C21
W 66th St - p404 B21/C21
W 68th St - p404 C20/D20
W 70th St - p404 B20/C20
W 72nd St - p404 B20/C20
W 74th St - p404 B20/C20
W 76th St - p404 B20/C20
W 78th St - p404 B19/C19
W 79th St - p404 B19/C19
W 80th St - p404 B19/C19
W 82nd St - p404 B19/C19
W 84th St - p406 B18/C18/D18
W 86th St - p406 B18/C18/D18
W 88th St - p406 B18/C18/D18
W 90th St - p406 B18/C18/D18
W 92nd St - p406 B18/C18/D18
W 94th St - p406 B17/C17/D17
W 96th St - p406 B17/C17/D17
W 98th St - p406 B17/C17/D17
W 100th St - p406 B16/C16/D16
W 102nd St - p406 B16/C16/D16
W 103rd St - p406 B16/C16/D16
W 105th St - p406 B16/C16/D16
W 106th St - p406 B16/C16/D16
W 107th St - p406 B16/C16/D16
W 109th St - p406 B15/C15/D15
W 111th St - p406 B15/C15/D15
W 113th St - p406 B15/C15/D15
W 115th St - p407 B14/C14/D14/E14
W 116th St - p407 B14/C14/D14/E14
W 119th St - p407 B14/C14/D14/E14
W 121st St - p407 B14/C14/D14/E14
W 123rd St - p407 B13/C13/D13/E13
W 125th St - p407 C13/D13/E13
W 126th St - p407 C13
W 127th St - p407 C13/D13/E13
W 129th St - p407 B13/C13/D13/E13
W 131st St - p407 B12/C12/D12/E12
W 133rd St - p407 B12/C12/D12/E12
W 135th St - p407 B12/C12/D12/E12
W 137th St - p407 B12/C12/D12/E12
W 139th St - p407 B11/C11/D11/E11
W 141st St - p407 B11/C11/D11/E11
W 143rd St - p407 B11/C11/D11/E11, p408 B11/C11/D11
W 145th St - p408 B10/C10/D10
W 147th St - p408 B10/C10/D10
W 149th St - p408 B10/C10/D10
W 151st St - p408 B10/C10/D10
W 153rd St - p408 B9/C9/D9
W 155th St - p408 B9/C9/D9
W 157th St - p408 B9/C9
W 159th St - p408 B9/C9
W 161st St - p408 B8/C8
W 163rd St - p408 B8/C8
W 165th St - p408 B8/C8
W 167th St - p408 C8
W 169th St - p408 B7/C7
W 171st St - p408 B7/C7
W 173rd St - p408 B7/C7
W 173rd St - p409 B7/C7
W 175th St - p409 B7/C7
W 177th St - p409 B6/C6
W 179th St - p409 B6/C6
W 180th St - p409 B6/C6
W 181st St - p409 B6/C6
W 183rd St - p409 C6
W 186th St - p409 B5/C5
W 187th St - p409 B5/C5
W 189th St - p409 C5
W 191st St - p409 C5
W 193rd St - p409 C4
W 201st St - p409 C3
W 203rd St - p409 C3
W 204th St - p409 B2/C3
W 205th St - p409 C3
W 207th St - p409 B2/C2/3
W 208th St - p409 C2/3
W 211th St - p409 C2
W 213th St - p409 C2
W 215th St - p409 B1/C2
W 216th St - p409 C1
W 218th St - p409 C1
W 219th St - p409 C1
W 220th St - p409 C1
W Houston St - p403 D29/E29
W Thames St - p402 D33/E33
Wadsworth Ave - p409 B5/6/7
Wadsworth Terr - p409 B5
Wagner Pl - p402 F32
Walker St - p402 E31
Wall St - p402 F33
Warren St - p402 D32
Washington Bridge - p409 C6
Washington Pl - p403 D28/E28
Washington Sq - p403 E28
Washington Sq East - p403 E28/29
Washington Sq West - p403 E28
Washington St - p402 E33, p403 C28/D29/30
Water St - p402 F32/33/G31/H31
Watts St - p403 D30/E30/H30
Waverly Pl - p403 D28/E28
West Broadway - p402 D31/32, p403 E29/30
West Drive - p405 D21, p406 D16/17/18
West End Ave - p405 B19-22, p406 C15-18, p407 C11-15
West Side Hwy - p402 D31, p403 C27/28/29/D29/30, p404 B23-26
White St - p402 E31
Whitehall St - p402 E34
William St - p402 E33/F32/33
Williamsburg Bridge - p403 H29/30
Wooster St - p403 E29/30
Worth St - p402e31
Wui Plaza - p402 E33

York Ave - p404 G21/22

Brooklyn

Map pp410-411

1st Ave - R13
1st Pl - S10
1st St - S11/T11
2nd Ave - R13/S11
2nd Pl - S10/11
2nd St - S11/T11, U6
3rd Ave - S11/T11
3rd Pl - S11
3rd St - S11/T11
4th Ave - R13/T10/11
4th Pl - S11
4th St - S11/T11
5th Ave - R13/S13/T10/11
5th St - S11/T11
6th Ave - R13/S13/T11
6th St - S11
7th Ave - S13/T11
7th St - T11/12
8th Ave - S13/T12
8th St - T11/12
9th Ave - S13
9th St - T11/12
10th Ave - S13/T12
10th St - S11/T11
11th Ave - T12
11th St - S11/T11
12th St - S11
13th St - S11/T12
14th St - S11/12/T12
15th St - S11/12/T12
16th St - S12
17th St - S12/T12
18th St - S12/T12
19th St - T12
20th St - T12
21st St - S12
22nd St - S12
23rd St - S12
24th St - S12
25th St - S12
26th St - S12
27th St - S12
28th St - S12
29th St - S12/V6
30th St - S12/V6
31st St - S12/W6
32nd St - S12
33rd St - S12
34th St - S12, W6
35th St - R12/S12/13/V13/W6
36th St - S12/13/T13

37th St - R12/S12/
13/W6
38th St - R13/S13/W6
39th St - R12/13/
S13/W6
40th St - S13
41st St - R13/S13
42nd St - R13/W6
43rd St - R13/W6/7
44th St - R13/S13/W6
45th St - S13
46th St - S13/W6
47th St - S13/W7
48th Ave - p411 W6
48th St - S13/W7
49th Ave - p411 W6
49th St - R13
50th Ave - p411 W6
50th St - R13
51st Ave - p411 V6/W6
51st St - R13
52nd St - R 13
53rd St - R13
54th Ave - p411 W6
54th Dr - p411 W6
54th Rd - p411 W6
54th St - R13
55th Ave - p411 U6/W6
55th St - R13
56th St - R13
57th Ave - p411 W7
57th St - R13
58th Rd - p411 W7
58th St - R13

Adams St - p411 T9
Adelphi St - U10/T9
Ainslie St - p411 V8
Albany Ave - V11/12
Albee Sq - p411 T9
Albemarle Rd - T13/U13
Amity St - S10
Anthony St - p411 V7/W7
Apollo St - p411 V7
Argyle Rd - U13
Ashland Pl - T10
Atlantic Ave - S10/U10

Bainbridge St - W10
Baltic St - S10/T10
Banker St - p411 U7
Bartlett St - p411 V9
Bay St - R11/S11
Beadel St - p411 V7/W7
Beard St - R11
Beaver St - p411 V9/W9
Bedford Ave - U10/13/
V10/U7/8/9
Bergen St - V11/W11
Berkeley Pl - T11
Berry St - p411 U7
Beverley Rd - U13/V13/
W13
Boerum Pl - S10/V8
Bogart St - p411 W8
Bond St - T10
Borden Ave - p411 V6
Bowne St - R10/S10
Bradley Ave - p411 W6
Bridge St - p411 T9
Bridgewater St - p411 W7
Broadway - W10/U8/
V9/W9
Brooklyn Ave - V11/12/13
Brooklyn Bridge - p411 S8
Brooklyn Queens Exwy -
p411 U8/9/V7/W7
Buckingham Rd - U13
Buffalo Ave - W11
Bush St - S11
Bushwick Ave - p411 V8
Butler St - S10/T10/11

Cadman Plz E - p411 S9
Calyer St - p411 V6/7
Cambridge Pl - U10
Carlton Ave - T10/U10
Carroll St - S10/T11/V12
Caton Ave - U13
Central Ave - p411 W9
Centre St - S11
Chauncey St - W10
Cherry St - p411 W7
Chester Ave - T13
Church Ave - U13/W13
Clarendon Rd - V13/W13
Clark St - p411 S9
Clarkson Ave - W12
Classon Ave - U10/U9
Claver Pl - U10
Clay St - p411 U6/V6
Clermont Ave - p411 U9
Clifton Pl - U10
Clinton Ave - U10/U9
Clinton St - S10/11
Clymer St - p411 P411 U8
Coffey St - R11
Columbia St - R11/12/
S10
Commerce St - R10/S11
Commercial St - p411 U6
Commercial Wharf - R10
Concord St - p411 T9
Congress St - S10
Conover St - R11
Conselyea St - p411 V8
Cook St - p411 W9
Cortelyou Rd - V13
Court St - S10
Cranberry St - p411 S9
Creamer St - S11
Crooke Ave - p410
Crown St - V12
Cumberland St - T10/T9

Dahill Rd - T13
Dean St - T10/U10/U11/
V11/W11
Decatur St - W10
Degraw St - S10/T10/11
Dekalb Ave - T10/U10/
V10/W9
Delavan St - R10/11
Devoe St - p411 V8/W8
Diamond St - p411 V7
Dikeman St - R11
Division Ave - p411 U8
Division Pl - p411 V7/W7
Dobbin St - p411 U7
Douglass St - T10/11
Downing St - U10
Driggs Ave - p411 U7/8/
V7
Duffield St - p411 T9
Dupont St - p411 U6/V6
Dwight St - R11

E 2nd St - T13
E 3rd St - T13
E 4th St - T13
E 5th St - T13
E 7th St - T13
E 8th St - U13
E 19th St - U13
E 21st St - U13
E 22nd St - U13
E 28th St - V13
E 29th St - V13
E 31st St - V13
E 32nd St - V13
E 34th St - V13
E 37th St - V13
E 38th St - V13
E 39th St - V13
E 40th St - V13
E 42nd St - V13/W13
E 43rd St - W13
E 45th St - W12/13
E 46th St - W12/13
E 48th St - W13
E 49th St - W12/13
E 51st St - W12/13
E 52nd St - W12/13
E 53rd St - W12/13
E 54th St - W12/13
E 55th St - W12/13
E 56th St - W12/13
E 57th St - W13
E 58th St - W12/13
E 59th St - W13
E 91st St - W12
E 93rd St - W12
E 95th St - W12
E 96th St - W12
E 98th St - W12
Eagle St - p411 U6/V6
East New York Ave -
V12/W12
Eastern Pkwy - V11/W11
Eckford St - p411 V7
Ellery St - p411 V9
Empire Blvd - V12
Engert Ave - p411 V7
Erasmus St - V13
Evergreen Ave - p411 W9

Fairview Pl - V13
Fenimore St - V12
Ferris St - R11
Flatbush Ave - U12/13
Flushing Ave - p411 U9/
V9/W8
Ford St - W12
Fort Greene Pl - T10
Fort Hamilton Pkwy - T13
Franklin Ave - U10/U9
Franklin St - p411 U6
Freeman St - p411 U6/V6
Frost St - p411 V7
Fulton St - T10/V10/11

Gardner Ave - p411 W7/
W8
Garfield Pl - T11
Gates Ave - V10
George St - p411 W9
Gerry St - p411 V9
Gold St - p411 T9
Graham Ave - p411 V8
Grand Army Plaza - U11
Grand Ave - U10/U9
Grand St - p411 U8/W8
Grand St Ext - p411 V8
Grattan St - p411 W8
Green St - p411 U6/V6
Greene Ave - U10/W9
Greenpoint Ave - p411
V6/W6
Greenwood Ave - T13
Guernsey St - p411 V7

Hall St - U10/U9
Halleck St - S11
Halsey St - W10
Hamilton Ave - S11
Hancock St - V10
Hanson Pl - T10
Harrison Ave - p411 V8/9
Harrison Pl - p411 W8
Hart St - p411 V9/W9
Hausman St - p411 V7
Havemeyer St - p411
U8/V8
Hawthorne St - V12
Henry St - S10
Herkimer St - W11
Hewes St - p411 U8/9/
V8
Heyward St - p411 U9/V9
Hicks St - S10
Hooper St - p411 U8/9/
V8
Hopkins St - p411 V9
Howard Ave - W10
Hoyt St - S10/T10
Hudson Ave - T10
Humboldt St - p411 V7/8
Huntington St - S11
Huron St - p411 U6/V6

Imlay St - R10
India St - p411 U6/V6
Ingraham St - p411 W8
Irving Pl - U10
Irving St - S10

Jackson St - p411 V7/8
Java St - p411 U6/V6
Jay St - p411 T9
Jefferson Ave - W10
Jefferson St - p411 W8/9
Jewel St - p411 V7
John St - p411 T9
Johnson Ave - p411 W8
Johnson St - p411 S9/T9

Kane St - S10
Keap St - p411 V8
Kent Ave - p411 U8/9
Kent St - p411 U6/V6
King St - R11
Kingsland Ave - p411
V6/7
Kingston Ave - V11/12
Knickerbocker Ave - p411
W9
Kosciusko St - V10/W9
Kossuth Pl - p411 W9

Lafayette Ave - U10/W9
Laurel Hill Blvd - p411 W6
Lawrence St - p411 T9
Lee Ave - p411 U8
Lefferts Ave - V12
Lefferts Pl - U10
Leonard St - p411 V8
Lewis Ave - W10/V9/W9
Lexington Ave - V10
Lincoln Pl - T11/V11/W11
Lincoln Rd - V12
Linden Blvd - V13
Livingston St - T10
Lombardy St - p411 W7
Lorimer St - p411 V8
Lorraine St - S11
Lott St - V13
Luquer St - S11
Lynch St - p411 U9/V9

Macdonough St - W10
Macon St - V10/W10
Madison St - W10
Malcolm X Blvd - W10
Manhattan Ave - p411
U6/V6
Manhattan Bridge - p411
S8
Maple St - V12
Marcy Ave - V10/U8/V8/9
Marginal St E - R12
Marion St - W10
Marlborough Rd - U13
Marshall St - p411 T9
Martense St - V13
Maspeth Ave - p411 W7
Maujer St - p411 V8
Mcguinness Blvd - p411
V6/7
Mckeever Pl - U12
Mckibbin St - p411
V8/W8
Meadow St - p411 W8
Melrose St - p411 W9
Meserole Ave - p411
U7/V7
Meserole St - p411
V8/W8
Metropolitan Ave - p411
U7/8/W8
Middagh St - p411 S9
Middleton St - p411
U9/V9
Midwood St - V12/W12
Mill St - S11
Milton St - p411 U6
Minna St - T13
Monitor St - p411 V6/7
Monroe St - V10/W10
Montague St - p411 S9
Montgomery St - V12
Montrose Ave - p411 V8
Moore St - p411 V9/W9
Morgan Ave - p411 W8
Moultrie St - p411 V6/7
Myrtle Ave - p411 U9/W9

N 1st St - p411 U8
N 3rd St - p411 U7/8
N 4th St - p411 U7/8
N 5th St - p411 U8
N 6th St - p411 U7
N 7th St - p411 U7
N 8th St - p411 U7
N 9th St - p411 U7
N 10th St - p411 U7
N 11th St - p411 U7
N 12th St - p411 U7
N 13th St - p411 U7
N 14th St - p411 U7
N 15th St - p411 U7
N Oxford St - p411 T9
N Portland Ave - p411 T9
Nassau Ave - p411 V7
Nassau St - p411 T9
Navy St - p411 T9
Nelson St - S11
Nevins St - T10
New York Ave - V12
Newell St - p411 V7
Noble St - p411 U7
Noll St - p411 W9
Norman Ave - p411 V7
Nostrand Ave - V10/11/
12/13/V9

Oak St - p411 U7
Ocean Pkwy - T13
Onderdonk Ave - p411 W8
Orange St - p411 S9
Orient Ave - p411 V8
Otsego St - R11

Pacific St - S10/T10/
V11/W11
Paidge Ave - p411 V6
Parade Pl - U13
Park Ave - p411 V9
Park Pl - V11/W11
Parkside Ave - U12/13/
V12
Patchen Ave - W10
Pearl St - p411 T9
Penn St - p411 U9
Pierrepont St - p411 S9
Pineapple St - p411 S9
Pioneer St - R10/11
Plymouth St - p411 T9
Poplar St - p411 S9
Porter Ave - p411 W7
Powers St - p411 V8
President St - S10/T11/
U11/V11
Prince St - p411 T9
Prospect Exwy - S12/T12
Prospect Ave - T12
Prospect Park Southwest -
T12/13
Prospect Park West -
T11/12
Prospect Pl - U11/W11
Provost St - p411 V6
Pulaski Bridge - p411 V6
Pulaski St - p411 V9
Putnam Ave - U10/V10

Quincy St - V10

Raleigh Pl - V13
Ralph Ave - W10/11
Randolph St - p411 W8
Reed St - R11
Remsen Ave - W12
Remsen St - p411 S9
Review Ave - p411 V6
Rewe St - p411 W8
Richards St - R11
Richardson St - p411 V7
River St - p411 U7/8
Rochester Ave - W11/12
Rock St - p411 W9
Rockaway Pkwy - W12
Rockwell Pl - T10
Rodney St - p411 U8/V8
Roebling St - p411 U8/V7
Rogers Ave - V11/12/13
Ross St - p411 U8/9
Rugby Rd - U13
Russell St - p411 V6/7
Rutland Rd - U12/V12/
W12
Rutledge St - p411 U9/V9
Ryerson St - p411 U9

S 1st St - p411 U8/V8
S 2nd St - p411 U8/V8
S 3rd St - p411 U8
S 4th St - p411 U8
S 5th St - p411 U8/V8
S 6th St - p411 U8
S 8th St - p411 U8
S 9th St - U P411 U8
S 10th St - p411 U8
S 11th St - p411 U8
S Elliott Pl - T10
S Oxford St - T10
S Portland Ave - T10
Sackett St - S10/T10/11
Saint Edwards St - p411
T9
Saint Felix St - T10
Saint James Pl - U10
Saint Johns PL - T11/
V11/W11
Saint Marks Ave -
U11/W11
Saint Marks Pl - T10
Saint Pauls Pl - U13
Sandford St - p411 U9/V9
Sands St - p411 T9
Schenectady Ave -
W11/12/13
Schermerhorn St - T10
Scholes St - p411 V8/W8
Scott Ave - p411 W7/8
Seabring St - R10/S10
Sedgwick St - S10
Seeley St - T13
Seigel St - p411 V8/9/
W8
Sharon St - p411 V8/W8
Sherman St - T13
Skillman Ave - p411 V8
Skillman St - U10/U9
Smith St - S10/11
Snyder Ave - V13/W13

Spencer St - p411 U9
Stagg St - p411 V8/W8
Starr Ave - p411 V6,W6
Starr St - p411 W8/9
State St - S10
Sterling Pl - V11/W11
Sterling St - U12/V12
Steuben St - p411 U9
Stewart Ave - p411 W8
Stockholm St - p411 W9
Stratford Rd - U13
Stuyvesant Ave - W10
Sullivan Pl - V12
Sullivan St - R11
Summit St - S10
Sumner Ave - V10/V9
Suydam St - p411 W8/9

Taaffe Pl - p411 U9
Taylor St - p411 U8
Tehama St - T13
Ten Eyck St - p411 V8
Terrace Pl - T12
Thomas St - p411 W7/8
Throop Ave - V10/V9
Tilden Ave - V13/W13
Tompkins Ave - V10/V9
Troutman St - p411 W8/9
Troy Ave - W11/12/13

Underhill Ave - U11
Union Ave - p411 V8
Union St - S10/V11/W11/12
Utica Ave - W11/12/13

Van Brunt St - S10
Van Buren St - V10/W10/W9
Van Dam St - p411 W6
Van Dyke St - R11
Vandam St - p411 W6
Vanderbilt Ave - U10
Vanderbilt St - T13
Vandervoort Ave - p411 W7/8
Varet St - p411 V9/W9
Varick Ave - p411 W7/8
Vernon Ave - p411 V9/W9
Verona St - R10/11
Veronica Pl - V13

W 9th St - S11
Wallabout St - p411 U9/V9
Walton St - p411 V9
Walworth St - p411 U9/V9
Warren St - S10
Washington Ave - U10/11/12
Water St - p411 S9
Waterbury St - p411 V8/W8
Waverly Ave - U10/U9
West St - p411 U6
Westminster Rd - U13
Whipple St - p411 V9
White St - p411 W8
Willoughby Ave - p411 U9/V9
Willow St - p411 S9
Wilson Ave - p411 W9
Wilson St - p411 U8
Windsor Pl - T12
Winthrop St - U12/V12/W12
Withers St - p411 V7
Wolcott St - R11
Woodruff Ave - U13
Wyckoff Ave - p411 W8
Wyckoff St - S10/T10
Wythe Ave - p411 U8

York St - p411 S9/T9

Queens

Map p412

1st St - W3
2nd St - U6
2nd St - W3
4th St - W3
8th St - W3
9th St - V4/5/W3
10th St - V4/5
11th St - V4
12th St - V4/W3
13th St - V4/W4
14th St - W3
18th St - W3/X2
19th Ave - Y2
19th Rd - Y3
19th St - W2/3/X2
20th Ave - X2
20th Rd - X2/3
20th St - X2
21st Ave - X3/Y3
21st Rd - X2
21st St - W3/4/X2
22nd Dr - X2
22nd Rd - X2
22nd St - V4/5/W3
23rd Ave - X3
23rd Rd - W2/X2
23rd St - V4/5
24th Ave - Y4
24th Rd - W3
24th St - V4/5/W4
25th Ave - X3/4/Y4
26th Ave - W3
26th St - X2/3
27th Ave - W3
27th St - X2/3
28th Ave - W3/X3/4
28th St - V5/W5/X2/3
29th Ave - W3
29th St - V5/6/W4/X3
30th Ave - Y4
30th Dr - W3
30th Rd - W3/X4
30th St - V5/W3/4
31 St St - X2/3
31st Ave - W4/X4/Y4
31st Dr - W3/4
31st Rd - W3
31st St - W5/6/X3
32nd Ave - Y4
32nd St - W4/X2/3
33rd Ave - W4
33rd Rd - V3/W4
33rd St - X3
34th Ave - W4
34th Ave - Y4/5
34th St - W4/5/6
35th Ave - W4
35th Ave - Y5
35th St - V6/W4/5/6/X3/4
36th Ave - W4
36th St - W4/5/6
37th Ave - W4/X5/Y5
37th St - W4/5/6/X3/4
38th Ave - V4/Y5
38th St - W5/6
39th Ave - W4/X5
39th Dr - X5
39th St - W5/6
40th Ave - V4/X5
40th St - W5/6
41st Ave - V4/X5/Y5
41st St - X3/Y3
42nd Pl - W5
42nd St - W6/X3/4/Y3
43rd Ave - V5/W5/X5/Y5
43rd Rd - V5
43rd St - W6/X3/Y3
44th Ave - V5/X5/Y5
44th St - W6/X3/4
45th Ave - V5
45th St - X3/Y3
46th Ave - V5
46th St - W6/X3/4/5/6/Y3
47th Ave - W5/X6/Y6
47th St - W7
48th Ave - U5
48th Ave - W6/X6/Y6
48th St - W7/X3/4/Y3
49th Ave - U5/V5/6/W6
49th Pl - X7
49th St - X4/5/6/Y3
50th Ave - W6/X6/Y6
50th St - X4
51st Ave - U5/V6/Y6
51st St - X5
52nd Ave - X6/Y6
52nd Dr - Y6
52nd Rd - X6/Y6
52nd St - X5
53rd Ave - W6/Y6
53rd Dr - Y6
53rd Pl - X4
54th Ave - X7
54th Rd - W6
54th St - X4/5/6/7
55th Ave - U6
55th Ave - X7
55th St - X4/5/6/7
56th Ave - W7/X7
56th Dr - W7
56th Rd - X7
56th St - X4-8
57th Ave - W7
57th Dr - X7
57th Rd - X7
57th St - X5/6/7
58th Ave - X7/Y7
58th Dr - X7
58th Rd - W7/X7/Y7
58th St - X4/5/6
59th Ave - X7/Y7
59th Rd - X7/Y7
59th St - X5/6/7
5th St - U5
60th Ave - Y7
60th Pl - Y8
60th Rd - X8/Y7
60th St - X5-8/Y5/8/9
61st St - X6/7/8/78
62nd Ave - Y7
62nd Rd - Y8
62nd St - Y4-9
63rd Ave - Y7
63rd St - X6/Y7
64th St - Y5-9
66th St - Y6/7
68th Rd - Y9
68th St - Y5/6/7
69th St - Y4/5
70th Ave - Y9
70th St - Y4-8
72nd P - Y6l
72nd St - Y3-7
72nd St - Y4/5
73rd St - Y4-7
74th St - Y3-7
75th St - Y7
76th St - Y3-7
78th St - Y3/4
79th St - Y6
80th St - Y3/4/Z5
81st St - Y4/5
82nd St - Y4
82nd St - Z5
84th St - Z4
86th St - Z4

Admiral Ave - Y8
Ainslie St - V8
Anthony St - V7/W7
Apollo St - V7
Astoria Blvd - W3/Y4

Banker St - U7
Baxter Ave - Z5
Beadel St - V7/W7
Bedford Ave - U7/8
Berrian Blvd - Y2
Berry St - U7
Blecker St - X8/Y8
Boerum St - V8
Bogart St - W8/9
Borden Ave - V6/W6
Borough Pl - X4
Broadway - U8/W4
Brooklyn Queens Expy E - Y4
Brooklyn Queens Expy W - X4/Y4
Bushwick Ave - V8/9

Caldwell Ave - Y7
Calyer St - V6
Catalpa Ave - Y9
Central Ave - Y9/Z9
Clay St - U6/V6
Clinton Ave - Y7
Commercial St - U6
Conselyea St - V8
Cornelia St - X9/Y9
Crescent St - W3/4
Cypress Ave - X8

Dekalb Ave - W8
Devoe St - V8/W8
Diamond St - V7
Ditmars Blvd - W2/X2/3/Y3
Division Pl - V7/W7
Dobbin St - U7/V7
Driggs Ave - U7/8/V7
Dupont St - U6/V6

Eagle St - U6/V6
Eckford St - V7
Eliot Ave - Y7

Fairview Ave - X8
Flushing Ave - W8/9/X7/8
Forest Ave - X8
Franklin St - U6/7
Freeman St - U6/V6
Fresh Pond Rd - X7/Y7/8
Frost St - V7
Frost St - V7/W7

Gardner Ave - W7/8
Garfield Ave - Y6
Gates Ave - X8
Gorsline St - Z6
Graham Ave - V8
Grand Ave - Y7
Grand St - V8/W8/X7
Grattan St - W8
Green St - U6/V6
Greene Ave - X8
Greenpoint Ave - V6
Grove St - X8
Guernsey St - U7/V7

Hamilton Pl - Y6/7
Harman St - X8
Harrison Ave - V8/9
Harrison Pl - W8
Hart St - X8
Hausman St - V7
Havemeyer St - U8
Hazen St - Y3
Henry Ave - Y6
Hewes St - U8/9
Hillyer St - Z6
Himrod St - X8
Honeywell St - W5
Hooper St - U8
Hope St - U8
Hull Ave - Y7
Humboldt St - V7/8
Hunter St - V5
Huron St - U6/V6

India St - U6/V6
Ingraham - W8
Ireland St - Y6

Jackson Ave - V5
Jackson St - U7
Jacobus St - Y6
Java St - U6/V6
Jay Ave - X7
Jefferson St - W8/9
Jewel St - V7
Johnson Ave - W8

Keap St - U8
Kent St - U6/V6
Kingsland Ave - V7/8
Kneeland Ave - Y6/Z6

Lee Ave - U8/9
Leonard St - V8/9
Linden St - X8/9
Lombardy St - V7/W7
Lorimer St - V8
Lynch St - V9

Madison St - X9/Y8
Main Ave - W3
Manhattan Ave - U6/V8/9
Manilla St - Z6
Marcy Ave - U8/9/V9
Maspeth Ave - W7/X7
Maujer St - V8
Maurice Ave - X6/7/Y6
Mcguinness Blvd - V6/7
Mckibbin St - V8/W8
Meadow St - W8
Menahan St - X8/9
Meserole Ave - U7
Meserole St - W8
Metropolitan Ave - W8/9
Milton St - U6
Monitor St - V7
Montrose Ave - V8
Moore St - V9
Morgan Ave - V7/W7/8
Moultrie St - V6/7
Mount Olivet Cres - Y8

N 4th St - U7/8
N 6th St - U7
N 8th St - U7
N 10th St - U7
N 12th St - U7
N 14th St - U7
N Henry St - V7
Nassau Ave - V7
Newell St - V7
Newtown Ave - W3
Newtown Rd - X4
Noble St - U7
Norman Ave - V7
Northern Blvd - Y4
Nurge Ave - X8

Onderdonk Ave - W8/X8/9

Page Pl - X7
Paidge Ave - V6
Palmetto St - Y8
Perry Ave - Y7
Pleasant View St - Z7/8
Powers St - V8
Provost St - V6
Pulaski Bridge - V6

Queens Blvd - W5/X5
Queensboro Bridge - U4
Queens-Midtown Tunnel - U5

Rene Ct - X8
Review Ave - V6
Richardson St - V7
Rikers Island Bridge - Y2/3
Rodney St - U8/V8
Roebling St - U8/V7
Roosevelt Ave - Y5/Z5
Russell St - V6/7

S 1st St - U8/V8
S 2nd St - U8/V8
S 4th St - U8
S 5th St - U8/V8
Saint Nicholas Ave - X8/9
Scholes St - W8
Scott Ave - W7/8
Seigel St - V8/9
Seneca Ave - X8/9
Sharon St - V8/W8
Shore Blvd - X2
Skillman Ave - V5-8/W5/X5
Stagg St - V8
Stanhope St - X8
Starr Ave - V6/W6
Starr St - W8/9
Steinway Pl - Y2
Steinway St - W3/4/Y2
Stewart Ave - W8
Stockholm St - X8
Sutton St - V7
Suydam St - W8
Suydam St - X8

Ten Eyck St - W8
Thames St - W8
Thomson Ave - V5/W5
Traffic St - Y8
Triborough Bridge - W2
Troutman St - W8/X8
Tyler Ave - X6/Y6

Union Ave - V8/9

Van Dam St - W5/6
Vandam St - V7
Vandervoort Ave - W7/8
Varet St - V9
Varick Ave - W7
Vernon Blvd - V3/4/5

Waterbury St - V8/W8
West St - U6/7
White St - W8/9
Willoughby Ave - W8/9/X8
Wilson St - U8
Withers St - V7/8
Woodbine St - Y8
Woodside Ave - X5/Y5
Woodward Ave - X8/9
Wyckoff Ave - X9

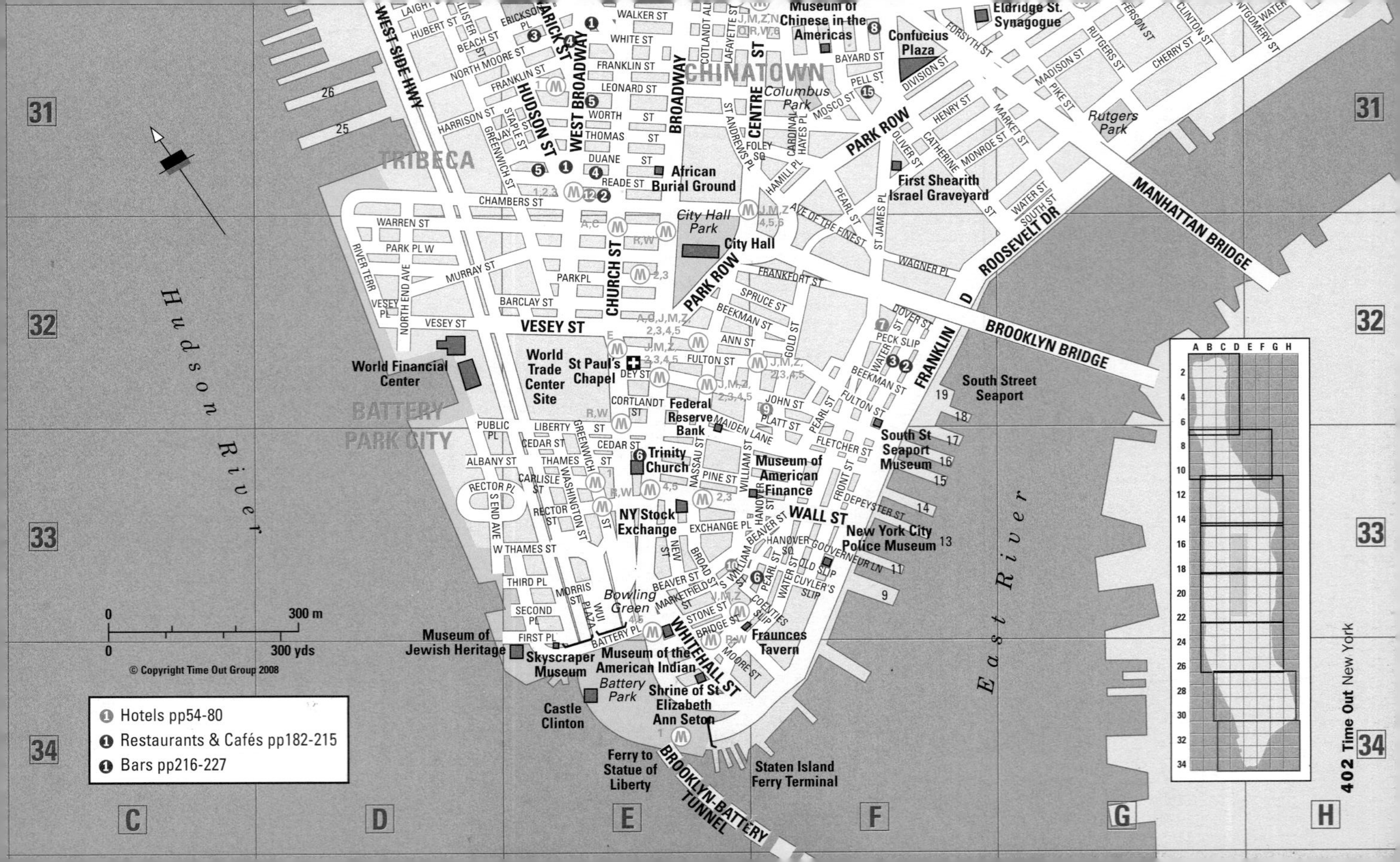

Hotels pp54-80
Restaurants & Cafés pp182-215
Bars pp216-227
© Copyright Time Out Group 2008
0
300 m
300 yds
Hudson River
East River
TRIBECA
BATTERY PARK CITY
CHINATOWN
World Financial Center
World Trade Center Site
St Paul's Chapel
City Hall Park
City Hall
African Burial Ground
Trinity Church
NY Stock Exchange
Federal Reserve Bank
Museum of American Finance
Museum of Jewish Heritage
Skyscraper Museum
Museum of the American Indian
Castle Clinton
Battery Park
Bowling Green
Shrine of St Elizabeth Ann Seton
Fraunces Tavern
Ferry to Statue of Liberty
Staten Island Ferry Terminal
New York City Police Museum
South St Seaport Museum
South Street Seaport
First Shearith Israel Graveyard
Columbus Park
Museum of Chinese in the Americas
Confucius Plaza
Eldridge St. Synagogue
Rutgers Park
WEST SIDE HWY
HUDSON ST
WEST BROADWAY
CHURCH ST
BROADWAY
CENTRE ST
PARK ROW
VESEY ST
WALL ST
WHITEHALL ST
FRANKLIN D ROOSEVELT DR
BROOKLYN BRIDGE
MANHATTAN BRIDGE
BROOKLYN-BATTERY TUNNEL

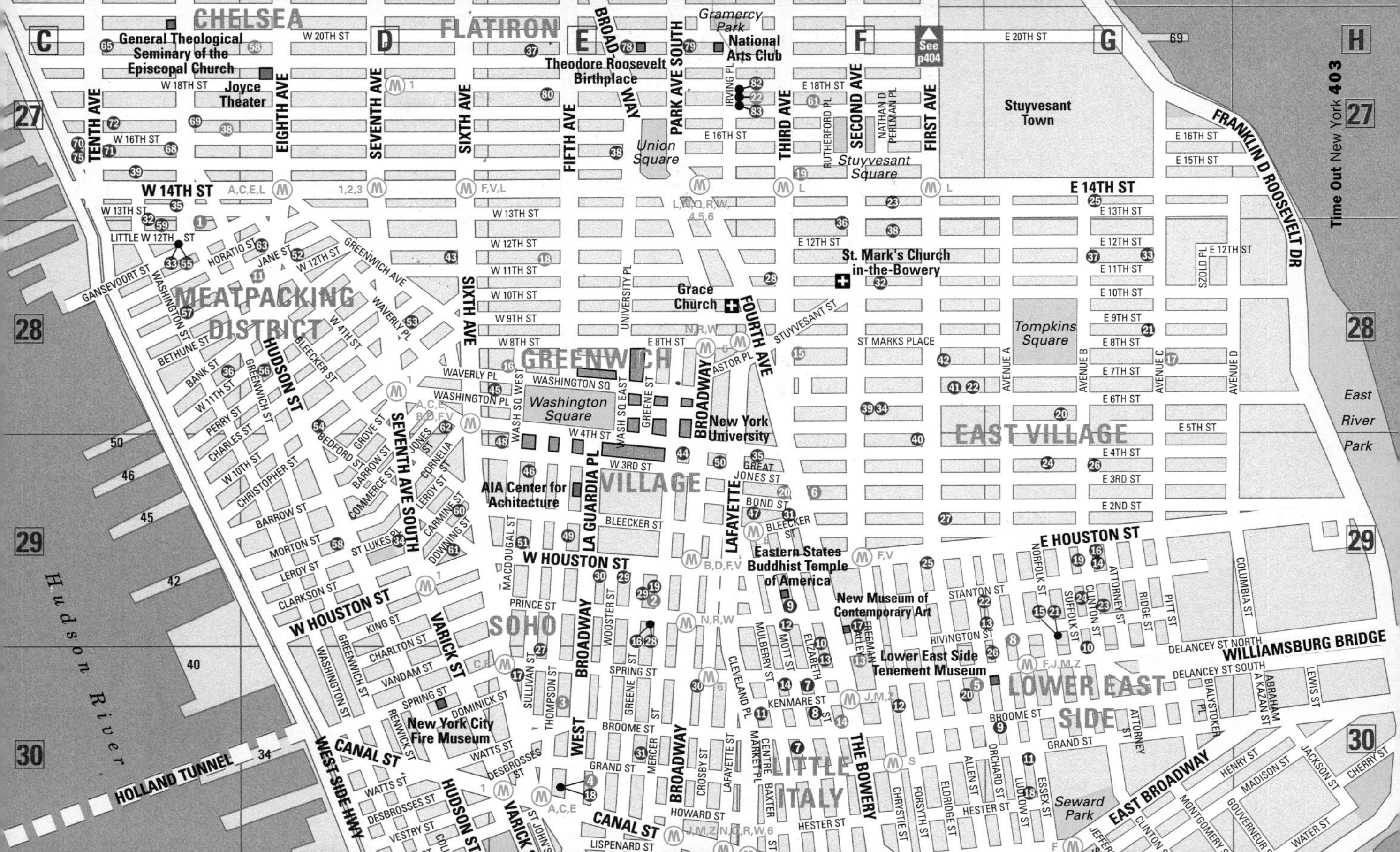

CHELSEA
General Theological Seminary of the Episcopal Church
Joyce Theater
FLATIRON
Theodore Roosevelt Birthplace
Gramercy Park
National Arts Club
See p404
Stuyvesant Town
W 20TH ST
E 20TH ST
W 18TH ST
E 18TH ST
W 16TH ST
E 16TH ST
E 15TH ST
TENTH AVE
EIGHTH AVE
SEVENTH AVE
SIXTH AVE
FIFTH AVE
BROADWAY
PARK AVE SOUTH
IRVING PL
THIRD AVE
RUTHERFORD PL
SECOND AVE
NATHAN D PERLMAN PL
FIRST AVE
Union Square
Stuyvesant Square
FRANKLIN D ROOSEVELT DR
W 14TH ST
E 14TH ST
W 13TH ST
E 13TH ST
LITTLE W 12TH ST
W 12TH ST
E 12TH ST
W 11TH ST
E 11TH ST
W 10TH ST
E 10TH ST
W 9TH ST
E 9TH ST
W 8TH ST
E 8TH ST
E 7TH ST
E 6TH ST
E 5TH ST
E 4TH ST
E 3RD ST
E 2ND ST
SZOLD PL
GANSEVOORT ST
HORATIO ST
JANE ST
GREENWICH AVE
WASHINGTON ST
MEATPACKING DISTRICT
BETHUNE ST
BANK ST
HUDSON ST
BLEECKER ST
W 4TH ST
WAVERLY PL
UNIVERSITY PL
Grace Church
FOURTH AVE
ASTOR PL
STUYVESANT ST
St. Mark's Church in-the-Bowery
ST MARKS PLACE
Tompkins Square
AVENUE A
AVENUE B
AVENUE C
AVENUE D
GREENWICH VILLAGE
WASHINGTON SQ
WASHINGTON PL
Washington Square
WASH SQ WEST
WASH SQ EAST
GREENE ST
New York University
W 3RD ST
GREAT JONES ST
BOND ST
EAST VILLAGE
East River Park
PERRY ST
CHARLES ST
CHRISTOPHER ST
BEDFORD ST
GROVE ST
BARROW ST
COMMERCE ST
SEVENTH AVE SOUTH
JONES ST
CORNELIA ST
LEROY ST
CARMINE ST
DOWNING ST
ST LUKES PL
MORTON ST
CLARKSON ST
AIA Center for Achitecture
LA GUARDIA PL
LAFAYETTE
MACDOUGAL ST
W HOUSTON ST
E HOUSTON ST
Eastern States Buddhist Temple of America
New Museum of Contemporary Art
STANTON ST
NORFOLK ST
SUFFOLK ST
CLINTON ST
ATTORNEY ST
RIDGE ST
PITT ST
COLUMBIA ST
Hudson River
KING ST
CHARLTON ST
VANDAM ST
VARICK ST
SOHO
PRINCE ST
WOOSTER ST
MULBERRY ST
MOTT ST
ELIZABETH ST
FREEMAN ALLEY
RIVINGTON ST
DELANCEY ST NORTH
WILLIAMSBURG BRIDGE
Lower East Side Tenement Museum
DELANCEY ST SOUTH
BIALYSTOKER PL
ABRAHAM A KAZAN ST
LEWIS ST
LOWER EAST SIDE
SPRING ST
DOMINICK ST
New York City Fire Museum
SULLIVAN ST
THOMPSON ST
WEST BROADWAY
CLEVELAND PL
KENMARE ST
CENTRE MARKET PL
BROOME ST
GRAND ST
HOLLAND TUNNEL
WEST SIDE HWY
CANAL ST
RENWICK ST
WATTS ST
DESBROSSES ST
VESTRY ST
MERCER ST
CROSBY ST
LAFAYETTE ST
HOWARD ST
LISPENARD ST
ST JOHN'S
LITTLE ITALY
BAXTER ST
HESTER ST
THE BOWERY
CHRYSTIE ST
FORSYTH ST
ELDRIDGE ST
ALLEN ST
ORCHARD ST
LUDLOW ST
ESSEX ST
Seward Park
EAST BROADWAY
HENRY ST
MADISON ST
JACKSON ST
CHERRY ST
MONTGOMERY ST
GOUVERNEUR ST
WATER ST

Hotels pp54-80
Restaurants & Cafés pp182-215
Bars pp216-227
300 m
300 yds
© Copyright Time Out Group 2008
Clinton Park
MIDTOWN
THEATER DISTRICT
GARMENT DISTRICT
CHELSEA
FLATIRON
GRAMERCY PARK
East River
WEST SIDE HWY
TWELFTH AVE
ELEVENTH AVE
TENTH AVE
NINTH AVE
EIGHTH AVE
SEVENTH AVE
SIXTH AVE
FIFTH AVE
MADISON AVE
PARK AVE SOUTH
LEXINGTON AVE
THIRD AVE
SECOND AVE
FIRST AVE
FRANKLIN D ROOSEVELT DR
BROADWAY
W 42ND ST
W 40TH ST
W 34TH ST
W 23RD ST
E 42ND ST
E 40TH ST
E 34TH ST
E 23RD ST
QUEENS-MIDTOWN TUNN
INCOLN TUNNEL
Intrepid Sea-Air-Space Museum
NYC Official Visitor Info Center
Museum of Arts & Design
Radio City Music Hall
Museum of TV & Radio
Rockefeller Center
NBC
Saks Fifth Ave
Christie's
Times Square Visitors' Center
TKTS
Helmsley Building
Japan Society
United Nations Headquarters
Times Square
Madame Tussaud's New York
International Center of Photography
Grand Central Terminal
Chrysler Building
News Building
Bryant Park
NY Public Library
TUDOR CITY PL
MITCHELL PL
Port Authority Bus Terminal
Javits Center
Scandinavia House: The Nordic Center in America
Morgan Library
Macy's
HERALD SQUARE
Empire State Building
General Post Office
Penn Station
Madison Square Garden
Manhattan Mall
Museum of Sex
Museum at FIT
Chelsea Park
Madison Square
MT CARMEL PL
ASSER LEVY PL
Manhattan Marina
Peter Cooper Village
Flatiron Building
General Theological Seminary of the Episcopal Church
See p403
Chelsea Piers Sports Complex

Great Lawn
W 82ND ST
See p406
Delacorte Theater
Goethe Institute
Metropolitan Museum of Art
UPPER EAST SIDE
E 82ND ST
EAST END AVE
W 80TH ST
W 79TH ST
American Museum of Natural History
Luce Nature Observatory
Belvedere Castle
79TH ST TRANSVERSE RD
E 80TH ST
E 79TH ST
W 78TH ST
E 78TH ST
John Jay Park
New-York Historical Society
W 76TH ST
RIVERSIDE DR
The Ramble
The Lake
Bow Bridge
Boathouse
Conservatory Water
Whitney Museum of American Art
E 76TH ST
W 74TH ST
VERDI SQUARE
E 74TH ST
The Dakota
W 72ND ST
Strawberry Fields
Bethesda Terrace
Naumburg Bandshell
E 72ND ST
Central Park
Asia Society & Museum
Roosevelt Island
W 70TH ST
The Frick Collection
E 70TH ST
HENRY HUDSON PKWY
FREEDOM PL
WEST END AVE
AMSTERDAM AVE
BROADWAY
COLUMBUS AVE
CENTRAL PARK WEST
WEST DRIVE
Sheep Meadow
EAST DRIVE
W 68TH ST
E 68TH ST
Rockefeller University
W 66TH ST
Tavern on the Green
China Institute
E 66TH ST
FIFTH AVE
PARK AVE
LEXINGTON AVE
THIRD AVE
SECOND AVE
FIRST AVE
65TH ST TRANSVERSE RD
W 64TH ST
E 64TH ST
Heckscher Playground
The Dairy
Zoo
MADISON AVE
Lincoln Center
W 62ND ST
Wollman Memorial Rink
E 62ND ST
RIVERSIDE BLVD
YORK AVE
W 60TH ST
Columbus Circle
E 60TH ST
Bloomingdales
Time Warner Center
Grand Army Plaza
W 58TH ST
ELEVENTH AVE
TENTH AVE
Museum of Arts & Design
E 58TH ST
SUTTON PL
W 57TH ST
Hearst Tower
Carnegie Hall
SIXTH AVE
Trump Tower
E 57TH ST
W 56TH ST
E 56TH ST
SUTTON PL SOUTH
NINTH AVE
SEVENTH AVE
Folk Art Museum
Museum of Modern Art
W 54TH ST
MIDTOWN
E 54TH ST
De Witt Clinton Park
CLINTON
NYC Official Visitor Info Center
Museum of Arts & Design
Museum of TV & Radio

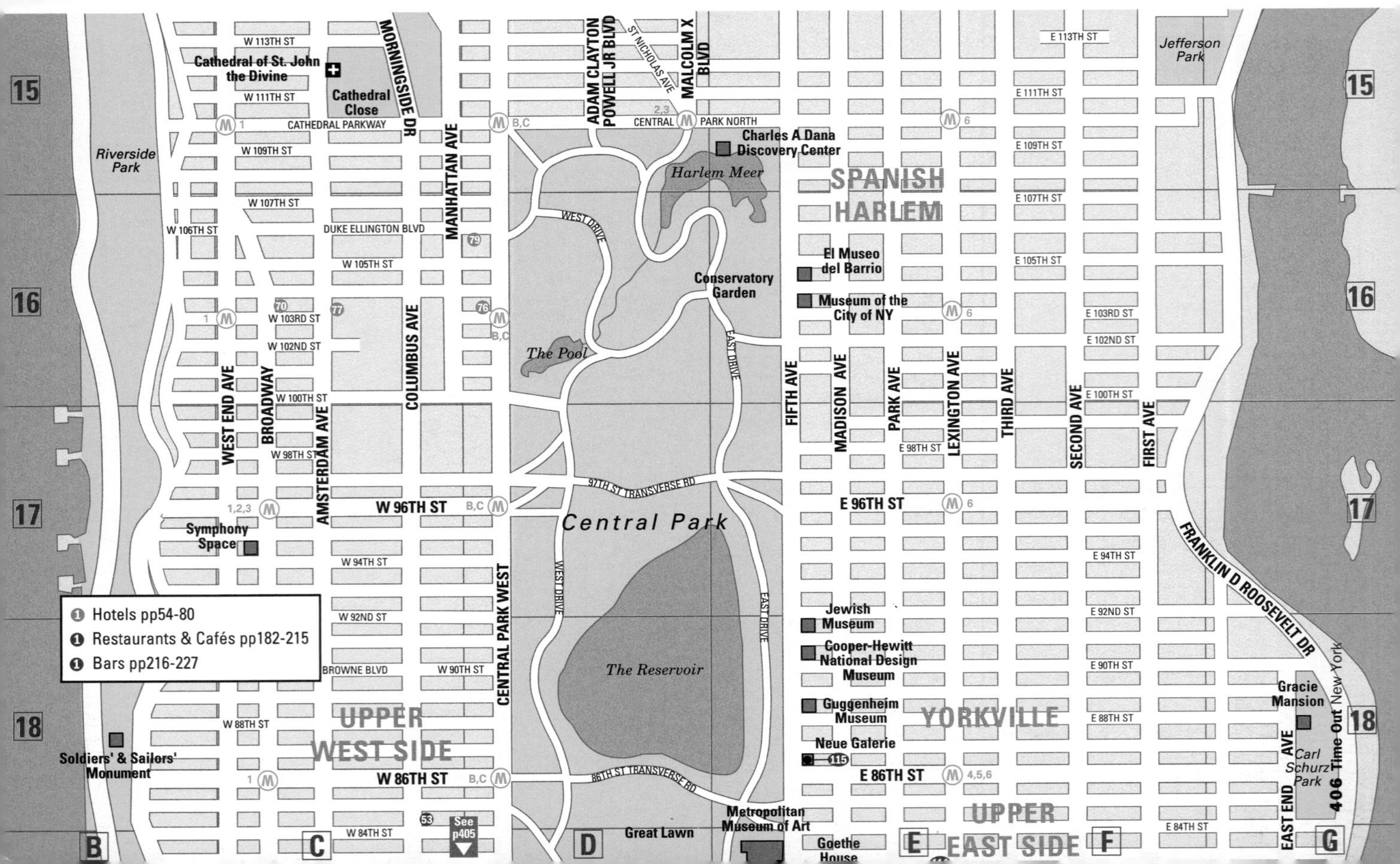

Hotels pp54-80
Restaurants & Cafés pp182-215
Bars pp216-227
Riverside Park
Cathedral of St. John the Divine
Cathedral Close
MORNINGSIDE DR
CATHEDRAL PARKWAY
W 113TH ST
W 111TH ST
W 109TH ST
W 107TH ST
W 106TH ST
DUKE ELLINGTON BLVD
W 105TH ST
W 103RD ST
W 102ND ST
W 100TH ST
W 98TH ST
W 96TH ST
W 94TH ST
W 92ND ST
BROWNE BLVD
W 90TH ST
W 88TH ST
W 86TH ST
W 84TH ST
WEST END AVE
BROADWAY
AMSTERDAM AVE
COLUMBUS AVE
MANHATTAN AVE
CENTRAL PARK WEST
Symphony Space
UPPER WEST SIDE
Soldiers' & Sailors' Monument
See p405
ADAM CLAYTON POWELL JR BLVD
ST NICHOLAS AVE
MALCOLM X BLVD
CENTRAL PARK NORTH
Charles A Dana Discovery Center
Harlem Meer
WEST DRIVE
EAST DRIVE
Conservatory Garden
The Pool
97TH ST TRANSVERSE RD
Central Park
The Reservoir
86TH ST TRANSVERSE RD
Great Lawn
Metropolitan Museum of Art
Goethe House
SPANISH HARLEM
El Museo del Barrio
Museum of the City of NY
Jewish Museum
Cooper-Hewitt National Design Museum
Guggenheim Museum
Neue Galerie
FIFTH AVE
MADISON AVE
PARK AVE
LEXINGTON AVE
THIRD AVE
SECOND AVE
FIRST AVE
E 113TH ST
E 111TH ST
E 109TH ST
E 107TH ST
E 105TH ST
E 103RD ST
E 102ND ST
E 100TH ST
E 98TH ST
E 96TH ST
E 94TH ST
E 92ND ST
E 90TH ST
E 88TH ST
E 86TH ST
E 84TH ST
YORKVILLE
UPPER EAST SIDE
Jefferson Park
FRANKLIN D ROOSEVELT DR
Gracie Mansion
Carl Schurz Park
EAST END AVE

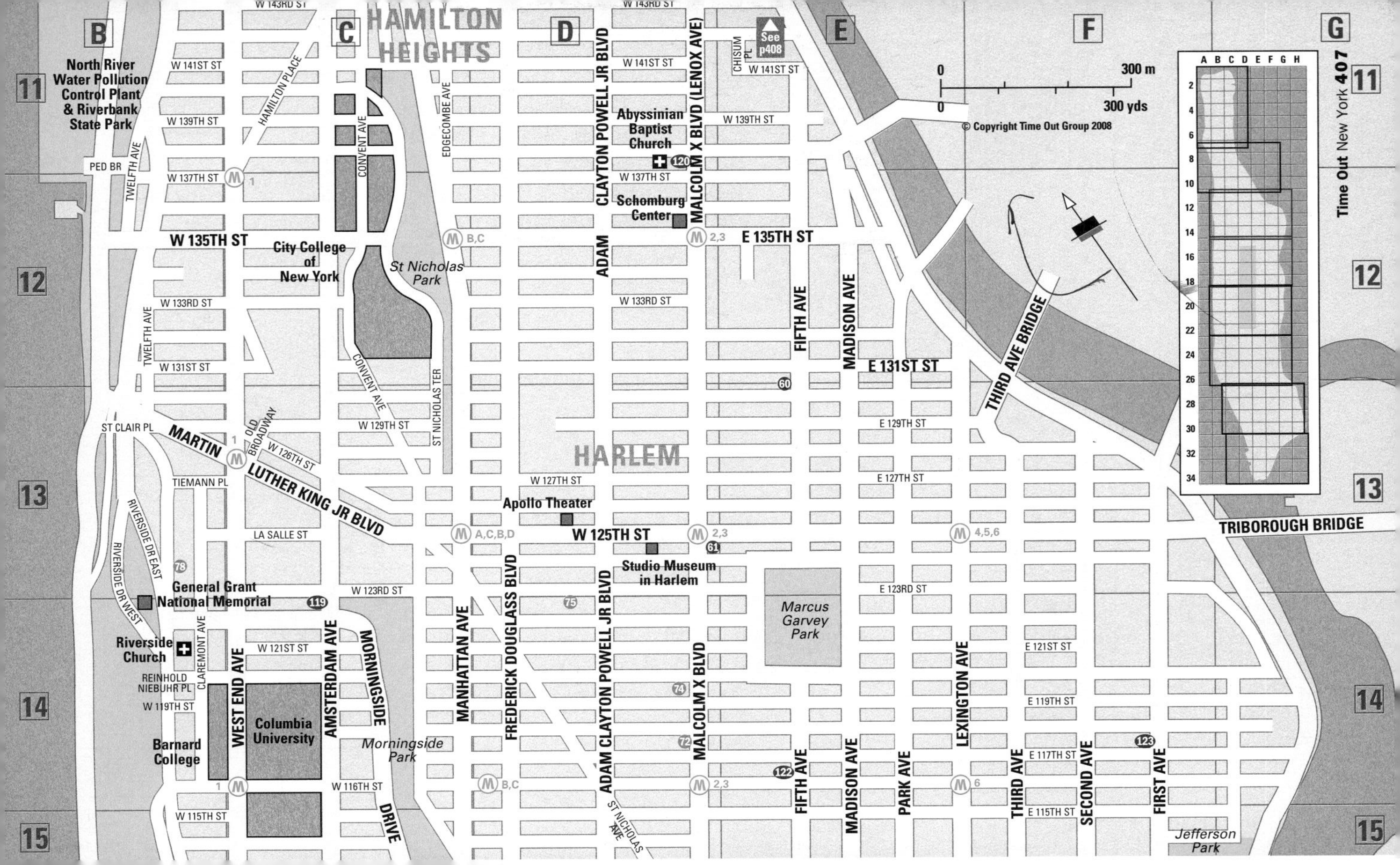

HAMILTON HEIGHTS
North River Water Pollution Control Plant & Riverbank State Park
PED BR
TWELFTH AVE
W 143RD ST
W 141ST ST
HAMILTON PLACE
W 139TH ST
W 137TH ST
CONVENT AVE
EDGECOMBE AVE
W 135TH ST
City College of New York
St Nicholas Park
W 133RD ST
W 131ST ST
ST NICHOLAS TER
W 129TH ST
ST CLAIR PL
MARTIN LUTHER KING JR BLVD
OLD BROADWAY
W 126TH ST
TIEMANN PL
LA SALLE ST
RIVERSIDE DR EAST
RIVERSIDE DR WEST
General Grant National Memorial
W 123RD ST
Riverside Church
CLAREMONT AVE
REINHOLD NIEBUHR PL
W 121ST ST
W 119TH ST
Barnard College
WEST END AVE
Columbia University
AMSTERDAM AVE
MORNINGSIDE DRIVE
Morningside Park
W 116TH ST
W 115TH ST
MANHATTAN AVE
FREDERICK DOUGLASS BLVD
ADAM CLAYTON POWELL JR BLVD
ST NICHOLAS AVE
Abyssinian Baptist Church
Schomburg Center
MALCOLM X BLVD (LENOX AVE)
MALCOLM X BLVD
CHISUM PL
See p408
E 135TH ST
HARLEM
W 127TH ST
Apollo Theater
W 125TH ST
Studio Museum in Harlem
Marcus Garvey Park
FIFTH AVE
MADISON AVE
E 131ST ST
E 129TH ST
E 127TH ST
E 123RD ST
E 121ST ST
E 119TH ST
E 117TH ST
E 115TH ST
PARK AVE
LEXINGTON AVE
THIRD AVE
SECOND AVE
FIRST AVE
THIRD AVE BRIDGE
TRIBOROUGH BRIDGE
Jefferson Park
0 300 m
0 300 yds
© Copyright Time Out Group 2008

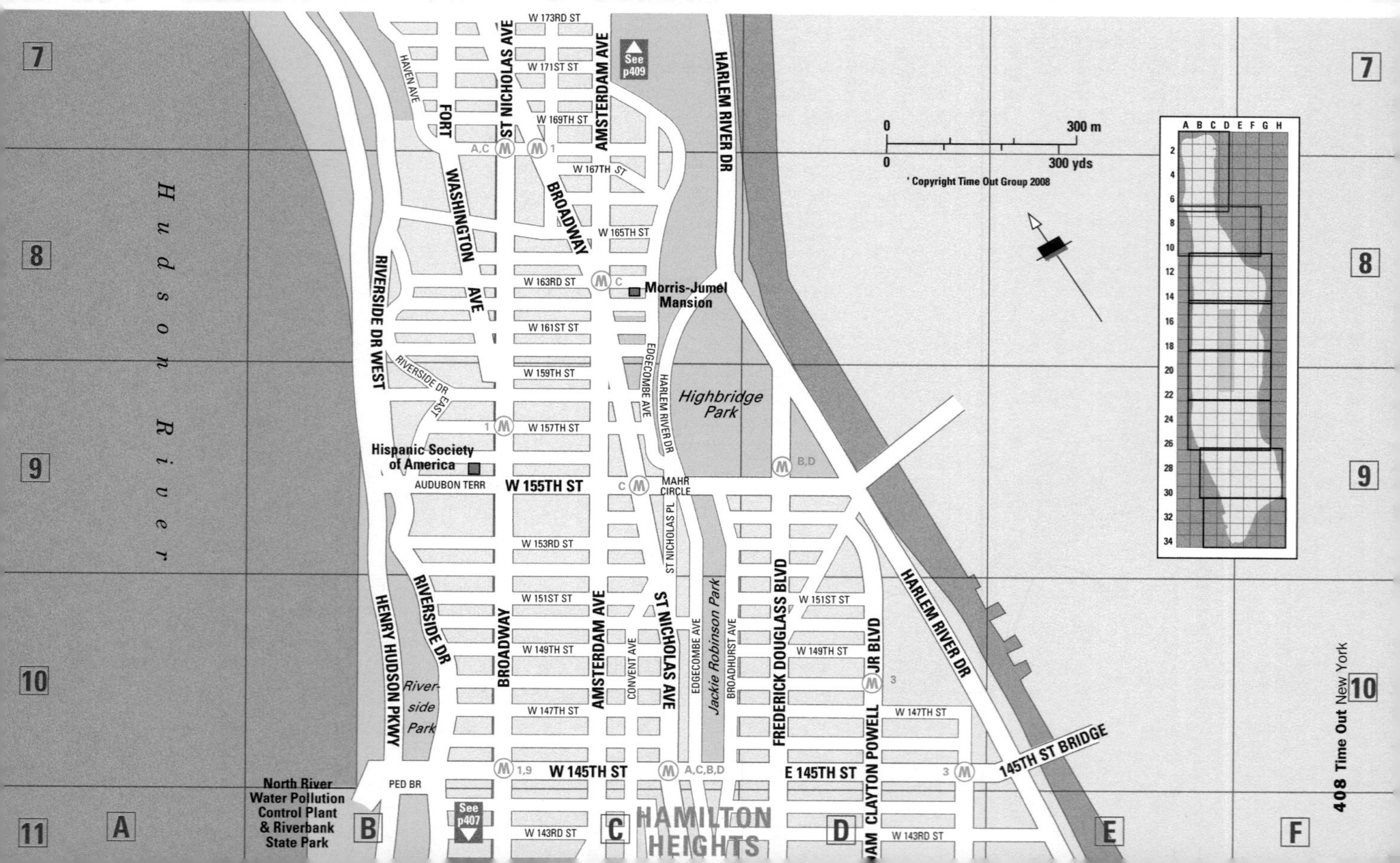

Hudson River
North River Water Pollution Control Plant & Riverbank State Park
HENRY HUDSON PKWY
RIVERSIDE DR WEST
RIVERSIDE DR EAST
RIVERSIDE DR
Riverside Park
PED BR
Hispanic Society of America
AUDUBON TERR
HAVEN AVE
FORT WASHINGTON AVE
See p407
See p409
BROADWAY
ST NICHOLAS AVE
W 143RD ST
W 145TH ST
W 147TH ST
W 149TH ST
W 151ST ST
W 153RD ST
W 155TH ST
W 157TH ST
W 159TH ST
W 161ST ST
W 163RD ST
W 165TH ST
W 167TH ST
W 169TH ST
W 171ST ST
W 173RD ST
AMSTERDAM AVE
CONVENT AVE
EDGECOMBE AVE
ST NICHOLAS PL
MAHR CIRCLE
HARLEM RIVER DR
Highbridge Park
Morris-Jumel Mansion
HAMILTON HEIGHTS
Jackie Robinson Park
BROADHURST AVE
FREDERICK DOUGLASS BLVD
E 145TH ST
ADAM CLAYTON POWELL JR BLVD
145TH ST BRIDGE
' Copyright Time Out Group 2008
0
300 m
300 yds

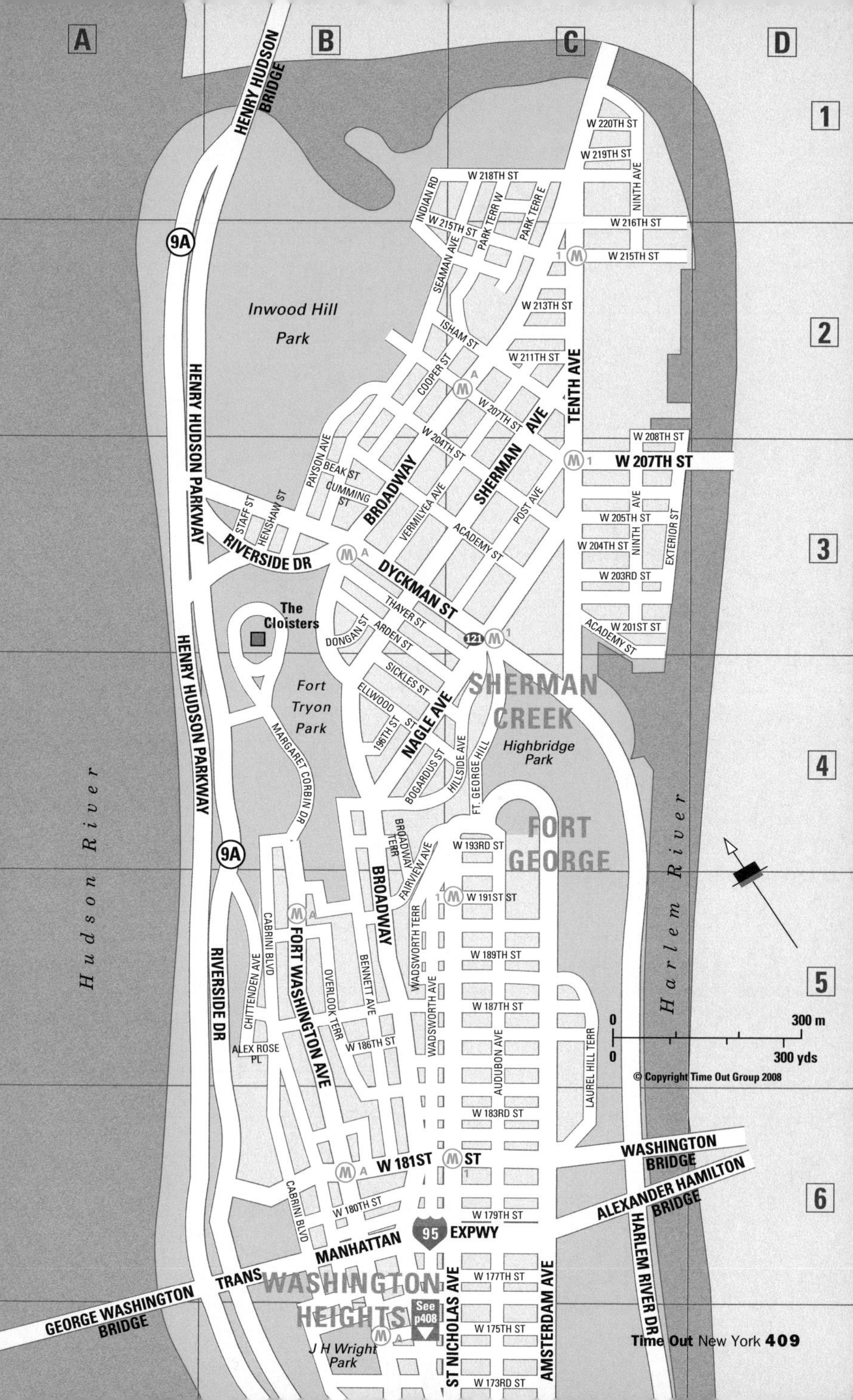
A
B
C
D
1
2
3
4
5
6
HENRY HUDSON BRIDGE
9A
W 220TH ST
W 219TH ST
W 218TH ST
NINTH AVE
INDIAN RD
PARK TERR W
PARK TERR E
W 215TH ST
W 216TH ST
W 215TH ST
SEAMAN AVE
W 213TH ST
Inwood Hill Park
ISHAM ST
W 211TH ST
TENTH AVE
COOPER ST
W 207TH ST
SHERMAN AVE
W 208TH ST
W 204TH ST
W 207TH ST
PAYSON AVE
BEAK ST
CUMMING ST
BROADWAY
VERMILYEA AVE
POST AVE
HENRY HUDSON PARKWAY
STAFF ST
HENSHAW ST
ACADEMY ST
W 205TH ST
NINTH AVE
EXTERIOR ST
W 204TH ST
RIVERSIDE DR
DYCKMAN ST
W 203RD ST
THAYER ST
The Cloisters
DONGAN ST
ARDEN ST
121
W 201ST ST
ACADEMY ST
SICKLES ST
SHERMAN CREEK
Fort Tryon Park
ELLWOOD ST
196TH ST
NAGLE AVE
MARGARET CORBIN DR
HILLSIDE AVE
FT. GEORGE HILL
Highbridge Park
BOGARDUS ST
Hudson River
Harlem River
FORT GEORGE
BROADWAY TERR
FAIRVIEW AVE
W 193RD ST
W 191ST ST
CABRINI BLVD
FORT WASHINGTON AVE
WADSWORTH TERR
W 189TH ST
RIVERSIDE DR
CHITTENDEN AVE
OVERLOOK TERR
BENNETT AVE
WADSWORTH AVE
W 187TH ST
AUDUBON AVE
LAUREL HILL TERR
0
300 m
0
300 yds
W 186TH ST
ALEX ROSE PL
© Copyright Time Out Group 2008
W 183RD ST
WASHINGTON BRIDGE
W 181ST
ST
CABRINI BLVD
W 180TH ST
ALEXANDER HAMILTON BRIDGE
W 179TH ST
95
EXPWY
MANHATTAN
TRANS
HARLEM RIVER DR
WASHINGTON HEIGHTS
W 177TH ST
GEORGE WASHINGTON BRIDGE
See p408
W 175TH ST
J H Wright Park
ST NICHOLAS AVE
AMSTERDAM AVE
W 173RD ST

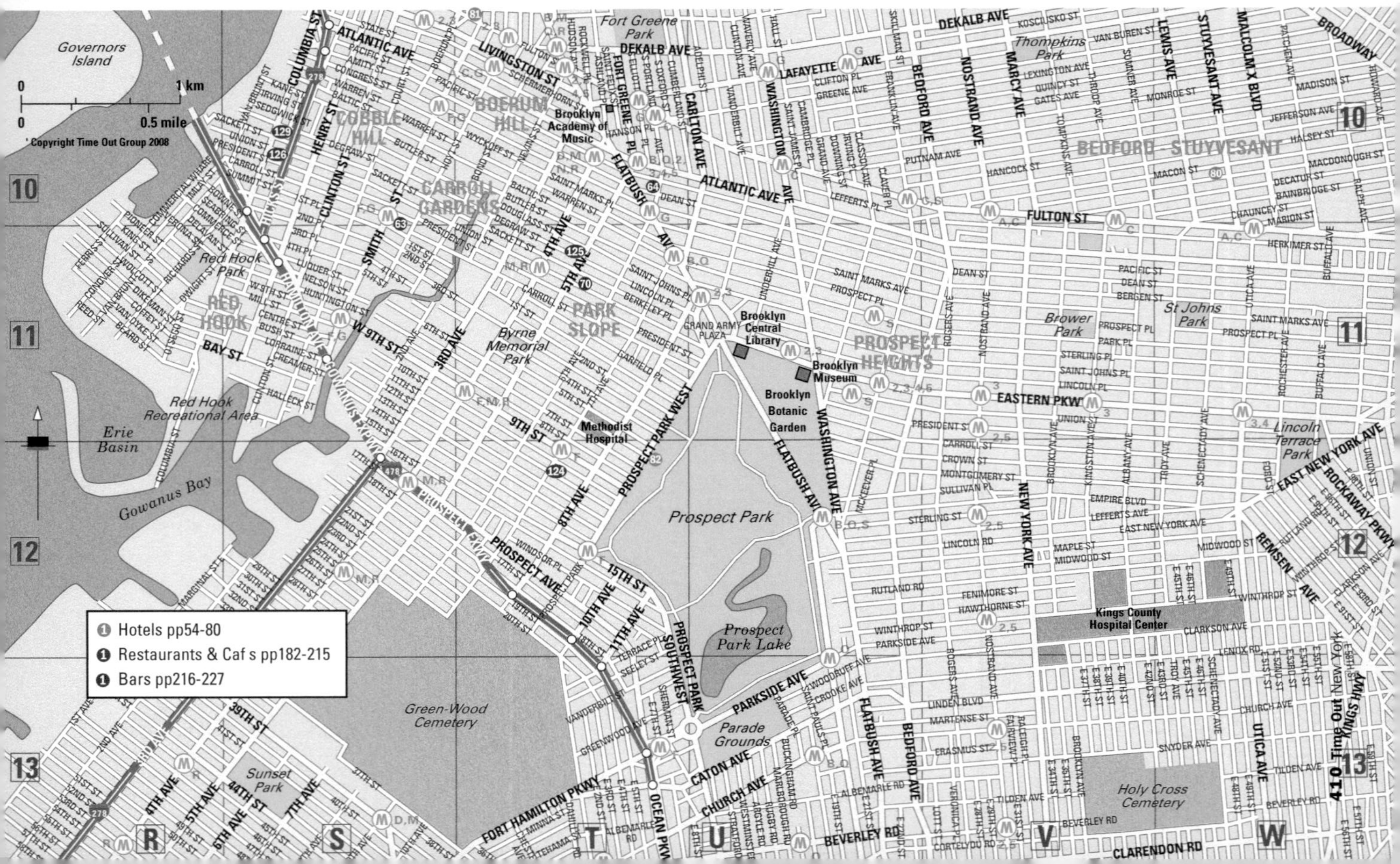

Hotels pp54-80
Restaurants & Caf s pp182-215
Bars pp216-227
0 0.5 mile
0 1 km
' Copyright Time Out Group 2008
Governors Island
Erie Basin
Gowanus Bay
Red Hook Recreational Area
Red Hook Park
RED HOOK
COBBLE HILL
BOERUM HILL
CARROLL GARDENS
PARK SLOPE
PROSPECT HEIGHTS
BEDFORD - STUYVESANT
Fort Greene Park
Thompkins Park
Brooklyn Academy of Music
Byrne Memorial Park
Methodist Hospital
Brooklyn Central Library
Brooklyn Museum
Brooklyn Botanic Garden
GRAND ARMY PLAZA
Prospect Park
Prospect Park Lake
Parade Grounds
Green-Wood Cemetery
Sunset Park
Brower Park
St Johns Park
Lincoln Terrace Park
Kings County Hospital Center
Holy Cross Cemetery
ATLANTIC AVE
FLATBUSH AV
FULTON ST
EASTERN PKWY
PROSPECT PARK WEST
PROSPECT PARK SOUTHWEST
PARKSIDE AVE
OCEAN PKWY
FORT HAMILTON PKWY
PROSPECT EXWY
GOWANUS EXWY
NEW YORK AVE
EAST NEW YORK AVE
ROCKAWAY PKWY
WASHINGTON AVE
BEDFORD AVE
NOSTRAND AVE
UTICA AVE
CLARENDON RD
BEVERLEY RD
CHURCH AVE
CATON AVE
KINGS HWY
BROADWAY
DEKALB AVE
10
11
12
13
R
S
T
U
V
W

Brooklyn

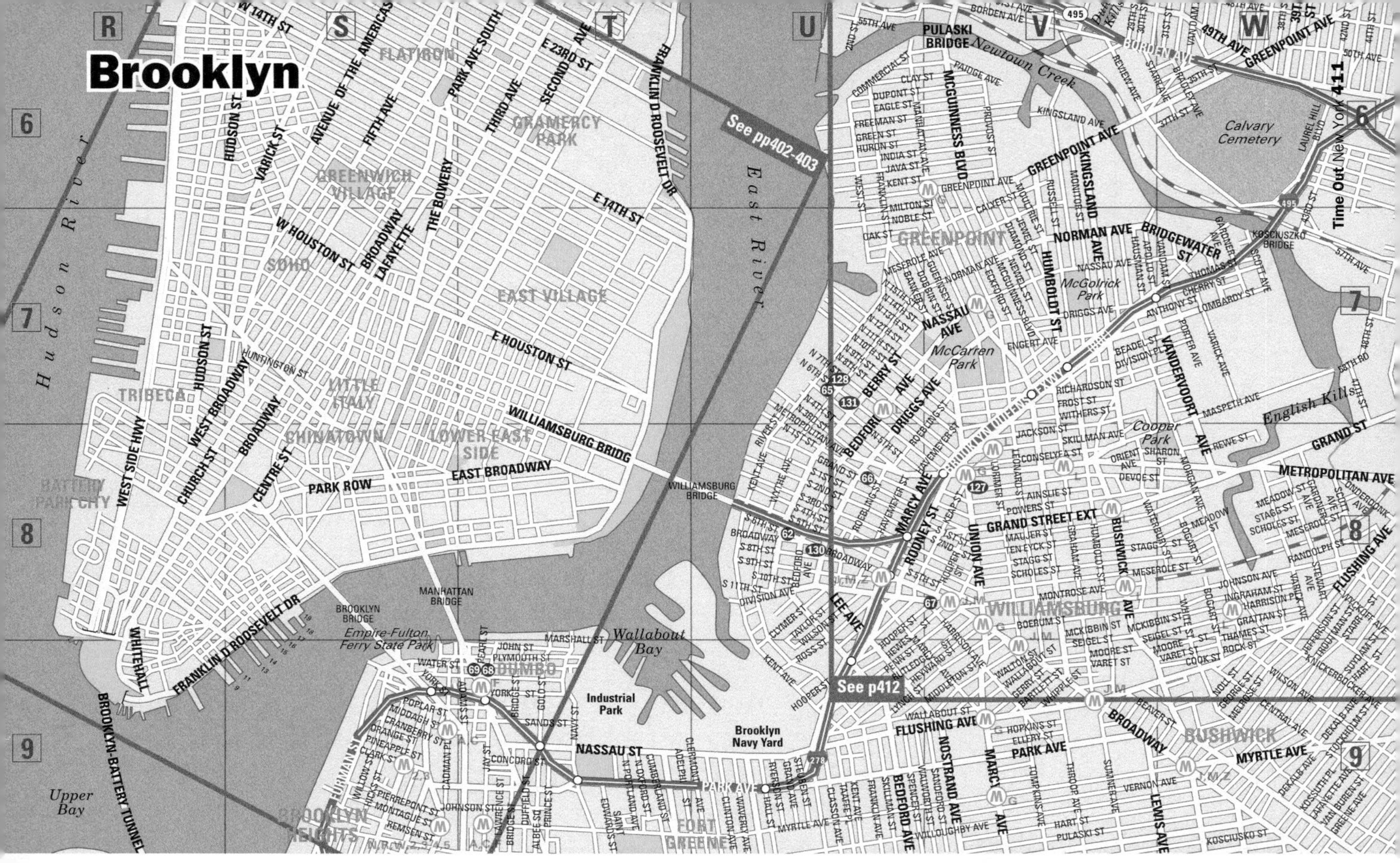

Hudson River
East River
Upper Bay
Wallabout Bay
Newtown Creek
English Kills
TRIBECA
SOHO
GREENWICH VILLAGE
FLATIRON
GRAMERCY PARK
EAST VILLAGE
LITTLE ITALY
CHINATOWN
LOWER EAST SIDE
BATTERY PARK CITY
DUMBO
BROOKLYN HEIGHTS
FORT GREENE
GREENPOINT
WILLIAMSBURG
BUSHWICK
Calvary Cemetery
McCarren Park
McGolrick Park
Cooper Park
Industrial Park
Brooklyn Navy Yard
Empire-Fulton Ferry State Park
BROOKLYN BRIDGE
MANHATTAN BRIDGE
WILLIAMSBURG BRIDGE
PULASKI BRIDGE
KOSCIUSZKO BRIDGE
BROOKLYN-BATTERY TUNNEL
WEST SIDE HWY
FRANKLIN D ROOSEVELT DR
WILLIAMSBURG BRIDG
BROOKLYN QUEENS EXWY
See pp402-403
See p412

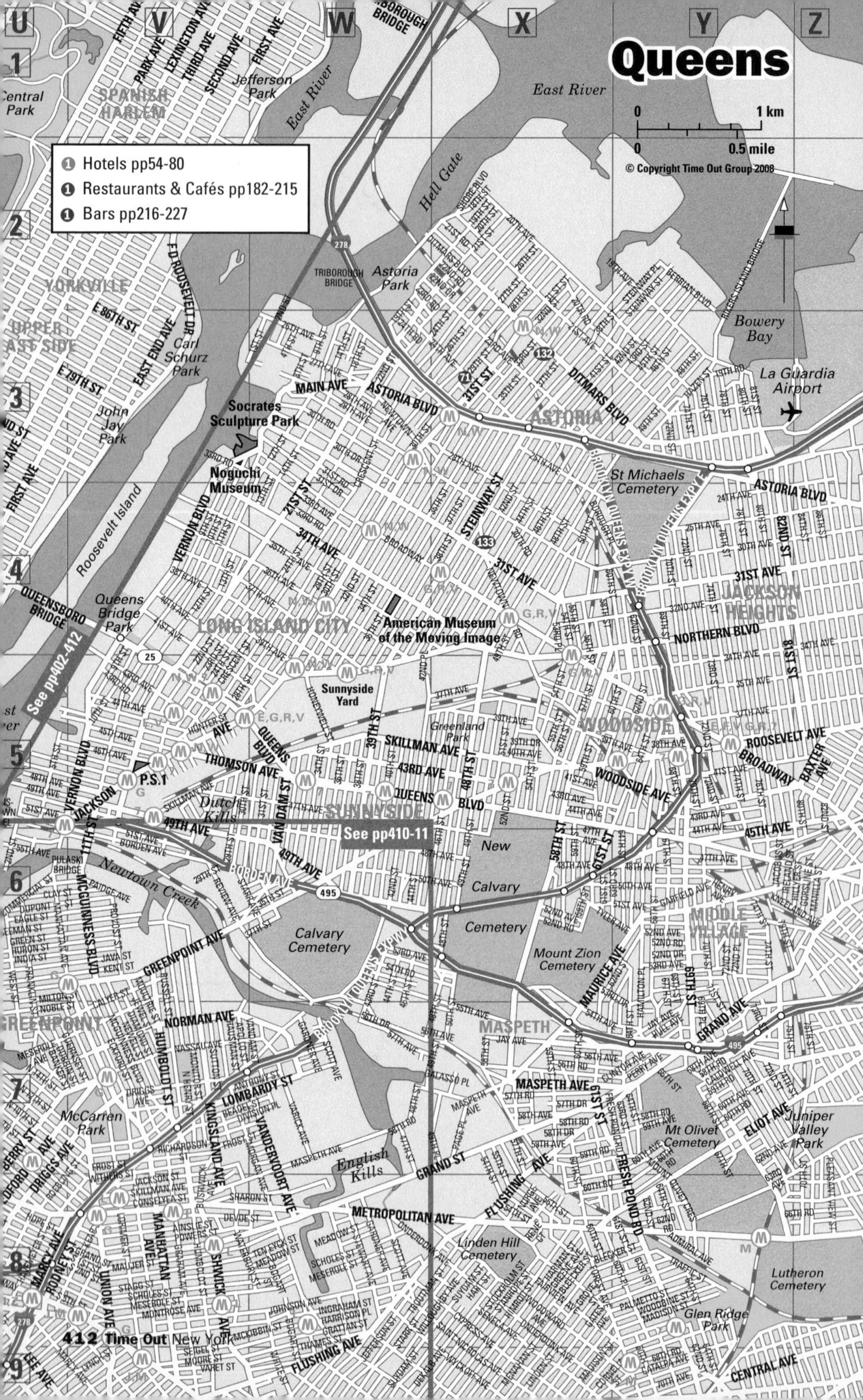

Queens
0
1 km
0
0.5 mile
© Copyright Time Out Group 2008
Hotels pp54-80
Restaurants & Cafés pp182-215
Bars pp216-227
U
V
W
X
Y
Z
1
2
3
4
5
6
7
8
9
East River
Hell Gate
Triborough Bridge
Astoria Park
Central Park
Spanish Harlem
Jefferson Park
Yorkville
Upper East Side
Carl Schurz Park
John Jay Park
Roosevelt Island
Queensboro Bridge
Queens Bridge Park
Socrates Sculpture Park
Noguchi Museum
Long Island City
American Museum of the Moving Image
Astoria
St Michaels Cemetery
Bowery Bay
La Guardia Airport
Jackson Heights
Sunnyside Yard
Sunnyside
Greenland Park
Woodside
P.S.1
Dutch Kills
See pp402-412
See pp410-11
Newtown Creek
Pulaski Bridge
Calvary Cemetery
New Calvary Cemetery
Mount Zion Cemetery
Maspeth
Middle Village
Greenpoint
McCarren Park
English Kills
Mt Olivet Cemetery
Juniper Valley Park
Linden Hill Cemetery
Lutheron Cemetery
Glen Ridge Park
Astoria Blvd
Ditmars Blvd
Northern Blvd
Queens Blvd
Roosevelt Ave
Broadway
Steinway St
Vernon Blvd
Jackson Ave
Greenpoint Ave
Metropolitan Ave
Grand Ave
Grand St
Flushing Ave
Eliot Ave
Woodside Ave
Skillman Ave
Thomson Ave
Borden Ave
Brooklyn Queens Expwy
Maspeth Ave
Fresh Pond Rd
Central Ave
Union Ave
Humboldt St
Kingsland Ave
Vandervoort Ave
McGuinness Blvd
Manhattan Ave
Marcy Ave
Lombardy St
Norman Ave
Rikers Island Bridge
FD Roosevelt Dr
First Ave
Second Ave
Third Ave
Lexington Ave
Park Ave
Fifth Ave
East End Ave
E 86th St
E 79th St

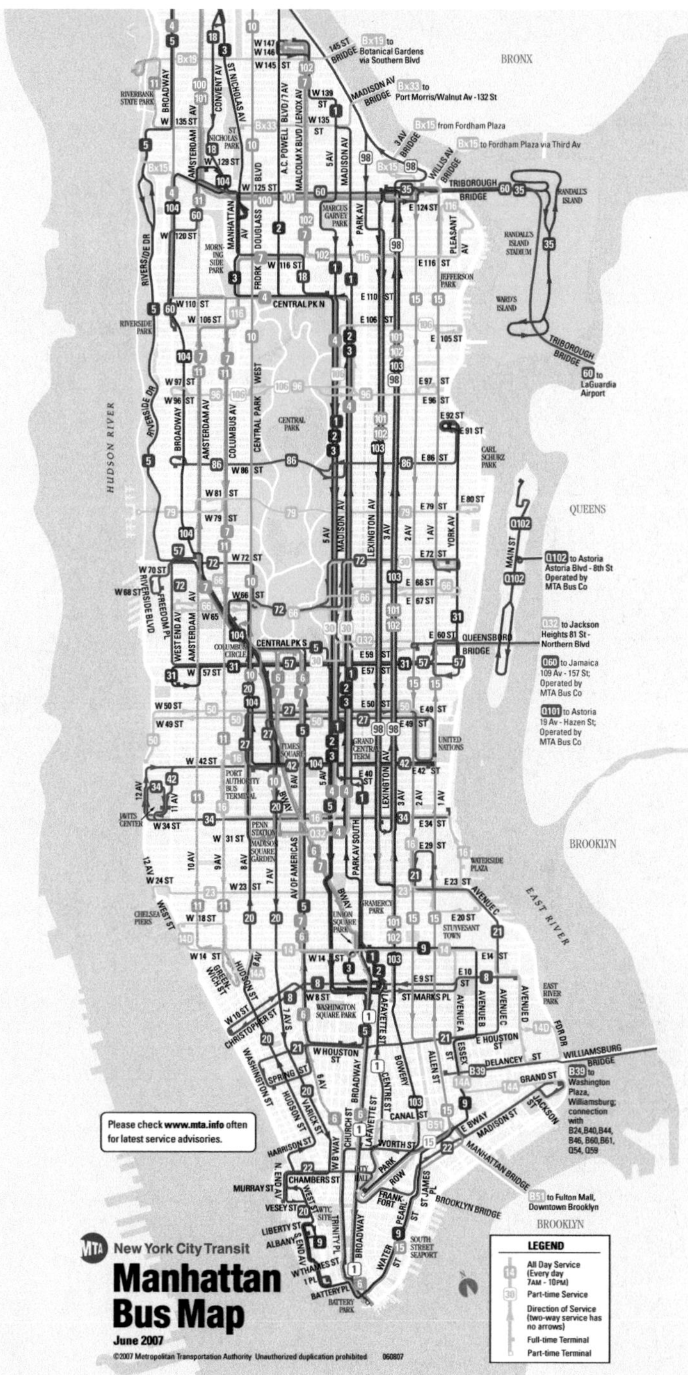
New York City Transit
Manhattan Bus Map
June 2007
©2007 Metropolitan Transportation Authority Unauthorized duplication prohibited 060807
Please check www.mta.info often for latest service advisories.
LEGEND
All Day Service (Every day 7AM - 10PM)
Part-time Service
Direction of Service (two-way service has no arrows)
Full-time Terminal
Part-time Terminal
BRONX
QUEENS
BROOKLYN
HUDSON RIVER
EAST RIVER
CENTRAL PARK
Bx19 to Botanical Gardens via Southern Blvd
Bx33 to Port Morris/Walnut Av - 132 St
Bx15 from Fordham Plaza
Bx15 to Fordham Plaza via Third Av
60 to LaGuardia Airport
Q102 to Astoria Astoria Blvd - 8th St Operated by MTA Bus Co
Q32 to Jackson Heights 81 St - Northern Blvd
Q60 to Jamaica 109 Av - 157 St; Operated by MTA Bus Co
Q101 to Astoria 19 Av - Hazen St; Operated by MTA Bus Co
B39 to Washington Plaza, Williamsburg; connection with B24, B40, B44, B46, B60, B61, Q54, Q59
B51 to Fulton Mall, Downtown Brooklyn
TRIBOROUGH BRIDGE
QUEENSBORO BRIDGE
WILLIAMSBURG BRIDGE
MANHATTAN BRIDGE
BROOKLYN BRIDGE
RANDALL'S ISLAND
WARD'S ISLAND
TIMES SQUARE
PORT AUTHORITY BUS TERMINAL
PENN STATION
GRAND CENTRAL TERM
UNITED NATIONS
WASHINGTON SQUARE PARK
BATTERY PARK
SOUTH STREET SEAPORT

STATEN ISLAND
BROOKLYN
Jamaica Bay
MTA Staten Island Railway
Staten Island Ferry
St. George
Tompkinsville
Stapleton
Clifton
Grasmere
Old Town
Dongan Hills
Jefferson Av
Grant City
New Dorp
Oakwood Heights
Bay Terrace
Great Kills
Eltingville
Annadale
Huguenot
Prince's Bay
Pleasant Plains
Richmond Valley
Nassau
Atlantic
Tottenville
South Ferry
Whitehall St
Bowling Green
Rector St
Wall St
World Trade Center
Chambers St
Franklin St
Canal St
Houston St
Christopher St Sheridan Sq
14 St
W 4 St Wash Sq
Spring St
Prince St
8 St NYU
Astor Pl
Bleecker St
Grand St
Delancey St Essex St
East Broadway
York St
High St
Jay St Borough Hall
Court St
Clark St
Borough Hall
Hoyt St
Nevins St
DeKalb Av
Atlantic Av
Bergen St
Carroll St
Smith 9 Sts
4 Av-9 St
Prospect Av
25 St
36 St
45 St
53 St
59 St
Bay Ridge Av
77 St
86 St
Bay Ridge 95 St
Coney Island Stillwell Av
West 8 St NY Aquarium
Ocean Pkwy
Brighton Beach
Sheepshead Bay
Kings Hwy
Avenue U
Avenue M
Avenue J
Avenue H
Newkirk Av
Cortelyou Rd
Beverley Rd
Church Av
Parkside Av
Prospect Park
Botanic Garden
Franklin Av
Nostrand Av
Kingston Av
Crown Hts Utica Av
Sutter Av-Rutland Rd
Saratoga Av
Rockaway Av
Junius St
Pennsylvania Av
Van Siclen Av
New Lots Av
Livonia Av
East 105 St
Canarsie Rockaway Pkwy
Broadway Junction
Howard Beach JFK Airport
Aqueduct North Conduit Av
Broad Channel
Beach 90 St
Beach 98 St
Beach 105 St
Rockaway Park Beach 116 St
Far Rockaway Mott Av
Beach 25 St
Beach 36 St
Beach 44 St
Beach 60 St
Beach 67 St